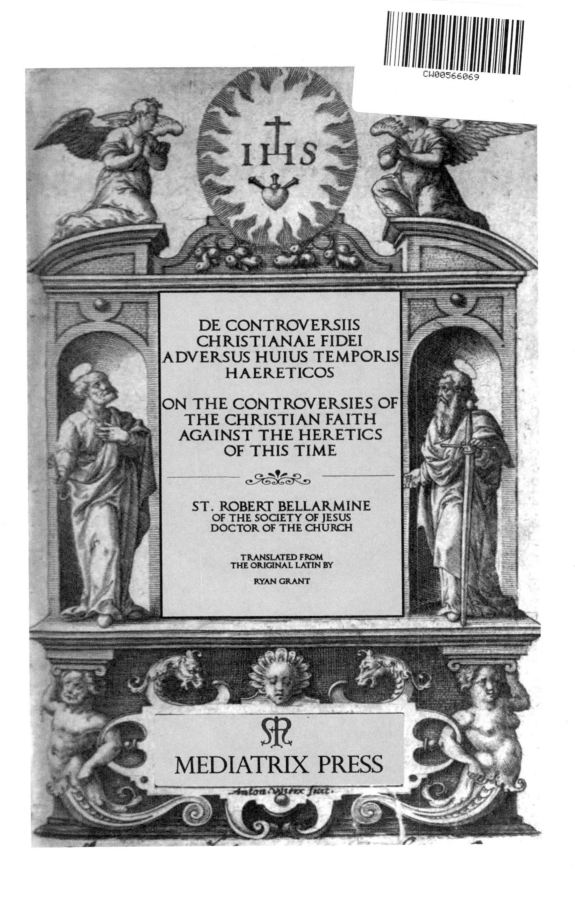

IHS

DE CONTROVERSIIS
CHRISTIANAE FIDEI
ADVERSUS HUIUS TEMPORIS
HAERETICOS

ON THE CONTROVERSIES OF
THE CHRISTIAN FAITH
AGAINST THE HERETICS
OF THIS TIME

ST. ROBERT BELLARMINE
OF THE SOCIETY OF JESUS
DOCTOR OF THE CHURCH

TRANSLATED FROM
THE ORIGINAL LATIN BY

RYAN GRANT

MEDIATRIX PRESS

Controversie Roberti
Bellarmini
S.R.E.
Presbiteri
Cardinalis
Archiepisc.
Cap.

Leodij I. Valdor sculpeb. C.J.

DE CONTROVERSIIS I
✠
ON THE ROMAN PONTIFF

St. Robert Bellarmine, S.J.
Doctor of the Church

In Five Books
Translated from the original Latin
of the 1588 Ingolstadt Edition
by
RYAN GRANT

MEDIATRIX PRESS

MMXVI

ISBN: 0692705708

Translated from *De Controversiis Fidei Christiani, contra haereticos nostri tempori.*
De Romano Pontifice.
Ingolstadt, 1588
Sartorius Publishers.
Revised according to the 1614 Paris edition, Tri-Adelphorum.

Second Edition, September 2017
First Edition, March 2016
Mediatrix Press
607 E. 6th St. Ste. 230
Post Falls, ID 83854
http://www.mediatrixpress.com

Table of Contents

BOOK IV
ON THE SUPREME SPIRITUAL POWER OF THE POPE

Translator's Preface

THE failure of the late medieval papacy to truly govern the Church had provoked a number of errors among those who would become flawed reformers as well as revolutionaries. Thus, became a consistent practice in Renaissance humanism to doubt many aspects of the Papal office.

Sadly, it can be said with Philip Hughes, a great Catholic historian of the Reformation, that the chief aim of the Popes was to make money.

Yet the Protestant reformers were not able to distinguish between the office and the man, and thus developed a number of arguments that in those days seemed rather compelling; that the Church should have no Pope; that the freedom of the Gospel means the Pope cannot impose laws; that Christ left no such office; that Peter even did not establish a See at Rome; and in fact, the Pope is the antichrist, meant to corrupt and destroy the Church.

At Trent, where the Church attempted to answer the many attacks of the early Protestants on Catholic teaching, one thing was notably absent: any particular refutation of their points on the Papacy. This glaring omission in Trent, however, was due not to an inability to answer the arguments, but to political pressure. Tied up with the question of the Papacy was also the pressing need of "reform of the head," which many Popes feared would touch their incomes as well as those of the Curia. Pope Paul III forbade his legates from permitting any discussion of "reform of the head" in the first period of Trent's sitting; just the same, the theologians and bishops who began trickling into Trent had the sense not to raise the issue. That reform would take saints, such as the great St. Charles Borromeo, St. Philip Neri, and above all St. Pius V, whose virtues later Popes could not ignore, and whose shining example bore down on more worldly Popes, preventing any return to business as usual.

For all that, little had been done at the magisterial level to clearly answer the questions of the time on the theological basis of the papacy. This task was left instead to the theologians as most things are before they ever reach the level of papal teaching. Today there are many who scoff at this, and relegate the teaching of the theologians, even in common, as mere opinions of no value. Yet were that true, the Church would never license works of theology. In fact, the great Jesuit theologian, Cardinal Franzelin (a peritus at Vatican I), wrote in his work *De Divina Traditione* the following about the work of theologians,

> "Bishops, both as individuals and in Councils to declare and define doctrine, employ the Academies and the teachers of the schools in counsel so that the common doctrine of the schools would be like a type of preparation of an authentic definition of Popes and Councils ... Although the schools and theologians of the

schools are not an organ constituted by Christ for the conservation of revealed doctrine under the assistance of the Spirit of truth, nevertheless, from the unanimous and constant opinion of those in the affairs of faith, when they teach thus it is to be believed not merely as something which is true, but by Catholic faith, we are led in recognition of Catholic understanding and of doctrine, which the very apostolic succession hands down and conserves as custodians and authentic interpreters of revelation."[1]

Among the theologians then, Bellarmine was perhaps the most prolific; no one is more quoted in the documents of Vatican I. There were, of course, other works in the scholastics and in Bellarmine's time, treatises such as that of Cajetan or Melchior Cano that were carried out along more scholastic lines, but as yet nothing systematic that would address all the Protestant arguments and defend the Church's traditional teaching—until this work.

Having become a distinguished scholar at Louvain, Bellarmine was recalled to Rome and placed in the Roman College (the future Gregorian University) to take up the chair of Controversial Theology. There it was seen that he not only had a perfect familiarity with the works of major Protestants, but he also had a seemingly photographic memory of the teachings of the Fathers. This also fit the current the counter-reformation, fired up by the spiritual example of St. Philip Neri, the thrust of humanism to highlight the teaching of the Church Fathers, and the focus on the early Church as well as martyrs given by Cardinal Baronius' work in the *Annales.*

Bellarmine takes up this with gusto, positing the objections of the Protestants, then refuting them systematically by an appeal to the Scripture and the teachings of the Fathers, resulting in a clear vindication of the Catholic side.

Bellarmine's treatise on the Papacy then, represents the first and—judging by the results—best attempt to address the questions over that office in an apologetic, rather than scholastic manner. He not only refutes Protestant teaching, but lays down the theological foundations which would make their way into the definitions of the First Vatican Council. Bossuet, the great French Bishop of the 17th century, notes that in his time, Bellarmine still reigned supreme, even among French theologians. References to Bellarmine fill the pages of later theological treatises of the great theologians.

Yet today some would think a treatise like this redundant, or, a waste of time, since Vatican I solemnly declared the Catholic doctrine on the papacy in 1870. Far from a mere antiquarian interest, however, this work is still valuable for us today. For irrespective of the recent ecumenical fervor, many Protestants

---

[1] *De Divina Traditione,* Thesis XVII, n.1.

still teach that Rome is the Antichrist, and oppose any dialogue with Catholics. The Eastern Orthodox, in spite of many favorable dialogue with theologians in the later 20th century, remain steadfastly against Catholic teaching and above all, the institution of the papacy. A browsing of the Wikipedia page on papal primacy reveals a number of arguments against the doctrine which Bellarmine refuted over 400 years ago! In Bellarmine's time, the Papacy was above all, *the* issue, as is clear in a debate held in London between Anglican Archbishop William Laud and an imprisoned English Jesuit named Fisher. Laud spent many hours trying to find errors in Bellarmine's arguments, and in the debate, he declared: "Indeed could I swallow Bellarmine's opinion that the Pope's judgment is infallible, I would then submit without any more ado. But that will never go down with me, unless I live till I dote, which I hope to God I shall not."[2] One of the members of his church 300 years thence, C.S. Lewis, shared the same sentiment in a letter to an Italian priest, which was part of a correspondence published today as *The Latin Letters of C.S. Lewis*. There, Lewis notes: "Where you write that the Pope is "the point of meeting" you almost commit (if your people will forgive my saying so) what logicians call a *petitio principii* (begging the question). For we disagree about nothing more than the authority of the Pope: on which disagreement almost all the others depend."[3]

Therefore, by the labor made to bring this work into good readable English, I hope that it will serve as a benefit to the Church. Some explanation as to the text is in order.

Those familiar with my recently published translation of *On the Marks of the Church* will note here the same format and style. Footnoting did not exist in Bellarmine's day and thus part of the labor is putting the voluminous references from the text into footnotes as well as formatting them as best I can into modern style. Many works do not have modern editions, and thus it is easier simply to give them as they are. Furthermore, all translations of the Scriptures, the Fathers, or others are my own.

Moreover, we have also tried as much as possible to stay true to the Latin, save for use of the passive voice which is used just as much as (and sometimes more than) the active voice. Still, when possible I have re-written the construction of the sentences from passive to active.

---

[2] Quoted in: Brodrick, Robert S.J., *Robert Bellarmine, Saint and Scholar*, The Newman Press, Westminster, 1961, pg. 72.

[3] *The Latin Letters of C.S. Lewis*, St. Augustine's Press, South Bend, IN, pg. 39.

Where necessary we have also added footnotes explaining some aspect of grammar or nuances lost in English and if necessary, a theological note of explanation, although we have kept these to a minimum, as of the two of us Bellarmine is clearly the brighter and there is little we could possibly add to this work.

Another word must be had on the term "canon". You will see this term used frequently by Bellarmine and his opponents. In the 16th century, "canon" had two basic meanings: matters dealing with faith, and matters dealing with Church law. In regard to the former, in the early Church, "canon" usually meant a summation of faith, and so canons were intended to define what the faithful would believe. After Constantine and the end of formal persecution, the practice developed of using a canon to refer to discipline rather than a statement of faith, though they often involved matters of faith or were held to be interpreters of divine law, hence, what must be believed. This is key in seeing why Bellarmine or his opponents cite various canons from councils and popes, and seem at times to get bogged down in them.

As to the latter, canon law was a complicated discipline, as it required a deep knowledge of the history of all canons, and which ones were in force or not, or overridden by others in this or that case. A compendium containing all applicable law would not be seen until 1917, with the culmination of the great work of Pope St. Pius X and Pope Benedict XV in producing the Code of Canon Law. We have done our best to bring clarity to something that is not as well understood today as it was then, so that one will not get lost in the seemingly endless ocean of "this canon says x, therefore," etc. The import is on what this or that canon says about the faith.

Lastly, this work would not be possible without the gracious assistance of my wife, who accepted many sufferings while I have labored on this project. Also, I would like to thank those who assisted in the editing for their perseverance through the rough grammar of my first draft. I would also like to thank Dr. Robert Sungenis, for his gracious assistance with the Hebrew that Bellarmine quotes, as I have little facility in that language. I would also like to thank Mike Church of the *Veritas Radio Network* who has graciously interviewed me to popularize this work. I also owe an unpayable debt to Maria Muckle who graciously took on the task of cleaning the Augean Stables of the first edition, which has allowed for this corrected second edition.

Finally, I would like to thank the gracious benefactors of the St. Robert Bellarmine translation project without whose financial assistance this work would not at all be possible. If you wish to contribute to that work, you can do so by visiting Mediatrix Press and going to the "Bellarmine Project" tab. May this work benefit the Holy Church, which once again has need of this great saint and teacher.

Ryan Grant
Mediatrix Press
http://www.mediatrixpress.com
Post Falls, ID
2015

Dedicatio

Omnibus benefactoribus laboris S.
Roberti Bellarmini votum esse, et praesertim
Joanni Schmieding et Josepho Gamez,
praesidio ejus remoto, hic liber fieri non
posset.

Dedicated to all the benefactors of the
St. Robert Bellarmine project, and most
especially John Schmieding and Joseph
Gamez, without whose assistance this work
would not be possible.

PREFACE

To the Books on the Supreme Pontiff
by
St. Robert Bellarmine, S.J.

Given in the Roman Gymnasium
1577

EFORE we approach the disputation on the Supreme Pontiff, I believe I must preface a few words. In the first place, on the utility and magnitude of the institution which is in dispute: thereupon, concerning those who attack the Roman Primacy in books, or even on the other side, those who fight in its defense; they have been zealous from the beginning of the Church even to our times, and at length, on the plan and order in which we should treat and also explicate the present Controversy, which is necessarily going to be long.

For indeed, the magnitude of the question on the Pope, and also its utility, are chiefly understood from two things: on the magnitude of the matter on which it is treated, and in like manner is called into doubt, and from the multitude and vigorous opposition of our adversaries. Furthermore, what exactly is treated on, when we treat on the primacy of the Pope? I will say briefly, we are dealing with the chief issue of Christian faith. Moreover, it is asked, should the Church exist any longer, or should it be dissolved and destroyed? For, what is it to ask, whether one ought to remove the foundation from the building, the shepherd from the flock, the general from the army, the sun from the stars, the head from the body, except to ask whether one should destroy the building, disperse the flock, empty out the army, darken the stars or kill the body?

Next our adversaries, that is, the heretics, since they generally disagree with themselves on doctrine no less than with us, nevertheless all agree on this, that with supreme opposition of their spirit they should oppose the See of the Roman Pontiff with their whole strength. There have never been any enemies of Christ and also his Church, who did not wage war together with this seat. It seems to me that the Prophet Isaiah foresaw and predicted these two things long ago, even in regard to the magnitude and the usefulness of the matter, when he said: *"Behold, I place in the foundations of Zion, a stone, a stone that is proved, the corner stone, precious, a foundation in the foundation.*"[1] Secondly, he foresaw the attack and opposition of the heretics, when he says of this stone: "*It is the Stone of offense, and the rock of scandal.*"[2] Although the latter citation from Isaiah is not contained in the same place as the former, (the latter are Chapter 8, the former contained in 28), nevertheless, the Apostle Paul in Chapter 9 to the Romans, and the Apostle Peter in his first epistle, Chapter 2, join all these words of the prophet together, so that no one can be in doubt whether they refer to the same end in the same manner: and although we are not ignorant that these words particularly fit Christ, nevertheless we reckon the same words are not unsuited to the vicar of Christ.

Therefore, what are the foundations of Zion? The Apostle John explains this in the Apocalypse; describing indeed all the parts of this same holy city, and also its decor, he says among the other things: "And the wall of the city, having twelve foundations, and in them the twelve names of the twelve apostles of the Lamb."[3] The foundations of Zion, therefore, are the Apostles counted among them, and a certain stone excels the rest: "Behold," he says, "I place a stone in the foundations of Zion." What this stone may be, no one is ignorant who reads the Gospel. Since, in point of fact, one of the twelve apostles was named Simon, and his name was changed by the Lord, Who willed, that he should be called Peter in place of Simon, I say a rock: accordingly in the Aramaic language, which our Lord most certainly used, this is none other than *Cephas,* that is *Petra,* or to be better accommodated to us Latins, *Petrus,* or *you are rock, and on this rock I will build my Church.* Behold the stone in the foundation of Zion. But of what sort do you reckon this stone? *The stone,* he says, *proved, the corner, precious, established in the foundation.* The proven stone: accordingly this rock is tested by every kind of proof, for all the gates of hell attack her.

And, while I will omit the persecutions of the Jews and also of the heathen, which were common both to this seat and with the rest of the Church; it must be noted in the first place, that all the heretics make war upon this seat, not just once, nor twice, but repeatedly and always with renewed armies. Thereupon the rivalry and pride of the Greeks has not yet ceased to wage war on this seat, whose religion with its dignity they have lost since being oppressed by the

---

[1] "Ecce ego ponam in fundamentis Sion lapidem, lapidem probatum, angularem, pretiosum, in fundamento fundatum." Isaiah 28: 16.

[2] "Lapidem offensionis, et petram scandali esse dicit." Isaiah 8: 14.

[3] "Et murus civitatis habens fundamenta duodecim, et in ipsis duodecim nomina duodecim apostolorum Agni." Apocolypse 21: 14.

Turkish emperor. Then the most powerful Christian emperors, and what is more, under the name of religion and piety, have tried to overturn and overthrow this seat, from whence they also obtained the scepter of the Roman Empire.

Moreover, you are not ignorant of the tragedies in the Church which Henry IV, Henry V, Otho IV, and above all, Frederick II and several others stirred up at different times. And, as if this were a little matter, Satan has stirred up the Roman people to rise up against Popes. The very serious epistle of Blessed Bernard to the Senate and the Roman people is still extant, in which he tried to calm their sedition against Pope Eugene which was counseled by the devil. However, very turbulent and pernicious seditions of this sort whose aims were to destroy the Roman Pontiff have endured not for days, nor months, but years, nay more, even centuries.

At the present very serious schisms have come about and many of them in themselves over the Roman Pontiffs, to whom they could not yield in any way, and at length labored even to destroy the See of Peter, as if it were not the strongest and most proven rock, established by God as the foundation of Zion, who said himself: "*Even the gates of hell will not prevail against it.*" Moreover, in the event that we might reckon that this seat has stood for so long on account of the incorrupt life and the untouched morals of the supreme pontiffs, we find that God permitted that certain popes who could scarcely be called good should at some time hold and reign in this seat. Rightly, such were Stephen VI, Leo V, Christopher I, Sergius III, John XII, and not a few others, if the things that we read about their lives and deeds in the writings of the historians of those times are true.

Therefore, such accounts that the heretics labor to collect on the vices of certain pontiffs ultimately comes to nothing. Truly, we recognize and affirm that their vices were not few: rather the glory of this seat was merely distant, obscured or diminished in their vices, in order that it could be more forcefully increased and magnified by the same. Here, we understand that the Roman Pontificate has existed for so long not by human counsel, prudence, or strength, but because this rock was so fortified by the Lord, divinely founded, surrounded by guards of angels, by a unique providence of God, and fortified by his protection, that the gates of hell should not be able to prevail against it by any means, whether by "those gates" is meant the persecution of tyrants, or the madness of heretics, the fury of schismatics, or sins and outrages. The proven stone, therefore, God placed in the foundation of Zion: not only proven, but even the corner stone, a stone which connects two walls. This seems to me to prove the distinction that was placed between the pontiff of Christians and of the Jews. The latter was indeed a foundation stone, but not a corner stone: nor indeed did it hold up two walls, but merely one. Rather, our stone is the corner stone; for both Jews and Gentiles are joined together like two walls, and they make one Christian Church which stand upon this one corner stone.

Isaiah adds, "*even precious.*" In one word, a treasure is meant, such that is derived most copiously in every Church from the See of Peter and in the greatest abundance. Indeed, from what place were the missionaries sent to Germany, France, England and other far away lands, that they might preach the gospel, except from this seat? Where did bishops, being cast out from their sees throughout the whole world, seek refuge, as the famous Athanasius, and Peter of Alexandria, Paul, and Chrysostom of Constantinople; where did they discover help and refuge, except in this See? From where do we have the explication of dogmas, the rites of the Sacraments, the communication of indulgences, except from this See?

Wherefore, that I should pass over the rest, which would take a very long time to enumerate, where is the consensus in doctrine, the bond of peace, the unity of Faith, where is the very salvation and life of religion, unless it is from this see? Otherwise, why is it that the heretics of our time, when they have sufficiently obtained many and even great lands, such as England, Scotland, Denmark, Norway, Sweden, Germany, Poland, Bohemia and not a small part of Hungary, have not yet been able to compel one general Council that they all might agree on one point of doctrine? Why even the Greeks, since the year 800, in which they cut themselves off from the See of Peter and the Roman Church, for almost 800 years have not once celebrated a Council to argue mutually among themselves for agreement and peace? When we, on the other hand, have had around ten general Councils, and at that very frequently, the last of which was in this time, in which the Lutherans bitterly contended among themselves, and publicly despaired of the unity and the supreme agreement of the celebrated fathers. What can be the reason for such a difference, except that all of them lack a leader and ruler, who alone can and ought to confirm all the brethren in Faith, and retain the whole Church in unity?

At length the prophet adds: "*It has been founded in the foundation.*" What, indeed, is founded in the foundation, except a foundation after the principle foundation, that is, a secondary foundation, not the first? Accordingly, the first and particular foundation of the Church we know to be Christ, about which the Apostle said: "*No man can place another foundation, apart from that which has been placed, which is Christ Jesus.*"[4] But after Christ, the foundation is Peter, and unless it is through Peter, one does not reach unto Christ. Although the heretics

---

[4]   1 Cor. 3:11.

talk about Christ, and boast that they follow his word and doctrine, nevertheless it is unavoidable that, as Leo the Great says, one is exiled from the divine mystery who will have dared to recede from solidity of Peter.

The See of Peter, therefore, is the proven stone, the corner stone, the precious stone, founded in the foundation, and it is indeed so for us: but on the other hand, to our adversaries, the heretics, it is nothing other than the stone of offense, and the stone of shame. Although they ought to build themselves upon it into a holy temple in the Lord, instead these, like truly blind and insane men, dash themselves against it. It goes against human wisdom, against their pride, for those who in their own eyes are experienced, that one mortal, in whom there is no erudition, nor goodness, nor any other reason they should judge themselves inferior to him, should be called the foundation of the Church, above which, a building has been placed, at the same time vast, sublime, and immense. For this reason it displeases them, because they do not understand, what may be not only easy for God, but even glorious to choose from the weak, that he might confound the strong. Nor do they seem to have noticed that this is God's way, that through faith and humility he leads to wisdom and glory.

Thus it is certain, without a doubt, that through the foolishness of preaching a crucified man, believers are saved: thus he chose fishermen, that he might convert emperors; thus in abject and common things, water, oil, bread and the species of wine, he bound the strength of the Sacraments, and the endless treasures of heavenly gifts: that while we are subjected to abject things by humility and faith, we are carried to the lot of the sons of God, and to the consort of the very divine nature. Nevertheless, the heretics close their eyes to all these things, and do not cease to fury and rage against the salutary rock, and against the counsel of God, that it should be to them the stone of offense and the rock of scandal. Indeed the Donatists named this seat the chair of pestilence: Berengarius called the pontiff of this seat the *pompificem* and *pulpificem*;[5] the Waldenses 'the whore clothed in purple'; Wycliff called it the synagogue of Satan; the Lutherans, Calvinists and Anabaptists contend it is the seat of Antichrist. And although they might disagree with us on many other matters, nevertheless, from this cause alone, have they wished to impose upon us a name. They call us nothing other than Papists, as if only, or particularly, they reckon we err in defending the supreme pontiff. And they do not reckon themselves to be able to give someone any greater insult, than if they might call him a Pope. On the other hand every place found to be filthy and sordid, and

---

[5] These are a Latin play on words for the word Pontifex (bishop or Pope), meaning "ostentatious Bishop" or "fleshy Bishop," roughly. They have no equivalents in English. -Translators note.

whatsoever is found to be foul and ugly in the nature of things, they begin to call according to some derivation of the term "Pope."

Therefore, this is the spirit of Luther and Calvin and the like against the Pope, that although they indeed write sharply and petulantly on all other matters, when it comes to the Supreme Pontiff, they do so violently, by loading on insults, calumnies, jeers: that he is driven by mad spirits, and is filled with a wicked demon, or rather, that he has lain aside human nature, and clothed himself with a demonic one. Besides, even if they would wish to establish a leader (naturally they refuse), they are weak and useless, but the supreme pontificate is the firmest rock, not them. For while they strike at this seat, that they should try to break it, instead they shall be broken by it: "Whosoever will have fallen" the Lord said, "upon this stone, will be broken; upon whom this stone should fall, it will break him."[6] And Pope Leo the Great declared: "Whoever thinks it wise to deny the first place to this seat, truly in no way can he decrease its dignity, but being puffed up with the spirit of his pride, he shall sink himself into hell."[7]

As some vast boulder, which stands out in the midst of the sea above the waves and tides is never thrown down nor moved, although again and again the blowing of the winds and the waves of the sea rush upon it with great force, but instead all these dissipated and broke: in like fashion when the See of Peter has been struck so many times already by the Jews, the heathen, heretics, rebels, and schismatics with incredible fury, nearly all of these were either consumed or conquered, or made prostrate, for over 1500 years she has stood immovable: and always (as St. Augustine said) while heretics howled around, it obtained the summit of authority. Since these things are so, unless I am mistaken, you will see the magnitude of this controversy we have proposed to explain.

I come now to it, which we have placed in the second point. The first ones who attacked the primacy of the Roman Pontiff in earnest appear to have been the Greeks. Truly, already then in the year of our Lord 381, they wished that the bishop of Constantinople, who as yet was not even a patriarch, should be set before the Eastern Patriarchs, and be made second to the Roman Pontiff. This can be seen in the second Ecumenical Council, Can. 5. Thereafter in the year 451, the Greeks, not being content with the matter, tried to make the bishop of Constantinople equal to the Roman Pontiff. For, in the Council of Chalcedon, act. 16, the Greek Fathers defined, although, not without fraud, since the Roman legates were absent, that the bishopric of Constantinople ought to be so close

---

[6] Matthew 21: 44.

[7] *Loc. Cit.*

to the Roman See, that still it should have equal privileges. Not content with this, in the times of St. Gregory, and of his predecessor Pelagius II, around the year 600 they began to call the Bishop of Constantinople "Ecumenical," that is, of the whole world, or universal bishop. The witness of this affair is St. Gregory himself in letters, many of which he wrote on this subject in a short time to John the bishop of Constantinople, to the Emperor Maurice, to the Empress Constance, and to the rest of the patriarchs of the East.

Next, in the year 1054, they openly pronounced that the Bishop of Rome had lost his position on account of the addition of the phrase *Filioque* to the Nicene-Constantinopolitan Creed, based on a judgment from the Council of Ephesus which had forbidden it, and further pronounced the Bishop of Constantinople to be the first of all the bishops.[8] There is even a little book extant in Greek written by Nilos Cabásilas, the archbishop of Thessalonika, against the primacy of the Roman Pontiff, which recently Illyricus brought into the light from unknown darkness, and translated into Latin.

On the side of the Latins, the first were the Waldenses, who removed themselves from obedience to the Roman Pontiff. The Waldensians arose in the year 1170, as Reynerius writes, and they flourished for 300 years. Then, in the year 1300, from the witness of Matthew Palmerio in his Chronicle, there existed those who were called the *Fraticelli*, who apart from other errors, held this: that the authority of Peter had long since ceased in the Roman Church, and was transferred to their sect.[9] Not long after, in the time of Juan de Torquemada who witnesses it, Marsilius of Padua arose, and John of Janduno, who held that not only are all bishops equal to the Roman Pontiff, but even all priests.

Thereupon, around the Year of Our Lord 1390, arose John Wycliff, and Jan Hus followed him, whose opinions against the Apostolic See can be read in the Council of Constance, sess. 8, and 15.

At length in our century Martin Luther, and so many heretics after him appeared, who tried to undermine the Roman Pontificate with all their strength and every effort of their spirit. And the summation of their doctrine is; the Roman Bishop was at some time shepherd and preacher of the Roman Church, and one from the rest, not one above the rest: but now it is nothing other than

---

[8] See also Sigebert in his *Chronicle*, and it is gathered otherwise from the epistles of Pope Leo IX.

[9] See Juan de Torquemada, lib. 4 *Eccles.* P. 2, cap. 37.

Antichrist.[10]

For a while now, those who wrote on behalf of the authority of the Supreme Pontiff have been found in all nations; but lest by chance someone might find himself passed over, I will not avail myself to enumerate them all, but merely those whose works I could get my hands on. From Poland we have one, which is like unto many others, obviously that of Cardinal Hosius, in his works *in explicatione Symboli*, ch. 26, and in book 2 *Contra Brentium*, and in his book *de auctoritate Summi Pontificis*.

From France we have two books: Reymond Ruffus in his book *adver. Carol. Molin. Pro sum pontif.* and Robert Arboricensis in *1. Tom. De utriusque glad. potest.*

From Germany we have John of Eck in three books *de prim. S. Petri*; John Faber *in refutat. Lib. Luth. de pontif. potest.* John Cochlaeus *in 4 Philippica*; Gaspar Schatzger *in Controvers.* Conrad Clingium *lib. 3 de loc. comm.*

From Lower Germany six: John Driedo *lib 4, ch. 3, pg. 2, de Scriptura et dogmata Ecclesiae.* Albert Pighius *lib. 3, 4, and 5,* Eccles. hier. John of Louvain *de perpet. Cath. Petri protect. Et firmit*; John Latomus in his book *de primatu Petri*; William Lindanus in his book *Panopliae*; John of Burgundy *in compendio Concert. tit. 31.*

From England six: Thomas Waldens in book 2 *doctrinalis Fid.* Art 1 and 3. John of Rochester [St. John Fisher] *in refut arctic* 25. Cardinal Reginald Pole in his book *de sum. Pontif.* and book 1 and 2 *to king Henry VIII*; Aalan Copum *Dialogo* 1. Nicolaus Sanders in his book *de visib. monarch.* Thomas Stapleton in book 6 *Controvers.*

From Spain seven: Juan de Torquemada book 2 *de Eccles.* Alphonse de

---

[10] See Luther in his book *de potestate Papae*, et in *assert*, art. 25. Cf. Philip Melanchthon (if he is indeed the author of the book) in *de potestate et primatu papae*, or *de regno Antichristi nomine* written in the name of the Smalkaldic Council. John Calvin in lib. 4 of the Institutes, Chapter 6, and the rest. Brenz *in Confessione Wirtemb.* Chapter on the Supreme Pontiff, and *in the Prolegomena against Peter of Soto.* Matthew Illyricus *in Cent.* 1, lib. 2, cap. 7, col. 524, et sequ. And ch. 10, col. 558, and thereupon in individual centuries, Chapter 7. For the same author, in the book on the primacy of the Pope, and in another *de hist. Concert. Papae* and *Concilii VI Carthaginens.*

Castro book 12 *contra haer.* Melchior Cano *lib. 6 de locis Theologicis*; Peter of Soto *in defens. Suae confess.* Ch. 74 even to the end. Francis Horantius, lib. 6, *de locis Cathol.* Francis of Toledo in *lib. contra Anthony Sadeelem.* And Gregory of Valentia who recently even wrote on the same argument in his *Analysi Fid. Cathol.* Par. 7 and 8.

From Italy 8: St. Thomas *in Opusc. cont. Graec.*; Blessed Augustine *Triumphum Anconitanum*, in sum. De potest. Papae; St. Anthony 3. Part. Tit. 22, *sum. Theol.*; Thomas Cajetan *de Instit. et auctor. rom. pontif.*; Thomas Compeggio in a book of the same title; John Anthony Delphinus lib. 1 and 2 *de Ecclesia.*

From Greece one: Gennadius Scholarius *in defensione cap. 5.*

Now, however, for what pertains to the order and disposition of the proposed disputation. It contains two particular parts; one on the institution of the supreme pontificate, *i.e.* the ecclesiastical monarchy, the other on the office and power of the Supreme Pontiff. And in the first part six questions are contained.
First: Whether monarchy might be the best form of government?
Second: Whether the rule of the Church should be through monarchy?
Third: Was St. Peter the first spiritual monarch of the Catholic Church?
Fourth: Whether the same Blessed Peter came [to Rome], and also established the same pontifical see to remain perpetually?
Fifth: Whether the Bishop of Rome succeeds St. Peter, not only in the Roman episcopate, but even in the primacy of the whole Church? Wherein, with respect to this question, certain other aspects [of the papacy] are also recalled, which when they are joined together, cannot be separated from it in any respect: such as, hearing the appeals from the whole world; establishing, confirming, transferring, punishing and even the duty of removing bishops, and several other attributes of this sort.
Sixth: Whether the same Roman Bishop could at some time have gone from being the vicar of Christ to being Antichrist?

The second part of the Controversy embraces six questions.
First: Should the Roman Pontiff make decisions on controversies of faith and Morals?
Second: Whether he can err in that judgment?
Thirdly: Can the Supreme Pontiff make laws which bind the consciences of men, and at the same time, punish those who break them?
Fourthly: Whether ecclesiastical jurisdiction was so consigned to the

Supreme Pontiff alone by Christ, that it is derived to the rest of the Church only through him?

Fifthly: Whether apart from spiritual jurisdiction the same Pope might have some temporal power, on account of the fact that he is Pope?

Sixthly: Whether he can have, and in the very matter does have, the rule by donation, of some temporal empire in certain provinces or regions?

Servo T. X.

Roberto Bellarmini.

ON THE ROMAN PONTIFF

BOOK I
ON THE ECCLESIASTICAL MONARCHY OF THE
ROMAN PONTIFF

CHAPTER I

The Question is Proposed: What Might be the best System of Government?[1]

HERE can be no doubt that our Savior Jesus Christ could and wished that his Church should govern by that plan and mode that would be the best and most useful. There are three forms of government: monarchy, that is, of one prince, the contrary vice to which is tyranny; aristocracy, that is the rule of the best men, to which is opposed an oligarchy; and democracy, that is, the rule by the whole people, which does not rarely fall into sedition.

The chief philosophers teach this, namely Plato, and Aristotle, and they do so for a good reason.[2] For, if the multitude must be governed, it cannot be done without being governed in some way according to those three modes: either one is put in charge of the commonwealth, or some from many, or everyone altogether. If one, it will be a monarchy, if some from many, it will be an aristocracy; if altogether everyone, then a democracy.

Moreover, although these three might only be simple forms of government, nevertheless, they can be mixed among themselves and from such a mixture four other forms of government are produced. One combined from all three; the second from monarchy and aristocracy; the third from monarchy and democracy: the last from democracy and aristocracy. That being so constituted, the first question arises, what might be the best form of government from those seven?

Now John Calvin, in order to altogether block every way in which one usually arrives by disputation to constitute ecclesiastical monarchy, places aristocracy and democracy before all other forms; an aristocracy from single forms, though in fact it is a mixed form, a government tempered according to his own mind. Most of all, he wished monarchy to be regarded as the worst of all, especially if it were constituted throughout the world or in the Church. His words from the *Institutes* are these: "Should it be as they would have it, that it is good and also useful that the whole world be comprised by one monarchy, which is still very absurd, but should it be so, still I will never concede that it

---

[1]   Here, the modern reader, particularly in the English speaking world where the benefits of "democracy" or "republicanism" are accepted *a priori,* should not become bogged down with a particular disagreement with Bellarmine on the issue of monarchy being the best form of government. In the first place, he is arguing largely from Aristotle in regard to what is objectively the best form of government, though he certainly was not a republican. Secondly, Bellarmine is using the argument for monarchy to buttress his defense of the monarchical government of the Church. -Translator's note.

[2]   Plato *in Politic.,* Aristotle book 3 *Polit.* ch. 5, and book 8.; *Ethic.* Ch. 10.

should flourish in the governance of the Church."[3] And again: "If in itself those three forms of government are considered which the philosophers posit, I myself can hardly deny either aristocracy, or a form combined with popular government, by far excels every other form of the state."[4] Thereafter he showed two arguments; one brought out from experience, the second from divine authority: "It was always sanctioned by experience itself, not only because the Lord confirmed it by his authority but even more, in that aristocracy is nearest to the form of government he established among the Israelites."

We, on the other hand, follow St. Thomas and other Catholic theologians in that, from the three simple forms of government we place monarchy before the rest, although on account of the corruption of human nature we reckon monarchy blended with aristocracy and democracy to be more useful for men in this time than a simple monarchy; provided the first parts should be of monarchy, it should have the second aristocracy, and in the last place should be democracy.

To be sure, in order that the whole matter can more easily be explained and confirmed by arguments, we will take up our teaching on the three propositions. The first proposition: among the simple forms the most excellent is monarchy. Secondly, blended government including all three forms, on account of the corruption of human nature is more useful than simple monarchy. Thirdly, after we have excluded all other circumstances, simple monarchy simply and absolutely excels.

---

[3]   *Instit.*, ch. 6, § 9.

[4]   *Ibid.*, 20 § 8.

CHAPTER II

The First Proposition is Proved, that Simple Monarchy is Superior to Simple Aristocracy and Democracy

LET us proceed from the first. We do not especially compare monarchy with mixed forms of government, nor do we place it before all mixed and simple forms; but we assert this; if some simple form of government must necessarily be chosen, without a doubt monarchy should be chosen. Now we will prove it by these arguments.

Firstly: all the old Hebrew, Greek, and Latin writers, theologians, philosophers, orators, historians and poets agree with this opinion. First we look to Philo from the Jewish theologians, praising the teaching of Homer: "That for many to command is evil, there should be one king, for [rule] pertains not to citizens and men more than to the world and God."[1]

Among the Greeks, blessed Justin teaches that the rule of many is harmful, and on the contrary, the rule of one is more useful and beneficial: "The rule of one is truly freed from wars and dissensions and is usually free."[2] Also St. Athanasius, "Truly we have said that a multitude of gods is a nullity of gods: so also, necessarily a multitude of princes makes it that there should appear to be no prince: however where there is no prince, there confusion is absolutely born."[3]

Among the Latins, St. Cyprian teaches the same thing, and he proves it most eminently from the very fact that monarchy should be the best and most natural government, because God is one. "For the divine authority, let us borrow from an earthly example: In what way has an alliance of power ever begun with trust, or ended without blood?"[4] St. Jerome says: "One emperor, one judge of the province. When Rome was built, she could not have two brothers as kings at the same time."[5] Lastly, one can consult St. Thomas.[6]

Now from the philosophers. Plato says: "One dominion has been arranged for good laws, the law of these is best; that governance in which not many command, we ought to esteem as the middle: the administration of many others

---

[1] *De confus. Linguar.*

[2] *In orat. Exhort. Ad gent.*

[3] *In orat. Adver. Idol.*

[4] *Tract. De Idol. Vanit.*

[5] Epist. Ad Rusticum monach.

[6] in I Q 103, art. 3; and book 4 of the Contra Gentiles, ch. 76.

in all matters is weak, and also frail."[7] Aristotle followed Plato, and after he enumerated these three forms of rule, he adds these words: "A kingdom is the best of these, a republic the worst."[8] Seneca said that Marcus Brutus did not act with sufficient prudence when he killed Julius Caesar in the hope of liberty; and giving the reason, he says: "Since the best state of the citizenry is to be under one just king."[9]

Next, Plutarch wrote a whole work on monarchy, and on the rest of the forms to rule the multitude, in which he expressed his opinion: "If the choice of electing were conceded, one should not choose anything else than the power of one." And again, Plutarch wrote the same thing on Solon of Athens, when he said that at Athens many seditions arose when democracy flourished, and immediately adds: "One method, however, appeared to be left over to safety and quiet, if matters would have been brought to the rule of one."

Among orators, Isocrates, in that oration which is entitled "Nicocles," contends to show this very thing for many reasons. But John Stobaeus marked it down in this title, ὅτι κάλλιστον ἡ μοναρχία; and also in that discourse of Hesiod, Euripides, Serinus, Ecphantus and many others, he produces testimonies to confirm this very thing.

Herodotus, in his *Histories* book 3, which is entitled *Thalia*, when he brought to light the slaughter of the Magi who had occupied the kingdom of Persia, also shows the disputation that was held among the princes on establishing a republic. He had departed from their disputation, and after shaking off the opinions of those who strove for aristocracy or a commonwealth, by the consensus of all, with only one exception, monarchy was judged to be the most useful and excellent, and on that account it was retained in Persia.

Thereupon among the poets, Homer in book 2 of the *Iliad*, advanced that opinion celebrated by nearly all writers, ὀυκ ἀγαθὸν πολυκοιρανίη, εἰς κοίρανος ἔστω εἰς βασιλεύς.[10] Calvin responds to that testimony of Homer, whose opinion alone, among so many, he objects to, says: "It is easy to respond: monarchy is not even praised in this sense either from the Homeric Ulysses, or from others, as if one ought to rule the whole world by means of authority; but they wish to indicate that a kingdom cannot take two and power (as he says) is an impatient

---

[7] *Politica* ultra med.

[8] *Ethica* book 8, ch. 10.

[9] *De benef.*, book 2.

[10] "It is not good that there be many; [in war] there must be one chief and one king." *Iliad*, book II, line 204-205.

consort."[11]

But certainly, if it was easy for Calvin to respond, it is easier for us to respond to Calvin. For, either he says nothing, or he says what we say, or he speaks falsity and contradicts himself. If, when he says one kingdom cannot have two men, he means to place the force on the word *kingdom* and means a kingdom properly so called cannot take two men since if there were two, there will not be a kingdom properly so called, (since a kingdom is properly the supreme power of one man), then really he says nothing altogether, but only spreads darkness over the inexperienced by the ambiguity of words. For to say in that sense, a kingdom does not take two, means the same as if someone would say, the rule of one is not the rule of two: and one man is not two men: nothing in this pronouncement is due to the wisdom of Ulysses.

Yet, if he does not put the force on that word, but rather he understands by kingdom the multitude who should be ruled, then he says the very thing which we are saying. On this we assert that monarchy excels a commonwealth and aristocracy, because the multitude is not ruled agreeably by many, and power is an impatient consort.

If therefore, he means for a kingdom to be understood not as a multitude but some individual province, or one scanty kingdom: that the sense might be, that one king is to be given to one province, nevertheless he is not to be judge of the whole world: then he speaks falsely, and contradicts himself. For the Homeric Ulysses does not dispute over establishing a republic in some individual province; rather he spoke to the whole army of the Greeks, who were then fighting at Troy, in which army there were many nations, many princes, and as many kings, and he affirmed it was not fitting for that whole multitude to be ruled by many, but by one. Therefore, the sense of this famous passage can be none other than; in whichever individual multitude you like, there ought to be one primary ruler; because he holds place equally in a scanty kingdom, and in the greatest command; for in one scanty kingdom there ought to be one king, not because it is scanty, but because it is one.

For this reason, if some kingdom was great, as was Assyria, or that of Cyrus, or even of Alexander or Augustus, it was one, it ought to have one prince, and seeing that the Church is one, "There will be no end of his kingdom,"[12] and, "In the days of their kings the God of heaven will rouse, because he is not overthrown;" on that account there even ought to be one king.

Next, Calvin even opposes himself. Accordingly, not only does he consider

---

[11]   *Instit.*, lib.4., ch. 6 §8.

[1]   *Doctr. Fidei*, lib. 2, art. 1, ch. 7.

that a monarchy over the whole world would not be advantageous, but not even over some individual city or the Church, as is clearly gathered from book 4 of the *Institutes*,[13] where he bestows all ecclesiastical power upon a body of elders; and from the same book,[14] where he praises those cities which having thrown off the yoke of princes, are governed by senate and people, as the republic of Geneva. Therefore, since Calvin leaves no place for monarchy, he himself saw how well he ought to respond to so many and such serious authors who praise the opinion of Homer.

Another reason is deduced from divine authority, which shows in three ways that monarchy is the best system of government. The first, by the establishment of the human race, God made from one every kind of man, as the Apostle says, indeed he did not produce both men and women equally from the ground, but man from the ground and the woman from the man. Showing the reason for this, St. John Chrysostom says that this is so that there should not be democracy among men, but a kingdom. And certainly if many men were produced from the ground at the same time they all would have been equally princes over their posterity; were that the case we could rightly doubt whether the rule of one pleased God. But now, since he made the whole human race from one, and he wished everyone to depend on one clearly, it appears to mean the rule of one is commended more than the governance of many.

Next, God showed his opinion not only when he inserted the natural propensity to monarchial rule among men, but even among nearly all things. There can be no doubt, whether the natural propensity must be referred back to the author of nature. Moreover, he even declares that in some house naturally the governance of the spouse, children, servants and all other affairs naturally pertains to one head of the household; it is, before all other forms of government, the rule of one. In like manner, a great part of the world is governed by kings. Apart from that, monarchy is by far older than the system of republics. "In the beginning, the rule of nations and empires was in the hands of kings."[15]

Therefore, it appears all living things aspire to the rule of one. St. Cyprian speaks thus: "There is one king for bees, one leader among flocks, and one rule among rams."[16] St. Jerome adds "And cranes follow one by the order of the

---

[13] *Instit.*, lib. 4, ch. 41, § 6.

[14] *Ibid.*, ch. 20, §8.

[15] Justin, lib. 1.

[16] *In tract., de Idol.* Vanit.

litter."[17] Calvin, however, mocks these testimonies, for he says: "On this matter, if it pleased God that they offer proofs from cranes and bees, who always choose one leader for themselves, there cannot be many proofs. Rightly, I accept the testimony they give, but do bees from all over the world merely choose one king? In their beehives are contained individual kings, so also in cranes, each flock has its own king; what else does this evince than that to each church ought to be attributed its own bishop?"[18]

This response from Calvin is easily refuted. For the Church is as *one sheepfold* (John 10), not many sheepfolds: thus it can also be called one beehive and one flock; and on that account, just as there is one king for bees, and cranes follow one in the rank of the litter, so the universal Church ought to have and follow one leader and primary teacher. Thereupon cranes and bees are not of that nature that they can unite when they are absent and placed far away from the union of spirit; and on that account it is little wonder that they do not flock together throughout the world to choose one king: and in this matter that each of their flocks have their own king shows clearly enough that the government of one is natural.

For if we evince from these examples brought from very authoritative Fathers, as Calvin says that to each church ought to be attributed its own bishop, why will he not suffer bishops except maybe in name only, but instead attributes all ecclesiastical power to a body of elders?

All of these aside, the form of rule which God himself wished to confirm by his authority, can be gathered here chiefly from that state which he established amongst the people of the Hebrews. He did not (as Calvin says but cannot prove), make the government of the Hebrews an aristocracy, or a government of many, but was plainly a monarchy. The princes among the Hebrews were first of all patriarchs, as Abraham, Jacob, Jude and the rest; thereupon generals, as Moses and Joshua; then judges, as Samuel, Sampson, and others; afterwards kings, as Saul, David and Solomon; thereafter again generals, as Zerubbabel and the Maccabees.

Further, the deeds of the patriarchs show they were provided with royal power. Abraham waged war against four kings,[19] and we do not read anywhere that he received full power from any senate, nor any decree from such a body. Judah judged his daughter in law who was accused of adultery, with fire,[20] and

---

[17] *Epist. Ad Rustic.*

[18] Lib. 4 *Instit.* Ch. 6 § 8.

[19] Genesis 14:13-17.

[20] Genesis 38:7.

he did not consult or ask any senate. Moses, as a true and supreme prince of the Jewish people, commanded many thousands of Jews to be killed on account of the golden calf,[21] which they had erected one day. We do not read of any decree of a senate, or that a plebiscite was held. The same thing can altogether be said of the judges, who received no faculty from a senate or the people, and waged wars that they wished and gave men over to be killed. Certainly Gideon, after the victory over the Medianites, killed seventy men in the city of Socoth, and destroyed the tower of Phanuel.[22]

Next, over the fields and those who attended them, the leaders of the Jews were entrusted with a supreme and also royal authority that is so clear that it is not necessary to prove. Therefore, it remains to be seen where Calvin read that the government of the Jews was by the aristocrats and the people, not usually governed by any one particular prince.

By chance, one will object that we have in the first book of Kings (Samuel), Chapter 8, where the Israelites are reproved by God, because they demanded a king. For, if God was not pleased to establish a king for their government, how believable is it that generals and judges were established by God with royal power?

We respond: someone can be put in charge of a state with supreme power in two ways: first, as a king and lord, who depends on no one; the second that for a king or a primary general, someone is indeed in charge of the whole people, but who, nevertheless, is himself subject to a king.

Therefore, God had in this second manner established the government of the Jews in the time of generals and judges that he should, without any doubt, be the proper and particular king of that people, and nevertheless, because they were men, and lacked a visible ruler, and one whom they could go to and appeal, he placed before them some man as for a king, who by no means depended upon the people who were subjected to him, but upon the true king, God alone. Hence, to Samuel: "They have not cast you off, but me, lest I should rule over them."[23] And with the Apostle: "Moses was faithful in the whole of his house as a slave."[24]

However, because the Jews were not content in this state of government, they wished to have a king in that prior manner, who not only should command all as one, but even make generals and judges, and even should possess the

---

[21]   Exodus 32: 26-28.

[22]   Judges 8: 8-10.

[23]   1 Kings (1 Samuel) 8.

[24]   Hebrews 3.

whole kingdom as his own, and transmit to his sons and grandsons the inheritance. On that account, they were rightly condemned and castigated by the Lord. Nor did that desire of having their own king so displease God that he commanded them to apply a rule by many, or to adapt to the spirit of aristocracy, rather he designated a king as the best for them, and afterwards saved and protected both their king and their kingdom for a long time, until it remained as a duty.

The last reason follows, which is deduced from the enumeration of those properties that everyone holds makes the best government in fact. That first property is order. In the very matter, if it is a better government, it is because it has been more ordered; however monarchy is more ordered than aristocracy, or democracy, thus it can be proved. All order has been placed in it that some man should be in charge, others should be subject: nor indeed is order recognized among equals, but rather among superiors and inferiors. Where there is monarchy, there all things altogether have some order, when there might be no man who is not subjected to someone, excepting he who has care of all things. For this reason there is supreme order in the Catholic Church, where the people are subject to their pastors, pastors to bishops, bishops to metropolitans, metropolitans to primates, primates to the supreme pontiff, the supreme pontiff to God. But where governance is in the hands of aristocrats, indeed the people have their own order when they are subjected to the aristocrats, but the aristocrats have none among themselves. Democracy lacks order in a far greater degree, since all citizens are of the same condition, and they are all judged to be of authority in the commonwealth.

Another property is the acquisition of its proper end. There cannot be any doubt, whether that form of ruling the multitude would be better that more fittingly and easily acquires its proposed end. The end of government, however, is the unity of the citizens among themselves, and peace, which that union appears principally to be centered on that all might think the same, wish the same and follow the same. They will obtain it much more certainly and easily if one must be obeyed, rather than many; for it can scarcely happen that many, of whom one does not depend on the other, might make judgments about matters in the same way. Therefore, when there are many who rule the multitude then one or another commands something or will not suffer someone, or in various pursuits the people necessarily become divided, but this can scarcely happen when it is the duty of only one to command.

Use confirms this same thing, and experience is the teacher of things. Accordingly, in Ancient Rome under the kings dissensions are rarely read amongst the citizens. After the kings were expelled, however, when a magistrate governed the republic for many years, it was a rare year in which the patricians did not contend with the plebeians, and at length they progressed even to civil strife so that in a certain measure that most powerful republic perished at its own hands. It even happened that there was never a greater and longer peace enjoyed in the roman state than under the emperor Augustus, who established the first stable monarchy at Rome.

The third property is strength and power of a state. That governance which in the judgment of all excels the rest, is the one which makes the state more powerful and stronger. It is a stronger state in which there is a greater peace and concord among the citizens, indeed the combined strength dissipated among them is itself stronger; but a greater unity is where all depend upon one, than where they depend upon many, as was proved above; consequently, monarchy makes both a stronger state, and is itself the best government.

Experience agrees: accordingly from the four greatest empires, three rose under kings, obviously the Assyrians, Persians and Greeks: the Roman Empire is the exception, which rose under popular domination, but even then they could not preserve it in great disturbances of affairs without a dictator that is, a king established *pro tempore*. Afterwards it flourished under Augustus more than it had at any time under the Republic.

The fourth property is stability and long duration. Certainly it cannot be denied that that government is better which is more stable and long lasting, but monarchy—not aristocracy or democracy—endured the longest. But if it is a question of external force, we already showed that without a doubt it is stronger than the rest.

Now it remains to be seen whether monarchy is less given to emergencies and change than any other form of government with there being no external force applied. It is so proved: "Every kingdom divided against itself will be destroyed,"[25] as Christ says in St. Matthew. But it is more difficult for monarchy to be divided than any other form of rule. It is divided less easily because it is more one; but being more one it is itself a simpler oneness than the multitude agreeing as one. Though truly the monarchy, is one in itself, and naturally, nothing other than one, still the multitude agreeing as one is only one from its character, in itself it is many; therefore, monarchy which depends upon one man, can be less easily torn asunder or destroyed than aristocracy or democracy, which depend upon the multitude agreeing as one body.

For example, the monarchy of the Assyrians from Ninus to Sardanaptum endured for 1240 years without interruption, as Eusebius teaches in his Chronicle; or 1300 as Justin gathers in book 1, or beyond 1400 as Diodorus

---

[25]   *Omne regnum in se divisum desolabitur.* Matthew 12:25.

wishes us to believe.[26] Thus, this kingdom so endured that there was always a son as successor of the dead king in the kingdom, if it is true what Vellejus Paterculus wrote in the first volume of his history.

But the kingdom of the Scythians, which is held to be the oldest of all, could not be destroyed by any external enemy, as Justin writes in book 2, nor was it dissolved in itself at any time, for around thousands of years that kingdom stood; there is no republic which was ever as long lived or as stable.

Certainly the most powerful republic of the Romans could scarcely count 480 years, as many years from the expulsion of the kings even to the reign of Julius Caesar. But under the monarchs in the east from Caesar even to the last Constantine, it endured for 1495 years without interruption; in the west, however, from the same Caesar even to Augustulus around 500 years, and from Charlemagne even to the present emperor it has been nearly 800. But for the 480 years that democracy flourished in the Roman Empire, the republic was not always ruled in the same manner: from the beginning yearly consuls were created, a little after they added tribunes, then the consuls and tribunes were taken up, creating the *decemviri*; after a year these were thrown out, and again the consuls and tribunes were recalled not rarely, even dictators and as many military tribunes were brought in with consular power. Therefore, no one form endured long, nor could they all reach the age of noble kingdoms together.

Some, by chance, bring up the Venetian republic, which counts about a thousand and ten years. Yet that has not even attained the years of the kingdom of the Scythians, or of the Assyrians; on the contrary, not even the kingdom of the Franks. And what is more it is not a republic, where aristocracy is mixed with rule by many, the form which Calvin praises; but an aristocracy mixed with monarchy: democracy has never existed in that city.

The fifth and last property is the facility of governance. Indeed, it relates more to whether it can be obtained easily and not with difficulty that the state should be well governed. That it is easier for the state to be ruled rightly by one rather than many can be proved from these reasons.

1) It is easier to find one good man than many. Thereupon, it is easier for the people to obey one than many. On that account, magistracies which take turns and govern a state for a short time are often compelled first to lay aside a duty than plainly recognize the business of the state; on the other hand, a king who always exercises the same office, even if from time to time he is of a meager intelligence, nevertheless by use and also experience is better than many others. 2) In like manner, yearly magistracies look after a business of the state,

---

[26]   *Lib.* 2, ch. 7.

which is not their own, but common and foreign; a king does so as properly his own. It is certain that it is not only easier, but even more thorough for one to care for his own things, than for others. 3) Where there are many who rule, it can hardly be the case that there would be no rivalry, ambition and contention present, and in point of fact it does not rarely happen that some impede others, and effect that those who govern the affairs at hand will administer the commonwealth badly. In such a case it is better for them to receive glory in abundance when they exercise the magistracy. But monarchy, which does not have anyone it might envy, or with whom to contend in governance, more easily moderates all things.

Lastly, to the extent that in great households, where many servants are assigned to the same duty, they manage their business badly because one shall leave behind a common duty to another; so even where there are many heads of state, one looks to another and while each one throws back the burden on his colleagues, no one sufficiently employs diligent care to the state. But a king that knows all things depend upon himself alone is compelled to neglect nothing. And also, hitherto, it is indeed proven that simple monarchy is better by far than simple aristocracy. Now let us proceed to prove the next proposition.

CHAPTER III

That Monarchy Mixed with Aristocracy and Democracy Should be More Advantageous in this Life than Simple Monarchy

THE NEXT proposition is such: government tempered from all three forms on account of the corruption of human nature is more advantageous than simple monarchy. Such a government rightly requires that there should be some supreme prince in the state, who commands all, and is subject to none. Nevertheless, there should be guardians of provinces or cities who are not vicars of the king or annual judges, but true princes, who also obey the command of the supreme prince and meanwhile govern their province, or city, not as someone else's property, but as their own. Thus, there should be a place in the commonwealth both for a certain royal monarchy and also an aristocracy of the best princes.

What if we were to add to these that neither the supreme king nor the lesser princes would acquire those dignities in hereditary succession, rather the aristocrats would be carried to those dignities from the whole people; then Democracy would have its attributed place in the state. That this is the best, and in this mortal life the most expedient form of rule, we shall prove from two arguments.

First, a government of this sort should have all those goods which, above, we showed are present in monarchy and should be on that account in this life more favorable and useful. And indeed, it is plain that the goods of monarchy are present in this our government, since this government truly and properly embraces some element of monarchy. It can be observed that this [government] is going to be more favorable in all things, however, because of this very fact that all love that kind of government more in which they can be partakers; without a doubt this our [form of government] is such, although this is not conveyed by any kind of virtue.

There is nothing we might say about the advantage, since it is certain that one man cannot rule individual cities and provinces by himself. Whether he wishes or not, he shall be compelled to entrust their care either for his vicars to administrate, or to princes as their own territory. Again it is equally certain that princes shall be much more assiduous and faithful over their own things than vicars who will look after someone else's territory.

Another argument is added from divine authority. God established a rule of this sort, such as we have just described, in the Church both in the Old and New Testaments. Furthermore, this can be proved from the Old Testament quite easily. The Hebrews always had one, or ten, or a judge, or a king, who commanded the whole multitude and many lesser princes, about which we read

25

in the book of Exodus: "With vigorous men being chosen from all Israel, he established them princes of the people, tribunes and centurions, both captains of fifty, and of ten, who judged the people at all times."[1] Also, one can see in the first Chapter of the book of Deuteronomy, there is clearly democracy in some manner.

On the Church of the new Testament the same thing will need to be proven, as evidently there is monarchy in the person of the Supreme Pontiff, and also in that of the bishops (who are true princes and shepherds, not merely vicars of the supreme pontiff); there is aristocracy and at length, there is a certain measure of democracy, since there is no man from the whole multitude of Christians who could not be called to the episcopacy, provided he is judged worthy for that office.

---

[1] Exodus 18:25-26.

CHAPTER IV

*That Without the Circumstances of this World, Simple Monarchy Would Excel
Absolutely and Simply*

HE THIRD proposition follows: Without the circumstances of this world,
simple monarchy is absolutely and simply better than all other forms of
governance. For, if the reason we prefer a mixed government to simple
monarchy is that one man cannot be present in all places and is necessarily
compelled, either through his administrative vicars or princes, to take care of
the business of the commonwealth, certainly, were this circumstance of person
as well as all others excluded, there will be no reason why simple monarchy
should not be preferred to all forms of government.

But we have besides that a more efficacious argument. Since simple
monarchy in the empire of God and Christ holds place, and moreover the best
things ought to be attributed to God and Christ, therefore, the best government
must be simple monarchy. If anyone, however, should wish to deny that, I do
not see in what way he could avoid falling into the error of the Marcionists and
Manichees, or even of the pagans. For, since the world is governed best by its
creator; and without controversy, if aristocracy were the best form of
government, many would be moderators of this world; therefore, it follows,
many creators, many first principles, and many gods.

Seeing that for the ancient Fathers, St. Cyprian, St. Justin, St. Athanasius, to
whom even the Jewish writer Philo can be added, there is one God who rules all
created things and governs them, they prove principally by this argument that
monarchy is the best government. Moreover, Justin and Philo even left written
books on the monarchy of God for that very purpose.

Since these things are so, the error of John Calvin cannot be excused, who
being completely blinded by his hatred of ecclesiastical hierarchy, prefers
aristocracy to all other forms of government, even if the question should be
considered with all circumstances removed. These are his own words: "And if
you compare these situations among themselves on the other side of the
circumstances, you may not easily discern what might be of more weight with
respect to utility, to that extent they contend in equal conditions."[1] And a little
after that: "Truly if those three were considered in themselves, that is the forms
of government which the philosophers put forth, I could hardly deny, either
aristocracy, or a state tempered by oligarchy, should by far excel all the others."[2]

But someone will say, read what follow, and you will discover the answer

---

[1]   *Instit.* Ch. 20 §6.

[2]   Ibid.

to your objection. Calvin adds: "Not in itself, therefore, but because it rarely happens that kings so control themselves that their will is never out of harmony with what is just and right; thereupon, as much as men are instructed with acumen and prudence, each one shall see to it that there is a sufficient quantity of both. Therefore, it happens that due to the vice or defect of men it is safer and more tolerable to have many heads of state."

I hear it, but what will become of the edition of 1554, where those words are not contained? Still, the objector will say: after he was admonished, he emended the error. I omit what it was never asserted against such a teacher in Israel that he erred so gravely. I marvel that Calvin could not correct that error, unless he opposed himself. For if, as he says, it is not easy to discern which state should outweigh the other even if they were compared *per se* apart from the circumstances of this world; if while these which the philosophers put forth were considered, aristocracy is shown to excel, then how true is what he adds right after: "Not indeed in itself, " etc. and: "Therefore, it happens that due to the vice or defect of men it is safer and more tolerable to have many heads of state"? Indeed these are opposed, unless I am mistaken.

No less are these statements opposed: "It cannot be discerned which one outweighs the other, if they should be considered beyond the circumstances of this world," and: "He commits the vices of men that aristocracy should be judged more useful." For, removing the question of the vices of men, and also all other circumstances, monarchy either excels or not: if it excels, for what reason will it be true that it cannot be discerned which state should outweigh the other, even if compared outside of the circumstances of this world? If it does not excel, by what argument do we defend the monarchy of God against the Manicheans and the pagans? Now, however, we are already coming to the next question.

CHAPTER V

The Second Question is Proposed: Should the Ecclesiastical Government be a Monarchy?

SINCE it has been shown that monarchy is the best government, the second question arises: whether the monarchical government is suitable to the Church of Christ. And also that we might separate certainty from doubt, we agree with our adversaries on three things. 1) That in the Church there is some government, for in Canticles we read: "As an army set in array."[1] In Acts, we have: "Attend to your own and the whole flock, because the Holy Spirit has placed bishops to rule the Church of God."[2] In Hebrews: *Obey those placed over you.*"[3]

2) That ecclesiastical government is spiritual and distinct from the political order. When Paul said: "Who presides in solicitude,"[4] and "Who carries out his duties well shall be held in honor twofold,"[5] and similar things, there were not yet any (or certainly very rarely were), secular princes in the Church. Those two things even Calvin teaches.[6]

3) That the absolute and free king of the whole Church is Christ alone, about whom it is said: "I have been established a king by him over his holy mountain, Zion."[7] And in Luke we read: "And of his reign there will be no end."[8] Therefore, an absolute and free monarch is not sought in the Church, or an aristocracy, or democracy, but such a quality can be of ministers and dispensers, since Paul said: "Thus a man esteems us, as ministers of Christ and dispensers of the mysteries of God."[9]

And our adversaries certainly reckon that the ecclesiastical government which was consigned to men by Christ is by no means monarchy, rather aristocracy and democracy, although they do not all agree among themselves.

---

[1] Canticles 6:3.

[2] Attendite vobis et universo gregi, quos Spiritus sanctus posuit episcopos regere Ecclesiam Dei. - Acts 20:28.

[3] Obedite praepositis vestris. - Hebrews 13:17.

[4] Qui praeest in sollicitudine. Romans 12:8.

[5] Qui bene praesunt duplici honore digni habeantur. 1 Tim. 5:17.

[6] *Instit.* Lib. 4, ch. 11 §1.

[7] Psalm 2:6.

[8] Luke 1:33.

[9] 1 Cor. 4:1.

Illyricus teaches that there is no one in the Church who is in charge of all, but the whole ecclesiastical authority is both in the ministers and in the people;[10] nevertheless, in another book[11] he attributed supreme power to the multitude of the whole Church, giving the first place to democracy in the Church, then the second to aristocracy that is the congregation of the elders. Calvin, on the contrary, grants supreme power to the body of elders, over whom he wishes a bishop to be in charge, as a consul of the senate.[12] He teaches the same thing clearly that the greater authority is the body of elders, rather than bishops. Calvin, however, attributes something to the people, but less than to a body of elders. Next, Brenz concedes supreme power to aristocrats,[13] but he would not have it that they are bishops, rather secular princes whom he contends are the most noble members of the Church. For a long time Catholic teachers have all agreed on the point that the ecclesiastical government which was consigned to men by God is indeed a monarchy, but tempered, as we said above, by aristocracy and democracy.[14] Following their footsteps, we now bring four propositions into the midst, and defend their strength. The first will be that the government of the Church is not in the power of the people. Second, it is not in the power of secular princes. Third, it is not chiefly in the power of ecclesiastical princes. Fourth, it is especially in the power of one supreme governor and priest of the whole Church.

---

[10]   *Cent.* 1 lib. 2, ch. 7.

[11]   *De episcop. elect.*

[12]   *Instit.* lib. 4, ch. 11, §6.

[13]   *In Prolegom. Cont. Pet. A Soto.*

[14]   The theologians who particularly treat on this are: St. Thomas, *4 Supra Sententias; Summa contra gentiles* ch. 76. Juan de Torquemada, lib. 2 *De Eccl.* Ch. 2; Nicholaus Sanders in the books on the visible monarchy of the Church.

CHAPTER VI

That the Government of the Church Should not be a Democracy.

ENCE, the first denial is proposed, namely of popular ecclesiastical government, and it can be confirmed by these arguments, firstly from four things which ought to be present in all popular government.

First, where there is popular government, magistracies are established by the people themselves, and also receive their authority from them. Since one cannot sit to declare a law of the people by himself, he ought at least to consult some who do so in their name. For that reason, Cicero calls the office of Consul, which was the greatest magistracy in the Roman Republic, the benefice of the people;[1] and he says in the same place that consuls were created to preserve the right of the people to vote.

Secondly, where there is popular government, one may appeal a decree of the magistrate in serious matters by bringing it to the judgment of the people: this custom was witnessed in the Roman Republic by Livy,[2] and Plutarch teaches the same thing about the Athenian republic in his work on Solon.

Thirdly, the laws by which the state must be governed, while indeed proposed by a magistrate, are commanded by the people, as is certain from Livy. The same can be seen in Cicero.[3]

Fourthly, magistracies are usually accused by the people, and indeed deprived of dignity and sent into exile, or even beaten to death, if it appears expedient to the people; there are many examples of this. The Romans, for instance, by the two first consuls whom they had created, deprived Tarquinius Callatinus of his magistracy before his time only on account of the odious name of the Tarquins, as Livy recalls it. Likewise, when they had created the *decemviri*, they deposed the same against their will, as Livy again witnesses in book 2 of his histories.

Now, it can easily be proved that none of these examples would be fitting to the Christian people. Therefore, to the first argument, it is certain enough in that in the whole Scripture there is not one word whereby, authority can be given to the people for creating bishops or priests; rather such authority is given to a bishop whereby, "For this reason I left you behind in Crete, so that you would correct those things which are wanting, and would ordain priests in every city, as I also appointed you."[4] And so the apostles, who were the first

---

[1]   *Init.* 2 Agr.

[2]   Livius lib. 2, and 4.

[3]   Livius, lib. 3; Cicero *de lege Manil.* and *de lege Agr. Ad pop rom.*

[4]   Titus 1:6.

ministers of the Church, were constituted by Christ, not by the Church, as we read in Mark 6. Also, the first bishops after the apostles, in that time when the Church was purest, were not made by the people, but by the apostles, as can be recognized even by the historians of Magdeburg themselves.[5] For the Centuriators witness, at Iconium, and Antioch, shepherds were given by Paul, and they teach, following Nauclero and other historians that Apollinarus was established a bishop by St. Peter at Ravenna, and likewise Majernum at Treveris, and Hermagora at Aquileiam.

Irenaeus asserted that Linus was made a bishop by the apostles Peter and Paul at Rome.[6] Tertullian wrote that Clement was made a bishop at Rome by Peter, and St. Polycarp of Smyrna by John the Apostle.[7] Eusebius affirms that Timothy was made a bishop at Ephesus by Paul, and Titus at Cretensis.[8] Nicephorus writes that Plato was made a bishop by Matthew the apostle in the town of the Anthropophagi, by the name of Mirmena. St. Mark was created a bishop by St. Peter and sent to Alexandria.[9] Dionysius, also the Areopagate, was made a bishop by Paul at Athens, which is gathered from Eusebius,[10] and Bede asserts the same thing in his martyrology. We could easily show the same thing concerning many others. Since these things are so, it appears sufficiently that in this first and purest age of the Church, there was no place for democracy, since not the people but the apostles established the ecclesiastical magistracy.

Nor is the second argument, on the appeal to the people, fitting for the Christian people. It has never been heard of in the Church that one might appeal from the bishops to the people, nor that the people should absolve those whom the bishop bound, or bound those whom the bishops absolved. Nor has it ever happened that the people judged on the controversies of Faith: and we advance many judgments of bishops, and especially of the Supreme Pontiff, which exist in volumes of councils. But our adversaries cannot advance even one judgment of the people.

---

[5]   Cent. 1, lib. 2, ch. 2, col. 13. The "Centuriators of Magdeburg", were a group of Protestant historians who attempted to show that Protestantism was the religion of the early Church. Cardinal Baronius and St. Peter Canisius completely disproved their work, to the extent that even amongst Protestants it is of a merely antiquarian interest. -Translator's note.

[6]   Irenaeus lib. 3, ch. 3.

[7]   *De praescript.*

[8]   Lib. 3, ch. 4.

[9]   Leo, *epist. 81* to Doscorum; Bede lib. *de sex aetat,* in Claudio.

[10]   Eusebius, ibid.

Add that, how innumerable are the Scriptures and the testimonies of the Councils, as well as Fathers, whereby it is proved that it is by no means fitting for the Christian people to exercise ecclesiastical judgment (which we have partly advanced in the question on ecclesiastical judgment, and partly in questions on Councils). But certainly, if in the Church a government of the people flourished, it would be a wonder that in 1500 years nothing ever was judged by the people.

Next, the third argument that imposing laws is even less fitting to a Christian people. All ecclesiastical laws are discovered to have been imposed either by bishops or by Councils; they have never awaited the vote of the people, as if it were reckoned that authority resided therein. Hence, St. Paul, traveling across Syria and Cilicia, commanded the people that they should guard the precepts of the apostles and elders.[11] However, there is no law whereby a plebiscite may be called in the Church, nor any such laws as there were in the Roman Republic.

Thereupon that last argument on judgment of a magistrate hardly fits at all. No bishop can be shown to have either been deposed or excommunicated by the people, although many are found who were deposed and excommunicated by the Supreme Pontiffs and general Councils. Certainly, Nestorius was deposed from the episcopacy of Constantinople by the Council of Ephesus, from the mandate of Pope Celestine, as Evagrius witnessed. Dioscorus was deprived of the bishopric of Alexandria by the council of Chalcedon, from the decree of St. Leo, which is clear from that Council, Act 3, and this indeed is the first reason.

Another reason is taken up from the wisdom of God. It is not credible that Christ, the wisest king, established in his Church that form of government which is the most degenerate of all: for the most degenerate government is democracy, as Plato teaches in his dialogue *Axiochus*: "Who can be happy living by the common will, even if he should be favored and applauded by it?" etc. Aristotle, from the three forms of ruling the multitude, pronounces monarchy the best, and democracy the worst. Plutarch reports that Anacharsides the Scythian marveled that in Greece wise men speak while fools judge, for without a doubt the orators were speaking, while the people gave judgment. Likewise, in Apophtheg, he says Lycurgus was asked, why Sparta had not established a democracy and he responded to his interlocutor that he should first establish it at home.

From our own authors, St. Ambrose says on the common multitude: "It does not pay merit to virtue, nor examine the benefits of public advantage, but

---

[11] Acts 15:23.

changes to uncertainty in disturbance."[12] St. Jerome adds: "The mob is always mobile, and is given to the manner of the blowing and diversities of the winds, going from here to there."[13]

St. John Chrysostom defines the people as full of tumult and disturbance, the greater part being constituted of foolishness, and also composed of a rash nature like the waves of the sea, changeable and repeatedly thrown in to contentious opinion; thereupon he adds: "Therefore, whoever is pressed into the servitude of this sort, is he not rightly the most miserable of all?"[14] Even right reason agrees. For, can it not be but the worst government where the wise are ruled by fools, the experienced by the inexperienced, the good by the bad? Yet such a government is democracy; for where democracy flourishes, all are established in suffrage; however it is certain that there will always be as many fools as wise, wicked as good, inexperienced as experienced.

To this, as Aristotle teaches, those who exert power from genius, these naturally are the lords of those who are less so.[15] Moreover, as St. Augustine says: "It is better that, where many foolish men live, they ought to be the servants of the wise."[16] Who cannot see what a disturbance of order it would be, to allow the governance of the state to be handed to the undisciplined multitude of the people?

Lastly, if the people should have some authority in the governance of the Church, or should have it from themselves, or from another, yet this power is not of themselves, because it is not from the law of nature or nations, rather from divine and supernatural law. Indeed, it is not the same as civil power, which is in the people, unless it should be transferred to a prince. Nor do the people have it from another, they ought, indeed, to have it from God if they have it from another, but they do not have it from God; accordingly in God's book that is in the Holy Scripture, there is no place where the power of teaching, shepherding, ruling, binding and loosing is handed to the people, rather the people are always called the flock which ought to be put to pasture. Moreover, it is said to Peter: "Feed my sheep," and again, "The Holy Spirit placed bishops to rule the Church of God."[17] Consequently, we do not have

---

[12]   *Hexameron*, lib. 5, ch. 21.

[13]   In ch. 21 Matth.

[14]   Hom. 2 in Joanne.

[15]   Lib. 1 *Politc.*, ch. 1 and 3.

[16]   *De. Utilit. Cred.*, ch. 12.

[17]   John 21:17; Acts 20:23.

popular government over the Church. Yet, against this proposition there are three arguments. The first is taken from the words of the Gospel of Matthew 18, "Say to the Church," where it appears the supreme tribunal of the Church is constituted in the power of the whole body of the faithful.

We respond: that phrase, "Say to the Church," means, bring to the public judgment of the Church, *i.e.*, to those who govern the public person in the Church. Thus also Chrysostom shows that "Say to the Church," means to the prelate, because the custom of the Church rightly confirms it; nor do we ever see or hear the cause of some criminal to be brought before the multitude of the people, but rather the case is judged by the bishop, as we often see and more often have heard.

The second argument is deduced from Acts of the Apostles, Chapters 1 and 6. For in Acts 1 the whole Church chose Mathias: and in Acts 6, the same Church chose seven deacons, and the Fathers in passing teach, the election of bishops pertains to the people.

We respond: on the election of ministers we must dispute in another place. Meanwhile, though, we deny it from that law which held the people were at some time involved in the election of ministers that this somehow proves there was democracy in the Church in any way. Accordingly the people did never ordain or create the ministers, or render to them any power, but merely nominated and designated, or as the Fathers say, asked for those whom they desired to be ordained through the imposition of hands made by bishops. Whereby the apostles say in Acts 6:3 "Consider seven men of good repute, whom we shall constitute for this work." Where they only grant to the people that they should find and offer some suitable to the office: but the Apostles created those who were offered as deacons, not the people. Cyprian also teaches this: "The Lord chose apostles, the apostles constituted deacons for themselves."[18] On that account, where, even if the people were truly to create bishops, the ecclesiastical government would not be a democracy. For indeed that some government should be a democracy it is required that the people should constitute the magistracy, but many other things are required; and that alone does not suffice in itself. The first kings were chosen by the people, and nevertheless, their government is monarchy, not democracy.

Proportionately, Roman emperors were once chosen by their soldiers, and now they are chosen by certain princes and just the same, the empire pertains

---

[18] Lib. 3, epist. 9.

to monarchy, not to democracy.[19] Should there be democracy, were it fitting, as was done in the election of a prince, still there would be a greater authority in the people than in the prince, and a judgment of the prince could be challenged by seeking a judgment of the people. This should not be in the Church, just as it should not be in a kingdom or in the empire of the Romans. Valentianus the elder, understanding this, as Sozomenus relates, when the soldiers wished to give him a colleague in imperium, responded: "It was you who chose to put imperium in my power, but already when I was chosen by you, you demanded someone as a consort of imperium; but it was not placed in your power to choose, but in mine."[20]

The third argument comes from the authority of saints Cyprian and Ambrose. Cyprian wrote to [his] priests and deacons on certain turbulent brethren: "Meanwhile, they should be forbidden to offer, and act both with us and with the whole people in their cause, etc."[21] Ambrose, arguing on a judgment of faith: "The people have already judged," and again: "Auxentius has run to your examination."[22]

I respond: St. Cyprian was accustomed to treat almost all major business in the presence of the clergy and the people, and did nothing without their consent. Moreover, he did this of his own will; he was not compelled by any law, as is certain when he said: "When I had decided from the beginning of my episcopacy to do nothing from my private judgment without your counsel, and without the consensus of the people, etc."[23] But Cyprian was not subject to the clergy or the people on that account: just as king Xerxes II was not subject to those wise men with whom he made all his counsels, as we read in the book of Esther, Chapter 1. Even if Cyprian had subjected himself to the clergy and the people, which is not in the least credible, he could not have immediately prescribed a law for the whole Church.

Yet for what pertains to St. Ambrose, he speaks in that place on a private judgment, in which each established that something should be followed for

---

[19] Translator's note: It is integral to his historiography to view the Holy Roman Empire as a legal continuation of the ancient Roman Empire, for reasons that will become clear later.

[20] Translator's note: Sozomen, lib. 6, ch. 6; "Imperium" has been left in the Latin, because it is a technical term in Roman law. When someone has imperium, they have the full authority to command troops, and choose their consorts.

[21] Lib. 3, epist. 14.

[22] In epist. 32.

[23] Lib. 3, epist. 10.

themselves, not on public judgment, which had authority to bind the rest. This much can be seen in the words of the same Ambrose, when he says in the same place: "They should come openly to the Church, let them hear with the people, not that each should reside as a judge, but that each should have an examination from his own disposition, let them choose which he ought to follow."

CHAPTER VII

That Ecclesiastical Government Should not be in the Power of Secular Princes.

ANOTHER proposition, which denies that ecclesiastical government pertains to secular princes, is opposed to two errors of Brenz. The first error is that aristocrats should be secular princes of the Church: for Brenz so disparages bishops that he would have it that they were the possession of princes. The second is that the care and government of the church particularly pertains to aristocrats. Such errors King Henry VIII of England also held; for he constituted himself as head of the English Church and in the same way reckoned that other princes should be the supreme head of the Church in their dominions.

Indeed, the first error is easily refuted from those prophetic words in the Psalms: "For your fathers sons are born to you, they established them as princes over all the earth."[1]

Thus St. Augustine teaches on this citation, *for fathers* (that is, apostles), sons are born (that is the many faithful), whom God established as bishops, and in this way they are princes over all the earth. Also, St. Jerome says on the same passage: "O Church, your fathers were apostles because they gave birth to you, but now because they have passed on from this world, you have for them bishops as sons." And further on: "The princes of the Church (that is the bishops), were established." The Greek Fathers say nothing different; Chrysostom and Theodoret express patriarchs through fathers; through sons they understand princes as apostles. Likewise the Apostle says: "In the Church he placed first apostles, second prophets, third even teachers."[2]

If the first are apostles who were bishops, and to whom bishops succeeded, certainly the first are not kings and secular princes. Rather, as St. John Damascene rightly noted, not only did the Apostle not place kings in the first place, but in no place, that he would show that kings are not the government of the Church, but only of the world.

The second is refuted from the Fathers. Ignatius says that nothing is more honorable than a bishop in the Church,[3] and he added that the first honor should be to God, the second to the bishop, the third to a king. St. Gregory Nazianzen says that they were precluded from fear.[4] St. John Chrysostom and

---

[1] Psalm 44:16.

[2] 1 Cor. 12:28.

[3] In epist. 7, *ad Smyrnen.*

[4] Orta. *Ad cives.*

St. Ambrose most certainly prefer a bishop to a king.[5]

In fact, Chrysostom subjects kings not only to bishops, but even to deacons; thus even to his deacon he speaks: "If any general you like, if a consul, if he is adorned with a crown, should come unworthily then restrain and punish him; you have greater power than he."[6] St. Augustine proves that Moses was a priest from the reason that Moses was greater, and nothing is greater than a priest.[7] And Gelasius says: "You know, O beloved son, that although you preside over earthly affairs with the dignity of the human race, nevertheless, you devotedly submit to prelates as heads of the divine."[8] And further on in the same letter: "It is supplied that you ought to recognize one in order of religion more than to be over them. Therefore, know that your judgment depends upon them, they cannot be ruled according to your will."

St. Gregory asserts that the first members in the body of the Lord are priests. And he teaches that priests are like gods among men, and on that account, must be held in honor by all, even kings;[9] Pope Nicholas I teaches and proves the same thing in his Epistle to Michael.

The third, from the deeds of bishops and kings. For Pope Fabian excluded the first Christian emperor from communion of the Sacrament of the altar on Easter, on account of some public sin he committed, nor would he admit him before he had purged it by confession and penance.[10] Likewise, Constantius openly professed that he could not judge concerning bishops, because they were gods: but on the other hand he was chiefly to stand subject to their judgment.[11]

St. Ambrose expelled Theodosius the elder from the threshold of the Church, and compelled him to undergo a public penance. Another time when the emperor in the Church ascended to the places of the priests and also wished to sit in the same place, Ambrose commanded him to descend and sit with the people, which he did gladly.[12]

Thereupon Sulpitius writes on the life of St. Martin that the emperor

---

[5] Lib. 3 de sacerdot., and hom. 4 in cap. 6 Isaiae; Ambrose lib. de dignit. Sacerd. Ch. 2.

[6] Hom. 83 in Matth.

[7] In. Psal. 98 (99).

[8] In epist. Ad Anastasium.

[9] Lib. 13 Moral. Ch. 19; lib. 4, epist. 31.

[10] Eusebius lib. 6, ch. 25, hist.

[11] Ruffinus, lib. 1, ch. 2, hist.

[12] Theodoretus, lib. 5, hist. Cap. 17.

Maximus, when he sat down to dinner where St. Martin was also sitting, and the cupbearer wished to offer the first chalice to the emperor, as to the most noble of all, he sent him to the bishop, who did not refuse but first drank and afterward handed the chalice not to the emperor, but to his priest: obviously he esteemed no one more worthy who should drink after himself; he did not prefer the whole group to himself, neither the king or those who were near him, but the priest.

Lastly, the same error is refuted by a two-fold reason. First, a bishop anoints a king, teaches, binds, absolves and blesses him; moreover, the Apostle says in Hebrews 7:7, "Without contradiction it is no less a thing to be blessed by a better man."

On that account, secular rule was established by men, and it is from the law of nations: but ecclesiastical rule was established by God alone, and is from divine law. The former rules men, as they are men, and more to the cause of the body than the soul; but the latter rules men, as they are Christians, and more to the soul than the body; the former has temporal rest and the safety of the people for his end; the latter has happy and eternal life for his end. The former uses natural laws and human institutions; the latter uses divine laws and divinely established Sacraments. The former wages wars with a few and visible enemies, the latter with invisible and infinite enemies.

But Brenz objects that bishops are servants of the Church. "We do not preach ourselves, but Jesus Christ, furthermore we are your servants through Jesus."[13] So much more should they be the servants of kings, especially when St. Peter spoke about kings thus: "Be subject to every human creature on account of God, whether king as though preeminent, or leaders as though sent from him."[14]

I respond: there is a twofold species of servitude; all who labor in the full measure of another are said to serve him, but really they labor and serve another by ruling him, and presiding over him; and there are those who labor and serve by submitting and obeying those who are properly in possession. bishops, however, are servants of the Church, but to the prior mode; just as even a magistracy serves the state, and a king the people (if he might be a king and not a tyrant), and a father his sons and a teacher his students.

Whereby St. Paul had said he was the slave of those whom he said he was their father, "I begot you through the gospel," and he added, "What do you want? Should I come to you with the rod, could it be in charity and the spirit of

---

[13]   2 Cor. 4:5.

[14]   1 Peter 2:13-14.

mildness? " And again: "Obey those who have been placed over you, and be subject to them," and "The Holy Spirit has placed bishops to rule the Church of God."[15] For this reason St. Gregory called himself the servants of the servants of God. And St. Augustine says: "Inspire, O Lord, in your servants my brothers, your sons and my lords, whom I serve by voice, heart and letter."[16] And St. Bernard says that Eugene, when he was made Pope, was elevated above nations and kings to minister to them, not lord it over them.[17]

But you will say, kings are kings, even in the Church, and Christians ought to be subject to them, *as though to ones preeminent.* Indeed it is true, but only in those affairs which pertain to the state. Certainly, Christian kings are preeminent over Christian men, not as Christians, but as men, just as they are even over Jews and Turks, but as men of state. For as Christians they are sheep subject to their pastors, the bishops, as St. Gregory Nazianzen and St. Ambrose taught, whom we quoted above, and St. Basil, who taught nothing can be said to be of more honor, than that an emperor should be called a son of the Church; indeed a good emperor is within the Church and not over it.

The second error of Brenz is easily refuted from the foregoing. If princes are not aristocrats of the Church, then aristocracy in the Church does not pertain to them. Nevertheless, these arguments can be added on that account.

First, the government of the Church is supernatural; it is fitting for no one except whom God has commissioned. Furthermore, we read in the Scriptures of what was entrusted to the apostles and the bishops, their successors. For it was said to Peter the Apostle, in the last chapter of John, "Feed my sheep." And on bishops, it is said in Acts, "whom God placed as bishops to rule the Church of God." We read nothing at all about kings.

Next, for the first 300 years there was no secular prince in the Church except for the emperor Philip alone, who lived for a very short time, and by chance someone else in provinces not subject to the roman empire; yet nevertheless, the same Church existed then which exists now, and it had the same form of government; therefore, secular princes did not rule the Church of Christ.

In like manner, those who have supreme power in the state can have all the things which lower officials can. In fact, can someone prohibit a king, if he wished to judge those reasonings in themselves, to recognize and judge what he entrusted to viceroys and magistrates and lower judges? But kings cannot usurp

---

[15]   1 Corin. 4:15; Hebr. 13:17; Act. 20:28.

[16]   *Confess.,* lib. 9, last chapter.

[17]   Bernard, lib. 2, *de consider.*

the duty of a bishop, priest, or deacon to themselves, as such things are to preach the Word of God, baptize, consecrate, etc. Therefore, kings are not the supreme magistracy of the Church.

Moreover that kings cannot invade the duties of priests we thus prove. In the first place, kings are not only men, but they can even be women: and the Apostle prohibits women to teach publicly,[18] and the Peputians are numbered among the heretics by Augustine and Epiphanius, because they attributed the priesthood to women.[19]

Therefore, Josaphat the greatest king says: "Amarias will preside as a priest and pontiff, in those things which pertain to God: next Zabadias will be devoted to those things which pertain to the office of king."[20] And when Uzziah the king wished to burn incense, the priest forbade him, saying: "It is not your duty, Uzziah that you should burn incense to the Lord, rather the priests'."[21] But since he persevered, immediately he was struck with a very serious leprosy by God. Yet, if in the Old Testament a king could not exercise the office of priests, how much less in the New, where there are by far more august sacerdotal offices?

Likewise, we read in the Synod of Autun (*Matisconensis*), and the Councils of Miletus as well as Toledo, that clerics are to be gravely punished if they would bring a subject of the Church to secular judgment.[22] And St. Ambrose says to Valentinian: "Do not weigh yourself down, O Emperor, that you should think yourself to have some imperial right in those things which are divine."[23] Likewise, as Theodoret relates, St. Ambrose said to the emperor Theodosius the same thing: "The purple makes emperors, not priests."[24] Theodoret also relates about a certain Eulogius, on an occasion when Modestus, the prefect of the Arian emperor Valens, said to him: "Join with the emperor;" but he responded with wit: "Do you also attend on the bishopric with the emperor? "

St. Athanasius also rebuked Constantius, because he had mixed himself in with ecclesiastical affairs, and adds that Hosius, the bishop of Cordova, said to the same emperor: "Do not instruct us in this way, but rather learn from us: God

---

[18]   1 Cor. 14:34, and 1 Tim. 2:11-12.

[19]   Augustine *haer.* 27; Epiphanius, *haer.* 49.

[20]   2 Chron. 19:11.

[21]   2 Chron. 36:18.

[22]   Synodo Matisconensi can 9; Concilio Milevitano; can. 19, Toledo 3, cen. 13.

[23]   Epist. 33 ad Sororem.

[24]   Theodoret, lib. 5, ch. 18, *hist.*

entrusted imperium to you, but to us those things which are of the Church."[25] Liontius the bishop said the same things to Constantius, as Suidas witnesses. Sulpitius relates that St. Martin said to the Emperor Maximus that it was unlawful, a novelty and unheard of that he might as a secular judge make determinations on the business of the Church.

St. Augustine teaches that the duty of pious kings is to defend the Church, and to punish blasphemies, sacrilege and heretics with severe laws and penalties: but in the same place he rebukes the Donatists, because they brought an episcopal plea not to their brother bishops, but to an earthly king to pass judgment.[26] St. Gregory the Great, when speaking about the emperor Maurice, said: "It is known, for most pious lords to love discipline and keep order, to venerate the canons and not get mixed up in the business of priests."[27] St. John Damascene amply teaches the same thing.[28] Thereafter, the emperor Basil, in the Eighth General Council, eloquently asserted that neither he nor any other laymen was allowed to treat on priestly business; because the same had been professed even by Valentinan the elder, as Sozomen witnesses above.

The arguments of Brenz are taken from examples of the Old Testament, where we read that Moses, Joshua, David, Solomon, and Josias, who were generals or kings, often mixed themselves in the business of religion. Brenz even adds to confirm the argument that the custody of divine laws had been entrusted to kings by God and therefore, the care of the Church pertains to them. Thus even the Apostle said: "He bears a sword not without cause. He is a minister of God, an avenger in anger to him who works evil."[29]

We respond: Moses was not only a general, but also the high priest that in a question on the judgment of controversies, which is shown in my work *de Verbo Dei*, lib. 3. The rest, however, now and then worked not just as kings, but also as prophets by an extraordinary authority. But not for that reason was that law to be blotted out from Deuteronomy, by which ordinarily in doubts on religion, men were remitted not to the king, but to a priest of the Levitical race.[30] What is more, as we said above, Oziah, the king, was punished by leprosy when he assumed the office of the priest.

---

25   Athanasius, epist. Ad solit. Vit. Agent.

26   Epist. 48, 50 and 163.

27   Lib 3, epist. 125.

28   1 and 2 Orat. Pro imag.

29   Romans 13:4.

30   Deut. 17:8-9.

Furthermore, we respond in confirmation of the fact that kings ought to be guardians of divine laws, but not interpreters; it is really for them to impede blasphemies, heresies and sacrileges by edicts. Moreover, since there are heresies, they ought to learn from the bishops what is in fact the Orthodox Faith, which pious emperors Constantine, Valentinian, Gratian, Theodosius and Marianus did, as can be recognized from history.

CHAPTER VIII
That Ecclesiastical Government Ought not Chiefly be in the Power of Bishops

HE THIRD proposition follows, which teaches that the government of the Church should not chiefly be in the power of bishops and priests, against two errors of Calvin. The first error of Calvin is that bishops and priests are equal by divine law, while the second is that supreme power in the Church resides in a body of elders. Jan Hus held to the same error, which can be understood from the condemnations of the Council of Constance.[1]

Now the first error in that disputation will be more appropriately refuted in the disputation *on Clergy*, and we will take it up in its place. In the meantime, it will be enough to refute the first error from the one that follows. Accordingly, these two errors are opposed among themselves. If the Church is ruled by aristocrats, as the second error would have it, certainly priests are not aristocrats. But if priests are aristocrats, then the Church is not ruled by aristocrats, since it is certain that there were never priests present in general Councils wherein the administration of the whole Church was conducted with authority to define, and where laws were imposed or abrogated whereby the Church is ruled, unless they were legates and they held the place of some bishops. That is not necessary to prove otherwise than from the very acts of the councils which are still extant.

Really the second error, which is more properly to this argument, is confounded for these reasons. First, it is never read in the Scriptures that supreme power was conferred upon a council of priests; whatever authority was conceded to the Apostles and the rest of the disciples by Christ, was conceded not only to all of them but even to them as individuals; and it was not necessary to exercise it in Council. Indeed individual apostles, and without a doubt, individual bishops, could and can even now teach, baptize, loose, bind, ordain ministers etc. The only passage is Matthew 18, where something is attributed to a Council, when it is said: "Where there will have been two or three gathered in my name, there I am in their midst."

What the power of a Council might actually consist of, however, whether it is supreme, medium or lowest, shall not be explicated here. Calvin himself does not make much of this reference in the gospel, to the point that he would say that it is nothing less than for whatever particular body you like to meet, and not a general Council. For that reason, we shall not labor much on this argument at present.

---

[1] Concilium Constantiensi sess. 15, art. 27, 28, 29.

Secondly, if supreme power of governance were in the hands of aristocrats, it would follow that the Church would almost always lack rulers, and most of all, there would be no one who would take care of the common good. Hence, the ecclesiastical commonwealth would be very miserable, as indeed, aristocrats would be equal among themselves, as is proper, and could not administer the common good unless they were either gathered together, or choose by a common consensus some magistrate whom they would all obey, in the fashion in which the Romans elected their consuls.

But in the Church, aristocrats are rarely gathered in a general Council. For the first 300 years there was no general Council, afterward scarcely every 100 years; but a magistrate, whom the universal Church would obey at least for a time, was never created by these aristocrats; for if they would create someone, he would most likely be one of the five patriarchs, who were always prominent in the Church. But our adversaries contend that the Roman Patriarch never had this power; from the other four this business is very certain. The Patriarch of Alexandria never had this power outside of Egypt, nor the others outside of their regions.

This is why, St. Jerome asks: "Tell me, what in Palestine pertains to the bishop of Alexandria?"[2] And Chrysostom, who was asked about Theophilus, the patriarch of Alexandria, who was conducting ecclesiastical business outside of his province, said, "It is not right that those who are in Egypt should judge those who are in Thrace."[3]

How absurd would this be if the Catholic Church, which is so truly one that in the Scriptures it should be called one city, one house, one body, but would have no one on earth who might take care of it? Who can't see it? For, if the particular Churches were not so united in themselves that they formed one body, it would suffice that each were its own ruler, but they could no more lack an individual ruler than one flock can lack a shepherd, and one body its head.

Thirdly, if supreme power should be in a body of aristocrats, in which there were a greater number compelled to attend a Council, so much greater would be the authority, in that it could never turn out that more authority could be given to a Council attended by fewer persons than one attended by more.

But the Council of Rimini was attended by 600 bishops, and has never been held to have had authority in the Catholic Church. The first Council of Constantinople on the other hand, had 450 bishops, and has always been held to have enjoyed the greatest authority. And we recall this for the sake of the

---

2   In epist. Ad Pammach., *Advers. Jo., episc. Hierosol.*

3   In epist. 1 to Innocent I.

present controversy, because that was called by the Pope, whose supreme power in the Church has been rejected by our adversaries. Moreover, those who grant supreme power of the Church to aristocrats can offer no reason why they condemn the council of Rimini, but embrace the Council of Constantinople. But, they say, the Council of Rimini erred while the first council of Constantinople did not; on that account, they embrace the latter and condemn the former. But what else is this than to make onself the judge of Councils and of the whole Church?

Fourthly, although democracy is absolutely the worst form of government, nevertheless, it appears more pernicious for the Church than aristocracy. Accordingly, the worst thing for the Church is heresy. Heresies, however, are more often excited amongst the aristocrats than among the common faithful. Certainly almost all heresiarchs were either bishops or priests; as a result, heresies are almost like factions amongst aristocrats, without which there would be no sedition in the Church of the people. But factions never arise more easily or frequently than when aristocrats rule, as can be proved not merely from example, and the testimony of philosophers, but even from the confession of Calvin himself.[4]

But our adversaries object based on the testimony of three Scriptures, joined even to three witnesses of the Fathers. The first is Acts XV, where we read that the first controversy of the Church arose, and was defined not by some individual supreme judge, but by the agreement of the apostles and elders: "They agreed, the apostles and the elders to consider on this word."

I respond: here, no argument can be asserted for aristocracy. In fact, in that very council where that first question was defined, Peter was the president and head, nor in reality would Peter, who was in someone else's diocese whose bishop, James, was present, dared to have spoken first, except that he was in charge of the whole council. Moreover it is not opposed to monarchy that something would be decided upon in public assembly by the common counsel and agreement of princes, in the same manner as it usually happened in imperial assemblies at this time.

The second testimony is Acts 20, where St. Paul admonishes the bishops with these words: "Attend also to your whole flock, wherein the Holy Spirit has placed you as bishops to rule the Church of God."

The third is in 1 Peter V, where St. Peter speaks thus: "I exhort the elders who are among you, as fellow elders and witnesses of the passion of Christ, pasture the flock of God which is among you."

---

[4] *Instit.*, lib. 4, Ch. 20 §8.

I respond: neither citation proves anything; truly we do not deny that bishops and priests come together that they should feed and rule the Church of God, but our question is on the supreme power of the whole Church; does it reside in the body of ministers, or in some individual man? In these citations, neither Paul nor Peter touches upon this question, rather they merely admonish bishops to vigorously exercise their pastoral office for the people.

They already brought from the Fathers that first citation of Cyprian, who so wrote to a cleric: "Such a matter, although I have determined that it considers the counsel and opinion of us all, I do not make bold to claim every matter to merely decide by myself."[5] I respond: Cyprian did not dare to render judgment because he had obliged himself of his own will, when he received the episcopacy, that he was to do nothing without the counsel and consensus of his priests and people, as we taught above from the same book.[6] Next, they bring Ambrose, who so said, "Both the synagogue, and afterward the Church, had elders, without whose council nothing was done."[7] I respond, no more from these words can ecclesiastical aristocracy be proved, than from the existence of a senate and royal counsel in a kingdom that there is no monarchy. Certainly, even Solomon had a body of elders by counsels,[8] and also Xerxes used the counsel of the wise in all affairs;[9] nevertheless, it does not follow that they were not kings. On that account, because the old bishops would do nothing without the counsel of priests with respect to what was of advantage and salutary, still, it was not necessary, nor can it be understood from that citation, that at the time of Ambrose were this not to be done that the Church would have ceased to exist.

Lastly, they produce Jerome, who said: "By the inspiration of the devil, some became zealous in religion, and even said among the people: 'I am of Paul, I Apollo, but I of Cephas,' they were governed by the common counsel of priests of the Church. Yet, afterward, when everyone began to consider those whom he had baptized as his own, not Christ's, it was decreed in the whole world that one chosen among the priests should be placed above the rest, to whom all the care of the Church belonged, and so the seeds of schismatics were abolished."[10]

---

[5] Lib 3, epist. 19.

[6] *Ibid.* Epist. 10.

[7] Comment. 5, ch. On the first epist. to Tim.

[8] 3 Kings (1 Kings) 12:6.

[9] Esther 1:13-14.

[10] In ch. 1 ad Titum.

Therefore, they argue, in the first period of the Church (which I readily grant was the purest), aristocracy flourished and priests were the aristocrats.

I respond: It seems that St. Jerome was of that opinion which reckons that, bishops, if it is a question of jurisdiction, are indeed greater priests, but with respect to ecclesiastical law, not divine law; such an opinion is false, and must be refuted in its place. Meanwhile, this in no way advances that aristocracy of priests which Calvin holds to, but considerably strikes against it. For Jerome does not say that in the first age of the Church an aristocracy of priests flourished, and that it was good government, but little by little afterward, through some abuse, monarchy was introduced by wicked men. Rather he affirms on the contrary that there was an aristocracy in the beginning, but since it was not advancing well, and thereupon many seditions and schisms arose, by the common counsel of the whole world, it was changed into monarchy.

Nor can there be any doubt whether Jerome would have taken notice that this change came to pass in the times of the apostles and from those apostolic authors. In this citation he says then a change occurred, when it began to be said: "I am of Paul, I of Apollo," as Paul witnesses what happened in his own time in 1 Corinthians 1. Next, Jerome says that James was created the bishop of Jerusalem by the apostles immediately after the passion of the Lord,[11] and asserts that St. Mark was the bishop of Alexandria.[12]

Add that Jerome does not speak about the universal government of the Church, but only of particular places, when he says that from the beginning the Churches began to be governed by the common counsel of priests. Besides, Peter was constituted as head of the whole Church, as the same Jerome teaches by means of eloquent words: "From the twelve one is chosen that being constituted as the head, the occasion of schism should be abolished."[13]

---

[11]   In lib., *de vir. Illust.* In Jacobo.

[12]   In epist. *Ad Evagr.*, 85.

[13]   In lib. 1 *cont. Jovinian.*

CHAPTER IX
Why the Ecclesiastical Government Should Particularly be a Monarchy

HE LAST proposition remains, which affirms that the government of the Church should particularly be a monarchy.

Certainly the first reason whereby the proposition is proved can be deduced from the aforesaid, for if there are three forms of rule, monarchy, aristocracy, and democracy, as has already been shown, the government of the Church ought not be either a democracy, or an aristocracy. Consequently, what else remains but monarchy? Thereafter, if monarchy is the best and most useful government, as we taught above, and is certain that the Church of God was established by the wisest of all rulers, Christ, to govern in the best way, then who can deny that his reign ought to be a monarchy?

Yet Calvin resists this and denies it, because for him, if monarchy were in fact the best form of government, it follows that the Church ought to be governed by some individual man, whereas it is certain that its king and monarch is Christ himself.[1]

But this is easily refuted, for although Christ is the one and proper king and monarch of the Catholic Church, and he rules and moderates invisibly and spiritually, nevertheless, the Church, which is corporeal and visible, needs some single visible supreme Judge, by whom controversies arising on religion might be settled, who would contain all lower prefects in office and unity. Otherwise, not only the supreme Pontiff, but even bishops, pastors, teachers and ministers, all would be redundant: for Christ is the shepherd "and bishop of our souls."[2] He is the single teacher, whom the Father of heaven bids us to hear.[3] He is the one "who baptizes in the Holy Spirit."[4]

Therefore, in the same way in which bishops, teachers and the remaining ministers are not redundant, even if Christ does what they do as ministers, so also one who, as a supreme steward, manages the care of the whole Church is not abolished from the midst even though Christ principally manages the same thing.

The second reason is brought in from the similitude which the Church of mortal men has with the Church of immortal angels. St. Gregory the Great also

---

[1] Calvin, *Instit.,* lib. 4, ch. 6 § 9.

[2] 1 Peter 2:25.

[3] Matt. 17:5.

[4] John 1:33.

uses this reasoning.[5] Accordingly this is a certain exemplar of it, and like an idea, as the Apostle appears to indicate.[6] St. Bernard eloquently affirms this when he speaks of the militant Church in that verse of the Apocalypse, "the new Jerusalem descending from heaven," he says has been addressed, and this is why it was established and conformed to the example of that heavenly city.

Nor has it been less certain and explored among the angels that besides God the supreme king of all, there is one who is over all others. But from the beginning that one was provided with this dignity, who now is called the devil; as many of the Fathers witness.[7] It can also be deduced from Scripture, in the book of Job where Behemot, that is, the devil, is called the prince of the ways of the Lord and in Isaiah,[8] where he is compared to Lucifer, that is, the greatest and most beautiful of the stars, at least in regard to appearance, and by common teaching, to which the Scriptures customarily accommodate themselves. Moreover, St. Jerome and Cyril teach on this passage that this Lucifer is the devil, as does Augustine.[9] There is also the book of Ezekiel, where it is said, "Every precious stone is your covering;"[10] and soon nine stones shall be enumerated, whereby it is meant, as Gregory expresses, the nine choirs of angels, which stood around this angel just as their prince.[11]

But after the fall of the devil, St. Michael is taken to be the prince of all the angels, from ch. 12 of the Apocalypse, where it is said: "Michael and his angels." Certainly, what does "Michael and his angels" mean, but Michael and his army? Since it is said the devil and his angels in the same place, we understand all wicked angels to be his subjects, just as soldiers are subject to their general. So also, when it says "Michael and his angels," we ought to understand all good angels acknowledge Michael as their prince, for which reason St. Michael has rightly been placed in ecclesiastical office of paradise, and has been named the prince of the heavenly host.

Calvin has nothing other to say than that it is not fitting to speak on

---

[5] St. Gregory, lib. 4 *epist.* 52.

[6] Hebrews 8:1-5.

[7] Tertull. Lib.. 2 *Contra Marcion*, Gregor. *Hom. 34; in Evang., and book 32 Moral*, ch. 24; Jerome, or rather more Bede in ch. 40 *of Job*; Isidor. Lib. 1 *De summa bona*, ch. 12.

[8] Job 40:15-24; Isaiah 14:12-15.

[9] Augustine, *de Civitate Dei*, lib. 11. Ch. 15.

[10] Ezechial 28:13.

[11] *Moral.* lib. 32, ch. 25.

heavenly matters except with exceeding temperance, and that no type of the Church must be sought than the one that is expressed in the Gospel and in the epistles of the holy Apostles.[12] But one need not speak with temperance, as it were, who says nothing from his own head, but follows the Apostles and the holy Fathers.

The third reason is taken from the Church of the Old Testament. It is certain that the Old Testament was a figure of the New, as the Apostle says: "All of these things were contained for them in figure."[13] In the time of the Old Testament there was always one who was over all in those matters which pertained to law and religion, especially from the time in which the Hebrews began to be rendered into the form of a people, and be governed by laws and magistrates, which was after the Exodus out of Egypt. Then indeed Moses ordered the commonwealth of the Jews; he wrote laws for them which he had received from God. He consecrated Aaron the priest and subjected all the priests and levites to one. And thereafter even to the times of Christ the one chief of the priests did not pass away, who governed all the synagogues of the whole world. That can be easily proved and it is even conceded by our opponents. So speak the Centuriators of Magdeburg: "In the Church of the Judaic people there was only one high priest by divine law whom all were compelled to acknowledge and obey."[14] Calvin affirms precisely the same thing.[15]

Therefore, since the Church of that time was a figure of the Church of this time, reason altogether furnishes that, just as the former had one visible ruler besides God the invisible ruler, so also the latter also should have these; accordingly there ought to be no perfection found in a figure which is not found more exactly in the embodiment [of the type].

Now Calvin applies two answers to this argument. The first is that the one meager Jewish people and all Christians of the whole world are not at all the same thing. He says: "The one people of the Jews ought, beset all about by the idolatrous, to have one high priest to maintain in unity lest they be dragged away by various religions. But to give the Christian people diffused throughout the whole world one head is absolutely absurd."[16] And he adds the similitude: "Just as for this reason the whole world ought not be committed to one man,

---

[12] *Institut.* Lib. 4, ch. 6 § 10.

[13] 1 Corinth. 10:11.

[14] *Cent.* 1, lib. 1, ch. 7, col. 257.

[15] *Instit.*, lib. 4, ch. 6 § 2.

[16] Ibid.

because one field is cultivated by one man."

To be sure, however, this first answer seems to not really answer the argument but to tie it more and more into a knot. For if the reason why the Jewish people had one head, as Calvin says, was so that it would be contained in unity and not defect to idolatry, those who took possession of it, for a greater reason, ought to have one head of the Church of Christians. For there it is more required to have one head where it is more difficult for unity to be preserved, where there is greater danger lest people be pulled away to different religions. Moreover it is more difficult for unity to be preserved in a greater multitude than in a lesser one, and the danger is greater where there are many enemies of the faith than when they were fewer. But the Christian people is much greater than ever the Jewish people was, and Christians have many enemies; they are not only besieged by Turks, Tartars, Moors, Jews, and other unbelievers, but they live among innumerable sects of heretics. Consequently, unity is much more difficult to preserve among Christians and a greater danger threatens from the enemies of religion than once threatened the Jews, either unity will be preserved or danger will threaten.

Hence, by that reason whereby Calvin attributes a head to the people of the Jews, he ought to attribute the same or greater to the Christian people. Secondly, the similitude on farming also effects nothing, nor do we wish that one man being put in charge should by himself rule the whole Christian world, to the extent that one farmer himself tills one field, yet we likewise commit to one supreme shepherd to rule the whole Christian world that he might rule through many other lesser pastors, just as one rich householder cultivates many fields through many farmers and one king administers many cities and provinces through many viceroys and governors.

Next, Calvin adds another response, saying that Aaron bore the figure not of a priest of the New Testament, but of Christ; hence, when Christ completed the figure in himself, there is nothing from it that the Pope can claim for his own.

Indeed, we do not only press the argument with the figure of Aaron, but of the whole Old Testament. Since the Old Testament is a figure of the New, just as there is monarchic rule in the old, so we say it ought to be in the new. I add besides, even Aaron himself not only bore the figure of Christ, but also of Peter to his successor: just as the sacrifices of the old law signify the sacrifice of the Cross, and at the same time they were a type of that sacrifice, which is now offered in the Church, so the high priest of the Old Testament both refers to Christ the high priest and at the same time was a type of his priesthood, which now we see in the Church; moreover, this is the same reasoning of sacrifice and priesthood.

Perhaps they will deny that the old sacrifices signify the passion of Christ, and at the same time our sacrifice, but St. Augustine teaches this: "The Jews in the victims of cattle, which they offered to God, in many and different modes, just as it was worthy by such a matter, they celebrated a prophecy of the future victim, which Christ offered up. For that reason Christians now carrying out the memory of his sacrifice, celebrate it by the most holy offering and partaking of the body and blood of the Lord."[17] He also says: "The whole, which the faithful know in the sacrifice of the Church what was foreshadowed by every kind of the first sacrifices ... The Lord himself commanded a leper to the same Sacraments, he sent to the priests that they would offer the sacrifice for him, since it had not yet succeeded them in sacrifice, which he wished to be celebrated afterward in the Church for all of those that he had pre-announced in all of them."[18]

There is no other reason why St. Gregory interpreted all the things which are said on the garments and decor of Aaron to concern his virtues, which are required among Christian pontiffs.[19] Likewise, why Cyprian expresses those things in the Old Testament about the Aaronic priests describe our priests (which all other Fathers frequently do), except that because the new priesthood succeeded the old, and the Christian pontiffs the Jewish ones, as much as they succeeded certain types and foreshadowings.

The fourth reason is sought from those similitudes, in which the Church is described in the Scripture. Moreover, they all show that necessarily there ought to be one head in the Church. The Church is compared with the "army in array" in the Canticles,[20] to a human body or a beautiful woman,[21] to a kingdom, a sheepfold, a house, a boat or the Ark of Noah.[22] Now there is no well-ordered camp where there might not be one general, many tribunes, and many lieutenants, etc. St. Jerome says: "In every powerful army they await the sign of one."[23] How therefore, is the Church a well ordered army, if all the bishops, nay more all the priests are equals, and by equal reasoning one head in every human

---

[17] *Contra Faustum*, lib.. 20, ch. 18.

[18] Augustine, *Contra adversarium legis et prophetae*, ch. 18; *de Baptismo*, lib. 3, ch. 19.

[19] Gregory, *De Cur. Pastor.* Par. 2, ch. 4.

[20] Song of Songs, 6:10.

[21] Ibid, 7:1-9.

[22] Daniel 2:44-45; John 10:1-18; 1 Timoth. 3:15; 1 Peter 3:20-21.

[23] *Epist. ad Rusticum monach.*

body?

Perhaps you might say: the Church has its own head, Christ, and this is why we cannot compare the Church with Christ in this place as the members with the head, even the bride with the bridegroom as the Scriptures use the similitude.[24] And certainly, if the Church which is on earth, with Christ being far off, is not ineptly compared to the bridegroom, even while Christ is absent, it ought to have one head, especially with the eloquent declaration of the Canticles, enumerating even the head among its other members, when the bridegroom says to the bride: "Thy head is as Carmel,"[25] and the bride concerning the bridegroom: "His head is the best gold."[26] And truly the bridegroom compares the head of the bride to mount Carmel, because even if the High Priest is as vast as a mountain, nevertheless, it is nothing other than the land that is man. The bride compares the head of the spouse to the best gold, because the head of Christ is God.

Now truly, was there ever a kingdom that was not ruled by one? And although the king of the Church is Christ, nevertheless, we gather from him that the Church ought to have someone apart from Christ by which it is ruled, because kingdoms are always royally administered that is, through one who is in charge of all. Accordingly, when the king is present he does it through himself; but if he is away, he does it through another, who is called a viceroy; often even with the king present, some general vicar is constituted.

Moreover, one sheepfold also requires one shepherd, as is gathered from the Gospel: "There will be one flock and one shepherd."[27] It must be noted in passing that "one shepherd" can be understood concerning a secondary pastor, namely Peter and his successors, as Cyprian expresses it. For when the Lord said he has other flocks and other sheep who are not of this fold, he speaks on the Gentile people and the people of the Jews, but he teaches that he has among the nations many elect, who either are already faithful, or certainly are going to be, and nevertheless, they do not pertain to that Judaic people.

If it is a question of the shepherd of God, the people of the Jews and gentiles were always one flock, and one God was their shepherd; nevertheless, there was not always one flock and one shepherd with respect to the governance of the human race, nor were the gentiles, or those among them pertaining to the Church, really ruled by the priest of the Jews. But Christ wished after his arrival

---

24 Apoc. 21:2; 2 Cor. 11:2; Ephes. 5:23-32; often in the Song of Songs.

25 Song of Songs 7:5.

26 Ibid, 5:11.

27 John 10:16.

that one flock be made from each people and all men to be governed by one shepherd. Hence, Cyprian says while speaking about Novatian, who wished to be made bishop of Rome while Cornelius had already been created such and sat: "Therefore, the Lord insinuating in us the unity coming from divine authority, so places it and says, 'I and the Father are one:' relegating his Church to such a unity again he says, 'And there will be one flock and one shepherd.' But if one flock, how can one be counted in the flock who is not in the number of the flock? Or how can the pastor be contained who, while truly remaining pastor, even in the Church of God succeeds to the presidency by ordination succeeding nobody, and beginning from himself be foreign and profane?"[28]

The similitude of the house and the boat remain, and indeed every house has one Lord and one steward, according to that passage of Luke's gospel, "Who do you think is the faithful dispenser, and prudent, whom the Lord constituted over his household?"[29] These words are said for Peter, and about Peter himself, since a little before the Lord had said to him: "Blessed are those servants whom the Lord will discover watching when he will have come." Peter asked: "O Lord, you speak to us this parable, can it be for all? The Lord responded to Peter: 'Who do you think is the faithful and prudent dispenser, whom the Lord constituted over his house'?" It is just as if he were to say, O Peter I say in the first place, it behooves you to consider what is required in a faithful and prudent steward whom the Lord will establish over his household.

And a little after that he might show himself to speak concerning one whom he will place over all that must be preserved and who shall be subject to the Lord alone, he adds, "What if that servant will have said in his heart, 'my Lord delays his arrival,' and begun to strike the servants and maidservants and to eat and drink and become drunk; the Master of that servant will come on a day he hopes not, and at an hour he does not know, and will divide him [from the rest], and will place him on the side of the treacherous." The Lord openly marks out with such words that he is intending to place one servant over the whole house, who can be judged by himself alone. Chrysostom eloquently teaches that this citation concerns Peter and his successors,[30] agreeing with Ambrose, or whoever is the author of that commentary on Chapter 3 to Timothy: "The House of God is the Church, whose ruler today is Damasus."

Thereupon, concerning the boat, St. Jerome says "In the boat there is one captain," and Cyprian a little after taught that the ark of Noah was a type of the

---

[28] Cyprian, *Epistula 6 ad Magnum*, lib. 1.

[29] Luke 12:42.

[30] *De Sacerd. Cir. Princ.*, lib. 2.

Church, and goes on to prove that Novatian could not be made captain of the ark, because Cornelius already had been, and one boat demands one ruler, not many.

The fifth reason is brought in from the first age of Church government. It is certain, therefore, that the Church gathered by Christ began from the first to have a visible and external monarchical rule, not an aristocracy, or a democracy. Indeed, Christ, when he lived on earth, visibly administered it, as its supreme shepherd and rector, as even the Centuriators affirm.[31] Even now the Church ought to have external and visible monarchical rule, otherwise what exists today would not be the Church. The same can be said of the city of God. As Aristotle teaches, a city is described by the same species as long as the same form of the commonwealth remains[32] that is, the same common mode of government, which, were it be changed, the state would also be changed.

The sixth reason is led in from a like thing. Individual bishops are rightly established in individual places, who are over all the rest of the ministers and pastors of the place. Now Calvin affirms this in these words: "What else will this bring to pass except that individual churches ought to be given their own bishops?"[33]

Again, in individual provinces individual metropolitans are rightly constituted that govern the bishops of their province, and in greater cities primates or patriarchs who, as St. Leo says, receive a greater care.[34] Even Calvin has not dared to deny this.[35] Therefore, it is equitable that there should be someone that is in charge of the whole Church, and to whom primates and patriarchs should also be subjected. For if monarchical rule is fitting for one city, one province, one nation, why not even for the whole Church? What reason demands that only parts should be ruled by monarchies, while the rest is governed aristocratically?

Thereupon, it is proven by such reasons as: there ought to be a bishop in charge of priests, an archbishop in charge of bishops, a patriarch over archbishops; by the same it can be proven that one supreme bishop ought to be

---

[31] *Cent. 1*, lib. 1, ch. 7, col. 268.

[32] *Politika*, lib. 3, ch. 2.

[33] *Instit.*, lib.. 4, ch. 6, § 7.

[34] St. Leo, *Epistula ad Anastas. Thessal. Archiep.*

[35] He so speaks in the *Institutes*, lib..4 ch. 4 § 4: "Moreover, individual provinces had one among the bishops as an archbishop: likewise in the Council of Nicaea patriarchs who were superior to archbishops were constituted by order and dignity; that pertained to the preservation of discipline."

in charge of the patriarchs. Why is one bishop necessary in individual churches, except that one city cannot be ruled well unless it is by only one? But the universal Church is also one. In like manner, why is one archbishop required except that the bishops might be contained in unity, that controversies may be quelled, that they should be called to a Council and compelled to exercise their office? But on account of the same causes one is required who is in charge of all archbishops and primates.

Now Calvin will respond that the greater primacy of bishops over priests, and archbishops over the other bishops is from honor and dignity, not authority and power.[36]

Certainly he is deceived or else deceives. For (that I might omit other passages), when the Apostle says, "Do not receive any accusation against a priest unless it is under two or three witnesses,"[37] he makes a bishop the judge of the priest. Further, one is not a judge without power. Besides, in the Council of Antioch, canon 16 states that if any priest or deacon should be condemned by his own bishop, and being deprived of honor comes to another bishop, he is by no means to be received. Therefore, a bishop can condemn a priest and deprive him of honor, because it is certainly of his power and jurisdiction.

Likewise, in the Third Council of Carthage, the Fathers asserted that it was lawful for primates of the bishops from whichever diocese to take up clerics and ordain them bishops where a need will present itself, even against the will of the bishop to whom the cleric was subject.[38] Here, do we not obviously see that there is a greater primacy with respect to power over other bishops? Thereupon, St. Leo and St. Gregory openly teach that not all bishops are equal in power but some are truly subject to others; St. Leo rightly deduces that the rule of the universal Church pertains to the one See of Peter.[39]

The seventh reason can be taken up from the propagation of the Church. For, the Church always grew and ought to grow, until the gospel has been preached in the whole world, as is clear from Matthew 24:14, "This gospel of the kingdom will be preached in the whole world, and then the consummation will come." But this cannot happen unless there would be one supreme prelate of the Church to whom the care of preserving and propagating this whole body depends, for no one ought to preach unless he is sent. "How did they preach

---

[36] *Instit.*, lib. 4, ch. 4 § 2.

[37] 1 T:19imothy 5.

[38] *Concilium 3 Carthaginensi*, ch. 45.

[39] Leo, *Epistula ad Anast. Thessal.*, no 84; Gregory, *Epist. 52*, lib. 4.

unless they were sent?"[40] But to send someone to foreign provinces is not a power of particular bishops; consequently, these have very certain boundaries of their own episcopacy, outside of which they have no right nor does the care pertain to them except of guarding the flock assigned to them.

Wherefore, in the history of the Centuriators of Magdeburg, we hardly discover a Church propagated after Apostolic times by any other than those whom the Roman Pontiffs sent to do the work of God. St. Boniface, being sent by Pope Gregory II, converted the Germans. St. Kilian, sent by Pope Conon converted the Franks; St. Augustine, being sent by Pope Gregory I, converted the English. Moreover, Pope Innocent constantly affirms, through all of Spain, France, and Africa, churches were founded through them whom Peter or his successors sent into this work.

The eighth reason is brought in from the unity of Faith. In fact it is necessary that all the faithful believe altogether the same thing in matters of Faith: "There is one God, one Faith, one Baptism."[41] But there can not be one Faith in the Church, if there were not one supreme judge, to whom all were held to acquiesce. The very fact of the dissension of the Lutherans, which we see, certainly teaches us sufficiently, even if there were to be no other reason that they do not have one to whom all are held subject as their judge, thus they have been divided into a thousand sects; still, they all descend from one Luther and yet they could not compel one council in which all would come together. Rather, even the most obvious reason persuades it. Since there are many equals, it can hardly happen that in obscure and difficult matters in their judgment any would wish to be placed before the other as a judge.

The Centuriators respond that the unity of the Faith can be preserved through the association of many churches, which would help each other, and treat on questions of Faith through letters amongst themselves.[42] But that certainly does not suffice since to preserve the unity of Faith counsel is not enough; rule is required. Otherwise what would happen if a bishop were erring and refuse to right to the others, or if after he had written he refused to follow their counsel? Was not Illyricus admonished by his colleagues that he should retract that Manichean error on original sin which he had aroused again from the pits of hell, and was never able to be persuaded or even patiently hear them? And if this meeting is so efficacious, why has peace and concord as yet still not been effected between soft and rigid Lutherans?

---

[40] Romans 10:15.

[41] Ephesians 4:5.

[42] *Centur 1* lib. 2 ch. 7 col. 522 et sequent.

You will say perhaps: The questions will be put to rest by a general council. They will accept everything from a greater part of the bishops. On the other hand a greater part of a general council can err if the authority of a supreme shepherd is lacking, as is proved by the experiment of the Armenians and that of the 2nd Council of Ephesus. Additionally, general councils can not always be compelled; in the first 300 years no general council could come about and nevertheless, many heresies existed then.

It remains that we should rebut the objections. First Calvin objects: "Contention happened among them [the Apostles], over who would seem to be greater, but the Lord said to them, 'Kings of nations lord it over their people; but it will not be so with you'." On that citation Calvin says: "The Lord taught that their ministry was not like that of a king, in which, one would not excel the rest in order that he might restrain this vain ambition of theirs."[43]

I respond: Both in this passage and in Matthew 20, the Lord does not remove monarchy from the Church, but rather more established it and advised that it would be different from the civil monarchy of the nations. Firstly, the Lord does not say you will not be in charge of others in any way, but rather "Thou will not be in charge *as* they," that means you truly will be in charge, but in a different way than they. Thereupon, is it not clearly added in this Matthew 20:26-27: "He who is greater among you, let him be as the younger, and he who is leader, (in Greek that is ἡγούμενος a general and prince), let him be made your servant"? Therefore, one was designated by the Lord.

Next, he declared the matter by his own example, "Just as I have not come to be ministered to, but to minister," and "I am in your midst, just as one who ministers." Nevertheless, he says about himself in John's Gospel: "You call me teacher and Lord, and you speak rightly, for I really am" (John 13:13). Just as Christ, therefore, did not lord it over, nor did he take charge even though he was the Lord, so also he wishes one from his own to truly be in charge, but without the lust for domination, such is in the kings of the nations, who are mostly tyrants, and command those subject to them like slaves and refer all things to their own pleasure and glory. Therefore, he wants his vicar to be over the Church as a shepherd and a father who does not seek honor and profit, but the good of his subjects, and that apart from the rest to labor and serve to the advantage of all.

Besides the kings of the nations, even those who are not tyrants, so administer their realms that they might leave behind a proper heir which is in their sons; but prelates of the Church are not so. Consequently they are not

---

[43] *Instit.*, lib. 4, ch. 20, § 7.

kings, but vicars; not householders, but viceroys. For this reason St. Bernard says, "Why do you not refuse to be in charge and reject lordship? Plainly thus, just as he does not rule well who rules in anxiety, you rule to provide, to consult, procure and serve; you are in charge to be so as a faithful and prudent servant whom the Lord has established over his household."[44]

The second objection of Calvin is that, "In Ephesians 4 the Apostle delineates to us the whole ecclesiastical hierarchy that Christ left behind after his ascension from earth. However, there is no mention of one head, rather the rule of the church passed to many in common. Moreover, the Apostle says himself, 'He gave some as apostles, some as prophets, but others evangelists, still others pastors and teachers.' He did not say that first he gave one as supreme pontiff, and others as bishops, pastors, etc."[45]

Likewise, "'Be solicitous to preserve unity of the spirit in the bond of peace, one body and one spirit, just as you were called in one hope of your calling, there is one Lord, one Faith,' and he did not say, there is one supreme pontiff to preserve the Church in unity." Again the same thing, "'To each one of us grace was given according to the measure of the gift of Christ.' And he did not say, to one was given the fullness of power and that in turn he governs for Christ, but his portion was given to individual men."

I respond: The supreme pontificate is eloquently posited by the Apostle in these very words, "And he gave some as apostles," and more clearly in 1 Corinthians 12, where he says, "And he placed in the Church first the apostles, secondly prophets." If ever a supreme ecclesiastical power was not only given to Peter, but even to the other apostles, therefore, all could say what Paul says, "My daily urgency is the care of all Churches,"[46] but to Peter it was given as an ordinary shepherd, to whom men would succeed others in perpetuity, while to the others it was just as delegated, to whom men did not succeed. There was, therefore, in those first days of the Church, a necessity to disseminate the faith quickly throughout the whole world that supreme power and freedom had to be conceded to the first preachers and founders of the Church. After the apostles died, however, the apostolic authority remained in the successor of Peter alone; indeed no bishop apart from the Roman Bishop ever had care of all the Churches, and he alone was called the Apostolic Pontiff by all, and his see the Apostolic See, both simply and by the *antinomasia* and office of his apostolate. We add here a few testimonies of this affair.

---

[44] *De Consider.*, lib. 3.

[45] *Instit.*, lib. 4, ch. 6 § 1.

[46] 2 Cor. 11:28.

Jerome says, "You who follow the apostles in honor, should also follow them worthily." And again, "I wonder how the bishops received something which the Apostolic See condemned."[47] Also, a great number of French bishops wrote to Pope Leo, which is number 52 among the epistles to Leo, "Let your apostolate give pardon to our lateness." And in the end of the letter, "Pray for me, O blessed Lord, to venerate the Apostolic Pope with merit and honor." Likewise, "I venerate and salute your apostolate in the Lord." Augustine declares, "The first place always flourishes in the Roman Church at the apostolic chair."[48]

Thereupon (that I should omit an infinite number of similar things), the Council of Chalcedon, in an epistle to Pope Leo, relates, "And after [having said] all these things, over and against the very one to whom the Lord had consigned care of his vineyard, he enlarged the insanity that is against thy apostolic sanctity." Hence, St. Bernard, speaking about all the apostles, concerning whom it is said in the Psalms, "You will constitute them princes over all the earth;"[49] he says to Pope Eugene, "You succeeded them in inheritance, so You, O heir, and inheritance of the world."[50] And below this very citation: "And he himself gave some as Apostles," he understands concerning the pontifical authority."

This response can also be made: The Apostle does not delineate the hierarchy of the Church in this citation, rather he merely enumerates the different gifts which are in the Church. Hence, first he places *Apostles* that is, those who were first sent by God. Secondly *Prophets* that is, those who predict the future, as the fathers Chrysostom, Oecumenius and Theophylactus put it. Thirdly, *Evangelists* that is, those who wrote the Gospels, as the same fathers show. Lastly, *Pastors and teachers*, and by that one saying he signified, albeit confusedly, the whole hierarchy of ministers of the Church. Also, he adds in 1 Corinthians the types of tongues, duties and other things which are not ecclesiastical ministries, but charisms of the Holy Spirit.

Next, to the objection on one body, one spirit, one Faith, one God, in which one Pope is not enumerated, I respond: one Pope is taken up in those words *one body and one spirit*: as indeed the unity of the members is preserved in the natural body that all obey the head, so also then in the Church unity is preserved when all obey the one.

And although the head of the whole Church is Christ, nevertheless, since he is away from the Church militant with respect to his visible presence, some

---

[47] Jerome, *Epist. 2 ad Damas. De nom. Hypost.*; *Contra Ruffinum*, lib. 2.

[48] Augustine, *Epistula 162.*

[49] Psalm 44 (45):16.

[50] *De Consider.*, lib.. 3, near the beginning.

one man is necessarily considered in the place of Christ that he may contain this visible Church in unity. This is why Optatus of Miletus calls Peter the head, and places unity of the Church in him, so that all adhere with that very head. John Chrysostom also speaks thus on the Church, "whose pastor and head is a fisherman and of low birth."[51]

Now I respond to that argument on the fullness of power. The supreme pontiff, if he might be compared with Christ, does not have a fullness of power, but only some portion according to the measure of the donation of Christ. Therefore, Christ rules all the Church, which is in heaven, in purgatory and on earth, as well as what was from the beginning of the world and will be even to the end; besides he can make laws from his own will, establish Sacraments, and give grace, even without the Sacraments.

But the Pope only rules that part of the Church which is on earth while he lives, nor can he change the laws of Christ or establish Sacraments, or remit sins outside of the Sacrament [of penance]. Nevertheless, if the supreme Pontiff is compared with the other bishops then he is rightly said to have the fullness of power, because they have definite regions over which they are in charge; even their power is defined. The Pope, on the other hand, has been put over the whole Christian world and he has the whole and full power, which Christ left behind for the utility of the Church on earth.

The third objection is of Calvin, where he uses this argument: "Christ is the head of the Church, as we read in Ephesians 4, therefore, one does an injury to Christ to call another the head."

I respond: No injury is made to Christ for the very reason that the Pope may be the head of the Church, rather his glory is increased by it. For we do not assert that the Pope is head of the Church with Christ, but under Christ, as his minister and vicar. It does no injury to the king if a viceroy should be called the head of the kingdom under the king, why it even increases his glory, therefore, all who hear the viceroy is the head of the kingdom under the king, soon they think that the king is the head in a more noble manner.

Add what Christ himself says concerning himself in the Scripture, "I am the light of the world," nevertheless, he does himself no injury. And the Apostle who said, "No man can place any other foundation apart from that which has been placed, which is Christ,"[52] also said "you are built on the foundation of apostles and prophets." Even though Christ may be the pastor and bishop of our souls, and the apostle of our confession and a prophetic man, and doctor of

---

[51] *Hom. 55 in Matth.*

[52] 1 Corinthians 3:11.

justice, nevertheless, Paul did him no injury when he wrote in Ephesians 4 that in the Church there are apostles, prophets, pastors and teachers. Thereupon, what name is there that is more august than that of God? Nevertheless, men are more than once called gods in Scripture without any injury to the true God. "I have said, ye are gods."[53] Why indeed will there be an injury to Christ the head of the Church if another might be said to be the head under him?

But they say, there was never any Church called the body of Peter, or of the Pope, but of Christ, I respond: the cause of the matter is that Christ alone should be the principle and perpetual head of the whole Church; that the kingdom is not said to be of a viceroy, but of a king, and the house is not of a steward, but of the Lord: thus the Church is not the body of Peter or the Pope, who only for a time, and governs it in place of another, but of Christ, who is the proper authority, and perpetually rules it.

Besides, when the Church is called the body of Christ that term "of Christ" can suitably be referred not just to Christ as head, but to the same Christ as a hypostasis of his body; just the same when we say the body of Peter is in that place, of Paul in that place, we do not mean Peter or Paul are bodies, but persons whose bodies these are. Therefore, Christ is not only the head of the Church, but he is a certain great body constituted from many and different members. St. Augustine notes because of the very thing which the Apostle says in 1 Corinthians: "Just as indeed there is one body that has many members, although the members are many, the body is truly one;" he does not add, "so even the body of Christ", but "so even Christ." Now, therefore, the Church is the body of Christ, not of Peter, because Christ, just as he sustains all the members by the hypostasis of this body, and works in all, he sees through the eye, hears through the ears, he is indeed the one who teaches through a teacher, baptizes through a minister, does all things through all; certainly that is not asserted about Peter, nor in any other man.

The fourth objection is of Theodore Beza, who argues that the burden of ruling the whole charge can be the duty of God alone;[54] hence, it is impossible for us to affirm the argument when we commit the rule of the whole Church to the supreme Pontiff. Luther says the same thing in his work *de Potestate Papae*, and a little book by the same name was written up during the Schmalkaldich synod agreeing with Luther's opinion.

I respond: It cannot be done without a miracle that one man alone could rule the whole Church in his own person, and there is no Catholic that teaches this:

---

[53]   Psalm 81 (82):6.

[54]   Beza, *Confess.*, ch. 5, art. 5.

yet that one man might see to it through many ministers and shepherds subject to himself is not only possible, but we reckon even useful and advantageous. For, in the first place, did not the Apostle say that he himself had "care of every church?"[55] He does not only speak about all the churches which he had planted, but simply about all. For Chrysostom writes on this passage that Paul took care of every church in the world and it can be proved from the epistles to the Romans, Colossians and Hebrews, where he writes to them whom he had not preached, and whom, nevertheless, he thought pertain to his care.

And although the apostles distributed among themselves those parts in which they would preach the word of the Lord with a peculiar zeal, nevertheless, they did not confine their care to the boundaries of this or that province, rather each one managed the concern of the whole Church, as if that care pertained to themselves alone.

Next, many secular princes have from God a very large kingdom, and certainly greater than the whole Christian world might be, which would never have been given by God unless they could administer it. We have the examples in Nebuchadnezzar, concerning whom we read in Daniel, "Thou art a king of kings, and the God of heaven hath given thee a kingdom, and strength, and power, and glory: And all places wherein the children of men, and the beasts of the field do dwell."[56] Likewise we read in Isaiah about Cyrus, "Thus saith the Lord to my anointed Cyrus, whose right hand I have taken hold of, to subdue nations before his face, and to turn the backs of kings, etc."[57]

How great was this kingdom is obvious from the first Chapter of Esther, where the king of Persia, Xerxes, is said to have ruled over one hundred twenty seven provinces from India even to Ethiopia. On Augustus we read in Luke, "An edict went out from Caesar Augustus that the whole world should be marked out."[58] And certainly the world was never more happily administered than in the times of Augustus. That kingdom had been prepared by God that the Gospel should more easily spread through the whole world, as Eusebius and Pope Leo prove.[59]

Therefore, since God willed almost the whole world to obey the rule of one man: why could he not also commend the universal Church to the prudence and

---

[55] 2 Cor. 11:28.

[56] Daniel 2: 37-38.

[57] Isaiah 45:1.

[58] Luke 2:1.

[59] Eusebius, *de Demonstr. Evang.* lib. 3, ch. 9; Leo, *Serm. 1 de Sanctis Petro et Paulo.*

care of one man? Particularly since ecclesiastical governance may prove easier than political and those kings did not have any other assistance apart from human prudence and the general providence of God, whereas our Pontiff has supernatural light of Faith, the sacred Scriptures, heavenly Sacraments and the particular assistance of the divine Spirit.

Add that by far, democracy or aristocracy in the Church is far more difficult than monarchy. For democracy in the Church is not such as it was for the Romans or Athenians, where men ruled one city alone, which is not difficult to come together as one, and they could establish the vote for many. In the Church, however, if there were to be popular government, every Christian in the whole world would have the right to vote; but who could gather all Christians to decide something for the whole Church?

For equal reasoning aristocracy would not be such in the Church as it is now for the Venetians, in which only one elite class rules the city, which can easily gather and determine what they wish. But such as it is it never was the type of thing in which every magistracy of the whole world, that is, every bishop and priest of the whole Christian world, would have equal right of governance, and even to gather them would either be very difficult or impossible without a miracle.

The fifth objection is from a little book which the Lutherans published at the Smalkaldic synod on the primacy of the Pope. They say that Paul equalizes all ministers, and teaches that the Church is over all ministers when he says: "All are yours, whether Paul, or Apollo, or Cephas."[60]

I respond: I am not of so keen an intellect that I perceive the force of this argument. For, if on that account the ministers are equalized, because they are numbered together when they are named, either Paul, or Apollo, or Cephas, then also all generals, consuls, and emperors will also be equal, for Chrysostom says: "If any general, if a consul, if he who is crowned with a diadem should go out unworthily, restrain and repress him."[61] And does it not follow that the Church is above the ministers in authority and power, because they are established on account of the utility of the Church? Otherwise, what Paul meant by those words "All are yours" would mean both boys would rule their tutors and the people would excel kings in authority, but tutors are so because of boys, and kings for the people, not the other way around.

The sixth objection is from the same book, "Christ sent all the apostles equally, as he says to them in John "I send you;" therefore, no one is in charge

---

[60]   1 Cor. 3:22.

[61]   Hom. 83 in Matth.

of the rest.

I respond: By those words one is not put in charge of the others, but we do not lack other citations whereby one man is put in charge. Certainly in John 21:17 it is said to only one man: "Feed my sheep."

Lastly, others object that if the world ought to be governed by one man in matters which pertain to religion it would be useful that it would be ruled by one in those matters which consider to the political order. But this has never happened nor is it expedient, as Augustine teaches: "With respect to human affairs all realms should be small and rejoice in the peace of small communities."[62]

I respond: The purpose of political rule and ecclesiastical rule are not the same thing. Accordingly, the world ought not necessarily be one kingdom, hence, it does not necessarily demand one who is in charge of all. The whole Church, nevertheless, is one kingdom, one city, one house, and therefore, ought to be ruled by one. That is the cause of this difference that it is not necessarily required for the preservation of political realms that every province should keep the same laws, and the same rites. They can indeed use laws and institutions for the variety and diversity of places and persons, and for that reason one man is not required to contain all in unity. Yet, it is necessary for the preservation of the Church that all should come together in the same faith, in the same Sacraments, in the same divinely handed down precepts which can not rightly be done unless they are one people, and contained by one in unity.

On the other hand, the question can be taken up whether it might be expedient that all provinces of the world are governed by one supreme king in political matters, although it may not be necessary. Nevertheless, it seems to me altogether expedient, if it could be attained by one without injustice and wars, especially if this supreme monarchy would have under it not vicars and viceroys, but true princes, just as the supreme pontiff has bishops under him.

Nevertheless, since it does not seem that such a monarchy could come into being except by applying great force and many terrible wars, then St. Augustine speaks rightly; maybe human affairs would be happier if there were small kingdoms with happy peaceful communities, than if every sort of king were to contend through lawful and unlawful means to extend and propagate their kingdom. Add to that, what St. Augustine proves is about small kingdoms, but he does not deny that it would be useful if one supreme ruler were over these

---

[62] Augustine, *de Civitate Dei*, lib.. 4, ch. 15.

very small kings; it seems he rather more affirms that when he says small kingdoms ought to be in the happy peace of small communities, just in the same way as there are many houses in a city. Therefore, it is certain that there is one man whom every house obeys, although each would have its own head of house.

CHAPTER X

A Third Question is Proposed, and the Monarchy of Peter is Proven From the Citation of the Gospel According to Matthew, Chapter XVI

HITHERTO it has been explicated and, unless I am mistaken, sufficiently and diligently proven that monarchy is the best of all governments, and a rule of this sort ought to be in the Church of Christ. Now the third question remains: Was Peter the apostle constituted head of the whole Church and its prince in place of Christ by Christ himself?

All the heretics whom we have cited from the beginning skillfully deny this. On the other hand, the Catholics whom we have cited affirm it. Really, it is not a simple error but a pernicious heresy to deny that the primacy of Peter was established by Christ. We shall undertake to confirm it by a threefold reasoning and manner. First, from two citations of the Gospel, in one of which it is promised, in the other it is given. Then from the many privileges and prerogatives of St. Peter. Lastly, from the clear testimony of the Greek and Latin Fathers.

Now to the first. We shall begin with the first citation of Matthew 16, where we read, "You are Peter, and upon this rock I will build my Church, and I will give to you the keys of the kingdom of heaven and whatsoever you bind on earth will be bound even in heaven, and whatever you loose on earth will be loosed even in heaven."[1] The plain and obvious sense of these words is, as we shall understand, a promise to Peter of the supremacy of the whole Church under two metaphors. The first metaphor is the foundation and building: indeed there is a foundation in a building that is a head in the body, a ruler in a city, a king in a kingdom, a head of house in a house. The second is that of the keys, one to whom the keys of the city are handed over, is established as a king or certainly the ruler of the city who may wish to admit some and exclude others.

But the heretics distort this whole citation in wondrous manners, for they neither wish Peter to be understood through the rock nor concede keys as promises to Peter. Likewise they are able to persuade themselves that the metaphors of the foundation and the keys do not mean supreme ecclesiastical power.

Therefore, we must explain four questions. 1) Whether Peter might be that rock upon which the Church shall be founded. 2) Whether that foundation might be the ruler of the whole Church. 3) Whether Peter might be the one to whom the keys are given. 4) Whether the full power to govern the Church

---

[1]   Matthew 16: 16-18.

should be understood through the keys.

On the first question there are four opinions. The first is the common teaching of Catholics that the rock is Peter, that is, the person called Peter. Nevertheless, not as a particular person, but as the shepherd and head of the Church. The second on this citation is of Erasmus that every faithful man is this rock. The third is of Calvin that Christ is that rock.[2] The fourth is of Luther and the Centuriators that faith or the confession of faith is the rock about which the Lord spoke in this place.[3]

The first opinion, which is most true, in the first place is obviously deduced from the text itself. For that pronoun, *this [hanc]*, when it is said "And upon this rock," proves some rock, upon which the Lord spoke of a little before. Next, the Lord called Peter the rock; in fact he spoke Aramaic, and in the Aramaic tongue Peter is called Cephas, as we have it in John I:26. Moreover, Cephas means rock, as Jerome teaches,[4] and the matter is most certain. In every place in the Hebrew text it is סלע [Selah][5] that is, *rock*, in Aramaic it is *Cepha*; hence the Hebrew word כפא, [Kepha] means stone or boulder, where we read in Jeremiah "They went up to the boulders," in Hebrew that is: נכפים עלו [Nakapiym elo].

Therefore, the Lord said: "You are Cepha, and on this "Cepha": or in Latin, *"Tu es petra, et super hanc petram aedificabo Ecclesiam meam;"* from which it follows that the pronoun *hanc* can not refer to anything but Peter who in this place was called "rock" [petra].

But then why did the Latin Translator not put it, *"Tu es petra, et super hanc petram"*? Because it should follow the Greek codex: therefore, it does not render it literally from Aramaic, rather from the Greek in which we read: σὺ εἶ Πέτρος, καὶ ἐπὶ ταύτῃ τῇ πέτρᾳ οἰκοδομήσω μου τὴν ἐκκλησίαν. Why doesn't the Greek use σὺ εἶς πέτρα καὶ ἐπὶ ταύτῃ πέτρα? The reason is because among the Greeks both πέτρος and πέτρα mean a stone; it has been seen as more agreeable to the interpreter to render the name for a man in the masculine rather than in the feminine. Thus, to explain the metaphor, he did not wish to say in the second place, ἐπὶ τῷ πέτρῳ, which would have been ambiguous, but ἐπὶ τῇ πέτρᾳ,

---

[2] *Instit.*, lib.. 4, ch. 6 §6.

[3] Luther, *de Poteste Papae*; The Centuriators, *Centur. 1*, ch. 4, col. 175, and *De primatu papae* of the Smalkaldic synod, lib. 1.

[4] *Ad Galat.*, ch. 2.

[5] The Selah used in our manuscript of the Hebrew Old Testament is rendered: סלזה, perhaps owing to a manuscript or printing error. -Translator's note.

which means nothing other than the rock.[6]

The consensus of the whole Church agrees, both of the Greek and Latin Fathers. The whole Council of Chalcedon which was made up of 630 Fathers, in its third act, appeals to Peter as the rock and the foundation of the Catholic Church. Likewise, today every mouth sings in the Church the verses of St. Ambrose which have been sung for 1200 years in a hymn of praises of the Lord's day: *Hoc ipsa petra Ecclesiae canente culpam diluit*. Moreover, St. Augustine witnesses in his time the beginning sung from the verses of St. Ambrose that Peter is the rock upon which the Lord built the Church.[7]

Besides, from the Greek Fathers Origen says, "Look to that great foundation of the Church and most solid rock, upon which Christ founded the Church, why else would the Lord say 'man of little faith, why did you doubt?'"[8]

St. Athanasius wrote both in his name and in that of the Synod of Alexandria, "You are Peter, and upon your foundation the pillars of the Church that is the bishops, are strengthened." Athanasius elegantly makes Peter the foundation, upon which the bishops rest and upon which as pillars, the whole building has been placed.

St. Basil says, "Peter, on account of the excellence of faith has received the building of the Church in his person."[9] Gregory Nazianzen says, "Peter is called

---

[6] Translator's note: To aid those untrained in Greek, I offer the following: English has largely lost the concept of grammatical gender. There is no rhyme or reason for why a noun might be classified as masculine, feminine or neuter (neither), except that they follow certain relationships or parent nouns which fall into those categories. Pronouns standing in place of a masculine or feminine noun, for example, will be translated into English as "it", as we have no grammatical gender. The noun πέτρα (petra) in Greek is feminine, but Peter is masculine. Unlike in Semitic languages, if one applies a feminine noun to a man, it has unhappy connotations (explored in drama, satire and other literary genres of Ancient Greek) that imply effeminacy or other vices, and so it was customary in any context to make the feminine noun masculine to suit who it is being applied to. Therefore, Bellarmine makes the exegetical commentary that changing the feminine noun *petra* into a masculine ending, *Petros* (2nd declension masculine), means it can only apply to Peter's name, whereas in Semitic languages like Aramaic, this is not necessary and would have been understood from the context. Thus the Greek interpreter in the 1st century (whether the original of Matthew's gospel was in Aramaic or Hebrew, or even if it was Matthew himself remembering what the Lord had said in Aramaic and rendering it into Greek) adjusted Peter's name to correctly render this into Greek usage.

[7] *Retractiones*, lib.. 1, ch. 21.

[8] Origen, hom. 3, *in Exod.*

[9] *In Eunom.*, lib. 2.

the rock, and he holds the foundations of the faith believed by the Church."[10] Epiphanius says, "The Lord established Peter as the first of the apostles, the strong rock, upon which the Church of God was built."[11]

St. John Chrysostom notes that, "The Lord said, 'you are Peter, and I will build my Church upon you'."[12] Again: "But why is Peter the foundation of the Church? He is a vehement lover of Christ; he, unlearned in discourse, is the victor over orators; he inexperienced, who stops up the mouth of philosophers; he who was not otherwise trained in Greek wisdom, dissolved it like a spider's web; he who sent a seine into the sea, and made a catch of the whole world?"[13] Cyril teaches: "Simon is not now his name, but Peter, he predicted, signifying fittingly by that word that in him, just as a rock and the strongest stone, the Lord was going to build his Church."[14]

Psellus, "His legs just as marble pillars: through the legs, understand that Peter is the prince of the apostles, upon whom the Lord in the Gospel promised he was going to build his Church."[15] The commentary of Psellus is contained in the canticles of Theodoret. Theophylactus in ch. 22 of Luke says, "After me, [Christ], you are the rock of the Church, and the foundation." Euthymius says, "I place you as a foundation of believers, I will build my Church upon you."

From the Latins, we begin with Tertullian in his work *De Praescriptionibus*: "Was anything hidden from Peter, the one said to be the rock upon which the Church must be built?"[16] St. Cyprian; "Peter, whom the Lord chose first and upon whom he built his Church..."[17] He repeats similar things in passing.

Hillary declares, "O happy foundation of the Church in the solemn vow of a new name! Its worthy building on the rock, which annuls the laws of hell. O happy porter of heaven!"[18] Still, here Erasmus makes the notation in the margin, "Faith is the foundation of the Church," as if the name of "Faith" (*Fidei*) were changed, and not Simon, and the faith were the happy porter of heaven. Why

---

[10]   *In Ora. De moderat. Servan. In disputat.*

[11]   *In Ancor.*

[12]   *Hom. 55 in Matth.*

[13]   *Hom. 4 in ch. 6 of Isaiah.*

[14]   Cyril, lib. 2, ch. 12 in John.

[15]   Psellus, *Cant.* In ch. 5.

[16]   *De Praescriptionis*, ch. 22.

[17]   *Epist. ad Quintum.*

[18]   *In Matth.*, ch. 16.

indeed did Hilary not say "faith" in this place? Ambrose says, "At length, for the solidity of devotion he is called the rock of the Church, just as the Lord said, 'You are Peter,' etc. Therefore, he calls that first placed the foundations of faith in actions him Rock, and the immovable rock of the Christian work should contain the framework and the building."[19]

Jerome adds in his commentary on Matthew, "According to the metaphor of the rock it is rightly said to him, 'I will build my Church upon you.'" And he also says, speaking on the See of Peter, "Upon that rock, I know the Church was built."[20]

Augustine also teaches, "Count the priests even from the very seat of Peter: that is the rock which the proud gates of hell do not conquer."[21] Note how both Jerome and Augustine not only call the see of Peter the rock but that upon which the Church is founded, and against which the gates of hell will not prevail, because Peter is the rock, not as a particular man, but as a pontiff. Likewise Augustine says, "Therefore, the Lord named Peter as the foundation of the Church; and so the Church adorns this worthy foundation upon which the heights of the ecclesiastical edifice rise."[22]

Maximus the Confessor says, "Through Christ, Peter was made the rock, when the Lord said to him: 'You are Peter, and upon this rock, etc.'"[23] Paulinus in his letter to Severus: "The rock is Christ, but he also did not refuse the favor of this word to his disciple, to whom he said: 'upon this rock', etc."

Pope St. Leo, "The disposition of truth remains and Blessed Peter, persevering in the fortitude received of the rock, did not relinquish the government of the Church which he had received. Thus, he was appointed apart from the rest, that while the rock is spoken of, while the foundation is pronounced, while he is constituted the porter of the kingdom of heaven, that there should be such society with Christ, through the very mysteries we recall the title."[24] St. Gregory, "Who does not know that the holy Church is strengthened by the solidity of the prince of the apostles?"[25]

From all this it appears how great is the impudence of the heretics. Indeed,

---

[19] Ambrose, *Serm. 47.*

[20] Jerome, *in cap. 16. Matth.; Epist. ad Damas.*

[21] *In Psalmis contra partem Donati.*

[22] *Serm. 15 de Sanctis.*

[23] *Serm. 1 de sanctis Petro et Paulo.*

[24] *Serm 2, de annivers. Assumpt. Suae ad pontif. Die.*

[25] Lib.. 6, epist. 37.

Calvin says in the place we already cited that he refuses to bring in the Fathers, not because he can't, but because he refuses to disturb the readers by disputing such a clear matter. Moreover, Erasmus marvels at this citation of Matthew; there have been some who would distort this reference to the Roman Church, and strive to excuse Cyprian and Jerome, because they said upon Peter the Church was founded, as if this were some unheard-of paradox; nevertheless, all the Fathers teach it, and many more recent theologians as well as canonists, and in fact the ancient pontiffs, Clement, Anacletus, Marcellus, Pius, Julius and others whom we have omitted both for the sake of brevity and because our adversaries do not receive them.

Now we shall examine the second opinion which is of Erasmus. He recommends that all the faithful should be understood by the name of Peter, from what Origen says on this citation, "Peter is everyone who is an imitator of Christ and upon every rock of this sort the Church of God shall be built. Therefore, the Church, against which the gates of hell shall not prevail, consists in individuals who have been perfected, who have in themselves the association of words and works, and the senses of all things."[26]

But Origen expresses this citation allegorically, not literally as Erasmus dreams up; Origen expressed this citation literally in what was quoted above. In fact, this citation could not be understood as concerning all the faithful if it were read literally. It is obvious because of the fact that the Lord described Peter in different ways to indicate that he was speaking to him alone. He called him Simon which was the name his parents had given him, and added the name of his father, calling him son of Jonah, or John, in order to distinguish him from Simon the brother of Jude. He says: "Blessed are you, Simon bar Jonah," then he adds the name of Peter, which he had given him. Besides he used pronouns distinguishing a certain person, saying: "I say to thee that thou are Peter, etc." Therefore, if it were permitted to still assert that here nothing peculiar was conferred upon Peter, or a promise which was not made to any others, certainly every place of Scripture could be twisted.

Hence, if all the faithful are this rock, upon which the Church shall be founded, then all will be a foundation. If all are the foundation, where will the walls and roof of this building be? In what organ, if the whole body is the eye, will it hear? Where are the remaining members?[27] Add the fact that the same Erasmus considered it to be absurd that the Church is built upon the man Peter, but if that is so how will it be built upon individual faithful? Are they not men

---

[26] *Tract. 1 in Matth.*

[27] 1 Corinthinas 12:12-30.

also?

The third explanation is of Calvin who, although he speaks more obscurely, nevertheless, appears to understand Christ as the rock. And indeed it is an important matter to consider upon which rock the Church will be built, since the Apostle says, "No man can place another foundation, apart from that which was lain, which is Christ Jesus."[28]

Augustine also agrees when he says, "Upon this rock, which you confessed, I will build my Church."[29] Likewise in the *Retractions* he had retracted what he had said elsewhere that upon Peter the Church was built and teaches rather that it ought to be said to have been founded on Christ,[30] and the citation which we are treating must be understood thus.

Nobody doubts whether Christ should be the rock, and the first foundation of the Church, and it is gathered in some way even from this citation. For if Peter is the foundation of the Church in place of Christ, Christ is much more the foundation. But by no means is it a more proper sense, and I should say that the Church is to be built upon Peter is immediate and literal. The proper arguments prove the reasons hitherto presented.

Firstly, the pronoun *this* (*hanc*) cannot refer to Christ as the rock, but to Peter as the rock; moreover, it ought to be referred to something nearby, not to something remote. Next, it was not said to Christ but to Peter: "Thou are Cepha," that is *rock*. Next, although Christ can be called the rock, nevertheless, in this place he was not called rock by Peter's confession, rather Christ, Son of the living God. Moreover, the pronoun "*this*" ought to be referred to the one being called "rock," not to the one who is not called by this noun. Likewise if it were to refer to Christ, to what end was it said: "I say to thee that thou are Peter?" Obviously it is in vain unless it follows that it refers to Peter. Finally, if it were to refer to Christ then the Lord would not have said, "I will build" but "I am building my Church:" for he had already built up the apostles and many disciples on himself. He says, "I will build," because he had not yet constituted Peter the foundation, rather he was going to do that after his resurrection.

Now I address the argument of Calvin: St. Paul speaks not on any particular person, but on the primary foundation; otherwise he would oppose himself when he says, "You are built on the foundation of the apostles and prophets."[31] Likewise, he would also be opposed to John, who describes twelve foundations

---

[28] 1 Corinthian 3:11.

[29] *Tract. In Joannem, ult.* CF. *Serm. 13 de verb. Dom.*

[30] *Rectract.* Lib.. 1 ch. 21.

[31] Ephesians 2:20.

in the building of the Church, and explains that the apostles are meant through these foundations.[32]

Now I speak to that objection made from Augustine. In the first place he does not condemn our teaching, but only places something before it. Thus he speaks in the *Retractions*: "I said in a certain place concerning the apostle Peter that on him, just as on the rock, the Church was founded, which sense is also sung by the lips of many in the verses of St. Ambrose, where he says on the cock crowing: 'This, while the very rock of the Church sings, purges his crime.' Yet I know that I had beforehand most wisely expressed thus that upon this Peter who confessed him should be understood; but it was not said to him: 'thou art rock' but 'thou art Peter:' the rock was Christ. Of these two teachings, let the reader choose which one is more probable."[33] Thus Augustine. Therefore, Augustine did not think it a blasphemy, as Calvin did, to assert that the Church was built on Peter.

I further add that Augustine was deceived only by his ignorance of the Hebrew tongue. For his argument (as he shows in this place) is that it was not said "Thou are rock" but "Thou are Peter." Therefore, he thought the rock, upon which the Church should be built, was not Peter, because he believed *Cepha* does not signify rock, but something derived from rock (*petra*) such as *petrinum* or *petrejum*,[34] just as "Christian" does not mean Christ, but something derived from Christ so the Church must be built upon the rock, not upon something *petrinum* or *petrejum*. Augustine reckoned that Peter is not understood by that rock. Yet, if he had noticed that *Cepha* means nothing other than rock, and the Lord said "You are rock, and upon this rock," he would not have doubted the truth of our opinion.

The fourth opinion remains, which is common among nearly all Lutherans, and at first glance appears to be confirmed by the testimony of the Fathers. Accordingly Hillary teaches, "The building of the Church is the rock of confession ... This faith of the Church is the foundation: through this faith the gates of hell are weak against it: this faith of the kingdom of heaven holds the keys."[35] St. Ambrose says, "The foundation of the Church is faith."[36] St. John

---

[32] Apocalypse 21:14.

[33] *Retractiones*, lib.. 1, ch. 21.

[34] Translator's note: Literally *stony* and *found among rocks*, in the Latin of St. Augustine's day.

[35] *De Trinitate*, lib. 6.

[36] *In Lucam*, lib.. 6, ch. 9.

Chrysostom: "Upon this rock I will build my Church, that is, faith and confession."[37] Likewise Cyril, explaining this citation, "I reckon he called the rock nothing other than unshaken and firm faith of the disciple."[38]

Illyricus adds: "If it is founded upon Peter, and rather not upon the confession of faith of the Church, then immediately it would have fallen. For Peter soon ran at the time of the Lord's passion, and he fell. Moreover in the same chapter of St. Matthew, it is said to him: 'Get behind me Satan, you are a scandal to me, because you do not have a sense of what is of God.' Thereupon he denied Christ a third time, and not without a great curse."

I respond: Faith, or confession, is considered in two ways. In one way it absolutely followed itself, and without any relation to the person of Peter; in the second way with relation to Peter. In the first way it appears our adversaries would have it that faith is the foundation of the Church, but certainly they are deceived. If it were so, why didn't the Lord say, instead of: "I will build upon this rock," "I am building," or "I have built my Church"? Many had already believed that he was the son of the living God, as early as the prophets, the Blessed Virgin, Simeon, Zachariah, John the Baptist, the apostles and remaining disciples.

Next, faith taken up absolutely, is rightly called the foundation of justification and of all strength, as Augustine says, "The house of God is founded by belief, erected by hope, perfected by love."[39] But the foundation of the Church is not properly faith. There ought to be a foundation of the same kind as the rest of the building. The Church is a congregation of men, just as of living stones;[40] thus, the stone, which is the foundation, ought to be also some man, not some virtue.

Last, the pronoun *this* most clearly showed that through the rock faith cannot be understood absolutely, for it is referred more closely to the one named rock; next, it had been said to Simon: "Thou are rock," not to faith; therefore, it behooves us to accept that faith is the foundation in the second way, and to say not any faith you please, but the faith of Peter, and not of Peter as a private man, but as the shepherd of the Church. It coincides with that which we said in this regard that Peter is the foundation.

Therefore, the faith of Peter is the foundation of the Church for a two-fold reason. First that on account of the merit of his faith Peter attained that he

---

[37] *In Matth.* Hom. 55; cf. *In Matth.*, hom. 83.

[38] *De Trinit.*, lib. 4.

[39] Augustine, *De verb. Apost.*, Serm. 22.

[40] 1 Peter 2:5.

should be the foundation of the Church, as Jerome, Hilary, Chrysostom and others show on this place. Secondly, because Peter is chiefly in the very matter the foundation of the Church that since his faith cannot fail, he ought to confirm and hold up all the others in faith. Thus, the Lord said to him: "I have prayed for thee that thy faith should not fail, and when thou hast converted strengthen thy brethren."[41]

Therefore, by reasoning of his indefectible faith, Peter should be the firmest rock, sustaining the whole Church. It is the same thing to say "upon Peter" and "upon his faith" the Church was founded, and the Fathers we cited speak in this manner. For St. Hilary, after he had said the faith of Peter is the foundation of the Church, and receives the keys of the kingdom, adds on Peter himself: "He merited a preeminent place by the confession of his blessed faith," and a little after: "Hence, he holds the keys of the kingdom of heaven; hence, his earthly judgments are heavenly, etc."[42]

Therefore, as he had said, "Faith is the foundation and holds the keys," so now he says Peter by reason of his faith merited a preeminent place that is that he should be the head, or foundation, and should hold the keys. And he says the same thing most beautifully about Peter: "O happy foundation of the Church by the solemn decree of a new name."[43]

For equal reasoning, when St. Ambrose says the faith of Peter is the foundation of the Church, notes the same thing: "He did not refuse to his disciple the favor of this word that he should also be Peter, who as the rock should have solidity of steadfastness and firmness of faith."[44]

Chrysostom, explaining in both citations why it is that the Church is built upon the confession of Peter, introduces the Lord speaking thus: "I will build my Church upon you."

Next, Cyril also says the foundation is not any faith, but that unconquerable and most firm faith of St. Peter, and he writes that Peter himself is the rock upon which the Church is founded.[45]

Now I respond to the objection of Illyricus, firstly with the commentary of Jerome for this chapter: when Peter was told: "Get behind me Satan" and when he denied Christ, he was not yet the foundation. Therefore, the place Christ

---

[41] Luke 22: 32.

[42] Hilary, *loc. cit.*

[43] *In Matth.*, ch. 16.

[44] *In Lucam*, lib. 6, ch. 9.

[45] *In Joannem*, lib. 2, ch. 12.

promised him, he had intended to give to him after the resurrection. Add that Peter did not err on the faith, but was merely ignorant of something, when he was told, "Get behind me Satan;" he was lacking in charity, not in faith, when he denied Christ. That we will teach in its proper place in the treatise on the Church.

CHAPTER XI
Why the Church is Built upon a Rock in Matthew XVI

NOTHER difficulty follows that must be explained, what it might be for the Church to be built upon a rock. Certainly our adversaries labor a little on this, for when they deny that Peter is the foundation of the Church, they suppose what that building signifies is but a little thing.

On the other hand, Catholics teach that what is meant by this metaphor is that the government of the whole Church was consigned to Peter, and particularly concerning faith. Therefore, this is proper to the foundational rock, to rule and hold up the whole building. The Fathers also explain it in this way. Chrysostom, explaining this passage in Matthew, says: "He constituted him pastor of the Church."[1] And below that, "The Father put Jeremiah in charge of one nation, while Christ put Peter in charge of the whole world." Ambrose says, "The rock is called Peter just as an immovable boulder that it should contain the unified structure of the whole Christian work."[2] St. Gregory says, "It is proven to everyone who knows the Gospel that care of the whole Church was consigned to St. Peter, prince of all apostles by the Lord's voice. By all means it was said to him: 'Thou are Peter, and upon this rock I will build my Church.'"[3]

Yet two arguments are usually given in objection against this. The first is that of Luther, who says: "That order does not avail, namely that the Church is built upon Peter, and so, Peter is the ruler of the Church. Just the same, it is rightly said that faith is built upon the Church, and nevertheless, it does not follow that therefore, faith is the ruler of the Church."[4]

I respond: We said the Church cannot properly be said to be built upon faith for that very reason. Next, although it might be said properly, it would never conclude the argument since all things must be understood as accommodated to their natures. Consequently, if one were to say the Church is built upon faith, the sense ought to be that the Church is understood to depend upon faith as by a principle of justification and by a certain gift, without which she could not be the spouse of Christ. Furthermore, if one were to say the Church is built upon Peter, the sense will be that the Church depends upon Peter as a ruler; thus, such is the dependency of one man upon another.

The second argument is more difficult. Just as Peter is called the foundation of the Church in this citation, so all the apostles are called foundations. "His

---

[1] *In Matth.* Hom. 55.

[2] *Serm. 47.*

[3] Lib. 4, ep. 32.

[4] *De Potestate Papae.*

foundations in the holy mountains,"[5] that is, as St. Augustine shows, in the apostles and prophets. Likewise in the Apocalypse we read: "And the wall of the city, having twelve foundations, and in them the twelve names of the twelve apostles of the Lamb."[6] Also in Ephesians: "Built up on the foundation of the apostles and prophets."[7] Alluding to such words, St. Jerome says, "But you say, the Church is founded upon Peter, although that is done in another place upon all the apostles, and equally upon them the strength of the Church is solidified."[8] Therefore, nothing near proper and particular was given to Peter.

I respond: All the apostles were foundations in three ways; nevertheless, without any prejudice to Peter. In the first way, because they first founded the Church everywhere, as Peter did not convert the whole world to the faith, but Peter led some regions to Christ, Paul some regions, James others, and still the rest others. This is why St. Paul says, "Thus I preached, not where Christ was named, lest I would build on someone else's foundation."[9] And again: "As a wise architect I placed a foundation, but another builds upon it."[10] Also in this manner the apostles are equally foundations; that which is signified we believe.

The second way apostles and prophets are said to be foundations of the Church is by reason of doctrine revealed by God. Accordingly, the faith of the Church rests upon the revelation which the apostles and prophets had from God. Moreover, new articles are not always revealed to the Church; rather the Church assents to that doctrine which the apostles and prophets learned from the Lord, as well as by preaching, or letters they entrusted to posterity. We are also built up by this reason as the apostle says to the Churches, "upon the foundation of the apostles and prophets." Peter is not greater than the rest in regard to those two ways, but as Jerome says, the strength of the Church is solidified equally in all.

All the apostles are called foundations in the third mode by reason of government. All were heads, rulers and shepherds of the whole Church, but not in the same way as Peter; they had supreme and full power as apostles or legates, but Peter as an ordinary pastor. Thereafter they so had the fullness of power that nevertheless, Peter should still be their head, and they depended

---

[5] Psalm 86 (87):1.

[6] Apocalypse 21: 14.

[7] Ephesians 2:20.

[8] *In Jovinian.*, lib. 1.

[9] Romans 16:20.

[10] 1 Corinthians 3:10.

upon him, not the other way around.

This is what is promised to Peter, in Matthew 16, since it is said to him alone in the presence of the others: "Upon this rock I will build my Church." In what Jerome teaches apart from the others cited above in his work against Jovinian, he explains why the Church was built upon Peter: "Although the strength of the Church is solidified equally upon all the apostles, nevertheless, in addition one was chosen among the twelve as the head, constituted so that the occasion of schism should be removed."

CHAPTER XII

To Whom it is Said: To Thee I Give the Keys in Matthew XVI

A THIRD uncertainty is over the person to whom it is said: "To thee I will give the keys." Although the sense of these words appears most obvious to Catholics, nevertheless, our adversaries so distort these words that they should now seem very obscure. Who, I ask that simply reads: "Blessed are thou, Simon bar Jonah," and immediately after: "I will give thee the keys," would not say, "the keys were promised to the son of Jonah?"

Just the same, Luther,[1] Calvin[2] and their followers, as well as the Centuriators,[3] the Smalkaldic council and all the other heretics of this time would have it that there is nothing specific promised to Peter the son of Jonah. Rather, whatever is said there pertains to the whole Church, the person of which Church Peter managed at that time.

Yet it must be noticed that Peter could manage the person of the Church in two ways, historically and parabolically. Historically he managed the person of another who, when he truly conducts some business by himself, signifies a matter that must be carried out by another. Thus Abraham truly had two sons; he signified God, who was going to have two peoples, as the Apostle explains in Galatians. Thus Martha who was anxious about the frequent service, and Mary sitting apart at the feet of the Lord, show two lives, of which one is action, the other is contemplation.

Parabolically, it is signified through one thing, when no deed is actually put forth, but something similar is exercised to mean something else: how in the gospel, the one who sows good seed signifies Christ preaching. In such a way, ambassadors usually receive the keys of the city, but meanwhile they do not properly acquire anything for themselves, but merely represent the person of their prince.

With that being so constituted, our adversaries reckon that Peter by the second reasoning signified the Church when he heard from the Lord: "I will give thee the keys." From which it follows, keys were given firstly to the Church itself, and through the Church they are communicated to pastors, and this is the literal sense of this place, as the Smalkaldic council says: "Therefore, he gave principally and immediately to the Church, just as also on account of it the right of vocation should have the origin of the Church."

But we believe that Peter managed the person of the Church in the first

---

[1] *De Potestate Papae.*

[2] *Instit.*, lib. 4, ch. 6, § 4.

[3] *Cent. 1*, lib. 1, and 2.

manner, and so without a doubt he truly and principally received the keys while at the same time he signified by their reception that he was afterward going to receive the universal Church in that specific manner. A little after we will explain which manner, but now we will briefly show the matter in itself.

First, Christ designated the person of Peter in so many ways that (as Cajetan rightly remarks) notaries who devise public documents do not usually describe some certain man by as many circumstances. For in the first place he expressed the substance of a singular person, through the pronoun *to thee* (*tibi*). Next, he adds the name given to him in birth, when he says "Blessed are you Simon:" he added the name of the father, when he said: "Son of Jonah:" nor did he wish to omit the name recently imposed by him so he says, "I say to thee that thou are Peter." To what end does he make so exacting a description, if nothing is properly promised to Peter himself? Next, Peter was not a legate of the Church at that time, or a vicar; who placed upon him a province of that sort? Therefore, we cannot suspect that he received the keys in the name of the Church, rather than his own.

Besides, the keys were properly promised by Christ to the one who had said: "Thou are truly Christ, the Son of the living God;" and as St. Jerome says, true confession received the reward, since Peter made known that excellent confession, and in his person, therefore, he received the promise of the keys in his person.

To this, if on that account it must be denied that keys were promised to Peter, because he managed a figure of the Church, by the same reasoning we will certainly deny that Abraham had two sons that represented two peoples, as the Apostle witnesses. Further, we would not be able to affirm that Martha being anxious for many things, while her sister Mary sat at the feet of the Lord, foreshadowed action and contemplation. But if it is so serious to call obvious history into doubt, it also ought to seem grave to doubt whether something unique was promised to Peter, since so singular an event is related in the evangelical history.

In the end, it was said to him by the Lord: "I will give thee the keys of the kingdom of heaven," and a little after he heard from the same Lord: "Get behind me Satan, you are a scandal unto me," and these second words are to Peter alone, and were said to his own person, as is clearly gathered from the Gospel, as even Luther himself teaches.[4] Therefore, who can deny that the keys were promised to Peter in his person?

Yet, maybe "I will give thee the keys," and "Get behind me Satan," were not

---

[4] *De Potestate Papae.*

said to the same man. But more correctly they are altogether to the same man, for in the same chapter of that Gospel both are contained, and the name of Peter is expressed by both, and in this opinion all the Fathers agree. Certainly Hilary, Jerome, Chrysostom and Theophylactus eloquently teach on Matthew 16 that "I will give thee the keys" and "Get behind me" are said to the same Peter.

Although Hilary does not dare in this place to refer the word "Satan" to Peter, nevertheless, he refers those which precede it to Peter, namely "Get behind me." And he also refers the word "Satan" to Peter in his commentary on the Psalms: "He had so great an obligation to suffer for the salvation of the human race that he reprimanded Peter, the first confessor of the Son of God, the foundation of the Church, the porter of the heavenly kingdom, the judge in the judgment of heaven, with the reproach of Satan."[5] And Augustine says: "Is it possible that Razias[6] should be better than Peter the Apostle, who, after he said: "Thou are Christ, the Son of the living God," was so blessed by the Lord that the latter declared that he merited to receive the keys of the kingdom of heaven, nevertheless, it is not believed that he must be imitated, where soon in the same moment he being condemned heard: "Get behind me Satan, you do not reckon the things which are of God, etc."[7]

St. Ambrose says a similar thing in his book on Isaac, where he expounds upon those words of the Lord to Peter: "You can not follow me now, but a little after."[8] Ambrose relates: "He had entrusted the keys of the kingdom of heaven; and showed it would not be meet for Peter to follow him."[9] So St. Ambrose altogether wished clearly to show the keys were consigned to the same man, to whom it was said "You cannot follow me now, but a little after;" it is certain that these words were said to Peter in his own person, and just the same when he will have been truly crucified in his own person, he followed Christ by dying.

Yet Luther objects against these arguments in the same book, *On the Power of the Pope.* First, he argues, it is certain that the Lord said to Peter: "Get behind me Satan, you do not reckon those things which are of God;" but these words are not fitting to the one whom the Father revealed the secrets of heaven, and who received the keys of the kingdom of heaven. Therefore, he heard the

---

[5] *De Trin.*, lib.. 6 and 10; Ps. 131.

[6] See 2 Maccabees 14: 37-46. In the context of this work St. Augustine is refuting Gaudentius who argues from the example of Razias who committed suicide rather than be captured. -Translator's note.

[7] *Contra duas epistulas Gaudnetii,* lib. 1, ch. 31.

[8] John 13:36.

[9] *Liber de Isaac,* ch. 3.

heavenly revelation not in his own person, but in the person of the Church, and received the keys of the kingdom of heaven.

We respond: all these are fitting to the same person, as now we have already proven, but not for the same reason. Peter indeed has revelation by a gift of God, and receives the keys. Yet scandal is caused by his own weakness concerning the passion and death of Christ. Nor should the name *Satan* trouble us: it does not signify the devil, but an adversary: accordingly שׂטן [sat-an] with the Hebrews is nothing other than adversary. Therefore, although the devil is here and there called "Satan," nevertheless, it does not indicate the devil everywhere.

The second objection. Peter said in the name of all the disciples: "You are Christ, the Son of the living God;" therefore, he heard in the name of all: "To you I will give the keys." Hence, it is certain that Peter responded to Christ in the name of all, not only from Chrysostom, who writes on this citation that Peter was the mouth of the apostles, but also from Jerome who says that Peter spoke for all, and Augustine, who says that one responded for all.[10] Even from that which Christ asked all the disciples: "Whom do you say I am?" For either all the disciples must be asked, which did not correspond to the question, or what is more believable, Peter responds in the name of all.

I respond: Peter responded in the name of all, not as some herald, but as the prince and head, as well as the mouth of the apostles, as Chrysostom says. Moreover, he alone responded, since the rest were ignorant of the chief thing they should say, but they approved the confession of Peter by their silence, and in that way through the mouth of Peter all responded. Just the same, Peter alone responded and the rest agreed with him; so Christ promised the keys to Peter alone, but after him they were communicated to the rest.

We prove that it is so by this reason. If Peter would have responded in the name of all or seen to it that the rest would have demanded this province from him, then he should know what they were to respond, but neither is true. Not the first, because he learned this by revelation of the Father, not from human consultation, as the Lord says: "Flesh and blood have not revealed to you, etc." Not the second, because revelation was made to him alone. Likewise, if he knew the mind of the others he would have indicated this in some way, just as he did when he said, "Where shall we go? You have the words of eternal life," and "We believe and we know that you are Christ, the Son of God."[11] In that citation, Chrysostom notes that Peter said for all, "We believe, etc." Therefore, Christ suggested that it is not true about all. For Judas did not believe: "Did not I

---

[10]   Serm. 13 *de Verb. Dom.*

[11]   John 6:68-69.

choose you, and one of you is a devil?" But when Peter said: "You are Christ, the Son of the living God," since he did not mention the others, the Lord simply approved the confession of Peter.

The testimonies of the Fathers agree, and they do not obscurely teach that Peter was the first who spoke, that he would not know what the others felt on the matter. Hilary on this citation says, "He was judged worthy that he should be the one to recognize something in Christ of God, etc." Therefore, if the first be true, then revelation was not made to the others at the same time. Hilary continues, "In the silence of all, understanding the Son of God by revelation of the Father, etc," and the same, "He spoke, what the human voice had not yet mentioned."[12]

Chrysostom says, "Seeing that he sought for their common opinion, they all responded; when he asked them about himself, Peter immediately rose up and arriving at it first said: "You are Christ, the Son of the living God."[13] St. Cyril says, "As the leader and head, he was the first from the rest to express: "You are Christ, the Son of the living God."[14] Augustine: "This Peter was the first of all of them to merit to confess by divine revelation, saying: 'You are Christ,' etc."[15]

St. Leo says, "The Blessed apostle Peter must be praised in the confession of this unity, who, when the Lord sought to discover what his apostles might think about him; it arrived first from his most excellent mouth: 'You are Christ, the Son of the living God.'"[16] And again in his sermon on St. Peter and Paul: "So long as the word of those responding is common, the fogginess of human understanding is expressed; but where something that may hold the sense of the disciples is examined, he is first in the confession of the Lord who is first in apostolic dignity." It is manifestly gathered from these testimonies that Peter responded for all by no other reasoning than that all the rest [of the disciples] assented to the opinion of Peter.

The third objection: the keys are promised to Peter, not as he is the son of Jonah, but as one who hears the heavenly Father; therefore, properly they are promised to anyone who is a hearer of the heavenly Father, therefore, they are not promised to flesh and blood. It is certain that a true disciple of the Father is not concerned with any particular man, rather that the Church depends

---

[12] *De Trinitate*, lib. 6.

[13] Hom. 55 *in Matth.*

[14] Lib. 12, *in Jo.* cap. 64.

[15] *De Tempore*, Serm. 124.

[16] *De. Pass. Dom.*, serm. 11.

assiduously upon the mouth of God the Father; therefore, the keys were promised not to some particular man, but to the Church.

I respond: this argument of Luther is amazingly opposed to the very words of the Gospel. Christ says, "Blessed are thou, Simon Bar Jonah." And a little after, "I will give thee the keys," but Luther says they are not given or promised to Simon bar Jonah. Again, Christ says, "My Father has revealed to you, who is in heaven." Luther says, however, "we are certain that it concerns no particular man whether he should hear the Father," hence, they do not concern Peter. Therefore, it is false or uncertain, when Christ says, "The Father has revealed to thee." Why, therefore, did the father reveal to Peter if Peter heard nothing? But if Peter also heard the testimony of Christ, it is also certain that the keys were given to Peter, the one who heard the Father of heaven.

Next, to be a listener of the Father is not a formal reasoning for why the keys should be given, otherwise ecclesiastical power would depend on the goodness of the ministers, which is the heresy of the Donatists that we see is even rejected in the Augsburg Confession.[17] Rather that excellent confession of Peter was the occasion or the meritorious cause why the keys were promised to him rather than to others, as is gathered from the commentaries of Hilary, Jerome, Chrysostom and Theophylactus.

The fourth objection is that St. Paul in his epistle to the Romans, Chapter 4, says, "Since the faith of Abraham was reputed unto justice," therefore, justice must be reputed to all who will have believed. So in the same way, if because Peter confessed Christ to be the Son of the living God he receives the keys, then certainly all the faithful who confess Christ have the keys. Luther says this argument is similar in form to the argument of Paul, and cannot be refuted, unless Paul's argument is likewise refuted.

I respond with Cajetan: this argument is similar in form, but unlike in matter, and on that account settles nothing. For faith leads to justice by its nature, and makes the just from the unjust, or more just from the just, if they would not fail in the remaining things which are required at the same time to be justified. But the confession of faith does not lead by its nature to receive the keys; rather, although the confession of Peter could have been rewarded in six hundred ways, it pleased Christ to make a gift of the keys. And we see something similar in the example of Abraham: accordingly Abraham was justified not by faith alone, but also he merited to become the father of many nations, as the Apostle says in the same place; nevertheless, not all who believe may be the father of many nations. Without a doubt, in itself there is not a

---

[17] ch. *De Eccles.*

natural connection between faith and the gift of the keys or fruitfulness; just the same it is naturally and in itself connected with justice.

The fifth objection: Either while Peter died the keys remained in the Church, or they perished with Peter: if the first therefore, they were given to the Church; if the second, men cannot now again be loosed and bound.

Likewise, in another mode, when a Pope is chosen, the keys will either be present with him, or not; if the first, therefore, he was already made Pope beforehand: if the second, whence, therefore, does he have the keys? Are they brought to him from some angel from heaven? Or rather does he receive them from the Church, to which they were handed by Christ from the beginning?

I respond: with the Pope being dead the keys do not perish, nevertheless, they do not remain formally in the Church, except insofar as they are consigned to lower ministers, but they remain in the hands of Christ. When, however, a new Pope is chosen, the keys are not brought by him, nor given to him by the Church, but by Christ, not in a new handing on, but in the ancient institution. Accordingly, when he gave these to Peter, he gave them to all his successors.

It would be similar if some king, when he places a viceroy over a province would publish at the same time, at his pleasure, that after the viceroy dies they should choose and nominate another and he concedes the same power as he had previously.

The sixth objection of Luther and of Calvin is in the noted citations of Matthew 16: so the keys of the kingdom of heaven are not given, but promised; but in Matthew 18 and John 20 they are given, but in those citations they are not given to Peter alone, but to all the apostles. For Matthew 18 says, "Whatever you will have bound upon earth, you will bind even in heaven, and whatsoever you will have loosed on earth, will be loosed in heaven," and John 20 has: "Receive the Holy Spirit; whose sins you remit will be remitted to them, and whose sins you retain are retained." Therefore, they were also promised not to one, but to all.

I respond: Concerning the second citation there is no difficulty: for it is certain that the whole power of the keys is not given through these words but only the power of order to forgive sins; accordingly the power in this citation is limited to sins. In Matthew 16 it is not so limited, rather it is said, "Whatsoever you bind on earth," but men are bound not only by sins, but even by laws. Thereupon, it is a lesser thing to retain sins than to bind the sinner, since to retain is to relinquish a man in his state, or not to loose, but to bind is to impose a new bond on him, which is done through excommunication, interdict, law, etc. Lastly, the Fathers eloquently assert that this power to remit sins is given through the Sacraments of Baptism and Penance. See Chrysostom and Cyril on this citation, and Jerome.[18]

On the earlier citation there is a greater difficulty, and indeed, Origen in his commentary on this citation contends that ecclesiastical power was not handed over, but merely fraternal correction. Moreover, in this passage, there is the phrase "to loose" which, by that admonition, is the occasion that should the sinner come back to his senses, the penance due shall be loosed from the bonds of sinner; that phrase "to bind" which is the occasion of denunciation that the sinner should be considered just as a heathen and a publican. Yet in the same place, Origen adds that it is not the same thing which is considered here; thus Origen's explication of Matth. 16 does not seem probable; nevertheless, it is sufficiently gathered from it that Origen in no way favors the Lutherans.

Another exposition is that of Theophylactus, who reckons the words of the Lord are directed to those who suffer an injury; moreover to bind them, while they retain the injury, and loose while they remit; which is not an exceedingly true opinion. For either one who receives an injury remits the penitent, or does not. If the first, then certainly he will have been loosed in heaven, but not besides that which he shall remit; for although he refuses to remit, he shall be remitted in heaven; if the second, then he is not remitted in heaven, whom he freed on earth: and also the same can be said on binding. Although the opinion might be true, nevertheless, nothing impedes our case; therefore, it is certain that something else was given to Peter than that he would remit injuries made to himself. Therefore, the exposition of Hilary, Jerome, Anselm and others on this place, not the least Augustine,[19] is common. The Lord spoke concerning the power of the keys, whereby the apostles, and their successors, bind and loose sinners.

And although this seems especially to treat the power of jurisdiction, whereby sinners are excommunicated, nevertheless, the Fathers we have named on this citation show both the power of order and of jurisdiction; certainly it seems that it can be deduced from the text itself, for here it is said so generally, "Whatsoever you will have loosed," etc. just as Matth. 16 has "whatever you will have loosed." But if these are so considered, what will we respond to our adversaries? Is it not so that what was promised to Peter alone is now given to all the apostles?

Thomas Cajetan teaches that it is not the same, the keys of the kingdom of heaven, and the power of loosing and binding; therefore, the keys of the kingdom of heaven include power, both ordinary and of jurisdiction, which is

---

[18] Jerome, *in epist., ad Hedibiam*, quest. 9.

[19] *Tract.* In Jo., 22 and 49.

signified by the actions of binding and loosing: and besides something further, it seems more obviously to mean to open and close than loose and bind.[20]

But this doctrine seems to us to be more mundane than true. For keys apart from those of order and jurisdiction are unheard of in the Church. And the plain sense of those words: "I will give thee the keys," and "whatever thou will have loosed upon earth, etc.," is that, the authority first should be promised or the power designated through the keys; thereafter even actions or a duty are explicated through those terms *to loose* and *bind*, so that altogether it should be the same as to open and close. Further, the Lord expressed the actions of the keys by loosing and binding, not by shutting and opening, in order that we should understand they are metaphorical sayings, and finally heaven is opened for men, since they are freed from their sins which forbade their entrance into heaven.

Therefore, with those opinions having been noted, we assert that by these words as they are contained in Matth. 18, nothing is given except inasmuch as it was promised or explicated and foretold that the apostles and their successors were going to have the power. Next, it is plain that the apostles were not made priests until the Last Supper, nor bishops and pastors until after the resurrection; hence, at the time in which the Lord said these things, they were private men, and they did not have any ecclesiastical power.

Thereupon, if by these words: "Whatever you will have bound in heaven will be bound," the power of binding is given in the very matter, it is also given by the former: "Whatever thou will have bound will be bound, etc." Power will be given, not promised, as the words are altogether the same. But our adversaries affirm that by the former words "whatever thou will have bound," nothing is given, but only promised; then by those words, "whatsoever you will have bound," nothing is given, but only promised. It was with a view to this promise that the Lord had said one should be reckoned for a heathen or a tax Collector if he would not listen to the Church, lest one should think that the authority of the Church can be scorned; he joined to it such power of prelates of the Church that what they might have bound on earth, shall be bound even in heaven.

No doubt you will say: If the keys were not given to the Apostles in this place, but only promised, then where were they given? I respond: They were given in John 20 and 21. For in John 20, when the Lord said to the apostles: "Peace be with you, just as the Father sent me, I send you," he attributed to them the power, or the key of jurisdiction; therefore, he made them just as legates by

---

[20] Cajetan, *de instit. et auct. Rom. Pont.,* ch. 5.

these words, and in his name governors of the Church; moreover in the following words: "Receive the Holy Spirit, whosoever's sins you forgive, etc." he gave to the same the power of order, as we said above.

Indeed, that we might understand that this supreme power was conferred to all the apostles as legates, not as ordinary pastors, and with a certain subjection to Peter, it is said to Peter alone: "Feed my sheep," just as in the same manner it had been said to him alone: "To you I will give the keys." Therefore, the keys of the kingdom as a principal and ordinary prefect, he then received alone, when he heard the words, "Feed my sheep;" then care of his brother apostles was consigned to him.

Besides, just as in Matth. 16 he is called "Simon bar Jonah" in the promise of the keys, so also it is shown in the last Chapter of John that he is called "Simon of John," or as it is in the Greek "Simon Jonah." And as in Matth. 16 the keys are not promised previous to his unique faith in Christ, so also in the last Chapter of John, "Feed my sheep," is not said before he would be asked whether he believed Christ more than the rest. And there is simply no reason why it should be said to Peter so uniquely: "To you I will give the keys," and "Feed my sheep," and that on account of his unique faith and love, unless he was going to receive something apart from the rest. Thus St. Leo writes correctly that the power of loosing and binding was handed to Peter apart from the rest.

The last objection of Luther and Calvin is taken from the testimonies of the fathers. St. Cyprian teaches that the keys were not given to Peter for any other reason apart from the rest, which later were given to all, so that it should signify unity of the Church: "In this the rest of the Apostles were assuredly endowed with an equal partaking of both honor and power as was Peter; but the beginning proceeds from unity, and the primacy is given to Peter so that the Church will be shown to be one."[21] Also St. Hilary so speaks: "You, O holy and blessed men, on account of the merit of your faith you were appointed the keys of the kingdom of heaven, and obtained the right of binding and loosing in heaven and on earth."[22]

St. Jerome also says, "You say the Church shall be founded upon Peter, although in another place it is made upon all the apostles, and they all received, etc."[23] St. Augustine teaches, "If in Peter there would not be the Sacrament of the Church, the Lord would not have said to him; 'I will give thee the keys of the kingdom of heaven.' If it was merely said to this man, Peter, he did not do this

---

[21] *De Simplic. Praelat.,* or *de Unitate Ecclesiae.*

[22] *De Trinitate,* lib. 6.

[23] *In Jovin.,* lib. 1.

for the Church; therefore, if this is not done in the Church, when Peter received the keys, it signified the Church."[24] Finally, St. Leo, explaining these words, says: "'To Thee I will give the keys, etc.' The force of this power passed to the other apostles, and to all princes of the Church the constitution of this decree passed."[25]

I respond: When St. Cyprian says the apostles were equal in honor and power he teaches nothing against our opinion since we certainly affirm the apostles were equal in apostolic power, and held the same authority over the Christian people, but it was not equal in itself. What St. Leo says explains these words of Cyprian, when he teaches, "Among the most blessed apostles there was a discretion of power in the similitude of honor, and although the choice of all should be equal, nevertheless, it was given to one that he should be preeminent over the rest."[26]

Moreover, St. Cyprian teaches the same thing in the same book and in other places. For when he says: "The beginning embarked from unity that the Church should be shown as one," he does not understand the logically prior order of time that this power was given to Peter alone, apart from the rest, that through it the unity of the Church should be signified; but that the Church began in the one Peter, just as in the foundation and head, that because of this very thing the Church should have one foundation and head, merely to show it is one: just as one house is described by one foundation, so also one body by one head.

But this opinion is proved first in the matter from the words of Cyprian, which is false by order of time; prior ecclesiastical power was given to Peter apart from the rest, for it was given to all in John 20. Moreover, after that it was said to Peter alone: "Feed my sheep;" therefore, the beginning is not understood to have embarked from one, because the keys should first be given to one, but because they were given only to one as ordinary, and the first pastor and head of the rest.

Thereafter, the same is proved from the words of Cyprian himself, for in this very book *On the Simplicity of Prelates*, he explains the unity of the Church and why the beginning was made by Peter alone. He writes that the Church is one in that manner in which all are called one light of the ray of the sun, as they spring from the one sun; and many rivers from one water, because they are derived from one source; and many branches from one tree, because they all

---

[24] *Tract. In Jo.*, final tractate; *in Psal. 108*, and *de doctrina Christiana*, ch. 18; *de agone Christi*, ch. 3.

[25] *Serm. 3, de annivers. Assumpt. Suae ad pontifi.*

[26] Epist. 84 ad Anasts. Episc. Thessal.

grow up from one root.

Next, this root and this source, whence the unity of the Church is taken up, is the seat of Peter, and Cyprian teaches this in many places: "They dare to sail to the chair of Peter, and the principal Church whence sacerdotal unity arises?"[27] What could be clearer? He also writes to Pope Cornelius, saying: "We know, we are exhorted that we should acknowledge the mother and root of the Catholic Church and hold fast to it."[28] And below that, explaining what this root might be, he says, "For the Lord first gave this power to Peter, upon whom he built the Church, and whence he established and showed the font of universality." Further down, "The Church, which is one, was founded by the voice of the Lord upon the one who received his keys." etc. There you see clearly that the Church is called one, because it was founded upon the one Peter.

Now we affirm the testimony of Hilary that all the apostles received the keys, but not in the same manner in which Peter had. Hilary writes the reason why in the same place: that Peter, because he alone responded while all the apostles were silent, rose above all by the confession of his faith, and merited the place; therefore, Peter had a preeminent place among the apostles, if we believe Hilary; and in Chapter 16 of Matthew, he speaks of Peter alone, "O blessed porter of heaven, to whose authority the keys of the eternal entrance are entrusted."

Now I respond to what Jerome says: the answer is in the same book, for Jerome says that though all the apostles had the keys still they needed to be subject to Peter the head.

Now I speak to the argument from St. Leo: Certainly that authority of loosing and binding passed to many others, but nevertheless, it was given principally to Peter. For the same Leo says in the same place, "If Christ wished something to be in common with him and the rest of the princes, he never gave except through Peter himself, anything he did not refuse to the others," and he also says: "The power of loosing and binding was entrusted to Peter apart from the rest."[29]

The testimony of Augustine remains, to which three things must be prefaced to explain it more diligently. First, when he says that Peter bore a figure of the Church when he receives the keys, speaks historically that he received this, not parabolically, so that in no way did he think it should be denied that Peter really received the keys in his own person. That is clear from

---

[27] Lib. 1, epist. 3 ad Cornel.

[28] lib. 4, epist. 8 ad Cornel.

[29] Leo, *epist. 89, ad Episc. Viennens.*

his tract on Psalm 108, in which place Luther objects: "There, Augustine says, Peter was a figure of the Church when he receives the keys, just as Judas was a figure of the ingratitude of the Jews when he betrayed Christ;" but it is certain that Judas really betrayed Christ historically in his person.

Likewise in the last tract on John, Augustine says that Peter bore the person of the Church militant and active life, when he heard, "Follow me:" and "Let another accompany you, and he will lead in which you do not wish;" and when he receives the keys of the kingdom, just as John bore a figure of the Church triumphant and contemplative life, when he reclined at the Lord's breast, and when it was said of him: "I wish him to remain thus." But it is certain that John historically and truly in his own person reclined at the Lord's breast, and fulfilled the letter in that: "I wish him to remain thus," whether he might die or not by a violent death, or another thing should be understood through those words. It is no less certain to the letter that Peter heard in his person: "Let another accompany you," etc.; therefore, it also ought to be understood historically that Peter received the keys.

Augustine says in *De Trinitate* that he bore a figure of the Church when he was baptized;[30] therefore, Augustine does not exclude a historical narrative when he says that one is a figure of another.

But you may say, Augustine seems to think that not everything in Psalm 108 can be understood concerning the person of Judas, and therefore, it is fitting to show many things about Judas bearing on his person of the impious. And in the last tract of John, Augustine expresses figuratively those things which are said of Peter and John, because they did not seem to agree properly with their persons. For it is written about Peter that Christ loved him more than John, and on the other hand it is written about John that he was loved by Christ more than Peter, which cannot be true to the letter, since Christ must be just, and always loved them more who loved him more; so, when Augustine expresses something on Peter as bearing the person of the Church, certainly he does that because he reckons that it does not properly fit Peter.

I respond: Augustine nowhere says that what is said about Judas is not true to the letter, or about Peter and John in the Scriptures; nor was Augustine so inexperienced or impious that he would wish to deny that John historically reclined at the Lord's breast, or that "this is the disciple whom Jesus loved;" or it was literally said to Peter, "Simon of John, do you love me more than these?" or: "Follow me." Therefore, Augustine does not deny that it can and ought to be understood literally about Judas, Peter and John, but he merely says that the

---

[30] *De Trinitate*, lib. 15, ch. 26.

literal sense is often obscure and is not easily understood; however, the mystical sense is much more illustrative and clear, and besides he wished to express these places figuratively with the literal sense being left out.

In the second place it must be observed that St. Augustine, when he says that St. Peter received the keys in the person of the Church, did not wish to signify that the keys were really and historically accepted by him, just as by a type of vicar or legate of the Church; but as the legate of a king, as such customarily receives the keys of some city in the name of his prince, but Peter rather more as from a prince and moderator of the whole Church, by which agreement we say it is given for a kingdom, which is given by a king, especially if that should be ceded for public advantage.

Furthermore, what the mind and opinion of St. Augustine are can be clearly gathered from the fact that in almost every place where he says that Peter was a figure of the Church, he explains that he says this by reason of the primacy. "Whose Church Peter the apostle bears the person of a figurative generality on account of the primacy of his apostolate," and also, "He is recognized to have born the person of which (of the Church) on account of the primacy which he had among the disciples,"[31] and: "Peter is named after the rock, blessed, bearing the figure of the Church, holding the rule of the apostolate."[32]

Lastly it must be observed that in Augustine, Peter bore a figure of the Church in two ways. First, Peter as the supreme Prelate of the Church receiving the keys signified all prelates that were going to have the same keys but from Peter, and they were not shared without measure, for Peter did not receive them so that he alone would use them, but that he would share them with all bishops and priests. Clearly, at any rate, the Apostles were merely excepted since they would receive them by a certain extraordinary plan immediately from Christ, as we spoke of in another place.

Therefore, Peter was first a figure of the whole body of ecclesiastical ministers, and in this Augustine would have it understood: "If this was only said to Peter, it gives no ground of action to the Church. But if such is the case also in the Church that what is bound on earth is bound in heaven, and what is loosed on earth is loosed in heaven,—for when the Church excommunicates, the excommunicated person is bound in heaven; when one is reconciled by the Church, the person so reconciled is loosed in heaven—then such is the case in the Church that Peter, by receiving the keys, signified the Holy Church." In that place Calvin omits the adverb *only* (*tantum*), in order to persuade us that

---

[31] In Ps. 108.

[32] Serm. 13 de verb. Domini.

nothing was said or given to Peter, except insofar as it signified the Church.

But Augustine does not say "If this was said to Peter, then such is the case in the Church," but, rather he says: "If this was only said to Peter, etc.," and the sense of those words is: If it had been so said to Peter alone, "I will give the keys" that he alone ought to bind and loose, it follows that the rest of the Church that is, the other ministers, do not do this; but if they also do this, as we see, certainly Peter when he received the keys represented the universal Church in figure.

In another manner, the same Peter receiving the keys was a figure of the whole Holy Church, that is, of all the just and living members of the body of Christ, for St. Augustine devised a new manner of speaking about the keys and the remission of sins on account of the Donatists. Hence, besides that mode of speaking, in which we say sins are remitted by the priests in the administration of the Sacraments of Baptism and Penance, is the manner of speaking he uses everywhere with the other Fathers. He frequently says sins are remitted by the charity of the Church, by the groans of the dove, by the prayers of the saints, and in this way the keys of the kingdom are merely of the just, and this was signified when Peter received the keys.

He says: "Charity of the Church, which is diffused by the Holy Spirit in our hearts, forgives the sins of his partakers; furthermore he retains the sins of those who are not his partakers."[33] Likewise Augustine says: "Whoever will baptize does not remit sins, which is given by the prayers of the saints, that is, through the groans of the dove, if he does not pertain to the peace of the dove whereby it is given. Therefore, would the Lord have said to thieves and usurers: 'When you forgive sins they are forgiven, but when you retain they are retained'? Indeed, outside [the Church] nothing can be bound or loosed, where there is no one who can either bind or loose: but he is loosed who makes peace with the dove, and he is bound who does not have peace with the dove."[34] And again: "For it is manifest that the Lord gave power to Peter in a type that whatever might be loosed on earth is something he loosed, because that unity even should be said to be perfected together with the dove."[35] And further down: "Through the prayers of the spiritual saints, who are in the Church, just as through the abundant cry of the dove, a great Sacrament is born, and a secret dispensation of the mercy of God that their sins should also be absolved, which are not through the dove, but by the hawk they are baptized, if they draw nigh to that

---

[33]   *Tract. In Joan.*, tract 121.

[34]   *De Baptismo*, lib. 3, ch. 18.

[35]   *Ibid*, ch. 17.

Sacrament with the peace of catholic unity." Similar things are in other works.[36]

For what remains, St. Augustine does not mean by these words that the Church of the just remits sins of its own authority; rather, no man's sins are remitted, except inasmuch as he will be baptized and reconciled, unless the charity of the Church is extended to him, and he is made a living member of the dove, and hence, a partaker of the prayers of the other just. Therefore, by the prayers of the saints, just as by the groan of the dove, interior penance is procured, as well as charity through which whoever is formally justified, is justified formally.

Again St. Augustine devised this manner of speaking on account of the Donatists, to whom it seemed a wonder that heretics can justify men through Baptism and be introduced into the Church since they are covered in sins and outside the Church. Augustine speaks to demolish this wonder both that he who baptizes does not remit sins, but the groan of the dove does, because he who is baptized is not justified because he is baptized by this one or that one, but because it is shown through Baptism, no matter who administers it, that the charity of the Church is extended.

---

[36] *De Baptisma*, lib. 5, ch. 21; lib. 3, and lib. 7, ch. 51.

CHAPTER XIII
What Should be Understood by the Keys in Matthew XVI

FOURTH remains: what forsooth should be understood by the keys? For Calvin contends that rule of the Church was not given to Peter, even if he could be convinced that the keys of the kingdom of heaven were given to Peter alone.[1] He attempts this argument by this reasoning:

What it may mean to loose and bind, the Lord shows in John Chapter 20, when he gave authority to the apostles to remit and retain sins. To loose therefore, is to forgive sins; to bind is to retain them. Further, the Scripture everywhere teaches how sins shall be remitted and retained since through the preaching of the Gospel men illuminated are witnessed to be freed from the depravity of their sins. "He has placed among you a word of reconciliation, we exercise legation for Christ, with God, as it were, exhorting us. We ask you, for the sake of Christ, be reconciled to God."[2]

Therefore, he is said to remit sins that converts men to God by announcing the Gospel; he is said to retain that declares those whom he sees are obstinate must be surrendered to everlasting punishment. For which reason it follows that to receive the keys of the kingdom of heaven is not to receive rule or power over others, but is the pure and sole Word of God. Calvin says that this exposition is not cunning, not coerced, not twisted, but germane, logical and obvious.

The Centuriators attempt to prove the same thing for another reason; to them if primacy was given or promised to Peter in these words, the apostles would not have doubted afterwards about who seemed greater among them.[3] On the contrary, when they sought the answer from him, the Lord at least would have responded: "Do not quarrel further, for I have established Peter as the chief." But the Lord said nothing of the sort; therefore that promise of the keys confers nothing with regard to the primacy.[4]

Yet we and all Catholics understand that power over every Church was given to Peter by the keys, and we confirm it for three reasons. First, the metaphor of the keys itself, as it is customarily received in Sacred Scripture; accordingly, Isaiah describes the deposition of one high priest and the establishment of another in these words: "Go, get thee in to him that dwells in the tabernacle, to Sobna who is over the temple: and you shall say to him: What

---

[1] *Institut.*, lib. 4, ch. 6 § 3.

[2] 2 Corinthians 5:19-20.

[3] Matth. 18; Mark 9; Luke 9 and 22.

[4] *Cent. 2*, lib. 2, ch. 7, column 526.

do you here, or as if you were somebody here? ... I will drive you out from your station, and depose you from your ministry. And it will come to pass on that day that I will call my servant Eliacim, the son of Helcias, and I will cloth him with your tunic, and will strengthen him with your belt, and will give your power into his hand, and he shall be as a father to the inhabitants of Jerusalem, and the house of Juda. And I will place the key of the house of David upon his shoulder and he shall open, and none shall shut: and he shall shut and none shall open."[5]

Here remission of sins obviously is not understood by the keys, but ecclesiastical rule. Isaiah 9 also pertains to such a purpose: "The rule was made upon his shoulders." Therefore, rule is said to have been placed upon the shoulders, because the keys, by which rule was designated, were customarily placed upon the shoulder. And one cannot deny that the keys signify the rule of Christ, if one reads this about Christ in the Apocalypse: "He who is holy and true says these things, who has the key of David, who opens, and no man closes, and closes and no man opens."[6]

Common custom also agrees, even in profane matters, for when cities are given to some prince, they offer him the keys as a sign of subjection, and the keys are usually handed over to one who is established as a steward in the house.

Secondly, it is proved by these words: "Whatsoever thou will have bound, etc.," for in the Scriptures one is said to bind who commands and punishes. The Lord speaks thus concerning precepts: "They bound heavy and unbearable burdens on the shoulders of men, etc."[7] And on punishments: "Whatever thou will have bound upon earth, etc."[8] Here, even Calvin witnesses that the Lord speaks about a censure of excommunication; therefore, the Church binds those whom she punishes with the penalty of excommunication. We also speak commonly to this that men are obliged to keep the law, and even obliged to undergo punishment should they fail to do so. Furthermore, one is said to loose who remits sins, who frees from a penalty, who dispenses from law, vows, oaths, and like obligations. Therefore, when it is said to Peter generally, "Whatsoever you loose, etc." the power of commanding is given to him, as well as of punishing, dispensing and remitting; hence, he is a judge and prince of all who are in the Church.

The third proof is from the Fathers: Chrysostom, while giving exposition on

---

[5] Isaiah 22: 17-20.

[6] Apocalypse 3:7-8.

[7] Matth. 23:4.

[8] Matth. 18:18.

this promise, says that the whole world was consigned to Peter, and he was made pastor and head of the whole Church.[9] St. Gregory said: "It is established that while all know the Gospel that care of the whole Church was consigned to Peter, the holy prince of all apostles, by the Lord's voice."[10]

The argument of Calvin does not conclude anything. For it is not especially true that the keys promised to Peter in Matthew 16 were given to him in John 20, since that is more to bind and loose than to remit and retain sins, as we taught above. And rightly in vain were the keys promised to Peter, as a reward for a singular confession, if nothing was singularly given to him afterward.

Then accordingly, it is also false that to remit sins is nothing other than to preach the Gospel. And it is a marvel that so obvious an exposition was obvious to none of the Fathers, but rather only occurred, at length, to Calvin. Certainly Chrysostom and Cyril, in this place of John, as well as Jerome,[11] understand by the authority of remitting sins the power of conferring the Sacraments of Baptism and Penance, not the power of preaching. Moreover it is not the same to preach and to baptize, as Paul teaches in 1 Corinthians I, where he says that he was sent by the Lord, "not to baptize, but to evangelize."[12]

Furthermore, to that which is said on the word of reconciliation, I respond: in that place a sermon is indeed understood by the word reconciliation, but Paul does not wish to say a sermon suffices to reconciliation, but through a sermon men can be moved to this that they would wish to be reconciled to God, so that afterward it happens through Baptism and Penance, as it is said in Acts 2. For after the sermon Peter says: "Do penance and be baptized, each and every one of you."[13]

To the argument of the Centuriators I respond: The apostles are obviously not understood by the promise of the Lord made to Peter, except after the resurrection of Christ; nevertheless, they mistrusted when Peter was constituted as the prince of all and contended among themselves. Nor is it a wonder that they did not understand that the Lord had spoken metaphorically; they were so unlearned that they did not understand many things properly. Therefore, Mark writes: "While they descended from the mountain he commanded them lest they would tell what they had seen to anyone, until that time when the Son of Man

---

9   Hom. 55 in Matth.

10   Gregory, lib. 4, epist. 32.

11   *In epist. Ad Hedibiam*, q. 9.

12   1 Cor. 1:17.

13   Acts 2:38.

will have risen from the dead. And they kept the word among themselves, seeking what it might mean that he was going to rise from the dead."[14]

Yet from that suspicion which they had about the primacy of Peter they contended amongst themselves, as Origen, Chrysostom and Jerome witness on Matth. 18. Nor is it true what the Centuriators say that the Lord did not already respond that he was designated a prince: Luke 22, "Who is greater among you, let him be your younger, and whoever among you is in authority (ἡγούμενος) among you, let him be as your master"? Did not he splendidly call one a greater and a leader?[15]

CHAPTER XIV

It was said to Peter Alone: Feed my Sheep (John XXI)

OW we treat in regard to those words of the Lord whereby supreme ecclesiastical power was promised to the apostle Peter. Now on those words there will be a dispute, that same power was given to the same Peter. These words are: "Simon [son] of John, feed my sheep." In the explication of such words, three things must be proven. First that it was said to Peter alone: "Feed my sheep," and that by the word "Feed" (*Pasce*) supreme ecclesiastical power was handed over. Lastly that by those terms: "my sheep" the universal Church of Christ was designated. Accordingly all our adversaries deny this.

Thus we proceed to the first where we prove, "Feed my sheep" was said to Peter alone. First by that name "Simon of John," for by that name only Peter was called, nor without a mystery, as we presaged above, in the same way inasmuch as Christ calls Peter and promises him the keys, so also he consigns the feeding of the sheep to him in the last chapter of John that without a doubt we might understand that the very thing which had been promised in Matthew XI is given to this same Simon, to whom it had been promised beforehand.

Secondly, it is proved by those words: "Do you love me more than these?" He said "Feed my sheep" to the same one to whom he said: "Do you love me more than these?" Furthermore, this is manifest that it is said to Peter alone, since the rest are excluded by those eloquent words given by way of comparison: "More than these." Next, they who are excluded are not every man, but particularly the apostles: they were indeed present then with Peter; Nathaniel, whom many think is Bartholomew, James, John, Thomas, and to other disciples, of which another is credible, namely Andrew; therefore, "Feed my sheep" was not said to all the Apostles, but to Peter alone.

Thirdly, it is proved from the threefold question. For we learn from Cyril, and Augustine, as well as others on this place of Scripture that Peter was asked three times whether he loved more than the rest, because he had denied three times, but *only he* denied him three times. Therefore, he alone is asked; hence, [the Lord] said to him alone "Feed my sheep."

Fourthly, it is proved from those words "Peter wept, etc." On that account, Peter wept, if we believe Chrysostom, because he feared lest by chance he had been deceived when he said: "You know O Lord that I love you." Just the same, it had been false when he had said: "And if it will be fitting for me to die with you, I will not deny you." But this origin of the sadness of Peter alone is fitting, since he had denied the Lord; therefore, *Peter alone was sorrowful,* and Christ spoke to Peter alone when he said: "Feed my sheep."

Fifthly, from those words: "When you will have grown old you will spread out your hands, etc." "Feed my sheep," is said to the one whose crucifixion is foretold: hence, death was predicted to Peter alone and in his proper person.

Sixthly, from those words, "But what hence?" and from the response of the Lord: "What is it to you? Follow me." Peter never would have asked what John was going to do, if he had understood "Feed my sheep," to have been said to all: nor would the Lord have said, "What is it to you? Follow me;" rather he would have said he will do the same thing which you do.

The seventh proof is from the Fathers. For apart from Chrysostom, Cyril and Augustine say on this passage of Scripture that it was said to him, "Feed my sheep" who had denied three times; which was, without a doubt, Peter alone. Ambrose has the same in the final chapter of Luke, explaining these very words: "Therefore that he alone will profess from all, should be born before all." Maximus the Confessor likewise says: "Now I judge it necessary that we speak of their proper and special virtues. This is Peter, to whom Christ, while he prepared to ascend into heaven, entrusted to feed his sheepfold and lambs:"[1] therefore, this was proper and special in Peter. Likewise, Pope St. Leo teaches: "The one whom the power of binding and loosing had been consigned apart from the rest, he commanded nevertheless, the more special care of feeding the sheep."[2]

But on the other hand, Calvin argues[3] that Peter exhorts his fellow priests that they should feed the flock of God;[4] therefore, either those words "feed my sheep" were said to all, or certainly Peter transferred his right to others.

I respond: Peter exhorts his fellow priests that they might feed the flock, not a universal one, but a particular one, when he says: "Feed the flock which is among you." Just the same, when St. Paul exhorts the Asian bishops that they should attend themselves to the whole flock he immediately adds, "in whom the Holy Spirit has placed you as bishops," that is, not simply a universal flock but to that whole flock which has been *commended to you.* Therefore, these words of Peter do not prohibit that general power to feed the whole flock would be consigned to Peter alone, and that he would not transfer his right full right to anyone.

Thereafter, Augustine and Chrysostom can be presented. For Augustine wrote: "When it is said to him (Peter), it is said to all, 'Do you love me? Feed my

---

[1] *Serm. de Sts Petro et Paulo.*

[2] Epist. 89, *ad Episc. Viennen. Prov.*

[3] *Instit.*, lib. 4, 6. § 3.

[4] 1 Peter 5:2.

sheep.'"[5] Chrysostom, trying to persuade Basil that he should take up the episcopate to which he was called, chose this citation, and said: "Then, going to show Basil his excellent speech in Christ, if he would feed his flock, since it was written: 'If you love me, feed my sheep.'" Therefore, Chrysostom would have it that these words of the Lord pertain not to Peter alone, but all bishops.

I respond: Although these words properly and principally pertain to Peter alone, nevertheless, it is fitting for them to pertain to all bishops in their own way, because all who are called into the lot of the solicitude by Peter ought to imitate the form of Peter in shepherding the flock. Therefore, what is said by the supreme pastor even in his manner, after his proportion has been preserved, is said about other lesser shepherds. And as the Lord was going to make Peter the shepherd of the Church, he asked him whether he loved him more than the rest that they would be reminded to whom pertains the right to choose and constitute shepherds, so that they would choose such men for the episcopate as excelled the others in charity. What Pope Leo says pertains to this: "Therefore, this is universally believed from Peter that the form of Peter is proposed to all rulers of the Church."[6]

---

[5] *De ag. Christ.*, ch. 30.

[6] Serm. 3, *de annivers. Suae assump.*

CHAPTER XV
What the word "Feed" Might Mean in John XXI

IN FACT, since it is certain that Peter is the one to whom it is said: "Feed my sheep;" it follows that we ought to see what this word *to feed* [*pascere*] means. Martin Luther contends that nothing new is given by that term *feed*, but only a duty of loving, preaching and teaching is enjoined upon Peter, who had already been constituted an apostle and pastor, though not of the whole Church, but of a certain portion just as the rest of the apostles and pastors.[1] He tries to prove it with these reasons.

First: "*To feed* is not to be in charge, but to offer food and minister, which can also be done by an inferior; consequently, he is not immediately established as a bishop to whom it is said "Feed." Next, the Lord does not command Christians to obey Peter, but he commands Peter that he should offer nourishment to Christians; therefore, a minister, not a prince, is constituted through this word "feed." Lastly, if the pontificate were established by these words, it would follow that those who neither love nor feed could be pontiffs; hence, often we would have no pope. Since, the greater part of popes neither love the flock nor feed with word and example, for that reason the institution of the papacy is not contained in this word *feed*, but a simple precept to love and teach."

Yet there will be little difficulty for us to show that by this term *feed*, the supreme power is attributed to whom it is said: "Feed my sheep."

First, *to feed* [*pascere*][2] does not properly mean to feed another, or one who ministers food for any reason, but one who procures and provides food for another, which an overseer or captain really does. "Who do you think is the faithful and prudent dispenser, whom the Lord constituted over his household that he would give them in due season a measure of wheat?"[3] Therefore, it is of this word *to feed* that one who is constituted over a household.

This is also understood by this word, *feed* [*pasce*], from the common use of speech, every for pastoral act: therefore, to feed is that which a shepherd does. Hence, a pastoral act is not only to offer food, but also to lead, lead back, guard, be in charge, rule and castigate. Why? Do shepherds of sheep only offer them

---

[1] *De Potestate Papae.*

[2]   Translator's note: *Pasco, pascere, pavi, patus* = to feed, to graze, to put to pasture. The original meaning of this term is pastoral, and as Bellarmine here argues, suggests one in authority, such as a shepherd, or a farmer who is over the animals.

[3] Luke 12:42.

fodder? Do they not also rule and compel them with a rod that they might obey? Hence, everywhere in the Scriptures "to feed" is received on behalf of one that is to rule, as we read in Psalm 2: "You rule them with an iron rod." In Hebrew חרעם [Tarem], that, is "feed them." Rightly they cannot deny that those who feed with an iron rod most truly have power as pastors. Also the Prophet Isaiah calls Cyrus רועי [Roey] that is, "you are my pastor." Nevertheless, in that place the aforesaid Cyrus was not in an office to offer food, rather over the greatest kingdom in the world.

Next can be more efficaciously shown in this place from that word which John places in his gospel. He wrote ποίμαινε, that is, "feed" by ruling and guiding. For even Homer frequently calls Agamemnon ποιμένα λαῶν, that is shepherd of the people.[4] We also read in Scripture: "A leader will go out from you, who shall rule [ποίμαινε] my people Israel."[5]

And it must be noted in the Hebrew of the prophet Micah, ch. 5, from where Matthew takes it up, there is no verb רעה [Raah] which means to feed, rather the word מֹשֵׁל [Mashal], which is to dominate. Therefore, "להיוה מושל בישראל ממך לי יצא" [Mamal Liy Yatsa Lahiyot Moshal Biysaral] - "Out of thee shall he come forth unto me that is to be the ruler in Israel." Later we read in the book of the Apocalypse: "And he will rule them with an iron rod;"[6] in Greek that is: καὶ αὐτὸς ποιμανεῖ αὐτοὺς ἐν ῥάβδῳσιδηρᾳ. Therefore, with ποιμαίνω does not mean to feed by any mode, but to rule and to be in charge of, and it was said to Peter by the Lord, ποίμαινε τὰ πρόβατα; it manifestly follows that Peter was constituted as the ruler and protector of the Church. Lastly, the testimonies of the Fathers agree. St. John Chrysostom not once calls the duty consigned to Peter a prefecture through that term "feed" and therefore expresses it by that other Scripture: "Faithful and prudent servant, whom the Lord set up over his household." St. Augustine says in this place: "The sheep themselves must be fed that is, he consigned them to be taught and ruled." Thereupon, Gregory calls pastors rulers, and the care as pastoral rule; nay more, the summit of ruling is interpreted itself to feed, rule and be in charge.[7]

Nor do these petty syllogisms of Luther bring anything to bear. To the first the response is: to feed is not the duty of a servant who waits on tables, but of

---

[4]   *Iliad*, lib. 2.

[5]   Matth. 2:6. In Greek it is εχ σοῦ μοι εξελεύσεται ἡγούμενος, ὅξις ποιμανεῖ τὸν λαὸν τοῦ Ισραὴλ.

[6]   Apocalypse 19:15.

[7]   *In lib. De cur. Pastor.*

a ruler: therefore, masters are not fed by servants, although these carry food to the tables of their masters, but on the other hand the servants are rather more fed by masters, by all means who are living at the expense of the masters.

I respond to the second: to be in charge and to be underneath as well as to rule, to be ruled, to feed and be fed, contain a certain relation amongst themselves, so that one cannot exist without the other. Hence, by such a word it is said to Peter that he should be put in charge, rule and feed. In the same manner we are bid to be under Peter, and also allow ourselves to be ruled and fed by him.

I respond to the third: "feed" is indeed a precept, but by that precept ecclesiastical rule is instituted, power itself is signified by the act, from where that act proceeds. Just the same, when God says: "Let the land sprout living grass:" and for the animals, "let them be fruitful and multiply," he attributes fertility to things, and established their natures suitable to regeneration. Not only God, but also men usually establish a prefect by a word of commanding in some manner. Thus if a king should say to someone: "Go, rule such and such a province," everyone understands that he is constituted a prefect of that province.

But Luther says: "If through that precept a pontificate is established, therefore, one ceases to be a pontiff if he does not fulfill the precept." I respond: by those words of precept a pontificate is so established that nevertheless, the power that was conferred does not depend on the observation of the precept. We see that also in human affairs: a viceroy does not cease to be a viceroy, as long as he is not recalled by the king, even if he does not rule the province rightly.

Lastly, what Luther assumes is not true that Roman Pontiffs have not fed the flock for a long time. For, although many of them did not preach, nevertheless, they exercise many other pastoral acts, while they bind, loose, dispense, judge controversies, create bishops, and what they do not do by preaching they do by others. Just the same, both Valerius, the bishop of Hippo, and several others, either impeded by old age, or by a hindrance of languge, fulfilled their duty of preaching through their priests.

CHAPTER XVI
How the Whole Church is Signified by Those Words "My Sheep" of John 21

A THIRD question remains, which is whether the whole Church may be understood by "My sheep." All Lutherans deny this, and especially Luther himself.[1] Likewise Illyricus[2] and the Centuriators,[3] the book of the Smalkaldic council on the primacy of the Pope, and Calvin.[4]

On the other hand, for us it has been explored and is certain that altogether all Christians, as well as the apostles themselves, are commended to Peter as the sheep of Christ's flock when it is said to him, "Feed my sheep."

Moreover it must be observed that Christ said twice, "Feed my lambs" and once: "Feed my sheep." However, in the Greek text he says once "Feed my lambs" and twice "feed my sheep." It seems that the citation was corrupted by the vice of copyists, who in the second place wrote πρόβατα, when they ought to have written προβάτια, that is little sheep or lambs: how easy it is for one iota to disappear![5]

And so I find it to be the case, firstly from Ambrose and Maximus the Confessor. Ambrose, on the last Chapter of Luke, says that Christ first entrusted to Peter the lambs (*agnos*) which in Greek is ἀρνία. Secondly, little sheep (*oviculas*) which in Greek is προβάτια. Thirdly sheep (*oves*) which in Greek is πρόβατα. Maximus the Confessor says that the *oviculas* and *oves* were consigned to Peter. Certainly he would not have said this except that he read προβάτια and πρόβατα. Next, I gather the same from our version: for if in Greek it was twice πρόβατα, unless some very unlearned boy would have altered it to lambs (*agnos*), who doesn't know that lambs are ἀρνια, not πρόβατα?

Therefore, although all Latin codices read *agnos*, this reading was never from Jerome, or disproved by any other; it is necessary to say that the interpreter read προβάτια, that is little sheep (*oviculas*) and turned it to lambs (*agnos*) because *oviculae* and *agni* are often received for the same thing.

---

[1] *De Potestate Papae.*

[2] *Contra Primatum Papae.*

[3] *Cent 1*, lib. 2, ch. 7, col. 525.

[4] *Institut.*, lib. 4, ch. 6 § 7.

[5] Translator's note: To clarify for readers not familiar with Greek, πρόβατα (probata) = sheep, while προβάτια (probatia) = little sheep, and is translated in the Vulgate by the Latin term *ovicula*. The difference is one letter "I" (iota).

With these having been noted, from this variation, which does not lack a mystery, we prove that all Christians were subjected to Peter. For, if by little sheep we understand lambs, we will say that lambs are repeated twice to mean two people, the Jewish people and the Gentiles: but the sheep being named once mean the bishops, who are just like mothers of the lambs. Therefore, the Lord consigned to Peter the care of the *lambs* (*agni*), that is, the Jewish people; and of the *lambs* (*agni*), that is the Gentile people; and of the *sheep* (*oves*), that is, of those who would give birth to those lambs in Christ, which are the apostles and bishops.

But if by little sheep (*oviculae*) we understand small sheep greater than the lambs, the smaller are perfected by the sheep; it will need to be said with St. Ambrose (loc. cit.) that the *lambs (agni), small sheep (oviculae) and sheep (oves)* were consigned to Peter; that is, those beginning, effecting and being perfected, so that there would be none in the Church no matter how spiritual, erudite and holy, who would not be under Peter. We will even understand by *lambs* the people who have no pastoral care; only each are sons, not parents. By *little sheep* we shall take up lesser priests, that is, priests and pastors, who thus are parents of the people that they may be sons of bishops. Through *sheep*, at length, we will interpret greater priests that is bishops, who are in charge of the lambs and the small sheep; and nevertheless, who are also subject to Peter himself. It seems Pope St. Leo regarded this when he says that Peter was put in charge of all nations, all the Fathers, and all the Apostles by Christ.[6] The nations are lambs, the fathers small sheep, the Apostles great and perfected sheep.

Thereupon, another reason and at that a characteristic one, he supplies to us with that pronoun "*my.*" For, when "my" is added without any restriction to the word "sheep" is manifestly meant that all these sheep are consigned to Peter to whom the pronoun "my" is extended. Moreover it is certain that word "my" extends simply to all, nor was there ever in the Church one who would not boast that he was a sheep of Christ; therefore, all Christians without exception the Lord commended to Peter.

We also see similar sayings everywhere in common speech. For he who says: "I leave behind my goods to my sons," without a doubt excludes nothing from his sons. And the Lord, when he says in John: "I know my sheep, and my sheep hear my voice, and I lay down my soul for my sheep,"[7] even though he does not say "all sheep," and "for all sheep," still, nobody can deny whether he spoke about all of them.

---

[6] Leo, serm. 3, *de anniver. assumpt. suae.*

[7] John 10:15.

Besides, what else is "Feed my sheep," than "have care of my sheepfold?" There is only one sheepfold of Christ: "There will be one fold and one shepherd."[8] Therefore, Christ consigned the whole flock to Peter.

To this end, when the Lord said "Feed my sheep," he either consigned all his sheep to Peter, or none, or some certain and defined ones, or some indefinite ones. But no man will have said none or certain ones were consigned; that is manifestly false: nor even certain indefinite ones, because it is not for a wise provider to relinquish indefinite care, when he could define it, especially when certain confusion and disturbance arises from that lack of definition.

Besides, to commend some, and not include some, appears to be the same thing as if none were to be consigned. Which ones, I ask, will he feed, who does not know his own flock? Therefore, it remains that Christ altogether assigned all his sheep to be fed by Peter.

Furthermore, this is the teaching of all the Fathers. Epiphanius says: "This is the one who heard, 'Feed my sheep,' to whom the sheepfold was entrusted."[9] There is one fold and one shepherd, as we proved a little before from the Gospel. St. John Chrysostom says on that citation: "While disregarding the others he spoke simply to Peter, and consigned to him care of the brethren." And further down: "For the Lord communicated to Peter, he entrusted to him the care of the whole world, etc."

St. Ambrose says on the final chapter of Luke that the Lord relinquished us to Peter by these words: "Feed my sheep," just as a vicar of his love, "needing to be lifted up into heaven he left behind one as the vicar of his affairs;" that without a doubt we should have Peter, who will maintain us in paternal and pastoral love, just as Christ himself had done. Likewise he says: "Because, he alone will profess among all, and is born before all."

Pope Leo the Great in the aforementioned sermon says: "From the whole world Peter alone is chosen that he should be put in charge of all nations, and all apostles, and all Fathers of the Church; so that although there may be many priests in the people of God, and many pastors, nevertheless, Peter properly rules all whom Christ rules."[10] St. Gregory says that the care of the whole Church was consigned to Peter, and he gives the reason saying: "Naturally it is said to him, 'Feed my sheep.'"[11]

Theophylactus, in the last chapter of John, says: "After the meal was ended

---

[8] Ibid.

[9] *In Ancor.*

[10] Loc. Cit.

[11] Gregory, lib. 4, epist. 32.

he consigned to Peter command of the sheep of the whole world, but not others, rather he handed it to this one."And in ch. 22 of Luke he says: "You, O Peter, being converted, you will be a good example of penance to all, since when you were an apostle, and denied, again you received the primacy of all, and command of the world." St. Bernard says: "There are, indeed, other porters of heaven, and other shepherds of flocks, but as you have received both names in a manner different from the rest, so for you they bear a more glorious meaning. Other pastors have each their several flocks assigned to them; to you all the flocks have been entrusted, one flock under one shepherd. Do you ask for proof of that? It is the Lord's word. For to whom (and I do not speak of bishops, rather of the apostles) have all the sheep been so absolutely and indiscriminately consigned? If you love me, O Peter, feed my sheep. Which sheep? The people of this or of that city, or region, or of some kingdom? He says 'my sheep.'"[12] In that place, is it not plain that he did not designate some, but assigned all? Nothing is left out where nothing is distinguished.

Now let us refute the arguments of our adversaries. First the objection of Luther. "Christ does not say: 'Feed all my sheep,' just as he said in another place: 'Teach all nations;' therefore, he did not hand all his sheep over to Peter to feed." I respond: the pronoun "My" exerts itself over a universal sign, as we showed above.

The second objection of the same Luther, and also of Illyricus, is that if the care of feeding all the sheep were consigned to Peter; Peter ought to feed all the sheep: that notwithstanding he does not do this; the rest of the apostles also feed their part of the Lord's flock, and they were sent by Christ, not by Peter. I respond: St. Peter fed the whole flock of the Lord, partly by himself, partly through others, as he had been commanded: for although the Lord sent all the apostles to preach and feed his flock, nevertheless, the very matter of their care (as Chrysostom says) he consigned to Peter; what they did, Peter did through them; they depended upon him just as the body on its leader.

The third objection is common to Luther and the rest, which we cited at the beginning of the chapter. The Apostle Paul in Galatians recognizes no subjection to Peter, or James, or John: "To whom we did not yield in subjection, not for an hour."[13] Likewise: "It is of no importance to me, of what quality some were, who appear to be something." Likewise: "Those who seemed to be something gave no commands to me." And again: "They conferred nothing upon me ... They

---

[12] St. Bernard, *de Consideratione*, ch. 8, n. 15.

[13] Galatians 2:5.

embraced me in friendship."[14]

I respond: What was proposed by Paul in the epistle to the Galatians was not to show he was not subject to Peter (that he attained governance; he makes no mention of this matter), but rather that his gospel was equally true and divine, and received immediately from Christ himself, just as the gospel of Peter, James and John. Therefore, the reality is the Pseudo-apostles boasted that since Peter, James and John were taught by Christ then Paul was a disciple of men; hence, it seemed to them that the gospel of the former was more true than that of Paul.

Therefore, against the calumnies of the Pseudo-apostles Paul arranged his epistle: "Paul, an apostle, not by men, nor through a man, but through Jesus Christ and God the Father, ... I make known the gospel to you that I preached, because there is no second man. Nor do I receive it from a man, nor did I learn it, rather I received it through the revelation of Jesus Christ."

It also pertains to this: "Those who seemed to be something, conferred to me nothing." Therefore, Paul means by these words that he received no doctrine from the rest of the apostles but he was diligently instructed in all things by Christ. Moreover he adds: "They received me in friendship." Indeed, he compels us that we should believe that Peter and Paul were companions in the same office of preaching, but he does not forbid that we understand Peter was greater than Paul in the office of governing. For also in the first book of Kings, the Scripture says: "Saul and his companions."[15] Nevertheless, the same Scripture makes Saul the king, and the rest his servants.

But that "to whom we did not yield in subjection" does not refer to Peter and James, but to the Pseudo-apostles. Thus we read: "But on account of the fact that false brethren were led in to investigate our liberty which we have in Christ Jesus that they might relegate us to servitude, to whom we do not yield in subjection."

Next, to that citation, "It is of no importance to me, of what quality were some who seemed to be something," it is not said in contempt of Peter and John, as the Smalkaldic book would have it, but in praise and honor. The reason Paul gives for why he wished to compare his gospel with the Apostles who were at Jerusalem, although at some time they were unlearned men and vile fishermen. He says it was of little importance what sort of men they were at one time because God does not receive persons, rather he goes out to them so that they who were already great apostles by the grace of God would seem like columns

---

[14] *Ibid.*, 2:9.

[15] 1 Kings (1 Samuel) 23:25.

of the Church.

Next that citation, "Whoever seemed to be something, they gave no commands to me;" no doubt the Smalkaldic Synod of the Lutherans saw some place where they read it, and from there copied out those words into their little book on the primacy of the Pope, for it is certain it is not found anywhere in Paul. Yet no doubt that is the familiarity which our adversaries have with God that they boldly add to his word, nor fear the wound which God threatens those who add to his word.

The fourth objection of the same. The Apostle teaches in Galatians that by divine and human law, jurisdiction was divided up between Peter and Paul, and to Peter was allotted the Jewish people, while to Paul the Gentiles, therefore, not all the sheep of Christ were consigned to Peter. These are the words of the Apostle: "Since they saw that the gospel for the uncircumcised had been entrusted to me, just as for the circumcised to Peter, it was for me also to labor amongst the Gentiles; thus they received Barnabas and me in friendship that we should labor among the Gentiles, and they amongst the circumcised."[16] Therefore, the apostolate of Peter does not pertain to us, for we are of the Gentiles.

I respond: the division of which Paul speaks in his epistle to the Galatians, is not of jurisdiction, but of provinces more suited to preach the gospel of Christ. Therefore, although all of the Apostles could (even as individuals) preach the Gospel in the whole world, nevertheless, to do it more quickly and easily a twofold distribution of provinces was made amongst the apostles. Origen says that the twelve apostles together so divided the world among themselves that Andrew should receive Scythia, Thomas Parthia and India, Bartholomew and Matthew Ethiopia, John Asia,[17] and the rest other places to imbue them with the gospel of Christ.[18]

A second distribution was made between Peter and Paul, without a doubt that Peter especially should work for the conversion of the Jews, though still he was not forbidden from the conversion of the Gentiles, while on the other hand, Paul was chiefly zealous for the conversion of the Gentiles. Still, it was not out of his power to seek the conversion of the Jews. We will confirm all of this from the divine letters with a little labor.

First, it was permitted to Peter to preach to the Gentiles, although he was

---

[16] Galatians 2:7-9.

[17] Translator's note: In the ancient world, Asia (also called Asia minor) usually meant Anatolia, which today is Turkey.

[18] Quoted in Eusebius, *Historiae Eccl.*, lib. 3, ch. 1.

an Apostle for the Jews, it is certain from many places. He preached to Cornelius and his whole house,[19] concerning which he says later, "You know because God elected that through my mouth from the earliest days the Gentiles should hear the Word of God, and believe."[20] Thereupon, in the last chapter of St. Matthew, the Lord said to all the Apostles: "Going therefore, teach all nations." And in the last of Mark: "Preach the gospel to every creature." Therefore, by divine law, all the Apostles could preach to all the Gentiles. And certainly the prince of the Apostles is not excluded from that law because it is given to all the Apostles.

Besides, Innocent I teaches that in the whole of Italy, Gaul, Spain, Africa, and Sicily, churches were established by Peter or by other men, some whom he chose and others whom he sent.[21] Yet it cannot be denied that these churches were mostly of Gentiles.

Therefore, if Peter was only an Apostle of the Jews and not of the Gentiles, why did he not make his seat at Jerusalem, which was the capital city of the Jews, but first at Antioch in Syria and afterwards at Rome, which were cities of Gentiles? And why did the Gentiles who were at Antioch not take their question on the laws to Paul, who was the Apostle of the Gentiles, but to Peter and James, who were Apostles of the Jews?

Indeed Paul could also evangelize the Jews, even though he received the principle mandate concerning the Gentiles, as is seen in his deeds. For wherever he went he evangelized in the synagogues of the Jews. He preached in a synagogue of the Jews at Salamis and in Antioch at Pisidia; likewise at Iconium, Thessalonika, Corinth, Ephesus and at Rome, the very first thing he did was announce the Gospel to the Jews.[22] And in 1 Corinthians he says: "I have been made for the Jews as a Jew that I should win them over."[23] Lastly he writes to the Hebrews, having care for them, and in 2 Corinthians 2 affirms that he bears the solicitude of all churches, and if of all, then certainly of the Jews.

Therefore, both Peter and Paul could preach by divine law, both to the Jews and Gentiles, even though Paul was especially the Apostle of the gentiles. For that reason the Lord himself said concerning Paul: "This one is my vessel of election that he should carry my name in the sight of the Gentiles, and kings,

---

[19] Acts 10.

[20] Acts 15:7.

[21] *Epistola I, ad Decentium*, ch. 1.

[22] Acts 13:13-43; 14:1-7; 17:1-9, 12-15; 18:1-19; 28:17-31.

[23] 1 Corinthians 9:20.

and the sons of Israel."[24] Here "sons of Israel" is placed at the end, Gentiles in the first. Moreover, it is said to Peter with the other Apostles: "You will be my witnesses in Jerusalem, in all of Judaea and Samaria, and even to the end of the earth."[25] There the Jews are placed first and the Gentiles last.

This is what Paul means in Galatians 2 that Peter was the Apostle of the circumcised, and he was of the uncircumcised. And thus Jerome expresses it in this place, where the question is proposed, whether it was not lawful for Peter to bring the Gentiles to the faith, and Paul the Jews. He responds that it was altogether lawful. Nay more, this was put forth to both that they should gather the Church in the whole world, but still Peter had the principle mandate for the Jews, and Paul the Gentiles.

Furthermore, it must be observed that the *munus* of Peter was more to be honored than of Paul, since the Lord himself willed for him alone to preach to the Jews; whereas through the other disciples to the Gentiles. "I am not sent except to the sheep who are lost from the house of Israel."[26] And the Apostle says: "The ministry of Christ Jesus was of the circumcised."[27] The same Paul compares the Jews to olive oil, and the Gentiles to a wild olive tree grafted onto a good olive that they might be made partakers of the fat.[28]

The fifth objection is that the same apostle in the same letter to the Galatians, chapter 2, says: "I resisted Peter to the face;" therefore, he was not subject to him, rather he was either superior to him or certainly equal to him, hence, not all the sheep of Christ are subject to Peter.

I respond: I know Clement of Alexandria suggests that it was not Peter the Apostle, but a certain other man condemned by Paul.[29] I also know that Jerome and many others would have it that it was not truly Peter, but some counterfeit Peter: but the opinion of Augustine is more probable that Peter was condemned in earnest; thus I say it is fitting for an inferior to condemn a superior, only when the matter demands it, and due reverence is preserved.

Therefore, Cyprian praises the humility of Peter, not because he had been condemned by Paul, but because he held the primacy and yet even more it was fitting for him to be submissive to the young and successors, where he indicates

---

24 Acts 9:15.

25 Acts 1:8.

26 Matth. 15:24.

27 Romans 15:8.

28 Romans 11:13-24.

29 As quoted by Eusebius, *Hist. Ecc.*, lib. 1, ch. 14.

that Peter was condemned by an inferior.[30] And Augustine speaks thus: "Peter offered a more rare and holier example to posterity, whereby they should not disdain to be corrected by inferiors: as Paul, by whom inferiors confidently dare to resist superiors for the defense of truth, with charity still being preserved."[31] Gregory also says: "He gave himself also to consensus from an inferior brother, and followed in the same matter business of his inferior that in this he would go before him, insofar as he was first in the summit of the apostolate, he should also be first in humility." And further down: "Behold he is condemned by his inferior, and he did not disdain to be condemned."[32]

The sixth objection, is that "the apostles, without any mandate from Peter, constituted deacons,[33] and again, they sent Peter into Samaria;[34] therefore, Peter was not the head and pastor of the apostles, but he rather was subjected to their command. Besides, Peter hesitated about whether it was lawful to evangelize the Gentiles,[35] and because he did that, he is condemned by the other disciples;[36] who, therefore, would easily believe that his sheepfold pertained to the Gentiles?"

I respond: The fact that all the Apostles took counsel amongst themselves to constitute deacons is nothing especially prejudicial to the primacy of Peter. It must be believed that it was done with Peter's authority, or certainly his consent. It would, however, derogate from his primacy if it could be proved that the deed was done when he refused and against his will.

To that argument on the mission of Peter and John which is in Acts 8, I respond: the term of "mission" (*missio*) does not necessarily mean subjection in the one who is sent. Thus, one is said to "send" who is the authority for someone that he should go, or that he should do it by precept; just as the Lord sent servants, on which it is said in John "The servant is not greater than the master."[37] One can also be said "to send" by counsel and persuasion: as an equal at some time sent to an equal, and an inferior to a superior. For in St. Matthew,

---

[30] Cyprian, *Epistola ad Quintum.*

[31] Augustine, *Epist. 19,* ad Hieronymum.

[32] Homilia 18 in Ezech.

[33] Acts 6:1-6.

[34] Acts 8:4-8.

[35] Acts 10.

[36] Acts 11:1-3.

[37] John 13:16.

Herod sent the Magi to Bethlehem, over whom he had no command; and the people of the Jews sent Phineas the priest to the sons of Ruben and Gad,[38] even though by divine law the high priest was over the whole people, as the Centuriators affirm. Therefore, the apostles sent Peter to the Samaritans by consultation and persuasion, because the matter was very great, to confirm that nation in the faith.

Now to those objections which are brought from chapter X and XI of Acts, I say many are deceived who think that Peter did not know the Gospel must be preached to the Gentiles, except that he had that revelation in Acts XI. Indeed it is very absurd, for in the last chapter of Mark and Matthew, the apostles are bid to teach all Nations, and lest someone would say the apostles did not understand, Luke says: "He opened the sense to them that they would understand the Scriptures." And next, while explaining he added some Scriptures: "because it was fitting for Christ to suffer and to rise from the dead, and to preach in his name penance to all the Gentiles." And Peter shows everywhere in Acts 1, 2 and 3 that he understood the Scriptures, citing the Psalms, Joel, Deuteronomy and namely that in Genesis: "In your seed every household in the land shall be blessed."[39]

Then Peter saw that in a vision partly because of himself and partly because of others: on account of himself, it was not that he should learn that it was lawful to preach to the Gentiles, but that he would understand that it was the proper moment to preach to them. For, the Lord had said: "You will be my witnesses in Jerusalem, in all of Judaea, and Samaria, and even to the ends of the earth." He had prescribed an order to the Apostles by those words that they should first preach in Jerusalem, then in the rest of Judaea, then in Samaria, lastly in the regions of the Gentiles. Up to that point, Peter was irresolute about the time when he should preach to the Gentiles, and whether it would be lawful for them to take the occasion to preach before it was preached to the whole of Judaea and Samaria. The Holy Spirit removed this doubt by showing that vision.

This is how St. Cyril explains the vision: "Immediately Peter understood that the time was at hand to transform shadows into truth."[40] On account of others, however, Peter saw the vision, because there were many converts from the Pharisees to the faith, who reckoned it was not fitting to preach to the Gentiles, and who also were going to blame the deed of Peter, if he had preached to Cornelius, just as they did after in Acts XI.

---

[38] Joshua 22:13.

[39] Genesis 22:18.

[40] Lib. 9 *in Julianum.*

Therefore that Peter should have the best reasons of treating the matter to those condemning him, God showed him this vision, as Chrysostom properly explains: "He said this for the sake of others, and that he should prepare satisfaction to those accusing him."[41] And in his commentary on this Chapter of Acts, Chrysostom says: "Did not Peter fear to eat? God forbid; rather, he said by divine dispensation this whole thing was done on account of them who were going to condemn him."

---

[41] Homil. 42 *in Matth.*

CHAPTER XVII

The First Prerogative of Peter is Explained from the Change of his Name

THUS far we have brought to bear those things which pertain to the promise and the establishment of the primacy of Peter. Now we bring to bear the singular and different prerogatives in confirmation of the same primacy. Yet we do this more joyfully than the Centuriators, who diligently labor to enumerate the fifteen sins and horrendous falls (as they say) of St. Peter, which they say are present in the divine Scripture by God's plan lest we might attribute too much to Peter.[1]

Although apart from the denial of Christ, which was a very grave sin, it cannot be denied that the rest of the fourteen sins of St. Peter are not to be abhorred, but rather the lies and blasphemies of the Centuriators should be, as we will prove a little later. Meanwhile, for the fourteen false crimes we bring to bear twenty eight true prerogatives.

The first prerogative is the change of name, for in the first chapter of John's Gospel the Lord says to Peter, "You are Simon son of John; you will be called Cephas." It must be observed in this place with Chrysostom that God never imposes new names except for very great reasons, and to signify privileges conceded to those whose names are changed. Thus with Abraham, since he was called אַבְרָם [Abram] that is, "lofty father," God wished him to be called אַבְרָהָם [Abraham] that is, "father of the multitude,"[2] that he should become the father of many sons, or rather more nations and peoples.

Additionally, there is a twofold prerogative in this change of name of Simon into the name of Peter. One that he changed the name of Peter alone among all the Apostles. For although he imposed a name on the sons of Zebedee, Boanerges [sons of thunder], nevertheless that was rather more a type of surname than a proper name, and they are never again called Boanerges by the Evangelists, but merely James and John as they were before. But Peter is thereafter almost always called Peter. Even Paul often names him Peter, and never calls him anything but Peter or Cephas, just as John often names him; but John is always John, never Boanerges.

The second is that the Lord gave a specific name to him. For in Aramaic Cephas means rock, as we taught above and St. Jerome witnesses.[3] Moreover in

---

[1] Cent. 1, lib. 2, ch. 10, col. 558.

[2] Genesis 17:5.

[3] Epist. *ad Galatos*, ch. 2.

Greek it means "head" [κεφαλή], as Optatus notes.[4] And at length it is one of the most famous names of the Christ. Nothing is more frequent in the Scriptures except that the Christ is called rock (*petra*).[5] Therefore, when Christ communicates this name to Peter alone, and that name which signifies himself, as a foundation and head of the whole Church, what else did he desire to show other than he made Peter the foundation and head of the Church in his place?

St. Leo says: "This, taken up in consort of undivided unity that which he was, would have him so named, by saying: 'You are Peter,' etc."[6] And in a sermon he so introduces Christ speaking to Peter: "Just as my Father has manifested to you my divinity, so even I make known to you your excellence, because you are Peter. That is, since I am the inviolable rock, I am the cornerstone, I am the one who makes each one, I lay the foundation apart from which no man can place another. Nevertheless, you are also rock, because you are solid by my power that those things which are proper to me may be yours by common participation with me."[7]

---

[4] *Contra Parmenianum*, lib. 2.

[5] Isaiah 8:14 and 28:16; Dan 2:45; Psal. 117 (118):22; Math. 21:42; Rom. 9:33; 1 Cor. 10:3; Ephes. 2:20; 1 Peter 2:4-8; and other places.

[6] Epist. 89, *ad Episcopos Viennensis provinciae.*

[7] Serm 3, *de anniversario die assumptionis suae ad pontificatum.*

CHAPTER XVIII

The Second Prerogative is explained from the manner in which the Apostles are enumerated by the Evangelists

THE SECOND prerogative of Peter is that when the Apostles are named by the Evangelists, whether all or some, Peter is always put in the first place. "These are the names of the twelve Apostles: first Simon, who is called Peter, etc."[1] We read the same in Mark 3, Luke 6, and Acts 1, but this was not done because Peter was called first by Christ that is certain. For the Lord first called Andrew, as John witnesses in Chapter 1.

But the Centuriators of Magdeburg oppose this and say: "Peter was called first either on account of his manifest gifts, or on account of age since he was exceedingly older than the others, not because he was the head of the others."[2] Moreover, they write in another place: "Peter was placed first in the catalogue because of his fall. Someone ought to be in the first place, and Peter comes to mind on account of his fall."[3] But nothing validates any of these reasons. Not the first, for either they speak concerning the characteristic gifts which Peter had in rank for the Church that he singularly receives the keys, which made him the foundation of the Church that he was constituted shepherd of all the sheep of Christ, etc. and thence they speak for our part. Or, they speak on his own personal gifts, that is, on his virtues, and then what they say is false. For the Evangelist could not easily know, nor would have dared to judge, who should be the best among the disciples, especially since he knew that John was a virgin while Peter was married; and the same John seemed to be so loved by the Lord that he was called, "The disciple whom Jesus loved." Nor would he be ignorant that James the younger was provided with such holiness that he should be called "just" and "a brother of the Lord" apart from all the others.

Now, when they speak of Peter's age, they oppose ancient tradition. For Epiphanius says: "Running to meet him, it came to pass that Andrew was first, since Peter was younger in age."[4] Indeed, Jerome says that John was not chosen as the head of the others, because he was almost a boy: but he does not say Peter was older than all the others.[5] Add what the Centuriators themselves say on the life of Andrew that it is probable that Andrew was older than Peter.[6]

---

[1] Matthew 10:2-4.

[2] *Cent 1*, lib. 2, ch. 7, col. 524.

[3] *Ibid*, ch. 10, col. 561.

[4] *Haeres. 51*, which is of Irrational things.

[5] *In Jovinianum,* lib. 1.

[6] *Cent 1.*, lib. 2, ch. 10.

Further, to the objection that the fact of his fall is the reason why one should be placed first in the *Catalogue*, and Peter comes to mind: Rather Peter may be placed first by reason of dignity, and it is clear from the manner in which he is made first among the twelve. Namely, when Matthew calls him first, then he does not call the others second, then another one third, etc., but without any observation of rank he names them.

Therefore, among Peter and the others, Matthew teaches there is an order; Peter is higher, the rest are lower, but among them he states no order, because they are all equal, as St. Albert the Great notes in his commentary on this citation. From this name *first* the Fathers deduce the primacy, a term the heretics hate so much. For just as rule (*principatus*) comes from prince, and a consulship (*consulatus*) comes from consul, so primacy comes from first (*primus*). Hence, Ambrose says: "Andrew followed the savior first, but he did not receive the primacy, but Peter."[7] And Augustine says on the last chapter of John: "Peter, on account of the primacy of his apostolate, etc." Certainly, primacy is not about the one who fell first in a written catalogue, but who duly and meritoriously is written first, on account of his degree and authority.

Secondly, the same is gathered from that which is changed in the order of the others: Peter is always put in the first place. For in Matthew 10, Andrew is put after Peter, in Mark 3, James is after Peter, in Luke 6, Andrew is named after Peter, but the order is changed for the rest: for Matthew puts Thomas ahead of himself, and Simon the Zealot ahead of Thaddaeus. Luke moreover, puts Matthew ahead of Thomas, and Thaddaeus before Simon. Acts of the Apostles places John after Peter, and in the others a great change is discovered.

For equal reason, where two or many are named, Peter is always put first. Mark 5 and Luke 8: "He did not admit any to follow him except Peter, James and John." And in Luke 22: "He sent Peter and John," while in Matthew 17: "He took up Peter, James and John." Mark 13: "Peter, James and John as well as Andrew asked him." In the last Chapter of John: "Simon Peter, Thomas, Nathaniel, and the sons of Zebedee were together, as well as two others from his disciples." Everywhere Peter is first which cannot be due to his fall.

Still, there is one citation where Peter is not named in the first place, Galatians 2, where it is said: James, Cephas and John. But it is not especially certain whether Paul spoke thus. For Ambrose, Augustine and Jerome read in this citation, both in the text and in their commentary, Peter, James and John. In addition, Chrysostom says in his commentary: "Peter, James and John;" showing that he so read it, therefore, it is credible that Paul spoke in that way.

---

[7] In 2 Cor. 12.

But if we admit it ought to be read James, Peter and John, it may be said, even with St. Anselm and St. Thomas on this passage that it was done because James was the bishop of Jerusalem, where the Apostles were then, from where Paul is speaking; or that Paul preserved no order in this passage.

For in any case, that Paul understood Peter to be greater than James is clear from the very same epistle, in Chapter 1, where he says: "Thereafter three years I came to Jerusalem to see Peter." He does not say, "I came to see James," although he was also the bishop of Jerusalem. He says: "Whoever says I am of Paul, I of Apollo, I of Cephas, I of Christ, etc."[8] Obviously he proceeds by ascending and constitutes Peter next under Christ.

Yet Peter is not only put in the first place and called first, rather he is also described everywhere in the Scriptures as a householder (*paterfamilias*), as a general and prince of the rest. For just as it is said in the Apocalypse, "The Devil and his angels, Michael and his angels," that is, a general and his soldiers, so also it is said in Mark 1:36 "And Simon followed after him, as well as those who were with him." Luke 8: "Peter and those who were with him spoke, etc." Luke 9: "But Peter and those who were with him." Mark 16: "Tell his disciples and Peter." Acts 2: "Peter standing with the eleven." And in the same place: "They said to Peter and the rest of the Apostles." Acts 5: "Peter and the Apostles said." 1 Cor. 9: "Do we not have the power to go about with a sister, just as the other Apostles and brethren of the Lord, and Cephas?" Now I ask, was not Cephas a disciple? Was he not an Apostle? Why, therefore, is it said Peter and the Apostles? To Peter and the disciples? The Apostles and Cephas? The only reason is that Peter was the prince and head of the others.

For that reason, St. Ignatius says that Christ came to them after the resurrection who were around Peter.[9] It pertains to the same prerogative that Peter almost always speaks in the name of all, as in Matthew 19: "Behold, we have left all things behind, etc." Luke 12: "Do you speak this parable to us, or to all?" John 6: "O Lord, to whom shall we go?" On that place, Cyril so writes: "Through one who was in charge, all responded." Hence, Chrysostom also calls Peter the "mouth of the Apostles."[10]

---

[8] 1 Corinthians 1:12.

[9] *Epist. ad Smyrnenses.*

[10] *Hom. 55.* In Matth.

CHAPTER XIX

Four Other Prerogatives are Explained from the Gospel of St. Matthew

HE THIRD prerogative is related in St. Matthew, where Peter alone walks with the Lord over the waters.[1] St. Bernard speaks concerning this prerogative: "He [Peter] is the counterpart of the Lord, walking over the waters; he designated him as the unique vicar of Christ that he should be in charge of not one people, but all people, and accordingly many waters, and many people."[2] A like thing is related in John, where while the rest of the disciples are coming in a boat to the Lord (who is waiting on the shore), Peter throws himself into the sea, and comes by swimming. St. Bernard says in the same place: "What is this? Truly a sign of Peter's singular Pontificate, by which he does not receive one boat as the rest, to be his own to govern, but the world itself, for the sea is the world, the boats the churches."

The fourth prerogative, is that peculiar revelation made to Peter alone in Matthew 16, a characteristic privilege that Peter, the first of all the Apostles, being thoroughly instructed by God, recognized the greatest mysteries of our faith, the distinction of the persons in God and the Incarnation. For, though often beforehand Christ had been called the son of God, as in Matthew 14, when the disciples said: "truly you are the son of God" and John I when Nathaniel said: "You are the son of God," nevertheless, they called Christ the Son of God in the way in which all the saints are called sons of God. But Peter understood that Christ was the true and natural Son of God. This is clear in the Greek text, where they are expressed by all the articles having emphasis: σύ εἶ ὁ Χριστὸς ὁ υἱὸς τοῦ Θεοῦ ζῶντος, and from the great approval of Christ, when he said: "Blessed are you, Simon bar-Jonah, because flesh and blood has not revealed this to you, but my Father who is in heaven," and even from the testimonies of the Fathers.

For Hilary calls Peter the first confessor of the Son of God,[3] and he also says that he spoke what the human voice had not yet brought forth.[4] He also says that Peter was made worthy, who is the first to have recognized something of God in Christ." Athanasius says[5] that Peter first recognized the divinity of Christ, and only after him did all the other disciples. Other Fathers say similar

---

[1] Matth. 24:29.

[2] St. Bernard, *de considerat.*, lib. 2.

[3] *In Psal. 131.*

[4] *De Trinitate*, lib. 6.

[5] Athanasius, *Serm. 4*, Contra Arianos; Chrysostom *in Matthew* ch. 16; Cyril, lib. *In Joannem* lib. 12, ch. 64; Augustine *de Tempore*, serm. 124; Leo *serm. 2* de natali Petri et Pauli.

things.

The fifth prerogative is in Matthew 16 where it is said: "And the gates of hell will not prevail against it." Whereby the stability of the whole Church is not only promised forever, but even of the rock upon which the Church is founded, as Origen notes in this place. Therefore, by a special privilege promised to Peter, his seat will never fall into ruin; a promise that, should the other Apostles have had it, the seat of James would still stand in Jerusalem, and John at Ephesus, Matthew at Ethiopia and Andrew in Scythia, but yet all these little by little gave their hands to the gates of hell. Hence, Augustine says against the Donatists, "Count the priests even from that seat of Peter that is the rock, which the proud gates of hell do not conquer."

The sixth prerogative is from Matthew 17, where the Lord bid that the tribute be paid for himself and for Peter: "Give to them for me and you." From which words was gathered the Apostles, and Peter was preferred before all the others, as Origen, Chrysostom and Jerome write. Furthermore, Chrysostom eloquently asserts in this place that Peter was placed before all the others, affected with such honor that he refused this to be written about himself by his disciple Mark. Therefore, Mark most diligently writes of Peter's denial in his Gospel, but those things which especially establish Peter's glory, either he omits or very briefly constrains them. In that matter there can be no other reason given, except that Peter wished it thus.

Lastly the author of the questions of the Old and new Testament, which is contained in the fourth volume of Augustine's works, q. 75, says that Christ paid two drachma, one for himself and the other for Peter, because just as in Christ, so also in Peter all are contained: "He set him up to be their head that he would be the pastor of the Lord's flock."

But Jerome, commenting on ch. 18 of Matthew after he had said the Apostles gathered drachma to pay, Peter was going to be the chief of all, he immediately adds: "The Lord, understanding the reason for the error, cleansed the desire of glory by the contention of humility." Therefore, the Apostles erred reckoning Peter to be the head.

I respond: Indeed the Apostles erred, but not in that they received Peter as one going to be their chief, but because they dreamed of temporal rule. Therefore, at no later time did they reckon something promised to them, since they had heard many things about the kingdom of Christ. The Lord corrected this error often, warning that the prefects of the Church would not be like the kings of the Gentiles, and that they should prepare themselves for persecutions and death in this world, not honor and glory.

CHAPTER XX

Three Other Prerogatives are Explained from the Gospel of Luke

THE SEVENTH prerogative is taken from Luke and John,[1] wherein two miracles of Christ are explained that took place while Peter was fishing. The first of which manifestly indicates, as St. Augustine shows us, the Church militant, and the second, the Church triumphant;[2] for on that account, the former was done before the resurrection of Christ, and the second afterwards.

Likewise, in the first miracle the nets are not cast to the right side of the boat, nor to the left, lest we would believe that only the good or the bad were to come into the Church; rather it is said indifferently: "Let go the nets," while in the second place, the nets are only cast from the right side of the boat, since only the good are gathered into eternal life.

Besides, in the first the nets broke, and the boat was almost sunk, which signifies schism and heresy, as well as scandal, which compel the Church to be restless: but in the second miracle the nets were not broken, as the Evangelist himself notes, as though looking back to the first fishing, in which the nets were broken. Nor is the boat restless, because in the next life there will be no schisms or scandals.

To this, in the first, the first are understood without number that it should be fulfilled what was written in the Psalms: "I announced and spoke, and they were multiplied beyond number."[3] But in the second miracle, they were not beyond number, rather a certain number, 153, for none were gathered apart from the number of the elect for the kingdom.

Lastly, in the first miracle the fish are introduced into the boat that is still restless; in the second they are brought onto the shore so as to designate by that stability an immortal and blessed life.

Therefore, the characteristic prerogative of Peter is that in each boat and each occasion of fishing (which certainly signifies the state of the Church), Peter is always found to be their chief. For in Luke V, when the Lord saw many boats, "he entered into one, which was of Simon," and from that one taught, so that we would understand through that boat the Church, whose captain is Peter, is where Christ teaches.

---

[1] Luke 5:1-11; John 21:1-14.

[2] *Tract. In Joannem,* Tract. 122.

[3] Psalm 39 (40): 6.

Ambrose says: "The Lord boarded only this boat of the Church, in which Peter was constituted as the master."[4] In the same place, it is said to Peter alone: "Cast out into the deep, and let down the nets for capture." Peter is bid just as a ship's captain, and a fisher, to lead others to fish. In the same place, the Lord explaining the figure, says to Peter alone: "Do not be afraid, from this moment you will be fishers of men." Thus even in John, Peter says: "I go to fish, and the others said to him: 'We are coming with you.'"[5] Also: "Simon Peter came up and dragged the net onto the land." What else is meant by these figures, than that Peter is the one who leads men from the world to faith and the Church militant, and who, reigning, leads and guides them to the Church triumphant?

The eighth is from Luke 22, where the Lord said: "Simon, Simon, behold Satan has asked for you that he might sift you just as wheat: but I have prayed for thee that thy faith shall not fail. And when thou has been converted, strengthen thy brethren." By such words, the Lord clearly shows that Peter is the prince and head of his brethren. Thus the Greek and Latin Fathers express it. Theophylactus says in this place: "Because I have you as a prince of the disciples, after you will have denied me, strengthen the rest, for it behooves you, who are the rock of the Church after me." Pope St. Leo says: "For the faith of Peter, he properly supplies that the future state of the rest would be more certain, if the mind of the prince were not conquered."[6]

The ninth is that Christ, after his resurrection, offered himself first of all to the Apostles for Peter to see him, which is gathered from the words of Luke: "The Lord has truly risen, and appeared to Simon."[7] There Ambrose notes that Christ appeared to Simon first before anyone else. For before he had appeared to Mary Magdalene, as Mark writes in the last chapter, this same thing is manifestly seen in the words of St. Paul: "I handed onto you what I had first received that Christ died, and was buried, and rose again on the third day according to the Scriptures that he was seen by Cephas, and afterward the eleven; next he was seen by more than five hundred of the brethren, thereafter by James, and all the Apostles: last of all he was seen by me, as one born out of time."[8] In which place St. John Chrysostom says: "Therefore, he was not seen by all in the beginning, nor even most, but only one, and to that prince worthy by

---

[4]   Sermon 11.

[5]   John 21:3.

[6]   *Sermon 3, de anniversario assumptionis suae ad Pontific.*

[7]   Luke 24:34.

[8]   1 Cor. 15: 1-8.

the greatest faith." And further: "Therefore, he first appeared to Peter, for since it was he who had first confessed Christ, for what reason would he not also be the first to see the risen one?" Theophylactus has similar things in this place.

CHAPTER XXI
Two Others are Explained from the Gospel of St. John

HE TENTH is that Peter was first to have his feet washed by the Lord, as Augustine shows in chapter 13 of John. And although Chrysostom and Theophylactus reckon in the same place that Judas was first and Peter second, nevertheless, they also gather the primacy of Peter from this place. Indeed, they say that no other was going to suffer apart from Judas that his feet should be washed before the prince of the Apostles: Moreover, Judas impudently constituted himself before Peter. But just the same, it seems the opinion of Augustine is more probable.

The eleventh is of John 21, where Christ foretold his death and death on a cross to Peter alone, that just as he had given him his name and imposed upon him a duty, so also he would have him as an ally in death: "When you are old, you will extend your hands and another will gird you, and he will lead you whither you do not wish. But he said this," adds the Evangelist, "meaning by what death he should give glory to God." Thereupon, in the same place the Lord adds, speaking to Peter: "Follow me." Such words they receive from the pastoral office, as Theophylactus shows; follow me, I who lead you to preach, and who hand the whole world into your hands. Others receive them as a similitude of death, as Euthymius, who explains that "*sequere me*" that is "imitate me" by suffering on the cross.

Yet there will be a full commentary, if we join each sentence. When the Lord consigned the sheep to Peter, and foretold the nature of his death, just as when concluding everything in one word, he says: "Follow me;" that is, be that which I was both living and dying, lead as a pastor of souls while you live, and afterward through death on the cross be carried over from this world to the Father. And lest we might suspect that these were said to all, the Lord eloquently excludes John, who then followed bodily: "Thus I wish him to remain, what of you? Follow me."

CHAPTER XXII

Another Nine Prerogatives are Explained from the Acts of the Apostles and the Epistle to the Galatians

THE TWELFTH prerogative is found in Acts 1, where Peter, just as a householder, gathers all into one body of disciples and teaches that one must be chosen in place of Judas. Chrysostom says concerning this: "How does Peter acknowledge the flock was consigned to himself? How is he the prince in this choir?" Oecumenius says: "Peter, not James rises, as one to whom presidency of the disciples had been consigned. Nor does anyone oppose the prayer of Peter, but soon they constituted two according to his precept, whom they reckoned most worthy in regard to degree that God himself should designate one of them."

The thirteenth is from Acts 2, where after they receive the Holy Spirit, Peter is the first of all to promulgate the Gospel, and he converted three thousand men by that first sermon. Chrysostom notes: "Peter was the mouth of all, but the eleven stood near, corroborating these by their testimony, which were taught by him."

The fourteenth is from Acts 3 where the first miracle in testimony of the faith is done by Peter. Although Peter and John were together, nevertheless, Peter alone said to the lame man: "Gold and silver I have not, but what I do have, I give it to you, etc." Ambrose remarks beautifully that Peter rightly published the first miracle by the strengthening of feet that he should show himself to be the foundation of the whole Church.

The fifteenth is from Acts 5, where Peter, just as a supreme and divine judge, discerned and condemned the hypocrisy and fraud of Ananias and Saphira, and slew them by his word.

The sixteenth is from Acts 9, where we read thus: "It came to pass, when Peter passed through all." In which place Chrysostom says: "Just the same, a general walking about in an army considers what part should be joined together, which drawn up, which needs him to come, and see wherever he goes he is found first."

The seventeenth is from Acts 10, where Peter first of all begins to preach to the Gentiles, just as he was first of all to preach to the Jews. And the vision was shown to him alone, whereby he was advised that it was the time to preach to the Gentiles, where it is also said to him: "Kill and eat." For it is of the head to eat, and through eating to drag down food into the stomach, and incorporate it into itself. Moreover it is signified by this metaphor that it is fitting that he as head of the Church should convert infidels, and effect them members of the Church.

But you might object: In Acts 8 did Philip not convert the heathen eunuch of the queen of Ethiopia? And Did Paul not in Acts 9 speak to the Gentiles, and dispute with the Greeks? Therefore, how is Peter said to be the first to have preached to the Gentiles?

I respond: The eunuch was a Proselyte, that is, he had already been converted to Judaism, so was not obviously a Gentile as Cornelius was. For Peter does not lie in Acts 15 when he indicates that he was the first to preach to the Gentiles. Thereafter in Acts 11, Luke writes that those who were dispersed by the tribulations which arose under Stephen walked abroad to different regions evangelizing, "speaking a word to no man, but to the Jews alone;" and one among them was Philip, as is clear from Acts 8. Besides, if Philip had already preached to a Gentile man, and no one had condemned him, why would Peter later hesitate whether it might be the time to preach to the Gentiles? Why is he inspired by a heavenly vision for this? Why, after this was heard, some from the Jews gaped, and others accused Peter as of bold insolence? Add that the eunuch himself went into Jerusalem to the Temple, and was reading Isaiah in his cart, which are obvious signs of Judaism.

Next, Jerome, speaking about Cornelius, says: "First baptized by the Apostle, he proclaimed the salvation of the gentiles."[1] And Chrysostom: "You see, from where the beginning of the gentiles was made? By a pious man who was held worthy in regard to his works."[2] But if, at some time, the Fathers say that the eunuch whom Philip baptized was a Gentile, they understand it to be so by nation and not by religion.

Concerning Paul there is no difficulty following the Greek manuscripts. In Greek it is not "He spoke to the gentiles", but only: "He spoke and disputed against the Greeks." But here he calls Jews Greeks that were born in Greece and spoke Greek, as Chrysostom and Oecumenius show. Besides, it does not have the appearance of truth that Paul would have preached to the Gentiles in Jerusalem itself, especially since no rumor was stirred up by the Judaizers, who afterward so forcefully rose up against Peter, because he had preached to Cornelius.

Nevertheless, seeing that the Latin manuscripts have it that he spoke to the gentiles and disputed with the Greeks, it can be said that he spoke and disputed with the Gentiles, not by bringing them to the faith, but by defending the faith from their calumnies. Therefore, Luke adds in the same place, not that some were converted, but so serious a hatred was roused against Paul that they sought to kill him. Therefore, the first Father of both Jews and Gentiles was

---

[1] *Epistola ad Salvinam.*

[2] *Hom. 22 in Acta.*

Peter.

The eighteenth is from Acts 12, where "Prayer was made without ceasing by the Church" for Peter after he had been shut up in prison. Wherefore he was also liberated by a characteristic miracle. We know before this, both when Stephen was in danger, who afterward was stoned and also James, who in like manner was shut up in the same prison and afterwards killed, that the Church did not make prayer without ceasing for them, as we now see it was done when Peter was in danger. What other reason can be assigned, except that there is a great difference between one member and the head itself when in danger? Therefore, Chrysostom says: "Prayer is a mark of great love and all beseeched the Father, etc."

The nineteenth prerogative is in Acts 15, where Peter speaks first in council, and James and all the rest follow his opinion, as Jerome teaches in a letter to Augustine. Furthermore, Theodoret, in an epistle to Pope Leo, speaks on the same affair: "Paul, the herald of truth, the trumpet of the most Holy Spirit, ran to the great Peter that he might bring resolution from him to those contending about the legal institutions at Antioch."

The twentieth is from Galatians I, where Paul says: "After three years I went up to Jerusalem to see Peter." In which place Oecumenius says, "Paul went up to Jerusalem to see Peter because he was greater." Chrysostom: "He was the mouth and prince of the Apostles, and on that account Paul went up to see him apart from any other."[3] Ambrose says: "It was worthy that he should desire to see Peter, because he was first among the Apostles, to whom the Savior had delegated care of the churches."[4] Jerome in an epistle to Augustine, cited above: "Peter had such authority that Paul wrote in his epistle, 'after three years I came to Jerusalem to see Peter.'"[5]

---

[3] Hom. 87.

[4] *Ad Galatos*, ch. 1.

[5] *Epistola ad Augustinum, 89.*

CHAPTER XXIII

The Other Prerogatives are Proposed from Various Authors

ITHERTO we have reviewed these prerogatives which are gathered from Holy Scripture: we shall now add another eight, which we take from various authors.

Therefore, the twenty-first prerogative is that Christ baptized Peter alone by his hands. Evodius writes about the successor in the Episcopate of Antioch, in a letter, which is titled τὸ φῶς, that among women, Christ only baptized his Virgin Mother, among men only Peter; and Peter baptized Andrew, James, and John, and the rest were baptized by them. Euthymius[1] refers to that, as well as Nicephorus.[2]

The twenty-second is that Peter alone was ordained a bishop by Christ: the rest, however, received episcopal consecration from Peter. That is what Juan Torquemada[3] proves with many reasons, but particularly two. The first is because either the Lord ordained no one a bishop, or all, or some, or one. It cannot be said he ordained no one. For if that were so, we would have no bishop now, since no man can give to another what he does not have himself. Therefore, a non-bishop cannot ordain a bishop, so if the Lord ordained nobody, and did not leave behind Peter ordained a bishop, who afterward ordained Peter and the others?

But that all the Apostles were not immediately ordained by the Lord is obvious. For at least Paul, whom he called from heaven, and made an Apostle, he did not ordain a bishop, but bid to be ordained through the imposition of the hands of ministers of the Church, as is clear in Acts 13, and from Leo's epistle to Dioscorus.[4] Moreover in the volumes of Councils, 79, Leo brings this example of Paul, and from Chrysostom, who says on this place of Acts that there was a true ordination of Paul, in which place they changed his name. It is immediately added, Saul, who is also Paul.

On that account that James the younger, one of the twelve, was ordained a bishop at Jerusalem by the Apostles, and not immediately by Christ, Anacletus teaches in an epistle,[5] where he writes that a bishop ought to be ordained by three bishops, just as James the younger was ordained a bishop by Peter, James

---

[1] *In cap. 3 Joannis.*

[2] *Hist.*, lib. 2, ch. 3.

[3] *Summae de Ecclesia*, lib. 2, ch. 32.

[4] Epistolae, 81.

[5] *Epist.* 2.

the elder and John. Likewise, Clement of Alexandria hands down the same thing that James was ordained a bishop by Peter, James and John.[6] Jerome says: "James, immediately after the passion of the Lord, was ordained a bishop by the Apostles at Jerusalem."[7] Nor can it be said this James was not the Apostle from the twelve, for Jerome opposes that in his book against Helvidius, and we showed the same thing in another place for the reason that it would not follow that the memory of an Apostle from the twelve was not preserved in the Church.

And the Lord did not ordain some and not ordain others, for that is proved because the Apostles, with the exception of Peter, were equals among themselves, and had no rights over another, and all power that was handed to them, was commonly handed to all, inasmuch as it can be gathered from the Gospels. Therefore, if the Lord did not ordain none, nor all, nor a portion of some, then it follows that he ordained only Peter.

The second reason is that the Fathers teach everywhere that the Roman Church is the mother of all Churches, and that all bishops had their consecrations and their dignity from her. But it would not seem that this could be the case except in the sense that Peter himself, who was bishop of Rome, ordained all the Apostles, and all other bishops, either by himself or through others whom he had ordained. Otherwise, when all the Apostles constituted many bishops in different places, if the Apostles were not made bishops by Peter, certainly a great part of the Episcopate would not deduce their origin from Peter.

Why is it, therefore that Anacletus says: "In the New Covenant after Christ the sacerdotal order began from Peter"? Furthermore, he cannot be speaking on a lesser order of priests, that is, of presbyters. For it is certain that the Apostles were all ordained priests together at the Last Supper; therefore, he speaks on the order of greater priests, that is, of bishops, whom he would not correctly say began from Peter, if all the Apostles were immediately ordained bishops by Christ.

Why is it that Cyprian also says that the Roman Church is the mother and root of the whole Catholic Church?[8] Why is it that Innocent I says in his epistle to the Council of Carthage,[9] "By whom (Peter) the episcopate and the whole

---

[6] Quoted in Eusebius, *Histor.* Lib. 2, ch. 1.

[7] *De viris illustribus*, in Jacobo.

[8] Lib. 4, epist. 8.

[9] Which is 91 among the epistles of Augustine.

authority of this name emerges?" Likewise what he writes in his epistle to the Council of Miletus: "As many times as the reasoning of faith is brandished, I reckon all our brothers and co-bishops ought to bring no authority except for that which pertains to Peter."[10] What of what Pope Julius I wrote to the Orientals: "How could you not incur blame, if the place from where you receive the honors of consecration, and whence you take up the law of the whole observance is also the seat of blessed Peter, which is for us the mother of sacerdotal dignity, and should be the teacher of ecclesiastical reason?"[11]

Lastly, what of that which St. Leo says: "If he wished for the other princes to be in common with him (Peter), he never gave anything he did not deny to the others except through Peter."[12] And again: "The Lord so willed the Sacrament of this office to pertain to the office of all the apostles that he principally placed it in Blessed Peter, the chief of all the Apostles, so that his gifts would flow into every body as if from a the head."?[13]

Yet our adversaries reject this specific argument by saying: "Episcopacy is included in the apostolate, otherwise it would not be true what Anacletus writes in the aforementioned epistle that bishops succeed the Apostles; but Christ made all of them Apostles, not just Peter. Therefore, Christ also ordained them bishops, not just Peter. In addition, how is what is said in the Psalms: 'Let another receive his Episcopate,'[14] understood concerning Judas the traitor, as Peter explains in Acts 1, when Peter did not ordain Judas; therefore, Peter did not ordain all."

I respond: Episcopacy is contained in the apostolate, and bishops succeed Apostles, not for the reason that someone who is an Apostle should also be a bishop (since the Lord chose twelve disciples in Luke 6, and named them Apostles, although it was before he made them priests, still less bishops). Consequently, the right of preaching properly pertains to the apostolate, to which was connected the fullest delegated jurisdiction. Such cannot also be said of bishops, because all the Apostles were bishops, nay more they were even the

---

[10]   93 among the Epistles of Augustine.

[11]   Julius I, *in Epist. 1 ad Orientales.* [The context of this letter is that St. Athanasius appealed to this Pope after being unjustly condemned by Eastern bishops, and Pope Julius I reversed their judgment. -Translator's note].

[12]   Serm. 3.

[13]   Epist. 89.

[14]   Psalm 108: 8.

first bishops of the Church, although they were not ordained.[15]

Now I respond to that part about Judas in Psalm 108 (109). It is not called an episcopate the way we now speak of episcopate, but any prefecture in Hebrew is פְּקֻנְדָה which means a visitation or a prefecture, and it is believable that Peter deputed this Psalm and that name to a prefecture to accommodate the apostolate of Judas.

Moreover, Luke, relating these in Greek, followed the interpreters of the Septuagint, which turned τὴν ἐπισχοπήν, which is a term that the Interpreters could not understand except as a prefecture in general, since in their time the establishment of the episcopate was still not properly so called. Add what even Cicero says in a letter where he uses this noun, when he says that he was constituted an *episcopus* by Pompey over the whole of Campania.[16]

This response can also be made: That Psalm speaks on a properly called episcopate, not the one which Judas had, but that which he was going to have if he had not betrayed the Lord.

The twenty-third is that Peter first detected the heresiarch, prince and father of all heretics who would come after, namely Simon Magus, as we read in Acts 8, and afterward he condemned and destroyed him. It was altogether fitting that the prince and father of the Church should conquer the prince and father of all heretics. Simon was indeed the father of all heretics, as Irenaeus writes.[17]

Yet we bring the testimony of the Fathers to bear on this matter, because Calvin holds the contest between St. Peter with Simon Magus to be a fable.[18] Egesippus, and Clement broadly explain the whole history as well as Arnobius, who says: "In Rome herself, mistress of all, in which, although men are busied with the practices introduced by King Numa, and the superstitious observances of antiquity, they have nevertheless hastened to give up their fathers' mode of life and attach themselves to Christian truth. For they had seen the chariot of Simon Magus, and his fiery car, blown into pieces by the mouth of Peter, and vanish when Christ was named. They saw him, I say, trusting in false gods, and

---

[15] Translator's note: There is something lost here in English, namely that the term ἐπισκωπός (episkopos) in Greek means an overseer, so St. Robert is trying to draw the distinction of the Apostles as overseers as opposed to their being actual bishops in the ordained sense.

[16] Lib. 7, *Epist. ad Atticum.*

[17] Lib. 1, ch. 20; and the beginning of lib. 3.

[18] *Instit.* Lib. 4, ch. 6 § 15.

abandoned by them in their terror, borne headlong by his own weight, lying prostrate with his legs broken."[19]

Damasus relates the same thing in the life of Peter, as well as numerous other fathers.[20] Augustine relates on the matter: "In the city of Rome, the blessed Apostle Peter destroyed Simon Magus by the true power of almighty God."[21]

Whereby we understand the same Augustine says: "Indeed this is the opinion of many, although many Romans hold that it is false, that the Apostle Peter intended to do battle with Simon Magus on the Lord's day, on account of the danger of a great trial, since the day before the church of the same city fasted, and after such a prosperous and glorious outcome followed, it kept the same custom, and several western churches imitate it."[22] Here he did not wish to say the opinion on the contest between Peter and Simon Magus was uncertain, as Calvin reckoned, but the opinion on the origin of fasting on the Sabbath. Although the authors cited hand down in unison that Peter fought with Simon at Rome, and conquered him, nevertheless, none hand down that this deed happened on the Lord's day, neither did they fast the day before, nor did they on that account institute fasting on the Sabbath, concerning which Augustine disputes in that epistle.

The twenty-fourth is that Peter placed his chief seat at Rome by divine command. The obvious sign of the Principate of Peter seems to be that when the Apostles were sent by him into the whole world, Peter was sent to that head of the world, the queen of cities. That is what St. Leo also teaches: "For, when the twelve Apostles, having received the speech of tongues of all from the Holy Spirit, took up the parts of the world distributed to them so as to imbue it with the Gospel, the most blessed Peter, prince of the apostolic order, was destined for the capital of the Roman Empire that the law of truth, which was revealed for the salvation of every nation, would be more efficaciously poured forth from that head through the whole body of the world."[23] Also, Maximus the Confessor: "In that place where the world had head of empire, there God placed the princes of his kingdom." But more on this in a following question.

---

[19]   Arnobius, *Contra Gentes*, lib. 2.

[20]   Cyril of Jerusalem, *Cateches.* 6; Epiphanius, *Haeresi.* 121. Theodoret, *haeret. Fabularum*, lib. 1; Ambrose *Oratine in Auxentium*; Jerome, *de Viris Illustribus*, in Simone Petro; Sulpitius, *Sacrae Historiae*, lib. 2. Gregory of Tours, *hist. ca.*, 25; Eusebius, *hist. Eccl.* Lib. 2, ch. 13; Maximus, *in Serm. Ult. De SS. Petro et Paulo.*

[21]   *De Haeres.* Ch. 1.

[22]   Epistle 36 *ad Casulanum.*

[23]   Serm. 1, *de natali sanctorum Petri et Pauli.*

The twenty-fifth is that at the end of the life of Peter, Christ himself appeared to Peter, and when the latter asked: "O Lord, where are you going?" he deigned to respond: "I come to Rome to be crucified again." Egesippus witnesses, along with Ambrose: "By night;" Ambrose says: "He began to enter by the wall, and seeing Christ in his place he ran to the gate, entered the city and said; 'O Lord, where are you going?' Christ responded: 'I come to Rome again to be crucified.' Peter understood that the response pertained to his own divine cross."[24]

Thereafter St. Gregory relates the same thing, in his explanation of the Penitential Psalms: "He said to Peter, 'I come to Rome again to be crucified,' he who had already been crucified in his own person, said he must be crucified in Peter." What did the Lord wish to show, when he said, to be crucified again in the crucifixion of Peter, except that Peter is his vicar, and that it should be done to Peter, just as it was done to himself? Thus, before he had said to Samuel: *"Non te abjecerunt, sed me, ne regnem super eos."*[25]

---

[24] Ambrose, *Oratione contra Auxentium*; Egesippus, *De Excidio Hierosol.*, lib. 3 ch. 2.

[25] "For they have not rejected you but me, lest I would reign over them." 1 Kings (1 Samuel) 8: 7.

CHAPTER XXIV
The Last Three Prerogatives are Brought to Bear

HE TWENTY-SIXTH prerogative is that only those churches that Peter had founded were always held to be Patriarchal and first. Accordingly, among the Fathers, only three churches were properly Patriarchal and first; Rome, Alexandria and Antioch.[1] Neither Luther nor Calvin deny that.

Of old, Jerusalem was held as a fourth patriarchal see for nearly 500 years, but in name, not in fact, which is to say in honor, not in power. For the Patriarch of Alexandria not only sat in a second place in Councils, but was even in charge of all archbishops and bishops of Egypt and Libya; and the bishop of Antioch not only sat in the third place, but was also in charge of all the Archbishops of the East. The bishop of Jerusalem was in the fourth place, but he was in charge of no archbishop or bishop; nay more, that see was subject to the Archbishop of Caesarea, who was the Metropolitan of Palestine, and besides that the Antiochene Patriarch was over the whole east, as we said. That is so clear from the council of Nicaea, can. 7, where it is discerned that the bishop of Jerusalem should have honor after Rome, Alexandria, and Antioch, but nevertheless, nothing is taken away from the authority of the metropolitan who was at Caesarea.

For this reason, St. Jerome thus speaks, "You, who seek ecclesiastical rule and use the canons of Nicaea, answer me this; does Palestine pertain to the bishop of Alexandria? Unless I am mistaken, there it is discerned that Caesarea is over the capital of Palestine, and Antioch of the whole East. Therefore, either you had ought to relate to the Archbishop of Caesarea, to whom, spurned from your communion, you had known communicated with us, or if it was judged far from expedient, rather more letters should have been directed to Antioch. But I know why you refuse to send to Caesarea and Antioch. You preferred to cause aggravation by means of busy ears, rather than to render due honor to your metropolitan."[2]

Here Leo also says: "Juvenal, the Bishop, so as to obtain rule of the province of Palestine, believed that he could suffice, and dared to strengthen the insolent through fabricated writings."[3] Lastly, neither Anacletus, nor Leo, nor Gregory cited above, where they enumerate the patriarchal sees, make any mention of Jerusalem.

---

[1]   Council of Nicaea, can. 6; Chalcedon act. 16; Anacletus, epistola 3; Leo ad Anatholium, epistola 53; epist. Gregorii ad Eulogium, which is number 37, lib. 6.

[2]   *Ad Pamachium contra Joannem Episcopum Hierosolymae.*

[3]   Epistle 62 *ad Maximum Antiochenum.*

After these, the Patriarchate of Constantinople arrives. For in the time of the Council of Nicaea, Constantinople did not yet exist, still less was it a Patriarchate. For in the twenty-fifth year of Constantine's rule, that is, in the fifth year after the Council of Nicaea, Constantinople had been dedicated, as St. Jerome writes in his Chronicle. Nevertheless, afterward, in the first Council of Constantinople, and thereafter at Chalcedon, the bishop of Constantinople tried not only to secure a patriarchate, but even to obtain second place among the Patriarchs. But not before the times of Justinian did he obtain it from the Roman Pontiffs. Moreover, at the time of Justinian, that is, after the year of the Lord and the works of the emperor, and by the permission of the Roman Pontiffs, the bishops of Constantinople and Jerusalem began to be considered in the number of the patriarchates, without further protest.

After these were so constituted, Calvin wonders, and not without cause, why so few, and why in this order the patriarchal sees were gathered.[4] For if you look to antiquity, the see of Jerusalem ought to be placed in the first place, and nevertheless, it is in the fourth. If you would consider the dignity of the first bishop, certainly after the Roman See, the see of Ephesus ought to be which was founded by St. Paul, and ruled by St. John even to his death. Jerusalem also, in which see James the Apostle the brother of the Lord first sat, and after him Simon, the brother of the Lord, ought to go before Alexandria, in which Mark, the disciple of the Apostles sat. Besides, why should Alexandria go before Antioch, when Antioch was more ancient than Alexandria and at Antioch Peter himself sat, while at Alexandria the disciple of Peter sat?

What if you were to say that Calvin suspected that in constituting the Sees of the patriarchs, the Council of Nicaea only had the purpose of listing the most noble royal cities?[5] St. Leo the Great would oppose him, who in an Epistle, responded to the argument of the Greeks who asserted that Constantinople ought to be a patriarchal see after Rome, because it was an Imperial See, and thus says: "Let the city of Constantinople have its glory, and while the right hand of God protects it, may it enjoy long-lasting rule in your mercy. Nevertheless, there is, on the one hand, the reasoning of secular matters, and on the other hand, of divine affairs. For apart from that rock, which the Lord placed in the foundation, no other construction will be stable."[6] And Gelasius says: "Concerning the royal city, some power is of the secular kingdom, the other distribution of ecclesiastical dignities. Just as each little city does not diminish

---

4   *Institut.* Lib. 4, ch. 6, § 13.

5   *Institt.* lib. 4, ch. 7, § 14.

6   *In Epist. 54, ad Martianum Augustum.*

the prerogative of the king, thus an imperial presence does not change the measure of religious dispensation."[7]

Thereupon, we ask, why there were only three patriarchal sees constituted, when there might be many more noble and royal cities? Then, the most noble and royal cities always were held to be where the seat of the emperor was; but in the times of the Council of Nicaea, the imperial seat in the East was at Nicomedia, which is by far the most famous city of Bithynia. In the West, there were Trier and Milan, of which Trier in Transalpine Gaul and Milan in Cisalpine Gaul were considered the most famous cities. Accordingly in the same time of Diocletian sitting at Nicomedia, thence he ruled the whole east. Maximian governed Italy from Milan, as well as Africa and Illyria; Constantius, the father of Constantine, moderated Gaul and Britain from Trier.

Hence, Gelasius says: "We laughed, because they wish a prerogative to be established in Acacia, because the bishop was of a royal city, but did not the Emperor constitute Milan, Ravenna, Sirmium and Trier such many times? Did not the priests of these cities surpass them in their dignities, reputed without measure, in antiquity?"[8] Why therefore, were Nicomedia, Trier and Milan not made patriarchal sees?

Add that the Council of Nicaea did not institute, as Calvin falsely teaches, patriarchal sees; rather it only confirmed them. Thus the Council has the words in Canon 6: "The ancient custom endures in Egypt, or Lybia, and Pentapolis that the bishop of Alexandria should have power over all these." And below: "Likewise, however, with Antioch, and the remaining provinces, the honor of each is preserved in the Church." And below in Canon 7: "Because ancient custom obtained the ancient tradition that in Heliae, that is, Jerusalem, honor be given to the bishop; consequently he ought to have honor."

Therefore, the true and only origin of that number of patriarchal sees is the dignity of Peter. Only those churches are properly held as patriarchates where Peter sat. Morever, Peter sat in his own person at Antioch and Rome, while in Alexandria he sat either in himself, as Nicephorus[9] witnesses, or through his disciple Mark, whom he sent in his place, and founded the church in his name, as St. Gregory teaches when he says: "Although there were many Apostles, nevertheless, for rule itself, only the seat of the prince of the apostles is valid in authority, which in three places, is one. He lifted up the seat in which even he deigned to rest and even end his present life: he honored the seat in which he

---

[7] *In Epist. ad Episcopos Dardaniae.*

[8] Ibid.

[9] Lib. 14, ch. 3.

sent his disciple the Evangelist: he strengthened the seat in which he sat for seven years, although left it. Therefore, since they are of one man the seat should be made one, to whom three bishops now preside by divine authority; whatever good I hear about you, I impute this to me."[10] In the same place he says: "He speaks to me about the chair of Peter, who sits upon a chair of Peter, etc." There he affirms that the bishop of Alexandria sits upon a chair of Peter, because Mark, the first bishop of Alexandria, sat in the name of Peter.

St. Leo gives the same reason in a letter: "Nothing should perish from the dignity of the see of Alexandria, which it merits through St. Mark the Evangelist, the disciple of St. Peter. Likewise the Antiochene Church, in which the name Christian first arose from the first preaching of the Apostle Peter, let it preserve in the paternal rank of constitution placed in the third level, and may it never become lesser."[11] Likewise Anacletus says in his third Epistle: "The Second See, at Alexandria, was consecrated in the name of Peter by his disciple Mark. Moreover, the Third See at Antioch of the same Blessed Peter the Apostle is held in the name of honor." Therefore, this is the reason of the number of these sees. But the reason for the order is that while all three were sees of Peter, nevertheless, he administrated the Roman See in his own person even to his death; while Alexandria was administered through Mark the Evangelist, and Antioch through Evodius.

Therefore, just as Peter is a greater Apostle than Mark the Evangelist, and Mark the Evangelist greater than Evodius, who was neither an Apostle nor an Evangelist, so also the Roman Church surpasses Alexandria, and Alexandria Antioch, in authority and dignity.

The twenty-seventh is the feast of the Chair of Peter. For the fact that a feast day is celebrated publicly in the Church in honor of the establishment of the Episcopate of Peter, and nothing such as that is done for the sees of the other Apostles, is an argument that the See of Peter singularly excels all the others, nay more, it is itself, the only and singular Chair, from which the whole world ought to be taught, as Optatus says.[12] Moreover that the feast of the Chair of Peter is very ancient, can easily be known from the Martyrology of Bede, and from a sermon St. Augustine gave to the people.[13]

The twenty-eighth prerogative is that in the style of letters, after the name of the Father, and of the Son, and of the Holy Spirit, the ancients joined the

---

[10] Gregory, lib. 6, epist. 37.

[11] Epist. 53 ad Anatholium.

[12] *Contra Parmenianum*, lib. 2.

[13] Serm. 15 de Sanctis.

name of the prince of the Apostles. The bishop of Nicepolis, Atticus, writes, as is read at the end of the Council of Chalcedon in this place: "What the Latin custom calls *formatas* must not be done in Canonical epistles, lest some fraud of falsity may rashly be presumed. It has been salubriously reached and constituted by the three hundred eighteen gathered here that letters so formed should have this layout of calculation, or computation must take up first the Greek letters that form "of the Father and of the Son and of the Holy Spirit, this is π, υ, α,[14] which respectively by number signify 80th, 400th and 1st. Additionally, the first letter of Peter the Apostle that is π, which means the number 80."

Optatus of Miletus also recalls the format of letters in these words: "The whole world communicates with him (Pope Siricius) and us in the same style of letters, in one society of communion."[15] And the Council of Miletus, Canon 20, forbids clerics, lest they might go without being accompanied by letters properly formatted.[16]

---

[14] Πατρος, υιου, αγιου πνευματος.

[15] *Contra Parmenianum*, lib. 2.

[16] See Burchard, lib. 2, ch. 227; Ivo, lib. 6, ch. 433 and 434; Sidonius Apoll., lib. 7 epist. 2.

CHAPTER XXV

The Primacy of Peter is Confirmed from Testimonies of the Greek and Latin Fathers

T REMAINS that we bring the testimonies of the ancient Fathers to bear for the primacy of St. Peter. Moreover, it must first be observed that if the Fathers said Peter was the head of the Church, or primate amongst the Apostles, or held the Church, that ought to be sufficient to show from the opinion of the Fathers that it is as we would have it. Our adversaries affirm by these two names, *head* (*caput*) and *primacy* (*primatus*), is meant supreme power in the Church. Thus the Centuriators say that it is a proper mark of Antichrist to have primacy [*primatus*] in the Church. [1] And Calvin says: "Certainly, as long as the true and pure face of the Church endured, all those names of pride whereby the Roman See afterward began to grow so haughty, were altogether unheard of."[2] He speaks there about the terms of "head" and "primacy". And in the same place he indicates, in the time of Jerome, the true face of the Church still endured.

Origen is the first to appear from the Greeks (for I must omit Dionysius, Clement the Roman, Anacletus and others like them, because our adversaries do not receive them), who speaks thus: "Since the chief affair of feeding the sheep was handed down to Peter, and upon him just as upon strong ground the Church was founded, the confession of no other power is extended except of charity."[3] Eusebius in his Chronicle of the forty-fourth year from the birth of Christ, says: "Peter the Apostle, a Galilaean by nation, and first Pontiff of Christians."[4]

There the distinction must be observed which Eusebius places between Peter and the bishops of other cities. For he does not say of Peter, "first bishop of the Romans" as he says in the same place about James: "James, the brother of the Lord, first bishop ordained from the Apostles of the Church of the people of Jerusalem." Moreover he says about Evodius: "Evodius ordained the first bishop

---

[1] *Cent 1*, lib. 2, ch. 7, col. 527.

[2] *Instit.*, lib. 4, ch. 7, § 3.

[3] *Ad Rom. Ch.* 6.

[4] Translator's note: *Pontifex, pontificis* (m) is a Roman term for a priest originating from the early Republican period. It was taken up early on to translate the Greek επισκωπός, along with the Latin term *antistis*, which is a literal translation of the Greek meaning "overseer," (which can be found in the Canon of the Mass), and the transliteration *episcopus*. We have retained "pontiff" here to stay as true to the Latin as possible.

at Antioch." He does not speak thus about Peter, rather "First Pontiff of Christians;" without a doubt that we would understand that James was the Pontiff of one city, but Peter of the whole Christian world. He calls Peter the same thing in the *Ecclesiastical History*, the most proved and greatest of all the Apostles, the prince and general of the first, and the master of the militia of God.[5] Moreover, what else is it to be the general of the militia of God, than to be the head of the Church militant?

St. Basil says, speaking on Peter: "That blessed man who was born ahead of the disciples, to whom the keys of the heavenly kingdom were consigned, etc."[6] St. Gregory Nazianzen, wishing to show that there ought to be an order in all things, takes the argument from the Apostles, who, although they were all great, nevertheless, had one put in charge: "You see in just the same way from the disciples of Christ: were all great and lofty, and worthy by election, this one is called the rock, and he holds the foundations of what is believed by the faith of the Church, and the remaining disciples bore themselves afterwards with a peaceful spirit."[7]

St. Epiphanius says: "He [Christ] chose Peter that he should be the leader of the disciples." And again: "This is the one who heard, 'Feed my lambs,' to whom the sheepfold was entrusted."[8] St. Cyril of Jerusalem calls Peter "the most excellent prince of the Apostles."[9] St. Cyril of Alexandria says: "As a prince, and head of the rest he first exclaimed: 'You are Christ, Son of the living God.'"[10] And in *Thesauro* (if we follow St. Thomas in a little work *Against the Errors of the Greeks*), he says: "Just as Christ received the scepter of the Church of the Nations from the Father, going forth as a general of Israel, over every principality and power, over everything whatever it is that all things would be bent to him: thus both to Peter and his Successors Christ plainly consigned, and to no other than Peter, Christ what was his in full, but he gave it to him alone."

St. John Chrysostom says: "He constituted Peter the pastor of the Church that was going to be," and a little further down: "God alone can concede that the future Church should remain immovable in the face of the attack of so many

---

[5] *Hist. Eccl.,* lib. 2, ch. 14.

[6] *Serm. de Judicio Dei.*

[7] *Oratio de moderatione in disputationibus servanda.*

[8] Epiphanius, *haeresi* 51; *in Ancorato.*

[9] Cateches. 2.

[10] *In Joannem,* lib. 12, ch. 64.

and so great waves rushing in, whose pastor and head [behold the name of HEAD (CAPUT) that is unheard of for Calvin], a fisherman and without nobility." And further down: "The Father put Jeremiah over one nation, but Christ put this one over the whole world."[11] And in a homily on the last chapter of St. John, he repeats it several times that care of the brethren, that is, the Apostles, was entrusted to Peter, as well as that of the whole world.

Euthymius repeats twice on the last chapter of John that Peter received presidency over all the Apostles. And he says in the same place: "If you were to say, how did James receive the see of Jerusalem? I respond, this one (Peter) was constituted the master of the whole world." There Euthymius teaches that just as James was the bishop of Jerusalem, so Peter was the bishop of the whole world.

Theophylactus says on that verse, "Strengthen thy brethren," in Luke 22: "The plain meaning of this verse is understood. Because I have you as a prince of disciples, after you will have wept on account of denying me, and will have done penance, strengthen the others; it is fitting for you, because after me you are the rock and foundation of the Church." And a bit further: "You, O Peter, having converted, you will be a good example of penance to all, who since you were an Apostle and denied, you again received primacy over all, and prefecture of the world." Here also you hear the name of PRIMACY [PRIMATUS] unheard of to Calvin. Next, Oecumenius says: "Peter rises, not James, and just as if more fervent and just as if that presidency of the disciples had been consigned to him."[12]

Hugh Etherianus, or Heretrianus, around the year 1160, in the time of the Emperor Emmanuel, wrote books on the procession of the Holy Spirit against his own Greeks, in which he speaks thus: "From the very evidence of the matter, it seems clear that Christ constituted Peter and his successors in perpetuity as prince and head not only of the Latins and Greeks, of the West, and the whole North, but even of Armenians, Arabs, Jews, Medianites and of the whole world, even over the southern climates."[13]

From the Latins, St. Cyprian says[14] that Peter refused to say when he was condemned by Paul that he held the primacy, and he was to be obeyed. From which words, he indicates that he had the primacy, and could command all

---

[11] *In Matt.*, hom. 11.

[12] *In Act.*, ch. 1.

[13] Lib. 3, ch. 17.

[14] *In Epist. ad Quintum.*

others. And, lest by chance our adversaries might say that Peter, in the opinion of Cyprian, did not say he had the primacy, because he would have spoken falsely, let us listen to Augustine explain this passage of Cyprian: "The same Cyprian, in his epistle to Quintus so speaks; 'For Peter (whom the Lord first chose, and upon whom he built his Church), when Paul disputed with him on circumcision, afterward did not haughtily vindicate himself, or arrogantly assume that he should say he held the primacy, and thus should be obeyed by newcomers ... Behold, where Cyprian records what we also learn in holy Scripture that the Apostle Peter, in whom the primacy of the Apostles shines with such exceeding grace, was corrected by the later Apostle, Paul, when he adopted a custom in the matter of circumcision at variance with the demands of truth. If it was possible for Peter at some point to not walk uprightly according to the truth of the Gospel, so as to compel the Gentiles to Judaize, etc."[15] The same St. Cyprian, in a book on the unity of the Church, or on the simplicity of prelates (as we cited it above) makes Peter the head, the font, the root of the whole Church. And he says on the same in an epistle to Juba: "We hold fast to one head and root of the Church." Therefore, Cyprian joyfully usurps these two terms which Calvin had said were unheard of in the ancient Church. St. Maximus the Confessor says: "Of how many merits was Peter with his Lord that later the rule of the little boat, the governance of the whole Church, should be handed over to him?"[16]

Optatus says: "The chair is one, and you would not dare to deny that you know it was to Peter, first in the city of Rome, that the chair was conferred, where Peter the head of all the Apostles sat, thence called Cephas; in such a one the unity of the chair is preserved by all, nor do the remaining Apostles defend individual chairs, each to himself that one would already be a schismatic and a sinner who should place another chair against that singular one. Therefore, the chair is one, which is the first from the dowry. In that Peter first sat, Linus succeeded him, then Clement, Linus, etc."[17] You see the name of HEAD and CHAIR [CATHEDRA] of Peter; and of successors, a unique chair of the whole Church is named, which was altogether unheard of to Calvin.

St. Ambrose on the last chapter of Luke calls Peter the VICAR of the love of Christ towards us, and says that he is the prelate of all. And again he says:

---

[15] *De Baptismo*, lib. 2, ch. 1.

[16] *In serm. 3 de Apostolis.*

[17] *Contra Parmenianum*, lib. 2.

"Andrew did not receive the primacy, rather Peter did."[18] Behold again that term unheard of to Calvin. He says the same about care of the Church of God entrusted to Peter by the Lord, in Chapter 1 to the Galatians, and at length in Sermon 11: "The Lord boards this boat of the Church alone, in which Peter is constituted the master, while the Lord says: 'Upon this rock I will build my Church.' Which boat so floats into the deep of this world that while the world lays waste all whom it receives, it will be preserved unharmed, the figure of which we have already seen in the Old Testament? Just as the ark of Noah, while the world shipwrecked, preserved unharmed all whom it had taken up, so the Church of Peter, while the world burns, will manifest unharmed all whom it embraces. And just as then, the flood carried on the dove brought the sign of peace, so even while the judgment is carried out Christ shall bring the joy of peace to the Church of Peter."

St. Jerome says: "Among the twelve one was chosen, constituted as the HEAD, so that the occasion of schism should be abolished. But why was John, a virgin, not chosen? It was conferred to age, because Peter was older, lest still an adolescent and nearly a boy should be preferred to men of age."[19] Thus you also hear the name of head, which was unheard of to Calvin.

St. Augustine says everywhere that Peter held the primacy, and especially in *De Baptismo*. Where he also adds: "I reckon it is no slight to Cyprian to compare him with Peter with regard to his crown of martyrdom; I rather ought to fear lest I show disrespect towards Peter. For who can be ignorant that the primacy of his apostleship is to be preferred to any episcopate whatever? Yet, granting the difference in the dignity of their sees, yet they have the same glory in their martyrdom."[20]

It must be observed in this citation, altogether much from the opinion of Augustine, that the chair of Peter excels the chairs of particular bishops; although he fears lest it would seem he makes some contumacy against Peter if he would compare Cyprian with him, who was still not only a bishop, but also the first of the whole of Africa.

It must also be noted that Augustine thought the martyrdom of Cyprian could be compared with the Martyrdom of Peter, although Peter's should be much more noble, because the palms of the martyrs are all of the same type: but the seat of Cyprian cannot be compared with the See of Peter, because the See of Peter is not only more noble than Cyprian's, but is, in a certain measure, of

---

[18] *In 2 epist. Ad Corinthios*, ch. 12.

[19] *In Jovinianum*, lib. 1.

[20] Loc. cit.

a different kind, for they differ, as a whole and a part. Not only was Peter the bishop of Rome, as Cyprian was of Carthage, but Peter was also the Pontiff of the whole world, while Cyprian was the pontiff of only one part of it.

Augustine says the same thing on the penance of Peter, saying: "It cures the plague of the whole body of the Church in its head, it composes the health of all the members in its crown, etc."[21]

The author of the questions of the Old and New Testament, which are found in volume four of the works of Augustine, says: "Just as in the Savior were origins of office, so even after the Savior all are contained in Peter. He constituted him as head of all that he should be the shepherd of the Lord's flock." And below that: "It is manifest, in Peter all are contained; therefore, asking for Peter, is understood to ask for all things. Therefore, the people are always either corrupted or praised in their leader."

St. Leo everywhere teaches this, especially in Sermon 3: "From the whole world, one Peter is chosen, who is put in charge both of the calling of all Nations and over all the Apostles and Fathers of the Church that each in the people of God might be priests, and many shepherds, nevertheless, Peter properly rules all, whom Christ principally rules."[22] And he also says: "It was provided in the great disposition, lest all should claim all things for themselves, rather that each one should be in each province, among whose brethren the first teaching might be held: And again, certain men among the elders were constituted in the greater cities that they might receive greater care, by whom the care of the universal Church will be brought to the one See of Peter, and nothing shall ever leave from his head."[23] Behold, you also have the name of head, and care of the universal Church.

St. Prosper of Aquitaine:

> O Rome, See of Peter, which for pastoral honor
> Made head in the world, whatever it doth not possess by arms
> It maintains by religion, etc.

Arator, in Chapter 1, of Acts, speaks thus on Peter:

> ... to whom the lamb had handed
> Having suffered, he saved such sheep, and the whole world
> He increases the flock by this shepherd,

---

[21] Serm. 124 *de temp.*

[22] Serm. 3, *de anniv. Ass. Pont. Suae.*

[23] *Epist. 84 ad Anastasium*, at the end.

In which office he rises supreme, etc.[24]

St. Gregory the Great says: "Since everyone knows the Gospel, it is clear that, the Lord's voice had consigned the care of the whole Church to the most blessed Peter, Prince of all the Apostles." And below: "Behold the keys of the heavenly kingdom he receives, the power of binding and loosing is given him, the care of the whole Church to him, and the rule is granted."[25]

Bede says: "He saw the simplicity of his heart, he saw the sublimity of the soul, of him who was rightly to be put over the whole Church."[26] And in another homily: "Therefore, Blessed Peter, who confessed Christ with true faith, but followed by love, specially receives the keys of the kingdom of heaven and the rule of judicial power that all believers through the world would understand that whoever would merely separate themselves from the unity of faith of that society in any way, such men are absolved neither from the bonds of their sins nor can they go in the door of the kingdom of heaven."[27]

St. Bernard teaches: "The place in which you stand is holy ground, the place of Peter, the place of the Prince of the Apostles, where his feet stood; it is his place, whom the Lord constituted as master of his house and the prince of his every possession."[28] And again: "The counterpart of the Lord walking over the water, he designated the unique Vicar of Christ, who ought not be over one people, but all, accordingly many waters, many people."[29]

By these twenty-four testimonies of the Fathers, just like the twenty-four voices of the Elders in the book of the Apocalypse, the consensus of the ancient Church is obviously shown, both Greek and Latin, against which no response can be made altogether, except what Luther and Calvin say about Pope Leo that they suffered the concerns of men and were deceived.

But if that were so, why did no man ever correct them? Certainly Epiphanius, Theodoret, Augustine and Damascene, detected the token bearers of heresies and heretics, and in their number they even placed Origen. But why, I ask, in the errors of Origen, did they not record what he said about Peter being

---

[24] The preceding quotations are in verse in the original Latin, and we have chosen to render them into English prose. -Translator's note.

[25] Lib. 4, epist. 32 *ad Mauritium.*

[26] *Homilia in Vigilia sancti Andreae; Intuitus eum, John 1.*

[27] Homilia in festo Petri et Pauli.

[28] *In Epistola 237 ad Eugenium.*

[29] *De considerat., lib. 2.*

handed the chief duty to feed the sheep by Christ? Why do they not number amongst the heretics Cyprian, Ambrose, Chrysostom, Optatus, Leo, and others, since they so clearly taught that Peter held primacy and was head of the whole Church and that the whole world had been entrusted to him? Certainly such an error, which is for Antichrist, as they say, which is so obviously favored by the pens of all their writers, would behoove them to turn up.

Why do the fathers shout as though with one mouth that ecclesiastical primacy was given to him by Christ; why do the same testify to so many characteristic prerogatives of Peter; why do we find in the sacred and divine scripture that this very primacy was so liberally promised, which we see was faithfully given? Certainly we will be exceedingly obstinate, if we were to close our eyes against so clear a light of truth.

CHAPTER XXVI
The Argument from a Comparison of Peter with James is Refuted

THE ARGUMENTS which our adversaries usually make against the primacy of Peter, are for the most part answered in the explication of two passages of Scripture, Matthew 16 and the last chapter of John, where we have treated on the rock, the keys and the sheep. Nevertheless, three things remain. One on a comparison of Peter with James: the second, from a comparison of the same with Paul: lastly, the argument on the foul falls of Peter to be abhorred, which the Holy Spirit wished to be committed to letter by divine counsel, lest we would render too much to the Apostle Peter.

Now the first argument is of Luther, from his book on the power of the Pope, where he tries to prove that James was greater than Peter for these reasons. First: "Christ was Bishop of Jerusalem, not Rome, and his apostles were priests, therefore, James, who after the passion of Christ was assigned the episcopate succeeded Christ, or certainly was his Vicar, not Peter." Thereupon, "Jerusalem is the mother of all Churches since 'the law will go out from Zion, and the word of the Lord from Jerusalem.' Therefore, James is father of all churches, not Peter." On that account: "The Council of Nicaea gave primacy to the bishop of Jerusalem, and confirmed that from ancient custom and tradition."

We can add two serious testimonies. One of Clement the Roman, quoted by Eusebius: "Peter, James and John, after the Assumption of the Savior, although given preference by him in nearly all things, nevertheless, they did not claim glory for themselves; rather James, who was called just, they established as bishop of the Apostles."[1] Luther regarded this in his book on the power of the Pope, when he said: "Peter, James and John, rejected the primacy, and they constituted James the younger.

Another is of Chrysostom, who says: "See the modesty of James. He received the duty of bishop of Jerusalem, and nevertheless, says nothing. Consider, moreover, even the singular modesty of the other disciples, they concede to him by agreement, lest disputing amongst themselves they might hesitate."[2]

I respond to the first argument: Christ was not the bishop of any particular city, rather, he was and is the Pontiff not only of Jerusalem, but of the whole Church. Nor does anyone succeed him, since he always lives. Next, it was more fitting for his general vicar that he should constitute somewhere else besides at Jerusalem, because just as through the coming of Christ the law and priesthood

---

[1] Clement, *Dispositionum*, lib. 6, which is found in Eusebius, *Hist.*, lib.. 2, ch. 1.

[2] Homilia 3 in Acts.

were changed, so even it was fitting that the place of the high priest should be changed, and truly all things would be made new. Moreover, by chance the temple and Jerusalem were to be overturned and burned in short order after the Ascension of the Lord.

To the second argument I say: the Church of Jerusalem is the mother of all Churches in antiquity, and distinguished by many privileges, on account of the presence of the Lord and the Apostles, which it had for a long time and especially on account of the mysteries of our redemption completed and consummated in that place; but still this is nothing prejudicial to the primacy of Peter. For just the same, James was the pastor and bishop of Jerusalem, so Peter was the pastor and bishop of the whole Church; and hence even of Jerusalem, which is a portion of the universal Church. Thus Chrysostom and Euthymius answer this argument,[3] whereby St. Bernard takes their arguments, saying: "James, content with one Jerusalem, yielded all to Peter."[4]

To the third argument of Luther, I respond: Luther did not read the Council of Nicaea correctly. For, as we proved above, in the Council of Nicaea, the fourth place is given to the bishop of Jerusalem among the patriarchs, inasmuch as it was an honorary concession, but no place was given in regard to true jurisdiction. Therefore, as a simple bishop he is subjected to the bishop of Caesarea, the metropolitan for the whole of Palestine.

Now I respond to the testimony of Eusebius: That citation of Eusebius has been corrupted without any doubt. For although it is in the Codex of Basel, the version of Ruffinus contains the words which we cited above; nevertheless, in the Cologne version, edited by a Catholic, the name "primacy" is not contained and in place of the words: "*Apostolorum Episcopum*," "*Hierosolymorum Episcopum*" are contained.[5]

Such a reading agrees especially with Nicephorus, and while alleging this citation in book 2, chapter 3, still it does not agree with the opinion of Eusebius in the same book of the *Ecclesiastical History*, where he says Peter was the

---

[3] Commentary on the last Chapter of John.

[4] *De considerat.*, lib. 2.

[5] Translator's note: What Bellarmine says here is also born out by the Greek versions in use today. Moreover, the Schaff and Wace edition of the Post Nicene Fathers from a century ago, (which was carried out by Protestants who feared that Anglican editions from the Oxford movement were too Catholic), translates the Greek with little difference from our own rendering of the Greek which Bellarmine quotes here: "Then James, whom the ancients surnamed the Just on account of the excellence of his virtue, is recorded to have been the first to be made bishop of the Church of Jerusalem."

greatest apostle, and the prince of the first.

Lastly it agrees with what is in the Greek Codex, both from the Vatican Library, and the recent edition of Paris. Thus the Greek is contained in each text: "Πέτρον γάρ φησιν καὶ Ἰάχοβον καὶ Ἰωάννεν μετὰ τὴν ἀνάληψιν τοῦ Σωτῆρος ὡς ἂν καὶ ὑπὸ τοῦ Κυρίου προτετιμημένους μὴ ἐπιδιχάζεσθαι δόξης ἀλλά Ἰάχωβον τὸν δίχαιον ἐπίσκοπον Ἰεροσολύμων ἐλέσθαι."[6]

Therefore, Clement of Alexandria does not say that Peter, James and John conferred primacy of the whole Church upon James the younger, and made him a bishop of the Apostles, which is most absurd, but he merely says the Apostles in particular did not seek their own glory, and therefore, did not assume for themselves the most noble episcopate of them all in that time, but conferred it upon James the younger. Therefore, although the episcopate of one city would not derogate from the primacy, nevertheless, it was no small glory to be made bishop of Jerusalem at that time, in which there was no particular episcopate more noble than it.

To the citation of Chrysostom, I say that he speaks about the seat of a particular bishop when he says: "The Apostles conferred the see upon James." For Chrysostom absolutely puts Peter ahead of James, which is manifest from many of his citations. For in his last homily of John on the words "Follow me," he says: "By such words, again he shows care and familiar affection for him. What if someone were to inquire how James received the seat of Jerusalem? I would respond that he [Christ] constituted this Peter teacher of the whole world."

Likewise, Chrysostom says, after these words which are thrown out in the objection, adding about Peter: "Rightly, he first seizes upon the authority of all in this business that he might have all in hand. Christ said to this one: "And when thou are converted, strengthen thy brethren."[7]

---

[6] Translator's note: There is a textual variant in the Greek which Bellarmine quotes in the 16th century Ingolstadt edition. Where Bellarmine has a genitive of agent in του κυριου (tou kuriou), modern editions of Eusebius have του σοτερος (tou soteros).

[7] Homilia 3 in Acta.

CHAPTER XXVII
On the Comparison of Peter with Paul

HE SECOND argument is taken from the fact that Paul is called an Apostle through an antinomasia; thence it appears to follow that he, rather more than Peter, was made Prince of the Apostles. "It happened that on ancient seals, whereby diplomas of the supreme Pontiff were signed, that images of Peter and Paul were discovered, but the latter on the right and the former on the left. But Thomas also observes this fact in the epistle to the Galatians, in the first *lectio*, as well as Peter Damian in a treatise on this matter."

I respond: Paul is called an Apostle by an antinomasia, not because he was greater than Peter with respect to power or authority, but for two other causes which never detract from the primacy of Peter. One was because he wrote many things, and was more learned and wiser in other matters. Then indeed we nearly call him an Apostle by an antinomasia, when we cite the letters he wrote. The second was because it pertains properly to the Apostle as it is for an Apostle to plant the faith. Moreover, Paul planted the faith in more places than any other. For the remaining Apostles were sent to certain provinces, while Paul was sent to the Gentiles, without any determination of province. And he speaks about himself: "I have labored more than all."[1]

Jerome also witnesses in Chapter 5 of Amos, concerning those words: "He who calls the waters of the sea, and pours them over the face of the earth," that not only did Paul plant the faith of Christ throughout that whole very long journey, which went from Jerusalem even to Croatia, as Paul himself also says,[2] but even from the Red Sea to the ocean, through nearly the whole world, as beforehand the earth had been wanting for the zeal of preaching. Therefore, in that matter, by what is proper of an Apostle, Paul excelled, and just as Peter is called the Prince of the Apostles, because he was established as the head and shepherd of the sheep, so also Paul can be called the Prince of the Apostles, because he carried out the Apostolic duty most excellently. In the same manner Virgil is called the prince of Poets, and Cicero the prince of Orators.

St. Augustine embraces each reasoning in a few words: "When he is called the Apostle, and some Apostle is not named, no one is understood apart from Paul, because he is more known in many epistles and labored more than all the others."[3]

Moreover, the objection on the images of Peter and of Paul, that they

---

[1] 1 Corinthians 15:10.

[2] Romans 15.:23-29.

[3] *Ad Bonafacium*, lib. 3.

customarily so arrange it that Paul is seen to the right of Peter, can be answered in many ways. Therefore, the first, although it is sufficiently certain that Peter was greater than Paul in regard to authority, as we taught above from the testimony of the Fathers,[4] still, it is certain that Paul is placed before Peter in all names; but this impedes nothing from the Roman Pontiffs or even from the pontificate of Peter himself. Not even from the Roman Pontiffs, because they acknowledge both Peter and Paul as a predecessor and parent. Accordingly, each Apostle founded a Church at Rome and governed it, as among others Irenaeus observes,[5] and each ended in the city by martyrdom. Therefore, all the glory of Paul pertains to the Roman Pontiffs. The supreme dignity and authority of Paul also does not check the pontificate of Peter, because it was extraordinary, such as it was.

For that reason, it is just like the people of Israel: Moses was older than Aaron, and just the same Aaron truly and properly was the high priest, and not Moses, but the children of Aaron, succeeded in that supreme dignity, because the power of Moses was extraordinary, but of Aaron it was ordinary: so also if we were to admit by an extraordinary privilege Paul was greater than Peter, we would not on that count deny that Peter was the ordinary and supreme Pontiff of the Church.

Thereupon, the response can be made that it is not perpetual that in the ancient images Paul takes up the right side. Accordingly, in those which are still in Rome, on certain ones Paul is discerned at the right, so in several others he is seen on the left; and as in charters Paul occupies the right, so also in coins he occupies the left.

And perhaps by design that which the Fathers observe that from the two supreme Apostles they put only one before the other. Without a doubt, the very manner should signify that these Apostles are either equal amongst themselves, or certainly they do not know whether one is better than the other. For although Peter is greater in power, Paul is greater in wisdom, or as St. Maximus elegantly preaches, Peter holds the key of power, but Paul holds that of wisdom.[6]

Hence, St. Leo says: "These, the grace of God has carried to such a height among all the members of the Church that they in the body, whose head is Christ, it constituted as a twin light of the eyes, on whose merits and virtues

---

[4]   Cyprian, *in epistola ad Quintum*; Augustine, *Epistola 19, ad Hieronymum*; Jerome, *epist. 89 ad Augustinum*; Gregory, *homil. 18 in Ezechiel*; Theodoret, *in epistola ad Leonem*; Oecumenius, *Ad Galatas*, ch. 1.

[5]   Irenaeus lib. 3, ch. 3.

[6]   Maximus, *Serm. Ult. De sanctis Petro et Paulo.*

there is nothing different, we ought to think distinguished, because them even by election are equal, and similar labor, and their end makes them equals."[7] And St. Maximus says: "Similarly, Blessed Peter and Paul are eminent among all, and they excel all by a certain peculiar prerogative; but among themselves, who is before the other is uncertain. I reckon indeed that these are equal in regard to merits, because they are equal in regard to their suffering."[8] St. Gregory says: "Paul the Apostle is the brother of Peter first in the Apostolic rule."[9]

The third response can also be applied. For, as Anthony Nebrissensis records in an annotation to five hundred passages of Scripture, when two fall together, it was once observed that the older and more honored should be at the left; but the younger would close his right side, and in some measure he would excel in a sign of attendance upon him. Thereupon, those who are at the sides [*laterones*] and by contraction, thieves [*latrones*] those who covered the right side of more noble men for the sake of their defense. He proves that by many arguments, but especially from the testimony of two famous poets. For Ovid says on an old man:

> Et medius juvenum non indignantibus illis,
> Ibat et interior si comes unus erat.[10]

Next, he is said to be more intimate who is at the left side, as we learn from Virgil, who says in the Aeneid about Cloantho, who sailed to the left side of Gyae:

> Ille inter navemque Gyae scopulosque sonantes
> radit iter laevum interior, subitusque priorem praeterrit.[11]

We can add the testimony of Eusebius, who writes in the life of Constantine that he saw Constantine as a youth in Palestine going to the province with the elder Augustus, and always marched along his right. Nor can there be any

---

[7] *Serm 1., de Natali Apostolorum.*

[8] Loc. Cit.

[9] *Dialog.,* lib. 1, last Chapter.

[10] "An old man walked between younger men, and they were not indignant, if he had only one companion, the elder walked on the inner side." -Ovid, *Fasti,* lib. 5, 67-68.

[11] "He between Gya's boat and the journey scraped the resounding boulders, on the inner left, and immediately passed by the first." -Virgil, *Aeneid,* lib. V, 168-172.

doubt, whether Constantine was a youth, and as a privatus he should be in a less honored place than the elder Augustus.

Nor is what Ambrose[12] says opposed to these, nor Jerome,[13] that to sit at the right is a greater sign of honor. For it is absolutely more honorable at the right, and especially in seats gathered by right order. That if two seats might be placed to the wall, and one does not cover the other, there can be no doubt whether the right ought to be held to be more excellent; nevertheless, there is a second reason from an assault, when one covers the side of another with his body.

Now, therefore, it is believable in the beginning that Paul began at the right of Peter, as a younger and lesser; for that reason in pontifical charters Paul is thus placed to the right of Peter that he should go before him, and nearly cover the whole, which is an argument on the obedience in Paul, and the dignity in Peter. Moreover, that later he began to be designated to the right, even when he did not cover Peter, or since Christ or the Blessed Virgin hold the middle place appears to have been done from inexperience. Without a doubt they had seen Paul depicted thus somewhere at the right, nor did they notice that he was at the right to cover Peter. The artist merely reckoned it was done on account of honor done for Paul, and for that reason, even in seats, or when they might stand amongst themselves, to give the right side to Paul.

It remains that it was not done by the Fathers on account of the honor of Paul, or thence could be proven that in all other matters Peter is put before Paul. If they must be named, Peter goes before, if they are invoked in prayers, Peter goes before, if a feast day is celebrated in their honor, Peter is first. Why therefore, in images, is that otherwise perpetual order changed?

Next, if this is not proved from someplace it can be admitted that for the sake of honor Paul is placed to the right of Peter in signs and images, and this seems to be for three reasons. First, because he appears to be of more profit to the Church than Peter, for he led many from the Gentiles to the faith of Christ; he traveled to more provinces with the greatest labor, and left behind many writings, and these are very useful to us.

But the Church in cultivating the memory of the saints does not so look upon the degree of honor which they had on earth as upon the advantage which they brought to the next generation. Therefore, since for the sake of gratitude she honors them, she brings a greater devotion to those to whom she owes more. Certainly Stephen and Lawrence the deacon were such; the former of which ministered more than St. James as a bishop and apostle, the latter, more

---

[12] *Serm. 61, De Pentecoste.*

[13] *In Comment. Ad Ephesos*, ch. 1.

than St. Sixtus, a Roman Pontiff, and still the Church honors Stephen more than James, and Laurence more than Sixtus, because these martyrs are the most famous of these deacons and marvelously light the way for the whole Church.

For equal reason, St. Jerome and St. Thomas Aquinas were simple priests; Anthony of the desert, Benedict and Francis were not even priests, and nevertheless, in regard to veneration, they are put forth by the Church ahead of many holy bishops, martyrs, and even Supreme Pontiffs because in their written works they are advantageous to the Church by the establishment of a great many of the religious orders.

The second reason is that Paul was so much the Doctor of the Gentiles, Peter of the Jews, that consequently, the Church would signify that the Gentiles were at length put ahead of the Jews by that which he said: "The greater will serve the lesser;" thus Paul was put ahead of Peter.

The third reason can be that Peter was called by Christ while he was still in this mortal life, and for that reason is placed on the left, while Paul was called from heaven by Christ in his glorified body, and while reigning and seated at the right of the Father. Moreover, this reasoning Peter Damian also touches upon in an epistle to Desiderius, when he writes on this very question; Innocent III and St. Thomas also speak on it.[14]

Peter Damian adds also a fourth reason, Paul was from the tribe of Benjamin and in the very matter Benjamin was shown and expressed by a type in the Scriptures. Hence, although Benjamin was last amongst his brothers, nevertheless, he was called to the right hand of his father, and was put before all the brethren by Joseph.[15]

---

[14] Innocent III, *Sermo de Evangelistis*; St. Thomas, *Commentaria in Epistola ad Galatas*, prima Lectio.

[15] Genesis 35:18; 43:34.

CHAPTER XXVIII

The Objection of the Fifteen Sins of St. Peter That is Preached by the Centuriators of Magdeburg is Refuted

HE LAST argument is taken from the dreadful falls of St. Peter, which the Centuriators of Magdeburg enumerate.[1] They also say that the memory of these were handed down by the counsel of the Holy Spirit, lest too much be granted to Peter, which God foresaw was going to happen in future ages.

The first fall that they bring is found in Matthew 14 from the curiosity of Peter; as they say, he sought from the Lord that he should be called forth onto the sea and thus, was later punished and fell into greater sins, such as wavering.

I respond: There is no sin of Peter in this place; rather more, singular faith. For if Peter had sinned by asking that he should be called forth onto the sea, he would not have obtained what he asked for. For the miracles of God do not cooperate with our sins. For this reason, St. Maximus says: "This is Peter, who was so trusting of Christ that the sea proved itself subject to his footprints. For new steps were given to him in the waves by his Lord, as faithful he asked, so beloved he merits. It seemed that he was afraid on account of this alone, that human frailty recognized how great a distance it was between the Lord and the servant." And below: "Truly blessed faith of Peter, and while he wavered, wondrous, whom dread of the danger could not disturb. Therefore, by shouting while he sank, 'O Lord, save me,' he despaired of himself, not the Lord when he doubted, lest someone would argue this fear of the most glorious Peter was a vice, etc."[2]

Secondly, they place what Peter said to Christ in Matthew 16: "Far be it O Lord, may it not be so for you." The Centuriators argue that by these words, St. Peter committed a foul and dreadful fall. "By these words a grievous fall is described for which he merited eternal damnation unless he were to be retrieved by the vastness of Christ's mercy. Nor is there a doubt whether what he had asked in earnest was a sin."

I respond: By far St. Jerome reckoned this event otherwise. For he says, commenting on the 14th Chapter of St. Matthew: "In all places, Peter is discovered with the most ardent faith. When the disciples were asked whom men said Jesus was, it was Peter that confessed that he was the Son of God; wishing to forbid him to continue to his passion, although he erred in sense, nevertheless, he did not err in affection." And he says in the sixteenth chapter,

---

[1] *Centur. 1*, lib. 2, ch 10, colum. 558-560.

[2] *Sermon 1, de natali Apostol.*

"It seems to me, this error of the Apostle comes from a feeling of piety since he will never appear in tune with the Devil."

The third sin they bring to the fore is what Peter says in Matthew 17: "O Lord, it is good for us to be here; if you wish, let us make here three tents, etc." Now the Centuriators say: "Peter sinned, because the memory of this thing and the cult he would think to establish outside the Word of God; nay more, even the voice of the heavenly Father castigates Peter's superstition."

I respond: that Peter in no way sinned is clear from Mark chapter 9, which says: "He did not know what to say, they were indeed extremely terrified." Therefore, Peter was taken up in some measure outside himself when he said these things, and although in such an excess of mind he could have erred, certainly he could not sin in any way. Nay more, Chrysostom teaches on this citation that Peter's words proceed from very great fervor: "You see with what fervor he burned for Christ, thus you ought not seek how prudently he exhorted, but rather how fervent he was in the charity of Christ, and how inflamed he was."

Besides it is a wonder how a new cult in memory of the transfiguration should smell of superstition to the Centuriators, since Peter clearly said: "It is good for us to be here," and hence "tents," not in memory of a past thing, rather he wished to erect tents for the present dwelling with the glorious Christ. Wherefore St. Leo says that what Peter asked was good, but of a lesser order, because it was not yet the time to come up into his glory.[3] Nevertheless, he did not sin in begging for the glory before its time, because he did not know what he said.

The fourth fall they bring is that Peter was the one and perhaps not the last from their number who agitated the question of who was going to be the greatest of them; the ignorance and ambition of which Christ was compelled to repress with a great discourse in Matthew 18.

Yet, Scripture nowhere says that Peter was in their number, and the Fathers commenting on chapter eighteen of St. Matthew, namely Origen, Chrysostom, Jerome and others, all eloquently teach that not Peter, but the other disciples advanced the question, because they suspected Peter was put before all the others, and this very thing is gathered from the Gospel. For when he said lastly in chapter seventeen that Peter was sent to the sea, they added in the beginning of chapter 18: "In that hour the disciples came to Jesus, saying, "Who do you reckon is greater?" By such words it indicates that while Peter was absent that question was advanced. Accordingly in that hour whereby Peter was sent away

---

[3] Leo, *Serm. De transfiguratione.*

to the sea, the rest of the disciples were present with the Lord.

The fifth fall the Centuriators bring is found in Matthew 18. Peter wished to restrict the remission of sins to the number seven, saying, "How often will my brother sin against me, and I should still forgive him? Even to seven times?" I respond: These are puerile trifles; nor did Peter wish to restrict anything, but asked a question of his master.

The sixth fall they constitute against him is in Matthew 19: Peter broke out in these words: "Behold we have left all things behind, what will we receive?" There it seems to them that Peter dreamed of certain carnal rewards, and even spoke arrogantly. Let us hear the commentary of Chrysostom: "He does not speak by ambition, or inane glory, but that he might lead in the people of the poor." The Lord himself also does not convict Peter as of sin, but rather, great rewards are promised to him.

They enumerate for the seventh fall what Peter says in John 13: "You will never wash my feet;" they say this is a certain ignorance and by a depraved devotion he denies that he is going to allow that Christ shall wash his feet."

I respond: The Fathers by far judge differently about the acts of Peter. St. Augustine says here that Peter acted as every other Apostle did in refusing it. St. John Chrysostom notes on this citation: "It was not an argument of small love or reverence, but on account of excessive love he spoke thus." Likewise, "By vehemently refusing, Peter was also more vehement in permitting; both were done out of love," and St. Basil, in a sermon on the judgment of God which was given on morals, says on the matter: "He gave nothing meaning sin or contempt, but rather he used the most excellent honor towards the Lord, showing the reverence agreeable of a servant and disciple." St. Cyril says: "Rightly, under such a weight of the matter, the faithful disciple became very frightened, and using for himself the fruit of the customary reverence, he refused."[4]

They would have it that the eighth fall is what Peter said in Matthew 26: "Even if I must die with you, I will not deny you." It seems that he alleged the Lord to be a liar, who had predicted he was going to deny him.

But let us hear Jerome on this citation: "It is not rashness, nor a lie, rather the faith of the Apostle Peter, ever burning with affection toward the Savior." And Chrysostom: "For what reason did this befall you? Certainly from much love, and much desire." Therefore, there was either no fall, or it was an excess of piety and love.

Now they would have it that the ninth is that he slept when he was bidden

---

[4] *In Joannem*, lib. 9, ch. 4.

to watch in the garden. But the Evangelist excuses him and the remaining Apostles, saying: "For their eyes were heavy." And rightly; although they should have watched much of the night, I do not see why it was so grave a sin to be conquered by sleep.

They enumerate the tenth fall, from Matthew 26. Peter cut off the ear of Malchus: "Against the command of Christ," the Centuriators say, "he boldly used a sword, and in an impious attempt, cut off the ear of Malchus, the minister of the High Priest." And further on they say: "With violent force, he [Peter] tried to impede the aforesaid counsel of God in Scripture, inasmuch as he could."

But in the first place it is a lie to say that Peter used a sword against the command of Christ. The Lord had said nothing about the use of the sword before, apart from that which is contained in Luke: "Whoever does not have a sword, let him sell his tunic and buy one."[5] And when the disciples said: "Behold there are two swords here," Christ responded: "It is enough," that is, two are sufficient. By such words, in reality he commanded nothing concerning the use of a sword, much less did he forbid it.

And even though the Lord afterward expressed disapproval of Peter's deed, because he did not lack defense, nevertheless, neither the Lord nor the holy Fathers blame Peter's intention; nay more, they praise it. Chrysostom says: "You consider love, piety and humility of the disciple. Therefore, it is one thing to strike Malchus from a fervor of love; it is another to put the sword back in its sheath, and to do so out of obedience."[6] St. Cyril says: "The intention of Peter, who took up the sword against enemies, was not foreign to the command of the law."[7] Ambrose tells us that: "Peter was well instructed in the law, and by the affect of need, who knew the repute unto justice of Phineas who destroyed the sacrilegious and struck the servant of the priest."[8]

Therefore, what the Centuriators say is blasphemous, that Peter impiously attempted that and violently impeded the counsel of God. Rather, he prepared that defense not from hatred against the counsel of God, but from love for his master.

For the eleventh, they place the denial of Peter, which we do not deny was a great sin, but far be it that such a sin should be against his primacy, as it rather more confirms it. So St. Gregory says: "It must be considered for us, why

---

[5] Luke 22:36.

[6] *Homil. 85 in Matth.*

[7] Cyril, *in Joan.*, lib. 2, ch. 35.

[8] Ambrose, *in Lucam*, cap. 22.

almighty God had arranged that he, born before the whole Church, should become frightened of a handmaid and permitted himself to deny him. Yet without a doubt we recognize in the act, by a dispensation of great piety, that he who was going to be shepherd of the Church, should learn in his own fault, how he ought to have mercy on others."[9]

They make the twelfth fault that after the Lord was taken by the Jews, "the excellent, courageous hero Peter picked up and fled." But first, not only did Peter do this, but as it says in Matthew 26: "All the disciples left him behind and fled." Thereafter, although Peter fled in the beginning, nevertheless, he soon returned, "And followed him from afar," as we read in the same place. Add the last that there does not seem to be sin in flight. For if they ought to have followed the Lord, or thrown themselves down to die for him, then they should have followed. But they already understood that the Lord refused any defense be made for himself; nor were they held to lay themselves down to die, since rather more they had received the command to flee: "When they persecute you in one city, flee to another."[10]

The thirteenth fall which the Centuriators enumerate, is that after the resurrection of the Lord, when Peter ran to the tomb with great ardor, still he had not yet rightly received the point of the resurrection as John shows.[11] But in the same place John defends himself and Peter together from that incrimination, when he says: "They did not yet know the Scriptures that it was fitting for him to rise from the dead." Therefore, Peter labored in a certain ignorance at that time, but without his own fault. Nor was he among those who refuse to understand that they might do well, but simply was ignorant.

The fourteenth fall they place in those words from John 21:21, where he asks curiously about John: "What of this man?" For which the Lord scolds him: "What of you? Follow me." In other respects, if that curiosity must be admitted, he deserves to be forgiven. For, as Chrysostom writes on this passage, it was from the exceeding charity of Peter toward John that Peter understood John to desire to ask concerning himself, but did not dare to do so; for that reason that he might oblige him, he asked the Lord.

The last fall the Centuriators constitute, is on the event at Antioch where he did not walk in the truth of the Gospel, and for that reason was rightly condemned by Paul. In referring to that as a sin, the Centuriators sufficiently imitate their elders, Marcion the heresiarch and the apostate Julian, who said

---

[9]   *Homil. 21 in Evangelium.*

[10]   Matthew 10:23.

[11]   John 20: 9.

Peter was marked and scolded on account of a very grave sin by Paul. Now their calumnies had already been refuted by Tertullian and Cyril.[12] The matter, however, is considered this way.

The Apostle Peter, when he had carried on at Antioch, took food with Christian liberty with the Gentiles. Now certain Jews came upon him who were sent by James the Apostle to Peter. Then Peter began to think that he could scarcely evade an offense, either of Gentiles or of Jews. For if he continued to eat food with the Gentiles, without a doubt he would offend the Jews, who still were weak in faith and could not yet persuade themselves that it was lawful for Jews to use the food of the nations. But on the contrary, were he to separate himself from the Gentiles, and eat food apart from them with the Jews, he should incur offense against the Gentiles, of course, who either would argue the shallowness of Peter, or begin to Judaize after the example of such a man. Therefore, in this disturbance of mind St. Peter chose that which he thought the least bad rather than offend the Jews, as it was plain to see he was especially Apostle to the Jews rather than the Gentiles. Now Paul ridiculed that choice, and sharply scolded Peter with sufficiency.

Now in regard to this deed of Peter, the Greek Fathers see it to be free from every sin, as is certain from their commentaries on Chapter 2 to the Galatians, and St. Jerome wrote under the Greeks, both in commentaries of the same epistle and in an epistle to St. Augustine,[13] but many of the Latins recognize some sin in this deed of Peter.[14]

It remains that though it was certainly a sin, it was either venial, that is, it was very light, or only material, that is, it was a certain error, without any fault of Peter. Accordingly, it is certain that he did what he did with the best intentions.

With respect to this, he erred in his choice. The reason was either some inconsideration, and thus the sin would have been venial, or from a lack of knowledge, and then it would be an involuntary ignorance, and consequently he committed no fault. Moreover, it is believable that divine providence was at work, so that in this business the mind of Paul would be made more clear than the mind of Peter, and we would be furnished with a very useful example both of liberty in Paul, and of patience and humility in Peter.

---

[12] Tertullian, *Adversus Marcionem*, lib. 4; Cyril, *in Julianum*, lib. 9.

[13] *Epistula 89.*

[14] Tertullian, *Contra Marc.*, lib. 4; Cyprian, *epist. Ad Quintum*; Ambrose, *ad Galatos*, ch. 2; Augustine *epist.* Ad Hieronymum, 8, 9, et 19; Gregory *moral.*, lib. 28, ch. 12, and several others.

BOOK II
ON THE SUCCESSORS OF THE SUPREME PONTIFF

CHAPTER I

A Question is Proposed: Whether St. Peter Went to Rome, Remained There as a Bishop, and Died There.

OW that those matters which pertain to the explication and defense of the primacy of Peter have been constituted, we turn to those which pertain to the primacy of his successors. We see that the right of succession of the Roman Pontiffs is founded on the fact that Peter placed his see with the Lord's permission in Rome, sat in that see and also died there. Therefore, the first question arises: Whether Peter was Bishop of Rome, and did not ever transfer his see from there to another?

Most of today's heretics call this into doubt that which has constantly been believed by the whole world for 1500 years; without a doubt St. Peter was a Bishop of Rome and gave up his ghost through martyrdom of the cross. Some of those who treat this argument are more modest, while others are more impudent.

The first that I know of who taught that St. Peter was neither Bishop of Rome or ever saw Rome itself was a certain William, the master of John Wycliff, as Thomas the Waldensian relates.[1] The Lutheran, Ulrich Velenus, followed him, who published a whole book on the matter, wherein by 18 persuasions (as he calls them) he reckons he has demonstrated that Peter was never at Rome, and both Peter and Paul were not at Rome, but were killed in Jerusalem. At the end of the book he tells us that for his labor, he, without any doubt, was going to receive the rewards of the unfading crown by God. Now truly, if God deigns to reward lies with a crown, then there can be no doubt Velenus will receive a very splendid one.

Illyricus also says in a book against the primacy of the Pope: "The proof is certain that Peter was never at Rome." John Calvin, after he shows that there is doubt about the whole matter, concludes: "Nevertheless, on account of the consensus of writers, I do not quibble over whether he died there, but rather whether he was a bishop, especially for a very long time; of that I cannot be persuaded."[2] The Centuriators hold similar things.[3]

Moreover, it must be observed, that there are four things which are called into doubt. First, whether Peter was at Rome? Secondly, whether he died at Rome? Thirdly, whether he was Bishop of Rome? Fourthly, did he ever move the Roman Episcopate once it was received?

---

[1] *Doctr. Fidei*, lib. 2, art. 1, ch. 7.

[2] *Instit.*, lib.. 4, ch. 6, §15.

[3] *Centur. 1*, lib. 2, ch. 10, col. 561.

From these four alone the last is necessarily required and suffices to constitute the primacy of the Roman Pontiff. That is the reason why Calvin could by no means admit only the fourth, while he made little trouble about the other three. This is because it is clear that the first neither requires nor suffices, since, although there are many Roman Pontiffs who never avoided that they should come to Rome, there are also many Roman Pontiffs who were never at Rome, such as Clement V, John XXII, Benedict XII, Clement VI, Innocent VI, and Urban V, all who were ordained in France, and all remained in the same place.

Likewise, the second is neither required nor suffices for it is seen that many Roman Pontiffs died outside of Rome; for Clement I died in Pontus, Pontianus in Sardinia, John I at Ravenna, Agapetus at Constantinople, Innocent III at Perugia, Innocent IV in Naples, John XX at Viterbo, and others in other places. The same is attested by the countless multitude, who daily die at Rome, and still are not Roman Pontiffs.

Moreover, the third is required, but does not suffice, for it is gathered from it that Peter was bishop at Antioch; and nevertheless, because he transferred that see to another place, the bishops of Antioch never thereafter held first place. Therefore, the fourth alone is required and suffices. Still, since all of them are true we will prove them individually by their proper arguments.

CHAPTER II
That Peter Was at Rome

S
O AS to begin from the first point at issue, we will show that St. Peter was at some time in Rome, first from the testimony of Peter himself. He says as much at the end of the first epistle: "The Church gathered in Babylon greets you, as well as Marcus my son."[1] Papias, a disciple of the Apostles, witnesses that this epistle was written from Rome, which is called Babylon by Peter. Eusebius witnesses this: "Papias also says this, because Peter in his first epistle, which he wrote from the city of Rome, made mention of Mark, whereby figuratively he named Rome Babylon, since he says; 'The Church chosen in Babylon greets you, and Mark my son.'"[2]

Jerome also witnesses in his book, *de viris illust.*, on Mark, that: "Peter, in his first epistle, meaning Rome figuratively by the name of Babylon says, 'the Church which is gathered in Babylon, greets you.'" Oecumenius, Bede and everyone else who published commentaries on this epistle express the same thing.

Additionally, John the Apostle calls Rome Babylon everywhere in the book of the Apocalypse, as Tertullian observes.[3] It is obviously gathered from chapter 17 of the Apocalypse where Babylon is called the great seat upon many hills, and has dominion over the kings of the earth. Now in John's time there was no other city which had rule over the kings of the earth apart from Rome, and it is known rather well that Rome was built upon seven hills.

Thereupon, our adversaries shout that Rome is Babylon from the book of the Apocalypse. Indeed, Luther himself titled his book: *de Babylonica captivitate*, and the Centuriators accept the Apocalypse in the number of the divine books for no other reason than that in this book many things were said against Rome, under the name of Babylon.[4] For which reason, if Rome is Babylon in the Scriptures, as they would have it, and Peter writes "from Babylon," he certainly writes from Rome.

Velenus however responds: "The true Babylon was only in two places, one in Assyria, the other in Egypt, which now is called Chayrum; from which it follows that Peter wrote from Assyria, or from Egypt, not from Italy when he said 'in Babylon.'" (loc. cit.)

---

[1] 1 Peter 5:13.

[2] Eusebius, *histor. Eccl.*, lib. 2 ch. 15.

[3] *Conta Marcionem*, lib. 3; *Contra Judaeos*.

[4] *Centur 1*, lib. 2, ch. 4, col. 56.

Yet Velenus says nothing of value, for we have shown from many writers that Peter speaks about Babylon not properly so called, but on that which in the Apocalypse is figuratively called Babylon, which we wills how from may writers. For this reason they must be believed more than one Velenus who could bring no author on behalf of his exposition. Otherwise, let Velenus tell us, if there was no Babylon outside of Assyria and Egypt, what indeed is that Babylon that is said in the Apocalypse to have rule over the kings of the earth? Indeed it is certain this fits neither Assyria nor Egypt.

Yet Velenus insists: "If with Peter they understand Rome by the name Babylon and even with John, therefore all who leave the Roman Church do so correctly. For in Apocalypse 18 we read thus: "It fell, it fell, Babylon the Great and it was made the habitation of demons and the confinement of every unclean spirit.' etc. And again: 'Go out from that, my people, that lest you be made partakers of her crimes, and that you do not receive her misfortune.'"

I respond: Babylon is not called the Roman Church, but the city of Rome, such it was in the time of John. For, as Tertullian expresses it, just as the true Babylon was the head of an empire and had a king, Nebuchadnezzar, who persecuted the people of God and led them into captivity so also in the time of the Apostles Rome was the head of an empire and had an emperor, Nero, who cruelly persecuted the people of God.[5]

John predicted that this Babylon would fall to ruin, because the Roman Empire had to be blotted out, which we now know was certainly done. Did not the Goths, Vandals, Huns and Lombards reduce the empire of the city of Rome almost to nothing?

He calls the same Babylon the dwelling place of demons, and the charge of every unclean spirit, because (as St. Leo says in his sermon on the birth of the Apostles) when she lorded over all the Gentiles, she served the errors of all the Gentiles. He says concerning this: "Go out from her, O my people," which is understood concerning the heart, not the body, as St. Augustine shows.[6] Indeed, John bids that the saints should not be joined with the heathen and idolaters in the similitude of their customs and life even if they might be able to be together with them in the same city. For which reason it is also certain that Christians never went out of the city on account of these words of John.

This is why St. Jerome, in an epistle to Marcella, in which he exhorts her in the name of Paula and Eustochia to migrate from Rome into Bethlehem, and after he brings to bear these words from the Apocalypse against Rome, he

---

[5] *Contra Marcionem*, lib.. 3.

[6] *Breviculo collationis*, Collatione 3.

immediately adds: "Indeed, the Holy Church is there, where the trophies of the Apostles and Martyrs are, the true confession of Christ, there the faith is preached by the Apostle, and there, with paganism trampled daily the Christian name lifts itself on high, etc." By such words he teaches that John was not speaking against the Roman Church, but against Roman paganism. And Jerome addresses Rome thus in another place: "I speak to you, who has blotted out the blasphemy written on the forehead by the confession of Christ."[7]

Secondly, this same thing is proved from the last book of Acts of the Apostles, as well as from the epistle to the Romans. It is established from those places that there were many Christians at Rome, nay more a full and flourishing Church, before Paul had come there. Therefore, I ask, who made these Christians, if Peter was not at Rome? For, many Fathers write about the fact that Peter preached to the Romans first of all, and founded a Church before Paul would have come there. Yet that someone else had done that cannot be shown by any firm argument.

Certainly, Irenaeus says that the Roman Church was founded by Peter and Paul; that is, first by Peter, thereafter by Paul and together with Paul.[8] Eusebius, speaking about Peter, says: "He *first* opened the door of the heavenly kingdom with the keys of the Gospel in the city of Rome with the word of salutary preaching."[9] Arnobius says that Rome converted to Christ because it had seen the fiery chariot of Simon Magus blow apart by the prayer of Peter and immediately vanish after the name of Christ had been invoked.[10]

Epiphanius says: "Peter and Paul were the first in Rome."[11] St. John Chrysostom says: "Peter the fisherman, especially because he occupied the royal city, shone more brightly than the sun after death."[12]

Paul Orosius writes: "In the beginning of the reign of Claudius, Peter the Apostle of our Lord Jesus Christ came to Rome, and taught salutary faith with a faithful word to all, and confirmed it by the most potent virtues, and thence Christians began to be at Rome."[13]

---

[7] *In Jovinianum*, book 2, near the end.

[8] Irenaeus, lib. 3, ch. 3.

[9] *Hist. Eccl.*, lib. 2, ch. 14.

[10] *Contra Gentes*, lib. 2.

[11] *Haeres.*, 27, which is of Carpocratis.

[12] *In Psal. 48 (49).*

[13] *Histor.*, lib. 7, ch. 6.

Pope St. Leo says, "When the Apostles received the charge to be distributed throughout the parts of the world to imbue it with the Gospel, the most blessed Peter, Prince of the Apostolic order, was destined to the capital of the Roman Empire."[14] Theodoret writes: "The great Peter first offered the evangelical doctrine to them (the Romans)."[15] Gregory of Tours in his *History*, after he had shown that Peter came to Rome under the rule of the Emperor Claudius, added: "From those days Christians began to be in the city of Rome."[16]

The Emperor Theodosius says: "The empire rules all people whom of our mercy we wish to live in such a religion as that religion which St. Peter the Apostle handed to the Romans, and still declares to be at work."[17] Add the prophecies of the Erythraean Sybil, which among other things predicted, that Christ was going to subjugate the city of Aeneas not in the sword or war, but on the hook of the fisherman. Antoninus refers to this prophecy also.[18]

Velenus responds that after the passion of Christ, which was still in the time of the Emperor Tiberius, Christians began to be at Rome, as he says Orosius hands down,[19] as well as Tertullian in the Apologeticus, Plantina in *Vita Christi*, and Tranquillus in *Vita Tiberii*. From which it follows that the Roman Church was not founded by Peter, who of course is said to have first come to Rome in the time of Claudius.

Let us add in favor of Velenus the testimony of Clement, where we read that Barnabas preached at Rome in the time of Tiberius.[20] In this Dorotheus Tyrensis followed, who says that Barnabas was the first who preached at Rome. I respond: It is false that any Christians were in Rome in the time of Tiberius, and what the Fathers say is very true, that Peter preached to the Romans, and that in the time of the Emperor Claudius. For, from four authors cited by Velenus, only two are ancient, Tranquillus and Tertullian, and they do not say this at all; thus Velenus clearly is lying, although in the preface he solemnly swears by his own conscience that he would thrust in no lie or deceit. Tranquillus does not mention Christians in the life of Tiberius, but in the life of Claudius, where he

---

[14] *Serm 1 de natali Apostolorum.*

[15] *Ad Romanos*, ch. 1.

[16] *Histor.*, lib. 1, ch. 25.

[17] *C. De summa Trinitate, et fide Catholica, L. Cunctos populos.*

[18] *Summa Historalis*, part 1, tit. 3, ch. 9, § 14.

[19] *Hist.*, lib. 7.

[20] *Recognitiones*, lib. 1.

says the Jews made a tumult over the instigation of Christ, and were expelled from Rome by Claudius. This certainly favors our teaching, for we contend that Christians began to be in Rome in the time of Claudius.

Now Tertullian in the *Apologeticus* indicates the contrary. For he says that Pilate wrote from Palestine to Tiberius about the resurrection of Christ, and that God was believed by many, which Tiberius related to the Senate, whether it seemed that Christ must be received as a God. Then the Senate refused, for the reason that he would have already been considered a God by the people, as Pilate had written, rather than that he should be consecrated by the Senate. From such a tale it cannot be gathered that Christians were then at Rome, but rather more that they were not. If indeed they were, it would be from them that Tiberius first recognized the report of Christ than from a letter of Pilate.

Next, Orosius, whom Platina followed, added to the words of Tertullian that the Senate decreed Christians to be banished from the city. Orosius eloquently teaches in the same seventh book that Christians were not at Rome until after the arrival of Peter, who came while Claudius ruled. Therefore the sense of the edict was this, that the Christian religion should not be received in any way, and should be banished from the city if ever one who was a Christian should arrive. Still such an edict would have no force, for, as the same Orosius relates, Tiberius established a penalty for the accusers of Christians.

Now I respond to that about Barnabas. It is not true that Barnabas preached to the Romans in the time of Tiberius. It is certain that no one preached to the Gentiles before Peter was admonished in a vision in Acts 10 and 11. From that time, Barnabas was always together with Paul, and carried through to the Council of Jerusalem, as is clear from Acts 11-15, and since Paul had not at that time gone to Rome, it is certain Barnabas did not go. The Council of Jerusalem, however, was celebrated in the eighteenth year after the passion of the Lord, as is gathered from Paul in Galatians 1 and 2, which was in the thirteenth year from the death of Tiberius; therefore, Barnabas did not come to Rome in the times of Tiberius.

Add to this point that the book of *Recognitions* is held to be apocryphal. Hence, Dorotheus Tyrensi is incorrectly reckoned to be the author of the *Synopsis*, a book that is filled with fabrications and lies. For (that I might pass over others), by what reason can that author be defended, since he numbers among the seventy-two disciples the eunuch of the Queen of Ethiopia, whom it is certain was converted by Philip after the Lord's Ascension, and he makes Junia a bishop, even though it is certain she was a woman? Furthermore he says that Caesar, of whom Paul makes mention in his letter to the Philippians, was a disciple of Christ and a bishop, even though it is clear that Paul is speaking about Nero Cæsar.

Lastly, add that if we were to receive the books of *Recognitions* and the *Sypopsis* of Dorotheus, it would profit Velenus little, or nothing at all. Likewise, therefore, Clement, whom Dorotheus followed, in the same place that he relates about Barnabas he says he accomplished nothing at Rome, and immediately after the first sermon held without fruit, he returned to Judaea.

Thirdly, the history concerning the Gospel of Mark is proven. Serious authors constantly write that Mark wrote his Gospel at Rome, exactly as he had heard Peter preaching; indeed Eusebius writes this, as well as many other Fathers.[21] Lastly, Tertullian says that the Gospel of Mark is ascribed to Peter, that in the very matter Mark was the interpreter and disciple of Peter, just as the Gospel of Luke is attributed to Paul: "What the disciples promulgated began to be seen to be of their masters."[22]

Velenus responds that they are all deceived because they failed to notice that there were two Marks. One, who was called John Mark, concerning whom a mention is made in Acts of the Apostles, 12-15; the second, who was called Mark Aristarchus, about whom Paul speaks in his epistle to Philemon. From these two, the first wrote the Gospel, and was the Bishop of Alexandria, and was a disciple and follower of Peter, yet never saw Rome. The second was at Rome with Paul, but did not write a Gospel. Next, the Fathers, who agree with the two Marks, attributed a Gospel to one, and hence, fell into that error that reckons Mark to have written a Gospel at Rome.

But our Velenus has committed three errors. The first is that he reckons in the Epistle to Philemon that Marcus Aristarchus is one man, when obviously they are two. Thus indeed Paul says: "Thus my fellow captives in Christ greet you Epaphras, Mark, Aristarchus, Demas, and Luke, my helpers." And more clearly in the last chapter of Colossians: "Aristarchus my fellow captive greets you, as well as Mark, a relation of Barnabus."

The second error is that he would have it that Mark the Evangelist was never at Rome, because he was the Bishop of Alexandria; as if he could not be sent from Rome to Alexandria by St. Peter, or even as if he could not come from Alexandria to Rome, and again return from Rome to Alexandria.

The third error asserts that the Gospel was written by John Mark. For John Mark was a relation of Barnabas, and a disciple of Paul, as is gathered from Acts 12-15, and from the last chapter of the Epistle to the Colossians, that he even

---

[21] *Histor.*, lib. 2, ch. 15, from Papias and Clement of Alexandria. Cf. Irenaeus, lib. 2, ch. 1; Jerome, *de viris illustribus*, in Marco; Damasus, *in Pontificali invita Petri*; Isirore *in vita Marci.*

[22] *Contra Marcionem*, lib. 4.

survived until the fourteenth year of Nero. Accordingly, Paul, in his second epistle to Timothy, which he wrote in the fourteenth year of Nero with his martyrdom imminent, bid Mark to be sent to him. Yet Mark the evangelist and the Bishop of Alexandria was killed in the eighth year of Nero, as Eusebius writes in his *Chronicle*, and Jerome in the book on Mark in *De Viris Illustribus*.

Fourthly, this same thing can be proven from the history of St. Peter's glorious conquest over Simon Magus at Rome, which is true from the testimony of many Fathers, as we proved in the previous book. Lastly, all the arguments agree with those which we will make plain in the following chapter, that St. Peter underwent martyrdom for Christ at Rome, nor could anyone die at Rome who had never been there.

CHAPTER III
St. Peter Died at Rome

T. PETER not only came to Rome at some point but also together with Paul laid down his life for Christ, as their tombs especially witness. For if Peter and Paul did not die at Rome, who brought their bodies to Rome? From where and when, and with what witnesses did someone bring them? If perhaps they would respond that the bodies of the Apostles were not at Rome, I ask where in the world are they? Certainly they were never said to be any other place. Nor does it have the appearance of truth that the bodies of the greatest Apostles would be so neglected since we see the bodies of so many other saints most diligently preserved.

Eusebius made this argument to such a degree that he thought it was superfluous to seek any others. He says, "Therefore Nero, as he openly declared himself a host of divinity and godliness, asked for the death of those Apostles who were really the generals and standard bearers in the people of God. Accordingly he condemned Paul to fall short by a head in the city of Rome itself, but Peter on the gibbet of the cross. I reckon it superfluous to seek testimony of them beyond this, since the deed is famous even to this day and their splendid *monuments* witness the event."[1]

Thereupon, the consensus of the whole world witnesses this same thing, which is especially gathered by the pilgrimage *ad limina Apostolorum*. Pope Nicolas I writes in his epistle to the Emperor Michael that so many thousand men from the whole world daily rush upon the source of religion, to the tombs of the Apostles, that the city of Rome alone would sufficiently show the Church of Christ to be Catholic or universal, since many from every race are always seen coming to the tombs of Peter and Paul.

Moreover, our adversaries cannot deny that all Christians were persuaded of this even to the times of John Wycliff, that is, even to the 14th century, that St. Peter was at and died in Rome. Furthermore it is not credible in any manner, that for such a long time there was never someone who unmasked this error, if it were one, especially since that which the whole world believed for so long, was not some deed made into a cornerstone and a monument without witnesses, which could easily be invented and refuted with great difficulty. Truly we say St. Peter carried out his pontificate for many years, and at length after Simon Magus was publicly defeated, it is well known that he ended his life crucified upside down by the command of a most powerful emperor, known for his cruelty. How believable is it that this affair, which we said was so famous, were

---

[1] Canticles 6:3.

to be in fact false, and there was no man for fourteen hundred years who would have refuted it?

Lastly, the testimonies of the Greek and Latin Fathers witness this same thing. Ignatius, who lived in the time of the Apostles, in his letter to the Romans (a great part of which is recited by St. Jerome),[2] asks the Romans not to impede his passion, saying, "I do not command you as Peter and Paul, etc." by which words he seems to allude to the passion of Peter and Paul, which came to pass a little before at Rome. Therefore, Roman Christians tried to impede their martyrdom. For they compelled Peter with tears to leave the city when he was sought for the punishment of Nero. Therefore, Ignatius says, although I cannot command you, as Peter and Paul were able, nevertheless I ask, lest you impede me, just as you tried to impede them.

Dionysius the Corinthian, who flourished a hundred years after the death of the Apostles, when he was at Rome, as Eusebius relates,[3] says among other things: "Together, both teaching in the same city, were equally one in the same martyrdom, and were crowned at the same time."

Cajus, who was nearly fifty years after Dionysius, says the same thing: "I have the trophies of the Apostles, which I shall show. If indeed you were to go forth on the royal road, which leads to the Vatican, or by the Ostian Road, you will discover the motionless trophy, whereby being constituted on each side, the Roman Church is fortified."

Egesippus, as he was very near to the times of the Apostles, lavishly recites the whole history, adding to those which had said before, that Peter was crucified upside down, as he had demanded.[4] Eusebius in his *Chronicle* for the seventy first year from the birth of Christ says, "First, Nero over all his crimes also made persecutions against Christians, in which Peter and Paul gloriously lie dead together."

Theodoret, speaking in an epistle to Pope Leo about Rome says, "It has the tombs of their fathers in common, the teachers of truth Peter and Paul, which illuminate the souls of the faithful." Origen, as Eusebius relates,[5] says, "And Peter, tarried to the last in the city of Rome; there he was also crucified, with his head down, which he so asked to be done, lest he should seem equal with the

---

[2] *De Illustribus Viris*, in Ignatio.

[3] *Hist. Eccl.*, lib. 2, ch. 25.

[4] *De Excidio Hierosolymae*, lib. 3, ch. 2.

[5] *Hist. Eccl.*, lib. 3, ch. 2.

Lord."[6] Athanasius says in his *Apologia pro fuga sua*: "Peter and Paul, since they had heard that it behooved them to undergo martyrdom at Rome, did not cast aside that departure, but departed with joy."

Chrysostom says: "The sky is not so bright that when the sun sends forth its rays, it would be as the city of Rome, sending out these two lights into all parts of the world. Paul will be caught up from there, and then Peter. Just consider and shudder at the thought of what a sight Rome will see, when suddenly Paul shall arise from that coffin, together with Peter, and they will be lifted up to meet the Lord."[7]

Now from the Latins. Tertullian says: "Since you are close upon Italy, you have Rome, whence comes even to us the authority itself. How happy is its church, on which the apostles poured forth all their doctrine along with their blood! Where Peter endures a passion like his Lord's! Where Paul wins his crown in death."[8] Lactantius says: "Christ, departing, opened all things to come to his disciples, which Peter and Paul preached at Rome ... Since Nero killed them, Vespasian extinguished the name and nation of the Jews, and did all the things which had been predicted were going happen."[9]

Ambrose says: "At night, Peter began to go out from the wall, and seeing Christ approach him at the gate, and go into the city, he said: 'Lord, where are you going?' Christ responded: 'I come to Rome to be crucified again.' Peter understood the divine response pertained to his own cross ... and immediately after being rebuked he honored the Lord Jesus by his cross."[10]

Jerome says: "Simon Peter proceeded to conquest Simon Magus at Rome, and held the sacerdotal chair there for 25 years, even to the end that is, in the fourteenth year of Nero, by whom he was affixed to a cross, crowned with martyrdom, with his head facing the ground."[11] St. Augustine says: "The merits of Peter and Paul, on account of the same day of passion, are more famous and Rome solemnly commends."[12] St. Maximus the Confessor says: "Peter and Paul endured martyrdom in the city of Rome, which as a head obtained the rule of

---

[6] *In Genesin*, lib. 3.

[7] *In Epistola ad Romanos*, Hom. 32.

[8] *De Praescript.*, ch. 36.

[9] *Divinarum instit.*, lib. 4 ch. 21.

[10] *In Oratione contra Auxentium*, which is contained in *epist.*, lib. 5.

[11] *De viris illustribus*, in Petro.

[12] *De Consensu Evangel.*, lib. 1, ch. 10.

nations, obviously that where the head of superstition was, there the head of sanctity should rest."[13]

Sulpitius adds: "Divine religion strengthened the city, while Peter managed the episcopate there, and Paul afterward was lead to Rome ... Paul and Peter were condemned to die, one by the severing of his neck, Peter was lifted up on the cross."[14] Paul Orosius, in book 7 of his *Histories*: "For the chief (Nero) at Rome, afflicted Christians by the penalty of death, and tried to root up that name; thus he killed the most blessed Apostles of Christ, Peter on a cross, and Paul by the sword." Eutropius says: "Thereupon, he added even this to all his crimes that he cut down the holy Apostles of God Peter and Paul."[15] Paulinus says: "Rome itself, made powerful by the heavenly and lofty monuments to Peter and Paul."[16] Isidore says on the life of Peter: "In the thirty-seventh year after the passion of our Lord, he was crucified by Nero Cæsar in the city of Rome, upside down as he wished."

St. Leo the Great says: "This very day, the feast must be venerated by a special and proper exultation of our city, apart from that reverence which it has earned from the whole world, that where it boasts in the death of the particular Apostles, there, on the day of their martyrdom, the first place should be given to joy."[17] Gregory of Tours says: "Nero bid Peter to be killed on the cross, Paul by the sword."[18] Pope St. Gregory, speaking about the Roman Church, says: "Peter made lofty the see in which he also sat and deigned to end the present life."[19]

Prudentius in a hymn on St. Laurence, speaks thus:

> Discede adulter Juppiter stupro sororis oblite,
> Relinque Romam liberam, Plebemque jam Christi fuge.
> Te Paulus hinc exterminat, te Sanguis exturbat Petri

---

[13] *Serm 5, de natali Apostolorum.*

[14] *Sac. Histor., lib. 2.*

[15] *In vita Neronis, lib. 7.*

[16] *Natali, 3.*

[17] *Serm 1, de natali Apostolorum.*

[18] Lib. 1, ch. 25.

[19] Lib. 6, epist. 37.

Tibi id, quod ipse armaveras, factum Neronis officit.[20]

Arator, at the end of Acts of the Apostles speaks thus:

> Dignaque materies Petri, Paulique coronae,
> Caesareas superare minas, et in arce tyranni
> Pandere jura poli, summumque in agone tribunal
> Vincere, ne titulos parvus contingeret hostis.[21]

Elipis, the wife of Boethius, in a hymn on the Apostles:

> O felix Roma, quae tantorum principum
> Es purpurata precioso sanguine,
> Non laude tua, sed ipsorum meritis
> Excellis omnem mundi pulchritudinem.[22]

I omit innumerable others, as Bede, Ado, Freculph, Bernard and the rest. Accordingly, these can suffice, since all lived in the first five centuries, and since our adversaries can not even advance one who taught the contrary. Lastly, add that the heathen authors, although they do not mention Peter and Paul by name, for they seemed contemptible to them, nevertheless agree with the cited Fathers in that, at Rome, Nero first commanded Christians to be killed, as is clear from Tacitus and Suetonius.[23]

To these testimonies Velenus makes no answer, except that what was said by some Fathers that Christ appeared to Peter at the gate of Rome and said "I come to Rome to be crucified again," is a horrendous lie and a blasphemy

---

[20] "Depart O adulterous Jupiter, forgetful debaser of thine own sister, give Rome back her freedom, and now flee the people of Christ. Hence Paul exterminates thee, the Blood of Peter drives thee away, that which you had equipped for yourself, impedes the deed of Nero." - *Liber Peristephanon*, hymn II.

[21] "Worthy matter for the crowns of Peter and Paul, to conquer Caesar's menaces, and to outstretch justice on a pole in the citadel of the tyrant, to conquer the supreme tribunal in agony, lest so small an enemy should lay hands upon thy honor." -Arator, *Actus Apostolorum*,

[22] "O happy Rome, thou empurpled by the precious blood of such princes, not by thy own laud but by their merits, excel the beauty of all the world." -*Decora Lux Aeternitatis.*

[23] Tacitus, *Annales*, lib. 15; Suetonius, *In Nerone*.

against Peter himself and the Holy Spirit. For he says Christ was never going to come down from heaven again except on the day of judgment as the Holy Spirit witnesses through the mouth of Peter: "Whom it is fitting heaven receives even to the times of the restoration of all things."[24]

Yet it is rather more Velenus that lies and blasphemes that he seeks to place shackles on Christ, lest he could move even to the Day of Judgment. For that I might omit other apparitions of Christ which are read in approved authors certainly in Acts of the Apostles Christ appeared to Paul while standing in the air.[25] What Paul truly saw then with his corporeal eyes was Christ present and near to himself, and it is clear both from the light which shone all around him, and from the blindness, which came after seeing the glory of Christ, as it is said in the words of Holy Scripture. For in Acts IX, Ananias says to Paul: "The Lord Jesus sent me, who appeared to you on the road." And in the same place: "Barnabas taking Paul lead him to the Apostles, and told them how he had seen the Lord." And Paul himself says: "Am I not an Apostle? Did I not see our Lord Jesus Christ?"[26] And again: "And lastly, to one as born out of time he was seen by me."[27] Where he enumerates witnesses of the resurrection, who saw the Lord with corporeal eyes, and places himself among them.

Now to that of Acts chapter 3, I respond: Peter wished to mean that Christ was not coming publicly and in the presence of all, except on the day of judgment; but hence it is not effected that he could not appear privately, and to whom he should wish.

---

[24] Acts 3:21.

[25] Acts 9:1-5.

[26] 1 Cor. 9:1.

[27] 1 Cor. 15:8.

CHAPTER IV
Peter Was the Bishop at Rome, Even to Death

NLY the last two points remain, which can be proven together. That Peter was a bishop at Rome, and that he retained his episcopate even to death, appears firstly to be recommended by the supreme dignity of the Roman Church. It is always held as first in the consensus of all, and over all the others, as even Calvin affirms. This excellence cannot, however, be accounted for by any reasoning apart from that the Prince of the Apostles was the proper pastor of that Church, as well as its bishop, as we showed above when we disputed on the twenty-six prerogatives of St. Peter.

Next, if Peter was not the bishop of Rome even to death, then let our adversaries show where Peter sat from that time in which he left Antioch. For Peter did not remain perpetually at Antioch, as the Antiochenes themselves confess, and that is sufficiently proved by the custom of the Church, which never attributes the first place to the bishop of Antioch. Moreover, there is no Church, nor was there ever one, which asserted Peter was its bishop with the exceptions of Antioch and Rome; therefore, for what reason will we say that Peter was not the bishop of any place?

But our adversaries cannot say this, of course, because they would have it that Peter was not the bishop of the universal Church, but only of some particular place, just as John was of Ephesus and James of Jerusalem. Thus, let them say where Peter was a bishop, or if he was bishop of Rome and afterward changed his see; let them say, if they can, to where he transferred it?

Let the testimony and consensus of all the Fathers be added, one so strong that Calvin is compelled to believe it unless he were to oppose himself. Really he says he refuses to oppose it on account of the consensus of the writers, whether Peter died at Rome; therefore, since the same writers say with supreme agreement that Peter was the bishop of Rome, and no one from the Fathers ever denied that, why can they not be convinced that Peter lead the episcopate of Rome?

St. Irenaeus listed a whole catalogue of Roman bishops, and in the first place puts Peter and Paul, secondly Linus, thirdly Anacletus, fourthly Clement and the rest even to Elutherius who sat; and from Clement, Sixtus and Elutherius he repeats that they succeed the Apostles, saying Clement was the third from the Apostles, Sixtus the sixth, Eleutherius the twelfth; but certainly it cannot truly be said that Roman bishops succeed Peter, if Peter was not the bishop of Rome.[1]

Tertullian says: "Let them unroll the order of their bishops, so through

---

[1] Lib. 3, ch. 3.

successions running down that the first bishop would be one from the Apostles, or apostolic men... Just as the Roman Church bears before it Clement, who was ordained by Peter."[2] Moreover, he does not reckon that Clement himself was ordained by Peter, but that Peter afterward transferred the see to another; as is clear from the same book where Tertullian writes that Peter was crucified at Rome, from which we understand that Clement was ordained by Peter while the passion of Peter threatened, and hence Clement succeeded after the death of Peter.

St. Cyprian very frequently calls the Roman See the Chair of Peter, which he would not be able to say rightly if he believed Peter had established his see somewhere other than Rome. He says: "They dare to sail to the chair of Peter, and to that principal Church, whence sacerdotal unity arises, bearing letters from schismatics and the profane. Do they not know that these are Romans, to whom treachery cannot have an entrance?"[3] And again: "It came to pass that Cornelius became the bishop when the place of Fabian, that is, when the place of Peter and the step of the sacerdotal chair was emptied."[4]

Eusebius says in his *Chronicle* for the year 44: "Peter, a Galilean, the first Pontiff of Christians, although he had first founded a Church at Antioch, set out for Rome, where, preaching the Gospel for twenty-five years, he persevered as the bishop of the same city." Epiphanius says: "In Rome, the succession of bishops has this sequence: Peter and Paul, Linus, Cletus, Clement, Evaristus, Alexander, etc."[5]

Athanasius, in a letter to those leading a solitary life, says: "First, they did not even spare Liberius, the Bishop of Rome, not at all moved by the reverence due to the Apostolic See ... [speaking of Liberius] We never received such a tradition from the Fathers, who received it from the blessed and great Peter, etc." There he numbers Peter amongst the predecessors of Liberius.

Dorotheus says in his *Synopsis*: "Linus, after Peter the head, was bishop of Rome." Sozomen: "It did not happen without divine providence that after Felix died, Liberius alone was in charge of the Roman Church, lest the see of Peter should be sprinkled with any stain of dishonor."[6] Eulogius the Alexandrian,

---

[2]   *Praescriptiones contra haereticos.*

[3]   Lib. 1, epist 3 ad Cornelium.

[4]   *Lib. 4, epist 2 ad Antonianum.*

[5]   *Haeres. 27,* which is of Carpocras.

[6]   Lib. 4, ch. 14.

quoted by St. Gregory,[7] says that "Peter sits at Rome even now in his successors." Optatus says: "Therefore, you would not dare to deny that you know that the first Episcopal chair is placed in the city of Peter."[8] And below that he enumerates the Roman bishops from Peter even to Anastasius, who sat in his time.

Ambrose says: "Indeed, Peter the Apostle is the author of this our assertion, who was the priest of the Roman Church."[9] Jerome says that Peter ruled the sacerdotal chair at Rome for twenty-five years.[10] He says the same thing in his first letter to Pope Damasus, on the term "hypostasis," saying: "I speak with the successor of the fisherman and disciple of the cross, I unite in your beatitude that which is in communion with the chair of Peter." Augustine says: "What do you suppose is the chair of the Roman Church, in which Peter sat, and in which now Anastasius sits?"[11] Likewise, in Epistle 16, he enumerates the Roman Bishops from Peter even to Anastasius.

Prudentius in a hymn on St. Laurence:

> Romae jam regnant duo
> Apostolorum principes:
> Alter vocator Gentium,
> Alter Cathedram possidens
> Primam, recludit creditas
> Aeternitatis januas.[12]

Prosper of Aquitane from *libro de ingratis*:

> Rome the see of Peter, which for pastoral honor
> Was made head of the world, etc.

---

[7] Lib. 6, epistl. 37.

[8] *Contra Parmenianum,* lib. 2.

[9] *De Sacramentis,* lib. 3, ch. 1.

[10] *De viris illustribus,* on Peter.

[11] *Conta literas Petiliani,* lib. 2, ch. 51.

[12] "At Rome now two princes of the Apostles reign: One the herald of the Gentiles, the other possessing the First Chair, he opens the gates of eternity to him entrusted." Loc. Cit.

Sulpitius says: "Divine religion strengthened the city while Peter was in charge of the episcopate."[13] Peter, the Bishop of Ravenna, in a letter to Eutyches which is contained among the proceedings of the Council of Chalcedon, says: "We exhort you, honorable brother, that you obediently attend to those things written by the Pope of the city of Rome, because blessed Peter, who both lived and presided in that seat as his own, supplies the truth of faith to all those seeking it."

Theodoret, in an epistle to Leo, after he had said that Peter and Paul died at Rome, adds: "They make your seat more famous; this is the chief of your possessions. Moreover, God also rendered that seat beautiful and famous when he placed Your Holiness in it, which sends forth the rays of the Orthodox faith." Isidore, in his life of Peter, says: "He, after founding the Church at Antioch, continued to Rome against Simon Magus under the rule of Claudius Caesar and there, preaching the Gospel, held the pontificate of the same city for twenty-five years." Bede[14] has the same, as does Freculph,[15] Ado of Vienna,[16] and all more recent authors.

Let them agree also, apart from the authority of so many Fathers, with the testimonies of the ancient Roman bishops who were martyrs or confessors. Pope Clement teaches that with his death approaching Peter handed on the Roman Episcopate to him.[17] Anacletus in Epistle 3 teaches that on account of the See of Peter, the Roman Church is the head of all others. Marcellus I, in a letter to the Antiochenes, says: "The See of Peter was begun with you, and was transferred to Rome at the Lord's command, etc." Pope Damasus says that Peter was the Bishop of Rome for twenty-five years, that is, even to his death.[18] Innocent I teaches the same thing, in a letter to the Council of Miletus.[19] Moreover, so do Pope Leo, Gelasius, John III, Pope St Gregory, Agatho, Adrian and Nicholas I,

---

[13] *Sacra histor.* Lib. 2.

[14] *De sex aetatibus.*

[15] *Chronicorum*, tomus 2, lib. 2, ch. 13.

[16] Chronicum, anno Christi XLV.

[17] *Constit. Apostolic.*, lib. 7, ch. 46.

[18] *In pontificali in Petro.*

[19] This is 93 among the epistles of Augustine.

and all others who wrote anything, affirm that their See is the Seat of Peter.[20] Their testimonies are still not received by our adversaries, because they say they wrote for their own purposes; yet certainly this is without cause, since these men were very holy, and none of the ancient Fathers ever condemn them in this regard.

Let the heretics of our time agree with the testimonies of the ancient councils, which they themselves receive. First, the Council of 300 bishops of Sardica: "We honor the memory of the holy Apostle Peter that these who would examine the case should write to Julius, the bishop of Rome, and if he will have judged that the judgment must be restored, let it be restored, and let him give judgment."[21] Likewise in the Council of Ephesus, the Roman Pontiff Celestine is called: "Ordinary successor and vicar of blessed Peter, Prince of the Apostles."[22]

In the second act of the Council of Chalcedon, when the epistle of Pope Leo was read, all shouted: "Peter has spoken through Leo;" and in the third Act, when sentence was imposed against Dioscorus, Leo is provided with the dignity of the Apostle Peter to have deposed Disocorus. And in an epistle of Leo the whole Council says that Leo is the interpreter of the voice of Peter; that is, Peter speaks through Leo. All of this obviously shows that it was the persuasion of the 630 Fathers at the Council that Leo, as Bishop of Rome, is the successor of Peter.

In the fifth council, first action, Menas, the Patriarch and president of the Council, bearing sentence against Anthimus and other heretics, says: "They had contempt for the Roman Church, in which there is succession of the Apostles, which bears sentence against them." In the sixth council, Act 8, the bishops titled a letter of Agatho in different ways. Among others, a certain one thus says: "Suggestions were directed by our father Agatho, the most holy Apostolic Archbishop, of the ancient and principal Roman see, just as dictated by the Holy Spirit, through the mouth of the Holy and most Blessed Prince of the Apostles, Peter, and written by the finger of the thrice most blessed Pope Agatho I receive and embrace." From these five most approved councils we have more than 1200 ancient bishops, mostly Greek, who witness that the Roman Pontiff succeeds Peter.

---

[20] Leo, *serm. 1 de natali Apostolorum*; Gelasius *Epistola ad Episcopos Germaniae et Galliae*; Gregory *lib. 2, epist. 33*; Agatho *in epistola ad Constantinum imperatorem*; Adrian *epistola ad Tharasium*; Nicholas I, *Epistola ad Michaelem*.

[21] Concilius Sardicensi, can. 3.

[22] *Concilium Ephesinum,* Tomus 2, ch. 16.

CHAPTER V

The First Argument of our Adversaries is Answered

LET us now rebut the objections of Velenus, which also contains arguments used by Calvin and Illyricus. His first persuasion is such: "The authors who say Peter came to Rome do not agree among themselves about the time in which he came; for Orosius says he came in the beginning of the reign of Claudius, Jerome says in the second year of Claudius, Fasciculus says in the fourth year of the same emperor, while the *Passionale* on the lives of the saints says in the 13th year of Claudius.

"Besides, a wonderful variety is discovered in the numbering of the successors of Peter. For one places Clement immediately after Peter, as Tertullian says (loc. Cit.), and Jerome,[1] others place Linus after Peter, and after him Clement in the third places, as Optatus and Augustine;[2] others place Linus and Cletus, or Anacletus, after Peter, and at length Clement in the fourth place, as Irenaeus and Jerome.[3]

"Add that all these make from Cletus and Anacletus one, therefore, nothing can be established for certain discord, and the argument of the authors is a falsity."

I respond to the first. The disagreement on the time (if there is such a disagreement) that Peter came to Rome, does not weaken our argument that Peter came to Rome. For it most often happens that one establishes on some business, and still does not establish on the manner or other circumstances. For it is certain among Christians that Christ died on the Cross for us. Nevertheless, there is very great disagreement on the time in which he died. Tertullian, Clement of Alexandria, and Lactantius teach that Christ died in the 15th year of the emperor Tiberius, in his 30th year.[4] Ignatius, Eusebius, and others say he was crucified in his 33rd year of age, in the 18th year of Tiberius. Onuphrius, Mercator, and a few other more recent authors would have it that Christ suffered in his 34th year of life. Irenaeus contends that Christ was almost fifty, hence he would have suffered under Claudius, not under Tiberius.

On the day and the month in which Christ died there is such a disagreement

---

[1] *Commnt. Isaiae*, ch. 52.

[2] Optatus, *Contra Parmenianum*, lib. 2; Augustine, *Epistol. 165.*

[3] Irenaeus lib. 3, ch. 3; Jerome *De Viris Illustribus*, in Clemente.

[4] Tertullian, *Contra Judaeos*; Clement, *Stromata*, lib. 1; Lactantius, *Divinarum isntitut.*, lib. 4, ch. 10.

of the Fathers (as well as more recent writers), that the jury is still out.[5] See for example, the many arguments which Clement of Alexandria relates;[6] but still, will we on that account deny that Christ suffered and died?

By equal reasoning, although it should be established that the weeks of Daniel are fulfilled by the passion of Christ, nevertheless there are many opinions on the time in which they begin, and in which they are defined; likewise, on the years of the kings of the Persians, on the years of Samuel, Saul and others, several leaders of the Jews, on the years of the Emperors and Roman Pontiffs; then on the years of the world, which have passed to this point, there are as many opinions as there are chronologies. Therefore, will we say on that account that there were never kings amongst the Persians, that Samuel and Saul did not exist, or that the Roman Emperors and Pontiffs never existed, and even that the world itself did not begin, or has not endured even to this day?

Therefore, the disagreement of writers is an argument for falsity, in regard to that in which they disagree, because necessarily some are mistaken by disagreements. But just as disagreement is a sign of falsity, so agreement is the greatest sign of truth, and there is agreement among all the Fathers that Peter sat at Rome, and died there.

Finally I respond: There is no disagreement among good authors. For Eusebius in his *Chronicle*, and Jerome in his book on Ecclesiastical writers, as well as Ado of Trier in his martyrology, they all say that Peter came to Rome in the second year of Claudius. Orosius does not disagree with this[7] when he says that he came in the beginning of the reign of Claudius. For if the reign of Claudius were divided into three parts, that is, beginning, middle and end, you will see that the second year pertains to the beginning. All those former authors agree with the latter and assert that Peter sat at Rome for twenty-five years, dying in the fourteenth of Nero, namely Damasus, Isidore, Bede, Freculph, Ado of Vienna, and the rest whom we cited above. Therefore, there are not twenty-five years even to the 14th of Nero, unless we begin from the second year of Claudius.

---

[5] Translator's note: This question belongs to those incidental questions of the 16th century that today no one takes up, such as the debate on whether there were 3 nails or 4, whether Christ was pierced in the wrist or in the hand, etc. Although to our knowledge there has never been a conclusive documentary settlement to the question, still at least since the 18th century there has been no doubt in the minds of Catholics that Christ died in 33A.D. Yet in the 16th century this was a serious question.

[6] *Stromata*, lib. 1.

[7] Lib. 7.

For this reason we duly scorn Fasciculus and the Passionale of the times, especially since Fasciculus followed Marianus Scotus, who is opposed to himself and the truth. Marianus Scotus says in his *Chronicle* that Peter came to Rome in the 4th year of Claudius, and died in the last year of Nero, nevertheless he sat in the Roman episcopate for twenty-five years and two months, which is in no way coherent in itself. For Claudius ruled for thirteen years, eight months and twenty days, while Nero reigned for thirteen years and seven months, twenty eight days, as Dio Cassius, Suetonius, Tranquilus, Eusebius and even Marianus Scotus himself witness. Truly, what is found in the *Chronicle* of Eusebius that fourteen years, seven months and twenty-eight days are attributed to Nero is plainly a copyist error; accordingly, since individual years are counted, they are not discovered to be apart from thirteen, and a little more.

Furthermore, these times of Claudius and Nero joined together do not make a point greater than twenty-seven years, four months and eighteen days, from which if you were to remove three years, five months and eighteen days, which Marianus Scotus would have vanish from the rule of Claudius, before Peter came to Rome, only twenty-three years and eleven months would remain. Therefore, either Peter died after Nero, or he did not sit for twenty-five years.

Now we move in regard to the second part of the argument to the succession of the first four Popes. To the first I respond, even if we were completely ignorant about who next succeeded Peter, still it would not be called into doubt whether someone had succeeded him. Just the same, as the greatest question is treated among the writers, who was the husband of Esther, since some think Xerxes the Mede, others Cambyses the Persian, others Darius Histaspis, while still others Artaxerses Longimanus, and still others that it was Mnemonem. Nevertheless no one ever thought there could be a doubt as to whether Esther had a husband or not.

Thus I respond: The whole matter can be thus arranged and explained. The Apostle Peter, while his passion was imminent, left the episcopal seat to St. Clement. Serious authors witness it, namely Tertullian, Jerome, Pope John III, and besides these Clement himself, Anacletus, and Damasus.[8]

But yet, after the death of Peter, Clement refused to sit in the Apostolic seat while Linus and Cletus lived, who were aids to St. Peter himself in the episcopal office. For that reason Clement was not the first Pope from Peter, rather Linus was. We so gather this, first from Epiphanius, who handed down from the

---

[8]   Tertullian, *de Praescriptionibus*; Jerome, *In Jovinianum*, lib. 1, and *Isaiae* ch. 52; Ruffinus, *praefatione recognitionum*, and *invectiva in Hieronymum*; John III, *in Epistola ad Episcopos Germaniae*; Clement, *Constit. Aposto* lib. 7, ch. 37; Anacletus *epist. 1*; Alexander *epist. 1*; Damasus *in Vita Petri*.

opinion of the Fathers that the seat was refused by Clement, while Linus and Cletus lived. Next from this ambiguity, if Clement or Linus or whoever else succeeded Peter without any contention, certainly no question would have existed about the first successor of Peter. Just the same, on the first successor of James at Jerusalem, and of Mark at Alexandria, and of Peter himself at Antioch, there was never any question.

But then a holy contention was born in the Roman Church after the death of Peter from humility, and there was one and another that ought to be the first successor of Peter. From there, some obscurity was discovered in this succession. Also, from these the authors can be reconciled, who either place Clement ahead of Linus, or Linus ahead of Clement; accordingly Irenaeus, Eusebius, Epiphanius, Optatus, Augustine and Jerome, when they assert that Linus was the next to have succeeded Peter, they assert what is true, but they do not deny that Clement had refused the episcopate. Next Tertullian, Jerome, Ruffinus and the rest, who write that Clement was left behind as a successor to Peter, they tell the matter truly. Furthermore, they do not deny that Clement in that time refused to receive the seat.

Nor do certain writings on the life of Linus matter much to me, such as the *Pontificale* of Damasus, the writings of Sophronius and of Simeon Metaphrastes, where they say that Linus died before Peter. Sophronius and Simeon are more recent, and the *Liber Pontificalis*, which is attributed to Damasus, is of doubtful authority in the matter. Yet the authors who write that Linus succeeded Peter, not only are most ancient, but even more they are many and esteemed.

Moreover after Linus, Cletus, or Anacletus sat, after whom Clement must be placed fourth. The authors are Irenaeus, Eusebius, Epiphanius, Jerome, and likewise, the most ancient Canon of the Mass, where we read of Linus, Cletus and Clement, and thereupon, Ignatius in his epistle to Maria Zarbensem, where he signifies Clement succeeded Anacletus. After Clement, another Anacletus must be added, as Optatus, Augustine, Damasus and others add.

Indeed there were two men named Anacletus, the second of whom is also called Cletus, although on account of the similarity in name, many Fathers make one from the two. First, the authority of the Catholic Church persuades us, which celebrates two feast days in their memory; certainly of Cletus in the month of April, and Anacletus in the month of July; Cletus was a Roman and the son of Emilianus, while Anacletus was an Athenian, and the son of Antiochus. It is not believable that in such a matter that the whole Church would be deceived.

Next, we gather the same from the fact that some Fathers place Anacletus before Clement, as Ignatius, Irenaeus and Eusibius. Others add, like Optatus, Damasus and Augustine; that is, by argument that they were two not one.

Hence the first Anacletus was also usually called Cletus; thence it is certian that the same was Pope, whom Ignatius, Irenaeus and Eusebius call Anacletus: Epiphanius, Jerome, Damasus, John III and the most holy Canon of the Mass itself name Cletus.

It ought to be no wonder, on account of the similarity of the name that one Anacletus was made from two by certain Fathers, since it is certain that the Greeks in many places confused Novatus with Novatian, and nevertheless it is quite certain that Novatus was a Carthaginian, while Novatian was a Roman priest. Eusebius and Nicephorus of Constantinople in their Chronicles made one person both Marcellus and Marcellinus, though it is altogether certain and proven that they were two separate men.

CHAPTER VI
The Second Argument of our Adversaries is Answered

HE SECOND persuasion of Velenus is also that of Calvin and the Centuriators. "Peter could not have come to Rome before eighteen years after the Lord's passion; for when the Council of Jerusalem happened in Acts XV, Peter was still in Judaea; but that Council came to pass in the eighteenth year from the Lord's passion, as St. Jerome gathers.[1] For Paul came to Jerusalem to see Peter three years after his conversion. Thereupon, it was after fourteen years he returned into Jerusalem to the Council, in which if you add one year which passed from the Lord's passion even to the conversion of Paul, they would be eighteen years.

"Add that Peter is said to have been in Judaea for five years, then seven years in Antioch, and as many years in Pontus, Galatia, Cappadocia, Asia, and Bythinia, and he could not preach in so many places in one day; consequently, at least eighteen years would have passed before Peter could have come to Rome.

"Besides, if before eighteen years Peter could have come to Rome then he would have come in the second year of Claudius, as we said above, and that cannot be both because in that year St. Peter was not yet freed from the prison in which Herod had thrown him in, and because his liberation happened in the third year of Claudius, as is gathered from Luke[2] and from Josephus.[3] Christ had also commanded his Apostles that they should not leave from Jerusalem before twelve years, but as Eusebius relates from Thrasea the martyr, this fell in the twelfth year from the resurrection of Christ, in the third year of Claudius. Therefore, Peter did not come to Rome in the second year of Claudius, but after the ninth year, which was the eighteenth from the passion of the Lord.

"Moreover Peter is said to have sat at Rome for twenty-five years, by Damasus, Eusebius, Jerome and others; therefore, he lived even to the 43rd year after the passion of the Lord, but then he would not have died under Nero, nor even Galba, Otho and Vitellius, but while Vespasian reigned. Therefore, Peter died in the reign of Vespasian. Yet Vespasian was a very meek emperor and he did not kill any Christians at Rome, as all witness.[4] Therefore, Peter died

---

[1] *In epistola ad Galatas*, ch. 2.

[2] Acts 12.

[3] *Hist.*, lib. 5, ch. 18.

[4] See Tertullian, *Apologeticus*, ch. 5; Augustine, *De Civitate Dei*, lib. 3, ch. 31; Eusebius, Sulpitius, Orosius and the other historians.

somewhere other than Rome."

I respond: First, although the Fathers could have erred when they said the Apostle Peter sat at Rome for twenty five years, nevertheless on that account it would not follow that Peter never sat at Rome, as we proved above by bringing many like matters. But there is no need to appeal to those arguments since Peter truly sat at Rome for twenty-five years as well as seven at Antioch, and all things still are consistent. This is, then, the true and brief history of the life of St. Peter.

St. Peter remained in Judaea for nearly five years for which reason St. Paul could easily meet Peter in Jerusalem three years after his conversion. And rightly, Eusebius places the journey of Peter to Antioch five years after the Lord's passion. This is also not opposed to that tradition of Thrasea the martyr: indeed the Lord did not command that all the Apostles should tarry in Jerusalem for twelve years; it is certain that this is false from the Acts of the Apostles, where we read that Peter set out into Samaria, Lydda, Jopah and Caesarea, before he was cast into prison and also to the point that, before the twelfth year from the passion of Christ. Rather, Christ commanded that not all should leave, so that some Apostles would always remain in Jerusalem according to the testimony of Hebrews. Therefore, in the 5th year after the Lord's passion, Peter set out into Syria, he set up his see at Antioch, and remained nearly seven years as bishop of that city.

Moreover, it is not probable what Onuphrius teaches in the additions to Platina that St. Peter did not sit at Antioch, unless it was after he returned from Rome. Accordingly, he could produce no Father as an author on his behalf. Rather, what we teach is what they taught before us.[5]

Still, this must not be so received, as if he never went out from Antioch in that whole time; nay more, that he traveled in the same time to nearby provinces, Pontus, Asia, Galatia, Cappadocia, and Bythinia. Thence he also set out in the seventh year of the Antiochene episcopate, which was the eleventh after the Lord's passion, returned to Jerusalem, and there was taken by Herod and thrown into prison, on the days of the unleavened bread.[6] But a little after was freed by an angel, in the same year, which was the second of Claudius, and at the same time he came to Rome, set up his see there, and held it for twenty-five years.

---

[5] Anacletus, ep. 3; Marcellus, epist 3; Innocent I, epist 14; Damasus, in Pontificali; Jerome, de viris illust.; Eusebius, in Chronico; Leo, Sermon 1 de sanctis Petro et Paulo; and at length, Bede, Isidore, Ado and all the rest.

[6] Acts 12:1-19.

Still, in that whole time in which he was the Bishop of Rome, he did not remain at Rome; rather, after that he preached at Rome for seven years, returned to Jerusalem, being expelled by Claudius from the city together with the rest of the Jews. Luke writes that Claudius had expelled all the Jews from the city,[7] and Suetonius writes the same thing about Claudius; likewise Josephus, as Orosius cites, and Orosius himself adds that this was done in the ninth year of Claudius that is the 18th from the Lord's passion. Therefore, they who were at Antioch heard that Peter came into Jerusalem; they sent to him Paul and Barnabas; and then the Council of Jerusalem took place. After Claudius died, however, Peter returned to Rome, and ended his life in the same place.

Nor does the fact that Peter was at Jerusalem a little before the death of Herod contradict this, for it is certain that Herod died in the 3rd year of Claudius. For St. Luke does not say Peter was in bonds a little before the death of Herod, but he rather more indicates the contrary when he says that after the liberation of Peter from prison, Herod set out for Caesarea, and there was delayed. This delay, no matter what extent of time, means that at the least it was a year. St. Luke relates the death of Herod immediately after the death of James and the imprisonment of Peter, that he might show the horrible ruin of Herod was a penalty for the sin he committed against the Apostles of the Lord.

---

[7] Acts 18:2.

CHAPTER VII
Another Five Arguments are Answered

HE THIRD persuasion of Velenus is thus: "Peter could not come to Rome even in the ninth year of Claudius, as we proved above, and he could not come afterward, for Claudius, who commanded the Jews to be expelled from the city, without a doubt commanded that they should not be received again; therefore, Peter never came."

Yet, we have already shown that Peter, in the 9th year of Claudius, did not come to Rome but left from Rome and afterward in the time of Nero returned, because in the time of Nero the Jews could be at Rome, as is clear from the last chapter of Acts where Paul preaches to the Jews at Rome.

His fourth persuasion: "When Paul condemned Peter at Antioch, the Council of Jerusalem had already been carried out and nevertheless Peter had not seen Rome." I respond: He had gone and come back.

The fifth persuasion: "Paul, writing to the Romans, bids greeting to many in the last chapter but he does not even mention Peter." This is not only from Velenus, but is also used by Illyricus to show that Peter was never in Rome.

I respond: in the first place, this argument concludes nothing, for otherwise it would follow that John was never a bishop at Ephesus, nor James at Jerusalem, because when Paul wrote to the Ephesians and the Hebrews he makes no mention of John and James. Next, I say, Paul did not bid Peter to be greeted, because he wrote the epistle in that time in which Peter returned from Rome and was living in Syria. Paul writes the epistle on a journey in which he set out for Jerusalem, where he was also seized. Thus indeed he writes: "And now, I set out for Jerusalem to minister to the saints, as Achaia and Macedonia have provided some alms to provide for the poor saints who are in Jerusalem."[1] In Acts 24, the same Paul, when he made his case at the tribunal of Felix, the governor of Syria, said: "I come intending to take alms into my nation, and offerings and prayers."

Next, this captivity of Paul happens in the middle of the period between the Council of Jerusalem and the death of Claudius. Accordingly, after that council, Paul adds Macedonia and Achaia, where beforehand he had never been, as is clear from Acts 16. He arrived in Jerusalem while Felix was governor, who was over Syria even to the death of Claudius, and in the beginning of Nero, as Josephus witnesses.[2] From which it follows that the Epistle to the Romans was written around the 11th or 12th year of Claudius, in which time St. Peter returned

---

[1] Romans 15:25-26.

[2] *Antiquit.* Lib. 20, ch. 9 and 13.

to Rome, and again traveled and visited the regions of Syria. What wonder, therefore, if Paul, writing to the Romans, does not greet Peter, who it is certain was not at Rome in that time.

The sixth persuasion: "Ambrose says in his commentary on Romans 16 that Narcissus, whom Paul bids greeting, was a Roman priest: but priest [*presbyter*] and bishop are the same in Paul's writings, therefore, this Narcissus was the Bishop of Rome, hence Peter was not the first Bishop of Rome."

I respond: Narcissus may have been a Roman priest but he was certainly not a bishop. Accordingly, Irenaeus, Eusebius, Optatus, Epiphanius, Jerome, Augustine, and the rest who wrote a catalogue of Roman Pontiffs make no mention of this Narcissus. Nor does that oppose the authority of Ambrose since Ambrose says in his commentary on 1 Timothy 3, "Every bishop is a priest, yet not every priest is a bishop." Moreover, Cornelius is quoted by Eusebius as saying that at Rome there was one bishop, but forty six priests.[3]

The seventh persuasion: "Paul struck an agreement with Peter that the latter should be the Apostle of the Jews, while he himself should be the Apostle of the Gentiles. Therefore, how can it have the appearance of truth that Peter should be so quickly forgetful of this pact, and invade another province that is Rome, which was the mother of the Gentiles?

"If you say Peter preached to the Jews who were there at Rome, we can say conversely that while Paul came there and began to preach, they marveled at the novelty of the doctrine, as can be understood from their words in the last Chapter of Acts: "This sect is known to us, because it is gainsaid everywhere, yet we ask to hear what you think;" and further down: "They believed these things which were said: but some did not believe, and when they say that they were not in agreement, they left."

I respond: Firstly, the "treaty" between Peter and Paul was not such that Peter could only preach to the Jews, or in Judea, while Paul could only preach to the Gentiles, or outside of Judaea; rather that Peter should preach to all in every place he would, but principally to the Jews, and Paul to all and in every place he wished, but principally to the Gentiles; otherwise Paul could be said to have invaded a foreign province when coming to Rome since he soon began to preach to the Jews, as is clear from the last chapter of Acts. Moreover, were this the case, Peter not only should not have come to Rome, but also neither to Antioch, Asia, Galatia, Pontus, Cappadocia and Bythinia, all places to which Velenus affirms that Peter went to.

Velenus is also wrong when he says that the Jews at Rome marveled at the

---

[3] *Hist. Eccl.,* lib. 6, ch. 33.

novelty of doctrine, on the occasion that Paul preached Christ to them, as though no one before had preached anything like it. For if no one had preached to the Jews at Rome before Paul came there, who converted the Roman Jews, to whom he wrote his epistle? Certainly, part of the Epistle to the Romans was written to the Gentiles, and part of it to the Jews who had converted to the faith of Christ since he disputes in the first four chapters on justification from faith without works of the law, against the pride of the Jews, who attributed the coming of the Messiah to their own merits. And in chapter 14 he treats on those who still Judaized, abstaining from certain unclean foods according to the law. And in chapter 16, he greets many Christians who were certainly converts from the Jews.

Yet maybe someone will say, if the Epistle to the Romans was written while Claudius, who expelled the Jews from Rome, was alive, who then are these Jews to whom Paul bids greeting? The Jews could scarcely return while Claudius lived.

I respond, it is not only believable that a little after the expulsion the Jews were able to return, but they did so without a doubt. For, Paul in Acts 18 discovered Aquila and Priscilla at Corinth, Jews who recently had come from the city, expelled by Claudius. Next, he stayed in Achaia for a year and six months, and in Asia for two years, then began a journey to Jerusalem; and also on that journey he wrote to the Romans and bid greeting to Aquila and Priscilla, who now had gone back to Rome.

Now to the question of the words of the Jews, "We ask from you to hear what you think, etc." I say these words were not of all the Jews who were at Rome, but only of those who were still not converted to the faith of Christ, apart from the many others living at Rome whom Peter converted. Nor is it shown by those words that they never heard the preaching of Christ, but that they still had not been persuaded, and therefore, wished to hear it from Paul. Although they were efficaciously convinced by him, some were persuaded that they should believe, and part of them remained in their obstinacy.

CHAPTER VIII
Another Eight Arguments are Answered

ERSUASIONS 8-15 are taken from the last chapter of Acts of the Apostles and the epistles which Paul wrote from Rome, without a doubt to the Galatians, Ephesians, Colossians, Philippians, Hebrews, Timothy and Philemon, and from letters of Paul to Seneca, and Seneca to Paul, for in all these writings there was an occasion of speaking about Peter, if he was at Rome; yet a marvelous silence is found everywhere.

Our opponents say that it so happens that not only is Peter not said to be at Rome in these places, but they even openly say he was not there. For Philippians 2 says about those who were at Rome: "All strive for what is their own." And in the last chapter of Collossians: "Aristarchus, my fellow captive, greets you, and Mark the cousin of Barnabas, and Jesus who is called Justus; these alone are my helpers in the kingdom of God." And in 2 Timothy 4: "In my first defense, no one assisted me, rather all left me behind." Therefore, either Peter was not at Rome, or Paul did him a very great injury since he numbers him among those who seek their own things, and who were not helpers in the kingdom of God and who deserted him in a tight spot. Now this argument is not only of Velenus, but also of Calvin.

I respond: Firstly, nothing is concluded from an appeal to a negative authority. Indeed, it does not follow that because Luke, Paul and Seneca do not say that Peter was at Rome, therefore, Peter was not there. Further, these three ought not to say everything, and something is more believed with three affirming witnesses than from a thousand who say nothing; they merely do not deny what others affirm. Otherwise, it would follow that because Matthew does not write in his Gospel that Christ was circumcised, Mark did not recall the presentation, Luke does not mention the new star and John does not say that Christ was born from the Virgin Mary, that all these will be false, which is absolutely absurd.

In regard to those three citations from Scripture, they do not deny that Peter was then in Rome; for although in Colossians Paul says: "Only these are my helpers in the kingdom of God," he is only speaking on his household that usually ministered with him. It is in the same manner how when he says in 2 Timothy 4 that, "Luke alone is with me," it is concerning his household and ministers. Therefore, it is certain from the last chapter of the Epistle to the Romans that many others, both Jews and Gentiles, were converted to the faith at Rome, who promoted the kingdom of God. And in the Epistle to the Philippians, when he says: "All seek what are theirs," it is understood figuratively; he speaks only on certain ones, not on all absolutely. For he had said in the same place a little before that Timothy was with him, who certainly was not seeking what was his own. He had also said in the first chapter that some preached the Gospel *from charity*, and hence did not seek what was their own, but that which is of Jesus Christ.

Lastly, in 2 Tim. 4, where he says: "No one assisted me, but all left me behind," which among other things, Calvin urges that he does not speak except about those who could help him with Caesar. For he says in the same place that Luke was then with him and nevertheless he speaks generally: "No man assisted me, rather all left me behind." Certainly Peter could not help him since he was no less hated by Caesar than Paul. Consequently, he only speaks about certain Roman nobles who could go to Caesar on his behalf but did not for fear of the tyrant.

Secondly, one could respond that in the time in which Paul came to Rome and in which he wrote his epistles, Peter was not at Rome. For, although he had set up his see at Rome, nevertheless he often left since it was fitting to establish the Churches in different places, as Epiphanius records.[1] For on that account, Peter took up for himself Linus and Cletus as helpers, who attended to his episcopal duties in his absence.

---

[1] *Haeres. 27.*

CHAPTER IX
The Sixteenth Argument is Answered

VELENUS gives as persuasion 16: "Ambrose says: '[Peter and Paul] died on the same day, in the same place under the sentence of the same tyrant.'[1] But Linus, in the passions of Peter and Paul, says that they did not suffer in the same time, nor in the same place, nor at the pleasure of the same tyrant.

"Besides, Josephus, who lived at the time of Nero, wrote a history at Rome on the Jewish war, and in that makes mention of those killed by Nero, yet still, he does not mention Peter, whom he certainly would not have omitted if he was truly killed by Nero. Josephus was a friend of Christians, and gladly mentioned them when the occasion was given. He writes about the death of Christ[2] and John the Baptist in the same place, as well as James.[3]

"Add that Peter was an old man when Paul was a youth, for after the passion of the Lord Paul is called a youth in Acts 7, in which time Peter already had a wife and, as the oldest of all the Apostles, was held to be first among them, until Paul attained old age, as he wrote in the epistle to Philemon; therefore that they died at the same time lacks the appearance of truth."

This argument can be easily refuted. In the first part of the argument, Velenus errs twice. First, he affirms elsewhere that the history of Linus was fabricated, and still from that he says the teaching of Ambrose is refuted. If indeed the history of Linus was fabricated, it lacks all authority. If it lacks all authority, how can it thence refute the teaching of Ambrose, an author of very great authority? Next, he errs, because in the same place Ambrose understands the same part of the city, and thence he would have it that Ambrose differs from others who say the Apostles were killed in different parts of the same city. Yet Ambrose in the same place understands the same city, not the same part of the city. Thus he adds: "In the same place, for another Rome would be wanting."

Now to the argument from Josephus. First I say, Josephus himself responded

---

[1] Serm. 67.

[2] Josephus, *Antiquitat.*, lib. 18. [Modern scholarship calls into question whether Josephus actually wrote favorably about Christ, or whether this was an addition of a copyist. The standard view is that Josephus did not write that, since he remained a Jew. On the other hand it could be argued that since Jewish understandings of the Messiah differed, Josephus could well have received Jesus as the Messiah and yet understood that in a different sense from Christians. Either way, Josephus' authorship was not in dispute by either Catholics or Protestants in the time Bellarmine wrote. -Translator's note].

[3] *Ibid.*, lib. 20.

in his work *On the Jewish War*,[4] where he says he wished to pass over in silence the crimes of Nero, that he killed his mother and wife and like things, since he knew the tale is troublesome; and he says these things rightly, for he dedicated the books to Roman emperors, who do not gladly hear their predecessors reproached. Next the argument on the author can be turned back upon on itself; for Velenus says in the same place that Peter was killed in Jerusalem, by the command of Ananus the Jewish High Priest. Therefore, I ask, how it is that Josephus, who writes on the deeds of this Ananus and the men whom he killed,[5] still makes no mention of Peter in that place? Thus Velenus is hoisted on his own petard.

Now in regards to age, I say that Peter was not old when Paul was said to be a youth, rather a man of mature age. That he had a wife and was first of the Apostles is no argument except that he was of virile age. It is not credible in any way that old men were chosen by Christ to carry out the greatest labors and journey through nearly the whole world. Just the same it is not believable that Paul as a teenager would be taken up to the Apostolic dignity, which pertained to the care of every Church.[6]

At length, Peter was not beyond fifty years when Paul was around twenty five that is, twice his age: nevertheless, they could still both be old and die together; indeed in the last year of Nero, Peter would have been about 86, and Paul 61.

---

[4] *De bello Judaico*, lib. 2, ch. 11.

[5] *Antiquit.* Lib. 20.

[6] Translator's note: To this could be added that in Latin, *adolescens* referred to someone from 18-30, as the Romans expected bad behavior from youths who would then get their act together about 30, particularly in the late Republican and early Imperial periods. See Adrian Goldsworthy, *Caesar*, Yale University Press. Thus the translators of the *Vetus Latina*, as well as St. Jerome, when they saw the Greek νεανίος, opted for *adolescens* to translate the concept of a youth early in his way to manhood, not a teenager as the word would lend itself in contemporary parlance in the 16th -Translator's note.

CHAPTER X
The Seventeenth Argument is Answered

THE SEVENTEENTH persuasion of Velenus. "Scripture and the Fathers openly teach that Peter and Paul were killed in Jerusalem by the scribes and Pharisees, not at Rome by the emperors. For Matthew 23 says: 'Behold I send to you Prophets and the wise, and scribes, and from them you will kill, and crucify and scourge them in your synagogues.' In which place Chrysostom says: 'He understands the Apostles, and those who were with them.' And Jerome on the same place: "Observe that according to each Apostle are different gifts of the disciples of Christ; some prophets, who were coming to preach; others the wise, who knew when they ought to advance a sermon; others, scribes, learned in the law, among which was Stephen whom they stoned; Paul was killed, Peter was crucified, the disciples were scourged in the Acts of the Apostles.' Likewise Nicholas Lyranus says on the same citation: 'From them you will kill, just like James the brother of John, and Stephen and many others, and you will crucify them, like Peter and Andrew his brother.'"

I respond: from the words of the Lord in Matthew 23, and the exposition of Chrysostom, one could gather nothing against our teaching. For the Lord and St. John Chrysostom do not say all the Apostles were to be killed by the Jews in Jerusalem, but only some. Indeed that is shown from the sentence: "From those you will kill and crucify, etc." And that was fulfilled in Stephen, whom they stoned in Acts 7, and in James the Elder, whom Herod killed for the sake of the Jews in Acts 12, and James the Younger, whom the Jews themselves killed in Jerusalem, as Josephus witnesses;[1] as well as Simeon the successor of James, who was crucified in Jerusalem, as Eusebius teaches in his *Chronicle*. To that we could add Matthias, whom many think probably was crucified in Judaea.

But if the Lord spoke about all the Apostles, as Velenus contends, then all histories must be denied which witness that Andrew died in Achaia, Philip and John in Asia, Thomas in India, Bartholomew in Armenia, Matthew in Ethiopia, as well as Simon and Jude in Asia.

As for St. Jerome, he does not mean that Peter and Paul were killed at Jerusalem, since he eloquently taught in *de Viris Illustribus* that they were killed at Rome by Nero; rather he deduces from the words of the Lord different gifts and different deaths of the disciples of Christ. Since the Lord had said that he was going to send prophets, and wise men, and scribes Jerome observed the different gifts of the Apostles, since again the Lord said: "Some you will kill, some you will crucify." The same Jerome observed that the disciples would pass

---

[1] *Antiquit.*, lib. 20, ch. 16.

from this life by different kinds of death, and places the examples of Stephen being stoned, Paul being beheaded, and Peter crucified. Therefore, they do not press these examples in order that we would understand that certain of the disciples were going to be killed by the Jews, but only in that, rather, that we might learn there were to be different kinds of martyrs.

Next, Nicholas Lyranus is not of such authority that he ought to oppose all the ancient Fathers and Histories, which hand down that Peter was killed at Rome by Nero, and Andrew in Achaia by Egaea. It so happened that Lyranus followed Jerome, and wished only to say that Peter and Andrew were crucified for Christ, however less carefully he spoke.

CHAPTER XI

The Last Argument is Answered

HE LAST persuasion of Velenus is thus. "Since errors are often fabricated about recent deeds, concerning both distant and disturbed times, could not flatterers of the Roman Curia fabricate the coming of Peter to Rome, his passion and pontificate?"

But if Irenaeus, Tertullian, Eusebius and thirty or forty other cited Fathers were flatterers of the Roman Curia, Velenus speaks rightly. But if it is the contrary then Velenus would be lying. In regard to Irenaeus and Tertullian, they are very ancient, and in their times the Roman Church was not yet so opulent that it could even have flatterers. Some were Greeks, as Eusebius, Theodoret, Sozomen and others, whose nation was rather more of the habit to envy than make obeisance to the Roman Church; most of them were nearly all holy men, such as Ambrose, Jerome, Augustine, Chrysostom and others, whose morals were far from the fawning of vices. Certainly then, it follows that Velenus, who calls these men flatterers of the Roman Curia, impudently lies.

Besides, the argument has no value. For errors are fabricated both from recent deeds as well as from ancient ones, when matters are carried out secretly and without witnesses, or in regard to the number of years, or like circumstances, which are easily given to oblivion. Yet, not in regard to the chief matter, as well as the substance of very famous matters, especially when, apart from the testimony of writers, there also exist stone monuments or much bronze, as in the matter on which we treat. And I have reckoned these can suffice for this disputation, from which I have received published in the famous book long ago of John of Rochester [St. John Fisher], a man of blessed memory, though I have never been able to see the book itself.[1]

---

[1] Translator's note: This book is titled: *Convulsio Calumniarum Ulrichi Veleni Minhoniensis, quibus Petrum Numquam Romae fuisse cavillatur,* and can be found in St. John Fisher's Latin Opera Omnia, published in 1597 at Metz, page 1299.

CHAPTER XII

That the Roman Pontiff Succeeds Peter in the Ecclesiastical Monarchy is Proved by Divine Law and by Reason of Succession

E have proven to this point that the Roman Pontiff succeeds Peter in the Roman episcopate; now we hasten to prove the matter on the succession to the primacy of the Universal Church. All of the heretics of our day deny this, and they especially oppose the primacy of the Roman Pontiff.[1] And before all these Nilos Cabásilas , the bishop of Thessalonica, in his book against the primacy of the Pope.

Nilus, however, does not deny that Peter was the pastor of the whole Church and that he managed the episcopate at Rome until his death, but contends this alone, that the Roman Pontiff does not succeed Peter in command of the whole Catholic Church, but only in the Roman episcopate. He adds that, afterward, a certain Roman Pontiff had first place in the decree of councils that he should be the first of bishops, the first to sit, the first to give his teaching; still, not that he should command the rest.

Now since the arguments of our adversaries are such that they are taken from the same fonts and chapters, we shall reduce all disputation to a few points or kinds of arguments and together we will prove the truth and refute the objections of others. First, it will be proved that the Roman Pontiff succeeds Peter in the Pontificate of the Universal Church, by divine law and reason of succession. Someone ought to succeed Peter by divine law: he cannot be any other than the Roman Pontiff therefore, he succeeds.

John Calvin denies each part of the argument. He argues: "Were I to concede what they ask with regard to Peter that he was the Prince of the Apostles and surpassed the others in dignity, there is no ground for making a universal rule out of a special example, or wresting a single fact into a perpetual enactment."[2] And again: "I will now bestow on them another [concession], which they will never obtain from men of sound mind, that the primacy of the Church was so constituted in Peter that it should always remain by means of a perpetual succession. Still, how will they prove that his See was so fixed at Rome that whosoever becomes bishop of that city is to govern the whole world?"[3]

Therefore, we shall prove each separately. First that it is fitting for someone

---

[1] Luther, *de Potestate Papae*; Illyricus *Contra primatum Papae*; The Smalchadic Council in a book by the same title; John Calvin, *Instit.*, lib. 4, ch. 6 and 7; the Centuriators *in Singulis Centuriis*, at the end, ch. 7.

[2] *Instit.*, lib. 4, ch. 8, §8.

[3] *Ibid.*, § 11.

to succeed Peter in the Pontificate of the Universal Church is gathered from the end of the Pontificate. For it is certain that there is a Pope because of the Church, not a Church because of the Pope. St. Augustine says as much: "That for which we are Christians, is on account of us; that which we are put in charge of, is on your account."[4] The Church at present requires a shepherd no less than in the time of the Apostles, rather even more now, since there are more and worse Christians. For that reason, when Peter was at the point of death, the Pontificate ought not to have ceased, seeing that it had been established not for the brief time of Peter, but for the advantage of the Church. Since it remains and perseveres, as long as the Church herself remains, or certainly as long as it sojourns on earth, it also has need of one supreme pastor for care and vigilance.

Secondly, it is considered from the unity of the Church. For the Church is one and the same in every time therefore, the form of rule ought not be changed, which is the form of the commonwealth and the state. Why, if in the time of the Apostles there was one supreme ruler and head of the Church, ought there not be now?

Thirdly, from the words of the Lord in the last chapter of John: "Feed my sheep." For the duty of a shepherd is an ordinary and perpetual duty; accordingly from the nature of the thing, the office of pastor ought to endure for as long a time as the sheepfold. Moreover, the sheepfold remains and will remain, even to the end of the world; therefore, in the matter it is necessary for the successors of Peter to remain in that supreme pastoral office.

Fourthly, from the same citation, for when the Lord says to Peter: "Feed my sheep," he consigned all his sheep to him, as we showed above; not only all by reason of the citation, but even by reason of time, since Christ ought to provide for us no less than the ancients; but Peter was not always going to live in the flesh, therefore, when the Lord said to him: "Feed my sheep," he spoke to all his successors in him. Therefore, St. John Chrysostom says: "For what purpose did he shed his blood? Certainly that he should acquire these sheep, whose care he consigned both to Peter and the successors of Peter."[5] And St. Leo says: "The disposition of truth remains, and blessed Peter, persevering in that strength of the rock which he had received, did not leave behind the governance of the Church that he had received. Obviously Peter perseveres and lives in his successors."[6] And St. Peter, the Bishop of Ravenna, in his epistle to Eutychus

---

[4] *De Pastoribus*, ch. 1.

[5] *De Sacerdotio*, lib. 2, near the beginning.

[6] Serm 2, *de anniversario assumptionis suae ad Pontificatum*.

says: "St. Peter, who lives in and is in charge of his own see, furnishes truth to those seeking the faith."

Fifthly, the Church is one body, and has its own head on earth apart from Christ, as is clear from 1 Corinthians 12. After Paul said the Church is one body, he adds: "The head cannot say to the feet 'you are not necessary to me;'" which certainly does not agree to Christ. He can say to all of yours, you are not necessary to me, no other head can be assigned there apart from Peter; nor ought the body of the Church to remain without a head with the death of Peter; therefore, it is necessary that someone should succeed Peter.

Sixthly, in the Old Testament there was a succession of high priests. For Eleazar succeeded Aaron,[7] and Phineas succeeded Eleazar,[8] and thus the rest. But the priesthood of the Old Testament was a figure of the priesthood of the New Testament; therefore, succession ought to be preserved in the see of Peter, the first and greatest of Christian bishops.

Next, all arguments whereby it is proved in the second question that the rule of the Church ought to be a monarchy, also prove this which we are now treating.

Moreover, that this successor of Peter should be the Roman Pontiff, can easily be proved. There never is or was one who asserted that he is the successor of Peter by any other way, or that he should be taken for such, apart from being the Bishop of Rome and Antioch. Yet, notwithstanding, the Bishop of Antioch does not succeed Peter in the Pontificate of the whole Church, for one does not succeed unless the place is yielded, either through natural death, or through legitimate death, that is, deposition or renunciation. But while Peter was still living and managing the Pontificate, he relinquished the Antiochene Church and set up his seat at Rome, as we proved in a question above. Therefore, it remains that the Roman Bishop, who succeeded Peter after he died in the city of Rome, succeeds to the same in its whole dignity and power.

Besides, if the bishop of Antioch succeeded Peter in the supreme Pontificate, it would be the first Church. But in the council of Nicaea, Canon 6, they declared the bishop of Antioch to be in the third place, not the first or second, just as it had always been, nor did the bishops of Antioch ever seek a higher place.

In order that this whole matter might be better understood, a few things must be observed. First, succession is one thing, while the cause of the succession is another. The succession of the Roman Pontiff into the pontificate of Peter is from the establishment of Christ; moreover, the cause of the

---

[7] Numbers 20:28.

[8] Judges 20:27-28.

succession whereby the Roman Pontiff, instead of the bishop of Antioch or someone else should succeed, has its beginning in the act of Peter. I say the succession itself was established by Christ, and is of divine law, because Christ himself established in Peter a pontificate that was going to endure even to the end of the world, and hence, whoever succeeds Peter, receives the pontificate of Christ.

But on the other hand, because the bishop of Rome, since he is the bishop of Rome, becomes the successor of Peter, he has his origin in the act of Peter, not from the first establishment of Christ. For Peter could have chosen no particular see for himself, just as he did in the first five years, and then were he to die, neither the bishop of Rome nor Antioch would succeed him, but he whom the Church would choose for itself. Peter could have always remained at Antioch, and then without a doubt the bishop of Antioch would have succeeded, but since he set up his seat at Rome, and held it even to death, thence it came to pass that the Roman Pontiff succeeded him.

Now, because Pope St. Marcellus writes in his epistle to the Antiochenes that Peter came to Rome at the Lord's command, as well as many other Fathers[9] that Peter endured martyrdom at Rome by Christ's command: it is not improbable that the Lord openly commanded that Peter should so set up his seat at Rome that the Roman bishop should absolutely succeed him. Yet, whatever the truth of that, at least the cause of the succession is not from the first establishment of the pontificate, which is read in the Gospel.

The second thing that must be observed, (although perhaps it may not be of divine law) is that the Roman Pontiff, because he is the Roman Pontiff, succeeds Peter in the rule of the whole Church; still, if anyone absolutely should ask whether the Roman Pontiff should be the pastor and head of the whole Church by divine law, it must altogether be asserted. For on this point nothing else is required than that the succession itself should be of divine law; this is that the ordinary office of governing the whole Church with supreme power is not from men, but was established immediately by God; besides, this was proven above.

Thirdly, it must be observed, although by chance it might not be by divine law, that the Roman Pontiff as Roman Pontiff succeeds Peter, nevertheless it pertains to Catholic faith. It is not the same thing, for something to be *de fide*, and to be by divine law. It was not by divine law that Paul had a cloak; still this

---

[9] Ambrose, *In oratione contra Auxentium*; Athanasius, *Apologia pro fuga sua*, etc.

is *de fide* that Paul had a cloak.[10] Although that the Roman Pontiff succeeds Peter may not be expressly contained in the Scriptures, nevertheless that *someone* succeeds Peter is deduced evidently from the Scriptures; that it is the Roman Pontiff is contained in the Apostolic Tradition of Peter, the same tradition declared by the general Councils, the decrees of Pontiffs, and the consensus of the Fathers, as we will show a little later.

The last thing which must be observed is that the bishop of Rome and the rule of the universal Church are not two Episcopates, nor two seats, except in power. For Peter was established as Pontiff of the whole Church by Christ, he did not add to himself the episcopate of the city of Rome, in the manner whereby the bishop of some place might add to himself another bishopric, or canonry, or abbacy; rather, he carried the episcopate of the city of Rome to the supreme Pontificate of the whole world, in the same way that a simple episcopacy is raised into an archepiscopate, or a patriarchate. Therefore, the archbishop or patriarch is not twice or three times a bishop, but only once, and in the sign of this affair, no more than one pallium is given to the Supreme Pontiff, even if he is a bishop, archbishop, patriarch and Supreme Pontiff. All these are one in act, and merely many things in power.

From which it follows that one who is chosen as the bishop of Rome, in the very matter becomes supreme Pontiff of the whole Church, even if by chance the electors do not express it. But now we shall respond to the objections of Nilos Cabásilas and Calvin.

The first objection of Nilos: "The Roman Pontiff has primacy from the Fathers because that city ruled the whole world, as we read in the Council of Chalcedon, action 16. Therefore, he does not have a perpetual succession from Peter." I respond: That decree was illegitimate, and was made by those protesting who presided over the Council. We will speak much more of this in Chapter 27.

The second objection of Nilos: "The Roman Pontiff is not an Apostle, but merely a bishop; as such, Apostles do not ordain Apostles, but pastors and teachers: therefore, the Roman Pope does not succeed Peter in apostolic power, which was over every Church, but only in the particular episcopate of Rome.

I respond: In the apostolate three things are contained. Firstly, that one who is an Apostle should be immediately a minister of the word, so that he should be taught by God himself, and can write holy books; and we affirm that this is not appropriate to the Roman Pontiff. Indeed it is not necessary that he should

---

[10] 2 Timothy 4:13 [This rather puzzling statement can be understood in that, because it is recorded in Scripture that Paul had a cloak, then it is *de fide* that he had one, although the matter is otherwise trivial. -Translator's note].

have new revelations daily, and write new holy books. Secondly, that one who is an Apostle should constitute the Church and propagate the faith in those places where it never was. Now this does pertain to the Roman Pontiff, which both reason and experience itself teach us. For, from apostolic times, those who founded Churches in different parts of the world, and still found them, were Roman Pontiffs. Thirdly, that one who is an Apostle should have supreme power over every Church, and we contend this also pertains to the Roman Pontiff, for this reason: because he succeeds Peter, in whom this power is ordinary, not delegated, as in the other Apostles.

Nor does Nilos Cabásilas conclude the argument when he says that Apostles do not constitute other Apostles, but pastors. The Apostles ought not create the Roman Pontiff as Pontiff of the whole Church, or Apostolic Pontiff, since Christ himself did this. This is why the seat of the Roman Pontiff is always called by all the Fathers the "Apostolic See," and in the Council of Chalcedon itself in the first action, which Nilos cites, the dignity of the Pope of Rome is called "The apostolate", and in the sixteenth action his see is called "Apostolic."

The third objection. "Peter was pastor and teacher of the whole world, but the Pope is and was only called the bishop of the city of Rome." I respond: That is false, and it can be seen from the Council of Chalcedon itself, omitting the rest. For in the third action, three epistles of the Eastern bishops to Leo are read, and in all Leo is called "Pope of the universal Church", and the same name is contained in the sixteenth action.

The fourth objection: "Peter ordained bishops at Antioch and Alexandria; but that is not permitted to the Roman Pope." I respond: Although in this time the obstinacy of the Greeks does not allow it, nevertheless this was formerly permitted to the Roman Pontiff. For in the Council of Chalcedon, seventh action, we read that Maximus, the bishop of Antioch, was received by the Council because he had been confirmed by Pope St. Leo. Liberatus and John Zonara[11] also write that Anthimus the bishop of Constantinople was deposed by Pope Agapitus, and in his place, Menas was ordained by the same Pope. But we will have many things to say about this in its proper place.

The fifth objection. "Whatever Peter said or wrote is an oracle of the Holy Spirit. But this is not fitting to the office of Pope. Therefore, the Pope does not have all the prerogatives of Peter." I respond: We do not contend that point.

The sixth objection: "It was said to Peter without condition, 'Whatever you bind will be bound, etc.' But Peter commanded the Roman Pope that he will only bind that or loose what rightly must be bound or loosed." I respond: Nothing is

---

[11] Liberatus, *Breviarium*, ch. 21; Joannes Zonaras *in Justiniano.*

proved by this argument other than Nilos was truly a Greek, that is, trifling and loquacious. Who ever heard that it was permitted to Peter to bind what should not rightly be bound? And where is that prescription of Peter to a Pope contained which Nilos advances?

Calvin objects firstly: "It does not follow that if Peter was in charge of twelve Apostles in the beginning that now someone ought to be in charge of the whole world, for a few may easily and advantageously be ruled by one man, but many thousands cannot be governed unless it is by many."[12]

I respond: In the first place, Peter was not merely in charge of the twelve Apostles, but also many thousands of Christians. In the last chapter of John, Christ consigned to Peter all his sheep, not merely the twelve Apostles. Moreover, we read in Acts 2 that the sheep of Peter increased to three thousand, and in Acts 4 to five thousand in Jerusalem alone. Thereupon, in a place where there are many men, so much more do they require one ruler, by whom they should be contained in unity. But this was spoken of at length in the first question.

Secondly, Calvin objects in the same place: "If therefore, the seat of the supreme pontificate is at Rome, because Peter the Apostle died there while managing the pontificate; therefore, the seat of the Jewish pontificate should always have been in the desert, because there Moses and Aaron died while managing their pontificate: and the pontifical see of Christians ought to be in Jerusalem, because there Christ, the High Priest [*summus Pontifex*] died."[13]

I respond, from the foregoing, the pontifical seat is not at Rome for the reason that Peter died there, but because he was the bishop of Rome, and he never transferred the seat from Rome to another place. Moses and Aaron, on the other hand, did not set up a seat in the desert, but died there while they were on a journey. Furthermore, Christ did not set up a seat at Jerusalem, nor in any particular place, as we said above.

The third objection of Calvin is from the same place: "This privilege concerning the primacy of the whole Church is either local, or personal, or mixed. If the first, then it was conceded once at Antioch; it cannot be taken from there, even if Peter left there and died somewhere else. If the second, therefore, it has nothing to do with place and Rome has no more right to the pontificate than any other city. If the third, then it does not suffice for this to be the bishop of Rome that someone should have the primacy. For if it is a privilege partly local, partly personal, it is not given to a place except for a time in which such

---

[12] *Instit.*, lib. 4, ch. 6, § 8.

[13] *Ibid.*, § 11.

a person is there, namely Peter."[14]

I respond: when it was first established by Christ the pontifical dignity was personal; nevertheless, by a deed of Peter, it was made afterward local, or rather mixed, not without divine assent. I say it was personal in the beginning, because it was not bound to any particular place by Christ, but absolutely conferred to the person of Peter: thus, although I affirm it was personal, still it was public, not private.

Personal privileges are said to be private which are given to some person merely for himself, but public privileges are those which are given for oneself and his successors. Still, since Peter set up his seat at Rome, it came to pass that this privilege was also local, and hence mixed. For it is bound to the city of Rome, as long as the successors of Peter retain the seat at Rome. For if the seat were to be transferred by divine law, then the Roman bishops would no longer be the bishops of the whole Church. If the seat itself were to be transferred, I say, so that those who are now Roman Pontiffs would be called bishops of some other place. Furthermore, it is not said that the seat is transferred if the Pontiffs are merely absent from the city. Whereas these have been said hypothetically, we do not believe it is ever going to happen that the seat of Peter will be transferred to another place.

The fourth objection of Calvin is from the same place. "If the Roman Pontiff, because he succeeds Peter, is the first bishop, then Ephesus ought to be second, Jerusalem third, and thus for the rest: but we see that Alexandria was second, where no one succeeded an Apostle; Ephesus could not even cling to the outermost corner."[15]

I respond: The order and number of the patriarchal sees does not depend upon the dignity of the first bishops, otherwise there would not be three, rather twelve for the number of Apostles; but solely from the dignity and will of Peter, as we showed above from Anacletus, Leo and Gregory on the third question on the prerogatives of Peter.

The fifth objection of Calvin is from the same book: "If the words which are said to Peter are also understood for his successors, then the Roman Pontiffs affirm that they are all Satans. For this was also said to Peter in Matthew 16, in the same place where it was said: 'To you I give the keys of the kingdom of heaven.'"[16]

I respond: The words which are said to Peter differ in a threefold manner;

---

[14]   *Ibid.,* § 12.

[15]   *Ibid.,* § 13.

[16]   Lib. 4, ch. 7, § 28.

some are said to him in regard to him alone, some in regard to him and all Christians, some in regard to him and his successors. Now that which is evidently gathered to have been said to him was for a different purpose. For those which are said to him, as to one from all the faithful, are certainly understood about all the faithful, as in Matthew 18 "If your brother will have sinned against you, etc." Those which are said for the purpose of his own proper person are said to him alone, such as: "Get behind me Satan," and "You will deny me three times." These were said due to his own imbecility and ignorance. At length, those which are said to him by reason of his pastoral office which hence are understood for all pastors, such as: "Feed my sheep," and "Confirm your brethren," and "Whatsoever you will have bound, etc."

Luther's arguments are mere trifles, and can easily be answered from the foregoing: and besides, they were carefully answered by Eck, Fabro, St. John Fisher and Cajetan, whose books are in everyone's hands; therefore, I pass them over.

CHAPTER XIII

That the Roman Pontiff Succeeds Peter in the Ecclesiastical Monarchy is proven from Councils

THE PRIMACY of the Roman Pontiff must be proved in the second place from councils. Indeed Luther,[1] Illyricus,[2] and Calvin[3] say that the Sixth Canon of the Council of Nicaea opposes us, in which a certain region is assigned to the Roman Pontiff to govern, and at that a scanty region. He is declared to be just one of the patriarchs, but not the head of the others; moreover, they could not discover the testimony of any council on our behalf. Just the same, there are as illustrious testimonies as there could be of the general councils for the primacy of the Roman Pontiff, from which nine were general, as in them, Latins and Greeks were present (with respect to which it must be remarked against the trifling and obstinacy of the Greeks).

First we have the Council of Nicaea, and that Sixth Canon which our adversaries are using to object, but this canon requires some explanation in order that the argument can be taken up from there. The Sixth Canon of Nicaea is thus held in the volumes of the councils which today are extant: "Let the most ancient custom endure in Egypt, or Lybia, and Pentapolis, that the bishop of Alexandria should have power over all of these, because at least the bishop of Rome also has a like custom."

Some things must be noted about this canon. First, from Nicholas I, in a letter to [the emperor] Michael, the Council of Nicaea stated nothing about the Roman Church, because its power is not from men but from God. Rather, it only constituted the state of other Churches according to the form of the Roman Church. Therefore, the Council does not say: "Let the bishop of Rome have administration of this or that region, but says: "Let the bishop of Alexandria have care of Egypt and Lybia, because the bishop of Rome is so accustomed." Obviously, the Roman Church should be the rule of the others, and nothing is stated about her properly. Therefore, Calvin, Illyricus, Nilos Cabásilas and the rest err when they say that certain boundaries were assigned to the bishop of Rome, that without a doubt he should only have care of the suburban Churches.

Secondly, it must be observed that the beginning of this canon is missing in the ordinary books, which is thus: "The Roman Church always has primacy, moreover let the custom endure, etc." Thus this canon is cited in the Council of Chalcedon, Act 16, by the bishop Paschasinus. Thus also it is altered in the

---

[1] *De Potestate Papae.*

[2] *Contra primatum.*

[3] *Instit.* lib. 4, ch. 7, § 1.

Greek about a thousand years ago by Dionisius, a certain abbot, as Alan Copus records in the first Dialogue. For that reason, in the same council of Chalcedon, Act 16, after a reading of this canon, namely the Sixth Canon of Nicaea, the judges said: "We carefully assess all the primacy and particular honor, according to the canons, preserved by our God-loving Archbishop of old Rome."

A third thing must be observed; the words "Because the bishop of Rome has such a custom," is usually explained in four ways. Firstly, as Ruffinus explains, the council decreed that the bishop of Alexandria should have care of Egypt, just as the bishop of Rome has care of the suburban Churches.[4]

But it is a false exposition, for if the bishop of Rome is the first and particular Patriarch, how believable is it that he is assigned a very narrow region, while to lesser patriarchs a very broad one is assigned? For Antioch had the whole East, and Alexandria three vast provinces, Egypt, Lybia and Pentapolis, but Rome would have had only the churches around the city that is six episcopates near to Rome. Next, that conjunction *because* [*quoniam*], is a measurable part of speech, but it is not a good cause for asserting that the bishop of Alexandria would have care of three provinces, because the Roman bishop has care of the churches near the city. Therefore, either the reasoning of the council avails to nothing, or Ruffinus did not correctly explain the opinion of the council. Finally, the churches around the city are not mentioned in the Council of Nicaea, neither as it is cited in the sixth Council of Carthage, nor as it is read in the Sixteenth Act of the Council of Chalcedon, nor as it is contained in its own place in the volumes of Councils, or even as it is with Abbot Dionysius, rather it says, "Let the most ancient custom endure in Egypt, or Lybia, and Pentapolis that the bishop of Alexandria should have power over all of these, because at least the bishop of Rome also has a like custom." Therefore, the opinion of Ruffinus is just pure divination, which Calvin follows, on the churches near the city.

The second explanation is of Theodore Balsamon,[5] in his explanation of these canons, as well as in the book of Nilos Cabásilas against the Primacy that the council decreed that the bishop of Alexandria should have care of all of Egypt, just as the bishop of Rome has care of the whole west.

This opinion is certainly more generous, but nevertheless false. For when the Council says: "Because the bishop of Rome has such a custom," it gives the

---

[4] *Hist. Ecclesiast.*, lib. 10, ch. 6.

[5] Translator's note: Theodore Balsamon was a Greek Orthodox Canonist in the 13th century. Bellarmine could only have read his works in Latin translation, since the Greek edition did not appear until 1615, nearly 30 years after he had composed the Controversies.

reasoning as we said about why the ancient custom ought to remain in Egypt, Libya and Pentapolis, because the bishop of Alexandria should have care of those places. Moreover, that the bishop of Rome has care of the west is not the origin of this affair. How does it follow that the bishop of Rome has care of the west, therefore, Alexandria ought to have care of Egypt, Libya and Pentapolis? Or why will the bishop of Alexandria, and not of Carthage, or someone else have care of it? Add, that the Council does not mention the West, nor the East, but it only says: "Because the bishop of Rome has such a custom."

The third explanation is of the great historian of the councils. He reckons from some ancient codex that in place of the phrase we have, "Because the bishop of Rome has such a custom," the phrase, "Because a metropolitan has such a custom" should be restored in place of it.

Yet this is not a solid explanation either. There are no better copies extant of the Council of Nicaea than those possessed by the ancient Roman Pontiffs, as we will show below when we will treat on titles; for the copies which were in Greek, were thoroughly burnt by the Arians, as St. Athanasius witnesses in his epistles to all the orthodox bishops; and therefore, it is no wonder if those which are cited by the Greeks and Ruffinus are mutilated and corrupted. Next, those contained by the Roman Church are the ones from which bishop Paschasinus brought as a legate to the Council of Chalcedon for Pope St. Leo, where this canon was read to the council, and likewise we read there: "Because the bishop of Rome has such a custom." Add that it is not good reasoning why the bishop of Alexandria ought to have such power that the metropolitans had such a custom. For metropolitans do not rule more than one province, and Alexandria had many provinces, and many metropolitans were subject to it.

Then the fourth explanation is the true one, that Alexandria ought to govern those provinces, because the bishop of Rome was so accustomed, that is, because the bishop of Rome customarily permitted the bishop of Alexandria to rule Egypt, Lybia and Pentapolis before the definition of any council; or it was his custom to govern those provinces through the bishop of Alexandria. Nicholas I understood this canon in that way in his epistle to the Empoeror Michael, nor does any other probable explanation appear.

The First General Council of Constantinople, in its letter to Damasus, which is extant in Theodoret,[6] says that it met in the city of Constantinople, from the command of the letter of the Pope, sent to it through the Emperor. And in the same place, it affirms that the Roman Church is the head, and it is among the members.

---

[6]   Theodoret, *Hist.*, lib. 5, ch. 9.

The Council of Ephesus, as it is found in Evagrius,[7] says that it deposed Nestorius by a command of a letter of the Roman Pope Celestine. Also, in the letter to the same Celestine, the same Council writes that it did not dare to judge the case of John, the Patriarch of Antioch, which was more dubious than the case of Nestorious, thus it reserved its judgment for Celestine. All of which especially indicates the supreme authority of the Roman Pontiff. The Council of Chalcedon, in Acts 1, 2, and 3, and in numerous other places, calls St. Leo, "Pontiff of the universal Church." And in an epistle to Leo: "And after all these things, and against him that was consigned care of the vineyard by the Savior, he extended insanity, that is, against your Apostolic Sanctity." You see that this great council confesses that the Roman Pontiff was consigned care of the vineyard by God himself, that is, of the Universal Church.

The Council of Constantinople, which was gathered before the Fifth Council on the case of Antimus, so speaks in Act 4 through Menas, the Patriarch of the Council: "We follow and obey the Apostolic See. We hold those communicating with it as communicating with us, and we likewise condemn those condemned by it." Now, if the whole Council professes itself to obey the Apostolic see, certainly the Apostolic see is over the whole Church with authority.

The Third Council of Constantinople, in Act 2, receives and approves the epistle of Pope Adrian to Tharasius, in which these words are contained: "Whose seat, it is becoming that it obtains primacy over the whole world and as the head arises over every Church of God; from where even the blessed Apostle Peter himself, feeding the Church by a command of God, altogether overlooks nothing, rather obtained and obtains supremacy everywhere, etc." Mark that it is said in the present: "it is becoming that it obtains the primacy;" and "As the head arises, etc."

The third Lateran Council under Innocent III, in which the Greeks and Latins were present, says in Chapter 5, "The Roman Church, by a dispensation of the Lord, obtains supremacy of ordinary power over all others, inasmuch as she is the mother and teacher of all the faithful of Christ." The General Council of Lyons under Gregory X, calls the bishop of Rome the Vicar of Christ, the Successor of Peter, the Ruler of the Universal Church, and in this council both Greeks and Latins were present.[8]

Next, the Council of Florence stated with the agreement of both Greeks and Latins, "We define that the holy Apostolic See and the Roman Pontiff hold primacy over the whole world, and the Roman Pontiff himself is the successor

---

[7] Evagrius, *Hist.*, lib. 1, ch. 4.

[8] VI, tit. De Electione, cap. *Ubi Periculum.*

of St. Peter, the Prince of the Apostles, and the true vicar of Christ, and is the head of the whole Church, as well as the Father of all Christians, and is proven to be a teacher, for our Lord Jesus Christ handed full power to him in the person of St. Peter to feed, rule and govern the universal Church." I omit five other general councils because the Greeks do not receive them, since they were not present, nor do the Lutherans since they were celebrated after the year 600.[9]

---

[9] These are Lyons, under Innocent IV, as is contained in the first Chapter *de Homicidio* in the Sixth; the Council of Vienne under Clement V, as is contained in *Clementina Unica, de summa Trinitate et fide Catholica.* Constance, sess. 8 and 15; Lateran V under Leo X, sess. 11, and the Council of Trent, sess. 14, ch. 7, and other places.

CHAPTER XIV

That the Roman Pontiff Succeeds Peter in the Ecclesiastical Monarchy is proven from the Testimonies of the Supreme Pontiffs

E take up the third argument from the teachings of the Supreme Pontiffs. It must be observed that the epistles of the Pontiffs can be distributed as though they were in three classes.

The first class contains epistles of the Pontiffs who sat to the year 300, in which the Centuriators and Calvin profess that truly the primacy is asserted and these Popes were saints and true Pontiffs, but they say their epistles were contrived and recent, as well as falsely ascribed to those Pontiffs.

The second class embraces the epistles of those Popes, who sat from the year 600 even to our times, in which our adversaries confess that truly the primacy was asserted and they were the authors of these in which they are entitled, but those Pontiffs were not worthy in regard to faith, and were pseudo-pontiffs, not true Pontiffs.

The third class takes up those epistles in which the primacy is openly asserted, and which it is certain were written by saints and true Pontiffs, who flourished from the year 300 to the year 600, namely Julius I, Damasus Siricius, Innocent I, Sozomen, Leo the Great, Gelasius, Anastasius II, John II, Felix IV, Pelagius II, and Gregory the Great. Therefore, in the testimonies of the first and second class, we will not devote attention to quotes, but it will be enough to mark the citations in parentheses and respond to the objections of the heretics; whenever they affirm in those epistles that our opinion is clearly asserted. The quotes will only be conveyed in the testimonies of the third class.

First: These holy Pontiffs openly assert the Primacy: Clement (Epistle 1) Anacletus (Epist. 3), Evaristus (Epist. 1), Alexander (Epist. 1), Pius I (Epist. 1 and 2), Anicetis (Epist. 1), Victor (Epist. 1), Zephyrinus (Epist. 1), Calixtus (Epist. 2), Lucius (Epist. 1), Marcellus (Epist. 1), Eusebius (Epist. 3), Melchiades (Epist. 1), Marcus, (Epist. 1).

To these testimonies they make no response except to say that they are recent and not genuine. But although I would not deny that some errors have crept into them, nor would I dare to affirm that they are indisputable, still certainly I have no doubt whatsoever that they are very ancient. Thus the Centuriators lie when they say that no worthy author before the times of Charlemagne cited these epistles.[1] For Isidore, who is two hundred years older than Charlemagne, says that by the counsel of 80 bishops he gathered the canons from the epistles of Clement, Anacletus, Evaristus, and the rest of the

---

[1] *Cent 2*, ch. 7, towards the end.

Roman Pontiffs. Likewise, the Council of Vasense, Can. 6, cites the letters of Clement just as they exist now and they are also cited by a council celebrated in the time of Leo I, that is, 350 years before the empire of Charlemagne. Lastly Ruffinus, who preceded Charlemagne by four hundred years, in a preface to the recognitions of Clement which he translated from Greek, recalls also the epistles of Clement to James, and says that he translated them out of Greek himself. Further, this version is truly of Ruffinus, as Gennadius witnesses.[2]

In the second class are the following Popes: Adrian I (epistle to Tharasius), Nicholas I (epistle to the Emperor Michael), Leo IX (epistle to Michael the bishop of Constantinople), Paschal I (epistle to bishop Panormitanus), Innocent III (Epistle to the Emperor of Constantinople). All of these avowedly and in earnest teach that the Roman Pontiff is over the whole Church.

Our adversaries respond to these by saying all these Pontiffs were Antichrists. Now we will refute this in a later question.[3] Meanwhile, we say this alone; if these Pontiffs were Antichrists, the whole Church would have perished, by nearly a thousand years; it is certain from the histories that the universal Church adhered to these Pontiffs and followed their teaching. But if the Church perished then Christ lied when he said in Matthew 16 that the gates of hell were not going to prevail against the Church. But on this we have said enough in the questions on the Church. Let us come to the third class, and we advance the twelve best and holiest Popes.

The first is St. Julius I, who in his epistle to the Oriental bishops,[4] speaks thus: "Why are you ignorant of the fact that it is customary that first it should be written to us so that what is just can be defined from here? For which reason, if a crime of this kind had been conceived against a bishop, it ought to be referred to our Church... What we received from blessed Peter the Apostle I signify to you; and I should not have written this, as deeming that these things were manifest to everyone, had not these proceedings so disturbed us."

In these words St. Julius affirms that the duty of judging the cases of bishops pertains to him, even in the East, although they are primary patriarchs (for he treats on the case of St. Athanasius the Patriarch of Alexandria); and this right he received from St. Peter, which is known to everyone. What response, I ask, can be made? The author is a saint, and very ancient; the epistle certain and the whole written down by St. Athanasius; and at length his words are clear and eloquent.

---

[2] *De viris illustribus*, in Ruffino.

[3] See Book III. -Translator's note.

[4] Which is extant in *Apologia Contra Arianos*, ch. 2, No 30.

The second is St. Damasus, who, in a letter to all the Eastern bishops, which Theodoret relates,[5] says: "Because your charity distributed the reverence due to the Apostolic seat, you most beloved sons excel, as many of you as there are." There, he recognized that due reverence and calls all the bishops sons. Likewise in Epistle 4 to the bishops of Numidia: "Do not cease to bring all those things which are in some doubt to us, just as to the head, as has always been the custom."

The third witness is St. Syricius, in an epistle to Himericus, the bishop of Tarragona, which Calvin also confesses is truly of Syricius: "For consideration of our duty, it is not for us to feign, nor to take the liberty to be silent, in which a zeal greater than all of the Christian religion depends upon. We bear the burdens of all who are weighed down. Indeed St. Peter carries these things among us, who protects and guards us as his heirs in all things, as we trust in his administration." And below that in Chapter 15: "We have explained, I believe, beloved brother, all the things which were set forth as being at issue, and we provided suitable replies to the individual cases that you relate tot he Roman Church, as to the head of your body, through our son the priest Bassianus." Next he commands the bishop that he would direct these, his decrees, to all other bishops.

The fourth is St. Zosimus, in an epistle to Hesychius the bishop of Solons: "We have chiefly directed these writings to you so that you will see to it that notice is given to all the brethren, our bishops ... Let each one know this, that laying aside the authority of the Fathers and of the Apostolic See, he will have disregarded that which we have defended in earnest; if he thinks he can attempt this after so many prohibitions, he should scarcely doubt that it is inconsistent in his regard with the rule of his see."

The fifth is St. Innocent I, in his epistle to the bishops of Macedonia: "Turn to the Apostolic seat, the relation to which, just as to the head of the Church, they did run, being sent when injury was done, etc."[6] Likewise, in an epistle to the Council of Miletus, which is among the epistles of St. Augustine, he says: "Diligently and agreeably consult the Apostolic honor. To the honor of that which is apart from those which are on the outside, care remains of all the churches; they followed the ancient form of the rule which you know is always kept throughout the world." Likewise, in an epistle to the Council of Carthage, which is 91, he says the Roman see is the *font and head of all churches.*

To this the Centuriators make no response, except that Innocent arrogates

---

[5] *Hist.* Lib. 5, ch. 10.

[6] *Epist. 22* ad Episcopos Macedonia.

too much for himself. For which reason, they contumaciously call him Nocentius.[7] But if that is so, why do the Fathers not condemn this error of Innocent? What does Augustine say about these two letters of Innocent: "He wrote on all things to us in the same manner, in which it was lawful, and also fitting for a bishop of the Apostolic see"?[8] Why does Augustine appeal to the "blessed memory" of Innocent in the same place?

Sixth is St. Leo. Because Luther and Calvin say the ancient Pontiffs had no authority outside of the West, we bring to bear the testimonies of Leo, in which the primacy is asserted and shown that the Pontiff exercised jurisdiction in that time in Greece, Asia, Egypt and Africa. Therefore, in Epistle 84 to Anastasius, the bishop of Thessalonika, he says: "That you too, just like your predecessors, should receive from us in our turn authority, we give our consent and earnestly exhort that no concealment and no negligence may be allowed in the management of the churches situated throughout Illyria. We have committed this to you in our stead, following the precedent of Siricius, of blessed remembrance, who then, for the first time, acting on a certain method entrusted them to your last predecessor but one, Anysius of holy memory, who had at the time well deserved of the Apostolic See that he might render assistance to the churches situated in that province which he wished kept up to discipline. ... We have so trusted your charity in our stead that you should be called into part of the care, but not in the fullness of power." At the end, where he had said that bishops, archbishops and primates were constituted with great providence, he adds: "Through which care of the universal Church flows to the one See of Peter, and should never be separated from the head." From this, not only the Primacy, but even the authority of Leo appears in the churches of Greece.

The same Leo, in his letter to Anatholus, the Bishop of Constantinople, said, "To you resident, in whom the execution of our disposition we enjoin, etc."[9] You see that he commanded the Patriarch of Constantinople. He also says, in Letter 62 to Maximus, the Patriarch of Antioch, advising him, that the latter frequently writes to him about what should be done concerning the churches. Leo writes in the same place: "Juvenal, the bishop, believed it could suffice for him to obtain rule of the province of Palestine. Cyril, of holy memory, rightly trembling at the fact, demanded much careful prayer that no approbation should be offered to illicit attempts, etc." You see how the Patriarch of Alexandria begged Leo, lest

---

[7] *Innocens, innocentis* should be obvious in English, it is the negation of *nocentius,* which means guilty one. -Translator's note.

[8] *Epistola 106 ad Paulinum.*

[9] *Epistola 46, Anatholl. Episc. Constantinop.*

he would permit Palestine to be subject to Juvenal? And when this province looked to the Patriarchate of Antioch, why did Cyril not rather seek the aid of the patriarch of Antioch than Leo?

Leo further writes to Dioscorus, the Patriarch of Alexandria: "What we know our fathers preserved with greater care we wish you also to safeguard, etc." Here we see Leo commands the Patriarch of the whole of Egypt and Lybia. Again, in Epistle 87 to the bishops of Africa: "What we suffer, no matter how venial, cannot remain altogether unpunished, if anyone should presume to usurp that which we forbid... there we command the case of Bishop Lupicinus to be heard." Therefore, Leo commanded the bishops of Greece, Asia, Egypt, and Africa. There are also extant letters to the bishops of Germany, France, Spain and Italy in which he clearly understands that he is their judge and head.

Lastly, in his first sermon he addresses the city of Rome thus: "By the holy Seat of Blessed Peter, head of the world, you were set up to preside over divine religion more extensively than earthly dominion. Although increased by many victories, the right of your empire you brought by earth and sea; still, has bellicose labor not supplied less to you than what Christian peace has subjected?"[10] What could be more clear?

Calvin responds to all these citations in two ways.[11] Firstly, he says that Leo was greedy beyond limit for glory and domination, and that many resisted his ambition. He cites proof of it in the margin of his Epistle 85.

But in that epistle, no such thing exists, nor do we discover in any of his epistles any who resisted St. Leo, with the exception of one French bishop named Hilary. This is only read in Epistle 89 of Pope Leo that this bishop wished to withdraw from obedience to the Apostolic See; nevertheless, we read in the same place that he came to Rome to make his case and was convicted in a council, and punished.

On the other hand, among the epistles of Leo are extant epistles to him from different councils, bishops and emperors, and specifically the epistles of the bishops of France, in which his piety and authority are wonderfully praised. I do not believe that there was anyone before Luther and Calvin who condemned St. Leo for pride and ambition.

Calvin responds in the second place: "Leo did not usurp the jurisdiction over other bishops, but as much as he interposed himself to settle their quarrels, so also the law and nature of ecclesiastical communion suffered." He attempts to prove this from the same epistle of Leo (84), where it seems as though he

---

[10] *Serm. I, de Natali Apostl.*

[11] *Instit., lib. 4, ch. 7 § 11.*

commands bishops; in fact Leo says that he would have it that all the privileges of metropolitans were preserved, as if he were to say that he advises from piety, to relinquish authority to those whom it belongs.

But if that is so then he was not more greedy of glory and domination, nor was he accused of ambition. Thereupon, the very words of Leo cited above teach clearly enough that he truly and clearly commanded bishops with authority.

Moreover, the fact that he would have it that the laws of the metropolitans be preserved does nothing to impede our case. For he wished them to be so preserved that at the same time they might be subject to the Apostolic See, and its Vicar. He says as much in the same epistle: "Therefore, according to the canons of the holy Fathers fashioned in the Spirit of God and consecrated in reverence of the whole world, metropolitan bishops of individual provinces, in which our care of your fraternity is extended by delegation, the right of antiquity of the dignity handed down for it we determine to hold undefiled, so that by predetermined rules they might withdraw neither by negligence, nor by presumption... If by chance, among those who are in charge of greater parts, were a case to arise from sins that cannot be defined by a provincial examination (which may God forbid!), the metropolitan will take care to instruct your fraternity on the quality of the whole business, and if in the presence of equal parties, the matter will not have been insensible in your judgment, to our understanding, let whatever it is be transferred to our examination."

The seventh is St. Gelasius. He says in an epistle, "All the churches throughout the world know that they are bound by the teachings of every Pontiff, for the See of blessed Peter the Apostle should have the right of resolving; inasmuch as he should have the sacred right to judge those matters in regard to every church, nor is it lawful for anyone to judge his judgment."[12] Nor can any response be given for these, it is certain that these are truly the words of Gelasius, and Gelasius was a holy man, who was in charge of the Church a thousand years ago.

The eighth is John II, who also sat a thousand years ago, who writes: "Among the clear praises of your wisdom and custom, O most Christian of princes, by a purer light, just as some star would twinkle, that is, by love of faith, being learned by zeal for charity you preserve the reverence for the disciplines of the Roman See, and are subject to it in regard to everything, being led to its unity, to its authority; this is the first of the Apostles, commanded by the Lord's words: 'Feed my sheep,' which is truly the head of the churches

---

[12] *Epistol. Ad Episc. Dard.*

which both the rules of the Fathers, and the statutes of princes decalre, etc."[13]

The ninth is Anastasius II, who wrote to the emperor: "Through the ministry of my humility, just as the seat of Blessed Peter is always in the universal Church, its rule should be held by yourself as designated by the Lord."[14]

The tenth is Felix IV, who wrote: "I joyfully received the writings of your sanctity, which you sent to the Apostolic Seat just as to the head that from there you would receive a response, whence every church of the whole religion takes its beginning."[15]

The eleventh is Pelagius II, who in an epistle to Eastern bishops, writes: "The Roman See, by the Lord's institution, is the head of every church."

The twelfth is St. Gregory the Great, who, no less than Leo, knew he was the Head of the whole Church. He writes in an epistle: "From the Council of Numidia, if anyone will have longed to come to the Apostolic See, permit him, and if some of them should wish to gainsay their ways, meet them."[16] From there it is clear what the authority of Gregory was in Africa. Likewise, he says in another epistle, "After the writings were directed to your beatitude, for the sake of my retirement in the cause of Honoratus the Archdeacon, that Honoratus uttered a condemned opinion on every side for his own degree is private. But if someone from the four patriarchs would so act, such contumacy could in no way pass without the gravest scandal." Certainly in these words St. Gregory obviously teaches that he was put in charge of all the patriarchs.[17]

Likewise he writes: "Know that We transferred the pallium of our brother John, the bishop of Corinth, to one that it is exceedingly fitting for you to obey." You see the authority of Gregory among the Greek bishops whereby he ordains the bishop and archbishop of Corinth by the transmission of the pallium? He also writes, "For concerning the church of Constantinople, who doubts it is subject to the Apostolic See? Or the fact that the Lord is the most pious emperor, which our brother Eusebius, bishop of the same city, assiduously professes."[18] And in Epistle 64, to the same archbishop: "For because he says he is subject to the Apostolic See, if some fault is discovered among the bishops, I

---

[13] John II, *Epist. ad Justin.*, which is contained in the Code of Justinian, Tit. 1.

[14] *Epist. ad Anastas. Imper.*

[15] *In Epist. I ad varios Episc.*

[16] Lib. 1, epist. 72 ad Gennad.

[17] Lib. 2, epist. 37, ad Natal.

[18] Lib. 7, epist. 63 ad Jo. Episc. Syracus.

do not know which bishop might be subject to him." What is clearer? I omit the letters to the bishops of Italy, France, and Spain, for there is no doubt concerning their subjection.

Calvin responds and says first: "Gregory granted to himself the right of correcting others; however, they did not obey him unless they wished."[19] But this cannot be said, for Gregory was very holy and exceedingly humble, for which reason even the Greeks commemorate his feast day; and Calvin likewise professes that Gregory was a holy man,[20] but usurpation of someone else's right is inconsistent with sanctity. Nor is it a venial blemish or stain to make subject all bishops to himself, but, as they frequently teach, intolerable pride, and the very mark of Antichrist; how therefore was Gregory a saint if he subjected all bishops to him unjustly?

Secondly Calvin responds, "Gregory judged the bishop of Constantinople by a command of the emperor, as is clear from lib. 7, Epistle 64 of the same Gregory." But in that epistle Gregory says the emperor wished that patriarch judged by him because the canons of Gregory himself require this. It is the same as if he were to say, the emperor refused to impede since according to the canons a bishop, though he be of a royal city, was to be punished by Gregory. This is the reason why in the previous epistle Gregory says the Emperor assiduously professes that the church of Constantinople was subject to the Roman Church.

Thirdly Calvin responds: "He [the emperor] punished Gregory just as others; Gregory was so prepared to be corrected by others, as he says himself,[21] and hence was no more in charge of them than subject to them." But Gregory, in that epistle, speaks on fraternal correction, not on a judicial censure, as he says, "Behold, your fraternity stands so sickly from banquets which I have condemned since, although I do not transgress this by life but by place, corrupted by all things, I am prepared to be corrected by all, and only I reckon this man is my friend by whose tongue before the apparition of a busy judge I wipe away the stains of my mind." Add that Calvin envelops the argument in contradiction, in asserting that at one and the same time the man is a prelate for all, and nevertheless subject to some.

Fourthly, he responds: "This state of the Pontiffs exceedingly displeases Gregory, hence he bewails," Calvin says, "and under the heat of the episcopate

---

[19] *Instit.*, lib. 4, ch. 7 § 12.

[20] *Institut.*, lib. 4, ch. 7, § 12.

[21] Lib. 2, epist. 37.

he would return to the world, as he says in an epistle."[22] But what Calvin misses here is that Gregory was given to exhaustion since he was brought from the quiet of the monastery to the episcopal burdens: moreover, he was not displeased that the Apostolic Seat managed the care of every church. For he opposed bitterly the same thing for the honor of his see against John the Bishop of Constantinople. He also says to Eulogius: "We shall maintain humility in mind, and nevertheless preserve our dignity in honor."[23] And in another epistle to John the Bishop of Panormus, he says: "We advise that the reverence due to the Apostolic See be disturbed by the presumption of no one. Thus, the state of the members remains whole, if no injury besets the head of faith."[24] And in his explanation of the Psalms he says, "In such a man he extends the rashness of his frenzy, that he will claim for himself the head of all churches, the Roman Church, and usurp for himself the right of power as Mistress of the Nations."[25]

---

[22] Lib. 1, epist. 5 and 7.

[23] Lib. IV, epist. 36 ad Eulog.

[24] Lib. XI, epist. 42 ad Joan. Panorm. Episc.

[25] *Explic. IV Psal. Poenit.*

CHAPTER XV

That the Roman Pontiff Succeeds Peter in the Ecclesiastical Monarchy is Proved from the Greek Fathers

ET US come to the testimonies of the Fathers who were not Supreme Pontiffs. Calvin and Illyricus make only three objections to us: Cyprian, Jerome and Bernard, about whom we will speak in their place. For the moment we will object to them from nearly thirty-three.

Therefore, the first should be St. Ignatius, who records in his epistle to the Romans: "Ignatius, to the holy Church, which presides in the region of the Romans." Why is the Church said to be presiding, except because it is the head of all others?

The second is St. Irenaeus: "The Church of Rome, of the greatest antiquity and recognized by all, founded and constituted by the two most glorious Apostles Peter and Paul, that which has tradition from the Apostles and heralding the faith to all through successions of bishops attaining even to us; we confound those men, who reveal that they gather it [the tradition] contrary to what is fitting by any manner or through their wicked charm, or vainglory, or through blindness and wicked knowledge. It is necessary for every Church to agree with this Church, on account of a mightier principality,[1] this is, those

---

[1] Translator's note: I insert here Cardinal Franzelin's commentary on these words *potentiorem principalitatem* from his text *De Divina Traditione*, Rome 1875: "Massuetus reads: *a more qualified* excellence, but affirms only the Claromont Codex to have *pontiorem* and the letter *n* being marked in *potiorem*; in the rest Codices. and editions *potentiorem* is read. Since the Greek text of Irenaeus is lacking, the erudite have proposed different conjectures: δια την ἱκανωτεραν ἀρχην (Griesbach); ἐξαιρετον πρωτειον (Salmasius); ὑπερτερον πρωτειον (Massuetus); διαφερουσαν πρωτειαν (Thiersch). But P. Shneemann, in his most excellent dissertation, proves the true sense of this citation and vindicates it against the shearing off made by Protestants (in *Ephermeride Der Katholik* 1867. T. XVII. p. 419), by comparing all the citations where expression *principalitas* occurs; but if it is less than certain at least he shows it the most probable, that the Greek was ἀυθεντιαν. Moreover, whatever is supposed from these or both nouns, from the context, the whole argumentation of Irenaeus is very clear; it cannot mean in the case of a greater power, but rather of preeminence, or primacy of the Roman Church. Therefore, in this *principalitatem*, Irenaeus establishes the foundation and principle of the unity of faith of all the churches or of the whole Universal Church. The only distinction, which the expression ἀυθεντια even considered in itself, and etymologically does not admit another meaning; ἀρχη and πρωτειον in themselves perhaps may be determined in an ambiguous sense from the very context for this meaning *principatus* and *primatus*, which certainly the most ancient express. Perhaps the translator who lived at the same time as Irenaeus thought "mightier pre-eminence" would suffice. Just as Irenaeus

who are faithful on every side, inasmuch as the tradition has been preserved in every way by these faithful men, which is the Tradition from the Apostles."[2] Mark that phrase *It is necessary*, and that, *for every Church to agree*. And also: *On account of a mightier preeminence*, as well as: *in which the Apostolic Tradition has always been preserved for all.*

For Irenaeus proves that he can confound all heretics from the doctrine of the Roman Church, because it is necessary for every church to agree with this church, and by it, just as by a head and font, the Church depends; and hence it is necessary that its doctrine is apostolic and true. He proves the fact that all Christians necessarily depend upon the Roman Church.

In the first place, *a priori*, because rule was given to this Church.

In the second place, *a posteriori*, because insofar as all always preserve the Faith in this Church, that is, in union and adhesion to this Church, as to a Head and mother.

The third witness is Epiphanius: "Ursacius and Valens doing penance, together with little books professed to St. Julius, the Bishop of Rome, so as to be restored from their error and crime."[3] Certainly they were bishops: therefore, why did they seek forgiveness from the Roman Pontiff, if the Roman Pontiff were not also the judge and head of bishops?

The fourth is Athanasius. In his *Second Apology*, he witnesses that certain bishops sought forgiveness for their crime from St. Julius I. And in his epistle to Pope Felix he says: "On account of that you, and your predecessors, clearly Protectors [*Praesules*], He [God] constituted in the capitol of the highest point and commanded to have care over every church, that you should come to our aid."[4] Lastly, in his book on the *Sentences of Dionysius of Alexandria*, he says: "Certain men from the Church thinking rightly, but ignorant of the case. That is why since it stood thus; it was written by him that they should go up to Rome, and there they accused Dionysius before the Prelate at Rome."

Why, I ask, is Dionysius the Patriarch of Alexandria accused by good men in the presence of the Roman Pontiff, except because they knew the Roman

---

appeals to the *principalitatem* of the Roman Church, so also Cyprian (ep. 55. p. 86) declares "the seat of Peter is also the *chief Church*.;" Augustine (*de Baptisma* 1. II. c. 1. n. 2.) "The Roman Church, in which the *chief (principatus) apostolic seat* always flourishes" (Ep. 443 n. 7); "The apostolate (of Peter) is preferred as *supreme (principatum)* to any episcopacy," as indeed "Grace stands apart from the Sees."

2 *Adv. Haeres.*, lib. III, ch. 3.

3 *Haeres. 68*, which is Meletian.

4 *Epist. ad Felicem Papam.*

Pontiff is the common judge of all?

The fifth is Basil the Great. In an epistle he says: "It appeared agreeable to write to the bishop of Rome that he might look to our affairs and impose a decree of his judgment. As that is difficult, some thence asked for a sentence of the council to be sent; these gave authority of the affair to wicked men, that they could not bear the labor of the journey, by a leniency and facility of morals. Then by a prudent and agreeable prayer they, who had returned by the right way, advised that every act of the Council of Armenia they should bear with them to get them rescinded, what was carried out with violence in that place." Basil attributes to the bishop of Rome authority of visiting the Eastern Churches, and from that authority of making and rescinding the general Conciliar decrees which were at Armenia.

The sixth is St. Gregory Nazianzen,[5] who says that the Roman Church always preserved the true teaching from God, as is fitting for the city which presides over the whole world. Nor is he speaking on the temporal empire, for in that time the capital of the Roman Empire was at Constantinople, not Rome.

The seventh is St. John Chrysostom, who says in Epistle 1 to Pope Innocent: "I ask that you would write the fact that these things were done so wickedly that they have no strength, moreover that those who behaved so wickedly ought to be subjected to the penalty of ecclesiastical laws." Theophilus the Bishop of Alexandria had deposed Chrysostom from the episcopate of Constantinople in a Council of many bishops; Chrysostom wrote to the Roman Pontiff, that he would discern with his authority that the judgment of Theophilus was void, and punish Theophilus himself. Therefore, Chrysostom acknowledged Pope Innocent as a the supreme judge even of the Greeks. Likewise, in his 2nd epistle to the same: "We thank you in perpetuity, because you have declared your paternal benevolence to us, etc."

Chrysostom acknowledged Innocent as a father, nevertheless he was older than Innocent, and the bishop of a royal city. Lastly, in the same epistle, he begs from Innocent lest he would excommunicate his enemies, even though they deserved it: "I pray your vigilance, that although they have filled everything with tumults, still if they may wish to be cured from the malady, lest they be afflicted, or cast from the body."

The eighth is St. Cyril of Alexandria. In his tenth epistle to Nestorius, and his eleventh to the clergy and people of Constantinople, he writes that Nestorius, unless he would rescind his heresies within a set time, ought to be shunned by all as one excommunicated and deposed. And in Epistle 18 to

---

[5] *Carm. De vita sua.*

Celestine, whom he calls "Most Holy Father" at the beginning, he asks from him whether he would have it that Nestorius was still to be communicated with at that time, or whether he was to be shunned by all. All of which sufficiently shows in what place St. Cyril held the Roman Pontiff, since in the condemnation and deposition of Nestorius, he showed that he was nothing other than the executor and administrator of the Roman Pontiff. Also in the book, *Thesauri*, he says: "Every head bows to Peter by divine law, and the primates of the world obey him just as they obey the Lord Jesus." Likewise: "We ought, as we who are members, adhere to our head, the Roman Pontiff, and the Apostolic seat."

Such words are not contained in the books *Thesauri* which are now extant, but they are cited by St. Thomas,[6] and by Gennadius Scholarius, a Greek author, in a book on the primacy of the Roman Pontiff. Moreover, it is certain that many books from the work *Thesauri* have perished, for the same phrase is cited in the Sixth Council, Act 10, lib. 32. Only fourteen books of the *Libri Thesauri* of Cyril are extant today. Besides, Andreas, the bishop of Colossensis, affirmed at the Council of Florence,[7] that in the *Thesauri* of Cyril the authority of the Roman Pontiff was wonderfully preached, and not one of the Greeks contradicted him.

The ninth is Theodoret, who in an epistle to Pope Leo says: "I await the judgment of your Apostolic See and I beg and entreat your holiness that you would impose the might of your just and right judgment to my appeal, and that it might bid you to hasten and show that my doctrine follows in the Apostolic footsteps."[8] Yet here was an Asian bishop who was in charge of 800 churches, as he says in the same place, nevertheless he acknowledges the Roman Pontiff as his supreme judge. He also says in a letter to Renatus, a Roman priest: "They have despoiled me of priesthood and thrown me from the cities; neither is age considered in religion nor reverence for grey hairs. This is why I beg you, that you might persuade the most holy Archbishop Leo, that he would use his Apostolic authority and that he might bid me to approach your council. That holy seat holds the reigns of government over every church of the world."[9]

The tenth is Sozomen in his *History*. He says: "Since on account of the dignity of his own seat he regards the care of all the faithful as his own, he restored each to their church."[10] He speaks concerning Julius I, who restored

---

6   *Opusculum contra Graecos.*

7   Sess. 7.

8   Theodoret, *epistola 113.*

9   *Epistula* 116.

10   *Hist.*, lib. 3, ch. 7.

Athanasius to his episcopate in Alexandria, and Paul to Constantinople.

The eleventh is Acatius, who says, in an epistle to Pope Simplicius, which is contained in a volume of the Second Council: "Carrying about the solicitude of all churches, according to the Apostle, you exhort us without ceasing, although watchful and anticipating of our own accord."

The twelfth. Concerning the bishop of Paterna, Liberatus thus writes in his Breviary: "When Sylverius came to Patara the venerable bishop of that city came to the Emperor and called to witness the judgment of God concerning the expulsion of a bishop of such a see, saying, 'There are many kings in this world, and there is not one, just as that Pope is over the Church of the whole world, being expelled from his see.'"[11]

The thirteenth is Justinian Augustus, the Elder, in a letter to John II, which is contained in the *Codex*, in the first title: "We will not suffer anything which pertains to the state of the churches that is not also made known to your holiness, who is head of all the churches of the world."

---

[11] Liberatus, *Breviarium,* ch. 22.

CHAPTER XVI

That the Roman Pontiff Succeeds Peter in the Ecclesiastical Monarchy is Proven from the Latin Fathers

OW from the Latins. St. Cyprian often teaches this [that the Roman Pontiff succeeds Peter]. But before we bring the proper citations to bear, the argument of his books on the *Unity of the Church* must be explained; from there his other testimonies shall be more easily understood. Therefore, in his book on the *Unity of the Church*, he proposes to show in what the unity of the Church consists, and he shows first from where division and heresy arise. "It happens in this way, that one does not return to the font of truth, nor seek the head, nor preserve the doctrine of the heavenly master."

There he proposes three things. Firstly, the font of truth is from the Church, that is, from the Church whereby doctrine will have begun. Secondly, the head of the Church is different from Christ; for a little before, he had said that all heretics seek Christ, and nevertheless here he says that all heresies are born because they do not seek the head of the Church. Thirdly, the doctrine of the heavenly Master is what the doctrine of Christ might be from the Church and its head.

After these were proposed, he soon declares these three matters, saying: "The Lord speaks to Peter, 'I say to you, that thou are Peter, and upon this rock I will build my Church, and the gates of hell shall not conquer it;' 'Feed my sheep, etc.'" In that place, Cyprian teaches that the font of truth is from the Church, which he had said must be sought in these words of the Lord. Therefore, this doctrine begins from the Church, and similarly, the head of the Church, which he had said must be sought, is Peter, and the doctrine of the heavenly Master are these same words. This is why, a little after, he adds and teaches that the Church is one in its root and head, although it is multiplied in propagation, and he places three examples, one of a light, of a font, and a tree. All these are one in root, and yet are multiplied in propagation. Therefore, we have from this place, that Peter is the head of the whole Church.

Moreover, this same thing is fitting for the bishop of Rome; Cyprian declares the same thing in a letter to Pope Cornelius, where, speaking on the schism of the Novatianists, who did not recognize Cornelius as Pope, he speaks thus: "Heresies do not arise from any other source, nor are schisms born, than in that because they do not obey the Priest of God, or one priest in the Church at a time, or it is not thought that there is one judge in the stead of Christ at a time. To which if all fraternity would comply according to the divine magisterium, no man from the college of priests would ever oppose anything, etc."[1]

Now our adversaries respond: "Here Cyprian speaks on individual bishops, and particular churches, and wishes to say in each Church there ought to be one Judge and priest at a time." But if this citation were matched against the previous one, it is obvious that Cyprian is speaking on the universal Church. For, just as in the first place he had said that heresies are born because the head is not sought, and he explained that the head of the whole Church is Peter, so here he says heresies are born because it is not thought that there is one judge in the stead of Christ in the Church, which without a doubt is Cornelius, for he is speaking about him. For that reason, a little below in the same epistle, he calls the Roman Church the See of Peter and the Principal Church, whence sacerdotal unity arises.

He also says in another letter to the same Cornelius: "We had recently sent our colleagues, that they might gather together the members of the torn body to the unity of the Catholic Church, but the obstinacy of different parties and their unbendable pertinacity not only refused the lap and embrace of the root and mother but even made an adulterous and contrary head outside the Church, etc."[2] Clearly this discourse is on the Catholic Church, of which the Novatianists are outside. But Cyprian says that the Novatianists not only refused to return to the Church and acknowledge the root and mother, or the head of this Church, but even set up for themselves an adulterous and contrary head. Therefore, just as Novatian was the head of all Novatianists, so Cornelius was the head of all Catholics.

Cyprian also teaches: "There is one God, and one Christ, and one Church, and one Chair founded upon Peter by the voice of the Lord. One cannot set up another altar, or make a new priesthood, apart from the one altar and one priesthood. Whoever does so gathers elsewhere, and therefore, scatters."[3]

Here, rightly, just as God is one and Christ is one, and the Church is one in number, not in species, so also the Chair is one in number; that is, there is a certain individual Chair which teaches the whole Church and that is of Peter, outside of which whoever gathers, scatters. Next, in another epistle,[4] he again calls the Roman Church the root and mother of the Catholic Church.

But our adversaries object. First, they bring up Cyprian's book *On the Unity*

---

[1]   *Lib. 1, epist 3 ad Cornel.*

[2]   Lib. 2, epistle 10, to the same Cornelius.

[3]   Lib. 1, epist. 8 ad plebem universam.

[4]   Lib. 4, epist. 8.

of the Church, where he so speaks: "The episcopate is one, part of which is held in solidity by individuals." Therefore, they say, there is not one bishop of the whole Church. Secondly, they object on the basis of Cyprian's epistle to Quintus, where Cyprian, while residing in council, says: "No one constituted our bishop that he should be of bishops, or compel his colleagues by a tyrannical terror to the necessity of obedience, when every bishop has the right of liberty and his power of his proper judgments, just as he can be judged by no other, since he cannot judge the other. But we await the judgment of our Lord Jesus Christ, who one and alone has the power of putting us in charge of the governance of his Church and judging it from our act."

I respond to the first: The episcopate is one in the same manner in which the Church is one. Furthermore, the Church is one in the same manner in which many branches of a tree are one tree, many rivers one water, and many rays one light. And in the same place Cyprian says that there is unity just as in the branches, rivers and rays by reason of the one head, that is of the root, font and the sun, even though the branches, rivers and rays are multiplied; so also the Church is one, and the episcopate one in the root and head, although there are many particular churches, and many particular episcopates. Therefore, part of one great episcopate is held by individual bishops in solidity, but not equally, nor in the same way. For Peter and his successors hold that part which is just as the head, and the root and the source; the rest hold the other parts which are like the branches and rivers.

This one episcopate is (as we said) similar to a heterogeneous body, not a homogenous body, from which it follows that individual bishops do not hold part of this episcopate in the same way. For just as the root, although it is a part, as the branch is also, nevertheless holds up and rules the branches as well as everything which is in the branches; they are virtually in the root, not the other way around; so also, although the Roman Church and the Roman Episcopate are part of the universal Church, and the universal episcopate, just like the Church at Tusculum[5] has its episcopate, nevertheless the Roman Church rules Tusculum, not the other way around.

Therefore, from the teaching of Cyprian it is rightly gathered that the Roman Pope is not only the bishop of all churches, as there are indeed other true bishops who received their part of the universal Church to rule; nevertheless it is not rightly gathered that the Roman Pontiff is not the head and pastor of all bishops, and hence also of the universal Church; seeing that the part which has been consigned to them to rule has that place in the Church which has the root

---

[5] Tusculum is a small suburb, by Mount Albano, not very far from Rome, and even in Roman times was a summer retreat for the wealthy. -Translator's note.

in the tree, the head in the body and the font in rivers of waters.

Now to the second objection I say: When Cyprian says: "No one makes himself a bishop of bishops," he speaks on those who were present at that Council in Carthage; he does not include the Roman Pontiff in that teaching, who truly is the bishop of bishops, and Father of Fathers, as we will show below when we treat on the titles of the Roman Pontiff.

Now when he says that a bishop cannot be judged except by God, just as he is constituted by God alone, I say: This ought to be understood in dubious and secret matters in the same way St. Augustine expresses it when recalling these very words of Cyprian, "I think in those questions which have not yet been discussed with very refined examination, etc."[6]

In that place he teaches that Cyprian meant that individual bishops in a council, while a matter is discussed, can freely state their opinion, nor ought they be compelled tyrannically by the president of the council to his opinion before a question may have been defined. For otherwise how could a Pope judge and depose heretical bishops or manifest schismatics, as is clear from Cyprian's letter to Pope Stephen[7] where Cyprian exhorts him to command the bishop of Arles to be deposed and to constitute another in his place.

The second from the Latin Fathers is Optatus of Miletus. He follows Cyprian's opinion on the singular chair of the whole Church in his work *Contra Parmen.*, where he says there are five dowries of the Catholic Church, and the first is the unique and singular Chair of Peter, in which unity ought to be preserved by all; but he showed that singular Chair is not only Peter's but also his successors' when he enumerated the Roman Pontiffs even to Siricius. At length he concludes, "Therefore, on the aforesaid dowries, that Chair is first, which we proved is ours through Peter."

The third is St. Ambrose, who says in his commentary on the first Epistle to Timothy: "When the whole world should be of God, nevertheless his house is called the Church, whose Ruler today is Damasus."[8]

He teaches likewise in his *Oration on Satyrus*: "Percunctatus is a bishop, if he should agree with Catholic bishops; that is, if he should agree with the Roman Church."

Why, I ask, are they not Catholic bishops unless they agree with the Roman Church, except that the Roman Church is the head of the Catholic Church? Ambrose says the same thing elsewhere: "Are we not ignorant that the Church

---

[6] *De Baptismo*, lib. III, ch. 3.

[7] Lib. 3, *epist. 13 ad Stephanum Papam.*

[8] I ad Tim., c. 3.

does not have some custom whose type and form we follow in all things?... In all things, I desire to follow the Roman Church, but still even we men have sense; therefore, what is rightly preserved elsewhere, we also rightly safeguard."[9]

In that place it must be observed that when Ambrose says that in all things he would follow the Roman Church and still that he refuses to follow the custom of not washing the feet of the recently baptized, that phrase *all things* must be understood on all necessary matters, and those pertaining to salvation, otherwise he would be opposed to himself.

The fourth is St. Jerome. He says in an epistle to Agemchiam of Monogamia: "A great many years ago, when I assisted Damasus, the bishop of the city of Rome, in ecclesiastical records and in synodal consultations of the East and West I responded, etc." You see how from the whole Church and the whole world responses were then sought from the Apostolic See? Jerome says in an epistle to Damasus on the term *hypostasis*: "Although your magnitude terrifies me, nevertheless your humanity invites, me, a sheep, to ask aid from the shepherd. I speak with the successor of the fisherman and disciple of the cross. I, following none first but Christ and uniting myself with your beatitude, that is in the communion of the Chair of Peter. I know that the Church was built upon that rock. Whoever will eat the lamb outside this house is profane. Whoever was not in the Ark of Noah perished while the flood reigned." And below, [speaking of schismatics]: "I do not know Vitalis, I spurn Meletius, and I ignore Paulinus. Whoever does not gather with you scatters; this is, who is not of Christ, is of Antichrist."

Observe firstly that Jerome, who was an Antiochene priest, nevertheless acknowledges himself as a sheep of the bishop of Rome.

Secondly, Jerome confesses Damasus to be the successor of Peter.

Thirdly, when he says: "I, following none first but Christ and uniting myself to your beatitude," he says that he would have it that he adhere first to Christ, then the Vicar of Christ. Therefore, it is the same thing as if he would have said: "I put no man before you, O Pope Damasus, except Christ himself."

Fourthly, the seat of the Roman Pontiff is made by Jerome the foundation of his [God's] house and boat, which is the universal Church, and hence the Roman Pontiff is made the head of the whole Church.

Lastly, Jerome prefers more to adhere to the Seat of the Roman Pontiff, than to his own bishop Paulinus, who was not one from a crowd, but the Patriarch of Antioch. Thus he says: "I do not know Vitalis, I spurn Meletius, I ignore

---

[9] *De Sacramentis*, lib. 3, ch. 1.

Paulinus."

For this reason, even Erasmus himself, who otherwise is usually more hostile to the Roman Church, says in an annotation on this citation, that it seems to him that Jerome asserts by these words that all churches are subject to the Apostolic See. This ought to be noted against the new heretics, who hold Erasmus for an oracle.

But Calvin objects to all this. Firstly, he brings the Epistle of Jerome to Nepotianus, wherein Jerome, while reviewing the examples of unity, says: "'Each bishop of the churches, each archpriest, each archdeacon, and every Ecclesiastical order depends upon its rulers.' Nor does he add," Calvin says, "that all the churches are tied together among themselves, just as by a bond, to one head."

Secondly not only Calvin objects, but also Illyricus and Melanchthon, and others, that in his epistle to Evagrius, Jerome says: "If authority is sought, the world is greater than a city. Why do you bring to me the custom of one city? Why do you defend the paucity, from which arrogance arose, against the laws of the Church? Wherever was there a bishop, whether at Rome, or Eugubius, or Constantinople, or Rhegium, or Alexandria, or Tanis, he is of the same merit, and of the same priesthood; the power of riches and the humility of poverty does not make one a more lofty or lowly bishop."

Now I say to the first: Jerome did not omit one head, for when he says: "And every ecclesiastical order depends upon its rulers," he indicates apart from one bishop, archpriest and archdeacon, that there are still other unities; without a doubt in each province one metropolitan; in greater particular regions one primate; in the whole Church one Pontiff. Otherwise, it will not be true that in every ecclesiastical order there is one ruler.

I say to the second: Jerome in that citation rebukes a certain wicked custom which was at Rome, but not in the whole Roman Church, or in the Supreme Pontiff, but only among the Roman deacons. Because there were few deacons, and they had care of the ecclesiastical treasures, little by little they began to put themselves before the priests, and to sit among them, since it was an ancient custom that while the priests and bishops were sitting, the deacons would stand not sit. Therefore, he says concerning these, "Why do you bring me the custom of one city? Why paucity, from which arrogance arises?"

Moreover, the Roman Pontiff did not approve of this custom, as Jerome shows in the same place; therefore, he says that only while the bishop was absent did a deacon dare to sit among the priests. But that which Jerome says: "bishops are of the same merit and priesthood," is true, yet it ought to be understood by reason of the episcopal rank, not jurisdiction. For Jerome did not wish to deny a greater authority of the bishop of Alexandria than that of Tanis, since it is certain that the former was in charge of three vast provinces, while the latter was but a tiny city.

The fifth from the Latin Fathers is St. Augustine. In Epistle 162 he says: "In the Roman Church the rule of the Apostolic Chair always flourishes." Likewise, in Epistle 92 to Pope Innocent: "Since the Lord placed you in that particular office by his grace in the Apostolic See and it furnishes so much in our times that were we to pass over, in view of your veneration, that which must be offered for the Church, we would rather depart in the fault of negligence than that you could either disdainfully or negligently receive the pastoral diligence of Christ, which we ask that you deign to apply to the great dangers to the weak members."

In such words Augustine asks, along with the whole Council of Milevitanus, that Innocent would apply his pastoral care to the Church, by coercing the Pelagians who particularly infested Palestine and Africa. But certainly he would not ask for this unless he also believed that Innocent was the pastor of Palestine and Africa. Next, why did Augustine not write to the Patriarch of Jerusalem, or the Metropolitan of Palestine, or rather more to the first bishop of the Church of Africa, namely Carthage, than to the Roman Pontiff, unless it is because he knew that the authority of the Roman Pontiff was greater in Palestine and Africa than that of their own bishops?

Likewise he says: "They came to me while present at Caesaraea, in which ecclesiastical necessity had derived for us what was enjoined upon up by the venerable Pope Zozimus, the bishop of the Apostolic Seat."[10] Without a doubt, Zozimus had commanded that the bishops of Africa should celebrate a council at Caesarea and St. Augustine reckoned it must be obeyed—necessarily Pope Zozimus must be obeyed. Likewise, he says to Pope Boniface, "Although you should preside more loftily, you do not have a taste for lofty things nor disdain to be a friend of the humble." And below: "It is common to all of us who exercise the office of the Episcopate, although you are preeminent in that as a lofty peak, the pastoral watchtower."[11] You see here all bishops are held by Augustine to be subjected to the loftier peak of the Roman Pontiff.

The sixth is St. Prosper of Aquitaine, who says in the *Liber de Ingratis*: "The seat of Peter at Rome, which was made head of the world for pastoral honor, holds by religion whatever it did not possess by arms." And on the *Calling of the Nations* he says: "Rome, through the rule of priesthood, was made more

---

[10]   *Epist. 157 ad Optat.*

[11]   *Ad Bonifacium*, lib. 1, ch. 1.

resplendent by the citadel of religion than the throne of power."[12]

The seventh is St. Victor of Utica, who calls the Roman Church the Head of all churches.[13]

The eighth is St. Vincent of Liren in his *Commonitorium*. "Then, certain epistles of St. Felix the Martyr, and of St. Julius, bishops of the city of Rome, were read to some. And that they should bear testimony not only as head of the city, but even the sides in that judgment, St. Cyprian applied from the south and St. Ambrose from the north." You see, the Roman Pontiff is called the head of the world.

The ninth is Cassiodorus, writing to Pope John: "You as a sentinel, preside over the Christian people; you love all in the name of the Father." And below: "On which account it behooves us to safeguard some things, but you everything."[14] (For Cassiodorus was commanded to have care of the city of Rome by King Theodoric). And below: "That wonderful seat cleanses its own inhabitants in the whole world with affection, which, although it is furnished in general in the whole world, it is also recognized by you and allotted locally."

The tenth is St. Bede. He writes in his *History of the English nation*: "When the foremost (Gregory) managed the Pontificate of the whole world, and long ago turning to the faith of truth was prelate over the churches, our nation which, to that point, had been held in the power of idols, he made the Church of Christ."[15]

The eleventh is St. Anselm. He dedicates his book on the Incarnation to Pope Urban II with these words: "To the Lord and Father of the universal Church journeying on earth, brother Anselm, a sinner in life to the Supreme Pontiff, Urban, a monk in habit, whether at the command or pleasure of God, called bishop of the city of Canterbury, giving due subjection with humble servitude, and devoted prayers. Because Divine Providence chose your Holiness, whose it is to guard Christian faith and life, he committed to rule his Church, it is more rightly related to no other, if something arises in the Church against the Catholic faith, that it should be corrected by its authority; by no other more securely, if something should be responded or shown against the error, that it should be examined by its prudence."[16]

---

[12] *De Vocatione Gentium*, lib.. 2, ch. 6.

[13] *De Persecutione Wandalica.*, lib. 2.

[14] Cassiodorus, lib. 11, *epistle 2 to Pope John.*

[15] *Hist. Gent. Angl.*, lib. 2, ch. 1.

[16] *De Incarnat. Verbi*, ch. 1.

The twelfth is Hugh of St. Victor. He writes: "The Apostolic See is given preference to every Church in the whole world."[17]

The thirteenth is St. Bernard, whom also Calvin relates on his behalf, and calls him a saint.[18] Bernard says in his book *de Considerationis:* "Well, let us still seek more diligently who you might be, what you are in charge of, for how long you are a person in the Church of God. Who are you? A great priest, the supreme Pontiff, you the prince of bishops, you the heir of the Apostles, you are Abel in primacy, Noah in captainship, Abraham in the patriarchate, Melchisedech by rank, Aaron in dignity, Moses in authority, Samuel in judgment, Peter in power, Christ by anointing. You are the one to whom the keys were handed, to whom the sheep were entrusted; indeed there are also other porters of heaven, and pastors of the flocks, but as glorious as you are, so much also are you more different and apart from the rest in the name you have inherited.

"The former have flocks assigned to them, individuals have their own; but to you all are entrusted, one over one body. You alone are not only shepherd of the sheep, but even of the shepherds... Therefore, according to your canons, of another care in part, you were called into the fullness of power. Power compels certain limits of the others; yours is extended on those, who received power over others. Could you not, if a reason existed, close heaven to a bishop; can not you alone depose him from the episcopacy, and even hand him over to Satan? Your unshakeable privilege stands to you, as in the keys which were given, than in the entrusted sheep."

This man, this holy man, as Calvin witnesses, and without Calvin innumerable miracles witness; but true holiness cannot be without true faith; therefore, St. Bernard believed with true faith that the Roman Pontiff was Pastor over the universal Church.

Moreover, many of the things that Calvin objects to, such as the vices and abuses of the Roman Curia, the same Bernard wrote against in the *liber de Considerationis,* that from the whole world the greedy, ambitious and simoniacal run to Rome, since they wish to be taken in authority to ecclesiastical honors. But this does not lack a solution, for St. Bernard expressly teaches that the bad morals of prelates do not impede to the extent that they be lesser prelates, and we are not less held to obey them, since the Lord said in St. Matthew: "Do what they say, but do not do according to their works."[19]

---

[17] *De Sacramentis,* lib. 2, p. 3, ch. 15.

[18] *Instit.* lib. 4, ch. 7, § 22.

[19] Matthew 23:3

Lastly, we bring the testimony of a Latin [Roman] Emperor, just as above we related the testimony of a Greek [Roman] Emperor. Valentinian says, in an epistle to Theodosius which is extant among the preliminaries to the Council of Chalcedon, "We ought to preserve the dignity of proper veneration to the Blessed Apostle Peter in our times, by far the most blessed of the city of Rome, to whom antiquity confers the rule of priesthood over all, let him have place and faculty concerning faith, and in judging priests."

Similar things are contained in the epistles of Gallia Placidia and Licinius Eudoxius Augustarum to the same Theodosius in the same place.

CHAPTER XVII

That the Roman Pontiff Succeeds Peter in the Ecclesiastical Monarchy is Proven from the Origin and Antiquity of the Primacy

O THIS point we have shown by divine law, the general councils, the testimony of the Pontiffs and from a consensus of the Greek and Latin Fathers, that the ecclesiastical rule of the Roman Pontiff was received from Christ; this type of argument, which is called *ducens ad impossible,* is what we now attempt to show. For if it is not, as we said, in any time or by any author that the ecclesiastical rule of the Roman Pontiff began—but no time is assigned, no author can be noted, for as we have shown this primacy was more ancient—then it is necessary that we should arrive at the fact that Christ was its author and it began in the time of Christ.

Our adversaries respond that they can assign a time and an author. Thus Juan de Torquemada places four opinions of the heretics.[1]

First are those who say that the authority of the Roman Pontiff is from the Apostles.

The second is the opinion of those who assert that it is from a general Council, which is the opinion the aforementioned Nilos follows.

The third opinion is of those who reckon it is granted by cardinal electors; which is also similar to what the book of the Smalkaldic council teaches on the primacy. Therein it tries to show that the Pope is not over the Church by divine law, because the Church elects the Pope.

The fourth opinion is of those who teach that this authority was introduced by the emperors, which is embraced by many heretics. Therefore, we shall briefly strike each one individually.

Now the first opinion has three testimonies on its behalf. One is of Anacletus, who says: "The rest of the Apostles with him (Peter) received an equal share of honor and power, and they wished him to be their prince."[2]

The second testimony is of Julius I, where, speaking on the Apostles, he says: "The Holy Roman Church would have primacy over all the Churches."[3] The third is from the Canon *I Louis,* dist. 63, where the Roman Pontiff is called the Vicar of St. Peter. From which it would seem to follow that not Christ, but Peter, bestowed authority upon the Roman Pontiff.

Yet this opinion is refuted with no trouble. For the same Anacletus in Epistle 3 speaks thus: "The most holy Roman Church obtained primacy not from the

---

[1]   *Sum. De Eccl.,* lib. 2, ch. 39.

[2]   In epist. 2.

[3]   Epist. 1.

Apostles, but from our Lord and Savior himself, just as he said to Blessed Peter: 'You are Peter, etc.'"

For this reason the same author writes that the Apostles would have Peter as their prince, but does not speak on the will to establish him, but rather, on the approval and acknowledgment that the Lord had instituted him. It seems that Pope Julius I spoke the same. Moreover the response can also be made to the testimony of Julius: Without a doubt, Peter has primacy from Christ alone. Nevertheless, the Roman Church, concerning which Julius is speaking there, has it in some manner from the Apostles.

For (as we taught above), the Roman Pontiff, as he is the successor of Peter, has the primacy from Christ; nevertheless, the cause of the succession arose from a deed of Peter. For which reason St. Gregory says: "He elevated the see in which he deigned to rest and end the present life."[4]

Furthermore, We can add that the name of *Vicar* presents no difficulty. For if in one place the Roman Pontiff is called the Vicar of Peter, because St. Peter still lives, and did not leave behind the government of the Church, as Leo says,[5] since nevertheless, St. Peter did not properly exercise pastoral office, but ruled and protected the Church by merits and prayers; these are improper locutions, and made only on account of the reverence for St. Peter that some time later was usurped. This is why St. Leo, in the noted place above, says that he is also an heir of St. Peter.

The second opinion, which teaches that the primacy was established by councils, Nilos tries to prove by two arguments. The first, is that in the Council of Chalcedon, Can. 28 (as he cites), or Action 16 in our codex, there he says the Council held the primacy of the Roman Church from the Fathers, for the reason that this city commanded the whole world in the time of the Empire.

Secondly, Nilos argues that in the law of Justinian we read: "We discern according to the decree of the holy councils that the most holy bishop of old Rome is first of all priests."[6] Such reasoning of Nilos can be confirmed from the Fourth Council under Symmachus, where we read: "In the first place of the Apostolic See, the merit of Blessed Peter, thereafter, the authority of the Councils, must be venerated, and handed on singular power in the Churches." Illyricus cites this same opinion in his book,[7] he proves with testimony from

---

[4] Lib. VI, epist. 37, *ad Eulog.*

[5] Serm 2 *de annivers. Assumt. Suae.*

[6] *Constit. Novel* 100, which still is 131 in our edition.

[7] *Lib. Cont. Prim. Et in hist. De Prim.*

four citations: epistle 301 (as he cites it, still it is 288) of Aeneas Silvias, afterward Pope Pius II; accordingly in that epistle Aeneas so speaks: "Before the Council of Nicaea everyone lived for himself, and scant respect was paid to the Roman Church."

But these arguments can be easily answered. That the Roman Pontiff, not by councils, but by Christ has the primacy, besides so many arguments already added, Gelasius witnesses in his 70th Council of bishops: "The Holy Roman Church was not given preference by any synods constituted in the other Church, but obtained the primacy from the evangelic voice of our Lord and Savior."

This is how I respond to the first argument of Nilos: that decree is indeed of a great council, but it was not done legitimately; hence it is of no strength or authority. For from the very Action 16 of the same council it is certain that the decree was made while the legates of the Apostolic See were absent, who presided over the council; it is likewise certain that the same legates clearly protested.

A decree of a general council which is made without the Roman Pontiff or his legate is not legitimate, as the Seventh Council witnesses (which Nilos also receives) in Action 6; that we would omit, meanwhile, other testaments. Not only did the legates of St. Leo resist the synod, inasmuch as it attained to that decree; but St. Leo himself, who confirmed the other decrees of that council, condemned and reproved that one, in Epistle 51 to the bishops of Anatolia.[8] Why? Because in that decree there are two manifest falsehoods. One is, that the Fathers of the Council of Nicaea allotted primacy to the Roman Pontiff. For the Council of Nicaea did not allot primacy to the Roman Pontiff, just as before it had not, for Canon 6 of Nicaea begins thus (as it is recited in Act. 16 of the same Council of Chalcedon): "The Roman Church has always had the primacy." Lastly, if before the Council of Nicaea the Pope did not have the primacy: by what law was Dionysius, the Patriarch of Alexandria, around 60 years before the Council of Nicaea, accused in the presence of the Roman Pontiff? And did the Roman Pontiff deny himself to be the judge, or did Alexandria refuse that judgment, since, nevertheless, each man was a saint? That these things are so, St. Athanasius writes.[9] Lastly, there is no word in the whole Council of Nicaea in which some new power is allotted to the Roman Pontiff, as we sufficiently showed above.

The other matter which is asserted in that decree is no less false, namely,

---

[8] Cf., *ad Martian, ad Pulcheriam, ad Maximam, ad Juvenalem.*

[9] *De sent. Dionys. Alexandr.*

that the reason why the Fathers had conceded the primacy of Rome is that this city was the seat of the Empire. For the eloquent words of St. Leo and St. Gelasius refute this, and the reason is in view. For, as Gelasius rightly remarked, Milan, and Ravenna, Sirmium, Trier and Nicomedia were the seats of the Empire for a long time:[10] nevertheless, the Fathers did not give any primacy to those bishops. Therefore, it should remain, that all the Fathers teach in a common consensus that the Roman See is the first of all Sees because it is the See of the Prince of the Apostles. The presence of the Emperor certainly does not confer it, any more than his absence could take it away.

Now to the second argument I respond: the canons of councils granted authority to the Roman Church in a certain measure, because they declared and asserted. It is even said that in a certain measure, the Council of Nicaea defined the Son of God to be consubstantial with the Father. For that reason, John II, in an epistle to Justinian, after he had said the Roman Church is the head of Churches, he added: "Just as the rules and statutes of the Fathers declare." And Nicholas I, in his epistle to the Emperor Michael: "These privileges were given to this Church by Christ, not by synods; yet they are celebrated and honored by the same."

And in the Fourth Council under Symmachus, three reasons are enumerated, if anyone would prudently draw his attention to it, for the primacy of the Roman Church. Thus we read, "His authority, that is, of Symmachus, remains first by the merit of Peter; next, following the Lord's command, the authority of the venerable councils handed over singular power over the Churches."

Firstly, "the merit of Peter" is posited, because Peter obtained the primacy on account of the merit of his confession.[11] Secondly, it is posited "by the Lord's command," whereby the primacy was established and conferred upon Peter, when it was said to him: "Feed my sheep."[12] Thirdly, the authority of councils is posited, which declared this command of the Lord.

Now to Illyricus' objection we can easily respond. For, Aeneas Sylvius in that epistle attempts to show nothing else but that the primacy of the Roman Pontiff

---

[10] Translator's note: The Roman Emperor Diocletian, 50 years or more before the Council of Nicaea, had divided the imperial administration into four emperors, known as the Tetrarchy, where there would be an Emperor for East and West, and junior emperors, all of whom would have different courts in different cities, thus they were royal. Even before the Tetrarchy, Diocletian had visited Rome only once out of fear of assassination.

[11] Matth. 16:13-20.

[12] John 21:15-19.

was established by Christ; thus the epistle begins to Martin Mayer, "There are several men of your nation, having little thought, in whom the authority of the Roman Pontiff seems to be neither necessary nor established by Christ. Therefore, we have resolved to write this epistle against them and transmit it to you, in order that if ever such men should come to you, you shall have it from us, whereby it shall be the sword with which you shall slay their boldness."

Although when he says "before the Council of Nicaea each lived for himself, and there was little regard for the Roman Church," he means nothing other than that on account of continual persecutions, the Roman Pontiffs could not freely exercise that authority which they had received from Christ; and on that account, the other bishops were compelled to look to themselves, and there was not much regard for the Roman Church. Now this opinion of Aeneas Sylvius is partly true, and partly false.

On the one hand, it is true that the authority of the Pope at that time was not a little impeded, as is clear from the persecutions which arose in that time; but on the other, it is not true that scant regard was held for the Roman Church, as the examples which we brought to bear above clearly declare.

The third opinion, from those four above, has almost no foundation. For it is certain that Pontiffs were earlier than cardinals, and at least some true Pontiffs were not created by cardinals. Certainly not the cardinals, but Christ created Peter Pope, and Peter, not the cardinals, chose Clement. Besides, if the cardinals conferred power on the Pope, they could also take it away; however this is false by the consensus of all; for even a doubtful Pope is not deposed by cardinals, but by a general council.

Yet you will say, that whatever is the case with cardinals, it is certain that the Roman Pontiff is chosen and created by men; consequently, he receives power from them. Moreover, the Supreme Pontiff is truly and properly made so by men, and it is witnessed in the decree of election of Gregory VII, which is contained in his life with Platina in these words: "We, cardinals of the Roman Church, clerics, acolytes, subdeacons, priests, with bishops, abbots and many others present, both of the ecclesiastical and lay order, we choose today, on the 23rd of April, in the Basilica of St. Peter in Chains, in the year of our salvation 1073, and so will that the archdeacon Hildebrand become the true Vicar of Christ. He is a man of much doctrine, great piety, prudence, justice, constancy, religion, modesty, sobriety, continence, governing his house, giving shelter to the poor, educated in the lap of Holy Mother the Church from his tender youth even to his present age, a learned man, whom indeed we will to be in charge of the power of the Church of God, whereby Peter was in charge by a clear command of God."

From which it appears two things can be deduced. One, the Pope is not above the Church but is subject to it, seeing that the Church makes a Pope, the Pope does not make the Church; which is the analogy of the book of the Smalkaldic synod in *Cont. Prim.* The second is that the Pontiff has all the power which he has by human law, not by divine law. And in the first there is no analogy, for electors of the empire create an Emperor, and the people create a king; yet an Emperor is above the electors, and a king is above the people. But nor does the second avail to anything.

I respond: It must be observed that in the Pontiff are three things: *the Pontificate itself,* which is just as a type of form; *the person,* which is the subject of the pontificate; and *the union* of one with another. From such things, the first is the pontificate itself, which is from Christ alone; but the person is indeed absolutely from natural causes; nevertheless as the *person* was chosen and designated to the pontificate from electors, it is theirs to designate a person. The true union is from Christ mediating the human act of the electors; while they choose and designate a certain person, they agree to the union of the pontificate with that person.

Therefore, the electors are truly said to create the Pope and to be the cause that there be such a Pontiff, and that he should have that power; nevertheless, they did not themselves give that power, nor are they the cause of its power. Just as in the generation of a man, because the soul is infused by God alone, and still the father, begetting by disposing the matter, is the cause of the union of the soul with the body, a man is said to beget a man; and still he is not said to produce the soul of man. Hence those words of the electors: "Whom indeed we would have it be in charge with that power, etc." only declare and express the perfect election of a man as the successor of Peter.

The fourth opinion is held by many heretics, who still do not agree among themselves. For Marsilius of Padua, and afterward John Wycliff and Jan Hus, said that the Pope received authority from Caesar. They appear to have understood by the name of Caesar, Constantine the Great, on account of the Canon which begins *Constantinus*, dist. 96, where Constantine decreed that the Roman Pontiff must be held in that place by all priests, like a king is held by lower judges of the whole kingdom.[13]

John Calvin says that the primacy of the Pope over the Greeks was given by the Emperor Phocas: over the Gauls and Germans by Pepin the short, and afterward by Charlemagne, king of the Franks.[14]

---

[13] See Juan de Torquemada, lib. 2, ch. 42, and book IV, last and next to last chapters.

[14] *Instit.* lib. 4, ch. 7, § 17.

Luther says that it was Constantine IV who conferred primacy on the Pontiff, and in testimony of this affair he cites Plantina in his life of Benedict II.[15] Nevertheless, the same Luther teaches in another place that the primacy of the Pope was introduced by the emperor Phocas;[16] which likewise the Centuriators teach,[17] as well as others.[18]

They can all be easily refuted. In the first place, the opinion on Constantine is of no harm to us. For Constantine the Great gave his palace at the Lateran and many other temporal possessions to the Supreme Pontiff; still he never gave any spiritual dowry, nor could he. For in the same Canon Constantine declares that St. Peter was the Vicar of Christ, and for that reason his successors ought to be held as princes and heads of the whole Church. Therefore, Constantine only declared an ancient law, and adorned the Pope with many added temporal gifts.

Add what the Lutherans and Calvinists contend must be supposed by this canon; hence in this time there is no edict from Constantine for us with the heretics, inasmuch as to spiritual jurisdiction. They affirm it did not begin with Constantine.

Next, the opinion of Luther rests upon a false foundation: Platina did not say that Constantine IV gave primacy to the Pontiff, but remitted his law that he had or thought he had in confirmation of the Pontiff. The predecessors of Constantine IV, from the times of Justinian, who freed the city from the Goths, did not permit the election of a new Pope, unless they had confirmed it; and the Popes tolerated this for the sake of the good of the Church, because they saw he could not exercise his office against the will of the emperor: that could be understood from St. Gregory.

For in the explication of the fourth penitential Psalm, he vehemently detests the temerity of the emperors, who usurped the right in the Roman Church to themselves.

And still St. Gregory himself, as his biographer John the deacon writes, since he was elected to the pontificate by the clergy and the people, he wrote secretly to the emperor, begging that he would in nowise give his consent; but the prefect of the city sent men knowing the affair, who seized upon the letter of Gregory en route, and tore up his letter, which they also did; and he directed

---

[15] *De potestate Papae.*

[16] *De supputat. Tempor.*

[17] *Cent. VI*, ch. 1.

[18] Illyricus, *hist. De Prim.*; the Smalkaldic Council *de Primatu Papae*; Theodor Bibliander, *Chron.* Tab. 11.

other messengers, who would point out the election of clergy and people to the emperor, and beg his confirmation.[19]

Therefore, Platina writes that Constantine IV, moved by the sanctity of Benedict II, sent to him sanction, whereby he would ask that he whom clergy and people chose should soon after be held as the true Vicar of Christ, without need to wait for any opinion of the emperor. Therefore, the sanction of Constantine IV was not concerning the power of the Pope, as Luther thought, but only in regard to his election.

Now to that argument about Phocas, I respond: Phocas published a sanction, in which he declared the Roman Church is the head of all churches, as Bede witnesses, as well as Ado and Paul the Deacon.[20] Yet it was not on that account that this primacy was introduced by Phocas, for Phocas ratified it by declaring and asserting, not by establishing a new thing; this can be proven by most certain reason.

Gregory says: "On the see of Constantinople, who doubts that it is subject to the Apostolic See, since our most pious Lord and Emperor, as well as my brother Eusebius, the bishop of the same city, profess it in earnest."[21] The epistle was written around five years before the reign of Phocas, as can be gathered clearly from a number of indications.

Next, Justinian the elder, who was around 70 years before Phocas, in an epistle to Pope John II, affirmed the Roman Church is the head of all churches, and Valentinian, who preceded Phocas by around 140 years, asserted in an epistle to Theodosius that the Roman Pontiff had the rule of priesthood over all. It is corroborated by the testimonies of Irenaeus, Athanasius, Cyril, Theodoret, Sozomen, and other Greeks whom we cited above.

The reason why Phocas reckoned that an affair so certain should be ratified again was the pride of the bishops of Constantinople, as Bede, Ado and Paul the deacon noted in the cited works. Since they wrote that they were "universal Patriarchs" and "first of all bishops" against all law and right, and the excommunications which Popes Pelagius and Gregory, the Roman Pontiffs, had imposed upon them could not break their obstinance, it seemed good to the emperor that he, whom the Greeks feared more, should interpose himself. Therefore, he declared that the Roman Church is the head of all Churches; hence the bishop of Constantinople was not a universal bishop, but a particular

---

[19] Joan. Diac., *Vita S. Greg.*, lib. 1, ch. 40.

[20] Bede, *de sex aetat.* In Phoca; Ado, *Chronicus*, Paulus Diaconus lib. XVIII de reb. Rom.

[21] *Lib. VII, epist. 63 ad Jo. Syracus.*

one and subject to the Apostolic See.

Now, I respond to the argument about Pepin the short: Calvin makes use of a wondrous artifice to summon a true historical account but roll it up in lies in defense of his heresies. For, on the one hand he says that by the suffrage of the Pontiffs, Pepin attained the kingdom of France, and Charlemagne the Empire of the Romans; it is true, and related by many historical letters. Yet what he says unjustly and wickedly, that the true king of France was despoiled of his kingdom by Pope Zachary and Pepin is false, and contumelious, not only against the Pope, but even the kings of France and the emperors of Germany, who both descend from that Pepin. But what he adds, that for that reason the primacy was conceded to the Pope by Pepin and Charlemagne over France and Germany as the custom of thieves to divide the prey, so that to Pepin and Charlemagne he would cede temporal dominion, but to the Popes, rule of priesthood, is not only false, but even contrary to the first lie, consequently, lies oppose themselves, and one destroyed the other.

And first, the fact that Zachary justly and legitimately deposed King Childeric, and bid Pepin be created, every historian who wrote anything about this event, both Greeks and Latins affirm[22] (with the exceptions of the Centuriators and Calvin).[23] They all relate that a little before the times of Pepin, the kings of the Franks had so degenerated from their elders, that nearly every care of the kingdom had been transferred to the Masters of Horse, or the Prefect of the Hall, and the king was only seen once a year on the first of May when they would show him to the people; the rest of the time, they devoted themselves to pleasure and delight; and on that account it was demanded from the Supreme Pontiff by the agreement of all the nobles to permit them to transfer the title of the kings to those who were truly in fact kings, and long ago had happily administered the business of the kingdom. What they rightly demanded was most just; really France labored on account of those monstrous infamies with all nations, and likewise the kingdom was replete with innumerable dissensions.

Not only this, (as these authors relate) but there was no business of the kingdom that these kings took care of; rather, even on account of their inertia,

---

[22] Einhart *in vita Caroli Magni,*; Aimonius, *de rebus gestis Francorum,* lib.. IV, ch. 61; Cedrenus *Vita Leonis Isauri*; Paul the Deacon, lib. VI, ch. 5 *de gest. Longobard.*; Blondus lib. X; Decadis, I. Rhegino lib. II Chronicor. Marianus Scotus, lib. III Chronol.; Otho of Frisia, lib. V histor.; Ado Viennensis in Chron. Aetat. Vi. Abbas Urspergensis in Chron. Sigebertus item in Chron. And Paulus Aemilius lib. 1 and 2 de gest. Francor.

[23] Magdeburgensibus, *Centur. VIII,* ch. 10 in vita Zachariae; Calvin loc. cit.

religion so labored in Gaul, that it had almost been extinguished, as is clear from St. Boniface,[24] who says for nearly 80 years, while this Sardanapalus reigned,[25] there was no synod celebrated. Episcopal churches were possessed by laity and tax collectors, clerics had four or five concubines at once, and religion had been tread upon and dissipated.

Therefore, since Zachary understood now that for many years the kings of France were so in name only, and Childeric, who then reigned, not only neglected all the custom of his ancestors, but even lacked altogether every quality, and truly was said to be (and was) stupid; at the same time, he saw the kingdom and religion in France come to ruin, and all the nobles of the kingdom desired Pepin, at length, as he looked to that which would provide safety for all; the Pope judged it to be lawful to transfer the kingdom of France from Childeric to Pepin, and also absolved them from the oath which they had been obliged to make to Childeric. That his decision was just, no man of sound mind would deny, especially when the event taught the change was most happy; never was the kingdom of the Franks more powerful or religion more flourishing than in the time of Pepin and Charlemagne.

Lastly, add the fact that nearly all the cited authors write, that the one who anointed and crowned Pepin as king at the Pope's command was a very holy man, namely St. Boniface, bishop and martyr, who certainly was never the author of any public injustice or crime.

But now, that it was never on account of Pepin or Charlemagne that the primacy of the Pope was brought into Germany and France can easily be shown.

First, because nobody writes this, apart from Calvin. Rather the cited authors, and especially Paulus Aemilius, say that the kings of the Franks received the protection of the Apostolic See against the Lombards and other enemies, and they gave to the Pope the exarchate of Ravenna, and certain other temporal things; but they never mention any spiritual dowry.

Next, if the nobles of the kingdom sought from the Pope by legates to be absolved from the oath, and that it would be lawful to transfer the kingdom from Childeric to Pepin, as Paulus Aemilius and others write; certainly they thought that the Pope was in charge of the whole Church and specifically France; otherwise why did they not seek from their own bishops, or why did

---

[24] *Epist. S. Bonifacii Episc. Mogunt., ad Zahar. Rom. Pontiff.*

[25] Sardanapalus was, according to Greek historians, the last king of Assyria, who dithered, dressed like women and failed to administer the kingdom. Bellarmine uses this somewhat mythical figure to describe the failure of the Merovingian kings. -Translator's note.

they not do what they wanted without a license from the Pope? Nay more, why did they wait that the Pope would command it, as Rheginus and others write? Therefore, if the Pope exercised the primacy in France before Pepin had been created king, how did he receive that primacy from Pepin? Do they not fight against themselves?

Next, before the times of Pepin it is certain that the Franks and Germans were subject to the Roman Pontiff in spiritual matters. For St. Boniface, the bishop of Moguntinus, wrote an epistle to Pope Zachary from the Prince Caroloman, as he indicates in the same place. Hence Pepin has already been made king; for it is certain that Caroloman, after laying aside his rule, became a monk before the exaltation of Pepin in the kingdom; but in that epistle he clearly professes the churches of Germany then were subject to the Pontiff and also among other things, sought from the Pope that he should erect three episcopates in Germany, and give him authority to call a council of bishops in France, and many other matters of this kind.

Likewise St. Bede, who preceded Pepin by about a hundred years, says: "Since Gregory leads the Pontificate in the whole world." I believe Calvin would not say that France and Germany are not part of "the whole world."

St. Gregory, who preceded Pepin by nearly 200 years, committed all 52 bishops of France to Virgilius the bishop of Arles in his stead, and commanded that more serious cases be referred to the judgment of the Apostolic See: "Insofar as it should be fitting without a doubt for opinion to be finished."

St. Leo, who preceded Pepin by 350 years, writes: "Your fraternity recognizes with us, that the Apostolic See, was to be consulted by the innumerable priests of your province, as well as for appeal of different cases, or retractions, or confirmation and judgments."[26]

St. Cyprian, who flourished more than 500 years before Pepin, writes to Pope Stephen so that he would depose the bishop of Arles, and put another in his place. St. Irenaeus, who preceded Pepin by 600 years, said: "To the Roman Church, on account of a mightier preeminence, it is necessary for every Church to agree, this is, all who are faithful on every side." He did not except France, since he was a French bishop, and we might not leave out the fact that when the Lord said to Peter and his successors: "Feed my sheep," without a doubt he numbered Germany and France among his sheep.

---

[26] Epistle 89 *ad Episc. Galliae.*

CHAPTER XVIII

That the Roman Pontiff Succeeds Peter in the Ecclesiastical Monarchy is Proven from the Authority Which the Roman Pontiff Exercised over Other bishops.

HE SIXTH argument is taken from the authority which the ancient Pontiffs always exercised over other bishops. Accordingly we read that bishops were established throughout the whole world by Roman Pontiffs, or deposed, or restored, the singular events of which should suffice in themselves to show this primacy.

And first, many examples can be brought to bear on the establishment of bishops. We read, for instance, in the Council of Chalcedon, Action 7, that Maximus was confirmed in the episcopacy of Antioch by St. Leo the Great. Likewise, Anatolius, the bishop of Constantinople, was confirmed by Leo, who writes thus: "It should be enough that by the aid of your piety, and the assent of my favor, he obtained the episcopate of such a city."[1]

Leo also writes in an epistle to Anastasius, the bishop of Thessalonika: "On the person of the bishop to be consecrated, and from the consent of the clergy and people, the metropolitan bishop relates to your fraternity, that each is well pleased in his province, that he should see to it to know you, that your authority should rightly strengthen the ordination which must be celebrated." And further on: "Just as we wish in no way to importune the just elections by delays, so we permit nothing to be presumed without your knowledge." And in Epistle 87 to the bishops of Africa; "Donatus Salicinensis, as we discovered, was converted from Novatian with his own, so we wish to preside over the Lord's flock, that he was mindful to send us the profession of his faith."

St. Gregory taught, in his epistle to Constance Augusta: "The bishop of the city of Salona was ordained without my knowledge and response, and the matter came to pass which happened under no earlier princes."[2] And everywhere he shows in his epistles that he sent the pallium himself, which is the insignia of an Archbishop, to different archbishops in Greece, France, Spain, etc. Still it must be remarked, the fact that although the primacy of the Roman Pontiff is proven from the confirmation of bishops, nevertheless, it is not necessary that he would have confirmed all bishops always; he could permit that this be done by patriarchs and primates, as it appears was the case in many places.

Now, on the deposition there are many examples extant, and in the first place from St. Cyprian. He writes to Pope St. Stephen saying: "Let your letters

---

[1] Epist. 54 ad Martian.

[2] Lib. 4, epistl. 34.

be directed to the province, and to the people of Arles, in which Marcianus being avoided, let another be substituted in his place."[3] And further: "You will make plain to us who should be constituted in place of Marcianus of Arles, in order that we may know to whom to direct our brethren, and to whom we ought to write."

Calvin takes up the argument on this citation: "I ask, if Stephen was then over Gaul, can it be that Cyprian was going to say to those being coerced that 'they are yours'? Yet by far, fraternal society is another thing, in which we have been subdued among ourselves, requiring that we advise each other."[4]

I respond: These words, which Calvin cites, are never discovered in Cyprian. So, if Cyprian thought that Stephen was not over Gaul, but could only advise in friendship, why did he not advise the Gauls himself?

Nicholas I enumerates eight patriarchs of Constantinople, in his epistle to the Emperor Michael, whom the Roman Pontiffs had deposed, among which was one Anthimus, whom Pope Agapetus deposed, not without the hindrance of the emperor and empress, and ordained in his place with his own hands Menas, as Liberatus and Zonaras write in their works.[5] Likewise, Pope Gelasius, in his epistle to the bishop of the Dardanelles: "The Apostolic See condemned Dioscorus, prelate of the Second See, by its own authority." And likewise: "The see of Blessed Peter did not receive Peter of Alexandria whom it had not merely condemned, but refused to absolve."

On that account Damasus deposed Flavian, the patriarch of Antioch, as Theodoret writes.[6] And although the Emperor Theodosius strove to stabilize Flavian in the episcopate, still he commanded him to continue to Rome to state his case. And Theophilus of Alexandria, though legates interceded with the Roman Pontiff on behalf of Flavian, as Socrates relates.[7] Sozomen witnesses that Chrysostom did his best to do the same.[8] Next, Flavian could possess that episcopate before him, which the Roman Pontiff, being pleased, agreed, and he promised that he was going to admit his legates, who soon after sent many bishops and especially priests of the Antiochene Church to the Pope, as the

---

[3]   Lib. III, epist. 13 ad Stephanum.

[4]   *Instit.*, lib. IV, ch. 7, § 7.

[5]   Liberatus, *Brevar.*, ch. 21; Zonaras, *Vita Justiniani*.

[6]   *Hist.* Lib. V, ch. 23.

[7]   *Hist.* Lib. V, ch. 15.

[8]   Lib. VIII, ch. 3.

same Theodoret writes.

Sixtus III also deposed the bishop Polychronicus of Jerusalem, after sending St. Leo while he was an archdeacon to Jerusalem.[9] Therefore, if the Roman Pontiff at some time deposed every patriarch, namely those of Constantinople, Alexandria, Antioch, and Jerusalem, certainly he is the supreme judge in the Church.

Next, there are many examples on the restitution of bishops deposed by others. For St. Cyprian says: "He cannot rescind an ordination legally carried out, because Basilides, after his crimes were discovered, continued on to Rome, where he deceived Stephen, our colleague, who is far removed and unaware of the affair and the truth, that he would solicit to be replaced unjustly in the episcopate, from which he had been justly deposed, etc."[10]

Next, Athanasius of Alexandria, Paul of Constantinople, and Marcellus of Ancyra, all bishops who were deposed by an Eastern synod, Pope Julius I restored, as Gelasius writes in the epistle to the bishop of the Dardanelles, and Sozomen records in his histories: "Since on account of the dignity of the seat which looks to the care of all, he restored each one to his own church." And further on: "Athanasius and Paul returned to their own sees, and they sent the letter of Pope Julius to the Eastern bishops."[11] Likewise, we read the following from the Acts of the Council of Chalcedon on the deposition of Theodoret by the Council of Ephesus: "Even let the most Reverend bishop Theodoret enter so that he may be a partaker of the synod, because the most holy Archbishop Leo has restored him to his episcopate."[12] Many similar testimonies can be brought to bear, to which our adversaries altogether cannot respond, nor do they attempt to.

On the other hand, NilosCabásilas proposes five arguments. The first argument is that the bishop of Rome is said to be first, because Constantinople is second from him, Alexandria is third from him, Antioch is fourth, Jerusalem fifth; but first and second are not said as one is superior and the other inferior, but only concerning those matters which are of the same rank and dignity; therefore, the bishop of Rome is not said to be first by reason of Tusculum or Tiburtinus, which are subject to her.

I respond: The Roman Pontiff is bishop, archbishop, patriarch and Pope at

---

[9] This is clear from Tom. I Concilior. In act. Sixti III.

[10] Lib. 1, epist. 4.

[11] Sozomenus, Hist., lib. 3 ch. 7.

[12] Council of Chalcedon, act 1.

the same time. As bishop, he is first in this province by reason of Ostia, which is second, and Portus which is third, and of the rest, which can be counted in that order. Yet, as archbishop, he is not first by reason of Ostia, which is not an archepiscopate, but a simple bishopric subject to the Roman archbishop. Nevertheless, it is first by reason of the Archbishop of Ravenna, Milan and of the rest of the western archepiscopates.

Furthermore, as the proper Patriarch of the West, he is not first by reason of Ravenna and the rest, which are not patriarchs, but by reason of Constantinople, Alexandria, Antioch and Jerusalem, which are patriachates. And in this way the five primary sees can be counted, each of which presides over many great provinces.

Lastly, as Pope and head of the universal Church, he is not first by reason of Constantinople, or of any other; rather he is Prince and Pastor of all, nor does he have any second in power as a colleague. For, just in the same way as there ought to be among the bishops of the same province one who is over the rest, and is called an archbishop, and among archbishops of many provinces, there is one who should be over the others and is called a patriarch, for equal reasoning, among the patriarchs of the Catholic Church, there ought to be one who presides over the rest and is named the Pope or the Vicar of Christ. And this is the Roman Pontiff, as we have shown by many arguments.

Now for the second argument of Nilos. He proposes that the Sixth Council in canon 36 renewed the constitution of the Second and Fourth Council, which granted the bishop of Constantinople equal privileges with those which the bishop of Rome has. Therefore, the bishop of Rome is not of greater authority and dignity than Constantinople, hence he cannot command all other bishops.

I respond: In the Second General Council the bishop of Constantinople was not equated to the bishop of Rome; rather, he was only placed before Alexandria and Antioch, as is clear from canon 5 of the same Council, whose words are these: "It is meet that the bishop of the city of Constantinople should have the honor of primacy after the bishop of Rome, due to the fact that it is the new Rome."

But in the Council of Chalcedon, Action 16, they added to the same canon that it is fitting for him to have equal privileges with the Roman Pontiff, but since the Legates of the Pontiff protested, the same council wrote an epistle to Leo, in which it asked him to confirm the decrees of the council. But the Fathers did not dare to make mention in that epistle of equal privileges; they merely wrote that they had renewed the canon of the Second Council in which second honor was attributed to the bishop of Constantinople.[13]

St. Leo also responded in an epistle to the council,[14] in which, as in all other places where he wrote on this case, he makes no mention of equal privileges, but only bitterly condemns the ambitious lust of the bishop of Constantinople because he wished to place himself before Alexandria and Antioch.

Nicephorus also writes in his history that when Pope John I came to Constantinople, the Pontiff was invited by the Emperor Justin that he would sit next to Epiphanius the Patriarch of Constantinople, so that it would appear as though they were equal. But the Pontiff did not wish to sit until a throne had been set up for himself over Epiphanius for the prerogative of the Apostolic See.[15] From that it appears that the canon on equal privileges was not admitted, even a long time after the Council of Chalcedon, and it had not force even in that council; otherwise Epiphanius could have cited the canon of that council, for he would not have suffered a throne to be set up for the Roman Pontiff over himself in his own church. Wherefore, there is only Canon 36 of the Sixth Council, which equates the bishop of Constantinople with Rome.

The rest of these canons are of no more force; for they are no canons of the true Sixth Council which was legitimate and ecumenical, but of another specific gathering, which was falsely named the Sixth Council. It is certain that the Sixth Council which was celebrated under Pope Agatho and the Emperor Constantine IV, published no such canons; rather five years after that synod had been dissolved, again they came together with I know not how many Greek bishops under the authority of the Emperor Justinian the Younger, and it published many canons in the name of the Sixth Synod.[16] The fact is manifestly gathered from the very origin of these canons, and from the confession of Tharasius the bishop of Constantinople in the VII Council, Action 4, that these same canons which Bede calls the "erratic Synod", and they were condemned by Pope Sergius

---

[13] This epistle is contained in act. Conc. Chalced. Act 3.

[14] Ep. 59.

[15] Nicephors, *Hist.*, lib. XVII, c. 9.

[16] Translator's note: This is also called the "Quinisext Council" from the Latin 5th-6th Council, as it was meant to complete the disciplinary work of the those two ecumenical councils. It is also called the Council in Trullo, from τρούλος meaning dome, or specifically the dome under which the 6th Ecumenical Council was held. The position of Nilos Cabásilas, whom Bellarmine is refuting, holding these canons as part of the Sixth Council, is still maintained by the Chalcedonian Orthodox Churches today.

who then sat, as Bede records.[17] From which it follows that same false Sixth Council, either was not general, or it was not legitimate: for it cannot be a legitimate general council, where the authority of the First See is lacking, as the Greeks themselves affirmed in the VII Council, act. 6.

And hence, for what reason can it be called a legitimate general council, to which not even one of the Latins was called? Furthermore, if it was not legitimate, it is plain that it could have no authority. But if it was legitimate, but particular, not general, it could not impose laws except upon men subject to it; it could not, therefore, reduce the position of the Roman See, and despoil it of privileges, which it tried in fact to do, when it attempted to equate the See of Constantinople with it, even though it was otherwise inferior and subject to it. For the Roman See was never subject to a Greek council; further in the very matter it is proved that there are no imperial laws or ecclesiastical canons, neither by reason or custom, that the Greeks could prove; ergo, there are no laws and canons, which subject the First See to the Second; it is contrary to all reason. Lastly, no testimony can be brought into our midst, whereby it is certain something was done from the authority of the Greek bishops in the Roman Church, or the rest of the Western Churches.

Next, the primacy of the Roman Church, was either given by Christ, as we believe, or by the Council of Nicaea, as Nilos himself teaches; therefore, by what law could this particular council in Trullo bring to bear upon that which Christ himself or a general council had given? It is manifest that the primacy of the Roman Church, through that communication of privileges which the council in Trullo ratified with its decree, would be abolished; for one who has equality with someone cannot be over all.

Besides, add that although the Second and Fourth Synod did not equate Constantinople to the Roman Pontiff, but made him only second to the Pontiff, nevertheless, that very canon was not ratified as long as the Apostolic See opposed it. For that reason, in the Fourth Synod, when the Greeks wanted to give second place to the See of Constantinople, and they suborned the decree of the Second Council from 80 years before to prove this, the Roman legates said: "If they used this benefice for 80 years, why do they require it now? If they never used it, why do they require it?" By which words they showed that it was in vain to appeal to that decree, because as it was never in use so also it was void.

The third argument. If the Roman Pontiff, because he is the first of patriarchs, has rule over the second, that is in Constantinople, therefore, for

---

[17] *De sex aetat.*, in Justiniano juniore.

equal reasoning Constantinople, because it is the second, will have rule in Alexandria because it is the third, and Alexandria the third in Antioch which is fourth, and Antioch in Jerusalem which is last. But no reasoning, no law and no custom admits this.

I respond: The Roman Pontiff has rule in Constantinople and the other patriarchates not because he is first patriarch, but because he alone is the Pope of the universal Church, the successor of Peter and the general Vicar of Christ. In the same way, each archbishop does not preside over the rest of the bishops of the same province because he is first bishop, but because he alone is an Archbishop of that province. But on that account, each patriarch is not eminent in power over all archbishops subject to him, but because he himself is the first archbishop, rather because he might be in that region the supreme and only patriarch.

The fourth argument. The Roman bishop does not ordain patriarchs, just as Patriarchs ordain their own metropolitans, and metropolitans their own bishops; therefore, he is not over the patriarchs, as they are over metropolitans, and metropolitans over bishops.

I respond: Indeed the Roman Pontiff did not customarily ordain Patriarchs, because it could not be suitably done, since either they would have to come to Rome, or the Pontiff himself would have to set out to them. Nevertheless, he confirmed it through letters; that we showed above from the example of Anatholius of Constantinople, and Maximus of Antioch. And this was no empty confirmation, as the case of Flavian clearly declares, because he could never obtain the Church of Antioch so long as the bishop of Rome would not agree. On this point, it is no less a thing to depose or restore than to ordain a bishop: moreover the Roman Pontiff did not once, but as often as it was necessary, either depose or restore patriarchs, as we proved above. Lastly, Menas, the Patriarch of Constantinople, was ordained by Pope Agatho, and Nilos cannot be ignorant of the fact, since Zonaras hands down the letters in his life of Justinian.

The fifth argument is that the Council of Nicaea, Canon 6, determined the regions assigned to all the patriarchs; and certainly handed the West to the bishop of Rome; Egypt, Libya and Pentapolis to Alexandria; Syria to Antioch, as well as Mesopotamia; therefore, the one Roman Pontiff ought not rule everywhere, and command the other patriarchs.

I respond: The Council of Nicaea assigned no region to the Roman Pontiff. What Nilos says about the West, he learned from the interpretation of Balsamon, not from the canon of the council itself; for in that canon there is nothing about the Roman Pontiff, except this little sentence, which Nilos himself cites thus: Επεὶ καί τῷ ἐν τῇ Ρώμη ἐπισμόπῳ ποῦτο συνηθές ἐστίν.[18] When such words render the reasoning why Egypt, Libya and Pentapolis ought to be subject to the bishop of Alexandria according to ancient custom, they cannot yield any another sense than that the Roman Pontiff customarily consigned the governance of those three provinces to the bishop of Alexandria.

Thereupon, if the Council of Nicaea wished to determine the dowry to the Roman Pontiff, why did it not begin from that? Why does it begin from Alexandria, which was second? And why did it not name the region which it gave to the Roman Pontiff? Add, lastly, that even if the Council of Nicaea spoke with eloquent words, that the West properly pertained to the Roman Pontiff, still Nilos would altogether gain nothing; for without a doubt, it was to be understood on the dowry of the patriarchate of the Roman Pontiff, apart from which he would still have the same supreme power over every Church. It must be observed in passing, what Nilos says, namely, that the West ought to be subject to the Roman Pontiff, is passed over by Illyricus in his very faithful translation, lest Illyricus would be compelled to be subject to the Roman Pontiff from the testimony of Nilos.

---

[18] "This is because that is the custom to the bishop of Rome." -Translator's note.

CHAPTER XIX

That the Roman Pontiff Succeeds Peter in the Ecclesiastical Monarchy is Proven from Laws, Dispensations and Censures

A SEVENTH argument can be introduced from the authority of imposing laws, dispensing them and punishing according to them, which the bishop of Rome exercised over the sons of the Church, although they may have been very great and noble. Numerous examples can be advanced from laws: it was a rare thing that there were any Pontiffs who did not decree something.

St. Leo the Great writes to the bishops of Campania, Piacenza and Thuscia, and constituted through all provinces, speaking thus at the end of the epistle: "After our admonition, let them give notice that if anyone of the brethren will have come against these constitutions, or attempts to do so, and will have dared to admit those things which are forbidden, he will know that he must be removed from his office ... All the decretals constituted by Innocent, of happy memory, which were ordained of all by our predecessors on ecclesiastical orders, and disciplines of the canons, so we command that your love ought to safeguard so that if anyone will have scorned them, thereafter pardon will be refused to him." In like manner, he prescribes two laws to Dioscorus the bishop of Alexandria, and in each uses these words: "We wish it also to be guarded by you."

Pope Hilary, presiding in a Roman council, said: "It shall be lawful for no one without danger to his status or divine constitutions, even to make bold the decrees of the Apostolic See." Pope Anastasius II said: "Let hard pride not resist the Apostolic commands, but through obedience to those matters which are commanded by the authority of the Holy Roman Church and the Apostolic See, may they be profitably fulfilled, if with the same holy Church of God, which is your head, you desire to have communion." St. Gregory, in a privilege which he gave to the monastery of St. Menard, also wrote at the end of a epistle: "If anyone, of kings, judges, bishops, or of any secular persons, will have violated the decrees of this apostolic authority and our command, let him be deprived of his honor."

On dispensations, we have an example in Epistle 1 of Gelasius (for we pass over the infinite more recent examples for the sake of efficiency): "We are constrained by the necessary disposition of things, and we are agreed upon the management of the Apostolic See, thus to balance the decrees of the paternal canons, and to measure the precepts of our predecessors, so what such necessity of the present times demands to be relaxed to restore the churches, after diligent consideration was applied, we refrained as much as it could be done." And he dispenses the same in many ways. Likewise, St. Gregory says in a letter[1] that he dispensed concerning matrimony with the English in prohibited degrees: and again, with the Siculi, that they may only once celebrate a Council in a year, since otherwise the rule commands councils to be celebrated twice in a year. Hence, this rule, which Gregory dispensed, is Canon 5 of the First General Council.

On censures there are many examples, and indeed they are very ancient. For Innocent I, when he heard that Chrysostom died, he excommunicated the Emperor Arcadius and Eudoxia his wife, who did not permit Chrysostom to be restored to his see, as Innocent himself had commanded. The epistle of Innocent on this affair is contained in Nicephorus' *Histories.*[2]

Nor can it be objected that even Ambrose, who was not a Supreme Pontiff, excommunicated the emperor. For Ambrose did that in his Church, when the Emperor had a seat at Milan, but Ambrose would not have dared to excommunicate someone outside of the diocese of Milan. Moreover, Innocent also excommunicated emperors at Constantinople, as well as those living there. Next, Gregory III, in like manner, excommunicated the Greek emperor Leo, as Zonaras witnesses in the life of Leo the Istaurian.

Nicholas I excommunicated Lothar the king of Gaul and his concubine, Vladrada, rather than his proper bishops, the archbishops of Cologne and Trier. On this point the Centuriators of Magdeburg tell the most impudent lies, when they say that King Lothar and the archbishops were unjustly harassed by Pope Nicholas. For as many historians write,[3] Lothar, from hatred toward Thietberga, his wife, and for love toward his concubine, suborned false witnesses to convict his wife of incest, and then, on the authority of the Archbishop of Cologne and Trier, repudiated her and led his concubine to wife, all of which those Archbishops confessed at Rome in council.

Therefore, if the Centuriators wish to make Lothar and the Archbishops just, as they do, it is necessary that they accuse Paul, who in 1 Corinth. 7 teaches that not even on account of the case of fornication could one marry another while the first wife is living. What about the fact that the wife of Lothar did not sin, but was only condemned by false testimonies; do the Centuriators justify false testimonies so they can scold the Pope in some way?

---

[1]   Lib. 12, ep. 31 to Felix the bishop of Sicily.

[2]   Lib. 13, ch. 34.

[3]   Rhenginus, lib. 2; Otho the Frisian, lib. 6, ch. 3; Sigebert *in Chronico* anni DCCCLXII.

But we have the example of the most illustrious and ancient. For, when Pius I decreed that Easter should not be celebrated on the fourteenth day of the first month of the Jews, but on the following Sunday, and the Asians refused to acquiesce, Pope Victor I excommunicated all of them around the year 190, as Eusebius writes.[4]

Calvin objects, however, that Victor was rebuked on this account by Irenaeus and rightly obeyed the one rebuking him, without a protest.[5]

I respond: Irenaeus, along with many others, rebuked Victor, because it seemed that he had cut such churches off from the unity of the Church for so trifling a cause (Eusebius witnesses the same thing), but the fact that Victor changed his sentence, *we read nowhere*. And even if Victor had changed his sentence, Calvin would gain nothing from that. We would say that the same power whereby Victor bound the Asians, he absolved them.

Next, the rebuke of Irenaeus and others does not diminish, but rather more increases the force of our argument. For in the same measure, whereby there were many displeased by the sentence of Victor, so they could more easily condemn or rather more preferably excommunicate Victor, if they thought he was one from the number of bishops, rather than the head and judge of all. But in reality, there was not anyone who taught that the sentence was void, or thought that Victor must be condemned or excommunicated; nor was there anyone who warned him lest he might exceed his limits and lest he might judge those not subject to him; in fact, they ought to have warned him if Victor truly was not the judge of all. Moreover, they reckoned Victor did what he could, not what he ought. Their words sound thus in Eusebius: "Their letters are extant, in which they more bitterly rebuke Victor, as if consulting him that it was unprofitable to what was fitting for the Church."

Moreover, this must be observed, that although Irenaeus and others then thought that Victor had acted imprudently, nevertheless, really he acted very prudently, as the whole Church judged afterward. For one from those particular authors of that opinion, on the celebration of Easter with the Jews, was Blastus, who in the very matter, little by little wanted to introduce Judaism, as Tertullian writes at the end of *De Praescriptiones contra haereticos:* "Blastus wanted to secretly introduce Judaism: indeed, he said Pascha should be kept in no other way than according to the law of Moses, on the fourteenth day of the month." Here, however, Blastus began to sow his heresy at Rome in the time of Pope

---

[4] Lib. 5, histor. Ch. 24.

[5] *Instit.* lib. 4, ch. 7 § 7.

Victor, as Eusebius witnesses.[6]

Therefore, because Pope Victor saw that truth on Easter was not only a diversity of observance, but bore the tallow of heresy, nay more, of Judaism itself, he reckoned the time was ripe to oppose it. Therefore, the Fathers of the Council of Nicaea approved of the judgment of Victor, as is clear from Eusebius,[7] and thereafter those who thought the contrary were held as heretics and called Quartodecimans,[8] as is clear from Epiphanius and Augustine.[9]

---

[6] *Hist. Eccl.*, lib. 5, ch. 15.

[7] *Vita Constantini*, lib. 3.

[8] Translator's note: From the Latin word for fourteen, since they thought Easter should only be celebrated on the 14th day of the Jewish month of Nissan, the calendar day that Christ rose from the dead. This heresy is also prevalent amongst certain Protestants today.

[9] Epiphanius *de Haeresi.*, 50; Augustine *haeresi*, 29.

CHAPTER XX

That the Roman Pontiff Succeeds Peter in the Ecclesiastical Monarchy is Proven from Vicars of the Pope

HE EIGHTH argument is taken up from the fact that the Supreme Pontiff had his vicars in various regions, either as an ordinary measure or only for a time, still with the reservation of greater cases.

For just in the very way that a king sends viceroys to provinces, and we understand those provinces subject to the king, and likewise, in the same way, the king enjoins judgments upon the governors of the provinces with reservation of certain cases, we yet understand that the king is the supreme judge, so also in the very matter the Apostolic See has vicars in nearly all far off regions, or consigns someone in their places for a time, and wishes more grave business to be referred to him; we rightly gather that the supreme judgement of the whole Church pertains to the Apostolic seat. There are many examples.

Pope Leo made Anastasius, the bishop of Thessalonika, his vicar for the East just as his predecessors were vicars for the predecessors of Leo, which he indicates in the same letter.[1] This appears to be the reason why the Council of Sardica declared in Canon 20 that clerics from outside Thessalonika should not be delayed there. Since the vicar of the Pope sat in that place, clerics met from the whole Greek world, and often stayed there longer than they should have. Leo also consigned their places to Potentius, the bishop of the regions of Africa.

Pope Celestine consigned the case of Nestorius of Constantinople to Cyril of Alexandria, as well as the rule of that church after the bishop was deposed.[2]

Gelasius, in an epistle to the bishops of the Balkans: "Why did Acacius not take care to relate this to the Apostolic See, by whom he knew care of those regions had been delegated to him?" Here he speaks of the bishop of Constantinople, Acacius, to whom the Roman Pontiff had consigned care of Egypt and commanded that he should depose the bishop of Alexandria.

Pope Hormisdas, in an epistle to Salustius the bishop of Spain, makes him his vicar for Granda and Portugal. Justinian writes that the bishop of Constantinople in certain places ought to be in charge just as vicars of the Roman Pontiff, because Vigilius constituted him such.[3]

St. Gregory constituted the Virgilius, the bishop of Arles, as his vicar throughout Gaul, and likewise reserved to himself more serious cases.

---

[1] Epistle 84 *ad Anastasium.*

[2] See the letter of Celestine to Cyril in volume 4 of al the works of Cyril, and in the same place the epistle of Cyril to the clergy and people of Constantinople.

[3] *In Authenticis* collat. 9, tit. 6, or *Novella Constitutione* 131.

CHAPTER XXI

That the Roman Pontiff Succeeds Peter in the Ecclesiastical Monarchy is Proven from the Law of Appeals

THE NINTH argument can be made from the fact that whenever something was legitimately called to the Roman Pontiff from any part of the Christian world, no appeal from his judgment was conceded. Thus, it is a very certain argument of rule, as our adversary himself confesses. Calvin says: "It is certain that supreme power is in the hands of the one before whose tribunal a man is called." But next he adds: "Often many appealed to the Roman Pontiff; he also tried to draw the examination of cases to himself, but was always mocked as often as he exceeded his boundaries."[1] Therefore, Calvin would have it that many called upon the Pontiff, that they might flee legitimate judgments, but appeals of this sort were derided. Now how truly would someone be mocked who being condemned by bishop of Florence, would appeal to the bishop of Milan; or being condemned by the king of Spain, might appeal to the king of France?

Thus it must be proved that one could rightly appeal to the Pontiff, and appeals were not derided, but rather, were received with honor and were efficacious. Firstly, it is proved from the Council of Sardica, which was general and always received in the Church. For Sulpitius writes that it was called from the whole world, and Socrates calls it a general Council.[2]

On that account, as Athanasius and Hilary write,[3] there were in that Council more than three hundred Catholic bishops, from thirty-six provinces of the whole Christian world, all of which Athanasius names: Italy, Gaul, Spain, Britain, Africa, Egypt, Syria, Thrace, Pannonia, and the rest. The legates of Pope Julius were there, as Athanasius relates in the same place. Likewise, the fact that this synod obliged every Church is clear from those words which are contained at the end of the council: "It shall safeguard every Church, which is constituted Catholic, diffused in the whole world."

Next, the Centuriators had described this Synod as legitimate.[4] In this Synod, two canons are contained on this matter, the fourth and seventh. The Fourth

---

[1] *Instit.*, lib. 4, ch. 7 & 9.

[2] Sulpitius, *Sacrae Historiae*, lib. 2; Socrates, *Hist. Eccleisasticae*, lib. 2, ch. 16. [It must be noted here that Sardica has never been received in the list of Ecumenical Councils of the Church, and Bellarmine will explain more on this later on. - Translator's note].

[3] Athanasius, *Secunda Apologia*; Hilary, *De Synodis*.

[4] *Cent. 4*, ch. 9.

Canon reads: "When some bishop was deposed by a judgment of the other bishops that abide in neighboring places, and proclaimed that he will argue the affair in the city of Rome, another bishop should not be ordained in the seat of the one who seems to be deposed, unless the case was determined by the judgment of the bishop of Rome."

The Seventh Canon: "However it has been agreed, that, if a bishop has been accused, and the assembled bishops of the same province have judged and deprived him of his office, and he appears to have appealed, and has taken refuge with the most blessed bishop of the Roman church and has desired to be heard, and he has thought it just that an examination be made anew, let him deign to write to these bishops who are in the adjoining and neighboring province so that they themselves may diligently make all inquiries and decide according to their pledge of truth. But if anyone asks that his case be heard again and by his plea moves the Roman bishop to send a presbyter from his own side, what he [the presbyter] wishes or what he determines will be in the power of the bishop; and if he decrees those ought to be sent who in person may judge with the bishops and who have the authority [of him] by whom they have been appointed, it [this decree] will be within his decision. But if he believes that the bishops suffice to put an end to the affair, he will do that which he decides in accordance with his own very wise deliberation."

Secondly it is proven from Pope Gelasius, who, in an epistle to Faustus says: "They are canons which would have it that appeals of the whole Church be related to the judgment of this see; from it, no appeal at all ought to be sanctioned." And in an epistle to the bishops of the Balkans: "To that place, from whichever part of the world the canons would have it appealed, yet no man is permitted to appeal thence."

The third is proven from the examples of those who have appealed. For even before the Council of Sardica, there was the custom in the Church of appealing to the Pontiff, as Leo deservedly relates in an epistle to the bishops of Gaul, that this is a very ancient custom.

In the year 142, Pius I being Pope, Marcion was excommunicated by his bishop in Pontus, and came to Rome that he might be absolved by the Roman Church, as Epiphanius relates.[5]

In 252, Cornelius being Pope, Fortunatus and Felix were deposed in Africa by St. Cyprian, and they sailed to Rome so as to appeal to Cornelius. Cyprian witnesses this.[6] Not long after, Stephen being Pope, Basilides was deposed in

---

[5] *Haeres.* 42.

[6] Lib. 1, epis. 3.

Spain, and appealed to Stephen.[7]

In the year 350, Julius I being Pope, Athanasius was deposed by the Oriental bishops, and appealed to the Pontiff, and was restored by him, as we showed above from Sozomen,[8] and this judgment came to pass before the Council of Sardica, as Athanasius witnesses in his Second Apology.

After the year 400, while Innocent I was Pope, St. John Chrysostom was deposed by Theophilus, and he appealed to the Pontiff, as is clear from his two epistles to Innocent. Likewise, in the same century, Flavian, the bishop of Constantinople, appealed to Leo, as Liberatus writes,[9] and Theodoret appealed to the same, as it appears from his epistle to Leo.

After the year 500, Gregory deprived John, a Greek bishop, from holy communion, because he had judged the bishop of Thebes who had appealed to the Apostolic See. I omit the testimony of later times, because these are scorned by the heretics. Rather, now the arguments of Nilos, Illyricus and Calvin must be answered.

---

[7] Cyprian, lib. 1 epist. 4.

[8] Lib. 3, ch. 7.

[9] Liberatus, *Breviarium*, ch. 12.

CHAPTER XXII

The Arguments of Nilos Cabásilas on the Law of Appeals are Answered

ILUS CABÁSILAS, in a book on the primacy, contends by two arguments that the bishop of Constantinople can be called in that mode in which the Roman Pontiff is likewise called, and hence they are equals, and not one Roman Pontiff presides over the whole Church.

The first argument is: Because the Sixth Council conceded to the bishop equal privileges with those which the bishop of Rome has. But we refuted this argument above. Nilos takes the second argument from the Council of Chalcedon, Canon 9, where it is stated that if a cleric should have cause against another cleric, let him be judged by his bishop; if against a bishop, then let judgment be given by an archbishop; if against an archbishop, by the one of highest rank of that jurisdiction, or by the bishop of Constantinople. Therefore, the last judgment is deferred to the ecumenical Patriarch of the royal city.

I respond: It is not altogether certain who is called the "one of highest rank of jurisdiction" [*primas dioeceseos*], and indeed Juan de Torquemada[1] teaches that the one of highest rank of a jurisdiction describes a bishop more dignified and greater than an archbishop, but lesser than a patriarch. But Pope Nicholas I, in his epistle to the Emperor Michael, writes that by *primas dioeceseos*, nothing else can be meant but the bishop of Rome. Such an opinion appears to be more true, both because the author has serious authority, antiquity as well as being more learned; and because it will not easily have been proved that in the time of the Council of Chalcedon there was in the Church, and especially in the East, any primates distinct from archbishops and patriarchs. Furthermore, the Greek term used in this canon is ἔξαρχος [exarchos], which does not properly mean a primate, but a prince, and such a term is more suitably squared with the Supreme Pontiff than primates. He alone is truly a prince of any Christian diocese you like.

With these having been noted, I respond: Firstly, that canon is rightly shown by Pope Nicholas I (loc. cit), that the council decreed that he who had cause with a metropolitan, should go to the prince of the diocese, that is the Roman Pontiff: or if he was near to the city of Constantinople, and wished to be content with the judgment of that bishop, let him go there. Therefore, it is such that first the general law was constituted on going to the Roman Pope, thereafter, a certain permission is present only for those who tarry near Constantinople.

Secondly, the response can be made that all of these canons have no force with us, except to the extent that they were renewed by the Roman Pontiffs. For

---

[1] *Super canon si clericus*, 11 q. 1.

Pope Leo writes to the Council of Chalcedon, that he approved that Council, only in regard to the explication of faith.[2] And Liberatus witnesses that all those Canons were constituted while the legates of the Pope were absent; nevertheless they otherwise governed the Council.[3] Next, custom, which is the interpreter of laws, obviously teaches that it was never lawful to appeal to the Patriarch of Constantinople, unless one was from those places subject to the same Patriarch. There is no example that can be proffered in which we might understand that from the West, or the South, or even the North appeals were made to the Eastern Church.

Thirdly, even if we were to concede that from the whole world one could have recourse to the judgment of the bishop of Constantinople according to these canons, still it would not follow that he were equal with the bishop of Rome. For from the force of that canon of Chalcedon, the bishop of Constantinople can only judge those who believe they have been wounded by their Metropolitan: but the Pope of Rome can judge even those who are wounded by Patriarchs, or by a council of bishops; whichever example you like shows this is especially and frequently the case, specifically those of Athanasius, Paul, Chrysostom, Flavian and Theodoret.

Lastly, add the fact that this canon of Chalcedon is not about an appeal, but on the first judgment, something that Nilos does not notice. Therefore, even if the bishop of Constantinople could judge any case you like from the whole world, nevertheless appeal could be made from him to the bishop of Rome, according to the Canons of the Council of Sardica. Nor could the Canons of Chalcedon be opposed in any way to those of Sardica; thus as always, the last judgment remains in the power of the bishop of Rome.

---

[2]   Epist. 59.

[3]   Breviarium, ch. 12.

CHAPTER XXIII
The First Argument of the Lutherans is Answered

OW we come to the arguments of the Lutherans. Our adversaries firstly object that St. Cyprian teaches: "For since it was established for all of us, and it should be right and equally just, that every case whatsoever should be heard in that place where the crime was carried out, etc.; it is indeed fitting that they, whom we are in charge of, should not go around us, etc.,"[1] and further on: "Except if the authority of the bishops constituted in Africa should seem less than a few desperate and lost men, etc." Where he condemns those who appealed to the Roman Pontiff, and he tries to show that appeal ought not be made both because it had been established in a council of bishops, and because the authority of the bishops of Africa is no less than that of the Romans.

I respond: The appeals did not sit well with Cyprian of those men who were manifestly judged and convicted of crimes; but he did not altogether abolish appeals. That is gathered from another epistle, where, speaking about Basilides, who was condemned in Spain but appealed to Pope Stephen, it says: "Nor indeed must the former (Stephen) be blamed, who indifferently received this surprise visit, but rather the latter (Basilides) be detested, who deceitfully dropped in on him."[2] But certainly, if it was not lawful for Stephen to admit appeals in any way, certainly he would have been exceedingly blamed because he did not reject the appeal, even if Basilides would have had a just case.

Therefore, to that which Cyprian says was constituted by all, "that the case should be heard in that place where the crime was carried out," I say it is constituted by this decree that the case should be judged first where the crime was committed; still it is not forbidden that it might be judged again in another place.

But you will say: Still, Cyprian proves from this decree that appeal ought not be made; therefore, appeals were forbidden. I respond: Cyprian does not argue from this decree alone, but from this decree concerning the circumstances of the manifest crimes of the guilty. So, Cyprian reasons this way: by the decree of the council every man's case should be heard in the very place where the crime was committed; their case has already been heard and their crimes made manifest. Therefore, why appeal to Rome, except that by chance they might impose upon the Pope, or at least annoy the bishops who had judged concerning them?

Add that, if by this decree it was meant to forbid all appeals, not only would it be forbidden to appeal to the Roman Pontiff, but also to any other judge; and

---

[1] Lib. 1, epist. 3.

[2] Lib. 1, epistle 4.

that is the very thing the Centuriators affirm.[3] They try to make these words general, but it would be a most absurd and ridiculous law which would forbid all appeal. Furthermore, in what inept state of this sort was a law ever tolerated which did not permit appeal to any judge? Therefore, the Centuriators, when they grant this law to the Church of God, which is arranged as the wisest state, show themselves altogether ridiculous and absurd.

Now, to that point which Cyprian adds, that the authority of the bishops of Africa is no less, I respond that *no less* does not refer to a comparison to the Roman Pontiffs, but to the case on wherein it was treated. The sense is that the bishops of Africa were not of a lesser authority than sufficed to judge that case.

---

[3]   Cent 3, ch. 7, column 176.

CHAPTER XXIV
Another Three Arguments are Answered

SECONDLY, they [the Lutherans] object that Pope Damasus, who in a letter to Theophilus and Anysius, which is 79 among the epistles of Ambrose, says: "When there was a judgment of this sort of the Council of Capua, as of the border with Bonoso, and also the judges voted for his accusers, we turn away, because the form of judgment cannot be relevant for us."

I respond: Firstly, that epistle is not of Damasus. In the works of Ambrose it is attributed to Ambrose, but it cannot be his, since in it mention is made of Ambrose just as if he were someone else. Therefore, its authorship is uncertain. Secondly, I say if it were a letter of Damasus, as many would have it, Damasus does not say he cannot judge, but that *it is not fitting* that he should judge, which was said rightly. Although the Pope is the Supreme Judge, nevertheless it is not fitting that when a provincial council established something, he should judge otherwise without reason.

Thirdly, Calvin objects[1] that the Council of Miletus, in Canon 22, states thus: "What if by them (that is neighboring bishops), they reckoned to challenge? Let them not challenge, except to the African councils, or to the primates of their provinces. Moreover, one who crosses the sea, because he thinks it must be appealed; let him be received in communion by no one within Africa."

Some respond with Gratian,[2] that he added to this canon the exception; unless by chance he should appeal to the Apostolic See. But this exception does not seem to square; for especially on account of the Roman Church the Africans had established that it was not lawful to appeal beyond the sea. Therefore, it was never the custom to appeal beyond the sea from Africa, except to the Roman See. Nor is it fitting to take refuge in these narrow exceptions, since the real answer is at hand.

Therefore, the response is that this canon is not in regard to a summons. For the question on appeals to the Roman Pontiff, it is not on appeals of priests and lesser clerics, but on the appeals of bishops. Accordingly, the Council of Sardica, which would have it that bishops can appeal to the Pontiff in Canons 4 and 7, would also have it that the cases of priests and lesser clerics be settled by neighboring bishops, so that it would be lawful for minor clerics to appeal from their bishop to other bishops of the same province, as Canon 17 has it. Pope Zozimus willed to renew those two canons, and commanded their execution in

---

[1] *Instit.*, lib. 4, ch. 7 § 9.

[2] 2 quest. 6, canon *placuit.*

Africa, as is clear from the Sixth Council of Carthage, and from the letter of the same Council to Pope Boniface.

Hence, this Canon 22 of the Council of Miletus speaks on priests and lesser Clerics, not on bishops, as is clear from Augustine, who was present at this Council, and still writes that it was lawful for African bishops to appeal beyond the sea, but not for lesser clerics.[3] And it is clear from the words of the council itself, it begins thus: "It was pleased that Priests, Deacons or other lower clerics in cases, which they had, etc." For this reason, Pope Innocent I approved the whole Council of Miletus in his epistle to the council, which is 93 among the epistles of St. Augustine. But certainly Innocent would not have done it, if there was something that derogated from the Apostolic See. Hence the ignorance and poor scholarship of Calvin appears, who says on the citation we noted, that Zozimus tried to cause it to be that this canon of Miletus would be corrected in the Sixth Council of Carthage. Yet it is certain on the other hand that Zozimus commanded that the canon should be confirmed, and rendered back to practice.

But you will say: If that is so, by what law did the Roman Pontiffs receive the appeals of the priests of Apia from Africa, and saw to it to restore their rank, as the African Fathers relate in an epistle to Boniface, and in another to Pope Celestine?

I respond: Although it was forbidden for clergy of a lower order to appeal from the bishops of their province, still it was not forbidden, nor could it be forbidden for the Supreme Pontiff, that he could not admit them if he wished. Besides, the Roman Pontiffs did not admit the appeal of the Apian priests, as much as listen to their complaints, and commanded the Africans that they should diligently examine their case, and faithfully judge it. Thus it appears from these two epistles that the priests of Apia twice came to Rome, and each time in turn were sent back into Africa, and there it was judged after they returned from the city.

Fourthly, Calvin objects using the epistle of St. Augustine, where we read the case of Caecilianus who was judged by the Pope, and certain others by the command of the emperor, and thereafter again, judged a second time by the bishop of Arles at the command of the same emperor, and thirdly judged by the Emperor. But if the Pontiff is supreme judge by divine law, why does he not judge himself instead of at the command of the emperor? Likewise, if there can be no appeal from him, how was there an appeal in the case of Caecilianus, and a judgment after the judgment of the Pontiff from the bishop of Arles, and again by the Emperor? Then, why did he suffer colleagues to be joined with him by

---

[3]   Augustine, Epist. 162.

the Emperor in the first judgment?[4]

I respond to the first point: the Pope did not judge, except when the emperor enjoined it upon him, because the case of the Donatists was not brought to the Pontiff first, as it ought to have been, but to the emperor. In this they acted wrongly, as St. Augustine teaches in the same work, where he also says Constantine the Emperor by far acted in a more orderly manner, since he did not dare to judge what was brought to him, but sent it to the Pontiff. To the second point, I say the Pope permitted himself to sit with others assigned by the Emperor, that he might satisfy the Donatists, by whom the Roman Pontiff was suspect. Now I say to the third, after the Pontiff judged the bishop of Arles later the emperor also did so, not because it was fitting, as Augustine says in the same place, but that the mouth of the Donatists should be altogether shut up. Therefore, the emperor, as Augustine says in the same place, was going to aim at forgiveness from the bishops, and became acquainted with the case unwillingly.

---

[4] *Instit.*, lib. 4, ch. 7.

CHAPTER XXV
The Last Argument on the VI Council of Carthage is Answered

ASTLY, Calvin,[1] the Centuriators,[2] and even the Greeks at the Council of Florence,[3] but above all Illyricus,[4] bring forth an argument that they believe is very strong from the history of the Sixth Council of Carthage, and this is the summary of the affair.

Pope Zozimus sought from the Africans through legates that they would command the execution of three canons from the Council of Nicaea. One, was on the appeals of bishops to the Roman Pontiff; the second, on appeals of priests and lesser clerics to neighboring bishops; the third, on not going to the constable, that is, lest the bishops of Africa might go to the hall of the emperor.

After the Africans received these commands, they gathered a national council of 217 bishops, and meanwhile, with Zozimus dead, Pope Boniface had succeeded him, and the Africans responded that they did not discover those Canons in the Council of Nicaea, and on that account, wrote to the Patriarchs of the East at Constantinople and Alexandria so that the latter would send to them authentic examples of the council of Nicaea. In the meantime, they were going to preserve those Canons save for more due diligence in the inspection of the authentic copies. Then, copies of the Council of Nicaea came from Cyril of Alexandria and Atticus of Constantinople, and in those these three canons were not discovered, rather only those twenty which are contained in the history of Ruffinus,[5] which Cyril also cites in his epistle to the Africans.

Therefore, since the Africans did not discover those particular canons in the copies sent to them, they wrote to Pope Celestine, who had succeeded Boniface, seeing that those canons were not discovered, that thereafter they would not easily admit appeals from Africa. This is contained in the Sixth Council of Carthage, and in those two epistles. What the Pope might have said as a response is not contained there.

Now, Illyricus and the Centuriators have heaped up over this history an immense pile of abuse, lies and besides that two arguments. In regard to abuse, Illyricus in his book on this history insolently perverts the names of nearly every Pope involved. St. Innocent he everywhere calls "Nocentium," St. Boniface

---

[1] Loc. Cit.

[2] Centur. 5, ch. 9.

[3] Sess. 20.

[4] *De Historia Concilii VI Carthaginensis.*

[5] Lib. 10, ch. 6.

"Malefacium", St. Celestine, "Infernalem;" St. Leo, in the manner of some hellish wolf, he merely calls the "roaring lion".[6]

The acts of the Council of Carthage itself will serve to blunt such petulance, as well as the epistles of the same Council to Boniface and Celestine, all of which Illyricus adds honestly to increase the size of his little book. The more scurrilously and rudely Illyricus speaks of these holy Pontiffs, the more the African Fathers speak of them with honor and seriousness. Besides, see Augustine on the praises of these Popes, as well as Optatus and Prosper of Aquitaine.[7]

On the other hand, there are as many lies as there are sentences in this book of Illyricus. I will bring up a few from the many. In the beginning of the book, he says that at the Sixth Council of Carthage, Prosper, Orosius and other characteristic men were present with Augustine. But Prosper and Orosius are not named in the Council, and they could not be present, since they were not in fact Africans and the Council consisted of African bishops alone.

A little after that, Illyricus relates that, together with Pope Boniface, a man in schism named Eulabius was elected; but Eulabius, who was chosen by a greater part of the clergy and people, was of such modesty, that he yielded of his own will, although in other respects he pertained to that pontificate by law. But Illyricus asserts this without any source, and we can produce against it Anastasius the librarian, who wrote on the life of the same Boniface, that Eulabium was thrown out from the council of 252 bishops, and unjustly ordained, while Boniface was confirmed by all.

Illyricus says to this, and often repeats, that the Roman Pontiffs demanded from the African Fathers that jurisdiction be conceded to them in Africa and in all other regions; and when it was deliberated on this affair for a whole five years, at length it was defined by the Council that no right should be conceded to the Pontiff. But that is not only a lie, because there was no such demand, nor can such a definition be found in that Council, but it is even impudent because it is asserted without any probability. Who would believe that Roman Pontiffs demanded jurisdiction from the Africans in Asia and Europe? Likewise who

---

[6] Translator's note: These names are all a Latin play on words. "Nocentium" means guilty, in place of Innocentium. Boniface means a good deed or someone who does good, thus "Malefacium," evil-doer; Celestine, which means heavenly, thus "Infernalem" means from hell, or hellish. As for Leo, what Bellarmine's remark is meant to show is that Illyricus lacked the sophistication to turn Leo's name on its head, so "roaring lion" is a direct quote from St. Peter's Epistle which means the devil.

[7] Augustine, epistle 157; Optatus lib. 1 ad Bonifacium; Prosper *Contra Collatorem.*

would believe that the African Fathers labored on this case for a whole five years, when they could respond in one word that the Popes had no right over outside nations, hence they could not concede it to anyone? Would someone not be laughed to scorn who sought jurisdiction from the king of France in Spain? And would not the king of Spain seem ridiculous, if he placed the matter in deliberation for five years?

Another lie, and it is the chief one repeated a thousand times in the book of Illyricus as well as by the Centuriators, is that Pope Zozimus busied himself in deception, and against his conscience, falsifying the Council of Nicaea that he might place a yoke upon the Africans by treachery. Concerning such a lie, we will give an answer by argumentation. Therefore, with these having been prefaced, let us proceed to the arguments [of Illyricus].

First, if the Pope is the supreme Judge of the whole Church by divine law, why would the Pontiffs strive to confirm their right of appeals, not from divine law, but from the Council of Nicaea? And why did so many Catholics, and the holy Fathers of the Council of Carthage, refuse to admit this right unless it should be found in the Council of Nicaea?

We respond to this argument briefly: one could always appeal to the Supreme Pontiff by divine law; still, whether it was expedient to use this power even in all places without cause was in doubt. For on every side reasons can be advanced. Indeed, if everywhere an appeal were conceded by all, it may easily happen that many would flee legitimate judgments, that they might trouble bishops who had first judged the matter without cause, that cases which are otherwise easy and clear might drag on for a very long time. And hence St. Cyprian, in the aforementioned epistles, does not once bemoan those who, being previously and legitimately judged and condemned, called upon the Roman Pontiff. Even St. Bernard enumerates many troublesome results which arise from an excessive frequency of appeals.[8]

On the other hand, if appeal were conceded to none, the occasion would be given to particular bishops that they might easily and boldly judge and tyrannically oppress the people; and still, that they might reckon they had no superior to themselves, and thus need render an account to no one. The result of that would be nothing other than that the one body of the Church should be torn in as many parts as there are episcopates.

Therefore, when the matter was in doubt, the General Council of Sardica declared that it was expedient that ordinarily priests and other minor clergy should be conceded an appeal from bishops to a provincial council, and bishops

---

[8] *De Consideratione*, lib. 3.

on the other hand, to the Apostolic See. This declaration was not a new concession, for the examples of those who appealed to the Roman Pontiff before the times of the Council of Sardica and Nicaea witness.

It is for that reason that in the Council of Carthage the Roman Pontiffs advanced not divine right, but the Council of Nicaea, to stabilize the law of appeals. This was the case because they wished to prove that not only could all appeal to them, but even that it was expedient for the Church that it should so happen, seeing that a general council had thought so.

For equal reason, the African Fathers desired to impede appeals of this sort, because they thought it was not expedient for their church, even though they were not ignorant of the fact, nor did they deny, that they could not absolutely impede appeals. Wherefore, in each epistle which they sent to the Roman Pontiffs on this case, they witness their subjection to the Apostolic See, when they relate the acts of the Council, and say they received its commands. Moreover, they do not command, but ask that he not offer his ears too easily to everyone making an appeal. But all these will be more clear in the answer to the second argument.

Thus, the second argument of the Centuriators and Calvin is of this sort: the Roman Pontiffs, Zozimus, Boniface, and Celestine, wished to prove the right of appeals to the Apostolic See from the Council of Nicaea. However, after the case was struck down, they were caught falsifying and corrupting the canons of Nicaea; therefore, not even human law, to speak nothing of divine, could call upon their judgment.

We respond: First, the African Fathers were deceived by ignorance, while the Centuriators and Calvin sin from malice. For the Africans repeat twice in their epistle to Celestine, that in no definition of the Fathers, and in no Synod did they discover those canons; from which it appears they did not have the canons of the Council of Sardica, in which those three canons are contained with eloquent words, and if they did have them, without a doubt they would have acquiesced. The authority of Sardica is no less than of the Council of Nicaea.[9] And it was not a greater error to cite Nicaea for Sardica than Matthew for John, or Jeremiah for Zachariah, as St. Matthew does in Chapter 27. Therefore, just as we cannot call Matthew a forger, because the same Holy Spirit spoke in Jeremiah and Zachariah, so also here. But the Centuriators knew about the Council of Sardica, and just the same conveyed it as legitimate in its account of the fourth century; therefore, it is necessary that they affirm the Africans

---

[9] Translator's note: To clarify Bellarmine's argument, he is speaking strictly on law, and in regard to canons dealing with law, Nicaea (which was an Ecumenical Council) and Sardica (which was not) are indeed, on equal footing.

284

were deceived, and the case comes to nothing; therefore, not withstanding that they obstinately claim victory with these, they oppose themselves, and sin from malice.

But you might say, in the Sixth Council of Carthage, ch. 6, they cite by name the Council of Sardica; therefore, the Africans were not ignorant of it.

I respond: those words whereby the Council of Sardica is cited are not of the Africans, but of the Papal legates. They cited these words from instructions given to them by Pope Zozimus. And besides, I believe, the citation was altogether corrupted, and either placed by copyists, Sardica for Nicaea; or what I rather more suspect, taken up from a margin in the text, that: "Ex Sardicensi Concilio." Therefore, the Council of Sardica is placed in the margin because really the words which are cited there are not now discovered except in that council. But, just the same, the name "Council of Sardica" ought not be in the text. Accordingly, the words that they cited were from the instructions of Pope Zozimus, which the legates brought from Rome. Moreover, these legates said they cited the canons from the Council of Nicaea. For which reason, soon after those words were recited, St. Augustine said: "We also profess that we are going to preserve this save for a more diligent inspection of the Council of Nicaea." Whereby he shows that he received the canon cited just as if it were from Nicaea.

Add that Augustine did not recognize another Council of Sardica apart from a certain heretical council of Eastern bishops against St. Athanasius.[10] There were two councils in Sardica, as is clear from the historian Sozomen.[11] One was a general Catholic council of over three hundred bishops, which Augustine never saw; the other was a heretical council of seventy-six bishops, which Augustine had seen.

Secondly, I say, the canons of the Council of Nicaea, which are found in Ruffinus,[12] and which were sent from the East to the Africans, without a doubt did not have all the canons which Nicaea published, and hence it is probable that these three canons which Zozimus cited from the Council of Nicaea really were in that council. The fact that these might not have been all, several prove from the epistle of St. Athanasius to Pope Marcus, in which he begs for a copy of the Council of Nicaea from the library of the Roman Pontiffs, asserting that the copies which were in Alexandria were burned by the Arians.

But this argument is ridiculed by the Centuriators, and truly it is not solid.

---

[10] *Contra Cresconium*, lib. 3, ch. 34.

[11] Sozomen, *Hist.*, lib. 3, ch. 10 & 11.

[12] Ruffinus, *Hist.*, lib. 10, ch. 6.

For that burning of books happened in the time of the Emperor Constantius, when Athanasius was expelled from Alexandria and a certain Arian named George was ordained in his place, as Athanasius himself witnesses in an epistle to all the faithful bishops. Moreover, it is certain from the *Chronicle* of Jerome, that Pope Marcus was already dead in that time. Next, if Pope Marcus had sent a copy to the Alexandrians from the Roman treasury, certainly the copies of Rome and Alexandria would have agreed with each other. Therefore, how in the copy sent by St. Cyril of Alexandra to the African bishops, would these three canons, which were found in the Roman copy, be wanting?

Nevertheless, it can be proven that these canons were not whole, even omitting the epistle of Athanasius. Firstly, because one from the particular canons of the Council of Nicaea, that Easter should be celebrated on the Lord's day,[13] is not extant among the canons of Ruffinus.

Secondly, St. Ambrose teaches that it was established in the Council of Nicaea, lest anyone married twice be received into the clergy. But this was not discovered among those 20 canons.[14]

Thirdly, Jerome asserts in the preface to his commentary on Judith, that the book of Judith was received into the canonical books by the Council of Nicaea. But this is not found among the canons of Ruffinus.

Fourthly, Augustine asserts on the designation of a successor, that it was forbidden in the Council of Nicaea that two bishops should sit together in the same church, against which he imprudently did, as he sorrowfully relates.[15] But this canon appears nowhere among those twenty.

Fifthly, in the African Council, the Fathers assert in canon 14 from a canon of Nicaea, that it is not lawful to offer the Eucharist without fasting. But where is this among those twenty canons?

Sixthly, at the end of the Council of Chalcedon, Atticus relates that in the Council of Nicaea, the origin of the format for how epistles were to be written was determined, and Optatus speaks on this, where he says: "With whom (the Roman Pope Siricius) the whole world communicates to us the business of forms in society of communion."[16] Likewise, the Council of Miletus, canon 20, where it forbids clerics to leave unless accompanied with formal letters. But this never

---

[13]   We know this canon was among those of Nicaea, from the epistle of Constantine that is contained in Eusebius, *de Vita Constantini*, lib. 3; Epiphanius, *Haeres.*, 69; Athanasius, *epistola de Synodis Armini et Seleuci.*

[14]   Epistle 82.

[15]   Epistle 110.

[16]   Optatus *contra Parmenianum*, lib. 2.

appears in those twenty canons of Ruffinus.

Seventhly, Luther, Calvin, the Centuriators and the other heretics everywhere object to us based on a canon of the Council of Nicaea found in the historian, Socrates,[17] in which they say wives are permitted to priests. But this canon is not discovered in those twenty. Therefore, if Zozimus is a corrupter and forger of the canons of Nicaea because he cited in the name of the Council of Nicaea one canon which is not discovered in those twenty, then by the same token, Constantine, Athanasius, Epiphanius, Ambrose, Jerome, Augustine, Atticus, Socrates, the African Fathers, as well as the Centuriators themselves and even Luther and Calvin are corrupters and forgers. For they all cite canons of the Council of Nicaea which are not found among those twenty.

Lastly, add that in the Council of Florence, sess. 20, a certain learned man named John asserted that he could show many testimonies of the holy Fathers, that at length the Fathers of the Sixth Council of Carthage knew that the canons of Nicaea were corrupted and false which were sent to them from Alexandria and Constantinople.

Now, in the third place, I say it seems to me very probable that in the Council of Nicaea these three canons were not expressly present, on which we are treating; rather, these were called Canons of Nicaea by Zozimus and Boniface because they held Nicaea and Sardica for one and the same; the canons of each council were joined in the same place in the Roman library just as if they were of the same Council. The ignorance of this affair disturbed the African Fathers.

The reasons which convince me are these. First, because these canons are contained in the same words in the Council of Sardica that the legates of Zozimus allege, and it does not have the appearance of truth that the same Canons were in the Council of Nicaea, and still the Fathers at Sardica do not indicate by any mode that they did not make the canons but renewed them. Therefore, I reckon that it was implicitly and obscurely decreed in the Council of Nicaea that one should appeal to the Pontiff, because without a doubt in Canon 6, the council commands the ancient customs to be preserved, and this one on appeals, as is clear from Pope Leo[18] and from the examples argued above: and also because the same council commands that once a case has been adjudicated it can be judged again in another place, as is clear from the epistle of Julius that is contained in the second Apology of St. Athanasius; but the Council of Sardica eloquently explained the whole business.

---

[17] *Hist.,* lib. 1, ch. 8.

[18] Epistle 89.

In the second place, because all the Canons of the Council of Sardica are contained in a translation of the Council of Nicaea made from Greek by Dionysius a thousand years ago, which is extant in the monastery of St. Vedasti Atrebati, where they are contained together just as if they were of the same Council.

In the third place, because otherwise a reason can not be given why the Council of Sardia, which is was certainly universal and approved, is not counted among the general councils. Certainly it ought to be called the Second Council, but it does not add to the number of councils, because it is held for one and the same with Nicaea. Moreover, the reason why the two Councils were joined together is because the same Fathers for the most part were present in each Council, and nothing new in regard to faith was defined at Sardica; rather it only strengthened the faith of Nicaea, since in other councils new heresies were condemned. Therefore, Zozimus did not cite Nicaea for Sardica by some deceit, but because they were held to be the same. I believe the same can be said for the letter of Pope Julius I to the Eastern bishops, Innocent in his epistle to Victricium, and Leo in Epistle 25 to Theodosius: they all cite this canon in the name of the Council of Nicaea. Just the same, the creed of Constantinople is everywhere called "Nicene," because it is an explication of Nicaea; so also the canons of Sardica, the Fathers usually call Nicene, because they are nothing other than an explanation and confirmation of the canons of Nicaea.

I add fourthly, the Fathers at Carthage never stated that no right was given to the Roman Pontiff in Africa, or that it was not lawful in any way for an African bishop to appeal to the Roman Church. Nor was there ever such a separation between the Roman Pontiffs and the African bishops, as Illyricus and Calvin say. For in the first place, a decree of this sort was never extant; next, the African Fathers themselves, in a letter to Pope Boniface, and in another to Celestine, very clearly witness their peace and subjection toward the Apostolic See. They write thus to Boniface:

"Since it has pleased the Lord that our humility should write concerning those things which with us our holy brethren, Faustinus a fellow bishop and Philip and Asellus, fellow presbyters, have done, not to the bishop Zosimus of blessed memory, from whom they brought commands and letters to us, but to your holiness, who is constituted in his room by divine authority, we ought briefly to set forth what has been determined upon by mutual consent; not indeed those things which are contained in the prolix volumes of the acts, in which, while charity was preserved, yet we loitered not without some little labor of altercation, deliberating those things in the acts which now pertain to the cause." Where, when they refer all things which were done to the Pope, and they affirm that they received the commands from Pope Zozimus, can it be that they do not openly indicate that they acknowledge him as a superior? But in an epistle to Celestine: "A due preface to the office of salvation, we ask for the expense; that afterward you would not easily admit those coming to your ears." In such words, they do not absolutely refuse that law on appeals, nor do they say that the Pontiff cannot, if he wishes, admit those making appeals, but they merely ask that he would not easily offer his ears to everyone making an appeal.

St. Augustine clearly preached the primacy of the Roman Pontiff in Africa and the whole Christian world, when he says, from the command of Zozimus, he and the other bishops came to Caesar; and when he wrote that the Pelagian heresy was condemned throughout the whole world by Innocent and Zozimus.[19] The same Augustine was subject to, and joined to Pope Boniface, as is clear from the beginning of his first book against two epistles of the Pelagians to the same Boniface. He also relates to Pope Celestine the case of a certain African bishop, and among other things says: "Work with us in piety, O most venerable blessed lord, and having received due charity, O most holy Pope, bid for yourself to recite all those things which are right."[20] And further on: "It arises in the example of the judgment of the Apostolic See itself, as well as what has been judged firm of other matters, etc." And on the other hand, Pope Celestine in a letter to the Gauls brings out Augustine with wonderful praise, and also says he has always remained in communion with the Roman Church; and that he was always held to be the greatest doctor by him and his predecessors.

Such a union of Augustine with the Roman Church convicts Illyricus of a manifest lie when he writes that the Roman Pontiffs had been excluded from power in all of Africa, refuted by Augustine and his colleagues as wicked corrupters and forgers.

Not long after that Council of Carthage, St. Leo wrote to the bishops of the province of Mauritania in Africa,[21] and says that he restored communion to Lupicinus, the bishop, because he had appealed to him from Africa. Likewise he sent bishop Potentius as his legate, so that he would discern African affairs in his place. Therefore, either the Council of Carthage did not forbid it, or certainly those Fathers changed their minds.

Again, around sixty years later, St. Eugenius, the bishop of Carthage, when he was compelled by the Arian king, Honoricus, to make a collation on the faith, he wrote to his colleagues across the sea. He could not establish something on the faith without a consensus of other bishops, and especially the Roman

---

[19]   Epistle 157.

[20]   Epistle 261.

[21]   Leo, Epistle 87.

Church. Victor of Utica relates the fact.[22] Therefore, the bishop of Carthage acknowledged the Roman Church to be the Head of all Churches even after the Sixth Council of Carthage, and if of all, certainly also of Africa, nor was he separated from the Roman Pontiff, to whom he declared he was going to write.

Not long after, when Thrasimundus, the successor of Honoricus, relegated nearly all the African bishops, that is 220, into Sardinia, the Roman Pope, Symmachus maintained that all of those bishops were members [of the Church] and liberally provided for their expenses;[23] which certainly is not an argument for separation but of communion and unity.

In the same time, St. Fulgentius was easily the prince of the African bishops, although he was most joined to the Roman Church, as is certain from chapter 12 of his *Life*. For when he wished in Egypt to set out for the solitude of the Monks, he was warned by the bishop of Syracuse not to do it, on account of the fact that all these monks were separated from the see of Blessed Peter, with which he was in communion. Therefore, after he left Egypt behind he came to Rome, to see the places of the saints. The same Fulgentius, as we see from Chapter 29 of his *Life*, faithfully written by his disciple, is assigned to the Church of Carthage, and had been joined to his bishop; from which it happens that the bishop of Carthage was also joined to the bishop of Rome, as St. Fulgentius could not lawfully communicate with two communions within himself.

After those times, Blessed Gregory manifestly declared his union with the bishop of Carthage, and the right of appeal and jurisdiction in all those provinces.[24]

Yet Illyricus objects against this from the epistle of Boniface II to Eulabius the bishop of Alexandria, as well as the epistle of Eulabius the bishop of Carthage to the same Boniface. From these epistles it is gathered, that after the Sixth Council of Carthage, the bishops of Carthage were separated from communion with the Roman Church for nearly a hundred years, and then at length reconciled when Eulabius subjected himself to the Apostolic See and anathematized his predecessors.

I respond: First, those epistles are exceedingly suspect. For in the first place, they seem opposed with those things which we said above on the union of Augustine, Eugene, Fulgentius, and other African bishops with the Roman Church. Next, Eulabius of Alexandria, to whom Boniface seems to have written,

---

22 *De persecutione Wandalica*, lib. 2.

23 Paul the Deacon, *Rerum Romanarum*, lib. 17.

24 Lib. 1, epist. 72, & 75; lib. 7, epist. 32.

did not exist, or at least not at that time, which is clear from the chronology of Nicephorus of Constantinople. Besides, Boniface shows in that epistle that he writes in the time of the emperor Justin; but Justin died before Boniface began to sit, as is certain from all histories. Still, this epistle, which is ascribed to Boniface, is almost certainly made from two fragments, one of which is taken from an epistle of Pope Hormisdas to bishop John of Constantinople, the other from an epistle of St. Gregory to the bishops of Gaul, which is the 52nd epistle in book four of the Registry of epistles. But St. Gregory was not yet born in that time, so it is believable that Gregory took the words from Boniface, although the style is altogether of Gregory.

Moreover, in that epistle which is attributed to Eulabius of Carthage, a certain Gregorian sentence is inserted, from Book 4, Epistle 36 to Eulogius. And there is nothing of the rest of the epistle, except a fragment of a letter of John, the bishop of Constantinople, to Pope Hormisdas.

Yet, if by chance these epistles might be true (which I can scarcely affirm), without a doubt they must not be received in the sense as if all the predecessors of Eulabius, even back to Aurelius who presided over the Council of Carthage were separated from communion with the Church of Rome, since that would be opposed to most certain and true history. Rather it would only mean that Aurelius first began to show disdain against the Roman Church, then by his example Eulabius himself, and maybe some others. In other respects Eulabius, after the truth was recognized, again subjected himself to the Roman Church. That much alone can be gathered from these epistles, should they be genuine.

CHAPTER XXVI

*That the Roman Pontiff Succeeds Peter in the Ecclesiastical Monarchy is Proven
from the Fact that the Supreme Pontiff is Judged by No One.*

HE TENTH argument is taken from the fact that the Roman Pontiff can
be judged by no man on earth. His rule cannot be more evidently shown
than if he should so be shown to be in charge of all, that he is subjected
to none. Thus, three things must be observed before we shall come to the proof.

Firstly, we do not dispute on this point about the Pontiff, as he is a temporal
prince, since in this mode not even our adversaries deny that he can not be
judged in temporal cases, as it is common to absolutely all princes that they
recognize no one superior in temporal business. Therefore, we speak on the
Pontiff by reason of the pontificate alone, and we say that, even if he had no
temporal power, he could not be judged in any way on earth by any Christian
prince, whether secular, or ecclesiastical, nor even gathered together in a
council.

Secondly, it must be observed, there were two errors on this matter. One is
of those who taught that the Pontiff can be judged by the emperor, punished,
deposed, if he would not exercise his office rightly. A certain Marsilius of Padua[1]
taught this, as well as Nilos.[2] Nilos differs, however, in that he teaches the
Pontiff cannot be judged by a secular prince, but rather, he contends he can be
judged and punished by a council of bishops. Next Calvin and the rest of the
heretics of our time join both errors together; they subject the Roman Pontiff to
a judgment of the princes as well as of the bishops.

The third thing which must be observed, the especial reason why the Pope
cannot be judged, is because he is the prince of the whole Church, and hence he
has no superior on earth. For because he is the supreme prince of the Church,
he cannot be judged by any ecclesiastical ruler, and again, because the
ecclesiastical commonwealth is spiritual, and hence greater and more sublime
than a temporal commonwealth. On that account, the Supreme Prince of the
Church can direct and judge a supreme prince of a temporal commonwealth; but
not be directed or judged by him; otherwise right order and the very nature of
the things would be perverted. I say this is the primary reasoning and, as the
Scholastics say, *a priori*. Still, because this reason assumes the fact that in the
whole disputation we strive to prove that the Roman Pontiff is the prince of the
whole Church, for this reason, even while omitting similar reasons, from the

---

[1] As he is quoted by Juan de Torquemada, *Sum de Eccl.*, book IV part 2, ch. 37; he
also refutes the same error in book II, ch. 93.

[2] *Lib. De Prim.*

testimony of councils, popes, emperors and doctors of the Church we will show that the bishop of Rome cannot be judged: that from there we might confirm our primary thesis, which is, that the Roman Pontiff is the head and prince of the universal Church.

Therefore, it is proved firstly from councils. At the Council of Sinvessanus, the Fathers said: "The First See will be judged by no man." These words are related from that council by Pope Nicholas in his epistle to the Emperor Michael. Likewise in the Roman Council under Sylvester, 280 bishops were present, and the last canon reads: "The First See will be judged not by the emperor, nor by kings, nor by any of the clergy or people."[3] Likewise, in the Roman Synod under Sixtus III, chapter 5, we read it was said: "It is not lawful to give sentence against the Pontiff." And Sixtus, who was accused, responded: "Although in my reckoning I may be a judge, whether or not I might judge, still the truth should not be hidden."

When Dioscorus, the bishop of Alexandria, at the Council of Ephesus dared to judge and condemn Pope Leo I, the Catholic Church so shuddered at this deed that the Council of Chalcedon, in an epistle to the Emperors Martianus and Valentinian, and in a second to Leo himself (which is contained in Action 3 of the same Council), wrote that it condemned Dioscorus for many reasons, but above all because he had presumed to impose judgment on the First See. Moreover, in the Second Council of Constantinople, under Symmachus, a book by Ennodius the Deacon was received, in which among other things had been written, "God willed the cases of men to be settled through men, but the bishop of this See, without question, reserves his own judgment."

The Roman Council under Pope Adrian II, whose words are related in the 8th Synod, Act 7: "We read that the Roman Pontiff has judged the prelates of every Church, but that anyone has judged him, we do not read." Such rightly must be understood on legitimate judgment. And the Eighth Council itself asserted, it is not lawful for any earthly prince to judge patriarchs, and above all, the Patriarch of Rome. Thereupon, in the Council of Milevitanus, Canon 19, clergy were grievously punished who wished to be judged by the emperor. Therefore, if the emperor could not judge clerics, how much less the Pontiff?

Secondly, it is proved from the testimonies of Popes. Gelasius, in an epistle to Anastasius the Emperor says: "There are two, O august Emperor, by whom this world is principally ruled: the sacred authority of the Pontiffs, and royal power. Wherein the weight of priests is so much more grave than even for kings themselves, when they go to render an account before divine examination.

---

[3] Nicholas also mentions this decree in the aforementioned epistle.

Know, therefore, that you depend upon their judgment; not that they can be reduced to your will." St. Gregory says: "If blessed Peter were to be censured at some time by the faithful, he would have attended to the authority which he had received over the holy Church; he could respond that the sheep would not dare to rebuke the shepherd." Nicholas I, in an epistle to Michael: "Enough is evidently shown that the Pontiff can neither be bound nor loosed by the secular power, that is, neither condemned nor absolved." Innocent III in an epistle to the Emperor, which is contained *ca. Solitae*, tit. *De majoritate*, expressly teaches this same thing. He also says it in *serm. 2 de consecrat. Pontif.* Boniface VIII acted in like manner in passing in his bull, *Unam Sanctam*. John XXII, again in passing, in his document *licet juxta doctrinam Apostoli*.

Thirdly, it is proved from the confession of Emperors. For Ruffinus writes about Constantine that he refused to judge bishops, but said he would rather that he was judged by the bishops.[4] The Emperor Basil made a similar confession in a speech, which he held at the end of the Eighth Synod, and among all the remaining laity, in rank of whom he had placed himself a head of, lest judges might wish to judge or command their own pastors. Thereafter, Nicholas, in the aforementioned epistle to the Emperor Michael, after bringing many testimonies, proves that pious emperors never commanded Pontiffs rather, they merely entreated them as fathers, if they wished something to be done by them.

Lastly, a few testimonies of the holy Doctors. Ambrose, in his *Oration on the handing over of the Basilicas*, says: "A good emperor is under the Church, not above it." Certainly, if it is not above the Church, how much less above the Father and Pastor of the Church.

Gregory Nazianzen, in an oration whereby he excuses himself because at length he had abstained from his ecclesiastical function: "You sheep, do not pasture the shepherds, nor elevate yourselves above their limits. It is enough for you, if you are rightly pastured; do not judge the judges, nor impose laws upon the legislators." And lest you think that emperors are excepted by Gregory, listen to what the same Doctor says in his oration to the citizens overpowered with fear, and the angry prince; he addresses the emperor this way: "Why do you not take up a free voice? Even because the law of Christ subjects you to my power, and my tribunal? Let us command him, I add, by both a greater and more perfect imperium. Receive a freer voice, I know you are a sheep of my flock, etc."

St. Bernard, in a letter to the Emperor Konrad, says: "Every soul should be

---

[4]   Ruffinus, *Hist.*, lib. 10, ch. 2.

subjected to the law by a more sublime power. How I desire you to guard the judgment in showing reverence to the Vicar of Peter, just as I command you to preserve the very thing of countenance from the whole world." Boniface the martyr is quoted by Gratian[5] speaking on the Roman Pontiff, saying: "He who is going to judge all must be judged by nobody." Lastly, Hugh of St. Victor says: "Spiritual power judges the earth, but the very thing was established first by God, and when it deviates, can be judged by God alone."[6]

---

[5] *Can. Si Papa*, dist. 40.

[6] *De Sacramentis*, part 2.

CHAPTER XXVII
The Arguments of Nilos are Answered

OW it remains that we answer arguments. The first is of Nilos Cabásilas; then of Calvin, lastly, that which Juan de Torquemada and others bring from the older heretics.

But before we propose the arguments of Nilos, we sense the reader must be warned that he ought not trust the translation of Illyricus. For in other places, and especially in this chapter, he distorts the words of Nilos not just once. Let the beginning of this citation be an example: Nilos has: ὅτι δὲ πάντα ἀναχρίνων αὐτὸς ὑπ' οὐδενὸς ἀναχρίνεται, τοῦτο καὶ ψεῦδος, τοῖς τῶν ἀποστόλων ἤθεσιν οὐ συμβαίνει. This is: "The claim, moreover, 'judging all things, he is judged by none,' is also false, and does not agree with the custom of the Apostles." Now, Illyricus renders it thus: "What our adversaries babble about, that the Pope judges all, and hence is judged by no one, is full of vanity and lies, and is not in accord with a great many just and modest canons of the Apostles."

But certainly, "they babble" [*blaterunt*] is not in the Greek and what Nilossimply says is false, Illyricus for his own eloquence adds: "In a word, is full of vanity and lies." Next, for *customs of the Apostles*, our faithful translator renders: "just and modest Canons of the Apostles." He failed to notice that he opposed that with the following words. For Nilostries to prove what he says not by Canons, but by reviewing the deeds of the Apostles.

Now, passing over this, let us see the argumentation of Nilos Cabásilas. He says: "Firstly, if Paul confers his doctrine with the Apostles, and Peter patiently bore to be rebuked bitterly by Paul, by what law would the Roman Pontiff have it to render an account on his deeds and life to no mortal?"

I respond: The example of Paul actually argues for our side; accordingly, he runs to Peter, and confers the Gospel with him, because he recognizes Peter is greater than himself, and he would give the example to posterity that they should run to the See of Peter in matters of this sort. Jerome marks this on our side in his epistle to Augustine,[1] and Theodoret from the Greeks in his epistle to Nero. Hence, Peter suffered to be rebuked by Paul, because that was not a judicial censure, but fraternal correction. For, as St. Augustine teaches, as well as St. Gregory, Paul did not rebuke Peter, as superiors judge inferiors from authority; but the way inferiors correct their superiors from charity.

The second objection: Pope Honorius was not only judged in the Sixth Council, but even condemned.

---

[1]   Which is 11 among the Epistles of Augustine.

I respond: On Honorius we will treat more profusely in another place, when we come to the question of whether the Pope could be a heretic. Meanwhile, we respond: Honorius was judged and also condemned in a case of faith (that is, if what was brought against him was in fact true), and we do not deny it, because the Church can judge a heretical Pope. Just the same, however, it is consistent with what we said, that the Pope can be judged by no one, and this will be made clear in the last argument.

Third; There are many broad laws about bishops, not only by the Apostles, but even more by councils, which certainly bind all bishops. Furthermore, the Pope is nothing other than a bishop, for that reason he is held by the laws. Hence, he has a superior by which he is judged.

I respond: The Pope is indeed restrained by ecclesiastical laws, but in regards to direction, not in regards to their restraint, as jurists usually speak about a prince. Although both general and local councils should speak about bishops universally when they impose laws, still, they ought be understood only concerning those bishops who are subject to the legislator and that fact can be made plain from particular councils. Accordingly, these councils often say: "If any cleric, if some bishop does that, etc."; still it is certain that none are bound to those laws except for clerics or bishops of that province.

Fourth: The Sixth Council prescribes laws for the Roman Church by name. For in the Canon 13, it condemns the Roman Church, because it did not permit a priest, deacon and subdeacon the use of wives, and also it commands that thereafter it should permit it. And Canon 55 condemns the same Roman Church, because in Lent it also fasts on Saturday, and it commands that it no longer be done.

I respond: We have already warned before about the canons falsely ascribed to that sixth Synod, since they were published afterward by a type of Ninth Synod, which the Roman Pontiffs not only did not approve, but even condemned.[2]

And rightly these two canons indicate enough of what sort this Synod was. For Canon 13 says that it proposes the doctrine of the Apostles and of the Fathers when it permits to clerics the cohabitation of wives, which is certainly quite false. For the Second Council of Carthage, by far more ancient and celebrated than that false Sixth Council, says in Canon 2: "All are pleased that bishops, priests and deacons, or those who handle the Sacraments, be guardians of purity, even that they should abstain from their wives, as the Apostles taught,

---

[2]   For more on this matter, see Francisco Turrianum in *De Sexta Synodo;* and Melchior Cano, *De Loci Theologicis,* lib. 5, last Chapter, in the answer to the sixth argument.

and antiquity itself preserved, and we also safeguard."

Likewise Epiphanius, who was a Greek and a most ancient and approved author, says: "But (the Church) does not receive a man living with one wife and begetting children, rather, he who restrains himself from one wife, or lives in widowhood, as a deacon, priest, bishop and even subdeacon, especially where the Ecclesiastical Canons are genuine. But you will say to me: in some places still, priests, deacons and subdeacons beget children; but this is not according to the Canon, but according to the mind of men, which it has lost its vigor through time."[3]

But Nilos says, the Sixth Synod cites Canon Six of the Apostles, which commands lest Clerics should abandon their wives under the pretext of religion.

I respond: It is commanded by that Canon that clerics who have wives, should provide for them those things which are necessary to live, not that they should live together with marital relations. Nilos cannot deny such an explanation, both because the very Council in Trullo which he cites explains the same canon in the same way,[4] and also, because otherwise that same Apostolic Canon, whose authority we do not reject, will be opposed to those canons of Trullo. For that Canon of the Apostles not only commands minor clergy, but even bishops, lest they abandon their wives. And still the Canons of the Council in Trullo permit marital relations to minor clergy, but not to bishops. Yet there will be much more on this matter in another place.

As to what he pertains to the canon on fasting on Saturdays, since the matter is indifferent, and each region can preserve its own custom, as St. Jerome and Augustine teach,[5] a council of Greeks ought not, nor could impose a law upon the Latins in this affair. Add the fact that Pope Innocent I takes our part in an epistle where he teaches one must fast on Saturday, and also the Greek Epiphanius who in a compendium of doctrine, only excepts Sundays from the fast of Lent.

Next, Canon 65 of the Apostles forbids fasting on Saturday. I respond: that canon appears substituted; the Church only receives 50 canons of the Apostles, as Cardinal Humbert testified in his book against Nicetas, and is quoted by Gratian.[6] Thereupon, if the Apostles truly commanded it, they certainly commanded it in hatred of heretics, who fasted on Saturday, lest they would

---

[3] Haeres. 19, Catharorum.

[4] Council in Trullo, Canon 48.

[5] Jerome, *Epistola ad Lucinium Boeticum*; Augustine, *Epistle 86 ad Casulanum*.

[6] Dist. 16.

appear to honor the creator, who rested on the seventh day. Therefore, after that heresy was long extinct, it would then have been lawful on Saturday, not only lawful, but even pious, on account of the memory of the Lord's burial, and so as to recede much further from Judaism.

Fifthly, Nilos objects against this answer in two ways. First, because although these canons may not be legitimate, still reason itself manifestly teaches that the Pope can be judged. All bishops, as bishops, are equal, as is clear from Dionysius, who says all are of the same order and dignity yet the Pope is nothing more than a bishop; that is certain both from the fact that he is ordained by bishops, and from the fact that Dionysius acknowledged no dignity in his *Ecclesiastical Hierarchy* greater than the episcopal dignity. Consequently, the Pope is held no less to the laws of the councils, and can be judged, as the other bishops.

Secondly, he argues, because those canons are legitimate and of a universal Council is proven in many ways: First, because the synod which made these canons is the Sixth Synod itself restored. The same Fathers who gathered from the beginning to explain the faith, are the same gathered afterwards to fashion the Canons. Secondly, because a legate of the Roman Pope was not lacking in this synod. Accordingly, Gortynae the bishop of Crete, held the place of the Roman Pontiff, as can be seen from the *History* of Basil. Thirdly; because the council which fashioned these canons is itself called a universal council, nor is it believable that so many Fathers would wish to lie. Fourthly, because the Seventh Council, Canon 1, receives the canons of the six universal synods, but the Sixth Council does not have other canons than those. Fifthly, because Pope Adrian, in an epistle to Tharasius, praises him with admiration because he constantly observed these decrees together with his own, and namely cited Canon 82 [of the Council in Trullo]. So, it follows that these canons were confirmed even by the Roman Pontiff himself.

I respond: That first argument on the equality of bishops proves entirely nothing. For the bishops are equal by reason of rank, as Dionysius says, but not by reason of jurisdiction. Accordingly even Nilos himself in this book affirms, that the bishop of Constantinople by far is no greater than the bishop of Caesarea, and others who are subject to the See of Constantinople. Hence, the Supreme Pontiff therefore, cannot be judged, not because he should have greater dignity or ordination than the episcopal rank; but because he has a fuller Episcopal jurisdiction, so that he is in charge of all, and subject to none.

Moreover, the canons of the Council in Trullo were not legitimate, and these arguments correctly prove the case.

To the first I respond: This synod cannot be called the "restored Sixth Council." For the presidents of the council were not the same, it was not the same emperor, and it was not the same number of bishops. For in the Sixth truly universal council, the Emperor Constantius was present, likewise, the legates of Pope Agatho, and 289 bishops, as we have it in the Seventh Council, in the third action. Yet at the time of this pseudo-sixth Council, Pope Agatho was already dead as well as the Emperor Constantius, and there were only 228 bishops.

Besides, from the beginning of the pseudo-sixth Council, they themselves said they restored the Fifth and Sixth Synod in a certain manner. Thus Theodore Balsamon called it not the Sixth, but the Quini-Sext Council. But how can this be called a council, or the Fifth believed to be restored, when no one from the Fifth Council was present? Accordingly, between the Fifth and "Quini-Sext" Council, *more than 130 years passed.* Thereupon, to what end did the Fifth and Sixth Synod need to be restored, and not preferably a new council called? Because, they said, they did not make canons. But they wished to make them. They were not convoked to make canons, but explain the faith.

To the second argument I respond: Whoever that bishop Gortyae was, and whoever gave him the place of the Roman Pope in that Synod, Nilos saw, because he does not express his name and he brings up an altogether unheard of history, as I do not know which Basil. At length, I say it does not lack suspicion of falsity. But whatever the case on this, it is certain to us that this Synod was condemned as wayward by Pope Sergius, who then sat; and as Bede and many others witness.[7]

This synod is the one which Sergius condemned, the one which fashioned the Canons, as is clear from Tharasius and Epiphanius, which in the Seventh Synod, Act. 4 and 6, speak. Five years after the Sixth Synod again, the Fathers came together and fashioned these canons; hence in that time it is certain, Sergius sat at Rome. Nor does the memory of any other council celebrated in that time exist; on which matter we will argue more profusely in book 1 *On Councils.*

Besides, Anastasius the Librarian, in his preface to a book on the Eighth Synod, writes that these canons are not contained either with the Roman Pontiffs, or with any patriarchs except that of Constantinople. From which he

---

[7] Bede, *de Sex Aetatibus,* in Justiniano juniore; Paul the Deacon, *de gestis Longobardorum,* lib. 6, ch. 4; Otho the Frisian, lib. 5, ch. 13; Ado of Vienne, Marianus Scotus, and Rheginus in his *Chronicle,* where he speaks on Justianian the younger.

rightly concludes that this council was compelled neither by the authority of the Supreme Pontiff, nor of the other patriarchs. Thus, Cardinal Humbert, a legate of Pope Leo IX, in a book against the Greeks, not only says that these same canons were not received by the Apostolic See, but even calls them nonsense.

To the third argument, I respond: It is not to be wondered at too much if these Fathers ascribed an invented title for themselves, when they call it a universal Council. They knew it could not prescribe laws under the color of the Roman Church, unless they would like to make it a universal Synod. Thereupon, when in Canon 2 they received the Synod held under Cyprian, which was judged as clearly erroneous by the universal Church, and in Canon 19 they openly lie about whether the use of wives for priests was permitted from Apostolic custom, and they have many other manifest lies, what a wonder if they would lie even in the title?

I respond to the fourth: When the canons of the six universal Councils were received in the Seventh Council, by the name of canons were not only understood the canons on morals, but all canons, whether they were decreed on customs, or on faith. For every Synod made canons for this reason. On customs, however, or on the ecclesiastical discipline, only the Council of Nicaea properly made any. For the Second and Fourth Councils published certain things, but they were not approved by the Apostolic See, as is certain from the Council of Chalcedon, action 16. Hence these are not properly called canons of the general Councils. Moreover the Third, Fifth and Sixth Council published no canons on customs.

To the fifth point, I respond: Tharasius was commended by Adrian, because he had seen him safeguard right faith, according to the decrees of the six general councils; the fact is that these canons of the Quini-Sext Synod are contained in the epistle of Adrian, recited from the epistle of Tharasius, and each is not refuted in its place by Adrian, because it was not an opportune time for doing so; still, he did not immediately approve them. But the fact that Adrian did, and after him, Nicholas, in an epistle to the Emperor Michael, they wished to cite certain parts from these canons, having learned from the Apostle even to use the testimonies of the heathen, when it was fitting.

Sixthly, and lastly, Nilos objects that it is intolerable, the fact that the Pope of Rome refused to be subject to the canons of the holy Fathers, since he had his dignity from the Fathers, and he also published many canons, and at length was unworthy that he should be honored as Father, since he condemned so many holy Fathers.

I respond: these reasons themselves prove that the Pope cannot be subjected to Canons, for he did not have his dignity from the Fathers, but from Christ, as we proved above. Hence he ought to be subject to Christ, not the Fathers. Next, when he may make canons, it is a sign that he is the prince and legislator: A prince, however, cannot be obliged to his own laws, since he would not be superior to himself, and laws are only imposed upon inferiors by a superior. Then, if all honor him as Father, he does not have any Fathers in the Church, rather they are all sons. Why is it a marvel if a father is not subjected to sons, but sons to the father? Add that, the Pope neither condemned the fathers nor their canons, although he could not be compelled by them.

CHAPTER XXVIII
The Objections of Calvin are Answered

ON the other hand, when Calvin condemns what we have said, that the Pope is judged by no one, he in turn proposes no argument[1] which would be proper for this place. Rather he merely says it can be gathered frm councils, histories and many writings of the Fathers wherein the Roman Pontiffs are compelled into regulation. At the same time, still nothing pleases him more than to pluck from such copious testimonies.

Moreover, he asserts that on the name of Supreme Priest and Universal bishop, it pertains to following the head. In another place,[2] he produces several citations of St. Gregory, who, although he was a Roman bishop, still he recognized the emperor as his lord. For in an epistle,[3] he calls the emperor his most Serene Lord, and calls himself his most unworthy servant. Furthermore, in the same letter, he even confesses the obedience that he naturally owes. Likewise in another epistle, he says: "Our Lord more quickly deemed the priests unworthy, not from earthly power, but by a consideration of excellence on account of it, whose servants they are, it is so lorded over them that it even expends true reverence."[4] In such a place Gregory speaks of himself, and numbers himself among those, over whom he affirms the emperor has dominion. Likewise in another epistle: "Having trusted in almighty God, the fact that he will grant long life to pious lords, and we will dispose under your hand according to his mercy."[5]

I respond: the fact that St. Gregory names himself the servant of the emperor ought not to appear a marvel. For, as John the Deacon writes, he called all priests brothers, all clergy sons, all laity his lords.[6] Still, it is not right to gather from there that Gregory could be judged by all the laity. The fact attains to obedience and subjection, wherein by humility he said he was the servant of the emperor, from the same, he requests just as commands, and he received commands. Nor did he hesitate to use the common manner of speaking, that we might say we obey when we do what the other desires, although he did not

---

[1] *Instit.*, lib. 4, ch. 7, §19 - 21.

[2] Ibid, ch. 11, § 12.

[3] Lib. 3, epist. 61.

[4] Lib. 4, epist. 31.

[5] Ibid, epist. 34.

[6] John the Deacon, *Vita D. Gregorii*, lib. 4, ch. 58.

command, nor maybe could command.

Add that Gregory spoke so humbly with the emperor not without reason, because in that time the emperor obtained temporal dominion over the city of Rome, and Gregory very much required his help and friendship, so that both he and the temporal goods of his Church, and the Roman people, would be defended from the swords and fury of the Lombards. In point of fact, the emperor, who was far away, used the works of Gregory much even in the administration of the temporal affairs of the state, and certainly on those affairs which Gregory did in the name of the emperor, he was held to account to the same emperor.

Nevertheless, should we compare absolutely person with person, the emperor of the sheep, the Pontiff as shepherd, we see that the Pontiff judges the emperor, not that the Pontiff ought to be judged by the emperor. That can be clearly gathered from the fact that pious Pontiffs often judged pious emperors; Fabian did Phillipas, Ambrose did Theodosius, Innocent did Arcadius; but pious emperors have never judged pious Pontiffs, nor is it read they commanded the same, which Pope Nicholas proves in a letter to the Emperor Michael with many testimonies. Nor was Gregory either ignorant or silent; for in that epistle 31 of Book 4 of the *Registry of Epistles*, which Calvin cites, although he says he is the servant of the emperor; still he adds that the emperor ought to show the reverence which is due to the priests, because certainly he is inferior to them, not superior. The example of Constantine offers the same, whom the bishops that were present begged to judge, and he did not dare to do so. Such an example certainly Gregory never would have brought forth if he believed the Pontiff ought to be judged by the Emperor.

Next, in the same place, although Gregory is called simple by the emperor, he was not silent, for a grave injury was made against him by that word; since simple and foolish seem to mean the same thing. But to what extent, I ask, would it be an injury if a master should call a servant, or a judge were to call a criminal, simple? Thus, St. Gregory understood which person ruled the Church, and what reverence was due to himself from the emperor; even if in the meantime he partly subjected himself from humility, and partly from necessity.

CHAPTER XXIX
Another Nine Arguments are Answered

NOW the following arguments are related by Juan de Torquemada and certain others from the ancient heretics. The first argument says that the Lord Jesus Christ Himself recognized imperial power over himself, when he said to Pilate: "You would not have power over me unless it were given to you from above."[1] Therefore, how much more should the Roman Pontiff, who himself is called the Vicar of Christ, be subject to the imperial power? It is confirmed by what St. Augustine says on this citation from the Gospel, where he openly teaches that Pilate had power over Christ from God, according to what was said by the Apostle, "There is no power except from God."[2] Likewise, St. Bernard agrees, who, in his epistle to Henry, the bishop of Sens, wrote: "Say, if you dare, to his Prelate that God does not know ordination, since Christ affirmed himself also that he was under the power of the Roman governor, which was of a heavenly order."[3]

I respond: Christ, without a doubt, was not subject to any human law, since he was God and the Son of God; rather, from his own will, he subjected himself to the judgment of Pilate on account of us, not by consigning some authority over himself, but by humbly tolerating the power which he had *de facto*, not from law. That fact St. Matthew shows,[4] when asked for the tribute, he taught first that he himself was not bound by it; and thereafter commanded it to be given to avoid scandal.

Now to that citation of John 19, the response is made in two ways. Firstly, with Sts. Cyril and John Chrysostom on this citation, the Lord does not speak on the power of jurisdiction, but on divine permission, without which sins could not even be done; that should be the sense: You cannot do anything against me, unless God decreed it was permitted, wherein the power is understood even that of Luke 22: "This is your hour, and the power of darkness."

But you might say: If the Lord spoke on permissions, why does he add right away, "For that reason those who handed me over to you, have the greater sin." Why did God permit Pilate to pass judgment on Christ and not the Jews, that they had to hand him over to Pilate; and still they handed him over while God was unwilling, and on that account sinned more?

---

[1] John 19:11.

[2] Romans 13:1.

[3] Epistle 42 ad Henricum, Episcopum Senonensem.

[4] Matth. 17:24-27.

I respond: It is best to follow the later opinion than the first. Accordingly when the Lord said: "For that reason," he did not only give the reasoning why the Jews sinned more than Pilate, but even why Pilate himself had sinned, although more lightly than the Jews. Therefore, this is the sense of those words: "Because not by extending justice, but only by the permission of God, you crucify me, for that reason you certainly sin; but still he sins more, who not only while not furnishing justice, but even impelled with hatred handed me to you, and threatened you with their rancor, so that you would crucify me."

The second exposition is of Augustine and Bernard, who teach, that Christ speaks on the true power of jurisdiction; according to such an opinion, they should join those words with the foregoing: "On that account, they who handed me to you have the greater sin." The sense is, "You crucify me, because you fear to offend Caesar, by whom you have your power, and you indeed sin, because you ought to obey God more than men; still the Jews sin more, who handed me to you, because, they crucify me not out of fear of a higher power, but from hatred and envy.."

And although the first exposition appears more literal, nevertheless, even this second holds nothing against our position. For Pilate is said to have had power over Christ, and he really held it, not *per se* but *per accidens*. He had power over all Jews *per se*, since they were subjects of the Roman Empire, hence the Lord had been offered to him as some one from a number of private Jews; for that reason also, in the very matter as he was so offered, so he had power. Even if Pilate caught sight of the fact that Christ is the Son of God, still he judged him not as the Son of God, but as a private Jew. Just the same, if in this time any clergymen you like, after changing his habit for a secular official, should be offered to be judged, the judge could punish him from his authority, and be excused from fault, if it were probable that he were ignorant.

The second argument. Paul appealed to Caesar: "I will stand before the tribunal of Caesar; it will be fitting for me to be judged there."[5] And again: "I appeal to Caesar." If Paul recognized Caesar as a judge, certainly Peter did also; for Peter and Paul were equal.

I respond: Firstly, it can be said that Paul appealed to Caesar because he had a judge *de facto*, even if he was not legally so. So Juan de Torquemada responds.[6] Secondly, it can be said even better with Albert Pighius, that there is a distinction between princes of the heathen and Christians, for at some time there were princes of the heathen, but not a Pontiff as their judge; but on the

---

[5] Acts 25:10.

[6] *Summae de Ecclesia*, lib. 2, ch. 96.

other hand, he had been subject to them in all civil causes, no less than the rest of men.

But the Pontiff would not be their judge, clearly, because he is not judge except of the faithful, according to that which is said in 1 Corinthians 6: "Why do you bring to me to judge concerning these who are outside?" But on the other hand that he would be subject civilly to them, both *de facto* and by law is also clear. For the Christian law deprives no man of his right and dominion; just as, before the Christian law, men were subject to emperors and kings, so also afterward. This is why Peter and Paul everywhere exhort the faithful that they be subject to princes, as is clear from Scripture.[7] Therefore, Paul appealed rightly to Caesar, and acknowledged him as a judge since he was accused of exciting sedition and a tumult amongst the people. But when princes are made Christians, and receive the laws of the Gospel of their own will, immediately they subject themselves just as sheep to the shepherd, and members to the head of the ecclesiastical hierarchy. So princes are judged by the shepherd, consequently, they ought not judge him.

The third argument. Paul says: "Let every soul be subject to higher powers."[8] 1 Peter 2: "Be subject to every human creature on account of God, just as to every distinguished king, etc." In such places the sermon is on secular powers, and none are excepted from subjection, not the clergy, nor a bishop, nor the Pope, when it is said: "Every soul should be subject." Nor can the response be made that the Apostles only speak on princes of this world who were heathen. For the Church, which always repeats the same readings, shows clearly enough that Paul and Peter speak on all princes who were then and who were going to come.

I respond: Both Peter and Paul speak generally, and exhort all be subject, that they might obey their superiors, whether spiritual or temporal. From such an opinion it cannot be deduced that the Pope is subject to a king, or a king to a Pope; rather, only that one who is subject owes obedience to his superior.

Because those opinions are general, it can be proved, for Paul says: "Let every soul be subject to the higher powers." In that place, he does not restrict his discourse to the secular power; rather, he speaks on every power. Nor does the example on kings who carry a sword impede our opinion. For Paul would have it speak more diligently and expressly on the king, because in that time Christians were accused of sedition as well as rebellion by their calumniators. For that reason he concludes generally in the end: "Render, therefore, to all what

---

[7]   Romans 13:1-7; Titus 3:1; and 1 Peter 2:13-17.

[8]   Romans 13:1.

is due; to whom tribute, tribute; to one whom honor is due, honor; fear, fear, etc." For equal reason, Peter speaks generally: "Be subject to every human creature;" that is, to every creature having power. Soon he shall place an example on a king, and leaders, on account of the same reason as Paul. Therefore, St. Bernard, (as we cited above) says: "It is read 'let every soul be subject to the higher powers,' which opinion I desire you to safeguard in showing reverence to the vicar of Peter, just as it is preserved for your countenance throughout the whole world."[9]

The fourth argument. In the old law the king judged and deposed a Pontiff, for Solomon deposed Abiathar, and constituted Zadok in his place; for equal reasoning in the New Testament, there will be a Christian emperor to judge a Christian pontiff.

I respond: Firstly, the similitude cannot be denied. Yet, although in the Old Testament there were only temporal promises, and in the New spiritual and eternal ones, as Sts. Jerome and Augustine teach,[10] it would not be a wonder if in the Old Testament the supreme power was temporal, but in the new it is spiritual.

I say secondly, even in the Old Testament the Pontiff was greater than the king, as Philo, Theodoret, and Procopius teach;[11] and it is deduced also from chapter 27 of Numbers, where it is said that at the word of Eliazar the priest [pontiff] both Joshua the prince and all the people should enter and depart, as well as from Leviticus 4, where four sacrifices are established, from the order of which, and the magnitude the order is gathered, as well as the dignity of persons for whom they were made. First there was the holocausts for the Pontiff. Second, even the holocaust for the whole people. Third of he-goats, that is, of a cheaper animal, for the king. Fourth of she-goats, for every private matter.

Now to the argument on Solomon, I say he, not as a king but as a prophet and executor of divine justice deposed Abiathar, after substituting Zadok. For in the same place, it is said that Solomon removed Abiathar, "that the word of the Lord might be fulfilled."[12]

The fifth argument. Christian emperors often judged and deposed Pontiffs.

---

[9] Epistl. Ad Conradum imperatorem, 183.

[10] *Contra Pelagianos*, lib. 1, et *in epistola ad Dardanum de terra promissionis*; Augustine *in Librum Numeri,* quest. 33, lib. 19; *Contra*

[11] Philo of Alexandria, *de Victimis*; Theodoret, *Quaest. 1 in Leviticum*; & Procopius in ch. 4 of Levitius.

[12] 3 Kings [Kings], 2:27.

For Constantius sent Pope Liberius into exile, Justinian Sylverius; King Theodoric threw John I into prison. Otho I deposed John XII, and substituted Leo VIII in his place. Henry III deposed Gregory VI, and commanded Clement II to be ordained. The histories of those times are full of such things.

I respond: These things certainly happened, but by what law, they themselves see. Certainly Liberius was unjustly sent into exile, as Athanasius witnesses in his epistle treating on the solitary life. Liberatus says the same thing in his *Breviary*, ch. 22. St. Gregory writes about John I,[13] and it is certain that Constantius and Theodoric were Arians, while Justinian was a Monophysite. Therefore, it is no more a wonder that the heretical princes would depose Christian Pontiffs by a tyrannical rule, than that the heathen emperors everywhere killed the same.

It is certain enough on Otho I, that he was motivated by good zeal, but he did not act according to knowledge when he deposed John XII, for this John was the most degenerate of all Pontiffs. And therefore, it is no wonder if the pious emperor, such as Otho I was (though less experienced in ecclesiastical matters), judged that he could be deposed, especially since many teachers sensed the same thing. For this reason, Otho of Frisia explains this history, and modestly evaluates the emperor: "Whether each did licitly or not, now is not the time to say."[14]

On Henry III there is a smaller difficulty, for as it is certain from the same Otho of Frisia,[15] the Emperor Henry did not depose Gregory, rather persuaded him that he should yield, because it appeared he had been elected by simony. In point of fact, he had yielded of his own will and Clement was elected. Besides, add that Leo of Hostia,[16] who flourished at that time, gathered a council of bishops, and the Pontiff was invited by the emperor that he should preside over the council. Whatever case of that Pontiff might be treated, still he was the supreme judge. Moreover, sorrowful for his faults, he asked forgiveness in earnest, and abdicated from the pontificate of his own will.

The sixth argument. The Pontiffs affirmed they were in subjection to the emperors. For Gregory, as quoted by Gratian, says: "If anyone should wish to refute us over these matters, let him come to the Apostolic See, that there he would justly dispute the issue with me before the confession of Blessed Peter,

---

[13]   *Dialogorum*, lib. 4, ch. 30.

[14]   Otho of Frisia, Historia, lib. 6, ch. 23.

[15]   *Hist.,* lib. 6, ch. 32.

[16]   *Chronicum Cassinensis,* lib. 2, ch. 80.

insofar as there one of our number there shall receive his opinion."[17] Likewise Pope Hadrian I conceded to Charlemagne the law of electing the Roman Pontiff, and ordering the Apostolic See, as is contained in dist. 63, Canon *Hadrianus*, and because Leo VIII conceded the same thing again afterward. The same dist. 63, as well as the canon, are contained in a Synod by Otho I. Likewise Leo IV asked judges from the Emperor Louis, and promised that he was going to obey their judgment, as is contained in the canon *Nos si incompetenter*, 2, quest. 7.

I respond: That quote of Gregory is not found in his works. Next, Gregory does not call upon the judgment of men, but of God. He seems to speak on the relation through the oath and on the expectation of a divine sentence, which is often imposed against perjurers. Hadrian and Leo did not concede to the emperor except that he would confirm or annul the election of a new Pontiff, and should order the Roman Church in regard to its temporal rule. It does not follow from that, that the emperor had power over the Pontiff. Moreover, those two privileges were conceded to the emperor on account of the frequency of schisms which occurred then; and on account of the frequent armies of the Lombards and Greeks, who continually disturbed the Roman Church; when all these causes ceased to be an issue, the privileges were recalled. Leo IV subjected himself to a distinguished judgment that was not forced by the emperor, as is clearly gathered from that very chapter.

The seventh argument. It is lawful for anyone to kill a Pontiff, if he invades any territory unjustly; for that reason, it will be much more lawful for kings or a council to depose the Pontiff, if he should disturb a commonwealth, or endeavor to slay souls by his example.

I respond: firstly by denying the consequent, because no authority is required to resist an invader and defend oneself, nor is it necessary that the one who is invaded should be a judge and superior of the one who invades; rather authority is required to judge and punish. Therefore, just as it would be lawful to resist a Pontiff invading a body, so it is lawful to resist him invading souls or disturbing a state, and much more if he should endeavor to destroy the Church. I say, it is lawful to resist him, by not doing what he commands, and by blocking him, lest he should carry out his will; still, it is not lawful to judge or punish or even depose him, because he is nothing other than a superior. See Cajetan on this matter,[18] and Juan de Torquemada.[19]

The eighth argument. The Pontiff was truly subjected in the forum of

---

[17] Gratian, *Can. Si quis*, quest. 7.

[18] *Tractatus de auctoritate Papae et Concilii*, ch. 27.

[19] *Loc cit*, lib. 2, ch. 106.

conscience to his confessor just as to a minister of God; why, therefore, could he not be subjected in the exterior forum as well, to some prince who is also a minister of God?

I respond: the reason for the diversity is because in the forum of conscience, the confessor is a worthy instrument of God, so that it is rather more God who judges through a man, than the man himself; the fact appears both from the fact that the confessor cannot altogether compel the penitent against his will to undergo punishment, and from the fact that in confession he judges even concerning occult crimes, which pertain to the knowledge of God alone. But in the exterior forum, a man is truly a judge, even as a man, although he may be constituted by God, and for that reason he only judges on manifest affairs, and can altogether compel one to punishment against his will.

The ninth argument. The Pontiff can give a certificate of repudiation of his own will to the Church through renunciation;[20] therefore, the Church can give a certificate of its own will to the Pontiff, and elect another in his place.

I respond: firstly, by denying the consequent. For the Pope is above the Church, not the other way around. For which reason even Deuteronomy 24 says that a man could give a certificate of repudiation to his wife whereas, that his wife could give a certificate to her husband is discovered nowhere. Secondly, I say, the Pope cannot renounce the pontificate without the consensus of the Church,[21] and hence if the Church *could* give a certificate of repudiation to the Pope, it could not without his consent; if he should consent, he would abdicate of his own will, he would not be compelled against his will.

---

[20] As is clear in Sexto, *de Renunciatione*, ch. 1.

[21] Translator's note: Even in Bellarmine's time this was hotly debated by canonists and theologians, (c.f. Suarez *de Summo Pontifice*, Distinction X, no 6), felt it was not necessary for anyone to receive a papal resignation. The 1917 Code of Canon law made it clear that it was not necessary for anyone to consent to the Pope's resignation in order for him to resign, and the 1983 Code follows it in this regard.

CHAPTER XXX
The Last Argument is Answered Wherein the Argument is Taken up, Whether a Heretical Pope can be Deposed

HE TENTH argument. A Pope can be judged and deposed by the Church in the case of heresy; as is clear from Dist. 40, can. *Si Papa*: therefore, the Pontiff is subject to human judgment, at least in some case.

I respond: There are five opinions on this matter. The first is of Albert Pighius, who contends that the Pope cannot be a heretic, and hence would not be deposed in any case.[1] Such an opinion is probable, and can easily be defended, as we will show in its proper place. Still, because it is not certain, and the common opinion is to the contrary, it will be worthwhile to see what the response should be if the Pope could be a heretic.

Thus, the second opinion is that the Pope, in the very instant in which he falls into heresy, even if it is only interior, is outside the Church and deposed by God, for which reason he can be judged by the Church. That is, he is declared deposed by divine law, and deposed *de facto*, if he still refused to yield. This is of Juan de Torquemada,[2] but it is not proven to me. For jurisdiction is certainly given to the Pontiff by God, but with the agreement of men, as is obvious. Because this man, who beforehand was not Pope, has from men that he would begin to be Pope, therefore, he is not removed by God unless it is through men. But a secret heretic cannot be judged by men, nor would such wish to relinquish that power by his own will. Add that the foundation of this opinion is that secret heretics are outside the Church, which is false, and we will amply demonstrate this in our tract *On the Church Militant*.

The third opinion is on another extreme, that the Pope is not and cannot be deposed either by secret or manifest heresy. Torquemada in the aforementioned citation relates and refutes this opinion, and rightly so, for it is exceedingly improbable. Firstly, because that a heretical Pope can be judged is expressly held in the canon *Si Papa*, dist. 40, and with Innocent.[3] And what is more, in the Fourth Council of Constantinople, Act 7, the acts of the Roman Council under Hadrian are recited, and in those it was contained that Pope Honorius appeared to be legally anathematized, because he had been convicted of heresy, the only reason where it is lawful for inferiors to judge superiors. Here the fact must be remarked upon that, although it is probable that Honorius was not a heretic, and

---

[1] *Hierarchiae Ecclesiasticae*, lib. 4, ch. 8.

[2] *Loc. Cit.*, lib. 4, part 2, ch. 20.

[3] Serm. 2, *de Consecratione Pontificis*.

312

that Pope Hadrian II was deceived by corrupted copies of the Sixth Council which falsely reckoned Honorius was a heretic, we still cannot deny that Hadrian, with the Roman Council and the whole Eighth Synod, sensed that in the case of heresy, a Roman Pontiff can be judged. Add that it would be the most miserable condition of the Church, if she were to be compelled to recognize a wolf, manifestly prowling, for a shepherd.

The fourth opinion is of Cajetan.[4] There he teaches that a manifestly heretical Pope is not *ipso facto* deposed; but can and ought to be deposed by the Church. Now in my judgment, such an opinion cannot be defended. For in the first place, that a manifest heretic would be *ipso facto* deposed, is proven from authority and reason. The authority is of St. Paul, who commands Titus,[5] that after two censures, that is, after he appears manifestly pertinacious, an heretic is to be shunned; and he understands this before excommunication and sentence of a judge. Jerome comments on the same place, saying that other sinners, through a judgment of excommunication are excluded from the Church; heretics, however, leave by themselves and are cut from the body of Christ, but a Pope who remains the Pope cannot be shunned. How will we shun our head? How will we recede from a member to whom we are joined?

Now in regard to reason this is indeed very certain. A non-Christian cannot in any way be Pope, as Cajetan affirms in the same book,[6] and the reason is because he cannot be the head of that which he is not a member, and he is not a member of the Church who is not a Christian. But a manifest heretic is not a Christian, as St. Cyprian and many other Fathers clearly teach.[7] Therefore, a manifest heretic cannot be Pope.

Cajetan responds in a defense of the aforementioned treatise, chapter 25, and in the treatise itself chapter 22, that a heretic is not a Christian simply; but is relatively. For since two things make a Christian, faith and the character, a heretic loses the virtue of faith, but still retains the character; and for that reason, still adheres in some way to the Church, and has the capacity for jurisdiction. Hence, he is still Pope, but must be deposed, because due to heresy and his final disposition he is disposed to not be Pope; as such he is a man, not yet dead, but constituted *in extremis*.

---

[4] *Tract. De auctoritate Papae et Concilii*, ch. 20, & 21.

[5] Titus 3.

[6] Loc. Cit., ch. 26.

[7] Cyprian, lib. 4, epist. 2.; Athanasius, *Contra Arianos*, serm. 2; Augustine, *de gratia Christi* ch. 20; Jerome *Contra Luciferianos*, and many ohters.

But on the contrary, since in the first place, were a heretic to remain joined with the Church in act by reason of the character, he could never be cut off and separated from her, because the character is indelible; yet everyone affirms that some can be cut off from the Church *de facto*. Consequently, the character does not cause a heretical man be in the Church by act; rather, it is only a sign that he was in the Church, and that he ought to be in the Church. While the character impressed upon a sheep when it was in the mountains does not cause it to be in the sheepfold; it indicates from which fold it fled, and to where it can be driven back again. This is also confirmed by St. Thomas,[8] who says that those who do not have faith are not united to Christ in act, but only in potency, and there he speaks on internal union, not external, which is made through the confession of faith, and the visible Sacraments. Therefore, since the character pertains to what is internal and not external, according to St. Thomas, the character alone does not unite a man with Christ in act. Next, either faith is a necessary disposition as one for this purpose, that someone should be Pope, or it is merely that he be a good Pope. If the first, then after that disposition has been abolished through its opposite, which is heresy, soon after the Pope ceases to be Pope. For the form cannot be preserved without its necessary dispositions. If the second, then a Pope cannot be deposed on account of heresy. On the other hand, in general, he ought to be deposed even on account of ignorance and wickedness, and other dispositions which are necessary to be a good Pope; and besides, Cajetan affirms that the Pope cannot be deposed from a defect of dispositions that are not necessary as one, but merely necessary for one to be a good Pope.

Cajetan responds that faith is a necessary disposition simply, but in part not in total, and hence with faith being absent the Pope still remains Pope, on account of another part of the disposition which is called the character, and that still remains.

But on the other hand, either the total disposition which is the character and faith is necessary as one unit, or it is not, and a partial disposition suffices. If the first, then without faith, the necessary disposition does not remain any longer as one, because the whole was necessary as one unit and now it is no longer total. If the second, then faith is not required to be good, and hence on account of his defect, a Pope cannot be deposed. Thereupon, those things which have the final disposition to ruin, soon after cease to exist, without another external force, as is clear; therefore, even a heretical Pope, without another disposition ceases to be Pope *per se*.

---

[8] III, q. 8, a. 3.

Next, the holy Fathers teach in unison that not only are heretics outside the Church, but they even lack all ecclesiastical jurisdiction and dignity *ipso facto*. Cyprian says: "We say that all heretics and schismatics have not power and right."[9] He also teaches that heretics returning to the Church must be received as laymen; even if beforehand they were priests or bishops in the Church.[10] Optatus teaches that heretics and schismatics cannot hold the keys of the kingdom of heaven, nor loose or bind.[11] Ambrose and Augustine teach the same, as does St. Jerome who says: "bishops who were heretics cannot continue to be so; rather let them be constituted such who were received that were not heretics."[12]

Pope Celestine I, in an epistle to John of Antioch, which is contained in volume one of the Council of Ephesus, ch. 19, says: "If anyone who was either excommunicated or exiled by bishop Nestorius, or any that followed him, from such a time as he began to preach such things, whether they be from the dignity of a bishop or clergy, it is manifest that he has endured and endures in our communion, nor do we judge him outside, because he could not remove anyone by a sentence who himself had already shown that he must be removed." And in a letter to the clergy of Constantinople: "The authority of our See has sanctioned that the bishop, cleric or Christian by simple profession who had been deposed or excommunicated by Nestorius or his followers, after the latter began to preach heresy, shall not be considered deposed or excommunicated. For he who had defected from the faith with such preaching, cannot depose or remove anyone whatsoever."

Nicholas I confirms and repeats the same thing in his epistle to the Emperor Michael. Next, even St. Thomas teaches that schismatics soon lose all jurisdiction; and if they try to do something from jurisdiction, it is useless.[13]

Nor does the response which some make avail, that these Fathers speak according to ancient laws, but now since the decree of the Council of Constance they do not lose jurisdiction, unless excommunicated by name, or if they strike clerics. I say this avails to nothing. For those Fathers, when they say that heretics lose jurisdiction, do not allege any human laws which maybe did not

---

[9] Lib. 1, epist. 6.

[10] Lib. 2, epist. 1.

[11] *Contra Parmenianum.*

[12] Ambrose, *de poenitentia*, lib. 1, ch. 2; Augustine, *Enchrid.*, ch. 65; Jerome, *Contra Luciferianos.*

[13] II IIae, q. 39, art. 3.

exist then on this matter; rather, they argued from the nature of heresy. Moreover, the Council of Constance does not speak except on the excommunicates, that is, on these who lose jurisdiction through a judgment of the Church. Yet heretics are outside the Church, even before excommunication, and deprived of all jurisdiction, for they are condemned by their own judgment, as the Apostle teaches to Titus; that is, they are cut from the body of the Church without excommunication, as Jerome expresses it.

Next, what Cajetan says in the second place, that a heretical Pope who is truly Pope can be deposed by the Church, and from its authority, seems no less false than the first. For, if the Church deposes a Pope against his will, certainly it is over the Pope. Yet the same Cajetan defends the opposite in the very same treatise. But he answers: the Church, in the very matter, when it deposes the Pope, does not have authority over the Pope, but only on that union of the person with the pontificate. As the Church can join the pontificate to such a person, and still it is not said on that account to be above the Pontiff; so it can separate the pontificate from such a person in the case of heresy, and still it will not be said to be above the Pope.

On the other hand, from the very fact that the Pope deposes bishops, they deduce that the Pope is above all bishops, and still the Pope deposing a bishop does not destroy the episcopacy, but only separates it from that person. Secondly, for one to be deposed from the pontificate against his will is without a doubt a penalty; therefore, the Church deposing a Pope against his will, without a doubt punished him; but to punish is for a superior and a judge. Thirdly, because according to Cajetan and the other Thomists, in reality they are the same; the whole and the parts are taken up together. Therefore, he who has so great an authority over the parts taken up together, such that he can also separate them, also has it over the whole, which arises from those parts.

Furthermore, the example of Cajetan does not avail on electors, who have the power of applying the pontificate to a certain person, and still do not have power over the Pope. For while a thing is made, the action is exercised over the matter of the thing that is going to be, not over a composite which does not yet exist; but while a thing is destroyed, the action is exercised over a composite; as is certain from natural things. Therefore, when cardinals create the Pontiff, they exercise their authority not over the Pontiff, because he does not yet exist; but over the matter, that is, over the person whom they dispose in a certain measure through election, that he might receive the form of the pontificate from God. But if they depose the Pope, they necessarily exercise authority over the composite, that is, over the person provided with pontifical dignity, which is to say, over the Pontiff.

Now the fifth true opinion is that a Pope who is a manifest heretic, ceases in himself to be Pope and head, just as he ceases in himself to be a Christian and member of the body of the Church; whereby he can be judged and punished by the Church. This is the opinion of all the ancient Fathers, who teach that manifest heretics soon lose all jurisdiction, and namely St. Cyprian who speaks on Novatian, who was a Pope in schism with Cornelius: "He cannot hold the episcopacy; although he was a bishop first, he fell from the body of his fellow bishops and from the unity of the Church."[14] There he means that Novatian, even if he was a true and legitimate Pope still would have fallen from the pontificate by himself if he separated himself from the Church.

The opinion of the learned men of our age is the same, as John Driedo teaches,[15] that they who are cast out as excommunicates, or leave on their own and oppose the Church, are separated from it as heretics and schismatics. He adds in the same work[16] that those who have departed from the Church maintain no spiritual power over those who are in the Church. Melchior Cano teaches the same thing when he says that heretics are not part of the Church, nor members,[17] and he adds in the last chapter, 12th argument, that someone cannot even be informed in thought so as to be head and Pope, who is not a member nor a part. He teaches the same thing when he says that secret heretics are still in the Church and are parts and members, so that a secretly heretical Pope is still Pope. Others teach the same, whom we cite in Book 1 of *de Ecclesia*.

The foundation of this opinion is that a manifest heretic is in no way a member of the Church; that is, neither in spirit nor in body, or by internal union nor external. For even wicked Catholics are united and are members in spirit through faith, and in body through the confession of faith and the participation of the visible Sacraments. Secret heretics are united and are members, but only by an external union; just as on the other hand, good catechumens are in the Church only by an internal union but not an external one; manifest heretics by no union, as has been proved.

---

[14] Lib. 4, epist. 2.

[15] *De Scripturis et dogmatibus Ecclesiasticis*, lib. 4, ch. 2, part 2, sent. 2.

[16] *Ibid.*, sent. 7.

[17] *De Locis Theologiis*, lib. 4, ch. 2.

CHAPTER XXXI

That the Roman Pontiff Succeeds Peter in the Ecclesiastical Monarchy is Proven from the Names, which Roman Pontiffs are Usually Given

THE LAST argument is taken from the fifteen names of the bishop of Rome, namely: Pope, Father of Fathers, Pontiff of Christians, High Priest, Prince of Priests, Vicar of Christ, Head of the Body of the Church, Foundation of the Building of the Church, Shepherd of the Sheepfold of the Lord, Father and Doctor of all the faithful, Ruler of the House of God, Watchman of the Vineyard of God, Spouse of the Church, Prelate of the Apostolic See, and Universal bishop. His primacy is obviously gathered from each individual one.

The first and most common, as well as most ancient name of the bishop of Rome is Pope [*Papa*]. For St. Ignatius, in his epistle to Mary the Proselyte near Zarbus, writes: "Since you are at Rome, with Pope Linus, etc." Moreover, Pope, or πάππας as it is in Greek, is a name which charming or babbling children usually call their fathers; as it appears in Philemon, the comic writer quoted in Athenaeum: "χαῖρε πάππα φίλατε,"[1] and in the Odyssey of Homer, where a daughter says to her father: "πάππα φίλε,"[2] while among the Latins, writers the likewise address a father or a grandfather. Juvenal for instance:

> *Mordeat ante aliquis quidquid porrexerit illa*
> *quae peperit, timidus praegustet pocula Pappas.*[3]

Ausonius likewise to his grandson:

> *Pappos, aviasque trementes*
> *Anteferunt patribus seri nova cura nepotes.*

Hence ecclesiastics began to call their spiritual father by the charming word, "Father."

This name was given by the Fathers now and then to a bishop; for Jerome in all his epistles to Augustine calls him Pope; just as even now every priest is called "Father". Still, just the same, from this name the primacy of the bishop of Rome is gathered in three modes. Firstly, by its use as a proper name, when Papa is absolutely pronounced, he alone is understood; as is clear from the

---

[1] *Athenaeum* Lib. VIII. The Greek means literally: "Hail! beloved Father."

[2] *Odyss.* Lib. VI.

[3] *Satyra* VI.

Council of Chalcedon, Action 16, where we read: "The most blessed and apostolic man, the Pope, commands this of us." "Leo" is not added, nor "Roman", or "of the city of Rome", or something else. Secondly, because he alone is called Pope of the whole Church, as is clear from the same act of the Council of Chalcedon, where Leo is called Pope of the universal Church; and from Liberatus,[4] where we read that no one is Pope over the Church of the whole world except the Roman Pontiff. Thirdly, from the fact that the bishop of Rome is called by the whole world, and by general councils, Father or Pope; but he calls no man Pope or father, rather sons or brothers, as is clear from the epistle to the Second Council,[5] and from the epistle of the Council of Chalcedon to Leo.

The second name is Father of Fathers, which is given to Pope Damasus by Stephen, the Archbishop of Carthage, in his epistle to Damasus which he wrote in the name of three Councils of Africa: "To the most Blessed Lord and lofty apostolic summit, to the Holy Father of Fathers, Pope Damasus, etc." Nor do we read any communication to anyone else with this name.

The third is Pontiff of Christians, quoted by Eusebius in his *Chronicle* for the year 44.

The fourth is Supreme Pontiff, which we read in the same epistle of Stephen of Carthage. It follows: "And to the Supreme Pontiff of all Prelates." Even St. Gregory uses the title.[6] St. Jerome, in a preface on the Gospels to Pope Damasus: "You, who are the high priest." And in the Sixth Council, Action 18, in an acclamatory sermon, the whole Council calls Pope Agatho: "Our most holy Father and Supreme Pope."

The fifth is Prince of Priests. We read concerning this in an epistle of Valentinian to Theodosius, which is contained before the Council of Chalcedon in Volume 1 of the Councils: "The most blessed bishop of the city of Rome, to whom the rule [*principatum*] of the priesthood all antiquity conferred over all, etc." And with Prosper of Aquitaine: "Rome, on account of the rule of the priesthood, was made greater in the citadel of religion, than in the lap of power."[7]

---

[4] *Breviarium*, ch. 22.

[5] Quoted by Theodoret, lib. 5, ch. 10.

[6] *Dialogorum*, lib.. 1, ch. 4. St. Anselm also uses it in his preface to *de Incarnatione Verbi* to Pope Urban, and St. Bernard uses it in all his epistles to the Roman Pontiffs.

[7] *De Vocatione Gentium*, lib. 2, ch. 6.

But Calvin objects[8] that at the third Council of Carthage it was forbidden for anyone be called Prince of Priests or High Priest; rather, only bishop of the First See.[9] I respond: That council only established on the bishops of Africa, among whom there were many equal primates, lest any of them would be called High Priest, or prince of others. Nor could this provincial council, or the bishops of any other provinces, oblige the Roman Pontiff. Therefore, Gregory, Anselm, Bernard and the Sixth General Council itself, not withstanding that canon, called the Roman bishop Supreme Pontiff.

The sixth is Vicar of Christ; St. Bernard uses such a title,[10] as well as the Council of Lyon under Gregory X.[11]

The seventh is Head of the Church, which the Council of Chalcedon uses in an epistle to Pope Leo: "Over whom you are in charge of, just as a head over the members," and Action 1 of the same council, it is said the Roman Church is the head of all churches.

But Calvin objects[12] that St. Gregory in a letter to John, the bishop of Constantinople, says: "Peter, the first member of the holy and universal Church. Paul, Andrew, James, what else are they than heads of individual peoples? Still all are members under one head of the Church."[13] There Gregory condemned John, who wanted to make himself head of the Church, and he uses this argument. Neither Peter, nor any other Apostle was head of the whole Church, but only heads of individual churches, and members of the universal Church.

I respond: That someone is the head of the whole Church can be understood in two ways. In one way, that the head should be such that he alone would be the head and prince, and all the rest of the lower would not be heads, but princes, and only of their office. In the second way, that he indeed should be the head, but general, so that he does not abolish particular inferior places, and true heads. For that reason universal cases do not take particulars, and that is why in the army the emperor does not remove particular generals of legions and cohorts.

And in the first mode, Christ alone is head of all the churches; accordingly

---

[8] *Instit.*, lib. 4, ch. 7, § 3.

[9] Council of Carthage III, can. 26.

[10] *De Consideratione*, lib. 2.

[11] Quoted by Sextus, *Titulo de Electione*, ch. *Ubi Periculum*.

[12] *Instit.*, lib. 4, ch. 7, § 21.

[13] Lib. 4, ch. 28, *ad Joannis Episopum Constantinopolitanum.*

being compared to Christ, all are vicars and administrators, nor can any be said to be his colleagues or fellow-bishops; and Peter in this mode is not the head, except of the particular Roman Church. Therefore, only of this Church is there a sole particular bishop and head; the other particular bishops are heads, bishops of their provinces, who are true princes, and of Peter, not of vicar, but of colleague and fellow bishop, and on this meaning St. Gregory treats in this place. In the other way, Peter was and now is the Roman Pontiff, truly the head of every Church, as the same Gregory himself teaches in these words: "The reverence of the Apostolic See will not be disturbed by presumption of any man; then if the head of faith will pulsate without injury, the whole condition of the members will persevere."[14]

The eighth is the Foundation. Jerome, in his first epistle to Damasus on the term *hypostasis*, says: "I know that the Church was built upon this rock." There he calls Damasus the rock of the Church.

The ninth is the Shepherd of the Lord's Flock: St. Ambrose says to Pope Siricius: "We recognize from the letters of your sanctity, the watch of the good shepherd, how you faithfully preserved the door entrusted to you, and that you guard the flock of Christ with pious care."[15]

The tenth is Ruler of the House of God: Ambrose says in his commentary on 1 Timothy 3: "The House of God is the Church, whose Ruler today is Damasus."

The eleventh is the Watchman of the vineyard, the Council of Chalcedon wrote in a letter to Pope Leo: "In addition, he extends insanity against him, to whom the care of the vineyard was consigned by the Savior, against your apostolic sanctity."

The twelfth is Father and Doctor of all Christians. We so have it in the Council of Florence, in the last session, by the same reasoning the Roman Church is called mother and teacher of all churches; as we have it in the Lateran Council under Innocent III, ch. 5 .

The thirteenth, is Spouse of the Church. The Pope is thus called in the Council of Lyons.[16]

But some object that St. Bernard[17] warns Pope Eugene, lest he should think of himself as the spouse of the Church; rather he should consider himself friend

---

[14] Lib. 2, epist. 42. He also has the same explanation on the fourth penitential psalm.

[15] Epistle 81.

[16] Quoted by Sextus, *de Electione*, in the Chapter "Ubi Periculum".

[17] Epistle 237.

of the spouse because it would seem absurd that the vicar of the king would be called the bridegroom of the queen.

I respond: Just as the Pope is called the Head, Ruler and Shepherd of the Church, in place of Christ, so also is he called the Spouse in place of Christ, or as the Vicar and Minister of Christ. For Christ is the true and principal spouse as it is said in John 3, he makes the Church fertile by his Spirit, and by his seed alone (which is the Word of God) are sons born. Popes are called spouses, because they cooperate extrinsically in the generation of sons, just as of a minister of the Word and of the Sacraments; and they generate sons not unto themselves, but unto Christ. Bernard, therefore, only intended to admonish the Pontiff, lest he would think that he was the Principal Spouse, and although it would be most absurd in the manner of carnal generation for the king to be assisted by a vicar, and one spouse to be of many; still in the spiritual order it is not absurd.

The fourteenth is Prelate of the Apostolic See. First it must be observed that not only was Rome called the Apostolic See by the ancients, but also Antioch, Jerusalem, Ephesus, and others which the Apostles founded, and in which they sat just as bishops. This is clear from Tertulian and St. Augustine.[18]

But the Roman Pontiff excels over those three in regards to this name. Firstly, because when it is purely said: "Apostolic See," and the name of Antioch, Ephesus or Rome is not added, it is always understood as Rome, which is called apostolic through an epithet. St. Augustine shows this when he says: "They were sent relating on this matter from the two councils of Carthage and Miletus to the Apostolic See."[19] He did not add Rome, and still he would have it so understood that certainly they were sent relating those affairs to Pope Innocent; is understood from other places of St. Augustine.[20]

Secondly, because the Roman Pontiff is not only said to hold fast to the Apostolic See, as the bishop of Antioch and Ephesus, but is even the rule of the Apostolic See.[21] Thirdly, because the Roman Pontiff is not only said to be the Prelate of the Apostolic See, as the bishop of Antioch and others, but even his office is called an apostolic office, as is clear from the Council of Chalcedon, Action 1, where we read that the vicars of Pope Leo said: "His apostolic office has deigned to command that Dioscorus should not sit in the Council." Likewise,

---

[18] Tertullian, *de Praescript.*; Augustine, Epistle 162, as well as in other places.

[19] Augustine, Epistle 106.

[20] Epist. 90 & 92. Similar examples of this occur everywhere.

[21] Augustine, Epist. 162.

the Emperor Honorius, in the epistle to Boniface: "We ask first, in order that your apostolic office would deign to focus by means of daily prayers and its devotion for salvation, upon our rule." Likewise an epistle of the bishops of Gaul, which is number 51 among the epistles of Leo, says: "Let your apostolic office give pardon to our lateness." Next, in an epistle of St. Bernard to Innocent we read: "It is fitting that we relate the emergence of dangers and scandals emerging in the kingdom of God to your Apostolic office, etc." Such a name, we read about no one else but the Roman Pontiff.

From that it is deduced that the bishops of Antioch and Ephesus and similar bishops were certainly bishops of Apostolic sees, that is, of those in which the apostles sat; but they did not succeed the Apostles in any sort of Apostolic office, otherwise their dignity would also be said of an Apostolic office. But the Roman Pontiff is the bishop of the Apostolic See and succeeded in some way in an Apostolic office, that is, in the care of the whole world, which was a certain part of the apostolic office, and on that account, it is called a position of the apostolic office itself. From which a certain objection of Nilos remains answered, which in his book on the primacy of the Pope he strives to prove, that the Roman Pontiff does not have primacy over other bishops, because the bishops of Antioch and Ephesus and Jerusalem were chosen to have apostolic thrones.

The fifteenth is Universal bishop. In the Council of Chalcedon, Act. 3, three epistles of different Greeks to Pope Leo were read, all of which begin thus: "To the most holy and blessed and universal archbishop and great patriarch, Leo of Rome." From such words, three lies of the heretics are refuted. One of Luther, where, when he said Gregory refused the name of Universal, he adds: "Why would someone speak of the name of Supreme and Most Holy?" Therefore, Luther[22] means that in the time of Gregory, the name of Most Holy and Supreme were as yet unheard of. In that, the incredible inexperience of Luther, or at least his malice, is uncovered, for all the Fathers call the Pope of Rome "most holy," and the citation clearly shuts the mouth of Luther.

What of the fact that in the second action of the same Council of Chalcedon, Aetius, the bishop of Nicopolis, calls St. Leo "Our Lord and most Holy Pope"? What title more displeases the heretics of our time although, it did not once displease a universal Council, and a senate, and the judges listening to Aetius say: "Because now the epistle of our Lord and most holy Pope has been read, etc."? Gregory himself uses the noun "supreme" [*summus*] as we cited above,[23] and the universal Council of Chalcedon says it (*summitas tua*) in its epistle to

---

[22] Luther, *de Potestate Papae.*

[23] *Dialogorum*, lib. 1, ch. 4.

Leo.

The second is of the Centuriators,[24] who say the Roman Pontiff was created a patriarch by Justin the Emperor in the year 700. But if that were so, how comes it that Leo is called Universal Patriarch very frequently in the Council of Chalcedon, which was celebrated in the year 454?

The third is of Calvin,[25] who relates the words of St. Gregory,[26] that the title of Universal was offered to his predecessors at the Council of Chalcedon, and then he adds: "This has no species of truth, for such a thing is not seen in the actions of that council." But of course this is an impudent lie, although certainly the council decreed nothing on this matter; still Calvin knows well enough that this name is given to the Roman Pontiff, and it did not displease the council, since in the third action, Pope Leo is most often called by this name, and no one in the council condemned such an appeal.

But Calvin objects against this name using the same words of Gregory, and very often repeats that the title of "universal bishop" is profane and a sacrilege, the forerunner of Antichrist, and therefore, no one from his predecessors ever wished to use it. Even Illyricus[27] objects, and likewise Luther,[28] that in a canon of an African council cited by Gratian,[29] *Prima sedis*, we read: "Moreover the Roman Pontiff is not called "universal"."

I respond: the name of "universal bishop" can be understood in two ways. In one way, as he who is called universal, should be understood to be the only bishop of all the cities of Christians; so that the rest might not be bishops, but only the vicars of the one who is called universal bishop; and in this manner, the name is truly profane, a sacrilege, and of Antichrist. Gregory speaks concerning this meaning, based on the reason which he gives. Even in that epistle cited by Calvin which is to Constantia: "It is very distressing, and must be borne with patience that my aforesaid brother and fellow-bishop, despising all others, should attempt to be called sole bishop."[30] And in a letter to Eulogius: "If one is

---

[24] *Cent. 6,* ch. 7, colum. 439.

[25] *Instit.* lib. 4, ch. 7, § 4.

[26] Gregory, lib. 4, epistle 32.

[27] *De historia Concilii VI Carthaginensis.*

[28] *De potestate Papae.*

[29] Dist. 99, canon Prima Sedis.

[30] Lib. 5, ep. 21.

called Universal Patriarch, the name of the other Patriarchs is diminished."[31] And in an epistle to Eusebius: "If one is universal, what remains is that you would not be bishops."[32] In another manner, a bishop can be called universal who has care of the whole Church, but generally not so as to exclude particular bishops. And in this manner, this name can be given to the Roman Pontiff, which is also proven from the mind of St. Gregory.

Firstly, because Gregory affirms that the name of universal bishop was given to the Roman Pontiff by the Council of Chalcedon, as well as to his successors,[33] which the same Gregory who was holy and Catholic teaches everywhere therefore, he thought that in some sense this title was fitting for the Roman Pontiff. Secondly, because Gregory asserts in the same epistle that care of the whole Church was consigned to Peter by the Lord, because it is the same thing as if he would have said: "Peter is the Universal universal bishop constituted by Christ." Thirdly, because even if the Roman Pontiffs, as Gregory correctly says, were never called universal bishops, still they often called themselves bishops of the Universal Church, as is clear from many Popes.[34] Such testimonies Gregory certainly read, nor was he ignorant in regard to the sense of a bishop of a Universal Church, and a universal bishop.

But you will say, if this name can have a good sense, why does Gregory absolutely pronounce it to be proud, sacrilegious, profane, and why does he absolutely avoid its use?

I respond: for two reasons. Firstly, for caution, just as the name, *Christotokos*,[35] has a good sense, and still the Fathers avoided the use of this name lest it would seem that the Nestorian heresy lurked under it; for Nestorius called Mary the mother of Christ, but not the mother of God. Secondly, because then the question was whether the name could be conceded to John, the bishop of Constantinople, but not whether it would be conceded to the Roman Pontiff: because then the name "Universal" would in no sense be fitting for that John, and still he usurped it to himself; therefore, Gregory simply and absolutely pronounced this name to be profane and a sacrilege. Without a doubt, the

---

[31] Lib. 4, epist. 36 ad Eulogium.

[32] *Ibid*, epist. 69.

[33] *Ibid*, ep. 32.

[34] Sixtus I, epist. 2; Victor I, epist. 1, Pontianus, epistle 2, Stephen I, epistle 1, St. Leo I, epistle 54, 62, 65.

[35] Translator's note: Χριστοτοκος, literally "Christ bearer," or "mother of Christ," as opposed to Θεοτοκος, God-bearer or "mother of God."

pronouncement was given in regard to the bishop of Constantinople. Just the same, Gregory also refused it, although it was fitting for him in some sense, because it was to better and more easily suppress the pride of the bishop of Constantinople. From these the argument of Calvin is answered.

To the second objection of Luther and Illyricus, I say, they did not notice that those words were not of a council of Africa, but of Gratian who after he relates the canon of the council of Africa, in which a bishop of the first See was forbidden to be called Prince of Priests, he adds on his own: "Nor is the Roman Pontiff called universal." Because such words are of Gratian, they do not have authority, and on that account can be understood in that manner which the words of St. Gregory are.

It is a worthy observation to make in this place, such was and is even in this time the pertinacity and pride of the Greeks, as well as how severely they were punished by God. For, although the see of the bishop of Constantinople had no place among the primary sees for more than 300 years, it not only elevated itself to the Patriarchate, but even ahead of the sees of Alexandria and Antioch, and wanted to make itself equal to Rome as well as universal. It could not be reduced to sanity by the censure of Pelagius II and of other Popes (more often for this reason they were excommunicated, as Leo IX writes in an epistle to the Emperor) nor even by the humility of St. Gregory, who, as John the Deacon writes in his life,[36] that he began on account of this affair to write, not that he was an Archbishop, nor a Patriarch, but a bishop and Servant of the Servants of God. Not even an edict from the Emperor Phocas, about which we spoke of above, could accomplish this purpose. At length, by a judgment of God from heaven, the Greeks were handed over with their Universal Patriarch into the hands of the Turks, which St. Birgitta had foretold was going to happen to them, as well as Pope Nicholas V, as Gennadius Scholarius relates in his book on behalf of the Council of Florence, ch. 5, § 14.

END BOOK II

---

[36] *Vita S. Gregorii*, lib. 2, ch. 1.

BOOK III
A DISPUTATION ON ANTICHRIST

CHAPTER I

A Disputation is Proposed on Antichrist

Up to this point we have proved that the Roman Pontiff succeeds Peter in the supreme rule of the whole Church. It remains that we should see whether at some time the Roman Pontiff might have fallen from that degree; certainly our adversaries contend that at this time, there is not a true bishop of Rome, whatever he might have been before. Even Nilos Cabásilas of Thessalonika, at the end of his little book against the primacy of the Roman Pontiff, says: "But the chief and principal point of my discourse is that as long as the Pope shall preserve the heavenly and agreeable order formerly instituted in the Church, as long as he shall adhere to Christ, the supreme Lord and head of the Church, I shall easily suffer him both as head of the Church and high Priest, even the successor of Peter or the Apostles; I will allow that all obey him, and that nothing should diminish that which pertains to his honor; but if he would have fallen from truth, nor wished to return to it, then rightly he ought to be held for one condemned and cast out." Thus Nilos.

But he ought to have shown into what errors the Roman Pontiffs have fallen, as well as both when and by whom they were condemned. Certainly we know that in the General Council of the Lateran under Innocent III, Lyons under Gregory X, and Florence under Eugene IV, the Greeks were convicted of error and returned to the faith of the Latins. Thereafter, they always went back to their vomit, and for that reason were gravely punished by God. Yet we read nowhere that the Latins ever came to the faith of the Greeks. Nor can any ecclesiastical judgment be brought against the Latins, as we have brought many against the Greeks.

On the other hand, Calvin says: "Let us grant all these things are true (although we have already forced the contrary from them): Peter was constituted head of the universal Church by the voice of Christ, and that honor being conferred upon him, he laid down in the Roman See, and it was ratified by the authority of the ancient Church, confirmed by long use, that the Roman Pontiff always had supreme power over all, and was in his person the judge of all cases and men, and was subject to the judgment of none; let them have many more if they want. I respond that still, in one word, it will avail them nothing, except that there ought to be a Church and a bishop in Rome."[1] And below that: "Let the Romans untie this knot: I deny that the pontiff is the prince of bishops,

---

[1] *Instit.,* lib. 4, ch. 7, § 23.

329

since he is not really a bishop."[2] And further: "Rome was rightly the mother of all churches once, but from the time it began to be the seat of Antichrist, it ceased to be that which it was."[3] And again: "We appear to some to be cursed and petulant since we call the Roman Pontiff Antichrist; but they who think so do not understand that they charge Paul with immodesty, after whom we speak; nay more, we speak thus from his own mouth. And lest anyone would cast before us words of Paul which might pertain to another matter and wrongly distort them away from the Roman Pontiff, I will show briefly that it can be understood in no manner other than that the papacy is the seat of Antichrist."[4]

All the heretics of this time teach similar things: Firstly, Luther, in his computation of the times, as well as in his *Assertions*, article 28 and 36, and often in other places. Likewise the Lutheran Centuriators in all of their *Centuries;*[5] Illyricus in his book on the Primacy; David Chytraeus in his work on the Apocalypse (the ninth and thirteenth chapters); Wolfgang Musculus in his work *de Ecclesia*, in common citations; Theodore Beza;[6] Theodore Bibliander;[7] Heinrich Pantaleon in his *Chronologia*; Henry Bullinger in his preface to his homilies on the Apocalypse, and above all, John Wycliff, who is among those condemned in article 30 of the Council of Constance, sess. 8. All of these pronounced that the Pontiff is the Antichrist.

Therefore, in order that this question should be carefully explained, it will be treated in nine chapters. The first will be on the name of Antichrist. The second on whether Antichrist might be one man, or a race of men. Thirdly, on the time of his coming and his death. Fourth, on his proper name. Fifth, from which nation he is going to be born, and especially by whom he will be received. Sixth, where he is going to set up his seat. Seventh, on his doctrine and morals. Eighth, on his miracles. Ninth, on his kingdom and battles. From all these it will appear very clearly with what impudence the heretics make the Roman Pontiff out to be the Antichrist, in which we will add a chapter proving not only that the Roman Pontiff is not Antichrist, but that he could by no means cease to be the bishop and shepherd of the whole Church, and such that no part of the objections of Calvin shall remain unanswered.

Now in regard to the first, some of our adversaries teach that the name "Antichrist" properly means Vicar of Christ, and hence the Pope, who asserts he

---

2   *Ibid.*, §24.

3   *Ibid.*

4   *Ibid.*, §25.

5   *Centur. 1*, lib. 2, ch. 4, column 434, and in all subsequent books of the centuries.

6   Beza, *Commentario 2 Thessalon.*, 2.

7   *Chronicum*, tabul. 10, 11, 12, 13 & 14.

is the Vicar of Christ, is himself Antichrist. Wolfgang Musculus teaches this in his citations, in the chapter on the power of ministers, and he tries to show that the word ἀντὶ means in place of, whence ἀντὶχριστος is in place of Christ, just as ἀντισρατηγὸς means he who thrusts himself in place of a leader, that is, one who would have it that he is the vicar of a leader. The Centuriators also teach that the Pope is the true Antichrist because he makes himself the Vicar of Christ.

But without a doubt they are deceived or are trying to deceive. The name "Antichrist" can not mean Vicar of Christ in any manner, rather, it merely means someone contrary to Christ; not contrary in any way whatever, but so much so that he will fight against that which pertains to the seat and dignity of Christ; that is, one who will be a rival of Christ and to be held as Christ, after he who truly is Christ has been cast out.

The meaning of this noun is proved in three ways. Firstly, because in Greek, the term ἀντὶ properly means opposition, and they are said to be opposed not only to those among whom they oppose, but even those whom they exert influence over. From there, it comes to pass that ἀντί, in composition, sometimes means contrariety and sometimes equivalence but never subordination, as is clear in the examples of all such names. For instance, ἀντίπαλος means imitation in mourning; ἀντίδοτον, a contrary remedy; ἀντιφρασις contradiction; ἀντὶσροφος equivalence; ἀντίθεος equal to God; ἀντιχειρις, that is the thumb, because from that region it is opposed and rules the rest of the hand, and so on and so forth. But "vicar" does not mean opposition but subordination to another thing, and therefore, cannot be expressed through the term ἀντὶ.

Hence, the term ἀντιστρατηγὸς does not mean the vicar of a leader but ordinarily a contrary leader just as ἀντισρατενομαι is a civil war. Moreover, sometimes one who is in place of a leader is not subject to him but rather equal to him in the way that the Latin words *Propraetor*, or *Proconsul*, do not mean the vicar of a praetor, or a consul, but one who is in some province, like that which a praetor or a consul is in the city. And in this Musculus was deceived because he read with Budaeus that ἀντισρατηγὸς means a propraetor, and he reckoned it meant vicar of a praetor, which is false.

Secondly, the same is proven from Scripture. Although there is some ambiguity about this noun still, as it is received in Scripture it is not ambiguous; our question ought not to be on the term ἀντιχριστος in an absolute sense, but as it is found in the Scriptures. Next, in the Scriptures the one who is called Antichrist is he: "who is extolled above everything which is called God."[8] That

---

[8]   2 Thessalonians 2:4.

is certainly not a Vicar of Christ but an enemy of Christ, the true God. In the First Epistle of John, Antichrist is said to be he "who denies Jesus is the Messiah,"[9] i.e. he who denies Jesus is the Christ, that he would claim for himself that which is for Christ. And in Matthew, it is said that Antichrist will affirm himself to be Christ,[10] which can hardly be a vicar but rather would be an imitator.

Thirdly, from all the authors who wrote on Antichrist and from the common consensus of all Christians, we understand by "Antichrist" a certain man as a distinct Pseudochrist. This is how St. John Damascene explains this term from the Greek Fathers,[11] and in the same manner Jerome explains it from the Latin Fathers,[12] and he was also an expert in the Greek language.

Next, Henry Stephan gives a similar explanation in his *Treasury on the Greek Language*, albeit he is from the number of the Swiss heretics. Thus, we have our first argument against our adversaries. Since the noun "Antichrist" means an enemy and imitator of Christ, and the Roman Pontiff is from the household of Christ declaring that he is subject to Christ in all things, it is clear that he would in no way say he is Christ, or that he makes himself equal to him; therefore, it is manifest that he is not Antichrist.

---

[9] 1 John 2:22.

[10] Matt. 24:5, 24.

[11] *De Fide,* lib. 4, ch. 28.

[12] *Quaestione undecima, ad Algasiam.*

CHAPTER II
Antichrist is Going to be a Certain, Specific Man

𝔑OW in what pertains to the second, we agree with our adversaries in one thing and differ in another. We agree in the fact that just as the name of Christ is received in two ways, sometimes properly concerning the specific and individual person of Christ, who is Jesus of Nazareth, and sometimes commonly concerning all those who have a similitude with Christ in regard to anointing, just as all priests, prophets and kings are said to be of Christ: "Do not touch my Christs;"[1] so also Antichrist is received properly sometimes for a certain distinct enemy of Christ, on which the Scriptures teach, and sometimes commonly for all who oppose Christ in some way. We read in the First Epistle of John: "You have heard, that Antichrist is coming, and now there are many Antichrists;"[2] in other words, you have heard Antichrist is going to come, and now, although that singular Antichrist has not yet come, still many seducers have come who also can be called Antichrists.

But we differ on Antichrist properly so called, whether he might be one individual man. All Catholics think that Antichrist is one specific man; but all the heretics cited above teach that Antichrist, properly so called, is not a single person but a single throne of a tyrannical kingdom as well as the seat of its apostasy that presides over the Church.

The Centuriators say: "The Apostles teach that Antichrist is not only one person, but a whole kingdom through false teachers in the temple of God that is presiding in the Church, in a great city, i.e. the city of Rome, whose works are compared to the deception and deceit of the devil."[3] The others we cited say similar things.

These are their reasons. First, Paul says that already in his time Antichrist began to live in the world: "The mystery of iniquity is now operating,"[4] and still he says in the same place that Antichrist must be killed by Christ at the end of the world. Hence, Beza concludes in his commentary on this citation in Thessalonians that: "They are clearly hallucinating when they think this can be understood about one man; unless they give me someone who remains alive

---

[1] Psalm 104 (105):15 We have rendered Christ directly to retain the sense of the original, the term in Greek (Χριστός) means "anointed", and thus Jesus, the anointed one, the culmination of every precursor of "anointing" in the Old Testament. -Translator's note.

[2] 1 John 2:18.

[3] *Cent. 1*, lib. 2, ch. 4, colum. 435.

[4] 2 Thessalonians 2:7.

from the age of Paul even to the day of judgment." Calvin argues in the same way from this passage. They confirm this reasoning from John who, in his First Epistle, says: "Every spirit that denies Jesus, it is not from God and this is Antichrist whom you have heard is coming, and is now in the world."[5]

The second reason is of Beza: because Daniel 7 does not understand individuals by the individual names of the beasts of bear, lion and leopard, but rather individual kingdoms, one of which contains many kings. Therefore, Paul, who wondrously agrees with Daniel, does not understand the man of sin and the son of perdition as one individual person but a figure as a body of many tyrants.

The third reason is of Calvin who argues from what is said in 1 John 2 that those who believe that one man is going to be Antichrist are mad and err of their own accord, since Paul in 2 Thessalonians 2 wrote that apostasy was coming and his head is going to be Antichrist. Accordingly, apostasy is a certain general defection from the faith which indeed makes one body and one rule, and is not a matter of a few years that it could be completed under one king.

With all of these not withstanding, the truth is that Antichrist is one individual man. The fact is proven from all the Scriptures and the Fathers who treat on Antichrist. There are five passages of Scripture. The first is in the Gospel of John: "I have come in the name of my Father, and you did not receive me, if another will have come in his own name, you will receive him."[6] Musculus and Calvin would have these words on false prophets understood in general, not on some individual, following Marloratus in his commentary on this passage. But their explication is opposed to the ancient Fathers and the text itself. For these words were spoken on one Antichrist, as Chrysostom, Cyril and all the Fathers witness on this citation.[7]

Besides this, the Lord opposes himself to another man, i.e. person to person, not kingdom to kingdom or sect to sect, as is clear from the pronouns and phrases: "I," another "in my name," that is in his own name, "me," etc. Therefore, just as Christ was one and an individual man, so also Antichrist will be one and an individual man.

Next, Christ says here that Antichrist will be received by the Jews for a Messiah. Moreover, it is certain that the Jews wait for one certain and singular man. All false prophets come not in their own name but in that of another.

---

[5] 1 John 4:3.

[6] John 5.

[7] Ambrose on 2 Thessal. 2; Jerome, *epist. Ad Algasiam*, quest. 11; Augustine, *Tract. In Joann.*, tract 29; Irenaeus, *Contra haeres.*, lib. 5; Theodoret, *in Epitome divionorum decretorum*, chapter on Antichrist, and others.

"Prophets that falsely prophesy in my name, these are not sent, etc."[8] But the Lord spoke about one specific man who will come in his own name, that is, who does not recognize some God, but "will extol himself," as Paul says, "over everything which is called God."

Next, many false prophets came before the coming of Christ and many were going to come after. Therefore, if he were speaking on false prophets the Lord would not have said: "If another will have come," but that many are coming.

The second passage is of Paul. "Unless first dissension will have come, and the man of sin will have been revealed, the son of perdition ... And then that wicked man will be revealed, whom the Lord Jesus will kill by the breath of his mouth."[9] Our adversaries understand these words on the true Antichrist, but the Apostle speaks on a certain specific and particular person, as is clear from the articles in the Greek: "ἀποχαλυφθη ὁ ἄνθρωποος τῆς ἁμαρτίας ὁ υἱὸς τῆς ἀπωλειας. . . καὶ τότε ἀποχαλυφθήσεταὶ ὁ ἄνομος; as Epiphanius teaches, the Greek articles draw together the meaning to one certain matter, that ἄνθρωπος will mean a man in common but ὁ ἄνθρωπος an individual man.[10] It is quite the wonder, that none of our adversaries who boast of their expertise in language happened to notice this.

The third citation is that of 1 John 2, where we read thus: "ἠκούσατε ὅτι ὁ ἀντίχρισος ἔρκεται, καὶ νῦν ἀντίχρισοι πολλὸι γεγόνασιν." or, "You have heard that *the* Antichrist is coming, and now there are many Antichrists." There, he places an article ahead of Antichrist properly so called, but without the article it would convey the name of Antichrist received commonly, clearly indicating that Antichrist properly so called is one certain person while Antichrist commonly received is not a certain person, but every heretic in kind.

The fourth passage is from Daniel chapter 7, 11 and 12, where he speaks on Antichrist, which Jerome and Theodoret as well as other Fathers teach on this

---

8   Jeremiah 14:14.

9   2 Thessalonians 2: 3, 7-8.

10   Translator's note: To make this clear for those who do not know Greek, the citation is the original for 2 Thessalonians, where a definite article is used for man [ἄνθρωπος]. In Greek there is a definite article before every noun; normally if it is not included, it means "a" thing instead of "the" thing, except in the case of a predicate nominative (linking verb) in what is called the attributive position. Therefore, by saying "the man" [ὁ ἄνθρωπος], St. Paul is identifying a specific man, not "a man" in general which he would have done by dropping the article. Lest anyone think this is a weak argument or a semantic point, in the Greek language the poets and dramatists make use of the articles for this very same purpose.

passage,[11] and even Calvin, the Centuriators, and Beza in their citations above. Moreover, in Daniel, Antichrist is not called one kingdom but one specific king from ten kings whom he will discover in the world; he will altogether abolish three from the midst and subject the other seven to himself. Add what Calvin says, that Daniel speaks literally on Antiochus Epiphanies[12] and allegorically on Antichrist whose figure was Antiochus, which Cyprian and Jerome also teach.[13] But Antiochus Epiphanius was a certain specific and singular person; therefore, Antichrist ought also to be a certain, specific person.

The fifth and last passage is in the book of the Apocalypse 13 and 17. Such passages are understood on Antichrist, as Irenaeus teaches, and it is clear from the similarity of the words to those places in Daniel and John. Each make mention of ten kings who will be on the earth when Antichrist will come and each predicts that the kingdom of Antichrist is going to endure for three and a half years. Just as Daniel speaks on one king so does John in the book of the Apocalypse.

The same is proven from the Fathers who teach in a common consensus on Antichrist. Firstly, that he will be the chosen instrument of the Devil to the extent that a plenitude of diabolic malice will inhabit him corporally, just as in Christ the man the plenitude of divinity dwelled in him corporally. Secondly, Antichrist will not reign more than three and a half years, and hence they teach Antichrist is going to be only one man.[14]

Now I shall respond to the first argument of Beza: In the time of the Apostles Antichrist began to live secretly, but not in his own person, rather in his precursors. Just as Christ began to come from the origin of the world in the patriarchs and prophets (who came before him and signified him so that it could be said the mystery of godliness began to operate from the beginning of the world), he did not come in his own proper person until the time when he received flesh from the Blessed Virgin Mary. In like manner, Antichrist began to come soon after Christ was assumed into heaven in his precursors, and the

---

[11] Irenaeus, lib. 5; Augustine, *de Civitate Dei*, ch. 23.

[12] Translator's note: Antiochus IV (*Epiphanies*, i.e. the Illustrious) was the successor of Alexander the Great's empire in Syria. After losing to the Romans in a war in Egypt he retired to Syria and began the persecution of, the Jews which lead to their uprising recorded in the books of the Maccabees in the Bible.

[13] Cyprian, *de exhortations martyrii*, ch. 11; Jerome in Daniel 11 and 12.

[14] See Irenaeus, lib. 5 near the end. Cyril of Jerusalem, *Catechesi* 15. Chrysostom, *in 2 Thessal. 2*; Theodoret, *hist.*, ch. 11; Ambrose *in cap. 21 Lucae*; Jerome, *in cap. 7 Danielis et quaest. 11 ad Algasiam*; Augustine, *de civitate Dei*, lib. 21, for many chapters, and *in Psalm 9*; Gregory, *Moral.*, lib. 32, ch. 12; Damascene, lib. 4, ch. 28; and Hippolytus the Martyr, *in oratione de consummatione mundi*.

mystery of iniquity began to work, namely in heretics and tyrants persecuting the Church; especially in Simon Magus, who said he was Christ, and in Nero who first began to oppose the Church. Just the same, he will not come in his own person until the end of the world. Therefore, the spiritual persecution of Simon Magus and the temporal persecution of Nero is called the mystery of iniquity because they were signs and figures of the persecution of Antichrist.

That this is the true explication of the Pauline passages can be shown in two ways. Firstly, from all the interpreters of this passage. Certainly, all understood through the mystery of iniquity in Paul either the persecution of Nero, as Ambrose and Chrysostom on this citation, as well as Jerome;[15] or heretics who secretly deceive, as Theodoret and Sedulius remark on this verse along with Augustine.[16]

Secondly, from reason, taken from the admission of our adversaries who say that Antichrist is properly the seat of the Roman Pontiff.

Therefore, if Antichrist, properly so called, was born in the time of the Apostles, it follows that Peter and Paul were properly said to be Antichrists, although in secret, and Nero and Simon Magus were the true Christ. It is certain that in the time of the Apostles there were no other bishops at Rome than Peter and Paul. Irenaeus eloquently affirms that the Roman See was founded by Peter and Paul and that they sat there as its first bishops.[17] All the Fathers whom we cited in the last book teach the same thing. It is also certain that Simon Magus and Nero battled with the Apostles Peter and Paul.

But if this does not please our adversaries, that Peter and Paul were Antichrists and Simon and Nero the true Christ, they are compelled to affirm that Antichrist did not exist in the time of the Apostles *per se*, rather only in his specific type. The consequence of that makes Beza's point, that Antichrist could not be one man unless we would grant that he lived from the time of the Apostles even to the end of the world, utterly ridiculous.

To confirm this, I say John spoke in that mode in which the Lord spoke on Elijah: "Elijah indeed is going to come and he will restore all things but I say to you that Elijah already came, and they did not recognize him."[18] In other words, Elijah was going to come in his own person but he already came in one like him, that is John the Baptist.

Now to the Second argument. In the first place, we must deny that Daniel always understands individual kingdoms for individual beasts. For sometimes

---

[15] *Ad Algasiam*, quaest. 11.

[16] *De Civitate Dei*, lib. 20, ch. 19.

[17] Irenaeus, lib. 3, ch. 3.

[18] Matthew 17:11-12.

he means one kingdom for one beast, as in chapter 7 where he understands the kingdom of the Assyrians for the lion; the kingdom of the Persians for the bear; the empire of the Greeks for the leopard; and through another unnamed beast the empire of the Romans. Sometimes he understands one king, as in the eighth chapter where he understands King Darius, the last king of the Persians, through the ram and Alexander the Great through the goat. Next, the consequent of the argument is denied. For Paul understands for "the man of sin" not someone from the four beasts described by Daniel, but that little horn which, in Daniel, prevails over the ten horns of the four beasts, i.e., that one king who rose from modest circumstances to subjugate all other kings to himself.

I respond to the final argument in several ways to show how impudent Calvin is when he writes that those who do not gather from his argument that the Roman Pontiff is the Antichrist err from their own will. Firstly, Antichrist can correctly be understood through "apostasy" in Paul's citation. Thus, the Greek interpreters understand it in a common consensus.[19] Moreover, Antichrist is called apostasy both through metonym,[20] because the case will be that many will recede from God, and through a certain excellence; there will be a characteristic apostasy that can be called apostasy itself.

Secondly, Apostasy can be taken up as the defection from the Roman Empire, as many Latins explain.[21] For as we will show in the following chapter, Antichrist will not come until the Roman Empire shall altogether fall to ruin.

Thirdly, if we were to admit that through apostasy defection from the true faith and religion of Christ is understood (as Calvin claims), still we would not be constrained by difficulties on that account. For Paul did not necessarily speak of the apostasy of many ages; he could speak on a certain great and singular apostasy that will only be in that brief time in which Antichrist will reign. St. Augustine writes that he was also understood in this way by many of the Fathers, and they taught that when Antichrist appears all secret heretics or false Christians will go to him and from that event the greatest apostasy is going to

---

[19]   Chrysostom, Theodoret, Theophylactus and Oecumenius. Additionaly, St. Augustine in *de Civitate Dei*, lib. 20, ch. 19.

[20]   Metonym is a linguistic device in classical languages such as Greek and Latin to use a name associated with a certain subject to indicate people carried out a verb in relation to it. Common examples would be "We were busy with Mercury" which would mean we transacted business, because Mercury is the god of commerce, or in the Aeneid book 4 it speaks of the keels of the ships to mean the ships themselves. Thus calling Antichrist Apostasy is to mean there will be a great Apostasy. -Translator's note.

[21]   Ambrose, Sedulius and Primasius.

occur, such as had never been before.

Fourthly, if we were to concede to Calvin that St. Paul speaks on the apostasy of many ages, he still gains nothing. Accordingly, we would be able say that apostasy does not necessarily pertain to one body and kingdom of Antichrist, nor demands one head, but is a defection to the kingdom of Antichrist that will happen in different places, under different kings and on different occasions. We now see that Africa defected to Muhammad, a great part of Asia to Nestorius and the Monophysites, and other provinces to other sects.

Fifthly and lastly, if we were to grant to Calvin a general Apostasy from the faith and that the kingdom of Antichrist endured for many years, it would not immediately follow that the Pope is Antichrist. For it still might be asked whether certain men have defected from the faith and religion of Christ; it could be us or them, that is, Catholics or Lutherans. Although they say we are the ones who have defected, nevertheless, they have not yet proved it, nor has it been declared by any common judge.

We can much more easily prove that it is the Lutherans that are the ones that defected than they can prove Catholics defected. Accordingly, they defected from the Church in which they were first and they do not even deny it. For (that I might pass over the rest), when Erasmus of Rotterdam says on that passage of 2 Thessalonians 2: "Then that wicked man will be revealed," he ingeniously confesses that nearly all the predecessors of the Lutherans and himself at one time obeyed the Roman Pontiff. Therefore, they defected from the Church and religion of their predecessors. On the other hand, they have not shown to this point that we have defected from some Church, nor could they ever show it. Therefore, since they read Paul: "Until a dissension will come, or apostasy and that wicked man will be revealed, etc.," and they know they have left the Church in which they were, while we have persevered in the same one that was always established, it is a wonder that they do not at least fear lest Paul might have spoken about them.

From this second chapter we have the second argument: to prove that the Pope is not the Antichrist. Therefore, if Antichrist is one person, yet there were and will be many Popes provided with the same dignity and power, then certainly Antichrist must be sought somewhere other than in the Roman See.

CHAPTER III
It is Shown That Antichrist has not yet Come.

ANY false suspicions and errors exist in regard to the third proposition, on the time of the coming of Antichrist both among Catholics and heretics. Yet with this distinction, Catholics know that Antichrist is not coming until the end of the world (which is true), but some err in that they think the end of the world is nearer than it really may be. On the other hand, the heretics err in the fact that they think Antichrist is coming long before the end of the world, and that he really already has come. Therefore, we shall speak on each error.

In the first place, all the Fathers who noticed the malice of their times suspected that the times of Antichrist approached. Thus the Thessalonians thought in the time of the Apostles that the day of the Lord approached, which the Apostle corrected in 2 Thessalonians 2. Likewise, St. Cyprian says: "Since Antichrist threatens, let the soldiers be prepared for battle, etc."[1] He also says in another epistle: "You ought to know, as well as believe and hold for a certain fact, that the day of persecution of the head has begun, and the end of the world and time of Antichrist approaches."[2] Jerome says: "He who held fast arises in our midst and we do not understand that Antichrist approaches?"[3] St. Gregory the Great: "All which has been predicted comes to pass; the proud king is near."[4] Gregory also boldly pronounced the end of the world.[5] But these were suspicions, not errors, since these holy Fathers did not dare to define a certain time.

Next, others more boldly constituted a certain time. St. Jerome relates in *de illustribus viris* that in 200 A.D., a certain Jude thought Antichrist was coming and the world was ending; clearly he was deceived. Again Lactantius says: "Every expectation is no more than two hundred years, etc."[6] There he teaches that Antichrist was coming and the world was to end two hundred years from his time. He also lived in the times of Constantine, around the 300th year of Christ; so he thought the world would by chance end in the year 500; but experience shows he was also deceived.

---

[1] Lib. 3, epist. 1.

[2] Lib. 4, epistle 6.

[3] *Epistola ad Ageruchiam de Monogamia.*

[4] Lib. 4, epistle 38.

[5] Homil. 1 in Evangelia.

[6] *Diviarum institutionum*, lib. 7, ch. 25.

St. Augustine relates the error of some who said that the world would end around the year 400 from the ascension of the Lord,[7] and also some who established the thousandth year. They were all deceived. It also happened even to the Pagans, who, as Augustine witnesses in the same book, gathered from I know not what divine oracle that the Christian religion would only endure for three hundred and sixty five years. There was a certain bishop, Florentinus by name, who asserted around the year 1105 that Antichrist had already been born, and hence the end of the world was closing in. The Council of Florence, having three hundred and forty bishops, was gathered for this reason by Pope Paschal II.[8]

Next, there was also a famous opinion that had many defenders,[9] that the world was going to endure for 6,000 years, since God had created the world in six days, and a thousand years is to God one day. The writers of the Talmud also agree with this opinion, and they say that they had a vision of the Prophet Elijah in which it is asserted that the world will endure for six thousand years.

This opinion cannot yet be refuted from experience, because according to the true chronology more or less 5600 years have elapsed since the beginning of the world. Ambrose rejects this opinion, asserting in his time that six thousand years had already elapsed, though obviously he is misled.[10] The moderation of St. Augustine is the best, since he thought the opinion probable, and followed it as probable.[11] From here, it does not follow that we know the last day. Moreover, we say it is probable, that the world will not endure beyond six thousand years, but we do not say that it is certain. On that account, St. Augustine bitterly rebuked those who asserted that the world is going to end at a certain time, when the Lord said: "It is not for us to know the time and the hour which the Father has placed in his power."[12] Laying all these aside, let us come to the heretics.

All the heretics of this time teach that the Roman Pontiff is the Antichrist, and now openly lives in the world, but they do not agree among themselves on the time in which he appeared. They have six opinions.

---

[7] *De Civitate Dei*, lib. 18, ch. 53.

[8] See the Chronicle of Matthew Palmeri, and Platina in *vita Paschalis II*.

[9] Justin, q. 71 *ad Gentes*; Irenaeus *adv. Haer.*, lib. 5; Lactantius, lib. 7, ch. 14; Hilary on ch. 17 of St. Matthew; Jerome in Ps. 89 to Cyprian.

[10] Ambrose *in Lucam*, lib. 7, ch. 2.

[11] *De Civitate Dei*, lib. 20, ch. 7.

[12] See Augustine, Epistle 80 *ad Hesychium*, in Psalm 89, and *de Civitate Dei*, lib. 18, ch. 53.

The First are the Samosatens, who bide their time in Hungary and Transylvania. They teach in a certain book which they titled: *Premonitions of Christ and the Apostles on the abolition of Christ through Antichrist*, that a little after the times of the Apostles Antichrist appeared; that is without a doubt when it began to be preached that Christ is the eternal son of God. They think, on the other hand, that Christ is a pure man, and that there is only one person in God, and this faith was preached by Christ and the Apostles. Thus, a little after the death of the Apostles, Antichrist came to Rome and after abolishing Christ the pure man, introduced another eternal Christ, and made God triune, and Christ twofold.

This opinion is easily refuted, apart from the arguments which we asserted above against all the heretics, and in two ways. Firstly, because when Antichrist will have come, *he will make himself God*, not someone else, as the Apostle says.[13] Moreover, they themselves claim that the Roman Pontiff does not make himself God, but preached Christ and made him God from a true man. Secondly, because they say that soon after Christ and the Apostles slept, the true faith of Christ was thoroughly extinguished and the whole world began to worship Christ as God. But Christ preached that the gates of hell were not going to prevail against the Church, and the Angel Gabriel preached that the kingdom of Christ would be forever.[14] David preached that all kings would serve Christ.[15] Therefore, how true is it that in the very beginning the nascent Church was destroyed by Antichrist?

The second opinion is of the Lutheran, Illyricus, who teaches in his Third *Catalogue* that Antichrist came when the Roman Empire fell into ruin. Moreover, it is certain that the Roman Empire began to fall after the tenth year of Honorius, when Rome was first taken, that is in the year of the Lord 412, as Blondus showed;[16] yet, Illyricus seems to understand this concerning the conception, not the birth of Antichrist. Accordingly he teaches the same thing in the *Centuries*,[17] that Antichrist was conceived in some manner at the beginning of the year 400, thereafter animated and formed in the womb of his mother, around the year 500; and at length was born in the year 606, when the Eastern Emperor Phocas conceded to the Roman Pontiff that he could be called head of the whole Church. He teaches the same thing in another place, that Antichrist was going to rule savagely with the spiritual sword for 1260 years,

---

[13] 2 Thess. 2:4.

[14] Luke 1:33.

[15] Psalm 71 (72):10-11.

[16] *Decadis Primae Historiarum*, lib. 1, ab Inclinatione Romani Imperii.

[17] *Cent. 6*, ch. 1.

but with the temporal sword for 666 years, and then the end of the world would come.

The first number he gathers from Apocalypse 11, where it is said the time of Antichrist would be 1260 days. Illyricus would have it that a day is taken as a year. The second number he gathers from Apocalypse 13, where the number of the beast is 666.

This opinion can be refuted in two ways. Firstly, it follows that Antichrist was not only born but also died, and hence the end of the world already came. For the Roman Pontiff took up the temporal sword, that is temporal dominion, at least in the year 699. Then Aripertus gave to the Roman Pontiff the Coctian Alps, where Genoa is now. Later, in the year 714, Luitprandus confirmed that donation, as Ado of Vienna and Blondus affirm, not to mention the Centuriators and Theodore Bibliander, who remarked for the year 714 that this province became the first Papist province.

Not long after, that is, in the year 760, Pepin gave the Exarchate of Ravenna to the Roman Pontiffs, along with a great part of Italy as many historians witness—even the Centuriators and Bibliander. Therefore, if Antichrist began to reign in the year 760, and endured for 666 years, then the end of the world happened in the year of Christ 1421, and now there have been more than 150 years after Antichrist died. But if the beginning of his reign is placed earlier, that is in the year 699, then the end will be placed in the year 1360 and now more than 200 years will have transpired from the death of Antichrist.

Perhaps they will respond that after the 666th year of his reign Antichrist did not die but only lost his temporal dominion. Thus, they might say that the spiritual kingdom of Antichrist endured for 1260 years, which still would not have ended, and if they were to begin from the year 666, consequently they ought to say that the spiritual kingdom of antichrist ought to endure considerably beyond his temporal kingdom. But that is certainly absurd and against all authors, and besides, it at least follows that the Popes ought to have lost their temporal dominion 200 years ago, which is opposed to the obvious fact.

Secondly, the same error can be refuted because it follows from the error of the Centuriators, who thought they discovered exactly when the world will end, which is against the words of the Lord in Acts I and Matthew 24. What should follow is clear since, if they know that Antichrist began to reign with the spiritual sword in the year 606, they know that he was going to reign only 1260 years and then the Lord is going to come to judge right after, as they gather from Paul in 2 Thessal. 2. Therefore, they know the last judgment is going to be in the year 1466. But if they do not know this, they are compelled also to not know whether Antichrist has come.

The third opinion is of David Chytraeus who teaches with Illyricus in his commentary on chapter 9 of the Apocalypse, namely that Antichrist appeared around the year of the Lord 600, and that this is sufficient to show that St. Gregory was the first Antichrist Pope. Chytraeus, however, does not agree with that which is asserted by Illyricus, insofar as the time and duration of Antichrist, but he prudently advises that it is not to be defined so boldly. He attempts to show with three reasons that Antichrist appeared in the year 600.

Firstly, because in that time Gregory established the invocation of the saints and Masses for the dead. Secondly, because in the year 606, Pope Boniface III asked the title of universal bishop from the Emperor Phocas. He adds the third reason in his commentary on chapter 13, that this time plainly and especially agrees with the number of the name of Antichrist, which contains 666 as it is contained in the Apocalypse, ch. 13.

Furthermore, Chytraeus adds that from this same number of the name Antichrist the time can be gathered wherein Pepin confirmed the reign of Antichrist. For as many years as there are from the year 97 in which John wrote the Apocalypse even to Pepin is without a doubt 666 years. Likewise, Jan Hus reckons the time from when the Roman Pontiff was declared Antichrist back to Pepin to be almost 666.

This opinion can be easily refuted, as it rests upon frauds alone. For in the first place Gregory was not the first who invoked saints and taught that Masses were to be offered up for the dead. All the Fathers taught this very thing as we showed in another place. For the present Ambrose suffices, who preceded Gregory by 200 years. He says in his book on widows: "The angels are to be observed, the martyrs prayed to."[18] He also says in his epistle to Faustus on the death of his sister: "Therefore, I deem that she is not to be wept for with tears but pursued with prayers; you ought not grieve for her but commend her soul to God with offerings."[19]

Next, Phocas did not give the title of "universal" to the Pope but addressed him as head of the churches. Even Justinian had already done the same long before, in an epistle to John II, and before that the Council of Chalcedon had done so in an epistle to Leo I. Therefore, there is simply no reason to place the coming of Antichrist in the time of the Emperor Phocas.

As to what Chytraeus adds on the number 666, it is altogether inept because that number does not agree precisely with the times that he would have it Antichrist appeared, or was confirmed, or declared to be so. For from Christ to the sanction of Phocas there are 607 years, not 666. From the revelation in the

---

[18] *De Viduis.*

[19] *Lib. 2 epist. 8 ad Fuastum de obitu sororis.*

Apocalypse to Pepin 658 years, and from Pepin to Jan Hus there are, as he says, 640. But certainly John the Apostle in the Apocalypse recorded a precise number since he also adds minute details. Moreover, Jan Hus was not the first to declare that the Pope is Antichrist; Wycliff had already done that. Nay more, Jan Hus never even said that the Pope is Antichrist. For in art. 19 of the Council of Constance, after being condemned, he says that the clergy, through their avarice, prepare the way for Antichrist. Next, all Lutherans boast that Luther was the first to unmask Antichrist, which brings us to the next opinion.

The fourth opinion is of Luther in his computation of time, where he places two arrivals of Antichrist. One, with the spiritual sword, after the year 600, when Phocas called the Roman Pontiff the head of all churches. He also says that Gregory was the last Roman Pontiff. The second is when he arrives with the temporal sword after the year 1000. Bibliander teaches the same thing.[20] Therefore, Luther and Bibliander agree in the first arrival with the Centuriators and Chytraeus—with the exception that Luther and Bibliander say that Gregory was a good and holy Pope while the Centuriators and Chytraeus say that Gregory above all did his best to introduce Antichrist and hence, he was the worst Pope, which is a horrendous blasphemy. In the second arrival, Luther and the Centuriators clearly disagree.

This opinion, apart from the common arguments which will be made afterward, is easily refuted. Luther places the arrival of Antichrist in the year 600 and 1000 altogether without reason. On the year 600 we have already spoken in refutation of Chytraeus. Concerning the year 1000, it can easily be shown, since Luther places the beginning of the temporal reign of Antichrist in that time when Pope Gregory VIII deposed the Emperor Henry IV, for then he ruled temporally as well as waged wars. Well now, all of these things already happened, as Gregory II excommunicated the [Byzantine] Emperor Leo, and deprived him of the rule of Italy in the year 715, as the historians Cedreno and Zonaras witness in the life of the same Leo. Furthermore, we already showed that the Roman Pontiffs had temporal dominion in the year 700, three hundred years before the first millennium.

Next, the Centuriators witness that Stephen III waged wars around the year 750,[21] and Adrian I could be said to have done the same thing, as well as other of their successors. In like manner, around the year 850, Leo IV, a holy man as well as famous for miracles, waged war against the Saracens. He reported a singular victory and fortified Rome with towers and ramparts still; he girded the Vatican hill with a wall, which thereafter was called after his name *civitas*

---

[20] *Chronicum*, tab. 11 & 13. ,

[21] *Cent. 8*, ch. 10.

Leonina, as nearly all historians of that time relate, and even the Centuriators themselves.[22]

The fifth opinion is of Henry Bullinger. In the preface to his homilies on the Apocalypse he wrote that Antichrist appeared in the year 753. Such an opinion disagrees with all those whom we cited above, and thence can easily be refuted because it rests upon a very weak foundation. Bullinger teaches in the Apocalypse, ch. 13, that the number found there of the name of the Beast, 666, means by that number the time of the arrival of Antichrist; in other words, so many years after the Apocalypse was written, Antichrist was going to come. And because it is certain from Irenaeus that the Apocalypse was written around the end of the reign of the Emperor Domitian, i.e., around the year 97, he gathers Antichrist was going to come in the year 753, by computing 666 years from the year 97.

To this point the opinion of certain Catholics can also be related, such as Jodocus Clicthovaeus, who reckoned from the commentaries of St. John Damascene[23] that Muhammad was Antichrist properly so called because he came around the year 666 according to what John had said before. But this reasoning amounts to nothing. In the first place, the Centuriators protest and contend that the number in the book of the Apocalypse does not mean the time of the birth of Antichrist, but of his death. Moreover, John the Evangelist, in chapter 13 of the Apocalypse, rejects the commentary both of Illyricus and Bullinger, since he explains himself that the number is not of the times but the name of Antichrist; *i.e.* Antichrist is going to have a name, whose letters in Greek form the number 666, as Irenaeus and all other Fathers explain.

Besides, no change is read in the Roman Pontiffs for that year 753. Moreover, Muhammad could not come then since he was born in the year 597 and began to call himself a prophet in the year 623. Next, he died in the year 632, as Palmerius witnesses in his *Chronicle.* Therefore, he did not make it to the year 666.

The sixth opinion is of Wolfgang Musculus, who in his works under the title *de Ecclesia,*[24] affirms that Antichrist came a little after the times of St. Bernard, i.e. around the year 1200. He attempts to show this because St. Bernard enumerates many vices of men, and especially of Churchmen, and very serious persecutions of the Church, adding: "It remains only for the man of sin to be revealed."[25] But this opinion is refuted without much effort: St. Bernard merely

---

[22] *Cent. 9,* ch. 10.

[23] St. John Damascene, *De Fide,* lib. 4, ch. 28.

[24] Chapter 12.

[25] Bernard, serm. 6, in Ps. 90.

suspected from the evils which he saw that Antichrist was near, just as we said many Fathers suspected it from their times, such as Cyprian, Jerome and Gregory, and Bernard was deceived in that suspicion just as they. Besides, the Popes from the year 900 to 1000 were without comparison worse than the Popes from 1100 to 1200. So if the former were not Antichrist, why would the latter be?

CHAPTER IV

The First proof: the Rule of Antichrist has not yet Begun.

HEREFORE, the true opinion is that Antichrist has not yet begun to reign, nor come, rather he is going to come and rule around the end of the world. Yet, inasmuch as he has not yet come he cannot be known. This opinion destroys all those mentioned above and clearly shows that the Roman Pontiffs are not Antichrists. It is proven by six reasons.

It must be known that the Holy Spirit gave us six certain signs of the arrival of Antichrist in the Scriptures: Two preceding Antichrist, namely preaching of the Gospel and the desolation of the Roman Empire; two accompanying it, certainly the preaching of Enoch and Elijah, and a great and remarkable persecution, so much that public religion would altogether cease; two subsequent signs, namely the desolation of Antichrist after three and a half years and then the end of the world, which we see presently still exists.

Hence, the first proof is taken from the first sign preceding Antichrist. The Scriptures witness that in the whole world the Gospel must be preached before the last persecution will come, which will be roused by Antichrist: "This Gospel of the kingdom in testimony to the whole world, in witness to all the Gentiles."[1] The fact that this should happen before the arrival of Antichrist can be proved by this reason: because in the time of Antichrist the cruelty of that last persecution will impede all public exercise of the true religion.

Yet, because our adversaries do not admit this reasoning (nor is it now the time to deduce from their own principles), we will prove it from the testimonies of the Fathers. Thus Hilary explains these words of Matthew: "The Gospel of the kingdom will be preached in the whole world, and then the consummation will come." Clearly he teaches that Antichrist, which he calls the abomination of desolation, is not going to come unless the preaching of the Gospel will precede him throughout the whole world.

St. Cyril, Theodoret, and St. John Damascene teach the same thing with eloquent words,[2] and besides, the same is gathered from the text because the Gospel says that before that greatest and last tribulation shall come, the Gospel must be preached such as it was not before nor will be afterward. The Fathers and above all, St. Augustine, teach that the persecution of Antichrist is meant by such a tribulation.[3] Yet the Gospel was not preached in the whole world in

---

[1] Matthew 24:14.

[2] Cyril of Jerusalem, *Catechesi 15*; Theodoret in 2 Thessal. 2; Damascene *de fide*, lib. 4, ch. 28; as well as many others.

[3] *De Civitate Dei*, lib. 20, ch. 8 & 19.

the time that the new Samosatens say Antichrist came, that is around the year 200 or 300. It is clear from Origen, who asserted at that time the Gospel was not yet preached everywhere.[4] Likewise from Ruffinus, who witnesses that in the time of Constantine the Emperor, that is, after the year 300, that the Gospel was preached in the furthest parts of India, since before they had never heard anything about Christ.[5] Next, we learn it from St. Augustine who says with some experience one would find that there were many nations in his time that had not yet heard anything about Christ.[6]

Now, it is clear that the preaching of the Gospel was not completed around the year 600 or 700, in which the Centuriators, Chytraeus, Luther and Bullinger place the arrival of Antichrist. This is so from the conversion of the Vandals, the Poles, the Moravians and similar nations, who it is certain had not heard the preaching of the Gospel until after the year 800, as the Centuriators themselves affirm in their histories.[7] Likewise, the preaching of the Gospel had not been completed in the times of St. Bernard, where Wolfgang Musculus places the arrival of Antichrist. This is clear from Bernard himself, who asserts in book 3 of *de Consideratione* that still in his time there were nations who had not heard the Gospel.

Next, experience teaches that even in our time the Gospel has not been preached in the whole world. Very vast regions were discovered in both the East and West in which no memory of the Gospel exists. Nor can it be said the faith was ever there but later extinguished, for at least some vestige would remain, either there or in the writings of the Fathers. Besides, we know where all the Apostles preached and the places were marked by many, though I would not say by all; but the new world was recently discovered; it was not known in Apostolic times or any other until a little before our age.

Only one objection can be made against this proof: That perhaps Scripture, when it says the Gospel must be preached in the whole world, does not speak absolutely but rather receives the whole for a part by a figure of speech, just as Luke 2 when it is said: "An edict went out from Caesar Augustus that the whole world should be enrolled." Otherwise what Paul says would be false, that already in his time: "The sound of the Apostles has gone out through all the earth,"[8] as well as what he says in Colossians: "The truth of the Gospel which has arrived even to you, just as it bears fruit and increases in the whole world...

---

[4] Origen, *homil. 28 in Matthaeum.*

[5] Ruffinus, *Hist.*, lib.. 10, ch. 9.

[6] Epistle 80.

[7] *Cent. 9*, ch. 2, col. 15 & 18.; *Cent 10*, ch. 2, column 18 & 19.

[8] Romans 10:15.

which has been preached to every creature which is under heaven."[9]

I respond: Without a doubt it is not through a figure that the Gospel ought to be preached and churches constituted, but properly and absolutely in the whole world, that is in every nation. In the first place, St. Augustine expressly teaches this,[10] as well as the other fathers we have cited, such as Origen and Jerome in their commentaries on Matthew 24.

Next, it can be proved by three reasons. 1) Christ said preaching in the whole world is a sign of the consummation of the age. Therefore, he adds: "And then the consummation will come." But if this is not properly, but synecdochically that the Gospel ought to be preached in the whole world, it avails to nothing as a sign. For in the first 20 years the Gospel was preached by the Apostles in the whole world. 2) Secondly, as Augustine reasons, all nations were properly promised to Christ; "All nations will serve him."[11] Christ generally died for all and as a result (as related in Apocalypse 7), the elect will be described as being from all nations, peoples, tribes and tongues. Therefore, even preaching properly ought to be general. For that reason, in Matthew 24 it is said that the Gospel must be preached in the whole world, "in testimony to all nations;" that is, lest any nation could be excused in the day of judgment for its infidelity on account of ignorance. So, before the general judgment, general preaching ought to precede.

Augustine responds to those passages of Paul in Epistle 80, and says that Paul, when he spoke in Romans 10, received the past for the future, just as David did who uses the same words. Moreover, when he says in Colosians: "The Gospel is in the whole world," he did not wish to say it was in act but in potency, because without a doubt the seed of the Divine Word was thrown out by the Apostles in the whole world, so that little by little in bearing fruit and increasing it was going to fill the whole world. Just in the same way that someone could suppose the flame from different parts of the city could truly be said to burn the whole of that city because the fire was applied little by little by burning and was going to take up the whole city; this is the same thing the Apostle indicates when he says: "In the whole world it is bearing fruit and increasing." Therefore, it did not plainly overtake the whole world since still it had to be propagated, but still has seized it in some way—that is, in potency not in act.

A response can be made with Jerome and St. Thomas that the Gospel arrived to the nations in two ways: in one way through report; in another through

---

[9] Collosians 1: 6.

[10] Epistle 80 to Hesychius.

[11] Psalm. 71 (72):11.

proper preachers and the foundation of churches. Indeed, in the first manner the Gospel arrived to all the Nations of the whole world then known in the time of the Apostles and in this way Paul could speak. Chrysostom should also be understood in the same way on Matthew 24. In the second manner it could not have arrived then but was going to in its own time, and on this the Lord speaks in Matthew 24 as well as in the last Chapter of Luke and Acts 1.

3) Lastly, add that it is not absurd were we to concede the Lord spoke properly but the Apostle figuratively, whereby we would be compelled to take the words of the Lord in their own meaning; they do not have the same force if they were to be accommodated to the words of St. Paul, especially when the Lord spoke on the future, while Paul spoke on the past.

CHAPTER V
The Second Proof: Desolation of the Roman Empire

HE SECOND proof is taken from another sign that will precede the times of Antichrist, which will be the *desolation* in every way possible of the Roman Empire. At length, it must be known that the Roman Empire was divided into ten kings, none of whom will be called "King of the Romans," although all will occupy some provinces of the Roman Empire in the same way that the King of France, the King of Spain, the Queen of England and by chance some others hold parts of the Roman Empire; at length they are not Roman kings or emperors, but until they cease to hold those dominions Antichrist cannot come.[1]

Irenaeus[2] proves this from Daniel, chapters 2 and 7, as well as from chapter 17 of the Apocalypse. In Daniel there is a description of particular kingdoms even to the end of the world, and a certain one is described whose golden head signifies the first kingdom, that is, of the Assyrians; its silver chest is the second kingdom, that is of Persia; the bronze mid-section is the third kingdom, that is of the Hellenistic Empires; the iron legs represent the fourth kingdom, that is of Rome. Now Rome was divided into two parts for a very long time, just as there are two legs and they are the longest part of the body. Next, ten toes arose from the two legs, and with these the whole statue ended; certainly this means that the Roman Empire was divided into ten kings, none of whom will be king of the Romans, just as no toe is the leg. But now, in chapter 7, Daniel clearly marks out through the four beasts the same four kingdoms which mean the last ten kings who will arise from the Roman Empire, yet they will not be Roman emperors; just as the horns begin from the beast but are not the beast itself.

Next, John describes a beast with seven heads and ten horns, upon which a certain woman sat, and explains the woman is a great city which sits upon seven hills, that is Rome;[3] the seven heads are those seven mountains, and also the seven kings, by which number all the Roman emperors are understood. He says the ten horns are ten kings that will rule together at one time, and lest we think these by chance will be Roman kings, he adds that these kings will hate the harlot and will make desolation, because they will so divide the Roman

---

[1] Although this is an attempt to interpret prophecy on Bellarmine's part combined with history it is not, strictly speaking, impossible even after the revolutions of the 18th and 19th century as there are still kings over England, the Netherlands, Spain and a few other areas once controlled by the Romans. -Translator's note.

[2] *Adv. Haere.*, lib. 5.

[3] Apocalypse 17: 1-5.

Empire among themselves that they will almost destroy it.

Next, Paul proves the same thing in 2 Thessal. 2:6 when he says: "And now you know what withholds, that he may be revealed in his time. For the mystery of iniquity already works, only that he who now holds should hold until he be taken out of the way. And then that wicked one will be revealed, etc." There, Paul does not dare to write openly on the toppling of the Roman Empire, because he still explained openly in the presence of Romans and he spoke as if to say: You know what should impede the arrival of Antichrist. I said to you, the Roman Empire impedes it, because its sins have not been filled and Antichrist, who shall abolish this empire on account of its sins, will not yet have come. Therefore, the one who now holds the Roman Empire should hold it, that is, he will rule, until it comes to pass from our midst, that is, it shall be abolished; then the wicked one will be revealed. The Greek and Latin Fathers explain it alike. Cyril of Jerusalem teaches on this passage: "The aforesaid Antichrist will come when the times of the Roman Empire have been completed."[4] St. John Chrysostom explains: "When the Roman Empire has been abolished from our midst, then Antichrist will come." Theophylactus and Oecumenius teach similar things.

From the Latins. Tertullian says that Christians prayed for the Roman Empire to long endure, because they know that when the Empire has been overturned, the supreme destruction of the world threatens.[5] Lactantius, explaining the signs which precede Antichrist and the end of the world, says: "The Roman name, which now rules the world (the soul shudders to say it, but I will speak on what is going to come), will be abolished from earth, and the Empire overturned in Asia, and again the East will rule and the West will serve it."[6] St. Ambrose, speaking on 2 Thess., says that Antichrist is going to come after the disappearance of the Roman Empire.

St. Jerome, explaining the same citation of St. Paul, says: "Christ will not come unless first there will be such a dissension that all the nations which now are subject to the Roman Empire will recede from it and unless the Roman Empire will already have been made desolate and thus Antichrist precede him."[7] Next, St. Augustine explains on this citation: "Such a one who merely commands, let him command, until he shall be taken from the midst; that is, abolished, and then the wicked one will be revealed, whom no one questions

---

[4] *Catechesis* 15.

[5] *Apologeticus*, ch. 32.

[6] Lib. 7, ch. 15.

[7] Quaest. 11 ad Algasiam.

means Antichrist."[8]

But this sign was not fulfilled in those times in which the Transylvanian Anti-Trinitarians say Antichrist came, that is, around the year 200, because then the Roman Empire particularly flourished and would do so long after.

But it is clear that this sign has never been fulfilled even to this point, because the succession still remains, and the name Roman Emperor—even by a wondrous providence of God seeing that the Empire failed in the west, which is one of the legs of the statue of Daniel—remained unharmed in the East, the other leg. But because the Empire of the East was to be destroyed by the Turks (and now we see this has come to pass), again God erected in the West the other leg, that is, the Western Empire through Charlemagne, and that emperor still endures.

Moreover, the fact that Rome itself, according to the prophecy of John, would fall in a certain measure, and lose the Empire, does not impede us. For the Roman Empire can stand well without the city of Rome, and the Roman Emperor can be so called when he lacks Rome, in the manner that he succeeds another Roman Emperor in the same dignity and power, whether he should have more or fewer provinces in his Empire. Otherwise Valens, Arcadius, Theodosius the younger, or their other successors even to Justinian, who all lacked Rome, could not be called Roman Emperors. Nor even would Charlemagne and his successors, who also did not possess the city of Rome, ever have been Emperors, which is false, and that is clear for two reasons.

First, by this reason alone the emperor, who now is, precedes all Christian kings, even if they are otherwise greater and more powerful than he is. Next, because it is certain that Charlemagne was created emperor with the agreement of the Romans, as Paul the Deacon witnesses;[9] and by the Greek emperor himself through legates sent to greet the emperor, as Ado witnesses,[10] as well as by the Persians and Arabs, that the emperor should be adorned with gifts, as Otho of Frisia relates.[11] Next, the Lutherans boast that they have three prince electors of the Roman Empire. Hence they cannot deny that the Roman Empire still endures.[12]

---

[8] *De Civitate Dei*, lib.. 20, ch. 19.

[9] *Rerum Romanarum*, lib. 23.

[10] Chronicum, for the year 810.

[11] *Hist.*, lib. 5, ch. 31.

[12] In this place it is worth noting that Greek Orthodox apologists often reject this and claim Charlemagne usurped the title. Modern research, however, bears out what Bellarmine is saying. Dimitri Vasilev, in his work *The Byzantine Empire*, notes that Charlemagne had proposed marriage to the Empress Irene and was

Orosius rightly compares the Empire of Babylon with Rome, and he says that God by far more agreeably managed things with the Romans than with the Babylonians. For after 1,064 years from which Babylon was founded, in one day Babylon, the head of the Empire, was taken, and the emperor killed, and the empire was destroyed and desolate. But after so many years, 1,064 from which Rome began, Rome was taken by the Goths; but the Emperor Honorius, who then ruled, was unharmed, and the Roman Empire was preserved.

Hence the deception of our adversaries appears. They think the decay of the Roman Empire suffices for the coming of Antichrist; but Paul, John and Daniel, as well as the Fathers we mentioned above did not say that decay was necessary, but desolation.

On the other hand, Luther, Illyricus and David Chytraeus object that this proof rather more makes their case, for it was preached by John in the Apocalypse, chapter 13, that the beast, which signifies the Roman Empire, was to be wounded to death, and was again healed by Antichrist. This certainly came about when the Pope restored again the Western Empire, which had already perished, in conferring upon Charlemagne the title and dignity of Emperor. Therefore, it is clearly understood from this translation or restoration of the Empire that the Roman Pope is truly the Antichrist.[13] Illyricus confirms this argument from Ambrose, who, while explaining the words of St. Paul, says that Antichrist is going to return freedom to the Romans, but under his own name. The Pope seems to have done this when he created an emperor for the Romans, who still depended upon him.

I respond: we read nowhere in John that when the beast is going to be healed by Antichrist that it signified the Roman Empire. But we read this, that one of the heads of the beast will die, and a little after is going to rise again, by the works of the dragon, that is the devil; which nearly all the Fathers explain concerns Antichrist himself, who makes himself dead, and again by some diabolic craft he himself raises himself, that he would imitate the true death and resurrection of Christ, and in that manner will seduce many.

St. Gregory so explains this, as do Primasius, Bede, Haymo, Anselm, Richardus and Rupertus on chapter 13 of the Apocalypse. And the text itself compels us that through the head of the beast, which was dead and brought back to life, we should not understand Charlemagne, but Antichrist. Accordingly, that head, as John writes, had power only for 42 months, and

---

honored by her and a subsequent emperor who acknowledged him as Emperor of the West. -Translator's note.

[13] See Illyricus, *Contra primatum Papae*; *Centur. 8*, ch. 10, col. 751; Chytraeum, *in Apocalyps.*, ch. 13.

blasphemed God and those who dwelled in heaven, and commanded in every tribe and people, tongue, nation, and all who dwelled on earth adored it but of such things we do not read on Charlemagne or any of his successors. Furthermore, Charlemagne ruled for more than 42 months and he did not blaspheme God and the saints, but rather more wonderfully venerated them, and many of his successors imitated his piety.

Next, neither Charlemagne himself, nor his successors, held power over every tribe, people, tongue and nation, as is known by all. Hence St. Ambrose did not speak on what the Pope did when he said a new Roman Empire that was to be created by Antichrist; rather after the Roman Empire had been overturned freedom was to be restored to the Romans, which it is not read the Pope ever did.

CHAPTER VI

A Third Proof: Enoch and Elijah

THIRD proof is taken from the arrival of Enoch and Elijah, who are still living and do so for the purpose that they might oppose the arrival of Antichrist, preserve the elect in the faith of Christ and finally convert the Jews; it is certain that this still has not been fulfilled. There are four Scriptures on this matter. The first, from Malach. 4: "Behold, I will send the Prophet Elijah to you, before the great day of the Lord will come, and convert the hearts of the fathers toward the sons, and the hearts of the sons to their fathers." The second, from Eccles. 68, where we read on Elijah: "You who were received in a fiery whirlwind, in the whirlwind of vast horses. You who are inscribed in the judgments of the times, appease the anger of the Lord, reconcile the heart of the father to the son, and restore the tribe of Jacob." And in chapter 64: "Enoch pleased God, and was lifted up into paradise, that he should bring repentance to the nations." Third, from Matthew 17: "Elijah is going to come, and will restore all things." Fourth, from the Apocalypse 11: "I will give my two witnesses, and they will prophecy for 1,260 days."

Even Theodore Bibliander relates all these citations in his *Chronicle*, but he says through Enoch and Elijah all the faithful ministers are understood, whom God rouses in the time of Antichrist; such were Luther, Zwingli and the others. At length, he concludes: "This is why it is a puerile imagination, or a Jewish dream, to await either Elijah or Enoch as definite persons in their properties." Chytraeus teaches the same thing in his commentary on that citation of the Apocalypse. And they attempt to show that the Lord taught that those passages in Malachi which speak about Elijah must be understood on John the Baptist: "He is Elijah who is going to come." And St. Jerome, in chapter 4 of Malachi, shows this to be about all the choir of prophets, that is on the doctrine of all the prophets.

Now, it does not seem to be a puerile imagination to us but a very true teaching, that Enoch and Elijah are going to come in their own persons—and the contrary is either heresy or an error proximate to heresy. Firstly, it is proved from those four Scriptures, since it is obvious that the words of Malachi could not be understood concerning anything at all, such as on teachers, like Luther and Zwingli and similar things, for Malachi says that the Jews must be converted by Elijah, and that they must be sent especially on account of the Jews which we see in that verse: "I will send to you," and in Sirach: "... to restore the tribe of Jacob." Yet, Luther and Zwingli have converted none of the Jews.

Moreover, it is certain that these cannot be understood on John the Baptist to the letter, but only on Elijah. We know that Malachi speaks on the second coming of the Lord because it will be to judge. For he says: "Before the great and terrible day of the Lord should come." The first coming is not called the great and terrible, but the acceptable time, and the day of salvation. For that reason it is added: "Lest by chance coming I shall strike the earth with a curse;" in other words, lest coming to judgment and discovering all the wicked, I shall condemn the whole world. Therefore, I shall send Elijah, that I should have others whom I shall save. But in the first coming the Lord did not come to judge, but to be judged; not to destroy, but to save.

I will respond a little later to the words of Matthew 11. Now I speak to Jerome; in his commentary on Malachi he also did not think that Malachi spoke about Elijah, but in his commentary on Matthew 11 and 17 he thought and taught the contrary. Next, this is the common interpretation of the faithful, as St. Augustine witnesses.[1]

Moreover, Sirach speaks on the very persons of Enoch and Elijah, not on others. It is proven because Sirach says about this Enoch, "He who was taken into paradise [is going to come] that he should give punishment to the nations." Also this Elijah, who was taken up in a chariot of fiery horses was going to come to restore the tribes of Israel. Certainly, such verses do not fit, unless they are about these particular persons.

I cannot marvel enough at what comes to mind from bishop Jansenius on this passage. He wrote on it that although it was the opinion of the Fathers that Elijah himself was going to come, still he is not convinced from this passage, for it can be said that the author of Sirach wrote that according to the received opinion of his time, wherein it was believed from the words of Malachi that Elijah was truly going to come in his person before the Messiah; although this would not be fulfilled in his own person, but in the one who was going to come in the spirit and power of Elijah. Yet, if that is so, as Jansenius says, it follows that Sirach erred, and wrote falsely. Rather, unless I am mistaken, Jansenius changed his opinion; writing on chapter 17 of Matthew he teaches that the passage of Malachi cannot be understood literally except concerning the true Elijah, which likewise would compel him to say the same on the verse in Sirach, which he expressed with no doubt on Malachi.

Now that the words of the Lord in Matthew 17 are understood on the true Elijah, not on John, is clear because John had already come and run his course, and still the Lord said: "Elijah is going to come." Moreover, it can be proved that all the Doctors only understand this to be on the true Elijah. Firstly, because the Apostles who advanced the question on Elijah were Peter, James and John, and they took up the occasion from the transfiguration of the Lord, where they saw

---

[1] *De civit. Dei*, lib. 20, cap 29.

Moses and Elijah. Therefore, when they ask: "What about what the scribes say, that Elijah must come first?" they spoke on that Elijah whom they saw on the mountain with Christ. Therefore, when Christ responded, "Indeed, Elijah is going to come and he will restore all things," he also spoke on that particular Elijah who had appeared in the transfiguration. Secondly, the same is clear from the words themselves: "And he will restore all things." Truly, John the Baptist did not do that, nor anyone else. For to restore all things is to recall all Jews, heretics and perhaps many Catholics deceived by Antichrist to the true faith.

But Bibliander insists that the Lord speaks of John the Baptist in Matthew XI: "He is Elijah who is going to come," that is, he [John] is the Elijah promised by Malachi. I respond: The Lord wanted to say that John was the promised Elijah, not literally, but allegorically. Therefore, he sent him ahead, although you wish to receive him, as if to say, indeed the Elijah promised in his person is going to come in the last coming. Still, if you also wish to receive some Elijah in the first coming, then receive John. For that reason he also added: "He who has ears to hear, let him hear," thereby showing it was a mystery that he had said John was Elijah.

Next, that the words of John in Apocalypse XI should be understood on the individual persons of Enoch and Elijah is clear not from all the doctors but for the very reason that John says in the same place that they will be killed by Antichrist and that their bodies will remain unburied on a street in Jerusalem, and after three days they will rise again, and they will ascend into heaven. No one has yet done that.

Still, David Chytraeus tries to respond in a commentary on this citation. He says first: John wanted to signify the many Lutheran ministers that would be killed by Papists, to whom God at length restored to life although he brought them into heaven, they were going to live forever. Secondly, he adds a little below that after the ministers were killed, life of the body was to be restored on the last day of resurrection. Thirdly, he adds in the same place that it can even signify through this restoration of life, and that we shall see many other ministers with the same zeal and power raised by God.

Yet these are very weak responses. The first cannot be defended, because the beatitude of the soul is not the restoration of lost life, but the acquisition of new life. Next, these two witnesses in the Apocalypse will rise in the sight of all and with their bodies restored; turning they will be lifted up, which certainly is not fulfilled in the beatitude of the soul. The second answer avails to nothing since John says that those two witnesses were going to rise before the last day, while the state of this world still endures. But John adds that it is to strike great fear to their enemies by their resurrection, and a little afterwords the movement of the world is going to happen, and seven thousand men are going to perish. Next, the third answer is not to the point. For the Scripture says that those same who were dead are to be roused to life, and taken up into heaven. Moreover, we have not yet seen any Lutheran minister resurrect, or be assumed into heaven. Why, John says that Enoch and Elijah are going to preach wearing sackcloth, and the Lutherans so hate sackcloth that if by chance Enoch and Elijah wear it while they are Lutherans, they will immediately be cast out.

Secondly, it is proved from the consensus of the Fathers that Enoch and Elijah are truly going to come in their persons in the time of Antichrist. For Hilary, Jerome, Origen, Chrysostom and all other interpreters of Matthew 17 assert this about Elijah. In like manner do Lactantius,[2] Theodoret,[3] as well as Augustine[4] and Primasius.[5]

On Enoch together with Elijah, many who write on the Apocalypse assert that they are going to come to oppose Antichrist, such as Bede, Richard, and Arethas. Arethas also adds that it is believed without exception by the whole Church. Moreover, John Damascene,[6] Hippolytus[7] the martyr, St. Gregory the Great[8] and Augustine[9] teach the same.

Thirdly it is proved because otherwise no reason can be given why these two should be taken up before death, and still live in mortal flesh who are going to die someday. Albeit the Jews say, as Rabi Salomon,[10] that Enoch was killed by God before his time, because he was light and inconstant, and they assert that Elijah, when he was born in the fiery chariot, was burned in his whole body by the flame. Perhaps the Lutherans who deny they are coming back think likewise; still all Catholics hold with certain faith that both live in their bodies. For the Apostle teaches that Enoch has not yet died;[11] Enoch was borne up lest he would see death, and that both he and Elijah were not yet dead but were going to die. Apart from those cited above, Irenaeus, Tertullian, Jerome, Augustine and Epiphanius clearly teach this.

Irenaeus, speaking abut Enoch and Elijah, says: "The priests who are

---

2 Lib. 7, cap. 17.

3 In cap. ult Malachiae.

4 Tracta. 4 in Ioannem.

5 In cap. 11 Apocalypsis.

6 Lib. 4, capite 28.

7 In oratione de mundi consummatione.

8 Moralium, lib. 21 36 & lib. 9 cap. 4.

9 Genes. ad litteram, lib. 9, cap. 6.

10 In cap. 5 Genes.

11 Hebrews 11:5.

disciples of the apostles say that those, who were born up thence (into early Paradise) were borne up and there remain even to the end, tasting incorruption."[12] Tertullian says about Enoch: "He has not yet tasted death, as glittering in eternity."[13] Epiphanius says about Enoch and Elijah: "These two remain in body and soul on account of hope."[14] Jerome in an epistle to Pammachius against John of Jerusalem says: "Enoch was borne up in the flesh; Elijah still was taken up in the flesh into heaven, and still has not yet died, being a tenant of Paradise, etc." Augustine says: "We do not doubt that Enoch and Elijah live in the bodies in which they were born."[15]

---

[12] Lib. 5.

[13] *Contra Iudaeos*, cap 1 de Henoch.

[14] In Ancorato.

[15] *De peccato Originali*, cap. 23.

CHAPTER VII
The Fourth Proof: the Persecution of Antichrist

HE FOURTH proof is taken from the fact that it is certain the persecution of Antichrist will be the most severe ever known, to the extent that all public ceremonies and sacrifices of religion will cease. We still do not see any of that. Now, the fact that the last persecution is going to be very severe is clear from what we read in Matthew 24: "Then there will be a great tribulation, such as has not been from the beginning of the world, nor will be." Moreover, we read in Apocalypse 20: "Then Satan must be loosed," who was bound even to that time.

St. Augustine, disputing on this citation, says in the time of Antichrist the Devil will be loosed, and hence that persecution will be much more severe than all the ones that preceded it;[1] the Devil can rage so much more cruelly loosed than bound. Therefore, he says, then the Devil is going plague the Church with all his own and their strength. Further, Hippolytus the martyr and St. Cyril say that the martyrs whom Antichrist will kill are going to be more illustrious than all the previous ones, because the old martyrs fought against the human ministers of the devil, but these will fight against the Devil himself prowling personally. But certainly we have experienced nothing like that from the year 600 or even 1000.

The heretics say that they suffer a great persecution from Antichrist because some of their number are burned. But what comparison is there of that sort of persecution with that carried out by Nero, Domitian, Decius, Diocletian, and others? Accordingly, for one heretic who is burned, a thousand Christians formerly were burned—and that was exercised in the whole Roman world, not only in one place. Furthermore, at present when the supreme penalty is given a man is merely burned, but in ancient times they exercised the most diverse and unbelievable torments.[2]

Pope Damasus writes in the life of Marcellinus that over seventeen thousand Christians were killed by Diocletian, and Eusebius, who then lived, writes that all the prisons were so full with martyrs that no place was left for criminals.[3] Moreover, in the whole of the book we cited, so many crowns were conferred for martyrdom in two hundred years that it would be impossible to undertake their number. Besides, the fact is that the heretics killed many more Catholics

---

[1] *De Civitate Dei*, lib. 20, ch. 8&9.

[2] From the pagan side, see Cornelius Tacitus on Nero, and from our side Eusebius in his *Ecclesiastical History*.

[3] Eusebius, *Ecclesiastical History*, lib. 8 cap. 6.

in the last ten or fifteen years in France and Flanders than inquisitors burned heretics in perhaps the last hundred. Therefore, they cannot call this persecution, but rather more civil war. For as Augustine teaches, when the true persecution of Antichrist will come, tribulation will only be upon the sons of the Church, but not upon their persecutors just as in the time of Diocletian and the princes of this world, Christians alone were slaughtered, but they did not slaughter.

For all that, were this to be called a persecution, then Catholics have a better claim to have suffered it than the Lutherans and Calvinists. For Catholics are the ones who were cast out from many areas and lost their churches, patrimony and even their country, without a doubt, to invaders seizing their things for the Ministers of this new Gospel; and as we said from the commentary of Laurence Surius and other historians of this time, it can be recognized that the fury of the Calvinists has taken up many more Catholics in a few years than heretics by the judgment of Catholic princes were given punishment for the denial of faith.

Nevertheless, Augustine proves the fact that the persecution is going to be well-known and manifest, while commenting on those words of Apocalypse 20: "And they surrounded the camp of the saints, and the beloved city."[4] By these words, it is meant that all the wicked were going to be together in the army of Antichrist, and were going to assault every church of the saints in open battle. For now there are many false men in the Church, who, concealing their malice, are outside the Church in heart but within the body. St. Augustine says: "But then they will all break out in open persecution from their hiding places of hate." Certainly, this has not yet been fulfilled in our time even though there never was a greater number of false brethren and feigned Christians. That this persecution is neither known nor manifested, neither they who say they suffer nor we who are alleged to cause it can say when this will begin.

Without a doubt the persecutions of Nero, Domitian and of other Roman Emperors were recorded diligently by Eusebius, Orosius, and Sulpitius. Nobody questions when these persecutions began and when they ended, just as no one questions when Christ came, because it was true and manifest and we absolutely know when it was and by whom it was made manifest. Nor are there any opinions on our side on the matter. But the heretics who say that Antichrist has come and now for so many years has exercised persecution still cannot advance one author who recorded when Antichrist came or to whom he appeared first, or when he began the persecution. They even disagree among themselves, so much so that one might say he came in the year 200, another in the year 666, while another in 1273. Another yet will say the year 1000, while another 1200,

---

[4] *De Civitate Dei*, lib. 20, cap. 11.

so they do not speak as men who are awake, but seem like men who dream in quiet.

Next, the fact that in the time of Antichrist, on account of the atrocity of persecution, the public office and daily sacrifice of the Church will cease, which Daniel clearly teaches: "From the time when the continual sacrifice will have been taken away for 1290 days." In that place, by the consensus of every writer, he speaks on the time of Antichrist. Furthermore, Irenaeus, Jerome, Theodoret, Hippolytus the martyr and Primasius all express the same thing, that Antichrist is going to forbid all divine worship which is now exercised in the churches of Christians, especially the most holy sacrifice of the Eucharist. That this sign has not yet been fulfilled is evident from experience.

From that we can gather three things. 1) Antichrist has not yet come, since the continual sacrifice is still in force. 2) The Roman Pontiff is not the antichrist, rather, he is quite contrary to him, since the Pope carefully honors and guards the sacrifice which Antichrist is going to take away. 3) The heretics of this time, apart from all other things, are precursors of Antichrist since no one more ardently desires to altogether abolish the sacrifice of the Eucharist than they.

CHAPTER VIII

The Fifth Proof: the Duration of Antichrist

HE FIFTH proof is taken from the duration of Antichrist. Antichrist will not reign more than three and a half years, yet now the Pope has reigned spiritually over the Church for more than 1500 years. Further, not one of them can be assigned that will have reigned precisely three and a half years so as to be accounted for Antichrist. Therefore, not only is the Pope not the Antichrist, but the latter has not yet come.

Now, that the reign of Antichrist is going to be for three and a half years is gathered from Daniel[1] and from the Apocalypse.[2] There we read that the reign of Antichrist is going to endure through time, times and half a time. For time is understood as one year, through times two years, through half a time, half a year. John argues this same thing, for in Apocalypse 11 and 13, he says Antichrist is going to reign for 42 months, which correctly corresponds to three and a half years. The Hebrews use years and lunar months, even if they reconcile them to the solar by adding one lunar cycle to the sixth year. Moreover, three and a half lunar years correctly makes 42 months, or 1260 days; correspondingly the lunar year is full and complete in 12 months, of which each has 30 days, as Augustine teaches.[3]

What Daniel 12 says, namely that Antichrist is going to reign for 1290 days is not opposed to us, even though it is 30 more days than John had said. This is because John speaks on Enoch and Elijah, who will be slain by Antichrist a month before Antichrist shall perish.

Our adversaries respond to this in three ways. First, Chytraeus[4] says that times (*tempora*) cannot be taken for three and a half years because it is opposed to experience; and Paul says Antichrist is going to endure even to the coming of Christ.[5]

Secondly, he says a certain time can be placed for an uncertain one; hence, more than a thousand years ought to be understood for 42 months or 1260 days. Bullinger says the same thing,[6] and his reason seems to be the one which Luther insinuates in his supposition of the times; because without a doubt it is certain from Apocalypse 20 that the Devil will be loosed for a thousand years. Thus, the

---

[1] Daniel 7:25 and 12:11-12.

[2] Apocalypse 12:6.

[3] *De Civitate Dei*, lib. 15, cap. 14.

[4] *In cap. 11 & 13 Apocalypsis.*

[5] 2 Thess. 2:6.

[6] *Sermon* 46 in Apocalypsim.

coming of Antichrist with the temporal sword was in the thousandth year from Christ and he has already reigned more than 500 years; therefore, it is fitting to receive those 42 months as an uncertain time.

Thirdly, the Centuriators respond that Daniel and John take a day for a year, and hence for 1260 days, 1260 years should be understood.[7] The reason can be that in Daniel 9, 70 weeks are understood to be 700 years, not days. And Ezechiel 4 says: "I gave you a day for a year." And Luke 13: "Today it is fitting for me to walk, and tomorrow as well as every day;" that is, to live for three years. Chytraeus puts this reasoning in chapter 11 of the Apocalypse, where he says the years and months of the same are called angelic years and months, not human.

Now, the common opinion of the Fathers is to the contrary. Let us look at those who assert that Antichrist will only reign for three and a half years due to the passages we have noted. Hippolytus the martyr, in his *Oration on the Consummation of the World*, says: "Antichrist will reign over the earth for three and a half years, afterward his kingdom and glory will be snatched away from him." Irenaeus said: "He will reign for three years and six months, then the Lord will come from heaven."[8] Jerome adds: "The time means a year; the times, according to the propriety of the Hebrew terminology, which has dual numbers, prefigures two years; half of the time, six months, in which the saints must be entrusted to the power of Antichrist."[9] St. Cyril said: "Antichrist will reign for merely three and a half years which we say not from some Apocryphal book, but from Daniel the Prophet."[10] Likewise St. Augustine said: "Even a man who is half asleep and reads these things can hardly doubt that reign of Antichrist against the Church will be very savage, although it is to last a scanty space of time. For time and times, and half a season is one year and two, and half which makes three years and a half; and through this, the number of days that were placed in the Scripture makes clear the number of months."[11] Theodoret says like things on chapter 8 of Daniel, as do Primasius, Bede, Anselm, Haymo, Arethas, Richard and Rupert on the Apocalypse.

Secondly, the same is proven from the fact that the Scriptures say that the time in which the Devil is unleashed, as well as of Antichrist, will be very brief. "Woe to the earth and sea, because the devil descends to you having great

---

[7] *Cent.* I, lib. 2, cap. 4, col. 438.

[8] Lib. 5, towards the end.

[9] *In Danielis*, cap. 7.

[10] *Catechesis*, 25.

[11] *De Civitate Dei*, lib. 20, cap. 23.

wrath, knowing that he has but a short time."[12] And again: "He bound him for a thousand years, and after these he ought to be freed for a short time."[13] How I ask, will this be true, if Antichrist will reign for 1270 years? For he will be free longer than he was bound.

Thirdly, because, as Augustine[14] and Gregory the Great[15] argue, unless that fearsome persecution were brief, many would perish who are not going to perish. This is why the Lord also says: "Unless those days would be brief, all flesh would not be saved."[16]

Fourthly, Christ preached for only three and a half years. Therefore, it would be fitting that Antichrist is not permitted to preach longer.

Fifth, the sum of those 1260 years, which our adversaries constitute, can in no way be accommodated to those words of Daniel and of John: "Time, times and half a time." For through time it ought to be understood without a doubt one certain number like one day, one week, one month, one year, one purification,[17] one jubilee,[18] one century, one millennium. But if we receive one millennium, then Antichrist will reign for 3500 years, which our adversaries do not admit. If we receive one century, then the time of Antichrist will be 350 years, which they also do not admit, and the same is clear concerning one jubilee, etc.

Sixth, when we read Daniel 4, we read that the number of times that will pass are seven in which Nebuchadnezzar will be going to be outside his kingdom, but for those times all understand seven years. If we would understand years of years, as our adversaries would have it in their treatment of Antichrist, it would behoove them to say that Nebuchadnezzar lived outside his kingdom for 2,555 years.

It is not difficult to answer their petty syllogisms. For when Chytraeus said that what Daniel and John spoke of cannot be received as three and a half years, nor properly for our usage of years, because experience witnesses that Antichrist has already been prowling for a longer time, he manifestly begs the question, as the logicians say. For he assumes what is in question. That very

---

[12] Apocalypse 12:12.

[13] Apocalypse 20:3.

[14] *De Civitate Dei*, lib. 20.

[15] *Morales* lib. 33, cap. 12.

[16] Matthew 24:22.

[17] Translator's note: The Romans had a purifying ceremony every 5 years (*lustrum*) and the word was used as a term for a period of 5 years.

[18] Translator's note: In the Old Testament, a Shemita (*Jubilaeus*) or Jubilee was every 50 years, and here would be used to denote a 50 year period.

thing is asked, whether Antichrist has come. But when he adds that by the opinion of St. Paul, Antichrist was going to rule even to the second coming of Christ, and concludes that he must reign longer than three and a half years, he does not see that he either again begs the question or says nothing. For no order can be made, unless it is assumed that Antichrist has already come—but that is what the very question is about.

But to that which both he and Henry Bullinger say, that a certain number is taken up for an uncertain period in this passage, I respond: a certain number is only placed for an uncertain one when some full and perfect number is placed, such as ten, a hundred, or a thousand, but not when different numbers are assigned where great and small are mixed. Then, a certain number must be taken up for an uncertain one, just as when the Scripture says in Apocalypse 20 that the devil was bound for a thousand years, as Sts. Augustine and Gregory say,[19] but not when it assigns time, times and half time, or 1260 days, or 42 months. For to what end are there a variety of numbers, if an uncertain time is meant?

Now I will address the argument of Illyricus. In the Scripture one does discover what can rightly be called weeks of years. Still, not days for years, or months for years. For weeks of years we read in Leviticus 25: "You will count for yourself seven weeks of years, etc." And certainly it is right to say that week is counted by the number seven in Greek, Latin and Hebrew. In Hebrew they say שבוע (sha-bo-ach, seventh) from שבע (sha-bach), which is seven, as is also said in Greek by ἑθδομὰς, and in Latin by *septimana*, through a number containing seven; just as seven days are called a week of days, so seven years are a week of years. But month of years, or day for year we never read, nor would it be correct to say it, because a month is not counted by some number, but by the cycle of the moon, which finished in thirty days. Hence the Hebrews call month ירח (ya-rech), that is moon, or חדש (ko-desh); that is the beginning of the moon, and in Greek month is μήν because moon is called μήνη.

In like manner, day does not mean a number, but a time of light, as in Genesis: "God called the light day, and the darkness night." Nor is the passage of Ezechiel opposed to this: "I give to you a day for a year."[20] There, he did not wish to say years are literally meant by days, otherwise it would behoove Ezechiel to have slept on his left side for 390 years, which is impossible. For God had commanded that he should sleep upon his left for 390 days and added: "I give to you a day for a year." So if those days were received for years, Ezechiel ought to sleep on his side for 390 years. Yet he did not live that long. Therefore,

---

[19] *Loc. Cit.*

[20] Ezechiel 4:5.

it must be said that in that passage a day is truly received for days, but can mean years through a type, because those 390 days in which Ezechiel slept were a sign of the sleep of God, through which he tolerated the sins of the Israelites for 390 years.

Now, to the objection made by Chytraeus from Luke 13: "It is fitting for me to walk today and tomorrow, as well as the day after," I respond: When Christ said this, he did not mean by these words that he was still going to preach for three years since the Lord said this in the last year of his life. For as Jerome notes,[21] the matter speaks for itself. Matthew, Mark and Luke did not write the deeds and words of the first two years of Christ's public ministry, rather only the third year. Therefore, the Lord either understood by those three days the triduum which was about to be taken up on the journey to Jerusalem (as St. Albert and Cajetan explain), or he certainly wished to show by that manner of speaking that he was going to remain and preach still a little while, as Jansenius rightly teaches. Lastly, where in the world did Illyricus and Chytraeus find days and angelic months? None are found in Scripture.

---

[21] Liber *de Scriptoribus Ecclesiasticis*, in Ioanne.

CHAPTER IX
The Sixth Proof: the End of the World

HE SIXTH proof is taken from the last sign following Antichrist, that the end of the world will come about. For the arrival of Antichrist will be a little before the end of the world. Therefore, if Antichrist would have come a long time ago, as our adversaries say, the world should have ended a long time ago. Daniel spoke twice about Antichrist,[1] once explaining the vision, adding each in turn; the second, that after Antichrist the last judgment immediately follows. "I considered the horns and behold, a little horn arose, and three from the first horns were torn from his face. I watched until thrones were placed, and the Ancient of Days sat, etc." And later, explaining the vision: "The fourth beast will be the fourth kingdom; the ten horns mean there will be ten kings and another kingdom will rise after them, and it will be more powerful than the first, and it will lay low the three kings ... And they will be betrayed into his hand through time, times and half a time, and he will sit in judgment, etc."

The prophecy of John is similar: "After these it will be fitting for him to be freed for a short time, and I have seen the seats, and they sat upon them and gave judgment upon them, etc."[2] Daniel said the same thing again afterward, in chapter 12. The reign of Antichrist will endure for 1,290 days, and he adds: "Blessed is he who waits and attains even to 1,335 days;" this is, even to sixty days after the death of Antichrist, because then the Lord will come to judge and he will render the crowns of justice upon the victors, just as Jerome and Theodoret show in their commentary on this citation.

Next, the same is gathered from Matthew 24: "This Gospel of the kingdom will be preached to all nations throughout the whole world, and then will come the consummation;" that is, the end of the world will be a little after. Then: "But immediately after the tribulation of those days the sun will be darkened, and the moon will not give its light; and then will appear the sign of the Son of Man, etc." St. Paul says the same thing: "Then that wicked man will be revealed, whom the Lord Jesus will kill with the breath of his mouth, and by the glory of his coming he will bring him to ruin, etc."[3] The Apostle teaches that almost immediately after Antichrist, Christ is going to come because he will intervene in that very short time, so that the frauds and deceits of Antichrist, which will have begun to be destroyed by Elijah and Enoch, will be utterly destroyed by the very arrival of Christ as well as the horrible preceding signs.

---

[1]   Daniel 7:20-22; 23-27.

[2]   Apocalypse 20:3-4.

[3]   2 Thessalonians 2:8.

Moreover, the same is seen in 1 John 2: "Little children, now is the last hour; and just as you heard that Antichrist has come, now there are many Antichrists, whence you know it is the last hour." In other words, John says that this time from Christ even to the end of the world is the last hour, that is, the last time or the last age, as St. Augustine says. And he proves this most beautifully from this principle that we know Antichrist is going to come at the end of the world. But now we have already spoken of his many forerunners, or lesser Antichrists. The sign is certain; this is the last hour, or age. It is in the same way that one could so argue about the last hour of night for we know the sun is going to rise at the end of the night. Furthermore, we see now many of its rays already illumine the sky so we know this is the last hour of the night.

Next, this is also the common consensus of the Fathers: Irenaeus,[4] Tertullian,[5] Augustine[6] and many others; we even see it in the testimony of our adversaries. They affirm that Antichrist is going to reign even to the end of the world, hence a little after his ruin it is going to be the end of the world. So from this sign, joined with that above, we make an unanswerable proof whereby it is proven both that Antichrist has not yet come and he is not the Roman Pontiff. For if the world is going to end immediately after the death of Antichrist and Antichrist will not be alive three and a half years after he appears, then it is clear that he will not appear or begin to reign except for three and a half years before the end of the world. But the Pope now, according to our adversaries, has reigned with both swords for more than five hundred years but still the world still endures.

---

[4] Lib. 5.

[5] *De Resurrectione.*

[6] *De Civitate Dei,* lib. 20, cap. 19.

CHAPTER X
On the Name "Antichrist"

OW the fourth disputation follows, which will be on the proper name and character of Antichrist. Everyone agrees that these words of John in the Apocalypse pertain entirely to Antichrist: "He will make all, small with the great, rich and poor, free and slave to have his mark on their right hand, or on their foreheads, so that no one will be able to buy or sell unless he shall have this mark, or the name of the beast, or the number of his name: 'this is wisdom'. He who has the knowledge will reckon the number of the beast. His number is of man, and that number is 666."[1]

Now, there are a great many opinions on this number. The first is of those who say that this number does not designate a name, but the time of the arrival or the death of Antichrist. Bullinger would have it thus in the preface to his homilies on the Apocalypse, that this is the time of the arrival of Antichrist. Similarly, the Centuriators say it designates the time of the death of Antichrist.[2] Still, some like Clisthoveus claim that in the writings of St. John Damascene,[3] it means the death of Muhammad, whom he calls the Antichrist. Lyranus, on this citation, agrees with those who do not quite think Muhammad is the Antichrist, but still believe this number means the death of Muhammad was going to be in the year 666 A.D.

This opinion is most absurd. Firstly, because John says that he speaks concerning the number of the name of the beast. Secondly, because the beast, whose number this is, will command all businessmen, so that they will use that number in contracts, as is obvious from Apocalypse 13. Therefore, the number does not pertain to the death of the beast, but rather to the period when he is living. The third is also false, that Muhammad died in the year 666. Some say he died in the year 637, such as Matthew Palmerius; others in the year 630 like Cedrenus in his compendium of histories; while others still in the year 638, as John Vaseus in his *Chronicle of Spain*.

The second opinion is of David Chytraeus, who teaches on this place in the Apocalypse that the name of Antichrist is λατεῖνος, or in Hebrew רומיית, (Rom-yi-yet) which is Roman. Hence the Pope, who is a Latin prince, since he rules in Latium, and is the Roman Pontiff, must be Antichrist. Theodore Bibliander teaches the same thing,[4] and for that reason the eleventh table of his

---

[1] Apocalypse 13:16-18.

[2] *Centur.* 1, lib. 2, cap. 4.

[3] Liber 4, cap. 28.

[4] Tabul. 10.

Chronology, which he begins from the year 600, he titles "the Latin Popes". There are two reasons: 1) what Irenaeus teaches in book 5 which has the appearance of truth, that this is going to be the name of Antichrist; 2) that really the letters of this name add up to that number, as follows:

ר 200	λ 30	τ 300
ו 6	α 1	ε 5
מ 40	τ 300	ι 10
י 10	ε 5	τ 50
י 10	ι 10	α 1
ת 400	ν 50	ν 50
666	ο 70	666
	ς 200	
	666	

This opinion is completely careless. In the first place, Irenaeus indeed says that the name λατεῖνος can probably be accommodated to Antichrist; but he adds it is much more probable that the name of Antichrist is not λατεινος, but τειταν, which also expresses that number, and the name is much more clear since it means the light of the sun.

Besides, the conjecture of Irenaeus, which was something at that time, is nothing now. For he says it is probable that Antichrist will be called Latinum, not because he ruled in Latium, but because the Latins then ruled so extensively and held almost the whole world. Since Antichrist ought to be a very powerful king, without a doubt he will seize the most powerful kingdoms that he will discover. Moreover, Irenaeus says that the kingdom of the Latins is the most powerful, since they really ruled then. Certainly that conjecture avails to nothing in our times, for the Latins no longer rule throughout the world; instead the Turks really rule, and among us the Spanish and the French, not the Latins.

Besides the name *Latin*, that it would mean Rome, is not written for ει, but through the simple Iota; and thence it does not render that number. In the same way the comment can be refuted on the word רומיית. For Roman can not end in a ת (tav), since it would be a masculine noun. For that ending is feminine in Hebrew. Without that letter ת, the number 400 is missing for the name of Antichrist. Moreover, the noun λατεῖνος, if it will be the name of Antichrist, will be proper to him especially in use, just as Arethas teaches, because it will need to be shown in a sign by all who buy or sell; yet the name λατεῖνος is common. Still, no Pope has ever been called Latinus either for their own name or for the name they take up; the Popes never call themselves Latins, only bishops or Popes.

Next, Romanus was a proper name of only one Pontiff, though still he could not be Antichrist since he did not live more than 4 months. Secondly, such a name is common.

Next, if only this name λατεῖνος or Romanus would effect the number 666, our adversaries would have an argument. But innumerable names are discovered that render the same number. Hippolytus the Martyr, in his sermon on the consummation of the world, recorded another name which renders that number, ἀρνοῦμαι; that is "I refuse." Arethas records seven: λαμπέτης, that is *renowned*; τειτὰν, that is *the sun*; ὀνικητὴς, that is *victor*; κακὸς ὁ δηγὸς, that is wicked general; ἀληθὴς βλαβερὸς, that is *truly wounding*; πάλαι βάσκανος, that is *once hating*; ἀμνὸς ἄδικος, which is a Gothic name, and in Latin comes out to DCLXVI, which makes 666 if we receive a D in Latin for 500, C for one hundred, L for fifty, X for ten, V for five, and I for one.

From more recent writers William Lindanus remarks that Martin Luther rendered the number 666 if Latin letters would be received for numbers after the customary usage of Greek and Hebrew in this way: A,1; D, 2; C 3; D, 4; E5, F, 6; G, 7; H 8; I, 9; K, 10; L, 20; M, 30; N, 40; O, 50; P, 60; Q, 70; R, 80; S, 90; T, 100; V, 200; X, 300; Y, 400; Z, 500. Gilbert Genebrardus remarks in the last book of his *Chronology* that even the name of Luther in Hebrew makes the number לולתר (Luliter).

I add two other things for the sake of Luther and Chytraeus, namely that דביד כיתריו, (David Chytraeus), and σαξόνειος, (the Saxon) render 666, and the latter agrees with Luther just as the name Latin does to the Pope.

ד	4	σ	200
ב	2	α	1
י	10	ξ	60
ד	4	ο	70
כ	20	ν	50
י	10	ε	5
ת	400	ι	10
ר	200	ο	70
י	10	ς	200
ו	6		
	666		666

The third opinion is of many Catholics who suspect Antichrist will be called ἄντεμος, both because this name properly agrees with him and also that it renders the number exactly, as Primasius, Anselm and Richardus argue.

This opinion is correctly refuted by Rupert, since the name which John insinuates will not be the name imposed on Antichrist by his opponents, but the name which he will take unto himself and boast in, so much so that he will command it be written on the foreheads of men. Moreover, it is not believable that he is going to take a name so odious and vile, such as ἄντεμος, and being mindful of all others noted above.

The fourth opinion is of the same Rupert, who believes this number does not mean the name of Antichrist but means the threefold prevarication carried out by the devil in Antichrist. For a series of 6 numbers, because it does not reach as far as the sevens, in which there is rest and beatitude, is the number of the creature perishing through prevarication from rest. But the devil incurs a threefold prevarication, or rather more, he makes one threefold. First he transgressed when he sinned in himself; next, when he made the first man sin he added 60 to a simple six; then thirdly he will transgress when he will seduce the whole world through Antichrist, and then will have added 600 to 60.

The fifth opinion is of Bede, who proceeds on a contrary path, and teaches the number six is perfect, because God created the heaven and the earth in six days. Sixty, then, is more perfect and six hundred the most perfect, from which he gathers that Antichrist is meant by the number 666 because he will usurp for himself the most perfect tribute which should be given to God alone. We read a figure of it in the Book of Kings, where a weight of gold, which is offered to Solomon each year, was six hundred and sixty six thousand talents.[5] These two opinions do not appear to sufficiently square with what John says, since that number is the number of a name, not a dignity or a prevarication. Yet these Fathers would hold their opinions on this passage with as much suspicion and conjecture.

Therefore, the truest opinion of this matter is of those who confess their ignorance and say that they still do not know the name of Antichrist. Such an opinion is of Irenaeus,[6] Aerthas and others on this place of the Apocalypse. If I may, I will ascribe the words of Irenaeus, because Chytraeus exhorts his readers to do the same, saying:

Being zealous I exhort you that you view the last pages of Irenaeus on this place of the Apocalypse, 333 and 334, which profitably and piously dispute on this number, and among the rest he judges that Latin or Roman is the name of Antichrist, that is λατεῖνος, etc. Now Irenaeus says the following: "It is more certain and less hazardous to await the fulfillment of the prophecy than to be making surmises and casting about for any names that may present themselves, inasmuch as many names can be found possessing the number mentioned and the same question will, after all, remain

---

[5]   3 Kings (1 Kings) 10:14.

[6]   Lib. 5, cap. 30, 3.

unsolved. For if there are many names found possessing this number, it will be asked which among them shall the man bear when he comes. It is not through a want of names containing the number of that name that I say this, but on account of the fear of God, and zeal for the truth. For the name εὐάνθας contains the required number, but I make no claim regarding it. Then also *Lateinos* has the number six hundred and sixty-six; and it is very probable, this being the name of the last kingdom [seen by Daniel]. For the Latins are they who at present bear rule. I will not, however, make any boast over this. *Teitan* too, the first two syllables being the Greek vowels ε and ι, among all names which are found among us, is rather worthy of belief.... Inasmuch, then, as this name "Titan" has such arguments to recommend it, that from among the many names we could gather lest perhaps he who is to come will be called "Titan", it has the greatest appearance of truth. We will not, however, risk the matter nor pronounce in earnest that Antichrist is going to have this name, knowing that if it were necessary for his name to be publicly revealed at the present, the one who beheld the vision of the Apocalypse would have made it known.

So, let Chytraeus hear the profitable, pious and erudite difference of Irenaeus, and not falsely impute to him what he never said. For Irenaeus judged that Antichrist might be Latin, or Roman, but he says that as often as it was repeated, the name of Antichrist could not be known in this time, and he proved this opinion with two reasons. First, because many names are discovered which make that number, nor is it permitted to divine the name from so many like it, because it happens that it will be one which has been predicted. Next, because if God wanted it known in this time, he would have brought this out through John himself. But he adds, that it is not due to any poverty of names, but from fear of God and zeal for truth. And for that reason he brings forth three names, εὐάνθας, λατεῖνος, and ταιτᾶν, whereby the second has a greater appearance of truth than the first, and he affirms the third to have more than the second, while he avows none of them for certain.

We could add a third reason from the same passage of Irenaeus. A little before we disputed against those who were gathering false names of Antichrist for their own purpose. For this reason, he says they fall into many troubles. For they express themselves with the danger of erring and deceiving others, and also of effecting that both they and many others will quite easily be seduced by Antichrist. When he will come, he will have some name which they will persuade him to have; he will not be held by them as Antichrist, and so he will not shun it. All such dangers without a doubt come upon the Lutherans, and especially this last one, because they have persuaded themselves that the Roman Pontiff is the Antichrist. When the true Antichrist arrives they will not easily recognize it and hence, will not avoid him.

Here we must remark that when he will have come, the name of Antichrist will be well known. Before Christ came, the Jews did not know for certain by what name he would be called, although the prophets preached much concerning his name. Even one of the Sibyls, in the first book of the songs of Sibyls, remarked that the number of the name of Christ was going to be 888, even as John writes that Antichrist's number is 666. But after Christ came, all controversy was abolished, and everyone knows he is called Jesus.

"But," says the Sibyll, "I will teach you what his number may be. For eight monads there are as many tens over it. And also 8 groups of ten, will mean faithless. But you bear in mind that is the name for the human race."	I 10
	η 8
	σ 200
	o 70
	υ 400
	ς 200
	888

It happens, that it is common to all prophecies of the prophets to be ambiguous and obscure until they are fulfilled, just as Irenaeus rightly teaches and proves.[7]

From these we take up the unanswerable argument to prove the Roman Pontiff is not the Antichrist and that Antichrist himself has not yet come. If Antichrist would have come and was the Roman Pontiff, his name would established for certain, as predicted by John, just as Christ for us —now there is no question—not even amongst the Turks, Jews, and Pagans, to the extent that he is named. But on the name of Antichrist there is still a great controversy, we make it plain by so many opinions that have been recited and refuted. Thus, the prophecy of John has not yet been fulfilled. Hence, Antichrist has not yet come nor is he the Roman Pontiff. Add the confirmation from the *Confession* of Augustine Marloratus, who in a great explication gathered from various Lutherans and Calvinists on the New Testament, so writes on this citation: "There are nearly so many explications of this passage whereby it appears it is very obscure and enigmatic." Yet if the prophecy is still very obscure and enigmatic, then it is not fulfilled; Antichrist has not come. Accordingly, all prophecies, when they are fulfilled are made evident. Therefore, why does Marloratus, lay down in his preface in the Apocalypse that it is so clear that the Roman Pontiff is the Antichrist, that if you were silent, the very stones would cry out?

---

[7] Irenaeus, lib. 4, cap. 43.

CHAPTER XI

On the Mark of Antichrist.

INDEED, there are also two or three opinions on the mark of Antichrist. Firstly, the heretics of this time teach that the mark of Antichrist is some sign of obedience and union with the Roman Pontiff, yet they do not explain in the same way what that sign will be. Henry Bullinger would have it that it is the anointing of Confirmation, in which all Christians are marked on their forehead as obedient to the Roman Pontiff.[1] Theodore Bibliander says the character of Antichrist is the profession of the Roman faith, because a true worshiper would not be considered a true Christian unless he professed that he adheres to the Roman Church.[2] Additionally, David Chytraeus adds the oath of fidelity, which many are compelled to furnish to the Roman Pontiff. In like manner the priestly anointing that they receive on their forehead and hand, saying: "He impresses, as the Papists call it, an indelible character." Therefore, he sinks down to statues and consecrated bread, as well as to be present at funeral masses. Now, what Sebastian Meyer and others along with Augustine Marloratus teach on this citation of the Apocalypse are not much different. But these petty arguments are easy to refute, both because they do not agree with the words of the text itself and also because all these signs were in the Catholic Church before their opinion holds Antichrist appeared.

1) We have from the text that there is going to be one mark, not many. For Scripture always speaks on an individual number both for a mark and for the name and number of the name of Antichrist. Therefore, the mark will be one. Likewise the proper name of Antichrist and his number are one. Hence, when our adversaries multiply so many marks they show that they do not know what it is that John is speaking about.

2) That mark will be common to all men in the reign of Antichrist and such is plain from the words themselves. He will make all the small and the great, rich and poor, free and slave receive his mark. But the oath of obedience and the priestly anointing agree with a very few individuals.

3) Scripture shows that the mark is of a type that could be borne without distinction on the right hand or on the forehead. He says: "He will make all receive the mark on the right hand or on their forehead." Moreover, this agrees with none of the arguments which our adversaries advance because the anointing of chrism cannot be received in the right hand and the profession of the Roman Faith can not be received in the hand nor on the forehead; it is made

---

[1] Serm. 61, *in Apocalypsim.*

[2] *Chronicus*, tab. 10.

by the mouth through profession and preserved in the heart by faith. The oath of fidelity is furnished by hand and mouth but in no way can it be borne on the forehead. Priestly anointing is received neither in the right hand properly, nor on the forehead, but above the crown and on the fingers of each hand. Then the last point, to be present at funeral masses and to kneel before statues and the Eucharist, are not obligations for the forehead or the hand, but rather of the whole body, and they are particularly felt in the knees.

4) The same Scripture says that in the reign of Antichrist, nobody will be allowed to buy or sell unless they show the mark, or the name, or the number of his name. But how many people buy and sell in the dominion of the Roman Pontiff who have not yet been anointed with chrism, nor furnished an oath of fidelity and are not priests? Are there not in Rome itself, where the Roman Pontiff has his seat, a great many Jews who publicly conduct business, buying and selling, yet none of them have these signs?

Let us come to the another account, whereby we prove all of these signs are older than Antichrist. Antichrist, in the opinion of our adversaries, did not come before the year 666. Yet Tertullian flourished around the year 200 and still called Chrism (Confirmation) to mind. He says: "The flesh is washed so that the soul will be cleansed, the flesh is anointed so that the soul consecrated."[3] Cyprian lived around the year 250, and he remembered the chrism: "It is necessary for anyone who has been baptized to be anointed, so that after he has received the chrism, that is, anointing, he may be able to be the anointed of God and have in himself the grace of Christ."[4] Augustine lived around the year 420, yet he says on John: "What is it that all believers know to be the sign of Christ, but the cross? What sign is it that is applied to the forehead of believers, or in the water, by which we are regenerated, or in the oil in which we are anointed with chrism, or the sacrifice whereby we are nourished, but the cross? Without it, none of these can be done rightly."[5]

For equal reason, *to adhere* to the Roman Church before the year 600 was a sign and mark of a truly Catholic man. Augustine writes about Cecilianus, who lived around the year 300: "He paid no attention to the multitude of his conspiring enemies since he saw himself through communicatory letters joined to the Roman Church, wherein the supremacy of the Apostolic See always flourishes, and with the rest of the world, whence the Gospel came into Africa."[6] Ambrose, who lived around 390, said: "It was inquired of the bishop whether he

---

[3] *De Resurrectione Carnis.*

[4] Lib. 1, epist. 12.

[5] *Tractatus in Joannem*, 118.

[6] Epistola 162.

thought with Catholic bishops, that is, whether he thought with the Roman Church."[7]

Victor of Utica, who lived around the year 490, writes of an Arian priest that wished to persuade the king not to kill a certain Catholic man using these words: "If you destroy him with a sword, the Romans will preach that he is a martyr."[8] In such a place, by the name of Romans he means African Catholics, for certainly the Arians would not speak on behalf of a Roman unless he meant the faith of the Roman Church, since they did not follow the Arian treachery.

The oath of obedience made to the Roman Pontiff is found in the time of St. Gregory,[9] and hence is before the year 606, since St. Gregory did not survive to that year.

On priestly anointing we have the testimony of Gregory Nazianzen, who lived around 380. In his *Apologetic* to his father when he became bishop of Sasimi he said: "When the anointing and the Spirit came over me, again I fell weeping and sad." There he calls to mind two anointings, one which he had received when created a priest, the other which he had to receive in the episcopal ordination. Speaking about Basil, who, after he was created a bishop refused a province, he said: "When he believed the Spirit and the business of the talents and the care of the flock was consigned to him, and he was anointed by the oil of priesthood and perfection, still he delayed to receive a prefecture from his own wisdom."

Now on the sacrifice for the dead, it will be enough to cite the testimony of Augustine, who says that it was a doctrine of the heretic Aërius that it was not fitting to offer sacrifice for the dead.[10]

Concerning the adoration of images, one testimony of Jerome, who lived in the year 400, will suffice for us. He said, in the life of Paul: "He worshiped, prostrate before the cross, just as if he discerned the Lord hanging there." Next, in the adoration of the Eucharist, St. Ambrose should be sufficient testimony. While explaining that verse: *adorate scabellum pedum eius,* he said: "Therefore, through a footstool the earth is understood; for the earth, the flesh of Christ, which today also we adore in the mysteries and which the Apostles adored in the Lord Jesus, as we said above."[11] Augustine says nearly the same thing in the same words in his explication of Psalm 98 (99).

So, since all these things which our adversaries suggest are marks of

---

[7] *De obitu Satyri.*

[8] *De Persecutione Wandalica,* lib. 1.

[9] Lib. 10, epist. 31.

[10] *De Haeres.,* cap. 53.

[11] *De Spiritu Sancto,* lib. 3, cap. 12.

Antichrist were in the use of the Catholic Church for many years before Antichrist would have been born in their reckoning, necessarily it must be that Antichrist either learned from the Church, and so to say this is to confuse Antichrist with Christ; or none of these pertain to the marks of Antichrist. Now follows what we contend. These suffice for that rash and absurd opinion of our adversaries, which they try to show with no witnesses and no proofs.

The second opinion is of some Catholics, who think the mark of Antichrist is a letter wherein the name of Antichrist will be written. So say Primasius, Bede and Rupert, who seem to have been deceived from something which they read: "Unless someone will have the mark of the name of the beast, or the number of his name." But John does not say this, rather he said: "Unless one will have the mark, or the name of the beast, or the number of his name." The Greek text agrees: εἰ μὴ ὁ ἔχων τὸ κάραγμα τὸ ὄνομα τοῦ θηρίου ἤ τὸν ἀριθμὸν τοῦ ὀνόματος αὐτοῦ.[12]

The third opinion is of the martyr Hippolytus, and of certain others. He thought that the mark of the beast was going to be that he would not use the sign of the cross, but rather would curse and abolish it. In this the Calvinists would be outstanding precursors of Antichrist. At any rate, I believe it is a positive character that will be devised by Antichrist, just as Christ had the sign of the cross made known to all. Yet no one will know what this character will be until Antichrist comes, just as we said on his name.

---

[12] Apocalypse 13:17. Translator's note: We have revised the Greek text Bellarmine made use of (where three printers errors were found) with the 1904 Nestle-Aland.

CHAPTER XII
On the Begetting of Antichrist

N the fifth, concerning the begetting of Antichrist, there are some things that are clearly erroneous asserted by some individuals, then some things that are probable, and others that have been investigated and are certain. Firstly, there were once many errors on Antichrist. The first error is that Antichrist was going to be born from a virgin by a work of the devil, exactly how Christ was born by a work of the Holy Spirit.

An author of a little work on the Antichrist relates this error, which is held under the name of Augustine in the end of volume IX (though it is probable that the work is of a rabbi, certainly it cannot be of Augustine). It is clearly erroneous, for to produce a man without the male seed is a work of God alone, who can supply all efficient causes, because he alone is of infinite power and contains every perfection of creatures in his essence. The devil, however, is a creature, certainly he can do wondrous works by applying active things to passive things in a short period; but he cannot supply the active power of a cause. For this reason St. Augustine says that to be born of a virgin was such a miracle in Christ, that greater things could not be expected from God.[1]

Still it would not be an error if someone would say that Antichrist was going to be born from the devil and a woman, the same way that certain people relate that men are born from liaisons with demons. Although the devil by himself cannot produce a man without the male seed, still he can exercise a carnal act with a man taking on the form of a woman, and take his seed; and then exercise a like act with a woman in the form of a man, and place the seed received from the man into the womb of the woman to beget a man in that manner. St. Augustine witnesses this,[2] and adds that experience has so proven it that it seemed to him that one would be impudent to deny it.

The second error was of the blessed martyr Hippolytus, who in his sermon on the end of the world, teaches that Antichrist is the devil himself, who will assume false flesh from a false virgin. For as the Word of God, which is truth itself, assumed true flesh from a true virgin, so Hippolytus thought it probable that the devil, who is the father of lies, was going to simulate that he had taken human flesh from a virgin. This opinion is refuted, both because in 2 Thessalonians 2 Antichrist is called a man, and also because the rest of the Fathers write in a common consensus that Antichrist is going to be a true man.

The third error is that Antichrist is going to be a true man, but at the same time also the devil, through the incarnation of the devil, just as Christ through

---

[1] Epist. 3 *ad Volusianum.*

[2] *De Civitate Dei*, lib. 15, cap. 23.

the Incarnation is true God and man. Several Fathers relate and refute this error.[3]

Origen believed this opinion is possible, inasmuch as he asserted that some angels were truly incarnate, which Jerome refutes in his preface to Malachi as well as in the first chapter of Haggai. And without a doubt, it is erroneous since a person cannot be created and thus sustain two finite natures in the way that the Word of God, who is infinite, can. There is no controversy on this amongst theologians, although some may teach that it altogether implies contradiction others teach it does not imply one. Nevertheless, all agree on the point that creatures, such as the devil, cannot do that by their power alone.

The fourth error is that Nero is going to rise from the dead and he is going to be the Antichrist, or certainly that he will still live and be preserved secretly in the vigor of youthful age and appear as he did in his own time. Sulpitius suggests this error;[4] but St. Martin writes that Nero himself will not be Antichrist, rather he is going to come with Antichrist and at length, must be destroyed by Antichrist.[5] Yet, because all these are said without any proof from reason, St. Augustine rightly calls this opinion a remarkable presumption.[6]

Apart from these errors there are two probable opinions of the holy Fathers on the begetting of Antichrist.

1) That Antichrist is going to be born from a woman by fornication, not from a legitimate marriage. St. John Damascene teaches this,[7] as well as certain others. Still, since it cannot be shown from the Scriptures it is not certain, although it is probable.

2) Antichrist will be born from the tribe of Dan, which many Fathers and Doctors assert.[8] They prove this from Genesis 49: "Let Dan be a snake on the path, let him be a horned snake on the path, etc." Likewise in Jeremiah 8: "From Dan we heard the growling of his horses, etc." Next, because in Apocalypse 7, where twelve thousand from every tribe of the sons of Israel is signified by the angel, the tribe of Dan is left out, which appears to be done in hatred of

---

[3] Jerome, *in Daniel.*, cap. 7; Bede, *in Apocal.*, cap. 13; Damascene, lib. 4, cap. 28.

[4] *Sacrae Historiae*, lib. 2.

[5] *Dialogus de virtutibus*, lib. 2.

[6] *De Civitate Dei*, lib. 20, cap. 19.

[7] Lib. 4, cap. 28.

[8] Irenaeus lib. 5; Hippolytus *in oratione de mundi consummatione.*; Ambrose, *de Benedictionibus Patriarcharum*, cap. 7; Augustine *in Iosue*, quaest. 22; Prosper of Aquitane *de promissionibus et praedictionibus Dei*, pars 4; Theodoret, *in Genesin.*, quest. 109; Gregory *Moralium*, lib. 31, cap. 18; Bede, Rupert, and Anselm, *in Apocal.*, cap. 7.

Antichrist.

This opinion is exceedingly probable on account of the authority of such Fathers; still it is not altogether certain, both because a great many of these Fathers do not say they know this but hint that it is probable, and because none of those passages of the Scripture clearly prove it. In the first place, in Genesis, Jacob seems literally to speak about Samson, when he says: "Let Dan be a serpent on the way, a horned snake on the path, and let him bite the hoofs of the horses so that the rider falls upon his back." For Samson was from the tribe of Dan, and was truly a serpent in the road for the Philistines. For he resists and plagues them everywhere. Jerome shows this in *Hebrew Questions*. It appears well enough that Jacob prayed well for his son when he said this, and hence did not predict evil but good.

Nevertheless, if this were to be accommodated to Antichrist allegorically, such as is brought in from the spiritual senses of Scripture, the argument could not be said to be more than probable. Moreover, Jeremiah 8 without a doubt does not speak on Antichrist, nor on the tribe of Dan, but Nebuchadnezzar, who was going to come to destroy Jerusalem through the region which was called Dan.[9] But why Dan, whose tribe was one of the greatest, is omitted in Apocalypse 7 is not sufficiently established.

Apart from these two probable opinions, there are two certain ones.

1) Antichrist will come particularly on account of the Jews, and will be received by them as if he were a Messiah;

2) He is going to be born from the nation and race of the Jews, be circumcised, and shall observe the Sabbath, at least for a time.

The first opinion is certain from the following. It is in John's Gospel where the Lord says to the Jews: "I have come in my Father's name, and you have not received me. If another will have come in my name, you will receive him." We proved that this citation ought to be understood to be about Antichrist in the second chapter above. Then, from the Apostle: "For the reason, since they do not receive the charity of truth that they may be saved, God will send to them the operation of error, that they would believe lies, etc."[10] Calvin and other heretics in commentaries on these words argue that these words are about us [Catholics], who, because we do not receive their Gospel, he permitted to be seduced by Antichrist. But we have all the interpreters on our side, who show it speaks about the Jews. See Ambrose, Chrysostom, Theodoret, Theophylactus, and Oecumenius.

Apart from them, Jerome says the following: "Antichrist will make all these

---

[9] Jerome, *in Hieremia.*

[10] 2 Thessal. 2:10-12.

things not with virtue, but from the concession of God on account of the Jews and because they refused to receive the charity of truth, the spirit of God through Christ, that having received the Savior they would be saved; God will send upon them not an operator, but the operation itself, that means the font of error, that they would believe lies, etc."[11] Even without so many commentaries of the Fathers the matter speaks for itself; the Apostle speaks about the Jews. For he says Antichrist must be sent to them who refuse to receive Christ. Moreover, who else is there that can be said to ought to have received Christ, but refused, more than the Jews? It also must be remarked, the Apostle did not say because they will not receive the truth but because they have not received it. Therefore, he speaks on those who refused to believe the preaching of Christ and the Apostles. It is certain in the times of the Apostles, the Gentiles eagerly received the Gospel, but the Jews refused to.

So apart from Jerome and other citations, all the other Fathers teach the same thing.[12] Even reason argues for it. For Antichrist, without a doubt, will join himself to those who are prepared to receive him; the Jews are of this sort, who await the Messiah as a temporal king and Antichrist will be such a king. For the Gentiles await no one. Moreover, Christians indeed wait upon Antichrist, but with fear and terror, not with joy and desire. Therefore, just as Christ first came to the Jews to whom he had been promised and by whom he had been awaited, and at length also joined the nations to himself, so also Antichrist will first come to the Jews, by whom he is awaited, and thereupon little by little subjugate all the nations to himself.

Now to the second opinion, that Antichrist is going to be a Jew and circumcised; this is certain and is deduced from the aforesaid. For the Jews have never received a non-Jewish man, or an uncircumcised one for a Messiah. Nay more, the Jews also await a Messiah from the family of David and the tribe of Judah; certainly Antichrist, although he could be from the tribe of Dan, will pretend that he is from the household of David. Next, all the Fathers very clearly teach that Antichrist will be a Jew, such as those twelve cited a little while ago, who say he is going to be from the tribe of Dan. Besides, Ambrose, *on 2 Thess. 2*, asserts that he will be circumcised; Jerome teaches in his commentary on Daniel 11 that he is going to be born from the Jewish people; St. Martin teaches that Antichrist is going to command that all be circumcised according to the

---

[11] Quaest. 11, ad Algasiam.

[12] Irenaeus, liber 5; Hippolytus *in oratione de consummatione mundi*; Theodoret in *Epitome divinorum decretorum*, capite de Antichristo; Suplpitius ex B. Martino, *libro 2, Dialogi*; Cyril *Catechesi* 15; Hillary, *in Matthaeum*, can. 25; Ambrose *in Lucam* lib 10, caput 21; Chrysostom, Augustine, and Cyril of Alexandria, in chapter 5 of John; Gregory *Moralium*, lib. 31; cap. 10; Damascene lib. 4, cap. 28.

law,[13] and St. Cyril asserts that he will be exceedingly zealous for the temple of Jerusalem to show himself to be from the progeny of David.[14] At length, even Gregory says that Antichrist is going to keep the Sabbath and all the other ceremonies of the Jews.[15]

From these we have the most evident proof that the Pope is not the Antichrist. For from the year 606, in which our adversaries say Antichrist came, it is certain that no Pope was a Jew, whether by race or religion or any other manner. It is also certain that the Pope to this point was never received by the Jews as a Messiah, but on the other hand is held as an enemy and a persecutor. For this reason they ask God in their daily prayers that God would give to the living Pope a good mind toward the Jews and that he might send a Messiah in their days who would liberate them from the power of the Pontiff, and a bishop such as the Supreme Pontiff especially is, which they call תנמון (tey-na-mon) but in Syriac means tail, and is opposed to head. For while we call a bishop the head of the people, they on the other hand call him a tail as an insult; the head is absent so that they might be prepared to receive a high priest as a head for their Messiah.

Therefore, R. Levi Gerson, in chapter 7 and 11 of Daniel, explains all those things which are said about Antichrist concerning the Roman Pontiff, whom he calls another Pharaoh and opposed to the coming Messiah. See the *orationes Mahasor*, fol. 26.

---

[13] Found in Sulpitius, *Dialog.*, lib. 2.

[14] *Catechesis* 15.

[15] Liber II, epist. 3.

CHAPTER XIII
On the Seat of Antichrist

E continue to the sixth. Our adversaries impudently affirm that the particular seat of Antichrist is Rome, or even founded upon the apostolic throne at Rome. For they say Antichrist is going to invade the See of Peter, and will carry off the summit to the highest place and thence tyrannically preside over and dominate the whole Church. They try to show that Rome is the royal city of Antichrist from Apocalypse 17, where John, speaking on the seat of Antichrist, says it will be a great city which will sit upon seven hills and which has rule over the kings of the earth.

Moreover, they try to show that Antichrist will have his seat at Rome, not in the palace of Nero but in the very Church of Christ, from what Paul says in 2 Thess. 2, that Antichrist is going to sit in the temple of God. For when he says absolutely, "in the temple of God," they understand the true temple of the true God. There is no such thing unless it is the Church of Christ, since the temples of the Gentiles are true temples, but of demons, not God. Moreover, the temple of the Jews was indeed for God but had already ceased to be a temple when the sacrifice and priesthood of the Jews ceased. For these three (the temple, the sacrifice and the priesthood) are so joined that you cannot have one without the other. Besides, that temple of the Jews was laid desolate and never in the future to be rebuilt, as Daniel says: "And even to the end of the world the desolation will continue;"[1] therefore, the Apostle does not speak about it.

The argument is confirmed from the Fathers. Jerome says: "In the temple of God he will sit, either in Jerusalem as some men think, or in the Church, as we reckon is more true."[2] Oecumenius: "He did not say the temple of Jerusalem, but the Church of Christ."

Theodore Bibliander adds the testimony of Gregory, who wrote in a letter to John of Constantinople: "The king of pride is near, and it is not unlawful to say that an army of priests is prepared for him." From such words he takes up a two-fold argument. One is thus; John of Constantinople is said to be a precursor of Antichrist, because he wished to be called universal bishop; so that will be Antichrist, who really will make himself a universal bishop, and will sit in the Church as the head of all. On the other hand, the army of Antichrist will be priests therefore, Antichrist will be a prince of priests. From this the heretics reckon that they have clearly shown that the Roman Pontiff is Antichrist seeing that he rules at Rome, he sits in the temple of God and he is called Universal

---

[1]   Daniel 9:26-27.

[2]   Quaest. 11 *ad Algasiam.*

bishop as well as Prince of Priests.

Just the same, the true opinion is that the seat of Antichrist will be Jerusalem, not Rome, and the temple of Solomon as well as the throne of David, not the temple of St. Peter or the Apostolic See. We can prove the fact by a two-fold argument: First, by refutation, then from the Scriptures and the Fathers.

First, I will establish the argument. Let us say that Antichrist will sit in the Church of Christ and he will be held as prince and head of the Church, and in that he will manage magistracy and offices, as Melanchthon, Calvin and other heretics teach.[3] Moreover, the Roman Pope is Antichrist, as these writers teach in the same places; therefore, the Roman Pope sits in the true Church of Christ, and is the prince and head of the Church. But there can only be one true Church of Christ, just as Christ is one, as even Calvin teaches;[4] therefore, the Lutherans, Calvinists and all others are foreign to the Church, which is under the Pope, that is outside of the true Church of Christ.

Calvin sees this argument and responds that the Church is not under the Pope as much as the ruins of the Church of Christ are seen there. He says as much in the *Institutes*: "Still, as in ancient times, there remained among the Jews certain special privileges of a Church, so in the present day we do not deny that the Papists have those vestiges of a Church which the Lord has allowed to remain among them amid the dissipation. ... He provided by his providence that there should be other remains also to prevent the Church from utterly perishing. Yet, when they pull down buildings the foundations and ruins are often permitted to remain; so he did not suffer Antichrist either to subvert his Church from its foundation, or to level it to the ground, but was pleased that amid the devastation the edifice should remain, though half in ruins... Hence, we scarcely deny that churches remain under his tyranny."[5]

But, his solution provides two arguments for us. 1) If only the ruins of the Church of Christ remain, therefore, the Church of Christ is ruined; hence Truth lied when it said: "And the gates of hell will not prevail against it."[6] 2) The Church is ruined as well as its ruins and foundation, so that the Papists also hold semi-ruined buildings; therefore, the Lutherans and the Calvinists have no Church. For they do not have the whole Church of Christ, since it is now a ruin, and still the ruins remain; but they do not even have the edifice, for that is with the Papists under Antichrist. Therefore, what is it that they have? By chance a

---

[3] Melancthon, *in apologia confes. Augustanae*, art. 6; Calvin, *Instit.*, lib. 4, cap. 2 § 12, and cap. 7 § 25; Illyricus, *Cent.* 1, lib. 2, cap. 4, col. 435.

[4] *Instit.*, lib. 4, cap. 1, § 2.

[5] Lib. 4, cap. 2, § 11-12.

[6] Matthew 16:18.

new building? But that which is new is not of Christ. But who, unless he were blind, does not see that he is safer in the true Church of Christ (even if an edifice), than to remain in nothing?

Now I come to the Scriptures whereby it is proved that the seat of the Antichrist is going to be in Jerusalem, not Rome. The first is in chapter XI of the Apocalypse, where John says that Enoch and Elijah are going to fight with Antichrist in Jerusalem, and must be killed there by the same Antichrist: "And they will throw their bodies in the streets of the great city, which is spiritually called Sodom, and Egypt, where even their Lord was crucified." Arethas in this citation says: "Their bodies he will cast out unburied in the streets of Jerusalem, for in it he will reign as King of the Jews." Likewise, all other interpreters show, and this can rightly be said to be Jerusalem, and it cannot be denied. For what City is it in which the Lord was crucified but Jerusalem?

This is why Chytraeus, who would rather this city were Rome, passes over the words "Where even their Lord was crucified," as if they did not pertain to the matter, or as though he had not read them. Nor is it opposed to what Jerome says, when he tries to show that Jerusalem cannot be called Sodom, since everywhere in Scripture it is called the holy city. For in that epistle he persuades Marcellus that, after leaving Rome behind, he should come into Palestine and there he can heap up all those places in praise of Jerusalem and in censure of Rome, and try to excuse Jerusalem in every manner. Nor does he do it in his own name, but in the name of Paula and Eustochius, to whom he thought forgiveness must be given, if they were to explain something a little differently than the matter stood. That the earthly Jerusalem can be called Sodom on account of the lust and the crimes of the Jews is also clear from Isaiah, who when he prefaced a title to the first chapter: "The Vision of Isaiah, which he saw over Judah and Jerusalem," he next added: "Hear the word of the Lord, O princes of Sodom! Perceive with your ears the law of God, O my people Gomorrah!"

Further, it is not a valid argument that Jerusalem is called holy, therefore, it cannot be called Sodom. For just as in the same epistle Jerome says that Rome is called Babylon by John, and the purple whore on account of the heathen emperors, and still, the same is holy on account of the Church of Christ, and the tombs of Peter and Paul; so also Jerusalem is the holy city, on account of the prophets and apostles who preached there, on account of the cross of Christ and his tomb and like things yet still it is Sodom and Egypt on account of the crimes of infidelity of the Jews and their blindness.

The Second place is Apocalypse 17, where John says there will be ten kings who divide the Roman Empire, and from such rulers Antichrist will come, having hatred for the purple whore, that is Rome, and are going to lay waste to her and even burn her with fire. How, therefore, will it be the seat of Antichrist, if he should overturn and burn it at that time?

Add that, as we showed above, Antichrist will be Jewish, and the Messiah of the Jews, and a king; therefore, without a doubt he will constitute his seat in Jerusalem, and he will hasten to restore the temple of Solomon. For the Jews dream of nothing other than Jerusalem and the temple, nor do they seem ever to be going to receive anyone for a Messiah who would not sit in Jerusalem and restore the temple in some way. Lactantius says for this reason, that in the time of Antichrist the supreme kingdom is going to be in Asia and the West will serve, the East will rule.[7] He also determines the part of Asia in which this kingdom will be and says it will be Syria, that is, Judaea, which is part of Syria, and which is always called Syria by the Latins.[8] In like manner, Jerome and Theodoret, commenting on chapter XI of Daniel, gather from Daniel himself that Antichrist is going to set up his tents in the region of Jerusalem, and at length it will end on mount Olivet. Further, Irenaeus clearly said that Antichrist was going to rule in Jerusalem.[9]

The third place is in the words of Paul: "So that he would sit in the temple of God."[10] Although different expositions are given by the Fathers, some also understand through the temple of God the minds of the faithful, in which Antichrist is said to sit after he will have seduced them, as Anselm expresses. Some understand through the temple Antichrist himself, with his whole people; Antichrist would want himself and his own to seem the true spiritual temple of God, that is, the true Church, as Augustine explains.[11] There, he deduces this exposition from the manner of speaking which Paul uses, who did not say in Greek ἐν τῷ ναῷ, (in the temple) but εἰς τὸν ναὸν, (into the temple), as if to say Antichrist will sit within the temple of God, that is, just as if he, with his own, were the temple of God. Although this annotation of Augustine is not necessary, for even if in Latin it is not correct when it says to sit within the temple, rather than in the temple, still in Greek it is not said incorrectly: καθέζουμαι εἰς τὴν ἐκκλησίαν, or εἰς τὸν ναὸν, as it is commonly read.

Some also understand the churches of Christians, which Antichrist will command to serve him, as Chrysostom interprets it. Still the exposition is the more common, probable and literal of those who teach that for the temple of God is understood the temple of Solomon, in whichever renewed temple that Antichrist will sit in. Especially in the New Testament, the churches of

---

[7] Lib. 7, cap. 15.

[8] Ibid, cap. 17.

[9] Lib. 5.

[10] 2 Thessalonians 2:4.

[11] *De Civitate Dei*, lib. 20, cap. 19.

Christians are never understood for Temple of God; rather that is always understood as the temple in Jerusalem. What is more, the Latin and Greek Fathers for so many centuries never called the churches of Christians temples, which in Greek are called ναὸς, as St. Paul says in this passage; rather they call them εὐχτήρια, that is oratories, as churches, or houses of prayer, or basilicas, or martyria.

Certainly neither Justin Martyr, nor Irenaeus, nor Tertullian, nor Cyprian use the noun "temple" when they treat on the Churches of Christians, and Jerome says that Julian the Apostate ordered that the basilicas of the saints either be destroyed or turned into temples.[12]

Further, the reason why the Apostles do not call the churches of Christians temples is two-fold. 1) Because then they did not have any temples, but only certain places in private houses that they set aside for prayer, a sermon and the holy celebration of the Mass. 2) Because while the memory of the Jewish temple still flourished, the Apostles were to introduce something similar to distinguish the church from the synagogue, so they avoided the use of the word "temple", just as on account of the same reckoning the Apostles in Scripture never call Christian priests "priests" [*sacerdotes*], but only bishops and elders. But after Jerusalem was destroyed and the temple burned, and the memory of the old temple and its priesthood abolished, everywhere the holy Doctors began to use the word "temple" and "priesthood".

Therefore, since the Apostle, writing that Antichrist was going to sit in the temple of God, said something which he wished to be understood by those to whom he wrote, and then they did not understand in the word "temple" anything else but the temple of Jerusalem, which appears for certain to be what the Apostle spoke about. But it is also confirmed from the common exposition of the Fathers.

Irenaeus says: "When Antichrist will have sat in the temple of Jerusalem, then the Lord will come."[13] Hippolytus the martyr (*loc. cit.*), says: "he will build a temple in Jerusalem." St. Martin (*loc. cit.*) teaches the same thing. Cyril of Jerusalem says: "What kind of temple does the Apostle speak of? In the temple that is the relic of the Jews. God forbid that it should happen in this, in which we are."[14] Hilary says on Matthew 25, "Antichrist, being received by the Jews, will stand in the place of sanctification." It is certain that he is talking about the temple of the Jews, for he calls it the place of sanctification, which is what Christ calls it in Matthew 24 when he said: "When you will have seen the

---

[12] Ep. *Ad Riparium.*

[13] Lib. 5.

[14] *Catechesi* 15.

abomination standing in the holy place." Ambrose says Antichrist, according to history, is going to sit in that temple in which the Romans threw in the head of a pig, in the time of the Emperor Titus; according to the mystical sense, he is going to sit in the interior temple of the Jews, that is, in their faithless minds.[15]

Sedulus explains, in this place of the Apostle, that in the temple of God, "He will try to restore the temple of Jerusalem, etc." John Damascene says: "In the temple, not ours, but the old Jewish temple."[16] Chrysostom, Theodoret, and Theophylactus (who say Antichrist is going to sit in the churches of Christians), also say he is going to sit in the temple of Solomon. Chrysostom says on this verse: "He will command himself to be worshiped as a God, and to be placed in the temple, not only in Jerusalem, but even in the churches." Theophylactus and Theodoret says the same thing; even Augustine and Jerome[17] do not deny Antichrist is going to sit in the temple of Solomon.

There is only Oecumenius, who denies that Antichrist is going to sit in the temple of the Jews, but he is the more recent of all of them, and by no means do we put him before the other Fathers. By chance his text might have been corrupted and lacked only one sentence, for it is strange that he would suddenly recede from Chrysostom, Theodoret and Theophylactus whom he otherwise always follows.

Now we respond to the arguments of our adversaries given above. To the first I respond in three ways. 1) It can be said with Augustine,[18] Aretha, Haymon, Bede and Rupert on chapter 17 of the Apocalypse, that for the whore which sits upon seven hills and has a kingdom over the kings of the earth, that Rome is not understood, but the universal city of the devil, which in scripture is always called Babylon and is opposed to the city of God, that is, the Church, which is called Jerusalem. Through the seven hills is understood the universality of the proud, and especially of the kings of the earth.

Secondly, it can be said, and in my judgment better, that for the whore is understood Rome, as Tertullian[19] and Jerome[20] explain it; but Rome ruling the heathen, worshiping idols and persecuting Christians, not Christian Rome, for the same authors explain it in the same way.

One must truly marvel at the impudence of the heretics, who, as they try and show the Roman Church to be the purple whore, use the testimony of

---

[15] In cap. 21 Lucae.

[16] lib. 4, cap. 28.

[17] Augustine, *De Civitate Dei*, lib. 20, cap. 19; Jerome, Quaest. 11 ad Algasiam.

[18] In Ps. 26.

[19] Lib. *Contra Judaeos; contra Marcionem*, lib. 3.

[20] Loc. Cit.

Tertullian and Jerome. For in that time when, heathen Rome was contrary to Christian Rome, which, I ask, do those Fathers call the purple whore? If heathen Rome, why therefore do the heretics abuse the testimony? If Christian Rome, therefore, already then the Roman Church had already sunk and then Antichrist already reigned, which not even they concede. Besides, if Christian Rome was then Babylon, why does Tertullian say: "O happy church, into which the Apostles poured the whole doctrine with their own blood."[21] And why does Jerome, speaking about Rome, say: "I shall say to you, O great Rome you have blotted out the blasphemy written on your forehead by the confession of Christ"? Next, the same is clear from John himself, who speaks about that Rome, which held empire over the kings of the earth and that was drunk in the blood of the saints and from the blood of the martyrs of Jesus. That certainly did not take place except in that Rome which cut down the martyrs under the rule of Nero and Domitian.

3) I say, although that woman could be Christian Rome, as the heretics would have it, still their argument has no force. As we showed above, Antichrist will have hatred towards Rome, in no matter what way he takes it up, and he will fight with it and lay it desolate, and burn it. From which it manifestly follows that Rome is not the seat of the Antichrist.

Now to the second argument: we have already said Paul treats on the temple of Solomon in that passage. Hence to the reasoning which we made, I respond: After the Jewish sacrifice and priesthood ceased that temple ceased to be a Jewish temple; but it did not immediately cease to be the temple of God. The same temple could have been the temple of Christians and really was so long as it remained. For the Apostles preached and gave praise there after the ascension of Christ and the arrival of the Holy Spirit, as is clear from the words of Luke: "They were always in the temple praising and blessing the Lord." We read the same in Acts 3: "Peter and John went up into the temple for the prayer at the ninth hour." And in Acts 5, the angel says to the Apostles: "Speak in the temple all the words of this life to the people."

To the argument from Daniel I respond: either Daniel would have it that the temple is not going to be rebuilt, except at the end of the world (which is true since Antichrist will be present at the end of the world); or it is going to remain desolate in eternity because although it will be rebuilt, still it will never be a temple not profaned after the destruction carried out by Titus. When it will be raised up by Antichrist, then the abomination of desolation will especially remain in it, i.e. either Antichrist himself or his image, or the temple will never be perfectly rebuilt, but will still be in the beginnings of rebuilding, and

---

[21] *Praescriptionibus contra haereticos.*

Antichrist is going to sit in that temple at its beginning stages.

We have already responded to the passages of the Fathers that either assert, or at least do not deny, that Antichrist is going to sit in the temple of Solomon. Many add the fact that Antichrist is also going to sit in the churches of Christians; that is true and not opposed to our position. The Fathers would not have it that Antichrist is going to sit in the Church as a bishop, like the heretics dream up, rather he is going to sit as a god. Antichrist will command all temples of the world to be converted to his worship, and he will make his own person worshiped. "He will command" (says Chrysostom on this citation), "himself to be worshiped as a God, and to be venerated and placed in the temple, not only in Jerusalem, but even in the churches." The rest speak in the same way.

Now to the arguments taken up from the words of St. Gregory the Great, I respond: from his words we deduce the contrary to those which the heretics have mustered. They argue thus: The bishop of Constantinople was a precursor of Antichrist, because he made himself universal bishop; therefore, Antichrist will be some universal bishop, who will usurp all things to himself. But the opposite is gathered, since a precursor ought not be the same with the one he foreshadows, but by far lesser, even if in some matter he is similar to him just as we see in John the Baptist and Christ. So if he is a precursor of Antichrist, who makes himself universal bishop, the true Antichrist himself will not make himself this, but something greater; without a doubt he will extol himself over everything that is called God. Or if the true Antichrist will only make himself a universal bishop, then John of Constantinople, who did this, was not a precursor of Antichrist, but the true Antichrist, which still Gregory never says, nor our adversaries. So the sense of the words of Gregory is that because Antichrist will be very proud, and the head of all the proud, so also he will suffer no equals; whoever usurps something not due to him and wishes to go beyond and be over others, he is a precursor to him. Such were the bishops of Constantinople, who, although in the beginning were only an archbishop, first usurped the title of patriarch, and then the title of universal.

With equal reasoning, when Gregory says: "an army of priests is prepared for him," he did not mean priests as in "priests pertain to the army of Antichrist", since he will gather his own in that army:; but priests as in the proud prepare an army for Antichrist, since he speaks on the same John and priests like him that elevated themselves unjustly above the rest. It does not follow that Antichrist will be a prince of priests, but prince of the proud.

From this chapter we have an outstanding argument that the Pope is not Antichrist, seeing that his seat is not in Jerusalem, nor in the temple of Solomon; nay more, it is believable that from the year 600 to the present (1589) no Roman Pontiff has been to Jerusalem.

CHAPTER XIV
On the Doctrine of Antichrist

N the doctrine of Antichrist there is a great deal of controversy between us and the heretics. It is certain from the Scriptures as well as from the testimony of our adversaries that there are going to be four points of doctrine of Antichrist.

1) He will deny that Jesus is the Christ and hence he will oppose all the things our Savior established, such as Baptism, Confirmation, etc. He will teach that circumcision and the Sabbath have not yet ceased, as well as other ceremonies of the old law. "Who is a liar, but he who denies that Jesus is the Christ? And this is Antichrist, who denies the Father and the Son, etc."[1]

2) After he will have persuaded the world that our Savior is not the true Christ, then he will assert that he is the true Christ promised in the law and Prophets. "If anyone will come in my name, you will receive him,"[2] that is as the Messiah.

3) He will declare that he is God and will demand to be worshiped as a god. "So that he shall sit in the temple, showing himself just as if he were God."[3]

4) He will not only say that he is God, but even that he alone is God and will oppress all other gods, i.e., both the true God and false gods, and all idols. "Who extols himself over everything which is called God, or that is worshiped."[4] And in Daniel: "He will not think God is his father, nor will he worship anything of the gods, because he will rise against them all."[5]

All of these are true in some manner and pertain to Antichrist; even our adversaries agree with us on this point. But the question is on the understanding of these four points. For Catholics understand simply according to the words of Scripture that Antichrist is going to deny the true Christ; he is going to make himself Christ; he is going to preach that he is God; and he will curse all other Gods and idols. From these four arguments we endeavor to show the Pontiff is not Antichrist. It is certain the Pope does not deny Jesus is Christ, nor has he introduced circumcision, or the Sabbath in place of Baptism, and the day of the Lord. In like manner, it is certain the Pontiff has not made himself Christ or God, and it is especially certain, that not only has he not made himself God (since he clearly worships Christ and the Trinity), but our adversaries maintain

---

[1] 1 John 2:22.

[2] John 5:43.

[3] 2 Thessalonians 2:4.

[4] Ibid.

[5] Daniel 11:37.

that he also worships idols and images and dead saints.

Nevertheless, our adversaries by far read it otherwise. They say in the first place that Antichrist is not openly going to deny Jesus is the Christ by word, but by work, because under the appearance of Christianity and the Church he will corrupt the doctrine on the Sacraments, on justification, etc. Calvin says: "We gather the tyranny of Antichrist is such that he abolishes not the name of Christ or the Church, but rather uses the name of Christ as a pretext, and lurks under the name of Church as under a mask."[6] The Centuriators of Magdeburg say: "Such is certain, that while professing Christ in doctrine he will still deny his office and merit... John shows that Antichrist is going to deny that Christ came in the flesh, this is, that Christ redeemed us wholly in his flesh and saved us; but that good works will confer salvation upon us."[7] Next, they say Antichrist is not going to make himself Christ or God by his own word, but by work, because he will take up the place of Christ and of God, making himself head of all the faithful in the Church, which is proper to Christ alone. The Centuriators remark: "He will show himself for God, that he might be vicar of Christ and head of the Church, and can set up and tear away the articles of faith."

Next, they say Antichrist is not going to reject idols; nay more, he shall openly adore them and they try to show from Daniel; after he had said Antichrist was going to rise against all gods, he adds: "He will venerate the god Moazim in his place, and a god whom their fathers did not know, he will worship with gold and silver and precious stones, etc."[8] For Moazim, however, the heretics understand the Mass, images, relics and like things of ornate temples. So Illyricus argues in his book *Contra Primatum*.

Moreover, when the Apostle says that Antichrist is going to elevate himself above everything which is called God or which is worshiped, they try to prove this was written about the Roman Pontiff, who makes himself vicar of Christ and usurps greater authority than Christ had. Illyricus tries to show it in his *Catalogue of Witnesses* (for I have not seen how the rest try to show it), page 3. Without a doubt, Christ declared nothing other than to show himself to be God; nay more, to effect that he and his cult is above God, which is to come in the name of Christ; from which it follows that the Pope, who offers himself for Christ's vicar, is himself the truest Antichrist. Likewise, Christ subjected himself to Scripture, he did and suffered such things that he would fulfill the Scripture, while the Pope said that he can dispense against the Apostle and the Evangelist, to make straight crooked and vice versa. This is the chief point especially of the

---

[6] *Instit.*, lib. 4, cap. 7, § 25.

[7] *Cent.* 1, lib. 2, cap. 4, col. 435.

[8] Daniel 11:38.

side of the doctrine of our adversaries on Antichrist which rests upon the Scripture alone through new glosses incorrectly explicated. It is a clear indication of the matter that they cannot even cite one interpreter or Doctor for their side.

Then let us begin from the first argument that Antichrist is going to openly deny Jesus is the Christ by public profession, and inasmuch as all his Sacraments will have been discovered he will trample them under foot. It is proved: 1) from the aforesaid, chapter 5 &6. For if Antichrist by nation and religion will be Jewish, and received by the Jews as a Messiah, as we have shown, certainly he will not preach our Christ, but will publicly oppose him. Otherwise, the Jews would receive our Christ through Antichrist, which is completely absurd. Besides, since there cannot be two Christs, how will Antichrist be able to thrust himself on the Jews as the Christ unless first he had taught that our Christ, who preceded him, was not really the true Christ?

2) It is proved from 1 John 2:22, "Who is a liar but he who would deny Jesus is the Christ? This is Antichrist." For all heretics who deny Jesus is the Christ are called Antichrists in some manner so, the true Antichrist himself will simply deny Jesus is the Christ in every way. It is confirmed because the devil is said to work the mystery of iniquity through heretics, because they deny Christ secretly, but the arrival of Antichrist is called revelation, because he will openly deny Christ.

It is also proved by the Fathers. Hilary says the devil tried to persuade men through the Arians that Christ was not the natural son of God, but adopted; yet through Antichrist he is going to try to persuade men that he was not even adopted, so as to utterly extinguish the name of the true Christ.[9] Hippolytus the martyr says that the character of Antichrist will be that men are compelled to say: "I deny Baptism; I deny the sign of the Cross," and similar things. Augustine asks whether men are going to be baptized at all while Antichrist rages. At length, he answers: "Certainly they will be strong, both parents to baptize their children, and these who shall then first believe, that they shall conquer that strong one, even though he has been unbound."[10] Here St. Augustine presupposes that Antichrist is not going to permit them to be baptized, and still some pious parents would rather suffer than that their sons should be unbaptized.

Jerome says in his commentary on Daniel chapter XI: "Antichrist will rise from a modest nation; that is, from the people of the Jews, and he will be so lowly and despised that he will not be given royal honor, but he shall obtain rule

---

[9]   *De Trinitate*, lib. 6.

[10]   *De Civitate Dei*, lib. 20, cap. 8.

both through treachery and deceit. He will do this because he will feign himself the leader of the covenant, that is the law, and the covenant of God." There, Jerome teaches that Antichrist is going to acquire rule over the Jews, because he will show himself zealous for the Judaic laws. Sedulius, commenting on 2 Thessalonians 2:6, says that Antichrist is going to restore all Jewish ceremonies so as to abolish the gospel of Christ. Gregory says: "Because Antichrist will compel the people to judaize so that he might restore the rite of the exterior law, he will want the Sabbath to be kept to place the faithlessness of the Jews in himself."

Then, in the time of Antichrist, all public offices and divine sacrifices will cease on account of the vehemence of the persecution, as we showed above in chapter III. It is evident from this that Antichrist is not going to corrupt the doctrine of Christ under the name of a Christian, as the heretics would have it. Rather, he will openly assault the name of Christ and the Sacraments while introducing Jewish ceremonies. Since the Pope does not do that, it is evident that he is not Antichrist.

Moreover, Antichrist will say openly that he is the Christ by name, not his minister, or vicar, as is clear especially from the very words of the Lord: "If another will come in my name, you will receive him."[11] There, the Lord seems to add on purpose "*in his own name,*" foreseeing that the Lutherans and Calvinists were going to say that Antichrist was not coming in his name, but in the name of our Christ as if he were his vicar.

Besides, the Fathers everywhere teach this. Irenaeus said: "He will try to show that he is Christ." Ambrose says: "He will argue from the Scriptures that he is Christ."[12] Theodoret says: "He will declare that he is Christ."[13] St. Cyril of Jerusalem said: "He will induce a certain man to falsely call himself the Christ, and through this title of Christ he will deceive the Jews who await him."[14] All the Fathers, as we showed above, say Antichrist will be received briefly as a Messiah by the Jews; thus he will openly and by name make himself the Messiah, that is, the Christ. Hence the Roman Pontiff, who does not do this, as is known, is not Antichrist. For this very reason that he calls himself the vicar of Christ, he asserts that he is not Christ, but his minister.

The fact that Antichrist will openly declare himself to be God and desire to be worshiped as God, not only by usurping some authority of God, but by the name of God itself, is proved from the express words of the Apostle in 2

---

[11] John 5:43.

[12] *In Caput* 21 *Lucae.*

[13] In 2 Thess. 2.

[14] *Catechesi,* 15.

Thessalonians 2: "So that he will sit in the temple of God, revealing himself as though he were God." Paul not only says that Antichrist is going to sit in the temple (for even we sit in temples yet still we are not Antichrists), but he even explains the manner in which he will sit, that he will sit as a god, the only one to whom the temple is properly raised. In Greek this is much more clear. For he does not say: ὡς θεὸς, as a god, but ὅτι ἐστὶν θεὸς; that is, revealing that he is God. All the Fathers so understand that verse.

Irenaeus says: "Proving to be an apostate and a robber, he will wish to be worshiped as if he were God." Chrysostom said on that verse: "He will command that he be worshiped for God, and be placed in the temple." He says elsewhere on this same verse: "He will confess himself as God of all."[15] Ambrose, commenting on 2 Thessalonians 2, said: "He will assert that he is God himself, not the Son of God." They all explain the verse similarly. From that we understand that the Roman Pontiff, who does not claim to be God, but the servant of God, is not Antichrist.

Furthermore, Antichrist is not going to permit any god, whether true, false or an idol, and this is proved from the very words of Paul in the same passage: "Who is extolled above everything which is called God, or that is worshiped." Here, we must remark that for "that which is worshiped," the Greek is σέβασμα which the Centuriators think means worship, that is, *the act of worshiping*, not *that which is worshiped*. From there, they try to show that the Apostle would have it that Antichrist is not going to adore idols, but is going to distort the worship of the true God by mutilating the Sacraments or by adding various ceremonies. Yet, certainly σέβασμα properly means not the act but the object, that is what is worshiped, such as an altar, shrines, idols, etc. Worship is σέβας, or θεοσέβεια, not σέβασμα. This is why the Paul himself says in Acts 17: "Διερχόμενος γὰρ καὶ ἀναθεωρῶν τὰ σεβάσματα ὑμῶν εὑρον καὶ βωμὸν, etc." He says "Disregarding and considering your idols, I discover the altar, etc." Here Paul clearly means through σεβάσματα the very things that are worshiped, such as the shrines, altars and idols. We also read in Wisdom: Κρεῖττον γὰρ ἐστιν τῶν σεβάσματων αὐτοῦ ων αὐτὸς μὲν ἔζησεν ἐκεῖνα δὲ οὐδέποτε. That is: "Man is better than the idols (σεβάσματων) which he made. For he lives for a time, but they do not."[16] I do not know from what source someone would so dare to twist things to deny that σεβασμάτων means idols themselves, or simulacra, which men make with their hands: things that seem to have life when they do not live.

Therefore, all Greek texts (even that of Erasmus, whom all the heretics celebrate, both in his version and in annotations), teach that σέβασμα ought to

---

[15] *Homil.* 40.

[16] Wisdom 15:17.

be rendered as a god. Next, the words of Daniel are rather clear: "He will not worship any of the gods, but will rise against them all." Jerome, writing on that verse, says this cannot be understood to mean Antiochus, as Porphyrius thought, because it is certain Antiochus worshiped the Greek gods; but it can be understood on Antichrist who will worship no god.

At last we come to the consensus of the Fathers. Irenaeus said: "Indeed he will put away the idols and will lift himself up as the one idol."[17] Hippolytus from the same sermon on the end of the world says: "Antichrist will not permit idolatry." Cyril of Jerusalem says: "Antichrist will hate idols."[18] St. John Chrysostom says on this place in Daniel: "He is extolled above everything which is called God, or divinity. For he will not induce to idolatry." Theophylactus, Oecumenius, and Theodoret all teach the same thing, and the last beautifully notes that the devil wondrously fools and is going to fool the sons of perdition. For of old he persuaded that there were many gods and that various idols must be worshiped, and in that way he took a great profit. In the time of Antichrist, however, because he will see that through the doctrine of Christ idols and the multitude of false gods have been expunged through nearly the whole world, he also will accuse idols and their multitude and in that way will still deceive men. In this it seems the Pope, who according to Catholics acknowledges God the Father and the Son and the Holy Spirit, and according to the heretics worships many idols, in no way can be called the Antichrist.

But they say Daniel chapter XI affirms that the God Moazim must be worshiped with gold, silver and precious stones.

The first response is that though the god Moazim, which is interpreted as strength (that is, very strong), Antichrist himself can be understood. Accordingly, that "He will be venerated," in Hebrew is not ישתחוה (yah-shea-ti-ka-veh), he will worship, but יכבד (ya-ka-bed), he will glorify. In the same way, in Psalm 90 (91) God says: "I will raise him and glorify him." In Hebrew that is אכבדהו (eh-ka-bey-day-hu), and certainly God is not going to glorify men by subjecting them to themselves but by exalting them. Therefore, Antichrist will glorify himself when he will be worshiped by all. For this reason the Septuagint renders this δοξάσει, and Theodoret expresses it in this way: "For this 'Moazim' means a strong and powerful god, and he will call himself this. For he placed it in his own place for himself. He will raise temples to himself, and adorn them with gold, silver, precious stones."

The second response, which I prefer, is that Antichrist is going to be a magician and by the custom of other magicians he will worship the devil

---

[17] Loc. Cit.

[18] *Catech.*, 15.

secretly, by whose work he will do wonders. He will call this one whom he is going to adore Moazim. Hence, for Moazim we do not think the name of a god, but of a certain strong and secret place in which the special treasures of Antichrist will be and where he will worship the devil himself. For it follows from Daniel that he will also see to it that he fortifies Moazim with a strong god whom he knows. And truly מעוז (ma-koz) means both a strong place and a citadel, as Nicholas Lyranus explains it. Moreover, it must necessarily be said that Antichrist is himself the god Moazim, or if he is someone else, Antichrist must worship him only in a very secret place, secret from all others. The very words of Daniel compel us that otherwise they would oppose themselves; if he will worship no god, how will he openly worship an idol?

Now, the two arguments of Illyricus are very weak. In the first argument he errs three times. First, he asserts that the words of Paul were explained by Christ, when it ought to be the other way around. Secondly, he errs in saying say in Matthew 24 that to come in the name of Christ means the same thing as to be the Vicar of Christ. For the very explanation of Christ is opposed to this argument of Illyricus. When the Lord says: "Many will come in my name," soon he adds: "saying, I am Christ." There, to come in the name of Christ is to usurp the name of Christ to one's own person. Once, Simon Magus did this very thing, as Irenaeus witnessed,[19] and in our times David Georgius. At length, Antichrist will do this very thing. But the Pope, because he calls himself the Vicar of Christ, does not make himself Christ.

Thirdly, Illyricus errs because he makes Christ an inept interpreter of Paul. For he does not rightly explain what Paul said: "Extol himself over every thing that is God" for the verse: "many will come in my name," that is, as he sees it, make themselves my vicar. The vicar of God is not over everything that is God, but below it, just as the vicar of a king is below everything of the king. It cannot be thought or pretended that one who professes himself to be the vicar of some king will boast to be above all kings. From that we see the blindness and impudence of our adversaries who babble this nonsense which they would abhor in its common meaning.

Now, I respond to the argument of Illyricus, where he argued that the Pope usurped a greater authority than even Christ had. The proposition and assumption of this argument involves two lies, and besides the consequence avails to nothing. 1) It is false that Christ subjected himself to the Scriptures since it should be certain that he is the author of the Scriptures, and hence above them. Moreover, when we read Christ did what he did so as to fulfill the Scriptures, the *that* is not a cause but means the event, as Chrysostom and

---

[19] Lib. 1, cap. 20.

Augustine teach in chapter 12 of John. Christ did not die because Isaiah wrote this, but Isaiah wrote this because it was going to happen.

Next, it is also false that the Pope ever said by word or deed that he can dispense against the Evangelists or Apostles. For even if he can dispense on some precept placed by the Apostles, still this is not against the Apostle but according to him, who without a doubt knew the Apostolic power whereby he, being put in charge of something, stood in the Church for a time; and that there were going to be successors, that they could moderate or change the same things so long as it would be expedient for the Church. But no Catholic ever said a Pontiff can dispense in any way from the Gospel, i.e., the divine precepts.

Then the consequent is bad. In the major proposition Illyricus speaks on the subjection of Christ to the Scriptures, not in regard to precept, but to prophecies, while Illyricus is not ignorant that Christ abolished the Sabbath and abrogated the ceremonial law. Yet in the minor he speaks about precepts, and so the argument has four ends, and thence nothing can be concluded.

This will be sufficient in this place on the doctrine of Antichrist.

CHAPTER XV
On the Miracles of Antichrist

HOLY SCRIPTURE contains three things about the miracles of Antichrist. 1) He is going to do many miracles. 2) These will be of some quality. 3) Three examples are posited. The Apostle teaches in 2 Thessalonians 2 that Antichrist is going to do miracles, saying: "His arrival will be accompanied by signs and wonders according to the operation of Satan." The Lord says in the Gospel of Matthew: "They will give signs and great wonders, so that, if it is possible, even the elect will be led into error." He said, "They will give," not "he will give." This is because not only Antichrist, but his ministers, will perform signs, to the extent that St. Gregory said even the torturers of the holy martyrs are going to perform signs and wonders at that time.[1] Next, in Apocalypse 13, "And he will perform great signs in the sight of men." Paul explains what type they will be in Thessalonians, saying in one word, they will be lies: "In all power, signs and lying portents."

Hence the signs will be lies by an account of all the causes, final, efficient, material and formal. For the end of those miracles will be to show Antichrist is God and the Messiah, which will be the most pernicious lie. Chrysostom teaches in this place, that these lies are called miracles because they will induce men to lie. And Ambrose in this place teaches that the purpose of the miracles of Antichrist are going to be that he will try to show himself to be God, just as our Christ proved his divinity with true miracles.

Next, the signs are called lies in regard to their efficient cause; for the principal efficient cause will be the father of lies, that is the devil. For the Apostle speaks thus: "His arrival according to the operation of Satan." And all the Fathers assert Antichrist is going to be an outstanding magician. Moreover, the devil is going to dwell in him in his very conception, or at least from infancy, and through him perpetrate signs.

St. Cyril of Jerusalem also teaches that Antichrist is going to be a magician, and instructed in sorcery, incantations and evil arts, he shall announce himself; his miracles are called lies because they begin from the father of lies.[2]

There will also be many lies from those by reason of the material cause, because there will be certain imaginary deceptions, as Cyril says above and Theodoret teaching on the same places of Scripture. For he will appear to raise the dead and heal the sick, but they will be illusions of demons, not true miracles. Due to the fact that in Apocalypse 13 Antichrist is said to be going to do miracles in the sight of men, i.e., appearances and delusions in the sight of

---

[1] *Moral.*, lib. 32, cap. 12.

[2] *Catechesis* 15.

men, not solid and true as Arethas remarks in the same place.

Next, there will be certain lies from those miracles by reckoning of the form, although they will be true from a reckoning of the matter, because it will seem that true things will be worked, but they will not conquer the power of the whole nature. Therefore, they will not formally be true miracles. True miracles are only called those which can be done by God, that is, which do not have natural causes, nor secret or manifest ones. Therefore, these miracles are not only in the sight of men, but even in the sight of demons and angels. But the miracles of Antichrist will all have natural causes, though they be secret from men.

In the Apocalypse,[3] they place three examples of the miracles of Antichrist. One, that he will cause fire to come down from heaven. The second, that he will make an image of the beast speak. Third, that he will feign himself to be dead and resurrect. Due to these particular miracles nearly the whole world will admire him.

From such miracles there will be two true earlier ones (true in regard to matter, not form), but the third will be no miracle at all.

Moreover, it could be objected against this that they do not all seem to be miracles attributed to Antichrist. For John, in that place, introduces two beasts, one which has seven heads, one of which seems to be dead and rises again. The second smaller one makes fire descend from heaven and the image speak. Therefore, if Antichrist will be before the beasts, these two miracles of the fire and image are not attributed to him; if he will be later than the beast, then the miracle of the resurrection cannot be attributed to him.

I respond: the first beast means either the Roman Empire or the multitude of the impious, as we said above, while one that is the head which seems to be dead and resurrects, is Antichrist. He will also be the supreme and last head of the impious; he will be the last king who will hold the Roman Empire, still without the name of Roman Emperor. And the Fathers teach that this feigned miracle of the resurrection is also certainly to be attributed to Antichrist.[4] St. Gregory argued in an epistle against Lyranus, who thought it was about the son of a certain Cusro, the King of Persia, whom he pretended was wounded in a battle but still not killed.[5] For no other proven history relates such a tale about the son of Cusro, nor can what follows in the Apocalypse agree with the son of Cusro: "And the whole world will admire the beast, saying who is like the

---

[3] Apocalypse 13:14-15.

[4] Primasius, Bede, Haymo, Richardus, Rupertus and Anselm interpreting Apocalypse 13.

[5] Lib. XI, epist. 3.

beast?"

Hence, the second beast in the Apocalypse, according to Rupert, means the same Antichrist. The same Antichrist is expressed through two beasts: The first by reason of royal power and tyranny, whereby he will violently compel men; the other by reason of magical arts whereby he will subtly seduce men. Still, according to Richardus, Anselm and others, the second beast means the preachers of Antichrist, who will try to show with miracles that Antichrist is the true Messiah. Therefore, all these miracles will be either of Antichrist, or of his ministers. Thus, it follows that the Pope is not Antichrist, seeing that no Pontiff has ever feigned that he was dead and risen again, nor has he or any of his ministers ever made fire come down from heaven or an image speak.

But the Centuriators object that the Pope has made many lying miracles: "Such as visions of souls talking from purgatory, and asking Masses to be said for them and the healing of plagues, such as happened to those worshiping statues or calling upon the saints."[6]

I respond: In the first place, these are not the miracles which John writes that Antichrist is going to do; he will die and rise, make fire fall from heaven and to give the power of speech to an image. Therefore, let them show any Pope who did these signs, let alone any bishop. Next, these three kinds of things that they say are the miracles of Antichrist were used in the Church before that time in which our adversaries said Antichrist came openly. St. Gregory writes about Paschasius the Deacon, who lived in the time of Pope Symmachus, around the year 500.[7] His soul appeared to St. Germain, the bishop of Capu,a asking the bishop to pray for him so that he might be freed from the torments of purgatory. Certainly, this miracle happened a hundred years before "Antichrist appeared," in the opinion of all the heretics of this time. For no man places the arrival of Antichrist until after the year 600 and around the death of Gregory I. The same Gregory relates other apparitions of souls, asking for Masses.[8]

On the miracles of healing from the veneration of images, Eusebius relates an example of a bronze statue made of the Savior in the spot where the Lord cured a woman from the flow of blood. A certain plant customarily grew under that statue which rose even to the fringes of the image, and it cured anyone who touched it of all types of evils.[9] It is evident from such a miracle that God wished to approve the cult of holy images.

On the healing divinely conceded to those who had vowed something to the

---

6   *Cent.* 1, lib. 2, cap. 4, co. 436.

7   *Dialog.* Lib. 4, cap. 40.

8   Ibid, lib. 4, cap. 55.

9   *Hist. Eccl.*, lib. 7, cap. 14.

saints, there are innumerable testimonies among the Fathers and an outstanding testimony is extant in Theodoret. He writes that in his own time the temples of the martyrs were full of pictures or simulacra of hands, feet, eyes, heads and other human members, whereby various gifts of healing were shown, which men received from the holy martyrs for a matter of devotion.[10]

---

[10] Theodoret, lib. 8 *ad Graecos*, which is on the martyrs.

CHAPTER XVI
On the Kingdom and Battles of Antichrist

WE READ four things in the Scriptures about the kingdom and battles of Antichrist. 1) Antichrist shall come forth from the lowest place and will receive the rule over the Jews by frauds and treachery. 2) He is going to fight with three kings, namely over Egypt, Libya and Ethiopia, and at length will occupy their kingdoms. 3) He is going to add to himself seven other kings, and in that way evade the monarchy of the whole world. 4) With a countless army he will persecute Christians throughout the world, and this is the battle of Gog and Magog. It manifestly follows that none of these things agree with the Roman Pontiff, so that he in no way can be called Antichrist.

Daniel speaks on the first point: "He will stand, despised in his place, and neither honor nor royalty will be given him, and he will come secretly and obtain a kingdom in deceit."[1] St. Jerome writes in this place that these are also understood as concerning Antiochus Epiphanies; still by far they are more perfectly fulfilled in Antichrist. In just the same way, the things which are said in Psalm 71 (72) about Solomon are understood on Solomon himself, but are more perfectly fulfilled in Christ. For that reason the same Jerome, after he had shown this place on Antiochus, having followed Porphryius, so added: "We, however, interpret better and more rightly that in the end of the world Antichrist is going to do this, who has his rise from a small nation, that is, the people of the Jews, and will be so lowly and despised that royal honor would not be given him, and through plotting and deceit he shall obtain rule, etc." Jerome means, this is the common exposition of Christians. Daniel in chapter 7 also compares Antichrist with a small horn because of its worthless and obscure beginning.

Yet this definitely does not agree with the Roman Pontiff in any manner, or it would be necessary for one to say that the Roman Pontiff, even to the year 600, was very obscure and of no name, and then quickly through deceit began to occupy some high place, but this is certainly false. For as Augustine says: "In the Roman Church the rule of the Apostolic See always flourishes."[2] Prosper of Aquitaine said: "Rome is made greater through the rule of priesthood in the citadel of religion, than in the throne of power."[3] And the Council of Chalcedon, in an epistle to Leo, asserted that at Rome the apostolic rays shine so that from there they expand to all and communicate their goods with everyone else. Next,

---

[1] Daniel 11:21.

[2] Epistle 162.

[3] *De vocatione Gentium*, liber 2, cap. 6.

even the heathen writer Ammianus Marcellinus, writing on the schism of Damasus and Ursicinus, says that he did not marvel if men contend with such zeal for the Roman Pontificate, since it has such power and importance.

Daniel speaks on the second point in chapter 7: "I considered the horns and behold, that small horn arose from the midst of the others, and tore out three from the first horns from his face. ... Hence the ten horns will be ten kings and another will rise after them. He will be more powerful than the first, and he will lay the three kings low." And explaining who these three kings are in chapter XI: "He will send his hand into the earth and the land of Egypt will not put him to flight, and he will be in control of the treasures of gold, silver and all the precious things of Egypt. He will also pass through Lybia and Ethiopia." St. Jerome, writing on these citations, and especially chapter 7, says: "Let us say what all Ecclesiastical writers hand down, that at the end of the world, when the kingdom of the Romans was to be destroyed, there were going to be ten kings who divide the Roman world amongst themselves, and an eleventh little king (Antichrist) was going to rise up who was going to conquer three of the ten kings, that is Egypt, Africa and Ethiopia; after they are dead, the other seven kings will submit their necks to the victor." Other Fathers writing on Daniel 7 and 11 teach the same thing on the three kings killed by Antichrist.[4]

This especially refutes the insanity of the heretics who argue the Pope is Antichrist. Let them say, if they can, at what time the Roman Pontiff slew the kings of Egypt, Lybia and Ethiopia, and occupied their kingdom? Theodore Bibliander, in his *Chronicle*, says that the Roman Pontiff is just as a little horn that first tore off one of the horns from the beast when Gregory II excommunicated the Greek Emperor Leo the Iconoclast, and forbade taxes to be rendered to him from Italy, and little by little occupied his territory, that is, he obtained the Exarchate of Ravenna. Second, he says the horn tore off another when Pope Zachary deposed Childeric, the king of the Franks, and commanded Pepin to be made king in his place. He does not say the third clearly, but seems to indicate that the third horn was torn off when Gregory VII excommunicated and deposed the Emperor Henry IV. There is a certain epistle extant from Emperor Frederick II, written against the Pope, in which he asserted three horns had been torn out by Antichrist, the kingdoms of Italy, Germany and Sicily, which the Roman Pontiff especially compelled to serve him.

But these are most untrustworthy. For in the first place, Daniel does not speak about France or Germany, but Egypt, Libya and Ethiopia. Next, no Pope has ever killed their kings, but Antichrist will kill three kings, as St. Jerome says. Besides, Antichrist will take possession of their kingdoms, not hand them over

---

[4] Irenaeus, lib. 5; Lactantius, lib. 7, cap. 16; Theodoret in cap. 7 et 11 Danielis.

to others. Yet the Pope did not take the kingdom of France for himself, but gave it to Pepin and after deposing the Emperor, bid another to be created; so he did not usurp the empire to himself. In like manner, when the Pope deprived Emperor Leo of the rule of Ravenna he did not take possession of it himself, but permitted it to the kings of the Lombards. Pepin, after the Lombards were conquered, gave it to the Pope. Next, if to depose princes is to tear out the horns, there will not be three, but many more torn out by Antichrist. For it is certain that apart from Leo III, Childeric and Henry IV, the Popes have deposed many others: Innocent III deposed Otho IV; Innocent IV deposed Frederick II. All six of these lost their empire.

On the third, we have the clear testimony of the Fathers. Lactantius and Irenaeus say that after three of the ten kings will be killed by Antichrist, the other seven will be subjected and he will be the ruler of them all.[5] Jerome remarking on chapter 9 of Daniel where it says, "And he will do what his fathers did not," says: "None of the Jews except for Antichrist will ever have ruled the whole world." Chrysostom asserts in his commentary on 2 Thessalonians 2 that Antichrist was going to be a monarch and succeed the Romans in Monarchy, just as the Romans succeeded the Greeks, the Greeks the Persians, and the Persians the Assyrians.

Next, St. Cyril of Jerusalem says that Antichrist is going to obtain the monarchy which beforehand was of the Romans.[6] This is sufficiently deduced from the opinion of the Fathers and Apocalypse, chapter 17, where we read: "And ten horns, which you saw, are ten kings. These have one plan, and power, and they will hand their rule to the beast." That this in no way agrees with the Roman Pontiff is certain. For the Pope was never a king over the whole world.

On the fourth, John says in the Apocalypse, chapter 20: "And the thousand years were ended; Satan was freed from his prison and went out, and seduced the nations, which are over the four corners of the earth with Gog and Magog, and he will gather them into battle, the number of which is like the sand of the sea. And they went up over the breadth of the earth, and surrounded the camp of the saints and the chosen city. And fire came down from heaven and devoured them, and the devil, who seduced them, was sent into the lake of fire and sulphur, where both the beast and the false prophets were tortured day and night for ever and ever." In these words the last persecution and its end are described. St. Augustine says the following about this: "This will be the last persecution before the impending judgment, which the holy Church will suffer throughout the world, the whole city of Christ by the whole city of the devil, in

---

[5] Lactantius, lib. 7, cap. 16; Irenaeus, lib. 5.

[6] *Catechisis* 15.

whatever degree each will be over the earth."[7] Similar things are in Ezechiel 38 and 39, which must be briefly explained on account of the many errors that arise from it.

---

[7] *De Civitate Dei*, lib. 20, cap. 11.

CHAPTER XVII
On Gog and Magog

THEREFORE, the first opinion, or rather error, is of the Jews, who teach that Gog is Antichrist, and Magog is the innumerable Scythian nations that hide within the Caspian mountains. Gog is going to come, that is Antichrist, with Magog, that is, with this army of Scythians, in the time which the Messiah will appear in Jerusalem; and then battle will be joined in Palestine, and there is going to be such a slaughter in the army of God, that for seven years the Jews will have no need to cut wood from trees to build fires because they will have spears, shields and like instruments thrown down everywhere with dead bodies, and then the golden age will come.

Jerome relates this opinion while commenting on chapter 38 of Ezechiel, as well as the writings of Peter the Galatian,[1] and Rabbi David Khimhi in their commentaries on the Psalms. Firstly, what they think is the coming battle of Gog and Magog that will take place is the first coming of Christ, confounding the first with the second, since the Scriptures clearly teach in the first coming Christ is going to come with humility, and finally will be immolated just as a tame sheep.[2] Secondly, that they think Antichrist is going to come to fight against them and with their Messiah is erroneous, since Antichrist really is going to be their Messiah, and will fight against the true Christ, our Savior, on behalf of the Jews.

The second opinion is of Lactantius, who thinks the battle of Gog and Magog is going to be a thousand years after the death of Antichrist.[3] He teaches that Antichrist is coming six thousand years from the beginning of the world and will reign for three and a half years. Then Antichrist must be killed; Christ will appear and the resurrection is going to happen, and the saints will rule with Christ there for a thousand years in the greatest peace and tranquility; meanwhile the infidels will not be exterminated, but will serve them peacefully. Again, after a thousand years the devil will be loosed again, and a most atrocious war will be aroused in all nations, where those who served the saints for a thousand years will fight against the same saints, and this is the battle of Gog and Magog, about which Ezechiel and John speak. But a little while later, all the impious will be slaughtered and then the second resurrection is going to take place, and the world will be completely renewed.

This opinion was also of many of the older Fathers, such as Papias, Justin Martyr, Irenaeus, Tertullian, Apollinaris and of a few others, as Jerome relates

---

[1] *Contra Judaeos*, lib. 5, cap. 12.

[2] Isaiah 53.

[3] Lib. 7, cap. 24-26.

in chapter 36 of Ezechiel, and Eusebius.[4] But for a long time it had been refuted as an investigated error. For the Lord clearly teaches that after the persecution of Antichrist the last judgment will immediately follow.[5] Then, all the good are going to eternal life, while all the wicked into the eternal fire, hence there is not going to be another thousand years, nor any battle.[6]

The third opinion is of Eusebius. He thought that Gog is the Roman emperor, and Magog his empire. But this rests upon a false foundation, for he deduces this opinion from chapter 24 of Numbers, where according to the Septuagint we read: "The kingdom of Gog will be lifted up, and his kingdom increased. God led him from Egypt, etc." There the Scripture seems to say that when Christ will return from Egypt in his time of infancy, then the kingdom of God will be lifted up. But it is certain that while Christ was an infant no kingdom was lifted up except that of the Romans.

But without a doubt this has been corrupted in this edition of the Septuagint. For the Hebrew does not have Gog, but Agag וידם מאגג מלכי (vey-ya-dom me-agag ma-ley-ko), "and it will be abolished on account of Agag," or his king before Agag. And the sense is, according to Jerome, commenting chapter 38 of Ezechiel, that the first King of Israel, Saul, was removed on account of Agag because he will sin by not killing him. Or according to others, Saul will be raised up before Agag, that is he will prevail and conquer Agag himself. Both are true, and that citation of Numbers is certainly understood to be about the kingdom of the Jews, not about Christ or the Romans. For it begins: "How beautiful are thy tabernacles, O Jacob, thy tents, O Israel, etc."

The fourth opinion is of others, who understand the wars of the devil through Gog and Magog and his angel, formerly completed in heaven with the good angels. Jerome refutes this, just as he refutes the literal argument in chapter 38 of Ezechiel.

The fifth is of Theodore Bibliander whom Chytraeus follows in his commentary on Apocalypse 20. Therefore, Bibliander in his *Chronology*, accurately treats on Gog and Magog, and at length teaches that the prophecies of Ezechiel and John do not pertain to the same time. Instead, the prophecy of Ezechiel was fulfilled in the time of the Maccabees, whereas Gog and Magog were Alexander the Great and his posterity that were kings of Syria and Egypt

---

[4]   *Hist.*, lib. 3, last chapter.

[5]   Matthew 24:9-14.

[6]   Translator's note: This opinion, common in some of the early Fathers, is called Chilism, or Millenarianism, and today, under a different form, the "Rapture." The early Fathers treat it as an opinion, and the later Fathers universally reject it, as do all later theologians. It appears to originate first in the early Father Papias.

that enjoined battles with the Jews and at length were conquered by the Maccabees. But the prophecy of John was fulfilled in the time of Pope Gregory VII and as many pontiffs who followed him, thus Gog and Magog were Popes, and other Christian princes and their armies, who so long fought against the Saracens for the holy land, and to recuperate the tomb of the Lord.[7] The first part of this opinion is also that of Theodoret in his commentary on Ezechiel 38, but it cannot be defended. Firstly, because without a doubt the prophecies of Ezechiel and John are one and the same, and hence each must be fulfilled after the coming of Christ. For John says the army of Gog is going to come from the four corners of the earth; Ezechiel says the same thing, namely showing the army of Gog is going to be Persians from the East, Ethiopians from the South, Tubal, that is, Spanish from the West, and Togorma, that is, Phrygians from the northern parts. Next John says that this army must perish from fire sent from heaven, and Ezechiel asserts the same thing at the end of chapter 36. "Fire and sulphur will rain above him and over his army." Next, John adds to this battle the renewal of Jerusalem, that is, the glorification of the Church and in a similar vein Ezechiel from chapter 40 even to the end of the book treats on nothing but the wonderful renewal of Jerusalem.

Besides it is proved in the second place that the prophecy of Ezechiel was not fulfilled in the time of the Maccabees. In Ezechiel 38, it is said to Gog "you will come at the end of your years." But Alexander the Great came in the middle of his years. Next, Ezechiel says that in the army of Gog there are going to be Ethiopians, Libyans, Spanish, Cappadocians, etc, who still never fought against Jerusalem, and particularly not in the time of the Maccabees. For the Syrians and Egyptians alone fought against them.

Next, Ezechiel describes such a victory against Gog and Magog, that afterwards there would be no fear of enemies; rather it was going to be the end of all battles. But such was not the victory of the Maccabees against the kings of Syria and Egypt. For the Jews never completely conquered the kingdom of Syria or Egypt, and a little after the Jews were again disturbed by the Romans, captured and never freed from their hands, as Augustine deduced from the history.[8] Therefore, the prophecy of Ezechiel was not fulfilled before the times of Christ.

The second part of the opinion of Bibliander, which is his own, is not only false but impious. For in the first place John speaks of the battle of Gog and Magog that is going to be against the camp of the saints, and the chosen city, that is, against the true Church of God. But the war of Christians to recover the

---

[7] *Chronologia,* tab. 14.

[8] *De Civitate Dei,* lib. 18, cap. 45.

Holy Land was wholly against Muslims, unless by chance Bibliander would have it that the Muslims are the true Church of God and the camp of the saints. Next, John says that men are going to be in the army of God from the four corners of the earth, but in the Christian army they were only from the West and the North, that is French, Germans and Italians. Besides, John says that after the war of Gog and Magog Jerusalem would be renewed and glorified; the devil, Antichrist and the false prophets are going to be cast out into the eternal fire. On the other hand, the war of the Christians for the Holy Land ended long ago, and still we have not seen any renewal of Jerusalem, nor the devil and the false prophets thrown into hell. For now, as even our adversaries affirm, the devil and the false prophets greatly flourish.

Besides, God himself manifestly showed by means of clear signs and wonders, both at Antioch in Syria, and on other places, that he was pleased by that war.[9]

Next, St. Bernard, whom the same Bibliander calls a saint in his chronicle, where he treats on the times of Eugene III, was one of many authors of this war. For he persuaded a multitude of French and Germans by words and miracles to set out for that war, as he himself shows.[10] The author of the life of St. Bernard writes that after the battle was completed Bernard gave sight to a certain blind man in testimony that the war he had preached was in the name of the Lord.[11]

The sixth opinion is of the Centuriators, who teach that Gog and Magog mean the kingdom of the Saracens or the Turks.[12] Such an opinion is plainly opposed to that of Bibliander and therefore, it is better or at least less bad. Yet still, it is absolutely false. Gog will come in the end of his years and will not endure for a long time, as is gathered from John and Ezechiel. But the kingdom of the Saracens began a long time ago and has endured for nearly a thousand years, which is by no means a little while.

The seventh opinion is of St. Ambrose. He taught that Gog represents the Goths, who had devastated many provinces of the Roman people.[13] St. Jerome calls to mind this opinion and says: "Whether it may be true or not, the end of the battle will show."[14] And now rightly the end of the battle shows that it was not true, since after the wars of the Goths we saw neither a renewal of the

---

[9] See William of Tyre, *de bello sacro*, lib. 6; Paulus Aemilius, *de rebus Francorum*, lib. 4.

[10] *De Consideratione*, lib. 2.

[11] *Vita B. Bernardi*, lib. 2, cap. 4.

[12] *Centur.* 1, lib. 2, cap. 4, col. 435.

[13] *De fide*, lib. 2, cap. ult.

[14] *Quaest. Hebraicis in Gen.*, cap. 10.

Church nor did all wars end.

The eighth opinion is of St. Jerome himself. While commenting on chapter 38 of Ezechiel he saw the difficulty of the matter and expressed it in the mystical sense on heretics after he omitted the literal sense. For he would have it that Gog, which in Hebrew means roof, signifies heresiarchs who have the character of a roof; they are elevated and proud. Magog, on the other hand, since it is translated "from the roof," means those who believe heresiarchs and are to them as a building is to its roof. This opinion, provided it is received in a mystical sense, is very true, but it is not literal. Ezechiel says that Gog is going to come in the end of years and John says in Apocalypse 20 that after a thousand years the same Gog is coming. (However, all Catholics understand the thousand years as the whole time which is from the arrival of Christ even to Antichrist.) Therefore, since Gog is not going to come until the end of the world, and the heretics began in the beginning of the Church while the Apostles were still alive, it is properly certain that Gog does not literally mean heretics. It must also be known that Jerome, when he says Gog means roof and Magog means from the roof, did not wish to say that Gog and Magog were the Hebrew for our words roof and from the roof. Rather, he meant they are almost the same. Properly in Hebrew roof is not Gog, but Gag גג and for from the roof they do not say Magog, but Miggag מגג.

The ninth opinion is of St. Augustine. He understands for Gog the devil, who is the character of a great roof, that is, of a great house in which many of the wicked inhabit; while for Magog he understands the army of Antichrist gathered from all the nations of the whole world.[15] Such an opinion without a doubt is the truest and must be embraced, insofar as it relates to Gog and Magog in the times of Antichrist. Both because all Catholic authors follow him, but also because everything which they say on Gog and Magog from Ezechiel and John rightly agree with Antichrist. For then, there will be truly the last and greatest persecution, and after it Jerusalem will be renewed, e.g. the Church will be glorified and no more wars are heard of. Insofar as he understands the devil for Gog it does not seem to be true. For John says the devil, being freed, is going to call Gog and Magog into battle; therefore, the devil is one thing, Gog is another.

Therefore, our opinion, which is the tenth, contains three things. Firstly, we assert that the battle of Gog and Magog is the battle of Antichrist against the Church, as Augustine rightly teaches. Secondly, we say it is probably quite true that Antichrist is signified by Gog while through his army, Magog. For Ezechiel perpetually calls Gog the prince, and Magog the land, or nation. Thirdly, we say it is probable that Gog is called by Magog, not the other way around, so that

---

[15] *De Civitate Dei*, lib. XX, cap. 11.

Antichrist should be called Gog, because he is the prince of the nation which is called Magog. Hence, the army of Antichrist is called Magog from the nation of Scythia not because it is certain to be made of Scythians, which the Jews mean by beyond the Caucasus and the Caspian Sea, but either because a great part of the army of Antichrist will consist of barbarians arising from Scythia (such as Turks, Tartars, and others), or what I rather more believe, because it will be an immense army and very cruel. For those whom we wish to say are savage, we call Scythian.

Now, that Magog really means a Scythian nation is clear from Genesis X, where we read that the second son of Japhet was called Magog, whereby it was called the region of Magog, which his posterity inhabited; which is Scythia as Josephus taught,[16] as well as St. Jerome.[17] This is the same as from the three sons of Cham, that is, Chus, Mizraim and Chanaan: Ethiopia was called Chus, Egypt was called Mizraim, and Palestine was called Chanaan; thus from the son of Japhet, Scythia was called Magog.

Moreover, when Ezechiel names Magog he regarded a nation denominated by Magog, the son of Japhet, because he adds as allies to it Gog and other nations denominated by other sons, or grandchildren of Japhet, such as Gomer, Togorma, Mosoch, Tubal, etc. Therefore, we conclude that the battle of Gog and Magog is the last persecution which Antichrist will excite against the Church in the whole world.

What Ezechiel says in chapter 38 is also not opposed to this, that the arms of Gog and Magog will be burned for seven years, since still it will be certain that after the death of Antichrist there will be but 45 days until the end of the world, as is gathered from Daniel. For Ezechiel does not speak literally, but figuratively as is the custom of prophets. He did not really mean that those arms would be burned for seven years, but that the slaughter would be so great that one could suffice for a very long time to keep the fires going with spears and shields of the slain men, if one needed to.

One doubt remains, whether on account of the savage persecution of Antichrist the faith and religion of Christ must be throughly extinguished throughout the world. Domingo de Soto believes that it is going to happen: "The loss and defection of the whole world from that see will be a sign of the end of the world. ... After the faith has been extinguished through the defection from the Apostolic See, the whole world will be empty and then continue in vain. ... Mortals will become frightened, as their love shall be pestilent. Thence its glorification and pride which under the leadership of Antichrist will at length

---

[16] *Antiquit.*, lib. 1, cap. 11.

[17] *Quaest. Hebraicis in Genes.*, cap. 10.

cause the city of God to shake."[18]

But, in my judgment, this opinion cannot be defended. For in the first place it is opposed to what Augustine says, that the Church is going to always be unconquered by Antichrist: "He will not desert his army which was called by the word 'camp'."[19] Next, it seems opposed to the Gospel, for we read in Matthew 16: "Upon this rock I will build my Church, and the gates of hell shall not prevail against it." But how will they not prevail, if they will utterly extinguish her? Likewise in Matthew 24, the Lord says on the ministers of Antichrist: "They will perform great signs, so that they will lead into error, and if it were possible, even the elect." There, the Lord meant the many chosen in that future time that will not allow themselves to be seduced by the miracles of Antichrist. Next, all writers who speak on the persecution of Antichrist, such as Ezechiel, Daniel, Paul, John and all the Fathers cited above, say that the victory of this war or persecution is going to be in the power of the Church. And the reasoning is evident. Who would believe that in this battle, in which the whole camp where God and the devil, Christ and Antichrist will fight, that God will be conquered by the devil, and Christ by Antichrist?

---

[18] *Sent.*, lib. 4, dist. 46, q. 1, artic. 1.

[19] *De Civitate Dei*, lib. 20, cap. 11.

CHAPTER XVIII

The Absurdities of the Heretics are Refuted, in Which They not only try to Show,
but Impudently Declare that the Roman Pontiff is Antichrist

LTHOUGH what we have treated up to this point on Antichrist could suffice, seeing that we have clearly shown that no place attributed to Antichrist in the divine Scripture agrees with the Supreme Pontiff, still so as to leave nothing wanting and because the impudence of our adversaries is so manifest, I propose briefly to refute that which Luther, Calvin, Illyricus, Tilman and Chytraeus assert trying to show that the Pope is the Antichrist.

1) Luther everywhere calls the Supreme Pontiff the Antichrist, and especially in his book *de Captivitate Babylonica*, in his work *Contra Execrabilem Bullam Antichristi*, in his assertion of articles, and in his book against Ambrose Catharinus.[1] Though he does this, only one argument can be found in all these books whereby he tries to prove this, namely in his assertion of article 27. He says: "Daniel foretold in the eighth chapter that Antichrist will be an impudent king by face, this is, as the Hebrew has it, powerful in regard to pomps and ceremonies of external works, meanwhile the spirit of faith is extinguished just as we saw fulfilled in so many religious orders, colleges, rites, vestments, deeds, churches, statues, rules and observances—and you can scarcely recite their number." And these same faces of Antichrist, as he calls them, he enumerates and profusely explains in his book against Ambrose Catharinus on the vision of Daniel.

For all that, this argument of Luther errs in three places. First, in the very foundation, since the Hebrew word שנפם (sha-panim)[2] means "robust in the face," and it is a Hebrew phrase that means a man with a smooth forehead who does not know how to be ashamed. For especially the Septuagint so renders it: ἀναιδὴς προσώπῳ, that is modest in the face. So also St. Jerome and Theodoret render it, and Francis Vatablus so explained it in the *Rules of Rabbis*: "Strong in face, that is he who does not blush, who has no shame."

Next, the same is gathered from Ezechiel 3: "The house of Israel has been rubbed clean in the forehead, and is hard of heart; behold I have given your face more vigor than their faces, and thy forehead is harder than theirs." The Hebrew for that is: "The house of Israel is robust in its forehead, and I gave your face to be more robust than theirs." The words have no other sense than this (as Jerome

---

[1] Translator's note: Lacelotto Politi, a Dominican canon lawyer.

[2] Translator's note: This is the Hebrew word as in the Ingolstadt and subsequent editions of the *Controversies*, but it is misspelled and we have not been able to discover the Hebrew word that Bellarmine intended.

rightly explains): They are indeed impudent, but you shall not yield to their impudence. Although they boldly and without shame do wicked things, you boldly and without shame shall rebuke them. Since that is so, Luther should see to it lest he shall be impudent in face if he would have his interpretation be put before that of the rabbis, Theodoret, Jerome, the translators of the Septuagint and Ezechiel himself.

2) The argument of Luther goes astray because from this opinion, whatever at length he means, he does not rightly gather that the Pope is the Antichrist. Even if it were certain that Antichrist is going to be powerful in pomps and external ceremonies, it is still not immediately gathered that Antichrist is whoever comes in pomps and external ceremonies. The logicians teach that nothing can be gathered from affirmative particulars. Otherwise Moses would be the Antichrist because he established so many ceremonies in Exodus and Leviticus that one can hardly begin to count them. And when the same thing is said about Antiochus, and in his figure of Antichrist, that understanding is perhaps enigmatic. If the reasoning of Luther would avail, it would follow that all who could answer the enigma are Antichrist. But that is certainly false and ridiculous.

3) Luther errs in attributing the institution of all orders and ecclesiastical ceremonies to the Roman Pontiff, when it is certain that a great many of these were established by the holy Fathers, not by the Roman Pontiff. The Greek Church has always had, and still has, monasteries, rites, observances and ceremonies which they received from St. Basil, St. Pachomius and the other Greek Fathers, not from the Roman Pontiff.[3] In the West also we have the orders of St. Benedict, St. Romuald, St. Bruno, St. Dominic, and St. Francis which, while approved by the Pope, were established and devised by these holy men with the teaching of the Holy Spirit. So, if orders pertain to the face of Antichrist, these holy Fathers must rather more be called Antichrist than the Pope.

I add, lastly, that the words of Daniel (except in regard to revealing Antichrist in his own time), agree more suitably to no man better than Luther. For he was impudent in his face above all, for as a priest and monk he openly married a consecrated virgin, when no example of such a thing can be shown in all of antiquity. Likewise, he wrote lies without number which have been recorded and published by many. John Cochlaeus writes in the acts of Luther for the year 1523, that in one book of Luther he noted fifty lies. From another Luther was found to have placed 874 lies. Next, how great was his impudence when, in his book against the Bull of Leo X, Luther dared to excommunicate his Pope when the universal Church adhered to him still? Who ever heard that a

---

[3] See the books of Cassian in the *Institutes*, and the *Constitutions of St. Basil.*

priest could excommunicate a bishop?

To be sure, the Council of Chalcedon abhorred the rashness of a certain Dioscorus, who, while presiding over the Second Council of Ephesus (that is, the robber council of Ephesis), presumed to excommunicate Pope Leo the Great. Yet, what comparison can there be between Dioscorus, the Patriarch of the second See, presiding in what was supposed to be a general council, and Luther, a simple monk writing in his cell? Nevertheless, leaving Luther, we come to Melanchthon.

CHAPTER XIX
The Trifles of the Smalchaldich Council of the Lutherans are Refuted

HERE is a little book extant on the power and primacy of the Pope, or the reign of Antichrist, published in the name of the Smalchaldich Council of the Lutherans, which seems to me to be the work of Melanchthon. At any rate, whoever wrote it, it has nothing but words and inane boasting. The author of the book says: "It is certain that the Roman Pontiffs, along with their members, defend impious doctrine and impious worship, and this plainly fits the mark of Antichrist in the rule of the Pope and his members." To this point we have seen the proposition, now let us hear the proofs: "For Paul, when describing Antichrist in his letter to the Thessalonians, calls him the adversary of Christ, extolling himself over everything which is called or worshiped as God, sitting in the temple just as God. Therefore, he speaks on someone ruling in the Church not on heathen kings; he calls this man the adversary of Christ because he is going to devise doctrine opposed to the Gospel and he will arrogate divine authority to himself."

Though all these things, even if they were true, would hardly impede us still, I ask on what foundation does this interpretation rest? Paul clearly says Antichrist is going to elevate himself over every god and is going to sit in the temple, not as a king or as a bishop, but plainly as God, and Chrysostom, Ambrose and the rest of the fathers interpreting this passage concur with this. Therefore, by what principle does he affirm without a witness or any reasoning that Antichrist is he who sits in the temple not as God, but as a bishop, and does not raise himself above every god, to such an extent that he not only worships God the Father, Son and Holy Spirit, but even prostrates himself before the Sacrament of the Eucharist in the sight of all, as well as before the tombs of the Apostles, martyrs, the cross and images of Christ and the saints, which the author himself, although impiously, usually calls foreign gods and idols? But let us see whether he can make this very thing fit the Pope.

"First, it is certain that the Pope rules in the Church and constituted this reign under the pretext of ecclesiastical authority and ministry. The pretext is these words: 'I give to you the keys'."

For certain he says that the Pope rules over the Church, but he does not prove it. On the other hand, we can show the contrary with little labor. One who rules suffers no superior, but the Pope professes that he is the vicar of Christ the King. And although in the whole house of God, and also in the whole kingdom of Christ he uses the fullest power, still this power is not in excess of the economy, rather it is the condition of a servant. For even Moses (as Paul says in Hebrews 3) "was faithful in the whole house of God," but just as a servant, while Christ is as a son in his own. But let us continue.

"Thereupon, the doctrine of the Pope is in many ways opposed with the Gospel and he arrogates to himself divine authority in three ways. First, because he takes for himself the right of changing the doctrine of Christ and the worship established by God, and wills his own doctrine and worship to be observed as though it were divine."

Likewise, he says this but does not prove it. Not only is this false, but it seems to be an impudent lie. Does he not know that in the Catholic Church the doctrine of Christ is taught by the mouth of all, and the worship cannot be changed not only by any man, but even by an angel, nor was there ever any question of whether what Christ taught or commanded should be believed or done. Yet it remains to be seen whether he or we interpret the doctrine and precepts of Christ better. In such a question he brings nothing other than his customary interpretation; but we bring the consensus of the Fathers, and of the Catholic Church, as well as decrees and customs. For we do not oppose the consensus of the Fathers and the decrees and customs of the Church (as he falsely boasts) let alone the Word of God, but only his interpretation and judgment. But let us hear the second proof.

"Secondly, because he takes power to himself not only to bind and loose in this life, but even the right over souls after this life."

Again, this is said but not proven. For the Supreme Pontiff does not take the right unto himself over dead souls. He does not absolve their sins or punishments by his own authority but only in a manner such as prayers of intercession, and he will also share the good works of the faithful with them. Moreover, prayers and fasting of the living benefit the dead, and especially the sacrifice of the Mass, as all the Fathers teach. On that matter we will dispute profusely elsewhere; in this place one testimony of St. Augustine will suffice. "It is without question that the dead are assisted by the prayers of the Holy Church and the salutary sacrifice, as well as almsgiving which is expended for their souls."[1] Still, let us go on.

"Thirdly, because the Pope refuses to be judged by the Church or by another and advances his authority in judgment of councils and of the whole Church. This is to make oneself God, to refuse to be judged by the Church or by anyone."

Here also, he says two things that he cannot prove. For particularly by what Scriptures, what councils, by what criterion ought the Pope be judged by councils or the Church? For we read (that I might pass over many other things which were disputed in the previous book) that Christ said to Peter: "Feed my

---

[1] Serm. 34.

sheep."[2] We believe, it cannot be doubted, that the sheep must be ruled and judged by a shepherd, not the shepherd by the sheep. We also read that in Luke the Lord said to Peter: "Who do you think is the faithful and prudent steward, whom the Lord constituted over his household?"[3] We see in that passage a specific steward was proposed for the whole household of Christ, and certainly that he would rule it, not be ruled by it.

Still, perhaps someone would object that if that steward were wicked, in the end who will judge him if the steward is in charge of all but subject to none? That is why the Lord added immediately after: "What if that servant would have said in his heart, 'My Lord delays his coming,' and began to strike the servants and maidservants, to eat, drink and be drunk; the master of the servant will come on a day on which he hopes not, and at an hour which he does not know, and he will divide his lot and share it with infidels."[4] Who does not hear that there is a judge of that wicked steward whom the Lord constituted over his household? Christ does not say that he will be judged by a council, but the "Lord will come on a day he hopes not, etc." Therefore, the Lord reserves judgment for himself over the one he himself constituted over his whole household. Hence, the Pope does not steal his authority from the judgment of councils and of the whole Church when he does not suffer himself to be judged by it. He cannot steal what was never given in the first place. Rather, councils duly gathered have never taken to themselves (outside the case of heresy), to pass judgment on the Supreme Pontiff. There is much to say on this matter in the proper place.

The second thing that he says and does not prove is that one makes himself God if he refuses to be judged by the Church or by anyone. For when he says "by anyone," he certainly understands any man; does Melanchthon not know that the Pope must be judged by Christ himself, and that he believes and professes this? By what arrangement does someone make himself God when he believes God must judge him?

Next, earthly kings attain judgment on earth in regard to matters of state; they recognize no one, and by his scheme, where he removes coercive power from bishops, these kings have no judge in ecclesiastical affairs. Will there not then be as many gods as there are kings? I do not think he is that insane that he would say this. Therefore, it remains that it is not true that one who would not be judged by any man thereby makes himself God.

Finally, he adds: "He defends such horrible errors and this impiety with supreme savagery, and he kills anyone who dissents."

---

[2] John 21:17.

[3] Luke 12:42.

[4] Luke 12:45-46.

Since he lies so impudently here, let him also, if he can, recognize that I myself who write this openly assert—and at that in the very city of Rome (and not without the Pope's knowledge)—that it is not lawful for the Pope to change Christ's doctrine, or worship, or establish new worship which should be held as divine, or which is opposed with the Gospel by any reasoning. I am not killed for that, nor do I suffer on that account. Without a doubt the Pope knows well that I speak the truth, but Melanchthon lies. Just the same he also adds a little after: "The doctrine on penance has been altogether twisted by the Pope and his members; for he teaches that sins are remitted on account of the dignity of our works; in like manner they never teach that sins are remitted by grace on account of Christ." These, however, are not our teachings but his lies. For we do not teach that, but altogether the contrary, as the Council of Trent clearly shows.[5] But enough has been said on this. Let us now turn to Calvin.

---

[5] Sess. 6, ca. 5-8

CHAPTER XX
The Lies of Calvin are Refuted

OHN CALVIN, explaining 2 Thessal. 2: "He who extols himself over everything that is called God," says many things with great flamboyance, but proves nearly nothing. "Paul means by these words that Antichrist was going to take as his own what is of the one God, that he will raise himself above everything divine and every god, that he might lay at his feet all religion and the whole worship of God. ... Now whoever will have been informed by the Scripture, even if he be a boy of but ten years, will notice certain things which are especially proper to God and which, on the other hand, the Pope usurps to himself, and he need not expend much labor to recognize him [the Pope] as Antichrist." This shows wonderful promise!

But let us, at length, hear by what reasoning he shall prove what he proposes. Perhaps it will be of the kind that even a boy of ten years will not labor much to refute it: "The Scripture proclaims that God alone is the legislator[1] who can preserve and destroy,[2] one king whose office is to rule souls by his word; it makes the same one the author of all sacred things; it teaches that justice and salvation depend upon Christ alone; and it assigns the mode together with the reasoning. The Pope asserts that every one of these pertains to his right; and he boasts that what seems fit to him he binds upon consciences by means of laws and subjects them to eternal punishments. He establishes Sacraments at his pleasure which are either new or corrupted from the ones which Christ had established, and he vitiates, nay more, altogether abolishes these so that in their place he substitutes the sacrileges that he had made. A foreign means of attaining salvation is devised that is altogether foreign to the Gospel. Lastly he does not hesitate to change the whole religion at a nod. What, I ask, is it to raise oneself over everything which is called divine if the Pope does not do it?"

Did I not say that Calvin says much, but proves little or nothing? For Calvin says all this, that the Pope boasts to bind men with laws upon their consciences as he sees fit, that he establishes new Sacraments but abolishes the old, that he devises a means of salvation foreign to the doctrine of the Gospel, that he changes all religion—but he does not prove any of it. In other words, for him to say something is to prove it; by equal reasoning to deny it ought to refute it.

Certainly, however, many of us are Catholic, and we obey the Roman Pontiff, the Vicar of Christ; we speak freely and without any injury to him that

---

[1]   Isaiah 33:22.

[2]   James 4:12.

he is not allowed to bind men with any law he pleases, i.e. pernicious and wicked ones, neither can he establish new Sacraments nor corrupt or abolish the ones established by Christ, nor is he permitted to confect a means of salvation foreign to the doctrine of the Gospel, or overturn the Christian religion, or change it. We, in truth, more gladly say that we know he also thinks and says the same thing. For if he did not think so, if he thought he was allowed to fashion wicked laws, establish new Sacraments or abolish the old or do other things of this sort, how would he knowingly and willingly suffer us, who are in his power here in Rome more than in I know not what corner of the world, to teach the contrary?

But they will say the Pope does not say he is permitted to do these things, but still in reality he contends that he is by his deeds. Therefore, it should be proven that he has done any of these things. Otherwise, that is to assume what must be proven, which although customary for our adversaries, the logicians call "begging the question."

Next, Isaiah 33 and James 4, the only two passages of Scripture that Calvin advanced, do not impede our position in the slightest. For Isaiah and James say: "One is king, judge and our lawgiver;" certainly that is not opposed with those words of Proverbs: "Through me kings rule and makers of laws determine what is just."[3] And with these, the Psalm: "And now understand ye kings, you are taught to judge the earth."[4] Another six hundred passages could be added. Therefore, Isaiah and James in whatever way do not make God the one king, judge and lawgiver, but only by reason that he alone is so King, Judge and Lawmaker that he ought to render an account to no one since he depends upon no one. He will rule and judge and impose laws by his own authority, i.e. he does not receive authority from another. Lastly, that he alone in regard to execution can destroy and save, as James says, we attribute none of that to the Pope or any other princes.

---

[3] Proverbs 8:15.

[4] Psalm 2:10.

CHAPTER XXI
The Lies of Illyricus are Refuted

OW we turn to Illyricus. In a book which he wrote against the primacy of the Pope, he says: "But among our other arguments it ought to be the most solid, truly and clearly proven that in this time, the Pope teaches and defends impious doctrine and is himself the very person of Antichrist, and I repeat the reasons of this matter here. 1 John 2 defines that Antichrist is he who denies Jesus is the Christ. The Pope clearly does this, not by words but by deed. Messiah is the Hebrew, Christ the Greek; it is a divinely sent person that he should be a perpetual priest and king over the people of God. The office of the priest is to teach, pray, sacrifice, but it is for a king to rule and defend."

Let us see how he will prove the Pope has snatched up these offices from Christ, and what testimony and proofs he advances. Still, unless I am mistaken, we will only see inane words. Therefore, he continues thus: "The Pope has seized the priesthood from Christ; not only does he wish to be heard as the beloved son, but what is more, he and his pseudo-apostles advance another Gospel. Likewise, he substitutes other mediators in heaven between us and Christ who intercede for us in the presence of the Father by neglecting the severe judge, Christ. Likewise, because he substitutes infinite sacrificing priests in place of Christ, who pleased God on behalf of the human race, to whom he says the priesthood passed from Christ through Peter. Thereupon, he wills us to be saved through their spiritual merits and those of the saints."

See how Illyricus conquers us with the clear proofs of Scripture! What if we were to show that all these things were merely lies? For where, I ask, have you read that the Pope wishes to be given more authority than Christ? We deny it and say: Prove it. Rather, we see that supreme honor is given to the Scriptures by the Pope and he holds for heretics those who teach something against Scripture. Next, is it not clearly a lie that the Pope has established other mediators for Christ and wants them to intercede with God the Father while neglecting Christ? Does our litany not begin with *Kyrie eleison, Christe eleison*? Are not all the prayers of our Church, which we read in Mass or in the Divine Office directed to God and do they not end: "through Christ our Lord"? Do we not acknowledge the mediation and intercession of Christ when, whatever we ask from God, or if we desire the saints to be asked on our behalf, we ask entirely through the merit of Christ? We do not have saints in place of God or of Christ, but we ask from them that they might join their prayers with our own so that whatever we wish of God we might obtain more easily through Christ.

By equal reasoning it is a lie that the Pope substituted sacrificing priests for Christ. Neither would we say the priesthood of Christ has passed to sacrificing priests through Peter. He has not proved any of these things, nor will he ever prove them. There can be no doubt whether if you had some means you would advance it. But it is as we say, Christ, who is a priest forever, and lives always to intercede for us, offered himself once to God in a pleasing sacrifice by death on the cross, but now he offers himself again and again and again in the liturgy through the hands of the priests.

Just the same, although many in our time baptize, still we read that: "This is he who baptizes in the Holy Spirit."[1] It does not follow that the office of baptizing passed from Christ to the priests, but that he is the one who always baptizes through the ministry of the priest; thus even though many priests today offer Christ in awe-inspiring mysteries, still, he is the primary priest and truly the high priest who through the ministry of all priests offers himself: "These works are not of human power. Who then in that supper consecrates, now also operates and perfects; we merely hold the rank of ministers."[2]

But I would gladly say to Illyricus, since all the ancient writers both Greek and Latin make mention of the sacrifice of the Eucharist and of the Christian priesthood (which no man denies unless he does not read), why at length does he attribute this to the Roman Pontiff, that he transferred the priesthood of Christ to sacrificing priests? But let us continue with the rest.

He adds in the last passage: "He wishes us to be saved through their spiritual merits, and of the saints." This is also a characteristic lie. Otherwise advance a place where the Pope will have said this. St. Peter says in Acts: "For we believe we are saved by the grace of our Lord Jesus Christ, just as even our Fathers were saved."[3] Nor do we acknowledge any other savior but Jesus Christ crucified who gave himself for the redemption for all.[4]

Hence, it cannot be denied that the merits and prayers of the saints benefit us according to their mode, unless one does not know or does not believe there is communication and connection among the members of the body of the Church. Although we will treat this matter in another place, it will suffice to add two testimonies here. St. Augustine says: "That we might be advised in that mode, should what we deserve so weigh us down that it seems we are not loved by God, we can relieve ourselves from it by the merits of those whom God loves."[5] He also repeats often in *City of God* that some obtained forgiveness by

---

[1] John 1:33.

[2] St. John Chrysostom, homil. 83 in Matth.

[3] Acts 15:11.

[4] 1 Tim. 2:5-6.

[5] Quaest. 149 *in Exodum.*

the merits of the saints.[6] This is what the Lord meant when he said: "Make unto yourselves friends from the mammon of iniquity, that when you falter, they might receive you in eternal dwellings."[7] St. Leo the Great says: "We believe and trust to obtain the mercy of God when we are oppressed by our own sins, that we are always, among all labors of this life in equal measure, in need of the help by the prayers of special patrons, we are raised up only by Apostolic *merits.*"[8]

Moreover, although we do not customarily so speak, as Illyricus says, that we are saved through spiritual merits, still, if anyone were to so speak and mean by the merits of the saints we are helped to obtain salvation through Christ, he could be no more rebuked than the Apostle Paul, who said: "I am all things to all men that I might save all."[9] And the Apostle Jude, who speaks in a similar fashion said: "And indeed reprove those that have been judged, but save others, pulling them out of the fire."[10] That is enough on the priesthood of Christ.

Nevertheless, Illyricus continues: "He steals the kingdom from Christ, because he wishes to be head of the Church on earth, but in heaven he constitutes other helpers and saviors for us, to whom he bids us to flee when in misery. Therefore the Pope denies Jesus is the Christ."

First I ask where in the world the Pope, or any Catholic, calls the saints "saviors"? I add this: If he asserts that he is head of the Church under Christ, as his vicar and minister, which the Pope does, is that to deny Jesus is the Christ? By the same reasoning does anyone who is a viceroy, or affirms himself as the governor of some province, thereupon deny his master is king?

Next, if to turn to the saints as helpers is to deny Jesus is the Christ, how, I ask, did Paul not deny Jesus is the Christ when he said: "I ask you, brethren, through our Lord Jesus Christ and through the charity of the Holy Spirit, that you help me by praying for me to God, that I might be freed from the unbelievers who are in Judea."?[11] How did Basil the Great not deny Jesus is the Christ when, in his *Oration on 40 martyrs*, he said: "Anyone who is oppressed in narrow straits, let him flee to them; again who rejoices, let him pray to them; that he may be freed from evils; that he would endure to prosperous times"? I omit the remaining Fathers, as I fear lest we might search too much and discover who else denied Jesus is the Christ.

Still, Illyricus continues. "In Daniel 11, Antichrist is distinguished by a great

---

[6] *De Civitate Dei*, lib. XXI, cap. 27.

[7] Luke 16:9.

[8] Leo I, *serm. 1 de natali Apostolorum*, Bellarmine's emphasis.

[9] 1 Corinth. 9:22.

[10] Jude 1:22-23.

[11] Romans 15:31.

many signs; first, that he will do what he wants, and the Pope does what is pleasing to him."

But when holy Daniel says of Antichrist, "He will do what he wishes," he means Antichrist will have no one greater than he, not even God. For it follows: "And will be lifted up against every God." Therefore, Antichrist will live for his own will in place of the law of God, and command and subordination. Certainly the Pope does not do this; rather he affirms that he is constrained by the law of God, and acknowledges Christ as his judge and superior.

Illyricus continues: "He confesses in canons[12] that he himself drags infinite souls with him into hell; still no man ought to say to him what he does? And the Gloss says the will of the Pope is held as the rule."

The Canon that begins *Si Papa* was not (as Illyricus falsely says) written by any Pope, but by St. Boniface, the bishop of Moguntium, Apostle of Germany and a martyr. He does not deny that the Supreme Pontiff, if he will have lived badly, must be corrected and also admonished by fraternal charity; rather, he denies that he can be convicted by authority and judged when he is the judge of every man. In those words which come before that canon (as is seen in the new edition of the decree), Boniface also calls the Roman Church the *Head* of all Churches with eloquent words, and affirms that the safety of the whole Church, after God, depends upon the safety of the Roman Pontiff.

I ask, therefore, from Illyricus, whether the teaching of St. Boniface, the apostle of the Germans, is true or not? For if it is not true, why object to us? If it is true, why does he not receive it? I will put the matter more plainly. If his teaching is not true, therefore, it is not true that the Roman Pontiff drags a great many souls with him to hell. What then? But if it is true, then the Roman Pontiff is truly the head of all Churches and the judge of all, judged by no one. For this reason, Illyricus should cease to argue with canons which can benefit him nothing. What pertains to the Gloss, Illyricus should know, that citation was either held by the Pope as false and thus purged from the new edition, or else it was never in that decree; I could not find it anywhere.

Illyricus goes on: "Secondly (Daniel) says that he will lift himself above God. The Pope did that as is clear from the foregoing. Likewise, because he wishes to make himself heard more than God, blaspheming he loudly proclaims the Scripture the font of all heresy, schism, ambiguity and obscurity, etc."

It would behoove him to at least relate the words of Daniel faithfully. It does not say he will lift himself above God, but "he will be lifted against every God." And below: "Nor will venerate gods because he will rise against all of them." This very clearly shows the Pope has nothing in common with Antichrist, since

---

[12]   Dist. 40, *si Papa.*

Antichrist will worship no gods but the Pope worships the one God, Father, Son and Holy Spirit. Not only that, but if we were to believe Illyricus then he openly worships as many gods as there are saints in heaven and images on earth, not to mention relics under the earth.

Moreover, when he adds: "The Pope loudly declares the Scriptures are the font of heresies and schisms," I have certainly never read that in the writings of any Pope; but I have heard the word of Luther, that Scripture is the book of heretics.[13] If that were received in the right sense then I do not see why it would be duly condemned. For St. Hilary also, in his last book on councils, shows that a great many heresies were born from bad understanding of Scripture. Tertullian also boldly stated: "Nor am I trying to say that the Scriptures themselves were so arranged by the will of God as to furnish materials for heretics when I read 'there must be heresies,' which could not exist without the Scriptures."

Not only does the Pope very truly teach that there is ambiguity and obscurity in a great many passages of Scripture, but so also do all the Fathers. Even Luther himself, whether he wished to or not, was compelled to affirm this when he wrote in a preface to the Psalms: "I would not have it presumed by any man in my regard that I have done what still none of the saints or the most learned could furnish, i.e. to teach and understand the Psalter in its legitimate sense in all places. It is enough for some men to have understood some things for their part, but the Spirit has reserved many things to himself so that we would always have students. It only shows many things so as to attract, and hands down many things to influence. ... I know that anyone who would dare to profess that he had perfect understanding of one book of Scripture in all its parts would be guilty of the most impudent temerity." Luther also writes the same thing in his book *de Conciliis et Ecclesia*, pag. 52. Does he not clearly affirm that he, with great sweat, sought the true and genuine teaching of Scripture? And, at length, are there not so many versions of Scripture, so many interpretations, so many different sects among our adversaries; why do they shout, on the other hand, how ambiguous and obscure the Scripture is?

"Third, [Daniel] says that things will go well for him [Antichrist] until the wrath of God shall put an end to them. The Pope oppressed as he willed both kingdoms and innumerable churches with his tyranny and impiety."

And this is the reason by which the author proves his case? Could not someone say what states and which churches the Roman Pontiff has oppressed? What if we were to show the contrary, that this mark of the Pope were plainly contrary to this third mark of Antichrist? In that time, in which according to Illyricus, the Pope began to be Antichrist, not only did his rule not increase, but

---

[13]   Luther, in a preface to the history that happened in Stasfort, in the year 1536.

in fact it decreased all the more. In the time of Leo the Great, that is, one hundred and fifty years before our adversary says Antichrist was born, the Roman Pope presided over as many nations as there were boundaries of the Roman Empire. For he thus writes: "Through the holy See of Blessed Peter, Rome was made head of the world; you preside more broadly in divine religion than earthly domination. Although by many victories the authority of your rule increased, you conferred it over land and sea; still what bellicose labor has subdued for you is less than what Christian peace has added."[14] And Prosper of Aquitaine says:

> Rome, the See of Peter, which for pastoral honor
> Was made head of the world,
> Whatever she does not possess by arms
> She holds by religion.[15]

Yet afterwards, while Antichrist was ruling (as Illyricus would have it) the Roman See little by little lost Africa, the greater part of Asia and all of Greece. In our own times they cry out that Antichrist is raging, yet all his affairs go so well that he has lost a great part of Germany, Sweden, Norway, all Denmark, a good part of England, France and Switzerland, Bohemia and part of the Balkans. Therefore, if things going well is a mark of Antichrist, it is not the Pope, who has lost so many provinces, but Luther, who by preaching carnal freedom has seduced so many people and for whom things go so well that from a private monk he became prophet of the whole of Germany; and just as the Pope evades it, he rightly can be called Antichrist. Nevertheless, continue.

"Fourthly, Daniel says 'he will have no care of the God of his Fathers.' This is truly said about the Pope, as we clearly proved above from the passage of John."

And we more clearly disproved it in the same place.

"Fifthly, he says he will have no care for the love of women: but the Pope became celibate both by instructing celibacy to his own, and by his homosexual lusts."

Here, I omit to say with what temerity Illyricus dares to say these things. Meanwhile, he has a simple task; either he could prove what he says or he cannot. I will not omit that the words of Daniel, although they sound this way in the Greek text, still in the Hebrew source are plainly contrary in the opinion of St. Jerome, who rendered the verse: "And he will be in lust for women." And although the Hebrew words רעל חמדת נשים (re-kal ke-me-dat na-shis), only

---

[14] Serm. 1 de natali Apostolorum.

[15] Liber *de ingratis*.

mean reeling from lust for women, they also do not have any other words joined to them whereby it could be understood whether it will be or not be Antichrist that will lust after women. Still there are two conjectures which the version of St. Jerome makes more probable.

1) It is certain that Antiochus, whom Daniel is literally speaking about, was exceedingly addicted to the love of women: "Antiochus," Jerome says, "is said to have been very lustful and so greatly disgraced the royal majesty through foul deeds and corruption, that he publicly had relations with mimes and harlots, and satisfied his lust in the presence of the people."[16] If this is so, how believable is it that Daniel was going to speak about such a king that will not be lustful for women?

2) Another conjecture is that since Antichrist is going to come as the Messiah of the Jews, and the Jews await a multitude of wives from the Messiah, apart from other goods, it is not in any way probable that Antichrist is going to command or praise celibacy.

Lastly, I add that if it is a mark of Antichrist that he will proclaim celibacy, then not only the Pope, but all the Fathers and even the Apostles themselves were Antichrists. For (that I might pass over the rest which will be advanced in its proper place) listen to what the Fathers of the II Council of Carthage say, in canon 2 of that council: "All are pleased that bishops, priests and deacons who confect the Sacraments ought to abstain from wives as guardians of chastity, that what the Apostles taught and antiquity itself preserved, we also would safeguard." But let us continue.

"Sixth, Daniel says that he will worship the god Moazim, and with gold and silver, which he did, while he placed his whole piety in it, so that many wonderfully splendid temples were built and rested upon every kind of precious ornament and songs would resound."

Many things were written above on the god Moazim, where we showed that he is either Antichrist himself or the devil whom Antichrist will secretly worship. But it seems to me that our Illyricus makes Jesus Christ the god Moazim, which is an intolerable blasphemy. For all the temples which the Roman Pontiffs have splendidly built and adorned with gold and silver are consecrated to Christ our God, and no man can be said to not know that. If, therefore, the one who is worshiped in temples of this kind is the god Moazim who does not see that Christ himself would be the god Moazim? Moreover, the building and adorning of temples did not begin in the year 666, the year our adversaries would have it that Antichrist appeared, but nearly three hundred years earlier.

---

[16] Comment. huius loci.

Listen to Eusebius (from Ruffinus' version): "From that fact joy was infused over us as if by a divine gift, especially at the sight of these places which a little before were destroyed by the treachery of the impious tyrants, that were now brought back to life with a more glorious construction, and high temples rose even higher for the humble assemblies."[17] St. Cyril of Jerusalem also says: "These who are now kings built this holy Church of the Resurrection, in which we are now, clothing it with silver and gold from their piety, and they made it splendid with silver monuments."[18]

See, if you will, the magnificence of the temples of Christians and the splendor of the vessels of the Church in Eusebius's *Life of Constantine,*[19] and Gregory of Nyssa;[20] Gregory Nazianzenus;[21] Chrysostom;[22] Cyril of Alexandria;[23] Damasus;[24] Ambrose;[25] Jerome;[26] Augustine;[27] Paulinus;[28] Prudentius in a hymn on St. Lawrence and Procopious in a book on the buildings of Justinian. Certainly, they all lived before the times of Antichrist, and still they witness that in each age their buildings were full of the ornaments of Christians, as we see these now, and they are beyond compare.

"Seventh, Daniel says that Antichrist will enrich his friends; the Pope has done that."

Clearly he so enriched John of Eck, John Cochlaeus, John Fisher of Rochester, Latomus, Driedo, Tapper, Pedro de Soto and so many other learned men, who, although they labored for days and nights to refute the frenzies of our adversaries, still, they received not even a penny from the Roman Pontiff. Although they expected no reward from men, they labored chiefly for the glory of God. But if the Roman Pontiff allots priestly opulence to cardinals and bishops, it is not as much that he believes they must be enriched as the piety of the faithful, who donate wealth to this purpose.

---

[17] *Hist. Eccles.,* lib. 9, cap. 10.

[18] *Catechesi* 14.

[19] *Vita Constantini,* lib. 3 et 4.

[20] *In oratione de sancto Martyre Theodoro.*

[21] Orat. 1 *in Iulianum.*

[22] Hom. 66 *ad populum Antiochenum.*

[23] *De recta fide ad reginas.*

[24] *Vita Sylvestri.*

[25] *De officiis,* lib. 2, cap. 21.

[26] *In comment.* cap. 8 *Zachariah.*

[27] *In Psalm* 113.

[28] *Natali tertio Sancti Felicis.*

Illyricus continues: "Paul places five marks of Antichrist in 2 Thessalonians 2. 1) That he will sit in the temple of God. The Pope does this. He, by styling himself vicar of Christ, reigns over the consciences of men. For if he were to profess that he is the enemy of Christ, as the Mohammadans, he would be outside the Church."

But Paul does not only say Antichrist is going to sit in the temple of God (for every bishop sits in the temple of God), but he explains in what manner he is going to sit in the temple, showing himself ὅτι ἐστὶν Θεός. The Pope, on the other hand, by Illyricus' own testimony, makes himself the vicar of God, not God himself. A vicar of God cannot be God unless he would fabricate lesser gods as well as greater ones. Thereupon, I ask, if the Pope is not outside the Church, as he says in this passage, and hence is within the Church, where, I ask, is Illyricus with his own? Is he outside the Church? For the Church is one, and the Pope sits in it. He who is not in it, is in no Church at all. But let us hear the rest.

"2) The fact that Paul says that now a great mystery is worked: I think it looks to the fact that the bishop of Rome, a little later, would begin to raise his head above that of others."

Without a doubt, as we wrote briefly above, following Nicholas Sanders who had already seen and written this very thing, Illyricus would make St. Peter the Antichrist, but Christ to be Simon Magus or Nero to be Christ. For Paul did not say the mystery of iniquity will be worked a little later, but was being worked in his time. Why, if this mystery pertains to the Roman Pontiff, is it necessary to pertain to St. Peter and if St. Peter, (the mind shudders to think and the hand fears to write) was the Antichrist, who does not see that Simon Magus and Nero, the enemies of St. Peter, were Christ and God? Let Illyricus have Gods and Christs of this sort for himself; we will not envy him.

"3) What Paul says, that Antichrist is going to come with characteristic lies, which the Pope has done, as experience witnesses.

4) That God will permit the efficacy of illusion: this manifestly happens in the papacy. For by far we believed the Pope more strongly than God."

We have already treated on the miracles of Antichrist above (chapter 15) and what Illyricus says is "from experience" is a very impudent lie. The Popes have never done either true or false miracles (not in this age nor in a previous one), whereby Antichrist is said to principally rule. What he adds on the efficacy of illusion, anyone should see how easily this has been twisted into an adverse meaning. What greater efficacy of illusion can be contrived than that in our time some are discovered who prefer to trust two or three apostates than the universal Church, all councils and all the Fathers, who apart from admirable doctrine and outstanding sanctity of life, are glorified with many miracles?

Moreover, what Illyricus advances in his fifth mark from St. Ambrose was refuted above in the second proof, in which we showed that Antichrist has not yet come.

Lastly, Illyricus adds a little from the epistle to Timothy: "In the last times many will leave the faith.[29] The Pope denies there is another faith apart from the historic one. They attend impostor spirits; the Pope proves all things by visions of spirits and souls. They forbid marriage, the use of food each of these from the Pope is very true and well known."

But, my good man, the Pope learned there is one faith from Paul; you seem to have learned from there something besides one faith; the Apostle says to the Ephesians: "One God, one faith, one Baptism."[30] Paul never defined this one faith as a trust resting upon the promise and Word of God, as you define it.[31] But he said to the Romans: "This is the word of faith which we preach, because if you shall confess the Lord Jesus in your mouth and will believe in your heart that God raised him from the dead, you will be saved."[32] He also said to the Hebrews: "By faith we believe the world was arranged by the Word of God."[33]

Who does not know that it pertains to sacred history that Christ rose from the dead and the ages are suited to the Word of God? Still, we do not call the one, only and true faith with which we certainly believe whatever God deigned to reveal by the Apostles and prophets historic faith, but Catholic faith. For we leave novelties of names to our adversaries.

What he adds, that the Pope proves all things by visions of spirits and souls, I do not know what spirit revealed to him. For to confirm those things which pertain to the state of souls, we apply something from apparitions of souls and from the approved writings of ancient authors. Such is what Eusebius writes on the apparition of St. Potamina[34] and that which St. Augustine relates on the apparition of St. Felix Nolan.[35] On the other hand, I do not know who ever advanced visions of Catholic souls to prove dogmas. But that is not his first lie.

What he advances in the last place on the prohibition of foods and spouses is easily refuted by St. Augustine: "So, again, if you were to encourage virginity just as the apostolic doctrine does, 'He who gives in marriage does well, and he who gives not in marriage does better;' if you taught that marriage is good, and

---

[29] I Timothy 4:1.

[30] Ephesians 4:5.

[31] Cent. 1, lib. 2, cap. 4, col. 262.

[32] Romans 10:9.

[33] Hebrews 11:3.

[34] *Hist. Ecclesi.* lib. 6, cap. 5.

[35] Lib. *de cura pro mortuis*, cap. 16.

virginity better, as the Church teaches (which is truly Christ's Church), the Holy Spirit would not have heralded you as forbidding marriage. What a man forbids he says is evil, but he does not do so when he places something better before a good.... You see, then, that there is a great difference between exhorting to virginity by proposing it as the better of two good things, and forbidding to marry by denouncing the true purpose of marriage; between abstaining from food as a symbolic observance, or for the mortification of the body, and abstaining from food which God has created for the reason that God did not create it. In one case, we have the doctrine of the prophets and apostles; in the other, the doctrine of lying devils."[36] It is not necessary to add anything.

Illyricus concludes: "Therefore, it is certain from these clear signs that the Pope is himself the true Antichrist, about whom the Scriptures prophecy."

But perhaps he would more suitably conclude in this way: Therefore it is certain from these clear lies, that Illyricus is one of his precursors, whom the holy prophet Daniel long ago foretold would have an impudent mouth.

---

[36] *Contra Faustum*, lib. 30, cap. 6.

CHAPTER XXII
The Ineptitude of Tilman is Refuted

ILMAN HESH wrote a book with the title *de Antichristo* that he subtitled "On six-hundred errors of the Popes" (which ought to be titled On six-hundred lies of the Lutherans). In it, he embraces four errors. Thus he says:

"The Popes say that Antichrist is going to come from Babylon from the tribe of Dan."[1]

Thanks are in order for Tilman, who teaches this is of ancient and holy Popes. If they are Popes who say Antichrist is going to come from the tribe of Dan, then certainly the Popes are Irenaeus, Hippolytus, Ambrose, Augustine, Prosper, Theodoret, Gregory, Bede, Arethas, Rupert, Anselm and Richard: all these, as we showed above,[2] teach in a common consensus that Antichrist is going to be born from the tribe of Dan. Still, we continue with Tilman.

"Secondly, the Papists deny that the Roman Pontiff, with his fellowship, are the true Antichrist, although it is proved and shown by very strong and clear testimonies of the divine word."

But we do not yet see these testimonies, nor are they extant in our Hebrew, Greek or Latin Bibles. For that which he advances as testimony for his side does not even name the Roman Pontiff.

"Thirdly, they teach Antichrist is only going to reign for three and a half years."

Here, immortal thanks are due to Tilman, because he affirms that not only all the Fathers, but even the Prophet Daniel and John the Evangelist are Papists. And he thus duly spares me his and his own, by which he reserves merely the dregs of the Scriptures, having abolished all learned and approved Fathers to the Papists. Please see what we taught above (chapter 8) and one will find those who taught this with eloquent words, whom Tilman affirms are Papists for teaching it, namely Irenaeus, Hippolytus, Cyril, Jerome, Augustine, Theodoret, Primasius, Aretha, Bede, Anselm, Richard, Rupert and even Daniel and John.

"Fourthly, they teach Antichrist is going to be killed on Mt. Olivet."

And here also he makes great men into Papists. Accordingly, Antichrist must be killed on Mt. Olivet, as St. Jerome gathers from Daniel and Isaiah.[3] Theodoret also, writing in the same place, even if he does not name Mt. Olivet, he affirms Antichrist must be killed not far from Jerusalem. But we shall see by what

---

[1] *Compendium Theologiae* lib. 7, cap. 8

[2] Chapter XIII.

[3] *In comment.* cap. 11 *Danielis.*

arguments he refutes the aforesaid errors. For he immediately adds the antidote in these words:

"The papist trifles on Antichrist that rest upon no testimony of Sacred Scripture must be rejected and detested. Jerome rightly says that he who does not place authority in Scripture is condemned by the same levity whereby he asserts something. And Paul warns that we should beware of the traditions of men.[4] I say this, however, lest anyone would impose upon you with false reasoning, etc. Likewise: 'See lest anyone would deceive you by philosophy, etc.' It must be sought from the Word of God what is thought about Antichrist, such as in 1 John 2. 'Who is a liar but he who denies Jesus is the Christ? This is the Antichrist.' Likewise, 2 Thess. 2, 'The man of sin and son of perdition will raise himself over every God, etc.' Likewise Matth. 24, 'Pseudochrists will arise, and Pseudoprophets, and they will give signs, etc.' Daniel 11: "And he will make offering to the god Moazim,' and in Apocal. 17: 'And I saw a woman drunk on the blood of the saints and from the blood of the martyrs of Jesus.' From these Sacred Scriptures, what the Christian faith holds about Antichrist, whom Christ and the Apostles foretold is coming, appears crystal clear in its testimonies. Since they are more clearly brought into the light, each individual mark agrees more clearly with the Roman Pontiff, so there should be no doubt that the Roman tyranny is the worst Antichrist."

It will not be tiresome, I believe, if we recall these cruder arguments to a syllogism and thence conclude the confutation of the clear errors above. Therefore the first error is refuted. The trifles of Popes, because they rest upon no testimony of Scripture, must be rejected and detested. But the Word of God declares: "He who denies Jesus is the Christ, he is Antichrist."[5] Therefore, it is an error to say Antichrist is coming from the tribe of Dan.

The second error is thus confuted. As Jerome rightly says, whatever has no authority in Scripture is condemned by the same levity whereby it is asserted. But Paul says: "the man of sin, and son of perdition will raise himself over every God."[6] Therefore the Papists err when they deny the Pope is the Antichrist.

Thus the third, and more powerfully because it is from two Scriptures; St. Paul says, "I say this, lest they place false reasonings upon you, etc."[7] And there will rise "Pseudochrists and pseudoprophets, and they will give signs, etc."[8] Therefore it is an intolerable error of the Popes when they say that Antichrist

---

[4] Coloss. 2:8.

[5] 1 John 2:22

[6] 2 Thes. 2:3-4.

[7] Coloss. 2:8.

[8] Matt. 24:24.

will rule for three and a half years.

The last and strongest of all because it is from three Scriptures. Paul warns: "See lest anyone deceive you with philosophy, etc."[9] Antichrist will make an offering to the god Moazim,[10] and John saw a woman drunk on the blood of the saints.[11] Therefore, the Papists err by the whole heaven when they say Antichrist is going to be killed on Mount Olivet.

Candid reader, forgive me for treating Tilman so ridiculously. Yet the impudence of the man compels me, since he has nothing worthy by way of refutation; but after writing such nonsense he still boasts as if he offered proofs as certain and as clear as in Mathematics.

---

[9] Coloss. 2:8.

[10] Daniel 11:38.

[11] Apoc. 17:6.

CHAPTER XXIII
The Lies of Chytraeus are Refuted

AVID CHYTRÆUS takes up in his commentary on the Apocalypse a vision of John where, as the fifth angel blows a trumpet, a vast star was seen to fall from heaven to earth, to which was given the key of the well of the abyss. After that a dense smoke was seen to rise from the abyss that darkened the sun and the air. Lastly, some strange locusts were seen to advance from the smoke; a little after they bore before themselves the appearance of horses, lions, scorpions and armored men.[1] Chytraeus explains that he thought this vision corresponded to the Roman Pontiff, and would also have it so thought by others when he says: "There is no doubt that this vision describes Antichrist, or the order of the Roman Papacy."

He also teaches that this vision begins in the year 600, and that star falling from heaven was Gregory the Great, the Roman Pontiff; his successors are those who abandoned the keys of the kingdom of heaven and received the keys of the well of the abyss. The smoke advancing from the well is the corruptions of doctrine and various traditions of the Roman Pontiffs. Next, he would have it that the swarms of locusts are bishops, clergy, monks; and to dissipate that smoke he proposes that the antithesis of pontifical doctrine is the evangelical doctrine, which is Antichristian opposed to Christian, and embraces twelve articles, as if it were another Apostolic Creed.

But this opinion can easily be refuted. 1) It rests upon no witness. Amongst the Fathers who interpreted this verse, such as Arethas, Bede, Primasius, Anselm, Rupert and others on this place, the star which fell from heaven represents the devil, not some bishop. In Isaiah it is said about the Devil: "How did you fall from heaven, O Lucifer, who rose in the morning?"[2] And because the devil fell much earlier than John's Apocalypse, the Fathers note that John did not say I saw a star falling from heaven, but "I saw the star that had fallen from heaven to the earth." For John saw that star that already was on earth, which formerly had shined with the brightest light in heaven. It very suitably corresponds to the Devil, just as what follows: "And the key of the well of the abyss was given to him." As Christ has and shares the keys of the kingdom of heaven with his own and rules over the minds of the faithful and the pious, so the Devil has the key of the well of the abyss and rules over the sons of infidelity; he is everywhere called in the Scripture: "the prince of Darkness; the

---

[1] Apocalypse 9:1-11.

[2] Isaiah 14:12.

prince of this world; god of this age."[3] He is also the one who, with God's permission, sends out the smoke of errors from the well and new swarms of locusts, that is heresiarchs with their armies, in nearly every age against the boundaries of the Church.

2) The opinion of Chytraeus is opposed to what John says in this same chapter on the sixth angel, and the sixth persecution. St. John describes six persecutions of heretics through the trumpets of the six angels, which were going to come from the time of the Apostles even to the end of the world. And even Chytraeus is not far off in that he understands by the first trumpet the heresy of the Ebionites, which was roused in the time of the Apostles. For the second trumpet he understands the heresy of the Gnostics that came after it; for the third the heresy of Paul of Samosata and his followers as well as the Arians; the fourth heresy is of the Pelagians, who were later than all the previous heretics.

Moreover, if through the fifth trumpet the persecution of the Roman Antichrist is understood, which all agree is the last persecution, then what shall we understand by the sixth trumpet? Chytraeus responds that the sixth trumpet signifies the persecution of Muhammad and the Turks. But this is not said rightly, both because the Muslims are not heretics but pagans and because the persecution of Muhammad will not follow that of Antichrist but will precede it, just as we think, or it will take place at the same time, as Chytraeus says. Therefore, Chytraeus is compelled to confound the fifth trumpet with the sixth, when still he related the others to different times. Catholics understand the sixth trumpet better; it is the persecution of Antichrist which truly will be the last and most fierce; but through the fifth some exceedingly pernicious heresy which will nearly precede the times of Antichrist. Yea, many guess with great probability it will be the Lutheran heresy.

3) But Chytraeus errs by the whole heaven when he teaches that St. Gregory was the star falling to earth, since St. Gregory, if any trust can be placed in historians, did not fall from heaven to earth but ascended from earth to heaven. He went from a judge to a monk, from a monk he was made a bishop; he never went back from the episcopacy to his magistracy, or from a monk back to the world. This is the same as what St. Basil, Gregory Nazianzen and John Chrysostom did amongst the Greeks, and Martin, Paulinus, and Augustine among the Latins, who went from seculars to monks, and were thereafter made bishops. No one ever said on that account that they fell from heaven to earth. Next, Gregory was second to none in regard to continence, sobriety and the love of heavenly things, but in humility he excelled all; and still Chytraeus would so

---

[3] John 12:31 and 14:30; 2 Cor. 4:4; Ephes. 6:12; Colos. 1:13 and other places.

boldly say that he fell from heaven, that is, from heavenly life to earth, nay more to an earthly life full of carnal delights.

Even Luther called Gregory a saint[4] and Luther followed Theodore Bibliander[5] in raising Gregory with the greatest praise; he said that the degree in which he excelled in zeal for piety and doctrine can be seen in his books, which is very true. For his writings breathe an admirable sanctity.

What he adds on the smoke from the well is no less vain. He interprets it as the corruption of doctrine introduced into the Church by Gregory and his successors. Yet, Gregory changed nothing which pertains to doctrine, instead what pertains to rites and discipline. He corrected many things which had crept in through abuse; he restored many things which had been forgotten by the negligence of time. Just so, he established a few new things, and those by mature counsel, as can be recognized both from the four books on his life, written by John the Deacon, and from his epistle where he explains the nature of the rites which he restored or instituted.[6] This matter will become especially clear if we review the very antithesis of evangelical and pontifical doctrine which Chytraeus proposes, not to mention by which he more often loses readers afterward.

I.

ON THE TRUE RECOGNITION AND INVOCATION OF GOD.

The Gospel teaches that only one God must be invoked and worshiped, just it is commanded to be done in his word. All trust in our salvation must be placed in the goodness and mercy of God alone. The Popes command men to invoke not only the true God, but also dead men or saints, to seek aid and help in perils and to wait for it, etc. This is plainly from a heathen custom; they bind the invocation and worship of God to certain statues, and thence if they come to this or that statue with invocation, God will be more merciful than to others.

Because we treat copiously on these controversies, which are touched upon in this *Antithesis*, in different places, here we will only show briefly that doctrine that Chytraeus calls "pontifical" is neither opposed with the Word of God nor began in the time of St. Gregory.

The Word of God teaches that only one God must be worshiped and invoked with that invocation and adoration which is due to God alone (who is also a

---

[4] *In supputatione temporum.*

[5] Tab. 10 *Chronol.*

[6] 63. lib. 7.

jealous God should we hold a creature for a creator). Nevertheless, the same Word of God commands us to honor more excellent creatures, even that we might invoke some, but not as gods, rather as beloved members of God's family. Just the same, kings suffer if they would see royal honors conferred upon their servants, but they rejoice when they see the same servants honored and observed. David says, "Adore[7] the footstool of his feet."[8] and Job says: "Call, if there is one to respond to you, then turn to one of the saints."[9] For that reason Abdias, a great and holy man, adored Elijah prostrate on the ground.[10] And the sons of the prophets when they heard the spirit of Elijah had passed to Elisha, coming they "adored him prostrate."[11] And the Apostle Paul implored the prayers of Christians for nearly all individuals, that through these he would be liberated from many dangers. No other reasoning can be given why it would decrease the honor due to God, if we were to demand from the souls of the saints to pray for us to God, just as it is not diminished if we will ask the same thing from the living.

Thereupon, St. Ambrose, who is 200 years earlier than St. Gregory, still so speaks in his book on widows: "The angels must be implored, who were given to guard us; the martyrs must be beseeched, of whom the pledge of the body seems to us to claim patronage. We are not ashamed to employ them as intercessors in our infirmity."

Moreover, we do not assign worship and invocation to statues of the saints, to memorials of the martyrs, and the remaining religious monuments any differently than God did to the sanctuary or to the temple of Solomon. Even if God hears us everywhere, and we can lift up our hands to God in every place, still, it is not without a reason that the Holy Spirit[12] and Christ call the temple of God the house of prayer.[13] Nor is it without reason that the most pious emperor Theodosius (as meanwhile I might pass over a great many examples

---

[7] Translator's note: We must draw the reader's attention to the fact that in Latin, terms like "worship" and "adore" are used in regards to the Blessed Virgin and saints, with the distinction that it is given with *dulia*, a Greek word indicating a lower level of dignity, whereas adoration with *latria* is given to God alone. In English this is generally accomplished with "veneration" and "worship", but we are hesitant to constitute ourselves the correctors of Bellarmine's Latin.

[8] Psal. 98 (99):5.

[9] Job 5:1.

[10] 3 Kings (1 Kings) 18:7.

[11] 4 Kings (2 Kings) 2:15.

[12] Isaiah 56:7.

[13] Matth. 21:13.

from antiquity) encompassed every place of prayer with the Priests and the people; before the reliquaries of martyrs and the Apostles they laid down prostrate on a rug and begged their faithful assistance from the saint's intercession. And certainly Theodosius who did this, and Ruffinus who wrote it[14] preceded St. Gregory by at least two hundred years.

II
ON THE OFFICE AND BENEFITS OF CHRIST

The Gospel teaches that eternal life and remission of sins be given on account of the unique and only Son of God, our Lord Jesus Christ, crucified, died and resurrected for our sake, not for any work or merits of ours. And indeed, this honor is proper to God alone, as is said in Isaiah 43: "I am, I am he who blots out iniquities." Likewise: "There is no salvation in any other." The Popes teach the contrary, not on account of the merits of Christ alone, but partly on account of Christ, and partly on account of our contrition, obedience or good works, that we are justified and saved, etc.

Catholic doctrine does not hold that sinners will be justified partly by Christ and partly by their works, as if their works would merit anything without Christ. Accordingly, we distinguish three kinds of works. One type is done from the strength of nature alone without faith and the grace of God. Concerning these, we plainly declare with the Apostle that a man is not justified from works but from faith, and if someone would be justified from works of this sort he would have glory, but not before God, as St. Paul says about Abraham.[15] Therefore, there is no controversy on these works, even if here and there it is attributed to us that we teach works are meritorious without the faith of Christ, which is an impudent lie.

The second type of works proceed from faith and the grace of God which disposes one to reconciliation with God and remission of sins. Of this kind are prayer, almsgiving, fasting, sorrow for sins and others. We do not say such works are meritorious from the justice of the reconciliation itself, but on the contrary we hear what was said at the Council of Trent,[16] that men are justified by grace because neither faith nor the works which precede justification merit it, but from justice, as if justification were due to works of this sort. Still, we affirm these works themselves, insofar as they proceed from faith and divine

---

14 Lib. 2 *hist. Eccl.* cap. 33.

15 Romans 4:2.

16 Sess. 6, cap. 8.

assistance, are divine works and merit in that manner, *i.e.* obtain remission of sins. Even if one would not concede it, nevertheless he concedes the Word of God. Why is it that Ezechiel says: "And when the evil man turns himself away from the wickedness that he has done and does judgment, and justice: he shall save his soul"?[17] Why does Daniel say, "Redeem your sins with almsgiving"?[18] Why does Jonah say: "God saw their works (fasting and hairshirts) and pitied them"?[19] Why does Christ say, "Much has been forgiven her because she has loved much"?[20]

Not only Gregory, but also many of the Fathers taught this very thing before him. Ambrose says, "Tears do not demand forgiveness, but they do merit it."[21] St. Jerome, "Those who simply confess their sins merit mercy from the humility of the Savior."[22] Augustine says: "Remission of sins itself is not without any merit if faith obtains this. For the merit of faith is not nothing; by such faith he said: 'God be merciful to me, a sinner,' and he went down justified, faithful and humble."[23] And in another epistle: "If someone will have said that faith of a work merits grace we cannot deny, but freely confess that it is so."[24]

The last kind of works is of those that make a man justified and proceed from the indwelling of the Holy Spirit in the heart of man as well as charity diffused in it. To such works, whether you like it or not, we attribute merit. Not in the manner that the remission of sins (which preceeds it) can properly fall under merit, but they truly and properly merit glory and eternal beatitude. Otherwise, why would Paul say: "I have fought the good fight, I have finished my course, I have kept the true faith, as to the rest there is laid up for me a crown of justice that the just Judge will render to me on that day"?[25] If eternal life is not truly the wages of good works, why does he call it the crown of justice, and not the gift of mercy? Why does he say it must be rendered, not given? Why from the just judge, not from a generous king? Therefore, St. Augustine says: "Even eternal life itself, which at any rate will be enjoyed without end and consequently is given for merits that precede it, nevertheless,

---

[17] Ezechiel 18:27.

[18] Daniel 4:24.

[19] Jonah 3:10.

[20] Luke 7:47.

[21] *In Lucam* lib. 10.

[22] Lib. 2 *adversus Pelagianos.*

[23] Epist. 105.

[24] Epist. 106.

[25] 2 Timothy 4:7

we are not sufficient in ourselves to furnish those very merits for which eternal life is given; rather we do these works by grace, it is even expressed by grace, but not because it is given by our merits, rather because the merits themselves are given, by which eternal life is given."[26]

Those two Scriptural testimonies that Chytraeus quoted hardly strike fear in us, namely: "I am the one who blots out iniquities... There is no salvation in any other." Testimonies of this sort exclude another God, another Christ, and another Savior and doctor of souls, which truly promise salvation without the true God and Christ Jesus the Savior. Nevertheless, they do not exclude faith, hope, charity, penance and the Sacraments, whereby the merit of Christ is applied to us, especially with God's operation. Otherwise, how could these two propositions adhere together: "I am the one who blots out iniquities; There is no salvation in any other," and "Your faith has saved you";[27] "He will save those who hope in him";[28] "He will save his soul";[29] "The fear of the Lord expels sin";[30] "He who will have believed and been baptized, will be saved";[31] "He who eats this bread will live forever?"[32] That is sufficient on this point; let us continue with Chytraeus.

III

The Gospel teaches that one who does penance and hears the promise ought to believe the promise and determine that the sins of others, such as Peter or Paul, and even his own are remitted on account of Christ. Such a man pleases God, is received and heard by God and by this faith he comes to God in daily invocation. The Popes contend that it always must be doubted whether we have remission of sins. Such a doubt is simply opposed to faith and is clearly heathen.

Our Gospel sufficiently teaches that it behooves one to have faith in the promises of God; all Catholics teach that there is no reason to doubt this. Still, there is no place in the Gospel where one can read that remission of sins is

---

[26] Epistle 105.

[27] Luke 7:50.

[28] Psalm 36 (37).

[29] Ezechiel 18:27

[30] Sirach 1:21

[31] Mark 16:16.

[32] John 6:51, 58.

promised to men by God. Much less can one find that each and every man should determine for certain that his own sins are remitted or that he pleases God, is received by God or heard by him. Rightly so, because it would overturn the other passages in which one can very clearly read the contrary. For what could be more clear than what the wise man writes in Ecclesiastes: "There are the just and the wise, and their works are in the hand of God; still no man knows whether they are worthy of hatred or love."[33] Likewise it is clear from Job chapter IX: "Even if I were simple, is my soul ignorant of this?" And again: "I feared all my works, knowing that you would not spare the offender."?

What of the fact that nearly all divine promises have an attached condition, which no man can know for certain whether he will have fulfilled them or not? "If you wish to enter into life, keep the commandments."[34] "If anyone comes to me and does not hate his father, and mother, and wife and children, brothers, sisters and still his own life, he cannot be my disciple."[35] "The Spirit himself gives testimony to our spirit, that we are sons of God; but if sons, then heirs, heirs of God, co-heirs of Christ, still, if we suffer it is so we will be glorified with him."[36] Next, St. Ambrose, who (as we said above) is much older than Gregory, says: "He wished the reproach that he suspected to be taken away from him, or else he thought in heart that God had not done so; although it was abolished by penance, still he suspected that his reproach still remained; and therefore he prayed to God that he would take it from him, because God alone knows what he cannot know even though he is the one who did it."[37]

IIII

The Gospel teaches that there is only one propitiatory sacrifice in the world (Hebrews 7:10), that Christ was offered once and for all to take away sins. The Popes teach that Christ is offered daily in the sacrifice of the Mass to God the Father."

Indeed the Gospel teaches that there is only one propitiatory sacrifice in the world because it was offered on the cross once and no Catholic denies that. Yet, the Gospel nowhere says that this unique sacrifice cannot daily be repeated in a mystery by Christ the High Priest through the hands of priests, and Catholics affirm this. Not only do they affirm it, those in all the centuries after Gregory,

---

[33] Eccl. 9:1.

[34] Matthew 19:17.

[35] Luke 14:26.

[36] Romans 8:16.

[37] *in Psalmum* 118.

but so do all the Fathers that preceded him by many centuries. Let us take Augustine in the name of all the others, who said: "Was not Christ immolated once in himself? And still, in the Sacrament he is immolated for the people, not only through all the solemnities of Easter, but every day."[38]

V

The Gospel teaches that sin is not only external actions opposed to the law of God, but even doubts about God, carnal security and contumacy, as well as the concupiscence born with us, and cast off in rebirth (Romans 7). The Popes deny that these evils are cast off in rebirth [Baptism] and claim these are sins opposed to the law of God.

No Popes, that is, Catholics, teach that only external actions are sins; rather this is a lie that Chytraeus learned from his father, who does not stand in the truth. Moreover, we do not question whether doubts about God, carnal security, contumacy and concupiscence are sins if they are voluntary; but if they are involuntary, such as the lusts of the flesh against the spirit, which Paul sensed, even if he did not share in them, these we steadfastly deny are sins. We do not relate this concerning the Pauline words to the heretics as if the words of Paul are true for them and not or us, but concerning the interpretation of the words. Chytraeus should not take it too badly if we propose Augustine and the whole chorus of the saints against these new men. Augustine says: "But concerning that concupiscence of the flesh of which they speak, I think that they are deceived, or that they deceive; for with this even he that is baptized must struggle with a pious mind, however carefully he presses forward, and is led by the Spirit of God. But although this is called sin, it is certainly so called not because it is sin, but because it is made by sin, as a writing is said to be some one's hand because the hand has written it.[39]

VI

The Gospel teaches that man can by no means satisfy the law of God in this imbecilic nature and that the just man in the perfect fulfillment of the law has committed every sin. (Romans 8). The sense of the enmity of the flesh is against God, for he does not obey the law of God, and cannot even do so. The Popes contend that man can satisfy the law of God and be just in this perfect fulfillment and merit eternal life.

---

[38] Epist. 23 *ad Bonifacium.*

[39] *Contra duas epistolas Pelagianorum*, lib. 1, cap. 13 (27).

The Popes, *i.e.* sons of the Catholic Church, do not say that man in this imbecility of nature has committed every sin. We acknowledge and profess it is very true what John says in the beginning of his epistle: "If we will have said that we have no sin, we deceive ourselves." Yet, these daily sins do not abolish justice, nor are against the law apart from the law of God, when for the remission of the same faults, "every spirit will pray in due season,"[40] and all the just sons of God and saints daily are taught to say: "Forgive us our sins."[41] For that reason, we do not fear to assert that man can be justified by the grace of God, and fulfill the law by the assistance of the same grace and in that fulfillment merit eternal life. We know who said: "And his commandments are not heavy,"[42] and likewise "Call the workers and pay them the wage."[43] And again: "Come ye blessed of my Father and possess the kingdom prepared for you, etc., for they hungered and you gave them to eat."

For this reason Augustine says: "For it is certain that we keep the commandments if we will; but because the will is prepared by the Lord, we must ask of Him for such a force of will as suffices to make us act by the willing."[44] And again: "Therefore, grace is given not because we fulfill the law, but that we can fulfill the law."[45] Nor do the words of the Apostle trouble us: "The sense of the flesh is enmity opposed to God." The same Apostle had already said: "Therefore, I myself serve the law of God in mind, while the flesh serves the law of sin."[46] What we do in mind, we truly do, but what we do in the flesh, if it is opposed to the mind, it is not ours, just as the same Apostle says: "If I do what I refuse, I do not work it."

VII

The Gospel teaches that good works are merely those that were commanded by God, according to the rule whereby he commands us only to those things ratified by the Lord, you shall not add nor take away. But the Popes ruin the whole Church with traditions, etc.

---

[40] Psalm 31 (32):6. Translator's note: Here it must be noted that the Vulgate was revised subsequent to this work to read: "Pro hac orabit ad te omnis sanctus in tempore opportuno." Every one who is holy will pray for this in due season. The original that Bellarmine used is maintained in the translation.

[41] Matth. 6:12.

[42] 1 John 5:3.

[43] Matth. 20:8.

[44] *De gratia et libero arbitrio*, cap. 16 (32).

[45] *De Spiritu et litera*, ca. 10.

[46] Romans 7:25.

As if this had not been repeated by them and refuted a thousand times already. When he says this is contained in the Gospel that good works are only those which God commanded, it is false. Where, I ask, does God command virginity? Doesn't Paul say: "Moreover, concerning virgins I have no precept of the Lord."[47] and still he says in the same place that it is good to remain a virgin, "Therefore, he who marries a virgin does well, but he who does not does better."

And that rule does not help him much; the things that I command you, let only these be done for the Lord. Moreover, in that place God does not forbid something other than that we should break his precepts; rather we should keep them whole, just as he commanded them, not turning to the left or the right. Therefore, St. Augustine, distinguishing precepts from counsels, says: "For it cannot be said: You shall not marry, as it is said 'you shall not commit adultery,' or 'you shall not kill;' the latter are demanded, so they are offered. If the former is done, it is praised, but if the latter two should happen, they are condemned. In the latter the Lord commands us what is due, in the former if you will have overspent, he will render to you upon returning."[48]

VIII

The Gospel teaches that each part of the Sacrament of the Lord's supper must be administered to all Christians, and expressly from the chalice (Drink from this, all of you.) But the Popes decreed and defined otherwise.

Still we do not see that passage of the Gospel where we are taught that each part of the Sacrament must be administered to all Christians. For the Lord does not say: "Drink from this, all Christians", but "drink from this, all of you." And Mark explained who "all of you" might be when he added: "And they all drank from it." Moreover, not all Christians drank, but all the Apostles, who then alone supped with the Lord.

IX

The Gospel teaches that true penance, or conversion to God, is a grave sorrow of heart for sins, and faith establishing that his sins were certainly remitted by Christ, etc. On the other hand, even though the Popes number contrition among the parts of penance, nevertheless they feign that this remission of sins is merited, and add auricular confession that was not commanded by God, and satisfaction or works due= in

---

[47]   1 Cor. 7:25

[48]   *De sancta virginitate*, cap. 30.

which they satisfy for the eternal punishments of sins, and this very thing they devise can be done for money. The whole doctrine is a blasphemy against the merit of the son of God, who alone satisfied for sins.

Here he proves nothing and advances no testimony of the Gospel. I see only inane words poured forth with an admixture of lies. For what he says on conversion and grave sorrow of heart he could omit. We truly require conversion and grave sorrow of heart among penitents, although he requires nothing else than I know not what terrors he has for contrition. What he adds on establishing faith for our sins to be remitted was refuted above. What he says about the Pope's contrition meriting remission of sins is a lie refuted above. When he says the Popes say that temporal satisfaction satisfies for eternal punishments it is equally a lie. For we do not think it satisfies for eternal punishments since we do not doubt it is remitted in justification, rather, God demands men who come to the Sacrament after Baptism to do penance for them either here or in purgatory. St. Augustine says: "The penalty is prolonged beyond the fault, lest, if the penalty were to end with the fault it would be accounted small."[49]

What he adds next about auricular confession not being commanded or that satisfaction is opposed to the merit of Christ is yet another case where he says it but does not prove it. Let him read, if he will, St. Cyprian[50] and he will discover the necessary confession of sin as well as satisfaction repeated in these very terms. Now, that money is paid out for satisfaction among Catholics (lest by chance here he might suspect some foul business) is nothing other than one kind of satisfaction, and it can be changed into a different kind by the judgment of the priest, such as fasting and almsgiving. Let us continue to the rest.

X

The Gospel teaches that one spouse is conceded to all men whether lay or priests, and it says eloquently that the prohibition of a spouse and of food is the doctrine of the devil. On the other hand the Popes forbid a spouse to a great part of men, priests and monks, and command them to abstain from certain foods on certain days.

Where, I ask, does the Gospel teach that a wife is conceded to those who have a vow of continence? Perhaps in Hebrews 13 where we read: "A spouse is

---

[49]   Tract. *in Ioan.* 124, n.5.

[50]   *de lapsis*, serm. 5.

honorable to all [men]." Moreover, if "in all" means absolutely every man, it will be honorable then for a father and daughter to marry, or mother and son, and brother and sister. Yet if Chytraeus does not like this, then he also should not like the idea that marriage would be honorable among a monk and a consecrated nun, or even with the rest of men to whom marriage is not lawful by vow. For the Apostle only means that we will honor marriage in all things when it is rightly and legitimately joined. Moreover it remains for Chytraeus to prove that those who make a vow of perpetual continence can duly and legitimately marry.

Listen to what Chrysostom wrote to a monk by the name of Theodore, who desired to marry or perhaps already had: "Honorable nuptials; but it is not now fitting for you to preserve the privilege of the married and although you frequently call this very thing nuptials, still, I reckon that it is worse than adultery."[51] Concerning that passage of the Apostle, 1 Timoth. 4: "Prohibiting to marry," etc., see what we said above in chapter 21 near the end.

XI

The Gospel teaches that there is one true and solid foundation upon which the Church of God is built, clearly our Lord Jesus Christ (1 Corinth. 3; Acts 4). That passage of Matthew 16 is so interpreted by St. Augustine (upon this rock), saying: 'You are Christ, the son of the living God; this is upon my very self, the son of the living God, I will build my Church; upon me I will build you, not me upon you. Yet the Popes cry out to the contrary that upon the rock of the Roman Church and the ordinary succession of Popes, the whole rest of the Church of the Christian world has been built.

But I believe he does not oppose Paul with himself, when he says: "We are built upon the foundation of Apostles and prophets."[52] Nor does he oppose Paul's assertion: "There is no foundation of the Church apart from Christ."[53] John, in the Apocalypse, ch. 21, when he says: "Twelve Apostles are the foundation of the twelve churches." For Paul speaks on the primary foundation in Corinthians, while he speaks in Ephesians (along with John in the Apocalypse) on the secondary foundations. Augustine speaks on the quality of the foundation in his *Narrations on the Psalms* against the position of the Donatists, where he says: "Count the priests, even from the See of Peter itself.

---

[51] Epist. 6.

[52] Ephes. 2:20.

[53] 1 Corinth. 3:11.

That is the rock which the proud gates of hell do not conquer." But much more was said about this above in book I, ch. X.

XII

The Gospel teaches that no Apostle or bishop, or any minister of the Gospel, is superior to another, or has greater power and dominion in what pertains to ministry. Rather all ministers have equal power to teach the Gospel, administer Sacraments, bind criminals and absolve those doing penance, as Scripture teaches the keys of the kingdom were consigned to all the Apostles equally.[54] On the other hand, the Roman Pontiff boasts that he has supreme power over all other bishops and the whole Church, and carries both the spiritual and political sword by divine law, etc.

Where does the Gospel teach that one bishop or minister does not have greater power than another? I still have not found it. The places that he cites clearly show the contrary. In Luke 22 the Lord exhorts them to humility and forbids them the rule of kings, and also tyranny to those who ought to be in charge of the Church; still among the Apostles one was greater than the rest, nay more, the Lord affirms himself to be the leader of the others. For he says: "He who is greater among you, let him be made the lesser, and he who is excellent (in Greek this is ἡγούμενος, which means a general), let him be just as an attendant." Moreover, the Apostle, where he says that he planted and Apollo watered, and again he laid the foundation just like an architect, and others built,[55] doesn't he mean clearly enough that he is greater than Apollo and the rest of his helpers?

Hence, in John 20 it is said to all the Apostles "Behold, I send you and whoever's sins you will have forgiven, etc."; but in chapter 21 the Apostles and the rest of the faithful are subjected to St. Peter, as sheep to their pastor, since to Peter alone in the presence of the other Apostles did the Lord say: "Feed my sheep." Next, even if in Matthew 18 all the Apostles are indicated with the words "whatever you will have bound, etc.," still, when he said, "I will give you the keys of the kingdom, etc." he said it to Peter alone, and without a doubt the Lord did not promise something to him singly unless he also meant to show something singular to him. But on this we have said much above in Book I, chapters 12-14.

Now, to his objection against the two swords in Bonfiace VIII's teaching

---

[54] Luke 22:24-30, 1 Corinth. 3:4, John 20:21-23 and Matthew 18:18.

[55] 1 Cor. 3.

where he mocks the arguments of that Pontiff, it is best to respond with just one thing in this place. We will take everything from St. Bernard who was a holy man even in the estimation of Chytraeus, as well as the customary plea of Melanchthon and Calvin that we have heard more than once. See book 2 and 4 of *De Consideratione*, or if he would like, he could refer back to the very matter when we dealt with it in the last book on the Pope,[56] and this will suffice for Chytraeus' teaching on Antichrist.

Now we must briefly show that this very vision of John squares better with Luther and Lutherans. In the first place that star which fell from heaven to earth can signify Luther. It is clear since he went from a monk to a secular, from celibate to married, from poor he was made rich, and from sober and modest living to sumptuous dinners and lunches. What else is this than to have fallen from a heavenly way of life to an earthly one?

Next, the smoke from the well of the abyss that follows the fall is clearly the blind and stupid who have no sense. In that before Luther defected from the Catholic Church, nearly the whole West was of the same faith and religion and in whatever direction a man might go, he would always find his brethren. All were then in the light. But after the fall of Luther such a smoke of errors, sects and schisms rose out that now even in the same province, nay more, in the same city or even house, one does not recognize another.

This smoke also obscured (as it says in the Apocalypse) the sun and air. By the sun we understand Christ, through the air the Scriptures, whereby we find, in a certain measure, our own as well as expose our adversaries. Indeed, Transylvania and its nearby regions are a witness of how vehemently this smoke has obscured, where they openly deny the divinity of Christ; Germany is also a witness, where Anabaptists openly and everywhere deny the humanity of Christ. Now truly there were once many heretics that attacked Christ in a similar fashion, but none more impudently than the heretics of this time. For not only do many of them deny that Christ is God, but they add he cannot be invoked nor can we do anything to know him. It is a horror to hear or read with what temerity the heretics of our age dispute the mysteries of Christ.

Again, it is incredible how vehemently this smoke has obscured the Scriptures. Now there are so many versions and commentaries extant that are opposed to one another that what was once clear now seems very obscure. What can be said more clearly than what Paul said, "I have no precept from the Lord on virgins, but I have counsel."[57] And yet all the heretics of our time constantly deny that there ever was a counsel of virginity and that Paul does not

---

[56] See Book V.

[57] 1 Cor. 7:25.

dare to counsel that one embrace virginity in this passage, but rather he simply wanted to discourage man. What can be said more plainly than the word of the Lord, "This is my body"? And yet nothing in this time is more obscure. What shall I say about the Transylvanians? They so pervert their commentaries on the Gospel of John (which was almost certainly written against Cherintus and Ebionis who denied the divinity of Christ) that they especially try to show from it that Christ is not God.

Now let us come to the locusts which come from the smoke of the well. Chytraeus understands through locusts bishops, clergy and monks, but he gets it all wrong, for even before the times of Gregory there were bishops, clergy and monks in the Church; nevertheless these strange locusts had not yet arisen. All the things that John says about the locusts square very suitably with the Lutherans and the other heretics of our time. 1) Locusts always come in great numbers and usually fall in squadrons. "A locust does not have a king and all go out in squadrons."[58] So the Lutherans do not properly have one head since they deny that there is a head of the whole Church. Just the same, they rose in a very brief period to be a vast multitude and no wonder, for they open the door to all vice-filled men; the gluttons run to them, because the Lutherans establish no fasts; the incontinent likewise because they reject all vows of continence. They concede marriage to monks and priests—even consecrated nuns. Likewise all apostates flock to them because all the cloisters are reserved for them and converted into palaces. Greedy and ambitious princes, because they add Ecclesiastical goods to their person and even Ecclesiastical power, they become not only lazy but enemies of good works because among them faith alone suffices; good works are not necessary. Next, all the reprobate and criminals flock to them because they have lifted them from the necessity to confess their sins and give an account to their own pastor, which is usually a bridle to sinners. Hence the locusts have so multiplied.

Moreover, these locusts are described by St. John in a paradoxical fashion. For they are said to have a human face, and even that of a women, the tail of a scorpion, the body of a locust, likewise they wear a crown on their head seeming to be of gold, but they have the teeth of lions and their chest is armed with an iron cuirass. Next, they seem just as horses prepared to battle and once they hear that the alarm has been sounded as the sound of chariots running to war, they had over themselves the king, the angel of the abyss, who is called the exterminator.

The charming faces mean the beginning of their preaching since it always begins from the Gospel. They promise to say nothing but the purest Word of

---

[58] Proverbs 30:27.

God. This is how they so easily attract the more simple. The tail of the scorpion means a poisonous and deadly outlet, for after they proposed the Word of God they foul it up with perverse interpretation, just as a recoiled tail drives in the sting and the lethal venom is found. The body of the locust is almost nothing other than the stomach (for it is a large-bellied insect) and therefore it can neither advance nor fly correctly, but raises itself high by jumping and soon falls to earth. This means the heretics of this time are men addicted to their stomach, enemies of fasting and continence, and therefore can neither advance to the way of the commandments nor fly to contemplate heavenly things.

Certainly they try to raise themselves at some point and amend their morals, but after the fashion of locusts, soon they fall back to earth. The Saxon visitation can serve as an example. Luther noticed that on account of the "gospel liberty" that they had preached all laws of the Church were abrogated and the people, deprived of that bridle, rushed into sin. Therefore, he established the visitation and advised pastors to preach penance, fear of God, obedience and good works. Still, this accomplished nothing.[59]

For equal reason they try to fly through contemplation and already have written everywhere books on the Trinity, on the Incarnation, and on other mysteries of this sort; but they fall into very serious errors, nay more, pernicious heresies, which is clear from the Ubiquists, who destroy the whole mystery of the Incarnation and the Trinity.[60]

The crowns on the head of the locusts mean the arrogance and pride by which they raise themselves over all men. There is a book of Luther extant which was written to Duke George, in which he says, "No doctor or writer from the time of the Apostles, nor even any theologian or canon lawyer has confirmed, instructed and consoled the consciences of those in the lay state as remarkably and beautifully *as I have*. Through a singular grace of God I know this for certain, because neither Ambrose nor Augustine, who are the best in this matter, are equal to me in this." What? Not only do Luther and Calvin make nothing of a thousand Cyprians and a thousand Augustines, but each Lutheran clergyman also holds Papists for asses and whipping posts! Were these the crowns that are just as gold—that is they seemed like gold but were not? They feign themselves full of zeal for the honor of God and moved by charity to say the things they say, when still they are less than acquainted with the zeal of God.

---

[59] See Cochlaeus in the life and acts of Luther, MDXXVII.

[60] Translator's note: The Ubiquists (*ubiquisti*) were a branch of Lutherans founded by Brenz that theld the Eucharist, the body of Christ was everywhere because Christ's flesh had been deified. This doctrine persisted until the Thirty Years War.

The teeth of the lion mean the detractions with which they assiduously slander the repute of Pope, clergy and monks by letters and sermons, as well as the saints themselves who rule in beatitude with God. And they seem to be nurtured by detractions since they make so many which are not, nor have been and perhaps never, that they appear to be utterly devoid of conscience. It is clear enough both from the other things which are read everywhere in their books and from those which a little before we cited in the Smalchaldich council, in Illyricus, Tilman, Calvin and Chytraeus.

The chest armed with an iron breastplate means obstinacy. Our adversaries are so obdurate that even if they were clearly beaten in argument, they will still never yield. Often they prefer to die than to recede from their obstinacy.

The similitude of the horses who seem prepared for war means boldness and temerity. They boldly challenge all to war, even though afterward they only advance a great many lies for argument. Luther said: "Come here all you papists, put together all of your studies and untie this knot if you can."[61] Nearly all the others speak in the same way. But the similitude of the swift chariots means the speed whereby that new heresy uses those possessed of different regions. In short order they occupied not only many kingdoms in the North, but even dared to sally to India, although God did not permit them establish themselves there, since the new and tender parts of the Church of Christ have not yet merited such a scourge.

Next, the angel of the abyss is called the king of these locusts, because even if locusts do not have a visible king, as we noted above, nevertheless, they have an invisible one since they cannot lack the devil as, "He is the king of all the sons of pride."[62] Moreover, the king of the locusts is called the exterminator because the devil never exterminated and devastated the Church through heresy as much as through Lutherans. For a great many of the other heresies destroyed one or another point of faith, but did not overturn all order and discipline in the Church. But the Lutheran heresy partly by itself, and partly by its daughters, Anabaptism, Calvinism, Trinitarianism and Libertinism, have altogether destroyed all goods of the Church in those areas where they prowl. They removed the Trinity from God through the new Samosatens, who also removed divinity from Christ; through the Anabaptists the whole cult and invocation from the angels and saints, the suffrage of the living in purgatory; nay more, they clearly dismissed purgatory itself. From the Church on earth, they removed books of the divine Scripture, nearly all the Sacraments, all traditions, priesthood, sacrifice, vows, fasting, feast days, churches, altars, reliquaries,

---

[61] *Assertio* art. 25.

[62] Job 41:34.

crosses, images, all monuments of piety and likewise Ecclesiastical laws, discipline, and they have also overturned all order.

Only hell remains, but perhaps it spared that lest it would do any injury to its king, the angel of the abyss. Not even this is the case, for many Lutherans deny that hell is a true place and fabricate I know not what sort of imaginary hell, but we spoke of this in Christ's descent into hell in another place.[63] Therefore, truly this can be called the exterminating heresy and a worthy title, which in Hebrew is אבדו‎ [Abadon], in Greek is ἀπολλύων, and in Latin *exterminans*. It should be no wonder if not even the Lutherans themselves marvel at this utter destruction except that, as we have said, they have been blinded by the smoke.

Still, there is one consolation amidst so many evils, that (as John says) these locusts do not harm the grass and the green trees; but only men who do not have the sign of the living God. Although that heresy may be wholly carnal, it cannot easily deceive good men in the souls of whom religion and piety have taken root and flourished. So we see rarely, or it has never happened, that some Church defected from the Lutherans that had not already begun to be corrupted among the lives of Catholics. But that is enough on this business.

---

[63] See Bellarmine, *De Christo.*

CHAPTER XXIV

The Arguments of Calvin and Illyricus are Refuted, Where the Former Tries to Show the Pope is no Longer a Bishop, and the Latter on the Fable of "Pope Joan"

IT only remains that we prove what we had proposed as the last place, that the Roman Pontiff is not only not Antichrist, but that he has not lost his pontificate in any way. Calvin attempts to show by means of a certain conjecture that today he is not a true bishop, saying: "I should like to know what quality of a bishop the Pope himself might have? 1) The office of a bishop is to instruct the people in the Word of God; 2) The next is to administer the Sacraments 3) admonish and exhort, to correct those who are in fault and restrain the people by whole discipline. Now, which of these things does he do? Nay more, which of these things does he pretend to do? Let them say then, on what ground they will have him to be regarded as a bishop when he does not even resemble any part of the duty with his smallest finger.

"It is not with a bishop as with a king. The latter, if he were not to execute the proper duty of a king, nevertheless, he retains the title and the honor. Yet, in judgment about a bishop, the command of Christ is regarded, which ought to always avail in the Church. Let the Papists then untie this knot. I deny that their pontiff is the prince of bishops, seeing that he is no bishop."

Unless I am mistaken, the whole argument can be reduced to a syllogism. Since there is this difference between a bishop and a king, that the king is the name of a power and a prefecture to which is connected the duty of ruling the people, whereas the bishop is the name only of an office to minister the Word of God and the Sacraments; certainly then, if neither king nor bishop exercise their office then the name of king retains its dignity while the name of bishop loses it. Moreover, the Roman Pontiff does not even exercise the episcopal office in any clear manner, seeing that he does not preach the Word of God to the people or administer the Sacraments; therefore the Roman Pontiff has lost the name and dignity and thus cannot be called a bishop.

Moreover, the Centuriators attempt to confirm this conjecture of Calvin's with a sign. They say that the evident sign of the change of the Roman Church into the whore of Babylon was something God willed near those times in which this change took place, that a certain woman who was a harlot would sit in the Papal seat, who was called Pope John VIII.

They attempt to show this, 1) from the authors Platina, Martin Polonus, Sigebert and Marianus Scotus; 2) from the vestiges of the affair which still remain in our time. Without a doubt there is a certain seat made of porphyry that is perforated on the inside, which remains in the palace of St. John Lateran that they say was established for use after the scandal was detected so that it would be discovered whether one recently created Pope was a man or not. Likewise, from a certain statue of a woman with a boy that remained even to our own times in that place, where it says the woman John VIII gave birth. Next, from the fact that the Roman Pontiffs, when they go from the Vatican to the Lateran, usually turn their head away at the place where this woman is said to have given birth in detestation of the fact; otherwise that is a straight road. It is not difficult, however, to untie these knots.

First we shall respond to Calvin. He is either talking about the signification of the name, or about the thing itself, when he says that *bishop* is the name of an office, but *king* is the name of a dignity. If the former, then he is clearly deceived, since a bishop is called from the Greek ἐπισκοπειν (to consider or inspect) and it means the duty of overseeing. In the same way a king (*rex*) is called from ruling (*regendo*) and means the office of ruling. Just as king is the name of a magistrate, so also is ἐπίσκοπος among the pagans, for whom the name meant a magistrate, that is a *praetor*.[1] What is more, the Holy Scripture attributes to a bishop the name of shepherd and king.[2]

But if Calvin speaks on the matter itself, then he is no less deceived. Just as royal authority is not a simple office to judge, as a judge of others, but is a true prefecture in political matters (the power to rule men subjected to him by commands and punishments); so also the episcopate is not a simple office to preach, as it is for others who preach yet are not pastors, but is a true ecclesiastical prefecture that has the power to rule men in spiritual and divine matters—hence to command and punish. We have spoken about that matter and many others above, and we will have much to say elsewhere. For the moment, a few passages will suffice to make the matter crystal clear. The Apostle Paul teaches: "As for the rest, when I come I will distribute it."[3] "Therefore, I write these things being absent because being present I will deal much more severely, according to the power that the Lord has given me."[4] And in Hebrews he says: "Obey those who have been placed over you and be subject to them."[5] Again, in 1 Timothy he says: "Do not receive an accusation against a priest unless it is with two or three witnesses."[6] Besides, it is also false that Popes do not exercise episcopal office. For they are not held to give sermons and minister the

---

[1] Aristophanes, *Birds*.

[2] Isaiah 44; Ephes. 4.

[3] 1 Cor. 11:34.

[4] 2 Cor. 13:10.

[5] Hebrews 13:17.

[6] 1 Tim.. 5:19.

Sacraments *per se*, if they are impeded by some just cause; rather it is sufficient if they will see to it that these things are done by others. Otherwise bishops would be obliged to do the impossible, since there is no place so scanty that a bishop can suffice by himself to preach and minister the Sacraments through the whole diocese. Therefore, just as it satisfies if he will preach through another in some place where he cannot be present, so also it satisfies if he will preach in every place through others when there is no way he could be present there. We do not lack the examples of antiquity. Possidius writes that St. Valerius, the bishop of Hippo, commissioned St. Augustine in the duty of preaching when he was still a priest, because being a Greek he could not preach to the people in Latin.[7] Possidius also relates that in the Eastern Church a great many bishops customarily demanded from their priests that they take up the office of preaching which they could not carry out by themselves. Nevertheless we cannot say that either S. Valerian or others who did not preach the Word of God themselves were not bishops.

Now what the Centuriators say, 1) That Sigebert, Marianus Scotus are more ancient than Martin Polonus, and, they place a "Pope Joan"[8] in their *Chronicles* is altogether false. Even if this is discovered in the printed versions of Sigebert and Marianus Scotus, it is not discovered in the most ancient manuscripts, it is certain that these authors' testimonies are corrupted. The most ancient example of Sigebert's manuscript is still extant from the monastery of Gembloux where he was a monk. It is reckoned to be in Sigebert's own hand and he makes no mention of a "Pope Joan." John Molanus, a Doctor of Louvain that is still alive, is a witness to the example of this manuscript. Likewise, in the most ancient copies of Marianus Scotus a "Pope Joan" cannot be found. The edition of the *Metropoli* of Albert Kranz published in 1524 at Cologne witnesses the fact.

2) Next, it is proved from his own narration that Martin Polonus fabricated this particular tale about "Pope Joan." a) He says this Joan was English from Moguntia. But Moguntia is not in England but in Germany. The Centuriators tell it the other way around, that she was Moguntian but raised in England. Moreover, Theodore Bibliander says in his *Chronicle* that she was not from England at all but merely educated there.

b) Martin and those who follow him says that she devoted herself to letters in Athens. But it is certain in that time there was no academy of letters in Athens or anywhere else in Greece. Synesius writes in his last epistle to his

---

[7] *Vita S. Augustini.*

[8] Translator's note: The Latin reads "*Papa Ioannes foemina*", but for the sake of ease we have rendered it with the more familiar "Joan" in English. In Latin Ioannes is a 3rd declension noun and will have the same endings for masculine and feminine.

brother that in his time Athens was nothing, but he lived just after the times of St. Basil and St. Gregory Nazianzen. Cedrenus and Zonaras write in the lives of the emperors Michael and Theodora, around the end of the reign of Michael when he ruled by himself after he banished his mother Theodora, that schools of philosophy and good letters were restored by Bardas Cesar, when even to that time all studies of wisdom had been extinguished in Greece for a great many years, so much so that not even a vestige remained. It is certain that the reign of Michael by himself fell in the times of Pope Nicholas I who succeeded Benedict III, who succeeded this pretended Joan, that is the woman John VIII which they allege. Furthermore, all histories, even that of Bibliander, place the beginning of the reign of Michael alone in the year 856, while the pontificate of this Joan would have been 854. It follows then that after the death of this Joan education was beginning to revive in Greece.

c) The Centuriators say that this Pope Joan gave birth on a journey from the Vatican to inspect the Church of the Lateran. But it is a certain fact, as Onuphrius proves in a book on the seven churches, that the Roman Pontiffs did not live in the Vatican, but in the Lateran palace even to the times of Benedict IX, that is even to 1390. How, therefore, if she lived in the Lateran, would she want to go from the Vatican to inspect the Lateran? Certainly if anyone were to write today that the Pope went from the Lateran to inspect the Church of the Vatican, it would be ridiculous, since everyone knows the Pope lives in the Vatican.

d) Martin and the others who follow him say this Joan gave birth during a solemn and public service. But this has no probability because a woman that was so many months with child would in no wise wish to proceed since there was a greatest danger of being detected.

3) This same thing is proven from an epistle of Leo IX, a very serious Pope, to Michael the bishop of Constantinople, where Pope Leo writes that the constant report is in the patriarchate of Constantinople that many eunuchs sat and among these a woman had crept in and was patriarch.[9] Leo IX certainly would never have mentioned this to the Greeks if such a thing had happened in the Roman See. Nay more, this is perhaps the root of the fable about Pope Joan. Since there was a rumor that some woman was the bishop of Constantinople, and then little by little, the name of Constantinople was dropped but the opinion and report of a female pontiff remained, and a universal Pontiff at that, some began to say in hatred of the Roman Church that the woman was the Roman Pontiff. And it has the appearance of truth that this rumor arose in the times of Martin. Certainly Martin Polonus, who first wrote this, relates no author but

---

[9] Cap. 23.

only says it is related. Therefore he has this only from an uncertain rumor.

Nor should it be any wonder if someone would fabricate this fable in hatred of the Roman Church, after the foundation about a female Pontiff had been laid amid the greatest contentions that existed in that time between emperors and Popes. For even now we see that the Centuriators fabricate more incredible things. Martin only wrote that this women was English from Moguntia, and added nothing about her parents, or even the woman's proper name. Nevertheless, the Centuriators have felt free to add in the rest of the details, saying that her father was an English priest and that at first she was called Gilberta, and raised in the habit of a man in the monastery of Fuldensis, and that she wrote many books on sorcery. These are all merely fabrications without any witness and devised without reason. Add that Martin Polonus appears to have been very simple, since he wrote many other fables as if they were attested history.

Now what they say about the perforated seat, the statute of the woman and the turning aside on the road are easily answered. It is certain from the book of sacred ceremonies that there were three stone seats in the Lateran Basilica in which a new Pope sat in the time of his coronation.[10] The first seat was before the entrance to the Church and this was low and abject; to such a seat a new Pope was lead and sat somewhat, to show by that ceremony that he ascends from the lowest place to the highest. From there elevating him they sung what we read in 1 Kings 2: "*Suscitat de pulvere egenum, et de stercore erigit pauperem, ut sedeat cum principibus et solium gloriae teneat.*"[11] And this is the reason why these were called the seats of the dung hill. The second seat was made of porphyry in the palace itself, and there he sat a second time in the sign of possession, and also sitting there he received the keys of the Church in the Lateran Palace. The third seat was similar to the second and not far from it, and also sitting it in after a short time, he handed the same keys to the one from whom he had received them, perhaps that this ceremony would remind him of death through which in a short time he was going to hand that power to another. From that seat, to the discovery of his actual sex, there is never a mention.

But the statue of the woman with the child without a doubt was not Pope Joan. For if our adversaries say that ancient historians refused to place the memory of this event in their books, how does it have the appearance of truth that the Popes themselves would have wanted to remember it with a statue?

---

[10] *Sacrarum Ceremoniarum,* lib. 1, sec. 2.

[11] "He raises the poor man out of the dust, the beggar out of the dung pile to sit among the princes and take hold of the throne of glory." 1 Kings (Samuel) 2:8.

Next, if the statue was of "Joan," it would represent a woman with a little infant just born, but the image relates neither a woman, nor an infant she was bearing in her bosom, but a boy sufficiently large and several years old as if going before a servant. For that reason some men think it was a statue of some heathen priest prepared to sacrifice which his minister went before. Next, why the Popes omit the shorter way when setting out for the Lateran is not in detestation of any scandal but because that way is narrow and bent and it is usually very busy. Add that, as Onuphrius witnesses, there are plenty of Popes that have never once traveled on this road.

Book IV
On the Supreme Spiritual Power of the Pope

CHAPTER I

Whether the Pope is the Supreme Judge in Controversies of Faith and Morals

ITHERTO, in spite of the lack of our own genius, we have proven that: 1) the bishop of Rome was constituted by Christ as the supreme pastor of the whole Catholic Church; 2) he has never degenerated into Antichrist; 3) he has not lost this supreme dignity in any other way. Now we must treat on his power both spiritually and temporally. In the present book we shall treat on the spiritual power; the following and last book will be on the temporal power, with the help of God.

Although many things in particular could be discussed on the spiritual power of the Pontiff, still there are four principal questions:

1) On the power of judging controversies of faith and morals; that is, whether this power is placed in the Supreme Pontiff.

2) On the certitude or, we might say, on the infallibility of this judgment, namely, whether the Supreme Pontiff could err in controversies of faith and morals.

3) On the coercive power of imposing laws, that is, whether the Supreme Pontiff not only judges and does not err in his judgment, but also whether he can impose laws that oblige men in conscience and compel them to believe and act according to how the Supreme Pontiff has judged.

4) On the communication of this power, or whether jurisdiction over all other ecclesiastical prelates was communicated to the Supreme Pontiff by them, or whether it was received immediately from God.

Besides these general questions theologians usually treat particular ones, such as whether the Supreme Pontiff can call, transfer, or dissolve general councils, whether he can confer indulgences; whether he can canonize saints; whether he can approve or condemn religious societies and whether he can choose or at least confirm bishops. All of these questions, however, and others of this sort are not proper to this place. The first group pertains to the disputation on councils, the second group to the disputation on Penance; the third to the disputation on the cult of the saints, the fourth to the disputation on vows and institutes of monks; the fifth to the disputation on the clergy. There, God willing, we will treat those questions.

We now take up the first general question on judgment of controversies, and we will spend a great deal of time on this point. For we already showed in the disputation on the Word of God that Scripture is not a judge of controversies, neither are secular princes or private men, whether approved or learned; rather ecclesiastical prelates. Now, in the disputation on councils it will be proven that councils indeed give judgment on controversies of religion (both general and particular) and that judgment is both firm and ratified, but only when the confirmation of the Supreme Pontiff comes. Hence, the Supreme Pontiff has the last judgment.

Therefore, in this disputation on the Pope we show the Supreme Pontiff is head and pastor of the whole Church. For what else do we show than that he is the supreme judge in the Church? There is either no one who ought to be a judge among men, or there ought to be one who is in charge of the rest. Nor do I think this ever could be recalled to controversy.

In the following this very question will become plain. For if we could show that the judgment of the Supreme Pontiff is certain and infallible then certainly it will establish that the same Pontiff is also the supreme judge of the Church. To what end would God have attributed infallibility in judgment to the Apostolic See except that he attributed supreme power in judgment to the same See? Lest we might say nothing on this point, let us advance a few testimonies from the law, the Gospel and the Fathers. In Deuteronomy there is a very famous testimony wherein doubts that arose on religion were referred to the judgment of the high priest. Moses says: "If you will have observed a difficult and ambiguous judgment between subject and subject, leper and leper, and you will see words of the judges differ within your gates; then rise and ascend to the place which the Lord your God will have chosen, and you will come to the priest of the tribe of Levi, and you will seek the judge who will be present in that time from them, who will judge the truth of your case, and you will do whatever those who are in charge of the place will have said, whom the Lord chose."[1] In that passage we must observe that two persons are distinguished: the priest and the judge, *i.e.*, the pontiff and the prince. The pronouncement of the sentence by the priest demands execution by the judge. Deuteronomy explains it this way: "Whoever will have been proud, refusing to obey the command of the priest, who in that time ministers to the Lord your God, will die by the judgment of the judge."[2]

In the Gospel, nothing is said more clearly than what the Lord says to Peter in the presence of the other Apostles: "Simon, son of John, feed my sheep." There we see two things: a) he speaks to Peter specifically, b) so much so that he does not exclude even the Apostles when he gives his sheep to him to be fed. Moreover, there cannot be any doubt whether it is among the duties of a pastor to discern the good pasture from the bad.

For this reason St. Jerome, a most learned man, in the question on the three hypostases did not trust his own erudition, nor the opinion of the Eastern bishops, nor even in the authority of his own bishop, Paul, the Patriarch of

---

[1] Deut. 17:8.

[2] Deut. 17:12.

Antioch. Rather he wrote to Pope Damasus, saying: "I, a sheep, demand assistance from the pastor. Please, discern, for I will not fear to say three hypostases if you bid it so."[3]

Theodoret, who was also very learned among the Greek Fathers, wrote to Pope Leo I, saying "If Paul, the herald of truth, the trumpet of the Holy Spirit, hastened to the great Peter to carry from him the solution to the difficulties of those at Antioch who hesitated from conformity with the law, much more do we, men insignificant and small, hasten to your Apostolic See in order to receive from you a cure for the wounds of the churches."[4]

Prosper of Aquitaine says in his *Chronicle* for the year 420: "In a council held at Carthage consisting of 216 bishops, the synodal decrees were advanced to Pope Zozimus; after they were approved, the Pelagian heresy was condemned throughout the world." Thus, the whole world recognizes a final judgment only from the Roman Pontiff. St. Gregory, whom everyone judges to have been very humble and never took something to himself unless it were just, spoke thus in an epistle to all the bishops of France: "If on the other hand (God forbid that his providence should allow it to come about), some contention or business would emerge where perhaps the force of it would cause something to come into doubt, and due to its magnitude it would require a judgment of the Apostolic See, then, after the truth has been more diligently examined, let all labor be spent from that relation to our examination, insofar as a suitable judgment from us will end the matter beyond any doubt."[5] The fact is that these holy Popes asserted the same thing before and after Gregory; yet we never read that anyone condemned this.[6]

---

[3] Epist., 15, n. 2 (ML, XXII, 355).

[4] Epistula 113 *ad Leonem I.*

[5] *Epistles*, lib. 4, epist 52.

[6] See also Innocent I, *in epistola ad Anastasium Thessalonicensem*; Gelasius I *epistola ad Episcopos Dardaniae;* Nicolas I *epistola ad Michaelem Imperatorem,* Innocent III *epistola ad archatensem Episcopum,* there the chapter is extent "Majores", and the one on Baptism.

CHAPTER II

A Question is Proposed: Whether a Judgment of the Pope is Certain?

NOW we come to the second question, but first it must be known at the outset that the Pope can be considered in four ways. 1) As a particular person or a private teacher; 2) As Pope, but by himself; 3) As Pope, but joined to a customary body of counselors; 4. As Pope together with a General Council.

Secondly, it must be observed that when it is asked whether the Pope could err, two things can be asked in all four of the ways that we have already considered. 1) Whether he could be a heretic. 2) Whether he could teach heresy. Then, it ought to be noted that 3) while on the one hand the judgments and decrees of the Pontiffs treat on all matters which are proposed for the whole Church, such as those decrees on faith and general precepts of morals; on the other there are particular matters that pertain to a few, such as nearly all controversies of fact; whether so and so should be promoted to the episcopate, or whether it was done lawfully, or whether he must be deposed.

With these things being noted, all Catholics and the heretics agree on two things. Firstly, that the Pontiff, even as Pontiff, can err in particular controversies of fact, even together with a general Council, because these depend especially on the testimonies of men. Secondly, the Pope can err as a private teacher from ignorance, even in universal questions of law concerning both faith and morals, just as what happens to other teachers.

Next, all Catholics agree on two other things, but only amongst themselves and not with the heretics. Firstly, the Pope with a general council cannot err when he issues decrees of faith or general precepts of morals. Secondly, the Pope, by himself or with a particular council, while stating something in a doubtful matter, whether he could err or not, must be obediently heard by all the faithful.

With such things being laid out, only four different opinions remain.

1) Should the Pope define something, even as Pope, and even with a general Council, it can be heretical in itself, and he can teach others heresy and that this in fact has happened thus. This is the opinion of all the heretics of this time, and especially of Luther, who in his book on councils recorded the errors even of general councils that the Pope approved. It is also the opinion of Calvin,[1] who asserted that at some time the Pope with the whole college of Cardinals manifestly taught heresy on that question of whether the soul of man is extinguished with the body, which is a manifest lie, as we will show a little later.

---

[1] *Instit.* lib. 4, cap. 7 § 28.

Next, he teaches in the same book[2] that the Pope can err even with a general council.

2) The second opinion is that the Pope even as Pope can be a heretic and teach heresy, if he defines something without a general Council, something that this opinion holds did in fact happen. Nilos Cabásilas has followed this opinion in his book against the primacy of the Pope; a few others follow the same opinion, especially amongst the Parisian theologians such as John Gerson, Almain[3] and still, Alonso de Castro[4] as well as Pope Adrian VI in his question on Confirmation; all of these constitute infallibility of judgment on matters of faith not with the Pope, but with the Church or a General Council.

3) The Third opinion is on another extreme, that the Pope cannot in any way be a heretic nor publicly teach heresy, even if he alone should define some matter, as Albert Pighius says.[5]

4) The fourth opinion is that in a certain measure, whether the Pope can be a heretic or not, he cannot define a heretical proposition that must be believed by the whole Church in any way. This is a very common opinion of nearly all Catholics.[6]

These authors seem in some way to disagree with themselves because some of them say the Pontiff cannot err if he should proceed maturely and listen to the counsel of other pastors, while others say the Pope can err in no way whatsoever, even by himself; but really they do not disagree among themselves. For the latter would not deny whether the Pope should be held to proceed maturely and consult learned men; rather, they only wished to say that infallibility itself is not in a body of counselors or in a council of bishops, but in the Pope alone. On the other hand, the former would not have it that they place infallibility in the counselors, but only in the Pontiff; rather they wished to explain that the Pope ought to do what is in himself by consulting learned men and experts in the matter which is treated. If anyone would ask, however, whether the Pope could err if he should rashly define something, then without

---

[2] Cap. 9 § 9.

[3] Libris *de potestate Ecclesiae*.

[4] Lib. 1, cap. 2, *contra haeres.*

[5] Lib. 4 *hier. Eccl.* cap. 8.

[6] St. Thomas Aquinas, 2 *Sentences*, 2 q. 1, art. 10; Thomas Waldensis, lib. 2, doctr. fidei cap. 37 and 48] Juan Torquemada, lib. 2 *Summae*, cap. 109, et sequentibus; John Driedo, lib. 4 *de Ecclesiast. dogmat.* cap. 3, part 3; Cajetan in *de Potestate Papae et Concilii*, cap. 9; Hosius *contra Brentium*, lib. 2, which is on legitimate judgments; John of Eck, lib. 1 *de primate Petri*, cap. 18; John of Louvain, lib. *de perpetua cathedrae Petri protectione et firmitate*, cap. 11; Pedro de Soto in his *apologia*, par. 1, cap. 83, 84, and 85; Melchior Cano, *De Locis*, book 6, cap. 7

a doubt the aforesaid authors would all respond that it cannot happen that the Pope would rashly define something, for God has promised the end, and without a doubt he promised also the means which are necessary to obtain that end. It would be of little benefit to know that the Pope was not going to err when he rashly defined something unless we also knew that the providence of God would not permit him to define something rashly.

From these four opinions, the first is heretical; the second is not properly heretical, for we see that some who follow this opinion are tolerated by the Church, even though it seems altogether erroneous and proximate to heresy. The third is probable, though it is still not certain. The fourth is very certain and must be asserted, and we will state a few propositions so that it can be understood and confirmed more easily.

CHAPTER III

The First Proposition is Established, On the Infallible Judgment of the Supreme Pontiff

THEREFORE we come to the first proposition. *The Supreme Pontiff can in no case err when he teaches the whole Church in those matters which pertain to faith.* This is against the first and second opinion we laid down in the last chapter, and in favor of the fourth. It is also proved by the promise of the Lord in Luke 22, as we find it in the Greek: "Simon, Simon, behold, Satan has asked for you that he might sift you like wheat, yet I have prayed for thee that thy faith would not fail, and that, thou later being converted, confirm thy brethren." This passage is usually explained in three ways.

1) The first exposition is of the Parisian theologians, that the Lord here prayed for the universal Church, or even for Peter who stood as a figure of the whole Church, and prayed that the faith of the Catholic Church would never fail. Such an exposition would be true, were it to be understood that he [Christ] prayed for the head of the Church and consequently for the whole body, which is represented by the head; but that is not how they understand it. They would have it that the prayer was only for the Church.

This exposition is false. Firstly, because the Lord designated only one person, saying twice "Simon," and adding, as often, the second person pronoun, "for thee," "thy faith," and "thou," "thy brethren." To what end would he do this? So that we would understand that Christ asked something special for Peter. Secondly, because the Lord began to speak in the plural: "Satan has asked that he might sift *you*," but soon after changes his manner of speaking and said: "But I have prayed for *thee*." Why did he not say for *you* as he had begun? Certainly if he were to speak on the whole Church, it would have been much more correct to say "for you."[1] Thirdly, the Lord prayed for the one to whom he said: "And later, being converted," but this certainly cannot agree to the whole Church unless we were to say that at some time the whole Church was corrupted and later converted again. Fourthly, he prayed for the one to whom he said: "Confirm thy brethren." Yet the Church does not have brothers whom she ought or can confirm for who, I ask, can be imagined as a brother of the universal Church? Are not all the faithful her sons?

2) The second exposition is from certain men who live in this time. They teach that the Lord only prayed in this passage for the perseverance of Peter in the grace of God even to the end. Yet against this, firstly the Lord prayed a little

---

[1]   Translator's note: We have intentionally used the early modern English singulars, *thou, thee, thine* to maintain the distinctions of Latin and Greek, which have different forms for the singular and plural 2nd person pronouns.

after for the perseverance of all the Apostles, nay more, even of all the elect, for in John 17 he said: "O holy Father, preserve them whom you have given me in your name." Thus there would be no reason why he should pray for Peter's perseverance twice. Secondly, because without a doubt the Lord asked something special for Peter, which is clear from the designation of a certain person; but perseverance in grace is a common gift of all the elect. Thirdly, because it is certain that the Lord at least mediately prayed in this place for the other Apostles. Therefore, he prefaced the purpose of this prayer: "Satan has asked that he might sift *you*," and afterward added just as the effect: "Confirm thy brethren." Therefore, the Lord did not pray only for Peter's perseverance but to grant some gift upon Peter for the use of the others. Fourthly, the gift asked for Peter in this citation also pertains to the successors. For Christ prayed for Peter to the advantage of the Church; but the Church always needs someone by whom she is confirmed, whose faith cannot fail. For the devil did not ask only to sift those who were at that time faithful but everyone altogether; nevertheless, certainly this gift of perseverance does not pertain to all the successors of Peter. Next, the Lord did not say I have prayed that your charity shall not fail but your faith, and really we know that Peter failed in charity and grace when he denied the Lord, but we know his faith did not fail.

3) Therefore, the true exposition is that the Lord asked for two privileges for Peter. One, that he could not ever lose the true faith insofar as he was tempted by the Devil, and that is something more than the gift of perseverance. For the Lord said to persevere even to the end; although Peter fell in the meantime, he still rose again in the end and was discovered faithful, since the Lord prayed for Peter that he could never fall because he held fast to the faith.

The second privilege is that he, as the Pope, could never teach something against the faith, or that there would never be found one in his see who would teach against the true faith. From these privileges, we see that the first did not remain to his successors, but the second without a doubt did.

Concerning the first privilege, we have the express testimony of the Fathers. St. Augustine said: "When he asked that his faith would not fail, he asked that he would have the freest, strongest, unconquered perseverance of the will in faith."[2] St. John Chrysostom says: "He did not say, 'You will not deny me,' but, 'that thy faith should not fail.' For by Christ's care and favor it came about that the faith of Peter did not altogether vanish."[3] Theophylactus said, commenting on Luke 22, "Although you must be struck for a short time, you have the seeds of reformed faith, even if the spirit will throw off the leaves of the first, still the

---

[2] *De correptione et gratia*, cap. 8.

[3] Homil. 83 in Matth.

root will live, and thy faith will not fail." Here, he explains with an elegant similitude that Peter, by denying Christ, lost the confession of the faith which is made with the mouth, which the words about the leaves mean; but the faith which is believed with the heart unto justice would not be lost. Prosper of Aquitaine explains this in the same manner.[4] Although the rest of the Fathers do not call to mind the other privilege, still they do not deny that, nor could they deny it, unless they would contradict many other Fathers.

On the second privilege, we have, in the first place, the testimonies of seven Fathers who were also holy Popes. Lucius I, a Pope and martyr said, "The Roman Apostolic Church is the mother of all churches and has never been shown to have wandered from the path of apostolic tradition; nor being deformed, succumbed to heretical novelties, according to the promise of the Lord himself, saying, 'I have prayed for thee, etc.'"[5] Pope Felix I, speaking on the Roman Church, said: "As it took up in the beginning the norm of the Christian Faith from its authors, the princes of the Apostles of Christ, she remains unsullied according to what the Lord said: 'I have prayed for thee, etc.'"

Pope Leo I said, "The special care of Peter is received from the Lord; he prayed for the faith of Peter in particular inasmuch as the state of the others would be more certain if the mind of the prince were not conquered. Therefore, in Peter the strength of all is fortified and the help of divine grace is so ordered that the strength which was given to Peter through Christ would be conferred through Peter to the remaining Apostles." In that citation, Leo recognizes both privileges; the first when he says: "If the mind of the prince was not conquered." The second, when he adds: "The strength which was given to Peter through Christ would be conferred through Peter to the remaining Apostles." For strength is not conferred upon others except by expressing the true faith.

Next, Pope Agatho said in a letter which was read in the Sixth Council, Act 4, and afterwards in Act 8 and approved by all, "This is the rule of the true faith, which both in prosperity and in adversity the Apostolic Church of Christ has vivaciously held fast, which has been shown to have never wandered from the path of Apostolic tradition, by the grace of God, nor being deformed, succumbed to heretical novelties since it was said to Peter: 'Simon, Simon, behold ... but I have prayed for thee, etc.' Here the Lord promised that the faith of Peter was not going to fail, and admonished him to confirm his brethren. The fact that the Apostolic Pontiffs, predecessors of my lowliness, always did this from the divine assurance is recognized by all."

Pope Nicholas I said: "The privileges of this see are perpetual, divinely

---

[4]   *De vocatione gentium*, lib. 1, cap. ult.

[5]   In epist. I *ad Episcopos Hispaniae et Galliae*.

rooted and also planted. One can strike against them but not transfer them; one can drag them but not tear them out. Those matters which were formerly your imperium remain, thanks be to God, insofar as they are inviolate; they will remain after you and so long as the Christian name will be preached, they will not cease to exist. ... For among other things, these privileges are especially conferred through us, 'Thou later being converted,' he heard from the Lord, 'confirm thy brethren.'"[6]

Leo IX said in an epistle to Peter of Antioch, "Without a doubt, it was for he alone whom the Lord and Savior asserted that he prayed that his faith would not fail, saying, 'I have prayed for thee, etc.' Such a venerable and efficacious prayer obtained that to this point the faith of Peter has not failed, nor can it be believed that it is ever going to fail in his throne." Pope Innocent III, in an epistle to the bishop of Arles said: "The Fathers, for the sake of the Church, understood especially in regard to articles of faith that those words refer to the see of Peter, who knew the Lord had prayed for him lest his faith would fail."[7] It seems that these pontiffs should be believed, both because they were saints, and because without a doubt the authority of their see must especially be noted.

Apart from these Popes, other authors are not lacking who express the point in the same way. Theophylactus, in chapter 21 of Luke, openly teaches that this privilege was given to Peter because he was going to be the prince and head of others; hence it was given to all the others that would succeed him in that supremacy: "Because I have you as a prince of the disciples, confirm the others. This is fitting for you, who are the rock of the Church after me, as well as the foundation." St. Peter Chrysologus said: "We exhort you, Honorable Brother, that you would obediently attend to that which has been written by the Pope of the city of Rome because Blessed Peter, who lives in his own See and presides there, is in charge of all those seeking the truth of faith." For although this author does not cite that passage of the Gospel: "I have prayed for thee, etc.," still, in the matter he considers without any doubt and faithfully affirms that the truth of faith is supplied to all those seeking it from the Roman See.

St. Bernard says, "It is fitting that every danger and scandal of the kingdom of God be referred to your apostolate and especially these which touch upon the faith. For I regard it worthy that there, above all, dangers to the faith are mended, where one cannot think the faith is lacking. For to what other see was it ever said: 'I have prayed for thee, that thy faith not fail?'"[8]

Our adversaries, however, object to this explanation. Firstly, because there

---

[6] Epistle to the Emperor Michael.

[7] Contained in cap. *Maiores, extra, de Baptismo et eius effectu.*

[8] *Epist. 190 ad Innocentium.*

was no Roman Church when Christ promised to Peter that his faith would not fail nor did the Lord ever mention the Roman See. Therefore, how can it be gathered that the Lord promised something to the Roman See when he said, "I have prayed for thee, etc."? Secondly, because if what is said to Peter, "I have prayed for thee, etc." is said to the successors, then: "And after thou being converted," was also said to the successors, then all the successors of Peter at some time denied Christ and later were converted.

I respond to the first: Christ is said to have prayed for the Roman See because he prayed for Peter and his successors, whose See was established at Rome.

To the second I say, 1) it is not absurd if we say that "being converted" is not referred to the penance of Peter but to the temptations of the others. Therefore, the sense should not be: *Being converted from sin to penance, confirm thy brethren*, but, *thou, whose faith cannot fail, when you will have seen the others wavering and vacillating, being converted to then confirm them*. For he had not yet preached to Peter about his fall, but he was going to a little after, so it seems absurd if he should first preach conversion rather than aversion, resurrection rather than the fall. 2) I say that if we were to explain "being converted" from negation, it does not necessarily agree with the successors of Peter to be converted from the sin of denial although necessarily "confirm the brethren" still would fit them. For being converted from sin does not agree with men except insofar as they are private persons, and therefore is a personal gift; to confirm brethren agrees with men as they are the head and prince of others and pass it on to their successors.

Secondly, the same conclusion is proven from that promise made to Peter in Matthew 16: "Upon this rock I will build my Church, and the gates of hell will not prevail against it." For as we showed above,[9] Peter is called literally the rock and foundation of the Church as the supreme ruler of the Church and hence his successor is similarly the rock and foundation of the Church. Thereupon we take up a two-fold argument.

First, why would the Pope be called rock, from the name of Peter, except because of constancy and solidity? Certainly if he is rock, he will not be broken nor carried around on every wind of doctrine. He will not err in faith at least insofar as he is the rock, that is, insofar as he is the Pope.

Second, by reason of the foundation holding up the building, which in no way can come to ruin. For if the building is such that it cannot fall to ruin, certainly its foundation cannot come to ruin. For it cannot be understood how the foundation would be destroyed and the house not fall. Nay more, for greater

---

[9] Book I, Chapter X.

reasoning the foundation cannot be destroyed if the house cannot fall. For the foundation receives nothing from the house, but the house receives strength from the foundation, and in this way all the Fathers express and deduce that Peter—and consequently the other Popes—cannot err. Origen says on this citation: "It is manifest, even if it were not expressed, because the gates of hell can prevail against neither Peter nor the Church, for if they prevailed against the rock on which the Church was founded, they would prevail against the Church."

Chrysostom says in this place, that only God could establish that the Church could be founded upon one fisherman, an ignoble man, and not fall through so many invading storms. Cyril (quoted in the *Catena Aurea* of St. Thomas) says on this point, "According to this promise, the Apostolic Church of Peter remains Immaculate from all seduction and heretical deceit, etc."[10] Theodoret said, "This Holy See holds the reign of the Churches of the world, not only on account of other things, but also because she remains free from the heretical stench."[11] There Theodoret seems to argue thus: the rule of the whole Church ought to be of that see which cannot fail in faith; we see, however, that only the Roman See is and was free of every heretical depravity; therefore, it is manifest that it is the one to which the rule of the churches was granted.

Jerome, in an epistle to Pope Damasus on the term *hypostasis*, just after saying: "I know that the Church was built upon this rock," he adds: "I ask that authority be given me by your letter either of not saying a word or else of saying three hypostases; I will not fear to say three hypostases if you bid it be said." There he asserts that he is going to safely follow the judgment of the Pope because he knows that upon him the Church was founded. It cannot happen that the foundation of the Church would fall. St. Augustine speaks in similar fashion against the Donatists: "Count the priests even from the very See of Peter; in the order of the Fathers who you see have succeeded the other, it is the very rock which the proud gates of hell shall not conquer."[12]

Gelasius, in an epistle to Emperor Anastasius, said: "This is what the Apostolic See guards against with all her strength because the glorious confession of the Apostle is the root of the world, so that she is polluted by no crack of depravity and altogether no contagion. For if such a thing would ever occur (which may God forbid and we trust cannot be), why would we make bold to resist any error?" Here Gelasius teaches that the Apostolic See cannot err because its preaching and confession is the root of the world; if it should err, the

---

[10] *Catena Aurea*, Matthew 16:13-19.

[11] *Epistola ad Renatum Presbyterum Romanum.*

[12] *In Psalmo contra partem Donati.*

world would err.

St. Gregory the Great shows that it cannot happen that the bishop of Constantinople could be a universal bishop, and hence the head of the Church, because many bishops of Constantinople were public heretics; nay more, even heresiarchs such as Macedonius and Nestorius. For it seems to follow that the whole Church would fall to ruin if he who is universal would do so.[13] He speaks likewise to Eulogius: "Who does not know that the whole Church was strengthened in the firmness of the prince of the Apostles, to whom it was said, 'Upon this rock I will build my Church, ... and thou, being converted, confirm thy brethren?'"[14] There Gregory clearly teaches that the strength of the Church depends upon the strength of Peter, and hence Peter is less able to err than the Church herself.

Thirdly, it is proved from that we read in John 21: "Feed my sheep." For what do we gather from these words but that the Pontiff was established as Pastor and Doctor of the whole Church, the proof of which was given above.[15] Hence the argument is thus: The Pope is the Teacher and Shepherd of the whole Church; thus, the whole Church is so bound to hear and follow him that if he would err, the whole Church would err.

Now our adversaries respond that the Church ought to hear him so long as he teaches correctly, for God must be heard more than men.

On the other hand, who will judge whether the Pope has taught rightly or not? For it is not for the sheep to judge whether the shepherd wanders off, not even and especially in those matters which are truly doubtful. Nor do Christian sheep have any greater judge or teacher to whom they might have recourse. As we showed above,[16] from the whole Church one can appeal to the Pope, yet from him no one is able to appeal; therefore necessarily the whole Church will err if the Pontiff would err.

Again, however, they respond that one can have recourse to a general Council. But this is also not so; as we will show in the treatise on councils, the Pope is above a Council and it is certain that general councils often erred when they lacked the judgment of the Supreme Pontiff; this is clear from the Second Council of Ephesus, the Council of Armenia, and others. Now they will respond again: one can have recourse to a general council in which the Pope is present, for a council with a Pope is something greater than the Pope alone. Still, in the first place the Lord said only to Peter: "I have prayed for thee, etc.," and "Feed

---

[13] Lib 4, epistol. 32 *ad Mauritium.*

[14] Lib. 7, epist. 37 *ad Eulogium*

[15] Lib 1, cap. 14, 15, 16.

[16] Lib. 2, cap. 13 et 14

my sheep;" he did not say this to Peter and a council. Likewise, he only calls Peter the rock and foundation, not Peter with a council; from which it appears that the whole strength of legitimate councils rests upon the Pope, not partly on the Pope and partly on a council. Next, a general council often cannot be gathered, just as it could not be done in the first three centuries on account of the persecutions of the heathen, and without a doubt the Church could persevere in that state even to the end of the world; therefore, there ought to be in the Church, even without a general council, some judge who could not err. Thereupon, what if in some council the Fathers should dissent from their president, that is, the council from the Supreme Pontiff while present and presiding, what would happen then? Would there be no remedy? Certainly there must be some judge. Moreover, the council could not be a judge in that case because when councils disagree with the Pope they can err, and have erred in fact, as we said about the Second Council of Ephesus and others; therefore it remains that the Pope must be a judge, and hence he cannot err.

Fourthly, it is proved from the Old Testament, which was a figure of the New. In Exodus 28:4 the Lord commands doctrine and truth to be placed in the judgment of the high priest, which is אורים ר תומים [or-eem tu-meem] (perfect lights) in Hebrew. Moreover, it must be observed that there is no agreement among the Jews nor even among Christians on what these two things might be. Rabbi Salomon would have it that it is the name of God יהוה [ye-cho-vach] (Jehova) written in a judgment, whose lightening the priests recognized as a divine response, since someone requested it. Arias Montanus teaches in his *Apparatus* that they are two very lucid stones that were produced immediately by God Himself and given to Moses. Josephus says that these are twelve stones in which were written the names of the twelve sons of Israel (Jacob) whom God commanded to be placed in the accounting, and he also mixes in many fables.[17] St. Augustine gives a more probable explanation that these very words were written in golden letters in the middle of the burse which hung before the breast of the priest.

What the Jews and Judaizers say does not hinder this explanation, namely that אורים [or-eem] does not mean doctrine, but splendors, from the root אור [or] (light); and תומים [tu-meem], does not mean to mean the truth, but perfection, from the root תמם [ta-maam] (perfect). Yet, Jerome must be believed more, who translates doctrine and truth along with the translators of the Septuagint, who likewise translate it: "δέλωσιν, καὶ αληθειαν," than the rabbis, and hence it must be said that אורים [or-eem] comes from the root ירת [ya-raat] which is *he taught*, and תומים [tu-meem] comes from the root אמן [a-man] *he*

---

[17] *Antiquitatum*, lib. 3, cap. 12.

believed.

Furthermore, why doctrine and truth would be written on the breast of the priest is explained in Deuteronomy 17, where the Lord commanded those who doubt the understanding of divine law should go up to the high priest, seek from him the solution and add, "Those things which he will show, let them be the truth of judgment to you." And therefore, by sign and word the Lord promised that on the breast of the high priest he was going to have doctrine and truth, and hence he was not going to err when he taught the people. But if this was fitting to the Aaronic priesthood, how much more fitting is it for the Christian priesthood? For this reason St. Peter Chrysologus, as was said a little before, exhorted Eutyches: "We exhort you, Honorable Brother, that you would obediently attend to that which has been written by the Pope of the city of Rome, because Blessed Peter, who lives in his own See, and presides there, is in charge of all those seeking the truth of faith."

Fifthly, it is proven from experience, and in that two-fold. For in the first place, it is certain that all patriarchal sees so fell from the faith that heretics sat in them teaching others their heresy, with the exception of the Roman See. The heresiarchs Macedonius, Nestorius, and Sergius sat in the See of Constantinople. The Arians Georgius and Lucis, along with Dioscorus the Monophysite, Cyrus the Monothelite, and many others sat in Alexandria. At Antioch there was Paul of Samosata, Peter Gnaphaeus the Monophysite, Macharius the Monothelite, and others. John the follower of Origen, and before him Eutychus, Irenaeus and Hilary the Arians sat in Jerusalem. No such thing can be shown from the Roman Church, from which it appears that the Lord truly prayed for it lest its faith would fail. For this reason, Ruffinus states in his exposition of the Creed: "In the Church of the City of Rome, no heresy ever had its beginning, and there the ancient custom is preserved."

The second thing which experience shows is that the Roman Pontiff has condemned a great many heresies without a general council, namely that of Pelagius, Priscillia, Jovinian, Vigliantius, and many others, whom the whole Church held as true heretics and shuddered at them simply because the Roman Church had condemned them. Therefore, it is a sign that the whole Church believes that the Roman Pontiff cannot err in matters of this sort. See also Prosper of Aquitaine in the last book against Collator and Peter the deacon.[18]

---

[18] *De Incarnatione, et gratia Christi ad Fulgentium.*

CHAPTER IV
On the Roman Church in Particular

HE SECOND proposition. *Not only can the Roman Pontiff not err in faith, but even the particular Roman Church cannot err.*

In this place it must be observed that the strength of the Roman Church in faith should be received in one sense, and the strength of the Pontiff in another. The Pope cannot err from a judicial error, that is, while he judges and defines a question of faith; but the Roman Church, that is, the people and the Roman clergy, cannot so err from a personal error so that everyone would err and there would be no faithful in the Roman Church adhering to the Pope. Even though individuals might err on their own, still it cannot happen that all will err as a body and the whole Roman Church become apostate.

Moreover, that the Roman Church cannot err in the manner explained can still be understood in two ways: In one way, that it cannot err while the Apostolic See continues to be at Rome; it would be otherwise if the See were to be transferred somewhere else. In the second way, that it simply cannot err or defect because the Apostolic See can never be transferred from Rome to another place. And indeed, following the earlier sense, our proposition is very true and perhaps as true as the first proposition concerning the Pope. For the authors we cited, such as Pope Lucius and Felix, martyrs, Agatho and Nicholas, confessors, and likewise Cyril and Ruffinus, all assert that not only the Pope but also the Roman Church cannot err.

Besides, St. Cyprian says, "They dared to sail to the chair of Peter and the principal Church, for they do not consider it is the Roman See, where treachery can gain no inroad."[1] St. Jerome said: "The Roman faith was praised by the apostolic voice; it does not receive deceptions of this sort. Even if an angel will announce differently than once was preached, by the authority of Paul, it cannot be changed." St. Gregory Nazianzen, in a poem about his life, around the middle said, "Old Rome has from ancient times held the right faith, and always retained it; just as it is fitting for the city which presides over the whole world, it always holds the faith whole from God."

I add even the testimony of two Popes, who also were condemned by heretics, but were received with the greatest honor by Catholics. One is Pope Martin VI, who in his Bull, which he published approving the Council of Constance, thought that they who thought differently than the Roman Church or the Sacraments or on the articles of faith should be held as heretics.

The other is Pope Sixtus IV, who first through the Synod of Álcala, then by

---

[1] Libro I, epistola 3.

himself, condemned the articles of a certain Peter of Oxford, one of which was that the Church of the city of Rome could err. And although this seems to be understood particularly on account of the Pope, still, because the Roman Church is not only the Pope but the Pope and the people, then when the Fathers or Popes say the Roman Church cannot err they mean that in the Roman Church there is always going to be a bishop teaching in a Catholic way and a people believing in a Catholic way.

But following the second sense, that the Roman Church cannot defect, is certainly pious and a very probable opinion; still it is not so certain that the contrary can be called heretical, or manifestly erroneous, as John Driedo teaches.[2] The fact is, it is not completely *de fide* that the Roman Church cannot be separated from the Apostolic See since neither Scripture nor tradition has the Apostolic See so fixed at Rome that it could not be transferred elsewhere. And all the testimonies of the Popes and Fathers (who say the Roman Church cannot err) can be related about the Roman Church as long as it shall remain in that Apostolic See, but not absolutely and simply.

Just the same, it is still a pious and very probable opinion that the chair of Peter cannot be separated from Rome, and hence the Roman Church absolutely cannot err or defect. It is proved firstly from the fact that the Apostolic See has remained in Rome for such a long time in spite of infinite persecutions as well as opportunities to move elsewhere. The first reason offered the greatest occasion to transfer the Roman See into another place in the times of the heathen emperors. They were very disturbed that the Apostolic See was in Rome, and for that reason whenever they heard a new bishop had been created, he was either killed or sent off into exile. Hence Cyprian praised the constancy of Pope Cornelius: "How great was the strength in the reception of his Episcopate? How great a strength of soul, what kind of strength of faith? Fearless he sat at Rome in the sacerdotal chair, in that time when the dangerous tyrant rounded up the priests of God by both lawful and unlawful means, although he heard that an envious prince had risen against him much more patiently and tolerably than that a priest of God had been constituted at Rome."[3]

The next occasion to transfer the see occurred in the time of the Goths, particularly during the time of Innocent I when Alaric took Rome, despoiled and burned it, as Jerome relates in his letter to Principia on the death of Marcella. Next, in the time of Leo I, when Genseric again took Rome and despoiled it, as Blondus writes,[4] in which period Rome remained for some space of time without

---

[2] *De Ecclesiasticis dogmat. et Scripturis*, lib. 4, cap. 3, par. 3.

[3] Lib. 4, epist. 2.

[4] Lib. 2 *decadis* 1.

an inhabitant. Again in the time of Pope Vigilius, Totila, having brought down a great part of the walls and burning nearly all the houses, nearly overthrew Rome, laid desolate the city and neither man nor women remained therein, as Blondus writes in the same work.[5] After that, in the whole time of the Lombards, the Roman Pontiffs were in the greatest misery, as is clear from many epistles of St. Gregory. Yet the Roman Pontiffs never thought of changing their Episcopate from Rome.

The third occasion of transferring the see was in the time of St. Bernard, on account of the persecution of the citizens of Rome. For so many years, Roman citizens had so troubled their Pontiffs that they were often compelled to leave the city into exile, as is certain both from historians and from St. Bernard.[6]

The fourth occasion was when the Roman Pontiffs remained in France for 70 years. Firstly, although they bided their time far away from Rome with the whole curia, why, I ask, did they not transfer the see? Why did they not exchange the Roman episcopate for that of Avignon? Since there were so many occasions to transfer it but still the see remained in Rome for more than 1500 years, it is very probable that it can in no way be transferred.

Secondly, this same thing can be proven from the fact that God himself commanded the Apostolic See of Peter to be established in Rome. Men cannot change anything that God commands. Blessed Marcellus, Pope and martyr, in an epistle to the people of Antioch, witnesses this command when he says that Peter, at God's bidding, transferred his seat from Antioch to Rome. St. Ambrose also witnesses this in his oration on the handing over of the basilicas, where he relates that Christ altogether willed that Peter should die at Rome. And for this reason when Christ met Peter fleeing from the city, he [Christ] said, "I am coming to Rome to be crucified again." It is a manifest sign that God wanted to confirm the See of Peter at Rome through his death. What Pope St. Leo I says also pertains to this: "The trophy of the cross of Christ you bore to the bitter Romans, where you, by divine pre-ordination, went ahead and obtained the honor of power and glory of the passion."[7]

Someone will say that it seems that this argument proves that the see cannot be transferred from Rome. For if it is of the faith, divine precepts cannot be changed by men; if therefore God commanded the see to be constituted at Rome, it would seem to be *de fide* that it cannot be transferred anywhere else.

I respond: That does not follow, for Marcellus and Leo do not define this matter as if it were *de fide*; rather they tell it as history. Moreover, they are not

---

[5]   Lib. 6.

[6]   Epistola 242 a*d populum Romanum*; epistola 243 *ad Conradum imperatorem.*

[7]   Serm. 1 *de natali Apostolorum Petri et Pauli.*

de fide accounts of the Pontiffs but only decrees. Next, what they themselves say, that at the Lord's command Peter transferred his see into the city, can be understood in two ways: 1) because the Lord commanded this when he appeared to Peter and then truly it was said by divine precept that the See of Peter was constituted at Rome; or 2) that Christ indeed did not clearly command it but that he said it was commanded because Peter did it by God's inspiration, just as all decrees and precepts of the Church can be said to be divine, which still are nevertheless changeable.

It happens that even if it were established that Christ commanded Peter that he should place his See in Rome, still it would not immediately follow that the command to do this was unchangeable. Because it is not certain how Christ commanded Peter that he should establish his see at Rome, therefore it is not *de fide* divine and immutable precept that the see was constituted at Rome. Still, as we said, it is very probable and is piously believed. Nor is it opposed that in the time of Antichrist Rome must be destroyed and burned, as is deduced from chapter 17 of the Apocalypse. For this will not be until the end of the world, and besides the Supreme Pontiff is called the Roman Pontiff and he will survive even though he will not live at Rome, just as he did in the time of Totila the king of the Goths as we said above. Besides, Augustine and many others commenting on that passage of the Apocalypse would not have it that Rome must be burned, but the multitude of the impious, which is the city of the devil.

CHAPTER V
On Decrees of Morals

HE THIRD proposition is thus: *Not only can the Supreme Pontiff not err in decrees of faith, but even in precepts of morals which are prescribed for the whole Church and which in matters necessary to salvation or in those matters treated which in themselves are good or evil.*

1) We say that the Pope cannot err in precepts which are prescribed for the whole Church since, as we said above, in precepts and particular judgments it is not absurd for the Pope to err. 2) We add in the second place that he cannot err in those matters which are necessary to salvation, or that are good and evil in themselves. Still, it is not erroneous to say the Pope in all his laws can err, without a doubt by fashioning a superfluous law, or one less discreet, etc. And we will declare the whole matter by examples. It cannot happen that the Pope would err by commanding some vice like usury, or by forbidding some virtue like restitution, since these are in themselves good or evil; nor can it happen that he would err by commanding something against salvation, like circumcision, or the Sabbath, or by forbidding something necessary for salvation, like Baptism and Eucharist. Although these things might not be good or evil in themselves, nevertheless, it is not absurd to say it can happen that he might bid something which is neither good nor evil in itself, or against salvation, but that is simply useless or he might command under some grave penalty; although it is not for subordinates to doubt on such a matter, but simply obey.

Now the proposition is proved: 1) It cannot happen that the Pope would err in precepts of morals necessary to salvation because then the whole Church would be gravely wounded in necessary matters, contrary to the promise of the Lord. "When the Spirit of truth will come, he will teach you all truth."[1] That is understood (at least) on a truth necessary to salvation. 2) Because then God would fail his Church in necessary matters, seeing that he would have commanded her that she should follow the Pope and yet permit the Pope to err in necessary matters. But if God is absent from no affair in regard to necessity, how much less from his Church? Moreover, that the Pope cannot err in morals that are in themselves good or bad is proved; for the Church could not be called holy as in the Creed. She is called holy chiefly due to holy profession, as we showed in another place, because without a doubt she declares a law and holy profession that teaches nothing false and commands nothing evil. Secondly, because then necessarily she would err concerning faith. For Catholic faith teaches that every truth is good, every vice is evil; but if the Pope would err by commanding vices or by forbidding virtues, the Church would be held to believe vices are good and virtues are bad, unless she would sin against conscience.

---

[1] John 16:13.

CHAPTER VI
On the Pope as a Particular Person

HE FOURTH proposition. It is probable and may piously be believed that not only as 'Pope' can the Supreme Pontiff not err, but he cannot be a heretic even as a particular person by pertinaciously believing something false against the faith. It is proved: 1) because it seems to require the sweet disposition of the providence of God.

For the Pope not only should not, but cannot preach heresy, but rather should always preach the truth. He will certainly do that, since the Lord commanded him to confirm his brethren, and for that reason added: "I have prayed for thee, that thy faith shall not fail," that is, that at least the preaching of the true faith shall not fail in thy throne. How, I ask, will a heretical Pope confirm the brethren in faith and always preach the true faith? Certainly God can wrench the confession of the true faith out of the heart of a heretic just as he placed the words in the mouth of Balaam's ass. Still, this will be a great violence, and not in keeping with the providence of God that sweetly disposes all things.

2) It is proved *ab eventu.* For to this point no [Pontiff] has been a heretic, or certainly it cannot be proven that any of them were heretics; therefore it is a sign that such a thing cannot be.[1]

---

[1] For more on this see Albert Pighius.

CHAPTER VII

The Objections are Answered by an Appeal to Reason

OW we take up arguments to the contrary, partly from reason and partly from the examples of various Pontiffs. 1) Many canons teach that the Pope cannot be judged unless he may be discovered to have deviated from the faith; therefore he can deviate from the faith. Otherwise these canons would be to no effect. This is clear from the preceding canon, *Si Papa*, dist. 40, from the 5th Council under Symachus, from the Eighth General Council, action 7, from the third epistle of Anacletus, the second epistle of Eusebius, and from Innocent III.[1]

I respond to the first: All of those canons speak on a personal error of the Pope, not a judicial one. For the Pontiff, if he could be a heretic, will only be so by denying some truth that has already been defined; he cannot be a heretic when he defines something new since in that instance he does not understand contrary to something defined by the Church. But the canons cited speak expressly on heresy; therefore they do not speak on the judicial error but personal error of the Pontiff. Secondly, I say those canons do not mean the Pope can err as a private person but only that the Pope cannot be judged; it is still not altogether certain whether the Pontiff could be a heretic or not. Thus, they add the condition 'if he might become a heretic' for greater caution.

2) If the Pope alone can infallibly define dogmas of faith then councils are in vain or at least unnecessary.

I respond: That does not follow. For even if infallibility might be in the Pontiff still he ought not condemn human and ordinary means whereby one can arrive at a truth of faith in the treatment of some matter. Moreover, a greater or lesser council is an ordinary medium for the magnitude or paucity of a matter that it treats. That is clear from the example of the Apostles. Certainly both Peter and Paul were able to infallibly define any controversy you like as individuals but they still called a council in Acts chapter 15.

Next, definitions of the faith especially depend on the Apostolic tradition and the consensus of the churches, but so that the opinion of the whole Church might be recognized when some question arises, they preserve the tradition of the Church of Christ. There is no better plan to do this than if the bishops from all the provinces should come together into one to relate the custom of his Church.

Besides, councils are very useful and often necessary to really put an end to controversies by not only making decrees on faith, but also preserving them. For

---

[1] *Sermon. 2, de consecration Pontificis.*

when a general council happens all the bishops subscribe and profess themselves to embrace that decree, and afterward they will preach in their churches; but if a general council does not happen, it is not so easy to reduce a decree made on faith to practice. It is possible that some may feign ignorance of the decree; others might complain they were not called and others even openly say the Pope could err, but on this matter we will speak more in the treatise on *Councils*, chapter X and XI.

3) If the Pope were infallible in a judgment of faith, they would be heretics or at least held in pernicious error and sin gravely who pertinaciously assert something against a definition of the Pope. But this is false, for St. Cyprian pertinaciously resisted Pope Stephen when he defined that heretics must not be rebaptized, as is clear from the epistle of the same Cyprian to Pompeius, and still not only was he not a heretic, but he did not sin mortally. For mortal sins are not blotted out except through Penance, even if one should die for the faith. Still, the Church venerates Cyprian as a saint, even though he does not appear to have ever repudiated his own error. This is confirmed by St. Augustine who says that the churches gave way on that question and Cyprian, as well as others, could dissent for the sake of charity among themselves until a definition of a general council would come about.[2] Therefore, Augustine did not think that a judgment of the Roman Pontiff was beyond doubt.

I respond to the example of Cyprian: Cyprian certainly was not a heretic, both because those who say that the Pope can err are not reckoned manifestly heretical, but also because there is no question that Pope Stephen did not define as *de fide* that heretics must not be rebaptized, although he commanded this not to be done, as is clear from the fact that he did not excommunicate Cyprian and others thinking the contrary. In like manner, Cyprian refused that it be held as *de fide* where he defined in the Council of 80 bishops that heretics must be rebaptized, protesting eloquently that he did not wish to separate himself from others because they thought differently.

Nor is this opposed to what Eusebius[3] and Augustine[4] write. Pope Stephen did not command lest those baptized by heretics should be rebaptized; but when he also opined that those who did not obey must be excommunicated, that was but a threat. For it is certain from St. Vincent of Lérin in his book on profane novelties of speech, and from Augustine (loc. cit.) that Stephen and Cyprian were always in union.

---

[2] *De Baptismo*, lib. 1, cap. 18 et alibi

[3] *Histor.* lib. 7, cap. 4.

[4] *De unico Baptismo*, cap. 14.

Through this a response can also be made to confirm it. For after the definition of the Pope he was still free to think otherwise, as Augustine says, because the Pope refused to make the matter *de fide* without a general council: rather he merely wished for the ancient custom to be preserved. Whether Cyprian sinned mortally by not obeying the Pontiff is not at all certain. For on his side it did not seem a mortal sin, because he did not sin but from ignorance; for he thought the Pope perniciously erred, and standing on that opinion, he felt obliged not to obey lest he would act against his conscience. But it does not seem the ignorance of Cyprian was crass, nor feigned; but it is probable and hence excuses from mortal sin. For he knew the Pope did not define the matter as *de fide* and saw that the Council of 80 bishops agreed with him. Why else would Blessed Augustine expressly teach that Cyprian only sinned venially and for the sake of charity; therefore it was easily purged by the knife of martyrdom?[5] Augustine also says that this sin was like a blemish in the glory of his holy soul, which the abundance of charity covered.

On the other hand, it seems he still sinned mortally since he did not obey the expressed apostolic precept, and disturbed the Pontiff without measure when he thought correctly. Even if Stephan did not define the matter as *de fide*, still he lately commanded that heretics should not be rebaptized, as Cyprian himself affirms in his epistle to Pompeius. Cyprian ought to obey his command and subject his judgment to the judgment of his superior, and at least ought not have advanced contumelious words, such as he advanced against Pope Stephen in his epistle to Pompeius, where he calls him proud, unlearned, blind and a fool, etc. Therefore, St. Augustine in his 48th Epistle to Vincentium, while he otherwise tries to defend Cyprian, asserted that where the contumelies are discovered these were either not his writings, or that afterward he did penance for his error and changed his opinion before death, although no retraction was discovered.

4) The African Council asserts in its epistle to Pope Celestine that a provincial council can err less in judgment than the Roman Pontiff: "Perhaps there is not anyone who would believe God can inspire justice of examination in each of us and reject the innumerable priests gathered in Council." But it is certain provincial councils can err; consequently the Pope can err much more.

I respond: The council speaks not on a judgment of faith but of fact, namely on the cases of bishops and priests who are accused of some crime. In cases like this, we affirm the Pope does not have the assistance of the Holy Spirit by whose assistance he cannot err. Additionally, we are not necessarily held to believe something these bishops say in that epistle, especially since it sufficiently appears that they were moved by the crimes of Apiarius who had

---

[5]   *Contra Donatistas*, lib. 1, ca. 18.

fled to the Roman Pontiff after he had in some measure exceeded the boundaries of polite speech. That the African Council was confirmed by Leo IV[6] does not oppose this since the decrees of the council were confirmed, but not of the epistle.

5) Nilos Cabásilas reasons this way in his little book on the primacy, "The Roman Pontiff can fall into any other vice, like avarice or pride, etc., therefore he can also fall into the vice of heresy. For Paul says some men were shipwrecked in regard to the faith, because beforehand they had lost a good conscience.[7] Likewise the Pope can deny God in deed by living badly, according to Titus 1: 'They confessed that they know God, but deny him with their deeds.' Therefore, he can also deny in deed for it seems easier to deny by word than by deed."

I respond to the first argument: Therein it is gathered correctly that the Pope by his own nature can fall into heresy, but not when we posit the singular assistance of God which Christ asked for him by his prayer. Furthermore, Christ prayed lest his faith would fail, not lest he would fall into vice.

To the second point, I say: The Apostle in that place does not understand any evil work you like, but works that proceed from infidelity of heart. For he speaks on the Jews that did not sincerely convert to the faith and profess that they know God but nevertheless, deny him by works because, by forbidding certain foods as unclean by their nature, they showed that they did not truly know the creator of all things.

Moreover, the Pope does not, nor can, do such works. But if by "deeds" we understand whatever sin you like, it would be false since it is easier to deny God by word than by deed. For who denies by word, denies simply and expressly, who denies by deed, denies him implicitly and in a certain measure, not simply.

---

6 Dist. 20, can. *de libellis.*

7 1 Tim. 1:19.

CHAPTER VIII

On the Errors Which are Falsely Ascribed to the Roman Pontiffs Peter, Linus, Anacletus, Thelesphorus, Victor, Zephyrinus, Urban, Pontian, Cornelius and Marcelinus, Who Were not only Popes, but even Martyrs

ET us now come to the individual Popes whom our adversaries contend have erred. The first is Peter. Nilos Cabásilas, in his book, *On the Primacy of the Roman Pontiff,* writes that Peter erred not only once but twice concerning faith. Further, he even supposes that by this argumentation he has proven that the Roman Pontiffs can err in faith. Certainly no Roman Pontiff received greater privileges from God than Peter. Moreover, it is clear from Scripture that Peter erred twice, both when he denied Christ,[1] and when he compelled the Gentiles to Judaize.[2] The Lutheran Centuriators of Magdeburg add, apart from these two errors, another thirteen falls of St. Peter, on which we wrote elsewhere.[3]

We respond: When St. Peter denied Christ, he had not yet begun to be the Supreme Pontiff, for it is certain that ecclesiastical rule was handed to him by Christ in the last chapter of John, since the Lord said to him after the resurrection: "Simon, son of John, feed my sheep." Therefore, that denial of Peter cannot be numbered among errors of the Roman Pontiffs. Besides, I add that Peter denied Christ with words, but not truly in his heart; hence Peter did not throw off the confession of faith, nor faith itself, as we showed previously.

Now, on the other hand, when St. Peter compelled the Gentiles to Judaize, this was not an error of preaching but of conduct, as Tertullian suggests in his work *de Praescriptionibus adversus haereticos.* St. Peter did not ratify by some decree that they must Judaize; rather, he formally taught the contrary in Acts XV. Nevertheless, when he was still in Antioch, he separated himself from the dinner table of the Gentiles lest he would give offense to those recently converted to the faith from the Jews, and by his example compelled them to Judaize in a certain measure, even Barnabas. But we do not deny that Popes can offer the occasion of erring through their own bad example; rather, we deny that they can prescribe the whole Church to follow some error *ex cathedra.* Moreover, the examples and doctrines of the Pontiffs are not equally pernicious

---

[1] Matthew 26:69-75.

[2] Galatians 2:11-14.

[3] *Cent.* 2, lib. 2, ch. 10, col. 558, 559, 560. (See: *On the Roman Pontiff,* book 1, ch. 28).

to the Church, seeing that the Lord instructed them, saying: "Do what they say, but do not do what they do."[4]

The second is Linus, who immediately succeeded St. Peter in the pontifical seat. He is mocked by the Centuriators because he had forbidden women to go into church without their heads covered.[5] He said: "It is established that no woman (certainly worthy of episcopal care) should enter into the Church with her head uncovered." But what if Linus would have added, that it were not fitting on account of the angels? Without a doubt they would claim that it is superstition. But the Centuriators have forgotten, I believe, that the Apostle Paul did not judge it unworthy of his care to command that women should veil their head on account of the angels;[6] St. Ambrose explains that this custom must be especially preserved in the Church on account of the reverence of priests, who are called "angels" in the Scripture.

The third is Anacletus, whom the Centuriators condemn in the same book,[7] because he built a memorial of St. Peter and adorned it. Certainly St. Peter merited so little from the Church that it was fitting for his memory to altogether cease! But if blessed Anacletus must be blamed because he established some monument for the bones of St. Peter, how much greater, I ask, was the sin of Constantine the Great, who built such a sumptuous basilica and adorned it with so many golden and silver gifts to the memory of St. Peter? But otherwise concerning all these things, all pious men judge differently than our adversaries judge them now. Certainly the very noble writer Gaius, so near to apostolic times, as Eusebius relates,[8] calls the tombs of Peter and Paul the trophies of the Apostles, by which the Roman Church is fortified as if by the firmest columns.

John Chrysostom expressed his supreme desire of coming to Rome so that he could fall prostrate at the tombs of Peter and Paul.[9] And I ask that you listen to the great honor with which he speaks about the city of Rome as well as the bodies and tombs of the Apostles: "Just as a great and strong body has two bright eyes, (Rome) has the bodies of those saints. Heaven does not so glitter, when the sun sends forth its rays; just as the city of the Romans pouring forth the light from those two lamps throughout the world. ... How great are those two crowns that adorn the city? What golden chains encompass her about? What fonts does she have? This is why I celebrate this city, not because of its

---

[4] Matth. 23:3.

[5] *Cent.* 1, lib. 2, ch. 10, colum. 627.

[6] 1 Corin. 11: 6-10.

[7] lib. 2, cap 20, col. 628.

[8] *lib.* 2 hist. ch. 25.

[9] In homily 32 on the *Epistle to the Romans*.

supply of gold, nor its many columns, nor on account of another fancy, but on account of those columns of the Church. Who will grant me now to throw myself around the body of Paul? To be fastened to his tomb? To see the dust of that body?" He further adds: "This body fortifies the city, which is more secure than innumerable towers, walls and ramparts; and with it is also the body of Peter. For Paul also honored him while he was alive, saying: 'I went up to see Peter.'"

Moreover, Theodoret not only praises Rome for many things, but most especially for the tombs of the Apostles, which he says illuminate the souls of the faithful. I pass over many other testimonies that can be added since they are proper to the disputation on the relics of the saints, which will be taken up in another place.

The fourth is Thelesphorus, who was the ninth Pope after St. Peter, and ended in a glorious martyrdom, as Irenaeus witnessed.[10] The Centuriators accuse him in these words: "He first commanded clerics that they should fast from meat for seven weeks before Easter, although it is against what is written: 'Let no man judge you in regard to food and drink.' Next, he increased the Masses and augmented their rites, and also bound it to the seasons, although the Lord's supper was not established on account of number, or ceremonies, or time. Likewise, he raised the dignity of clerics and their sanctity exceedingly above the people, as if it were not written that all are one in Christ Jesus. Moreover, he would not have priests charged or accused by the people, and he calls that law the firmest wall of his order, constituted by himself and the Fathers against persecutors."[11]

These clearly are the errors of Thelesphorus, which are judged to be errors by the Centuriators because such are against the rule of Luther; but if we judge justly, would it not rather more be said that the dogmas of Luther, which do not suffer the choice of foods, nor Masses, nor the rank of priests above the people, are erroneous and false, because they disagree with the rule of Thelesphorus? For since Thelesphorus was a saint and a martyr, and very close to the times of the Apostles, and even could have spoken with Peter, Paul and John, is it not more believable that he could better recognize the doctrine of Christ than Luther, who was not a martyr and lived 1400 years after the times of the Apostles? These are petty arguments of the Centuriators, and answered a thousand times.

For what they advance from Paul: "Let no man judge you on food and drink," are not opposed to taking up abstinence from meat, or having such

---

[10] lib. 3, ca. 3.

[11] *Cent.* 2, cap. 10, col. 212.

abstinence appointed to a season to subdue the wantonness of the body; rather they are opposed to those who never use certain foods for the very reason that they were unclean according to the Old Law. Thus the same citation of Paul applies to them: "Let no man judge you in food or drink, or on the day of the feast, or a new moon, or the Sabbath, which are shadows of things to come."[12]

They add that the Lord's Supper was not established in regard to number, nor in regard to rite or time; we do not deny this. But what happens from there? Did Telesphorous err on that account, when he wished three Masses to be celebrated on Christmas, and added other rites, and established the times in which Masses were to be celebrated? For although the Lord's supper was not established in regard to number, rite and time, still the number, rite and time ought to be determined in regard to celebrating the very supper of the Lord rightly, unless perhaps order would be less fitting to such a Sacrament than disorder.

Next, they add from the Apostle: "All of you are one in Christ Jesus."[13] This proves nothing less than that priests are no more worthy than laity. Paul explains precisely how we are all one in Christ when he says we are one body, where there are various members, eyes, hands, feet, and some are more noble and worthy than others.[14]

The fifth is Pope Victor, the fifteenth Pope from St. Peter. He was once infamously accused by certain heretics, as though he had taught that Christ was only a man, as Eusebius relates.[15] Yet, Eusebius proves this was a false calumny in the same place; it is certain that the prince of that heresy, Theodotus, was excommunicated by Victor.

The sixth is Pope Zephyrinus, the successor to Pope Victor, who seems to have ratified the heresy of the Montanists. Tertullian writes in his book against Praxea, that the Roman Pontiff, recognizing the prophecies of Montanus, advanced the peace to the churches of Asia and Phrygia by that recognition and was persuaded by Praxea to recall the letters of peace which he had already sent out. It is certain from the histories that Zephyrinus was the bishop of Rome at that time. For that reason, Rhenanus, in his annotations to Tertullian, placed this remark in the margin, that the bishop of Rome accepted Montanism. Nor can it be said that in this period this heresy was not yet condemned by the Church, since, as Tertullian says in the same place, Praxeas persuaded the Pope to recall

---

[12] Coloss. 2: 16.

[13] Galat. 3: 28.

[14] Rom. 12:4-8; 1 Cor. 12:4-31.

[15] Lib. 5, hist. ch. 28.

the letters of peace, for the very reason that his predecessors had already condemned that heresy.

I respond: Trust is not to be altogether placed in Tertullian on this question, as he was a Montanist himself at this time. Just as a little earlier Artemon had falsely claimed that Victor, the Roman Pope, agreed with him (which we have already shown from Eusebius), so at this time when Tertullian was a Montanist he tried to drag the Roman Pope into the opinion of Montanus. Otherwise, why did neither Eusebius, nor anyone else, record this error in the Roman Pontiff?

Still, because often it is the case that lies are founded upon some truth, it is believable that Pope Zephyrinus was persuaded by the Montanists that the doctrine of Montanus was not different from the doctrine of the Roman Church, and therefore, the same Pope wished to restore peace to them which his predecessors had taken away. He did not even approve the error which his predecessors condemned; rather, he thought the Montanists were falsely accused concerning these errors. This is not, however, to err concerning faith nor to accept the error of Montanism, as Rhenanus pretends, but to err in his person, which happens also to many other holy men. Ruffinus writes in his book that Arius, so that he might persuade the Emperor Constantine that he was Catholic, wrote his belief by a careful artifice so that he should be reckoned as a Catholic, yet still be recognized for what he was by his own followers.[16] Moreover, Pope Leo I warns that bishop in no uncertain terms to command the Pelagians returning to the Church to abjure heresy, because most of the time they deceive the Church with a confession of their faith that is so composed that they might appear Catholic, when they are not.[17] This very thing appears to have also happened to Pope Zephyrinus.

The seventh is Urban, the eighteenth Pope from St. Peter. The Centuriators condemn him in these words: "He established Confirmation after Baptism, but blasphemously says, through the imposition of the hands of bishops Christians receive the Holy Spirit and become fully Christian."[18] They also condemn Pope Cornelius for the same error.[19]

Yet, in the first place, they are lying when they say the Sacrament of Confirmation was established by Pope Urban. For its use exists in the Acts of the Apostles 8 and 19, where the Apostles impose their hands over the baptized, so that they would receive the Holy Spirit. And besides, Tertullian, who is older than both Urban and Cornelius, mentions Confirmation in many places. In his

---

[16] Lib. 10, hist. ch. 11.

[17] *Epist.* 86 to Nicetas of Aquileia.

[18] *Cent.* 3, ch. 10, col. 277.

[19] *Ibid*, col. 282.

work, *de Resurrectione Carnis,* he says: "Flesh is washed, so that the soul will be without stain; the flesh is anointed, that the soul be consecrated." And in *de Praescriptiones contra Haereticos,* speaking about the Devil, who imitates our Baptism and Confirmation: "He imbues, at any rate, certain believers and his faithful; he signs his soldiers there on the forehead." And in *de Baptismo*: "Furthermore, going out from the laver we are anointed with blessed Unction." And a little further: "Next the hand is imposed, calling forth through blessing and inviting the Holy Spirit." Do you not see with Tertullian Unction, a sign on the forehead, imposition of hands, arrival of the Holy Spirit? Therefore, what could Urban establish? It is certain that Tertullian was older than Urban. For Tertullian lived in the times of the Emperor Severus, and his son Antoninus, as the Centuriators teach basing themselves on Jerome in the same volume of the *Centuries.*[20] What of the fact that the same Centuriators number among "the blemishes of Tertullian" that he recognized anointing after Baptism as well as the necessary sign of the Cross? Therefore, how can they embrace this idea that Confirmation was established by Urban, when they already placed it among the "blemishes of Tertullian," who is older than Urban?

Next, when the Centuriators add that what Urban says is a blasphemy, namely that men receive the Holy Spirit and are made fully Christians through the imposition of hands of bishops, they do not require refutation, since they advance no proof. Especially when Cornelius also says the same thing, as they affirm, and even Cyprian,[21] Cyril,[22] Augustine[23] and other Fathers frequently do.

The Eighth Pope who is said to have erred is Pontianus, the successor of Urban. The Centuriators accuse him of writing that priests confect the body of the Lord by their own mouth, and give it to the people, and that God receives the sacrifices of others as well as forgives their sins and reconciles them through the priests.[24] The Centuriators so greatly call this teaching a blasphemy, but they advance nothing whereby they prove it is a blasphemy. They ought not take it so badly if we believe a holy martyr and what was established by the Apostles more than what was established by Luther, especially since we read the same thing in the writings of all the ancient Fathers.

Listen to Jerome in his epistle to Heliodorus: "Far be it that I would speak evil about anyone who, succeeding to the apostolic step, confects the body of Christ with his own holy mouth, through whom we are also Christians; who,

---

[20] *Cent.* 3, ch. 10, col. 277.

[21] lib. 1, epistle 12.

[22] *Catechesis* 3, mystagogica.

[23] *in epistolam Ioannis,* tract 6.

[24] *Cent.* 3, ch. 10, col. 278.

having the keys of the kingdom of heaven, in a certain measure, judge before the day of judgment."

Listen to Augustine, where he speaks about captive women among the barbarians: "Pray to God for them, and entreat that he would teach them to say such things as St. Azarias poured forth to God in his prayer and confessions among other things. They are thus in the land of their captivity, just as they [the Israelites] were in that land, where they could not sacrifice to the Lord in their custom; just as they cannot offer oblation at the altar of God, or discover there a priest, through whom they might offer it to God."[25]

Listen to Chrysostom, in the third book on priesthood, where he says: "To purge the leprosy of the body, or that I might speak more truly, not even to purge, but to show one has been purged, it was lawful to do so to the priests of the Jews alone. On the other hand, to our priests, I do not say to prove they have been cleansed, but that it has indeed been conceded to them to cleanse not the leprosy of the body, but the filth of the soul." Therefore, when Pontianus says that through the priests the body of the Lord is confected, the offerings of others are received by God and the sins of men are forgiven, he says what even the most approved authors said, Jerome, Augustine, Chrysostom, and still all the rest, whom I pass over for the sake of brevity.

The ninth is Pope Cornelius, whom the Centuriators claim taught that only water was to be offered in the chalice of the Lord.[26] Such an error was shown to be against the Gospel, but this is a very impudent calumny. They prove this only from what Cyprian relates to Cornelius where he makes many arguments against this error.[27] But Cyprian does not say this is Cornelius' error, but that of others. Next, that epistle was not written to Cornelius, but to Caecilius, a certain African bishop, as other examples show. But the Centuriators then by chance drank more liberally and with sparkling and heavy eyes read one for another. Add that Pope Alexander, the predecessor of Cornelius, already published a decree lest anyone would offer anything other than wine mixed with water in the chalice of the Lord.

Next, if from this epistle they condemn others, why do the Centuriators not condemn themselves? Accordingly, Cyprian, more often in this epistle, calls the Eucharist a sacrifice, and does not teach that only water or only wine must be offered, but water mixed with wine. The Lutherans, however, obstinately deny that the Eucharist is a sacrifice and judge that only wine must be consecrated in the chalice without water.

---

[25] Epist. 122 *ad Victorianum.*

[26] *Cent.* 3, ch. 6, col. 145 and ch. 7, col. 165.

[27] Lib. 2, epist. 3, *ad Cornelium.*

The tenth is Pope Marcelinus, who sacrificed to idols, as is certain from the Pontifical of Damasus, the Council of Sinvessanus, and from the epistle of Nicholas I to the Emperor Michael. But Marcelinus neither taught something against faith, nor was a heretic, or unfaithful, except by an external act on account of the fear of death. Now, whether he fell from the pontificate due to that external act or not, little is related; later he abdicated the pontificate and shortly thereafter was crowned with martyrdom. Still, I believe that he would not have fallen from the pontificate *ipso facto*, because it was certain to all that he sacrificed to idols only out of fear.

CHAPTER IX
On Liberius and Felix II

HE eleventh Pope who is accused of error is Liberius. Now, although the Centuriators do not dare to define anything on Liberius,[1] still, Tilman Hesh boldly affirms that he was infected with the Arian heresy.[2] And, of course, he has serious authors as witnesses for his opinion; St. Athanasius,[3] St. Jerome and Pope St. Damasus.[4]

I respond. There are two things certain concerning Liberius, and one in doubt. Firstly, it is certain that from the beginning of his pontificate even to exile, he suffered for the Catholic faith and was a keen defender of the Catholic religion. All writers who spoke on those times witness this fact, such as Ammianus Marcelinus, Athanasius in both *Apologies*; Ruffinus, Sulpitius Socrates, Sozomen, Theodoret, and Nicephorus.[5]

Secondly, it is certain that Liberius, after he returned from exile, was also truly orthodox and pious. As the Church historian Socrates writes, after he returned from exile, Liberius refused to receive the Macedonians into the Church unless they would openly lay aside heresy.[6] Besides, after his death, he was held as a saint, as is clear from the words of St. Ambrose: "It is time, sister, to return to the precepts of Liberius, of holy memory, that the holier the man, the more pleasing conversation should approach."[7] Likewise, we see in the words of Epiphanius that: "Eustathius lead a legation to blessed Liberius, the bishop or Rome, together with many bishops."[8] Basil also says in epistle 74 to the western bishops: "Certain things were proposed to us by the most holy Liberius."

Next, Siricius, who was the third [Pope] after Liberius, declared in an epistle to Hymericus that Liberius was his predecessor of revered memory. How I ask, could these Fathers call Liberius most blessed after his death, if he had died in heresy? Therefore, only one doubt remains: whether in the middle period, that is, in the very return from exile, he did something against the faith. And

---

[1] *Centur.* 4, ch. 10, colum 1284.

[2] *De Ecclesia*, lib. 1 cap. 9.

[3] Epist. *ad solitariam vitam agentes.*

[4] *Chronicus et Catalogus scriptorium*; in Fortunatiano; *In vita Liberii.*

[5]   Marcellinus, *Historiae suae*, lib. 15; Ruffinus, *Hist.* lib. 10 cap. 22; Socrates, *Sacrae Historiae*, lib. 2.; Sozomen, *Hist. Ecclesiastic.*, lib. 2, cap. 29. Thedoret, Lib. 4 cap 10. Lib. 2, ch. 16 and 17.; Necephorus, Lib. 9 ch. 35, 36, and 37.

[6] Lib. 4, ca 11.

[7] *De Virginibus*, lib. 3, in principio.

[8] *Haeres.* 75.

certainly, Sulpitius, Socrates, Sozomenus and Nicephorus show in the citations we have noted, that Liberius was always the same and never diminished in the constancy of the faith. On the other hand, Athanasius and Jerome obviously say the opposite; that being tired of exile he at length bent and subscribed to heresy. To which it can be added St. Hilary, who says against the Emperor Constantius: "You turned your war even to Rome, you snatched from there the bishop, and you are so miserable that I do not know whether you banished a man with greater impiety than you sent him back."[9] Ruffinus, however, affirms that he could not discover for certain whether Liberius had subscribed to heresy.[10]

From such opinions there seems to us to be a second truer one. For Athanasius, Hilary and Jerome are both more ancient and important than the rest, and they relate the matter not as dubious but rather as certain and investigated. Besides, epistles written in the hand of Liberius can be read from the Vatican Library, which were written partly to the Emperor, and partly to the Oriental bishops; therein he sufficiently showed that he would acquiesce to the will of the Emperor. To this, unless we should affirm that Liberius at some time defected from the constancy that must be guarded in the faith, we are compelled to exclude Felix II, who managed the pontificate while Liberius was alive, from the number of the Pontiffs, although still, this very Felix was venerated by the Catholic Church as a Pope and martyr. Next, Sozomen[11] and Nicephorus[12] hint more obscurely that Liberius, in the Council of Sirmium, agreed with Valens and Ursacius (the Arians) and made peace with them, received back his see, aided even by letters of the same council. But although they would have these matters thus, still Liberius neither taught heresy nor was a heretic, but only sinned by an external act, just as St. Marcellinus, and, unless I am mistaken, he sinned less than Marcellinus.

St. Athanasius teaches that he was not truly a heretic,[13] when he says that Liberius was compelled against his will by the force of the rack to do what he did. Nor must it be though to be truly his opinion which had been twisted from him by threats and terrors, especially given what he advanced when he was freely disposed; that he did not teach heresy can easily be proved. It is gathered from the words of Athanasius as well as from the epistles of Liberius himself, that Liberius committed two faults: 1) That he subscribed to the condemnation of Athanasius; 2) That he had communicated with heretics; but in neither did

---

[9]   *Adversus Constantium.*

[10]   *Hist.*, lib. 10, ch. 27.

[11]   *Hist.*, lib. 4, ch. 14.

[12]   Lib. 9, ch. 37.

[13]   *Loc. cit.*

he expressly violate the faith. For although heretics persecuted Athanasius for the faith, nevertheless, they pretended it was not due to the faith but morals, and Liberius consented to the condemnation of Athanasius on that basis, not on account of the faith. For equal reason he communicated with heretics, because they feigned that they were Catholics. In his epistles, Liberius says that he communicated with Oriental bishops because he discovered that their faith agreed with the Catholic faith, and was foreign to the Arian treachery.

Besides, Sozomen and Nicephorus[14] say that in the peace which Liberius made with the Arian bishops, nothing was demanded from him except that he would subscribe to the Confession of Sirmium published against Photius and the Confession of Antioch published in Enceniis. These confessions also do not have the word ὁμοούιος; still they are Catholic, and Hilary, in his book on councils, shows that they are Catholic. It happens that Liberius not only did not subscribe to the Arian confession, but even published a *Confession* before he left from Sirmium wherein he excommunicated those who denied that the Son is the same as the Father in substance, as well as in all other matters, as Nicephorus and Sozomen relate in the works we have cited. The reason he did this is because the Arians spread a false rumor that Liberius began to teach that the Son is not consubstantial with the Father.

Now someone will say: If that is so, then why does Jerome say that Liberius bent and subscribed to heresy in the end? I respond: Although Liberius did not expressly consent to heresy, still he was interpreted as having done so since he permitted Athanasius to be condemned, whom he knew suffered persecution for the sake of the faith, and communicated with Ursacius and Valens whom he knew were heretics although they feigned otherwise. Therefore, this is what Jerome meant.

The twelfth who is accused of error in faith by the heretics is Felix II, whom Tilman Hesh contends was an Arian[15] and attempts to show it from the testimony of St. Jerome, who in the catalogue of writers, on Acacius, says thus: "Acacius, whom they named μονόφθαλμου (*monophthalmou*) because he had one eye, was the bishop of Caesarea in Palestine. Under Constantius the Emperor he became famous because the Arian bishops constituted him Felix at Rome in place of Liberius." But we respond that Felix was never an Arian, although he communicated with the Arians in the time in which he was not the true Pope. Still, when he began to be a true Pope, not only was he not an Arian but he even publicly detested the Arians, and on account of their persecution he received the crown of martyrdom from the Lord.

---

[14] Sozomen, Lib. 4, ch. 14.; Nicephorus, Lib. 9 ch. 37.

[15] *De Ecclesia*, lib. 1 ch. 9.

Therefore, it must be explained as briefly as it can be done, the history of the pontificate of Liberius and Felix, from which a marvelous providence of God will appear in the Apostolic see. After Liberius departed into exile on account of the Catholic Faith, the Roman Clergy swore never to admit another man as Pope while Liberius lived. Jerome witnesses that in his *Chronicle*, although his words have been transposed. These words "Who, being in exile, all the clergy swore, etc.," which are placed in the year 351 ought to be placed after these: "Liberius, the bishop of the Romans, is sent into exile," which are placed in the year 361.

Next, by a work of the Arians, and especially of Acacius, the bishop of Caesarea, Felix a Roman deacon was created a bishop in place of Liberius; on account of this good deed he freely communicated with him although he was not an Arian. Thus Ruffinus writes: "In Liberius' place, Felix his deacon was substituted by the heretics and he was not tainted by diversity of sect, but agreement of communion and ordination."[16] Theodoret says: "Liberius was succeeded by a faithful deacon named Felix, who, although he preserved the whole faith expressed in the Council of Nicaea, still he freely communicated with those who labored to subvert the same. And for that reason no one living at Rome wished to enter the Church if he was inside."[17]

Sozomen also writes the same thing.[18] Jerome does not disagree in his catalogue of writers on Acacius; for that term [Arian] is added to the name of Felix, and it seems to have crept in from somewhere else. Accordingly, the ancient manuscript codices do not have that term, as Marianus Victorius remarked on this place, nor does the translation into Greek made by St. Sophronius have it. Now what I find most important is that Freculph[19] and Ado of Vienna,[20] when referring to the whole sentence in this citation of Jerome, do not have the term "Arian".

Next, it is not at all credible that Jerome and Ruffinus could have such a discrepancy in their history, that one would deny something and the other affirms it. Even if Felix were an Arian (which still to this point is not proven) he did no harm to the Apostolic see. At that time Felix was an anti-pope, not a true and legitimate Pope, as two cannot be Pope together. The true Pope was still alive, namely Liberius. Wherefore (as we related from Theodoret above) no Catholic in Rome wanted to communicate with Felix at that time.

---

[16] *Hist.*, lib. 10, cap. 22.

[17] *Hist.*, lib. 2, cap. 17.

[18] *Hist.*, lib. 4 ch. 10.

[19] Lib. 4, ch. 80.

[20] *in Chronico.*

Next, two years after the fall of Liberius, concerning which we spoke above, then the Roman clergy abrogated Liberius from the pontifical dignity and conferred it upon Felix, whom they knew to be Catholic. From that time Felix began to be a true Pope. Although Liberius was not a heretic, still it was considered that, on account of the peace made with the Arians, that he was a heretic, and from that presumption his pontificate could rightly be abrogated. For men cannot be held to thoroughly search hearts; yet when they see one who is a heretic by his external works, then they judge simply and condemn him as a heretic. Jerome shows this in his *Chronicle*, when he says that many from the Roman clergy perjured themselves and went to Felix. They are said to have perjured themselves, because they did not keep the oath that they had taken to not receive another Pontiff.

Next, Felix, now a true Pope, noticing the danger to the Church and the faith, without a doubt inspired by God who did not desert his Church, not only receded from communication with the Arians, but even compelled a council and declared the Emperor Constantius, as well as the bishops Ursacius and Valens with whom Liberius had made peace, to be truly heretics. And for that reason, when Liberius returned to the city, Felix was ejected with his own by the Arians, and died not long after, whether beheaded, or consumed in labors. That is not known for certain. This, however, bears on the matter, that Felix, after the fall of Liberius, was a true Pope, and died for the Catholic faith, which is proved by these arguments.

First, Damasus (or whoever is the author of the *Pontifical*), clearly witnesses the life of Felix. St. Jerome appears to mean the same in the *Chronicle*, when he says on the Roman clergy: "After a year with Felix they were thrown out, because Liberius, conquered by the exhaustion of exile and subscribing to a heretical depravity, entered Rome as a victor." These words mean persecution moved against Felix, and it was moved by those who favored the Arians. From that it follows that Felix himself suffered persecution for the Catholic faith.

Secondly, all ancient Martyrologies, both those lain down by Bede, Ado and Usuard, and even the manuscripts for the fourth day before the Kalends of August (29 July), place the memory of St. Felix II, Pope and Martyr, who declared Constantius a heretic. Add that St. Gregory I, both in his antiphonary and in his Sacramentary, places the whole ecclesiastical office that must be read for Mass in the day of St. Felix, Pope and martyr, on this same day, the fourth before the Kalends of August. Moreover, this Felix was a Roman Pontiff, and hence, the one about whom we are speaking, as Micrologus witnesses.[21] Therefore, since the Catholic Church has venerated this Felix for a thousand

---

[21] Lib. *Ecclesiast., observationum*, cap. 43.

years as a Pope and martyr, he ought not be excluded from the number of Pontiffs, even if we could advance no other reason.

Thirdly, Pope Felix, the grandfather of St. Gregory, is called Felix IV by very ancient writers, such as by John the Deacon[22] and by Leo Hostiensis.[23] But he could not be fourth, unless the Felix about whom we are writing would have been the second. There were no more than two Felixes, apart from this our Felix, before the fourth. Therefore, a thousand years ago this Felix was held in the number of Pontiffs, and they did not make him in the number of the schismatics.

Fourthly, when there was some ambiguity in Rome in the year 1572 whether this St. Felix ought to be placed in the new Martyrology a marble box was discovered in the Basilica of Sts. Cosmas and Damian, with this inscription in the marble in ancient characters: "Hic Iacet Corpvs Sancti Felicis Papæ, et Martyris, qui Constantivm Hæreticvm Damnavit."[24]

At any rate, after the death of St. Felix, Liberius again reconciled the Roman clergy to himself, and was an outstanding Catholic prelate, as we showed above from the history of Socrates on the case of the Macedonians. For that reason in the consensus of all he began to sit legitimately again, and sat even to death. This is the reason why in the catalogue of Popes, some of the Fathers like Augustine[25] and Optatus,[26] could not place Felix, because clearly, the whole time of Felix was rolled into the pontificate of Liberius.

The thirteenth is a certain Pope (anti-Pope) Leo, whom several say succeeded Felix II and was plainly Arian; he died by the same type of death in which Arius perished, namely by the effusion of all his intestines, while at the toilet. Vincentius relates this,[27] as well as Conrad Halberstatensis in his Chronicle. The Centuriators do not reckon this improbable.[28]

There is no doubt that this Leo was an anti-pope. It is certain that Leo I was the one who sat in the time of the Council of Chalcedon; this is, around a hundred years after the times of Felix II. Next, all ancient writers, such as Jerome, Augustine, Optatus, Theodoret, Ruffinus, and still more recent writers, like Sigebert, Martin Polanus, Platina and everyone else, place Damasus after the death of Liberius and Felix.

---

[22] *De vita B. Gregorii*, lib. 1, ch. 1.

[23] *Chronici Cassiensis*, lib. 1, ca. 1.

[24] Here lies the body of St. Felix, Pope and Martyr, who condemned Constantius as a heretic.

[25] Epist. 165.

[26] Lib. 2.

[27] *Speculi histoiralis*, lib. 15, ch. 23.

[28] *Cent*. 4, ch. 10, in *vita Felicis II*.

Perhaps this false story arose from the imagined opinion of the heresy of Liberius, and the persecution against Catholics after Felix II was expelled. After the expulsion of Felix, leisurely men falsely reckoned that Liberius began to take on the nature of a fierce lion against Catholics and imagined an Arian Pope Leo sat after Felix II.[29] But these are numbered among the fables.

---

[29] Translator's note: To be clear, not only historians but even the Church has not followed Bellarmine's judgment on Felix II. On the one hand Bellarmine brings credible arguments; still it muddies the waters even more. Modern historians know that the 2nd formulary of Sirmium, which Liberius signed, was not in itself heretical but could be interpreted as such. But when Bellarmine argues that, essentially, a Pope can be removed from the Pontificate by the Roman Clergy because it appeared that he was heretical, he creates a problem in that by his own admission Liberius was not a heretic. Therefore, how does Liberius cease to be Pope, unless it were by the will of the Church? This too is contrary to what he says in Book II, ch. 30 as well as in this book. Thus we have one possibility: Bellarmine correctly sees in these writings that Felix II was not a heretic, and was received temporarily by the Roman clergy, whether he was intended to be a puppet of the Arians or not, but then defended the faith by an act of God's providence though he was not a true Pope. Thus, Liberius did not so much become true Pope again (as if he could cease to be Pope while in exile) as resume his control of the Roman Church. This would seem to satisfy the issue, although we would leave it for experts in this area to clarify further.

CHAPTER X

On Siricius, Innocent and Seven Other Popes

HE fourteenth Pope is Siricius, whom John Calvin accuses of error because in his letter to the Spanish he calls the union of spouses pollution.[1] But Calvin impudently lies, which is his custom. For Siricius did not appeal to the pollution of true and legitimate spouses; rather, their illicit unions where, union after carrying out a public penance again returned to the same union, on account of which they had done penance. No one ever did penance for a legitimate marriage.

The fifteenth is Pope Innocent I, whom the Centuriators,[2] in the life of Innocent, say gravely erred because he had commanded that a consecrated virgin, already veiled, who will have married or committed fornication, was not to be received to Penance while the man with whom she had sinned was alive.[3] It seems wicked, they say, that a woman doing penance ought not be absolved, unless first the one who seduced her should die. Likewise, in epistle 18, he wrote to Antiochenus at Alexandria that the baptisms of Arians were certainly valid, but that the Holy Ghost was not conferred through them, because they are separated from the Church. There, it seems, he would have it that the efficacy of holy baptism depends on the goodness of the minister, which is against the common doctrine of the Church. Moreover, he taught[4] that a man cannot be a priest who receives a widow as a wife, since the law of Moses commanded in Leviticus that a priest should receive a virgin as a wife, as if Christians were still held to the judicial laws of the Old Testament.

I respond: Firstly, Innocent wished to say that virgins should not be received in Penance who refused to be separated from the adulterer, except after his death, and this is most just. Those who persevere in their sins ought not be absolved by the Church.

I speak now to the second point. Innocent speaks in that place about those who were baptized or ordained by heretics, when they were polluted by the same heresy. Those of this sort receive the Sacrament of baptism, or of ordination, but they do not receive the grace of the Holy Spirit, which cannot be present in heretics. And in ordination, not only do those ordained by heretics not receive grace, but they do not have the right to exercise Orders. The

---

[1] *Institutes,* lib. 4, ch. 12 §24.

[2] Epist.2, cap.12.

[3] *Cent.* 5, cap. 10.

[4] Epistle 22, ch. 1.

ordaining bishop loses that right through heresy, nor can he give what he does not have.[5]

Now I address the third argument. Innocent did mean that we are bound by the laws of the Jews; rather he wished to argue from a similar thing, or rather more, from a better thing in this mode. Priests in the Old Testament were held by divine precept not to marry a widow. Therefore, it is much more fitting that in the priesthood of the new law, the Church should require that they be not husbands of widows, on account of the excellence of Christian priesthood.

The sixteenth is Celestine I, whom Lorenzo Valla asserts was infected with the Nestorian heresy, in his *declamatione de falsa donatione Constantini*. But what Laurence says is false, since not only was it never recorded that Celestine was infected with this heresy, but he is the one who especially condemned that heresy, which is clear from Prosper of Aquitaine[6] as well as from the whole Council of Ephesus. Valla was deceived by the equivocation of the name. For there was a Celestine that was a Pelagian heretic who held certain things in common with the Nestorians.

The seventeenth is St. Leo I, who said that those women who think that their husbands are dead, or because they never return from captivity, marry another, do not sin; still, if the first should return, they are held to renew the first marriage. If however, the men do not wish to do so, they are not bound.[7] Here there are two errors: 1) That a woman would not sin if she married another man when she thinks the first husband is alive but simply never returned; 2)That a woman can remain with the second husband if the first refuses her. The Centuriators have much to say about this error.[8]

I respond: in neither case did Leo err. For when he says that a woman who marries would not sin while the prior husband is still alive, he spoke only on a woman who will marry because she supposes that the first husband is dead, and he eloquently explained the same thing. He said, in regard to a woman who will marry because she thinks her husband is never going to return, not that she sins nor that she does not, because he thought the matter was known in itself, for without a doubt she sins. However, when he says a woman ought to return to the first husband, if he wishes it, consequently he wishes to be understood that a man ought to return to the woman, if she wills him, even if otherwise he does not want her. Husband and wife are equal in this matter. Therefore, if one of the spouses should wish to return to wedlock, the other is necessarily bound to

---

[5] See the *Glossa*, 1, quaest. 1, can. Arianos.

[6] *Chronicum* anni CCCXXXI.

[7] Epist. 79 ad Nicetum.

[8] *Cent.* 5, ch. 10, in *vita Leonis I.*

obey: if, however, neither wishes to return, they can remain separated, in regard to the use of marriage, and this alone is what St. Leo permitted. From that it does not follow that a woman can remain with the second husband, for the same Leo clearly says in the same place that the first marriage is indissoluble, and necessarily must be reformed, while the second may be dissolved because it could not be a true marriage.

The eighteenth is Pope Gelasius. The Centuriators note that he has two opinions, which are erroneous according to Catholics.[9] One is in the book against Eutychus, where he says that true bread remains with the flesh of Christ in the Sacrament. The second we discover with Gratian that one cannot consume one part of the Sacrament of the Eucharist while not the other without great sacrilege.[10] Thus, either Gelasius erred in these two, or we err who teach and follow the contrary.

I respond to the first: That book is not of Pope Gelasius. It is either of Gennadius, who wrote a book of the same title to Pope Gelasius, or of Gelasius Caesar, the bishop, whom Jerome calls to mind near the end of this *Catalogue of Ecclesiastical Writers*. Accordingly, Pope Gelasius wrote five volumes against Eutychus, as Trithemius relates; but this one, however, is only one scanty book. Next, this author promises that he is going to gather the teachings of almost all the Fathers, on the Incarnation of the Lord, and when he adds fifteen Greek Fathers he only advances two Latin authors, Ambrose and Damasus. Yet he omits Cyprian, Hilary, Jerome, Augustine, Innocent, Leo, Prosper, and the like, whom Pope Gelasius never omitted; nay more, nor did any Latin author do so. Therefore, it seems manifest that this author was Greek and not Latin. To the second, I say that Gelasius speaks in that canon only on the priest offering the sacrifice, who cannot take only one species without sacrilege, because he would render an imperfect sacrifice.

The nineteenth is Pope Anastasius II, who is accused of three errors. Firstly, because he communicated with Photinus, who had communicated with the heretic Acacius without a council of bishops, priests and clergy of the whole Church. Secondly, because he wanted to secretly recall Acacius, whom Felix and Pope Gelasius had condemned. Thirdly, because he approved baptism and orders confirmed by the same Acacius; on account of such errors and sins the same Anastasius, after a divinely constituted plague had set in, immediately died. Not only does the author of the *Pontificalis* write these things in the life of this

---

[9]   *Cent.* 5, ch. 4, *de coena Domini*; cap. 10 *in vita Gelasii*.

[10]   *De consecrate.*, dist. 2, canon.

Anastasius, whose account Tilman Hesh followed,[11] but even Gratian,[12] and the Centuriators.[13]

I respond: It is quite false that Anastasius wished to recall Acacius. This is certain from Evagrius[14] and from Nicephorus[15] as well as Liberatus. Acacius died in the time of Pope Felix, from whom Anastasius was third. How, therefore, did Anastasius wish to recall someone to his see who had long been dead? But, some would say, he at least wished to restore his name. On the other hand, an epistle of this Pope Anastasius is extant, sent to the emperor by the same name, in which he asks the Emperor to command the name of Acacius be held in silence in the Church, seeing that he had been most justly condemned by his predecessor Pope Felix. What Gratian says, namely, that Anastasius erred in this epistle because he wanted the Sacraments of baptism and order which Acacius had conferred to be held as valid,[16] does not show Anastasius a heretic, but Gratian inexperienced. Who does not know that Catholics that are baptized by heretics are truly baptized, and likewise those who are ordained by them are truly ordained, even when the ordaining bishop was a heretic and remained so, at least in regard to the [Sacramental] character?

Now, that part on Photinus is probably a lie, just as the revocation of Acacius, but even if it were true, would Anastasius not be Catholic for that reason? Or is it not lawful for the Supreme Pontiff to absolve one excommunicated without a council of all bishops, priests, and clerics of the whole Church? Now the matter which they add, that Pope Anastasius immediately died by a heaven sent plague, seems to arise for the reason that the heretical emperor Anastasius died from being struck by lightning at the same time, as the historians relate in his life.[17] Otherwise it is without doubt a fable.

The twentieth Pope is Vigilius. Liberatus relates in chapter 22 of his *Breviary* that Vigilius wrote an epistle to Theodora the Empress and other heretics, whereby he confirmed their heresy and declared anathema on those who confessed that there are two natures in Christ.

I respond: Many reckon that heretics corrupted this citation of Liberatus, for the reason that it seems contrary to what is said in the *Pontifical*. But since no

---

[11] *De Ecclesia* lib. 1, cap. 9.

[12] Can. Anastasius, dist. 19.

[13] *Cent.* 6, cap. 10, in *vita Anastasii*.

[14] Lib. 3, cap. 23.

[15] Lib. 15 and 17.

[16] Canon. *Ita Dominus*, distinction 19.

[17] Bede, Cedrenus, Zonaras and Paul the Deacon.

vestige of corruption appears in the book of Liberatus, and really, the relation is not opposed to that of the *Pontifical*, another response must be given. Therefore, I say that Vigilius wrote that epistle, and condemned the Catholic faith, at least from exterior profession, but this does nothing to obstruct our case. For he did that when Pope Sylverius was still living and at that time Vigilius was not Pope, but an anti-Pope. For two men cannot be true Popes at the same time, and it was certain then to all that Sylverius was the true Pope, although he abided in exile.

It must be known, that Anthemius, the heretic, was deposed from the Episcopate of Constantinople by Pope Agapetus. Then the empress [Theodora] sought from Sylverius, the successor of Agapetus, that he would restore Anthemius. Yet when he refused, Vigilius, then an archdeacon, promised the empress that he would restore Anthemius, if he could be made Roman Pontiff: immediately, by the command of the empress, Belisarius, his general, expelled Saint Sylverius from his own see and sent him into exile, and created Vigilius Pope, or, rather, an antipope. In that period it would be no marvel if he erred in faith, and could even plainly be a heretic. Still, he did not even define something against the faith as Pope, nor was he a heretic in spirit. Accordingly, he wrote that nefarious epistle, and it was unworthy of a Christian man; still, he did not openly condemn the Catholic faith in it, nor manifest a heretical spirit, but secretly, on account of the lust for control, just as Liberatus says in the aforementioned citation, which also appears from the epistle of Vigilius himself. He writes that they should be careful lest anyone should see that epistle, and that all should be secret for a time. Vigilius then was upon the very narrow straights that his ambition had thrown him. For if he openly professed heresy, he would fear the Romans, who were never seen to suffer a heretic to sit in the chair of Peter; if, on the other hand, he would profess the Catholic faith, he feared the heretical Empress, whose work had secured for him the pontificate. Therefore, he devised the plan that he would be a Catholic at Rome, and meanwhile through, his letters feign that he was a heretic to the emperor.

It happened a little afterward, that Sylverius died and Vigilius, who to that point sat in schism, now began to be the sole and legitimate Pontiff for certain through the confirmation and reception by the clergy and the Roman people.

From this time neither error nor feigning of error was discovered in Vigilius, but rather, supreme constancy in the faith even to death, as it shall appear. For he received with the pontificate the strength of faith and he was changed from a weak chaff into the most solid rock. When the Empress Theodora, having relied upon the secret letters as well as the promise of Vigilius, asked from him that he would restore the aforementioned Patriarch Anthemius, as he had promised, he wrote back that he had promised rashly and gravely sinned in that

513

promise. Therefore, he could not nor would fulfill what he had promised, lest he would add sins to sins. For that reason, when the Empress became angry, he was sent into exile, and miserably tortured even to death. That much is not only written in the *Pontifical*, but Paul the Deacon also annotated it in the *Life of Justinian*, as well as Aimonius.[18] Even the Centuriators themselves,[19] as well as the same Liberatus who was cited earlier, say that Vigilius was later miserably afflicted by the adherents of that very heresy which he had secretly fostered in the beginning.

Next, Vigilius, after the death of Sylverius, was a true and holy Pontiff, as all witness who lived in those times and wrote something on him. Pope Gregory I says: "The memory of Pope Vigilius must be recalled, constituted in the royal city, who promulgated the sentence of condemnation against Theodora, then the empress."[20] Cassiodorus says: "It is certain that Origen was condemned at that time by Blessed Pope Vigilius."[21] Arator wrote a preface to the Apostolic Acts, which he dedicated to Pope Vigilius, and begins thus: "To the holy, most blessed, Apostolic, Pope Vigilius, first of all priests in the whole world." Next, it is certain from Evagrius that the Fifth General Council was confirmed by Vigilius, in which that heresy that Theodora favored and which the adversaries of Vigilius accused him of adhering to, was condemned.[22]

It could be said that the epistle of Vigilius, which Liberatus calls to mind, was fabricated by heretics. Liberatus, moreover, may have believed false rumors that the heretics had spread. That the heretics fabricated a certain epistle in the name of Pope Vigilius to Theodora and Justinian can be recognized by certain indications in the Sixth Council, action 14; but whatever the case on this, it is enough for us that when he was a true Pope, he made no error in faith.

The twenty-first is St. Gregory I. Durandus accused him of error because in an epistle[23] he permitted priests to confer the Sacrament of Confirmation, which is fitting for bishops alone to confer by divine law. On account of this citation of Gregory, Adrian asserts that the Pope can err in defining dogmas of faith.[24]

I respond: Firstly, it is not St. Gregory, but rather Durandus and Adrian who have erred. The Council of Florence, in the *Instructione Armenorum*, and the

---

[18] *De gestis Francorum* lib.. 2, ch. 32.

[19] *Cent.* 6, cap. 10, in vita Vigilii.

[20] Lib. 2, epist. 36 ad Episcopos Hyberniae.

[21] Lib. *de divinis lectionibus*, cap. 1.

[22] Lib. 4, cap. 37.

[23] Lib. 3, epistle 26 to John the bishop of Caralitanum.

[24] In *quaest. De Confirmatione*, last article.

Council of Trent, in the last canon of its 7th Session, teach that the ordinary minister of Confirmation is the bishop. Wherein it follows that extraordinarily, even a non-bishop can be the minister of this Sacrament. Next, Gregory did not publish some decree on the matter, but only conceded to certain priests, that in the absence of the bishops, they may confirm. Hence, if Gregory erred in this matter, it was not of doctrine but an error of example or fact. There is another error which is attributed to St. Gregory but falsely, and we will speak on it below when we treat on Gregory III.

The twenty-second is Boniface V, whom the Centuriators grievously condemn[25] because he taught that Christ redeemed us only from original sin.[26] I respond: The Centuriators added that term *only* on their own. For Boniface says: "Therefore, hasten to acknowledge him, who created you, who breathed the breath of life into you, who sent his only-begotten son for your redemption, so that he would deliver you from original sin." The reason why he did not call to mind other sins is because original sin is the principal one, and it was for the purpose of destroying it that Christ principally died. Wherefore, in John I we read: "Behold the Lamb of God, behold he who takes away the sins of the world. In Greek: "Τὴν ἁμαρτιαν τοῦ κόσμου" that is, the sin of the world; this is original sin, because it alone is common to the whole world. For many have no other sin, such as all children.

---

[25] *Cent.* 7, ca. 10.

[26] Epistle to King Edwin of England, c.f. Bede, lib. 2, *Hist. Anglorum*, cap. 10.

CHAPTER XI
On Honorius I

HE TWENTY-THIRD is Honorius I. Nilos Cabásilas contends that he was a Monothelite heretic in his book on the primacy of the Roman Pontiff. The Centuriators assert the same thing and place him among manifest heretics.[1] Not just heretics, but even several Catholics contend Honorius was a heretic, such as Melchior Cano.[2] There are six arguments that they bring to the fore.

1) From the epistles of Honorius himself, for there are extant two epistles of Honorius to Servius; one in the Sixth Council, action 12, the other the same, act 13. Furthermore, they say that in each Honorius approves the doctrine of Servius, the leader of the Monothelites, and bids it not to be said, that Christ had two wills, or operations [*operationes*].

2) From the Sixth Council, act 13, where Honorius was condemned as a heretic and his letters were burned, and in the following acts the condemnation was repeated by all.

3) From the Seventh Council, last act, where the whole Council declared anathema to Honorius, Sergius, Cyril and the other Monothelites, and repeated the same in an epistle which it wrote to all clerics.

4) From the Eighth Council, act 7, where the letter of the Roman Council under Pope Adrian II was read and approved. In that letter the Pope asserts with the Council that Honorius was judged after his death by the Sixth Council, because he had been accused of heresy.

5) From the epistle of Pope Agatho, who in a letter to the Emperor Constantius (which is contained in the 4th act of the Sixth Council), he declares Anathema to Honorius, just as to the Monothelites.

6) From Leo II, who in an epistle to the same emperor, which is contained at the end of the council, the same Honorius is cursed; just as one who had contaminated the Apostolic See with heresy.

7) From various Greek and Latin writers who witness that Honorius was a heretic. Thrasius, the bishop of Constantinople, asserts this, in an epistle to the Patriarchs, which is contained in act. 3 of the Seventh Council. Likewise Epiphanius, a Catholic deacon, in a disputation with a heretic named Gregory, which is contained in act 6 of the Seventh Council, volume 2. Psellus relates it

---

[1] *Cent.* 7, cap. 10 in vita ipsius, and cap. 11, col. 553.

[2] *De Locis,* lib. 6, last chapter.

in a poem about the Seventh Council, as does Bede,[3] and it is in the *Liber Pontificalis* concerning the life of Leo II.

Yet several wrote on behalf of Honorius: Albert Pighius,[4] Cardinal Hosius[5] and Onufrius in an annotation to Platina in the life of Honorius. Their reasoning is much more efficacious than of the other side, as will be clear in the answers to the arguments.

To the first: I respond in two ways. It is possible that these two epistles were fabricated and inserted into the general council by heretics. Certainly one should not say this rashly, yet in this matter it is certain that in the Fifth Council heretics inserted fictitious epistles of the Roman Pope Vigilius, as well as Mennas, the Patriarch of Constantinople. That was detected in the Sixth Council,[6] while the acts of the Fifth Council were re-read. They discovered three or four groups of things inserted and placed in these epistles by heretics. What wonder would it be if they carried out the same plans in the Sixth Council?

To the second I say, no error is contained in these epistles of Honorius. For Honorius confesses in these epistles what pertains to the matter of two wills and operations in Christ, and he only forbids the name of one or two wills, which then were unheard of, and he did it with prudent counsel. That he confessed the matter itself is clear from the words of the second epistle: "We ought to confess both natures in the one Christ, joined in a natural unity, working in harmony with the other, and also confess operations. And certainly the divine operation, which is of God, and the human operation, which is of God, carrying it out not in division, nor confusion, informing the other but not changing the nature of God into man, nor the human into God, but confessing the different natures whole, etc." This confession is very Catholic, and altogether destroys the Monothelite heresy.

Moreover it can be shown that Honorius acted with great prudence when he forbade the names of one or two operations. For then it was the beginning of this heresy, and nothing on these terms was yet defined by the Church. Then, Cyrus of Alexandria began first to preach one operation in Christ, while conversely Sophronius of Jerusalem opposed himself to Cyrus, preaching two operations in Christ. Cyrus related this contention both to Sergius of Constantinople and to Honorius of Rome. Therefore, Honorius, fearing that which later would happen, wanted to conciliate each opinion, and at the same

---

[3] *De Sex Ætatibus*; in vita Constantini IV Imperatoris.

[4] *Hierarchiae Ecclesiasticae*, lib. 4 cap. 8.

[5] *Contra Brentium et Joannes a Lovanio*, lib. 2; in de perpetua cathedrae Petri protectione et firmitate, lib. 2 ch. 11.

[6] Actione 12 et 14.

time abolish the matter of scandal and contention from sight. He acted to prevent this contention from becoming a serious schism, and at the same time he saw the faith would be preserved without these terms. Therefore, he wrote in the first epistle that they ought to abstain from the term "one operation," lest we would seem to place one nature in Christ with the followers of Eutychus, and again from the term of two operations, lest we seem to place two persons in Christ with Nestorius. "Let no one, being offended by the term 'of two operations' think by some madness that we agree with the Nestorian sects, or certainly if again we sensed that one operation must be affirmed, that we would be reckoned by itching ears to confess the foolish madness of the Monophysites."

In the second epistle, while teaching the manner of speaking and reconciling the opinions: "Therefore, bearing the scandal of a novel invention, it is not fitting for us to preach defining one or two operations; but for one which they mean by 'operation,' it is fitting for us to confess there is one operator, Christ the Lord, truthfully in each nature; and for two operations, after the term of twin operations has been removed, or rather more of two natures, that is, of divinity and flesh taken in one person of the only begotten Son of God the Father unconfusedly, indivisibly, and also inconvertibly to preach his proper workers with us." Certainly, this can only be praised.

Then they say, however, that a little below he clearly preaches only one will in these words: "Wherefore, we profess one will of our Lord Jesus Christ." I respond: In that place, Honorius spoke only on the human nature, and meant that in the man, Christ, there were not two wills opposing each other, one of the flesh and the other of the spirit; but only one, namely the spirit. For the flesh in Christ desired absolutely nothing against reason. Moreover, this is the mind of Honorius, and that is plain from the reason that he gave. Thus he says: "Wherefore, we affirm one will of our Lord Jesus Christ, because certainly our nature was assumed by the divinity there is no fault, certainly that which had created sin, not that which was damaged after sin." This reasoning is null, if it is advanced to prove in Christ, God and man, there is only one will; it is very efficacious if thence it must be proved that in Christ the man there were not contrary wills of the flesh and spirit. That contrariety is born from sin, but Christ has a human nature without sin.

Next, because someone could have objected with the citations of the Gospel, "I have not come to do my will," and "Not what I will, but what you will," where Christ seems, as a man, to have contrary wills, indeed one wicked, whereby it wished not to suffer; and the other good, whereby it did not wish to fulfill the first will, but the contrary which was conformed to the will of God. Honorius responds a little later: "It is written, 'I have not come to do my will, but the will of Him who sent me,' and 'Not what I will, but what you will Father' and other things of this sort. They are not of a different will, but taken up from the dispensation of humanity. This was said on account of us, to whom he gave an example, in order that we might follow in his footsteps, the pious teacher imbuing his students, that each one of us should not do his own will, but rather more that he would prefer the will of the Lord in all things." In other words, Christ did not have contrary wills, so that it would be fitting for him to conquer and mortify one. Instead he so spoke as if he had contrary wills, that he would teach us to mortify our own will, which often strives to rebel against God.

St. Maximus, who lived in the time of Honorius, confirms this with serious testimony. He wrote a dialogue against Pyrrhus, the successor of Sergius, which is still in the Vatican Library. In that *Dialogue* he introduces Pyrrhus the heretic, advancing in front of him the testimony of Honorius, then he responds that Honorius was always Catholic, and proves it with another source, from the testimony of the secretary of Honorius himself, who wrote those epistles dictated by Honorius, and who was then still living, and said that. Moreover the Secretary witnesses the mind of Honorius was never to deny two wills in Christ, and whenever it seems to deny two wills, it must be understood on two contrary and opposed wills in the same human nature, which is discovered in us from sin, but was not in Christ. St. Maximus records these very words:

> PYRRHUS: What do you have whereby you could respond about Honorius, who wrote in his letters to Sergius in previous times that he clearly professed one will in our Lord Jesus Christ?
>
> MAXIMUS: I reverence each of these letters, and a more certain interpretation must be given. Did not his scribe, who wrote those epistles in the name of Honorius, who still lives, say that he adorned the West with the splendor of every virtue and discipline in religion; or the citizens of Constantinople, who will have nothing but what is pleasing to them?
>
> PYRRHUS: I reverence what he wrote.
>
> MAXIMUS: But he [the secretary] wrote to Emperor Constantius about that epistle, at the command of Pope John, saying "We rightly said one will of our Lord Jesus Christ, it must not be taken up as if it spoke on two wills of divine and human nature, but only of one in human nature." Since Sergius wrote to preach that there were two particular contrary wills of Christ, we wrote back that Christ did not have two contrary wills.

Furthermore, in the whole epistle, Honorius contends it must not be said that in Christ as God and man there is one or two wills, how did he so forget himself that he would then clearly affirm one will? Therefore, he did not say there is one for God and man, but one for Christ as man alone, as the words which follow and the secretary witness. Therefore, we hold that there is no error in these epistles.

I say to the second: without a doubt, the name of Honorius was inserted among those who are condemned by the Sixth Council by rivals of the Roman Church, and likewise whatever else is said against him. I prove this, a) because Anastasius the Librarian witnesses this in his history drawn from Theophanus the Isaurian, a Greek; and b) it was nearly an ordinary custom of the Greeks to corrupt books. For (as we said) in the Sixth Council itself, act 12 and 14, many corruptions were discovered made by heretics in the Fifth Council. And Pope Leo[7] sought from the Greeks why they had corrupted his epistle to Flavian even though he was still living? Pope Gregory asserted that at Constantinople they had corrupted the Council of Chalcedon, and he suspected the same about Ephesus.[8] And he adds that the codices of the Romans by far had greater veracity than those of the Greeks: "Because the Romans, just as they do not have frauds, so also they do not have impostures."

Next, Nicholas I, in his epistle to Michael, referring the emperor to the epistle of Adrian I, said: "If still, it has not been falsified in the hands of the church of Constantinople from the custom of the Greeks, but is just as it was sent from the Apostolic See, so far it will have been preserved." He did not say this without cause, for the things he alleges in the epistle to Photius from the epistle of Adrian to Tharasius, are not contained in that epistle, as it is read in the Seventh Council. Therefore the Greeks cut out that citation, because it took action against the honor of Tharasius. Therefore, if the Greeks corrupted the Third, Fourth, Fifth and Seventh Council, would anyone be surprised if they had corrupted the Sixth also? Especially since it is certain that a little after the Sixth Council concluded, many bishops again went up to Constantinople and published the canons in Trullo; the purpose of the said bishops seems to have been nothing other than to revile and condemn the Roman Church.

Thirdly, the council could not condemn Honorius as a heretic, unless it opposed the epistle of St. Agatho, nay, more even itself; plainly it asserts the contrary. For Pope Agatho in Epistle I to the Emperor, which was read in that very council (sess. 4), says: "This is the rule of the true faith, which vigorously remains steadfast in good times as well as bad. This spiritual mother defended the affairs of your most peaceful empire, namely, the Apostolic Church of Christ, which through the grace of almighty God is proved never to have erred from the course of apostolic tradition, nor succumbed to the depravities of novel heretics. From the beginning of the Christian faith she has secured by means of

---

[7] Epist. 83 *ad Palaestinos.*

[8] Lib. 5, epist. 14 *ad Narsem.*

the authoritative princes of the Apostles of Christ, with the unimpaired goal remaining in her power, according to the divine promise of our Lord and Savior himself, which was confessed by the prince of the disciples in the holy Gospels, Peter, saying 'Peter, behold, Satan has asked to sift you like wheat, but I have prayed for thee, that thy faith shall not fail, and thou, when thou has been converted, strengthen thy brethren.' Let your tranquil mercy consider that the Lord and Savior of all, whose faith it is, who promised the faith of Peter was not going to fail, admonished him to strengthen his brethren, which the Apostolic Pontiffs, the predecessors of my scanty [Pontificate] have always done, and which has been acknowledged by all."

Here, note that Agatho not only says the faith in the see of Peter did not fail, nor could fail, and hence the Pope cannot, as Pope, settle something against the faith; but even that all his predecessors, one of which is Honorius, always resisted heresies and strengthened the brethren in faith. And further on, after Agatho enumerated the Monothelite heretics, Cyrus, Sergius, Pyrrhus, Paul, Peter and Theodore, he said: "Hence, the holy Church of God must be delivered and freed from the supreme endeavors and errors of such teachers, in order that the evangelical and apostolic rectitude of the Orthodox faith, which was founded on the firm rock of this Blessed Peter, Prince of the Apostles and of the Church, which remains inviolate by his grace and protection from every error, every number of prelates, clergy and people will confess and preach with us." The whole council in the eighth action, and in the 18th approved this epistle, where the Fathers not only said that Agatho spoke, but that St. Peter spoke through Agatho.

Therefore, from these testimonies I argue: If Honorius was a Monothelite heretic, then how could Agatho, disputing in the face of this very heresy, write that none of his predecessors ever erred? And when the other churches were stained by the errors of their Prelates, only the Roman Church remained intact? Then, if the council affirmed that Peter spoke through Agatho, and said: "the Roman Pontiffs always confirmed their brethren in faith, and never succumbed to heresy," with what temerity would the same Council in nearly each action say anathema to the heretic Honorius? Therefore it must be that either the council was falsified; or the epistle of Agatho, or that the council is opposed with itself and with Agatho. Now, noone has ever asserted this last one, not even the heretics; on the second there was never any suspicion; therefore it is necessary to hold the first.

Nilos responds to this last argument, but in vain: "Perchance Agatho was moved, both from the fact that the reasoning of the question demanded, as often happens, that he should so write; and because really that Church had erred from the truth more rarely."

But the reasoning of the question certainly demanded that he would say something on his authority, and on the praises of his predecessors. But would it demand that he would impudently lie? Would it not also have been a very impudent lie for Agatho to say that all his predecessors always resisted heresy, if Honorius, whom he was speaking about, was contaminated with that heresy? It is not enough to say that the Roman Church erred more rarely in order to maintain that it had truly never erred. But let us listen to the rest. Nilos continues: "Otherwise, if this were true, simply and without exception (that no Roman Pontiff erred), how would that agree with what [Scripture] says; 'All have sinned and we are all guilty; there is not one who does good, not even one?'"

Certainly outstanding reasoning, as if David spoke on faith and not on morals. The Psalmist does not say that there is not one who believes rightly, rather "There is not one who does good," and James says: "For we all have offended in many things." Otherwise, if he meant on faith, it would follow that even Paul, and John and all the Apostles could err, even after the reception of the Holy Spirit.

Nilos continues: "It may be that this is rightly said that when Agatho spoke, he meant that in past times the Roman Church did not err, but not that it would be impossible to err in the future." But Honorius, O good Nilos, was in past times. He preceded Agatho by many years. Moreover, did not Agatho speak on the future, when he said that the faith in the See of Peter *would* never fail?

Lastly, Nilos adds: "Agatho certainly wrote these things before the Sixth Council, for then he was not sufficiently acquainted with the matters on which the Sixth Council treated. It would be no great wonder if that holy council examined matters which one man alone could not sufficiently discern."

But if this is so, then Agatho erred from ignorance. Yet why did the whole council in the 8th and 18th action approve that epistle, as though it were written by St. Peter? Why is this anything else than to say the whole council either approved error, or is clearly opposed to itself? I will pass over the fact that no one better understood the doctrines of Honorius than Agatho, since the matter is made plain by John IV. It was more often examined by Theodore, Martin and other predecessors of Agatho, the successors of Honorius.

Fourthly, it is proved from the epistle of Nicholas I to the Emperor Michael, where Nicholas says on the Roman Pontiffs: "For at no time has even a wicked rumor ever defiled us; and when perverse things are discerned with the wise, do they not dispute them all the more?" But how is this true, if in a public, celebrated and well attended general council, it was so often acclaimed 'anathema to the heretic Honorius'?

Fifthly, it is proved because it is either necessary to say that this council, where it condemns Honorius, was corrupted by rivals, or it is fitting to assert this same council labored under intolerable error and impudence; but this second has never been said even by heretics, therefore the first must be said. Moreover, the council could not condemn Honorius for a heretic without intolerable impudence and error, since it is certain it had no other indication of the "heresy" of Honorius except from his epistles to Sergius, where Honorius forbids one or two operations to be said in Christ. But those epistles very clearly witness that Honorius considered and taught two operations in Christ and he only wished for Sergius to abstain from the use of those words "one", or "two" to remove scandal and pacify contention. Moreover, he cannot be condemned as a heretic when he confessed the matter itself, although he thought the name could be kept silent for a just cause, especially before a definition of the Church. Otherwise, St. Jerome could now be condemned as a heretic because in his epistle to Damasus he sensed it must not be said in God there are three hypostases, the contrary of which the Church later defined, and not only once.

Lastly, it happens that a well-attended Roman Council (which was celebrated by Pope St. Martin I, a Pope and a martyr, before the Sixth Council), took up the case of the Monothelites. Sergius, Cyrus, Pyrrhus and Paulus were condemned by name, but no mention was made of Honorius. This cannot be attributed to human respect, since these bishops were very holy men, and especially St. Martin, who presided over the council. Much less can it be attributed to ignorance or forgetfulness. Who would better know the deeds of their successors? Therefore, if the Roman Council did not condemn Honorius, which had his epistles in its own hand as well as living witnesses of his words and deeds, how credible is it that the Sixth Council would do it from his epistles alone?

What if someone were brought in that could not believe that the Sixth Council would be corrupted; he could look to another solution, which is in Juan de Torquemada.[9] He teaches that the Fathers of the Sixth Council condemned Honorius but from false information, and hence erred in that judgment. Although a legitimate general council could not err in defining dogmas of faith (and the Sixth Council did not), still it could err in questions of fact. Therefore, we can safely say that those Fathers were deceived by false rumors and did not understand the epistles of Honorius, and wrongly enumerated Honorius with the heretics.

You will say: Therefore, you understand the epistles of Honorius better than so many Fathers? I respond: Certainly not me, but by John IV, Martin I, Agatho

---

[9] D *de Ecclesia* lib. 2, cap. 93.

and Nicholas I, the Supreme Pontiffs, and by the Roman Council gathered under Pope Martin, these epistles were better understood than by the Greeks in the Sixth Council.

Why, therefore, you will ask, did the legates of Agatho not protest when Honorius was condemned? I respond: It would have been done to avoid a greater evil. The legates feared if they would have protested that a definition of right faith would be impeded, and a schism which had endured for sixty years, would not be healed. For in that council many patriarchs were condemned, of Constantinople, Alexandria and Antioch, whose successors would not easily have acquiesced unless also Honorius were condemned, who had been accused together with them. And thus the second argument.

Now I respond to the third: The Fathers of the Seventh Council followed the Sixth, and only repeated what had been read in it. Hence they were deceived from the Sixth Council, which was either corrupted or had condemned Honorius in error.

To the fourth I respond: Adrian, with the Roman Council, did not clearly say that Honorius was a heretic, but only that anathema was said to him by the Orientals, because he had been accused of heresy. There it seems Adrian, on that account, had said Honorius was anathematized by the Oriental bishops, because he knew he was not anathematized by the Western bishops, that is by the Council of St. Martin. Moreover, Adrian added that even in the case of Honorius, the Eastern bishops would not have dared to pass judgment on Honorius unless the Roman See had already given its consent, because he knew the legates of Agatho consented to the condemnation of Honorius, and indeed we say this if the acts of the Sixth Council are to be defended as if they are intact; if we were to say they were corrupted, then the response will be that Adrian was deceived by those corrupted acts of the Sixth Council.

You might say: But certainly these Councils believed that the Pope could err. I respond: Those Fathers only believed that the Pope could err as a private man, which is a probable opinion, although the contrary seems more probable to us. That is all that Honorius is accused of, that he fostered heresy in *private letters*.

To the fifth I say: Melchior Cano errs twice in this argument. First, when he says Agatho said anathema to Honorius; it is not discovered in his epistles. But Cano seems to have been deceived by the work *Summa Conciliorum*, for the author of that work added the name of Honorius against the faith of those epistles which are contained whole in the second volume of councils. Next, when he says this epistle of Agatho was written to the Sixth Council. Both epistles were not written to the council, but to the emperor.

To the sixth argument I say: The same men who corrupted the Sixth Council also corrupted the epistle of Leo. If that epistle were to be thought of as some part of the council, it is fashioned with that council. Or else Leo followed the judgment of the legates of Agatho, lest he would disturb a business that was already settled. But we are not held anymore to follow one Leo than so many other Popes, especially in a question of fact, which does not pertain to the faith.

To the seventh argument: I object authors to authors, many to a few, and more ancient to more recent; for in the first place, St. Maximus (who lived in the time of Honorius), in the *Dialogue against Pyrrhus*, as well as Theophanes the Isaurian in his history which Onuphrius and Emanuel Calleca cite in a book (which he wrote for the Latins against the Greeks), always witnesses the fact that Honorius was Catholic. Next, even Photius, a Greek, and hostile to the Roman Church, in a book on the seven councils, where he comes to the Sixth Council, says that those who were condemned were Cyrus, Sergius, Pyrrhus, Paul and Peter, but he says no such thing of Honorius. Likewise, Zonaras, in his life of Constantine IV, relating the names of those condemned in the Sixth Council, omits Honorius, just as Paul the Deacon in the life of the same Constantine IV. Lastly, almost all Latin historians such as Bede, Anastasius the Librarian, Blondus[10] Nauclerus, Sabellicus, Platina and others have it that Honorius was a Catholic and holy Pope.

I have added even Bede, even if Melchior Cano refused. I do not doubt whether he thought the same thing, although in his book *de sex ætatibus*, the name of Honorius crept in among those who were condemned in the Sixth Council. It seems some scribe added the name of Honorius in the book of Bede, for the reason that in the Sixth Council everywhere he is discovered with the names of Cyrus, Sergius etc. That Bede held Honorius for a holy man, even after his death, is clear from book 2 of his *History of the English People*, chapters 17-19, where he speaks often of Honorius as the best of shepherds.[11]

---

[10] *Decadis primae*, lib. 9.

[11] Translator's note: As with the case of Liberius, it is important to note that Bellarmine is not infallible even though he was a great theologian and historian. While nearly all theologians at his time argued this based on the work of Cardinal Baronius and others, theologians in the later 18th and 19th centuries judged that Bellarmine's second opinion is more probable, namely that Honorius was condemned but this was by way of concession. When the case was reviewed at Vatican I it was judged that Honorius was condemned for not having done enough to stop heresy. Therefore, while Bellarmine's argument is still possible, since councils can err in points of fact (and we add that he brings many good testimonies that make his case), nevertheless, it has been superseded in the estimation of theologians and Church historians.

CHAPTER XII
On Seven Other Popes

HE TWENTY-FOURTH Roman Pontiff who is accused of error is St. Martin I, whom the Centuriators[1] accuse because he taught that forgiveness is not to be given to priests or deacons after their ordination for sins,[2] which seems to be a species of Novatianism.

I respond: Martin did not speak on forgiveness of sins, but on the restitution to their sacred ministries. He wished priests and deacons who grievously sinned to be deposed from their state, and if they should come to their senses and seek forgiveness, they should be absolved from their sins, but never restored to their state, which is what all the Fathers teach.

The twenty-fifth is Pope Gregory III, whom the Centuriators accuse, 1) that in an epistle to St. Boniface, he commanded all of those who had been ordained by anyone apart from those whom the Roman Pontiff had sent to be consecrated again.[3] But this is clearly a lie. Gregory only commanded those that were not ordained by true bishops must be consecrated again.

2) They accuse him, in another epistle to St. Boniface, of permitting a man to marry another woman, if, on account of some disease, his own wife is not well enough to render the marriage debt. Gratian also records this.[4] St. Gregory the Great is also accused of the same error by several, on account of his epistle to Augustine of Canterbury, in which the same words are found.

I respond: In the first place, one must marvel why the Lutherans would hold this for an error, since Luther taught the same thing, as John Cochlæus shows.[5] Next, I say that Gregory did not speak on any sort of imbecility, but on perpetual and natural impotence, through which a woman is unsuitable for marriage. Such marriages, if they were contracted from error, are not reckoned to be marriages and they are dissolved in the judgment of the Church as we see it in the decretals,[6] and the Glossa responds in like manner.[7]

---

[1] *Cent.* 7, ch. 20.

[2] Epist. *Ad Amandum.*

[3] *Cent.* 8, ch. 10, in the life of Gregory III.

[4] Canon: *Quod proposuisti*, 32, quest. 7.

[5] *Septicpite*, cap. De Matrimonio.

[6] Tit. *De frigidis*, cap. ex literis. Translator's note: In the event that the reader is confused, the Church teaches that one must have the capacity to engage in marital relations in order to truly have a Sacramental marriage.

[7] In 20. D. can. E libellis.

But against this, Gregory seems to judge that the first was a true matrimony, and not dissolved as much as added according to it. He writes that a man ought not to take away the subsidy from the first wife; that is, he ought to still support and sustain her as a wife. Therefore, it could also be said with the same Glossa,[8] that the Pope spoke on each infirmity, but not to concede another spouse as though it were just, but rather less bad. It seems less bad that someone should have one concubine, than that he should consort with many harlots. Or, certainly, the Pontiff fell from ignorance. But we do not deny that it could happen to the Popes when they do not define something as *de fide*, but only declare an opinion to others. Gregory seems to have done this in this citation. Moreover, it must be noted that this opinion was not of Gregory I, but only of this Gregory III, since it is not discovered among the works of St. Gregory, but only in the volumes of councils. There, the Roman Council, on the prohibited degrees in regards to matrimony, is attributed to Gregory I and III, when still really it could not be so unless it originated from Gregory III. Such is clear from names of the emperors who appear in the beginning and end of the council.

The twenty-sixth is Nicholas I, whom several condemn, because he taught that baptism conferred in the name of Christ, without expression of the three persons, was valid.[9] That is contrary not only to the evangelical institution, but even to the decrees of other Popes, namely, of Pelagius and Zachary, who condemned the baptism of those who are only baptized in the name of Christ and not expressly in the name of the Father, and of the Son, and of the Holy Spirit, and is clear in the same place.[10] Nor can the response be given that in the time of Nicholas, it was still not defined whether baptism was invalid if conferred in the name of Christ, for that was defined in the English Council and confirmed by Pope Zachary who preceded Nicholas.[11]

I respond: Nicholas was not defining a question on faith when he spoke; rather, he only expressed his opinion in passing as a private teacher. For what he intended to teach in that canon was not on the form of baptism, but only on the minister concerning which he had been asked. Therefore, after he responded and defined that baptism was valid, even if given by a Jew or a pagan, which the question was especially about, he added in passing that baptism is valid whether it is given in the name of the three persons or in the name of Christ alone. In this he followed the opinion of Ambrose as he says himself.[12] Still, in my

---

[8] In 32 quaest. 7, can. *Proposuisti.*

[9] As is related *de consecr.* Dist. 4, can. *A quodam Judaeo.*

[10] Dist. 4, can. *Mulsti*; and can. *In Synodo.*

[11] Canon "in Synodo", de consec. Dist. 4.

[12] *Sententiam* lib. 1, de spiritui sancto, cap. 3.

judgment, this opinion is false, but not heretical. There is no certain definition of the Church that is discovered on this affair, and various opinions are discovered among the Fathers.

Now those canons of Pelagius and Zachary also do not obstruct the case. In the first place, Pelagius did not define anything, but in his epistle to Gaudentius explains his opinion only as a teacher. Moreover, the canon of Zachary is exceedingly suspect. In the first place, Gratian cites the epistle of Zachary to Boniface, when he places this canon, but such an opinion is not discovered in the epistles of Zachary to Boniface, which are extant in the volumes of councils.

Next, Bede makes no mention of this English council in his history, where he always makes mention of other English councils. Nay more, Bede himself follows the contrary opinion,[13] as he approves the opinion of Ambrose on baptism in the name of Christ. Still, one could not ignore a decree of an English council, if it were real, which Zachary mentions, since he lived in the same time and still outlived Zachary. It does not seem at all believable that he would wish to contradict a council celebrated in his own country and confirmed by the Apostolic See.

Yet, if we admit the authority of this council and Zachary, we can respond twofold. Firstly, with St. Peter Lombard that in this council it was only defined that baptism was not valid without the invocation of the three persons. Still, it was not defined whether the three persons ought to be named explicitly, and hence this cannon is not opposed to the opinion of Ambrose and of Nicholas, who taught that it sufficed to implicitly name the three persons in the one name of Christ.[14] St. Bernard also understood that canon of the council in this manner[15] as well as Hugh of St. Victor and all other teachers of that age, who taught, not withstanding the canon of the English Council, that baptism in the name of Christ was valid.

It can be said secondly, that the English Council was not truly and properly approved by the Apostolic See, and therefore does not make the matter *de fide*. Zachary certainly praised the English Council, and cited its decrees for his proposition; still, he did not properly approve it as Pope and with the intention of confirming the acts of the Council. It is one thing for the Pope to confirm the decrees of Councils in earnest, and another to commend something that other [Councils] proposed.

---

[13] Actor. cap. 10.

[14] 4 dist. 3.

[15] Epistle 340.

The twenty-seventh Pope is Stephen VI, who can be joined with the twenty eighth Pope accused of error, Sergius III. It is certain from Platina and others, that Stephen invalidated the acts of Pope Formosus, his predecessor, and commanded those ordained by him to be ordained again. Hence he thought that the Sacrament depended upon the virtue of the minister, which is a manifest error in faith. For that reason, Pope John IX afterward invalidated the acts of Stephen VI and approved the acts of Formosus. But a little afterward, Sergius III again invalidated the acts of Formosus, and hence also of John, and approved the acts of Stephen. Necessarily, one of these Popes was opposed to the others and erred, as the Centuriators diligently observed.[16]

I respond: Stephen VI and Sergius III erred in a question of fact, not of law, and gave a bad example, not false doctrine. This is the history. Formosus, the Cardinal bishop of Portus, was deposed by Pope John VIII, and demoted and returned to the lay state, after which he swore that he would never return to the city, or the episcopate. A little after the death of John VIII, his successor, Martin II, absolved Formosus of his careless oath, and restored him to his original dignity. Not long after that, Formosus was created Pope. He lived for five years and died.

Stephen VI succeeded him who, being enkindled with great hatred against Formosus (or else unaware or not believing that he was absolved of his oath by Pope Martin), decreed publicly in a C\council of bishops that Formosus was never a legitimate Pope and therefore, all his acts were invalid. He compelled all those who had received orders from him to be ordained again, just as if they had received nothing. This deed displeased everyone, and therefore three Popes in succession, Roman I, Theodore II and especially John IX, after calling another Episcopal Council, judged that Formosus was a true Pope and invalidated the sentence of Stephen VI. Next, Sergius III succeeded him and imitated Stephen VI in all things. The particular question was whether Formosus was a legitimate Pope. We do not deny that in such questions Popes can err, and Stephen and Sergius erred in fact.

But you will object: Stephen and Sergius not only judged that Formosus was not a true Pope, but even the sacred orders which he conferred were not valid; such is a manifest error against faith. Even if Formosus was not a Pope, and always remained deposed and demoted, still, because he was at one time a true bishop, and insofar as the character and power of orders cannot by any means be taken away, it is an error in faith to say that the sacred orders he conferred were not true orders.

---

[16] *Cent.* 9, ch. 10, in the life of Stephen VI, and *Cent.* 10, ch. 10 in the life of John IX and Sergius III.

I respond: Stephen and Sergius did not publish some decree whereby they determined the orders by a demoted bishop, or the orders that Formosus by name conferred after he had been demoted, must be conferred again; rather, they only *de facto* commanded them to be conferred again. Such a command proceeded not from ignorance or heresy, but from hatred against Formosus. Sigebert remarks in his *Chronicle* for the year 803 that Stephen VI was forcefully opposed by all those who were ordained by Formosus.

The twenty-ninth Pope is John XIII, or as some say, the XIV, whom the Centuriators accuse of a horrendous error and sacrilege, because he began to baptize bells against the institution of Christ, which other heretics frequently use in their objections against us. I wonder why they do not also say that we used to catechize and instruct the bells so that they could ring out the creed! They either condemn the matter itself, or the name "Baptism of Bells." In the matter, clearly they are deceived, or else they are lying, for bells are not really baptized but only blessed and dedicated for divine worship, in the manner that churches, altars, chalices and other sacred vessels are blessed, as is clear from the pontifical where the blessing of bells is contained. Yet no mention is ever made there of baptism, and it is not said: "I baptize you in the name of the Father, and of the Son and of the Holy Spirit." Rather, only prayers to God are found there, just as in all other blessings. If they condemn the name, let them know the name of baptism is not from the Popes, but from common speech; as it is metaphorically accommodated to the blessing of bells because the people see the bells are sprinkled with holy water, and meanwhile names are given to them so that some may be distinguished from others.

The thirtieth Pope who is said to have erred is Sylvester II, whom Martin Polanus relates was a magician and sorcerer, and mangled by the devil in the Church of the Holy Cross at Jerusalem (Santa Croce). The Centuriators[17] and Tilman Hesh[18] relate this narrative. It is a fact that sorcerers, just as the great part of infidels, worship the devil in place of God.

I respond: These are, without a doubt, fables which are told on the witchcraft and death of Sylvester II. For no author of good faith affirms that for certain, and the tomb of this Pope still exists in the Lateran Basilica, with an inscription placed on it by Pope Sergius IV, a holy man by the agreement of all writers, who was only five years after Sylvester. The inscription praises Sylvester as the best Pope. The occasion of making this story on the witchcraft of this Sylvester was because Sylvester was an expert in geometry and also wrote books on the subject. In that age, however (that is the 900s), which was

---

[17] *Cent.* 10, ch. 10.

[18] *De Ecclesia*, lib. 1, ch. 9.

more unlearned and infelicitous, anyone who devoted himself to mathematics or philosophy was reckoned commonly to be a magician. See Onuphrius in his annotation to Platina.

CHAPTER XIII
On Gregory VII

HE THIRTY-FIRST who is accused of error by our adversaries is Pope Gregory, the seventh of that name. The Centuriators condemn him as a heretic,[1] a wizard, seditious, guilty of simony, an adulterer and the worst, not only of all Popes, but of all men. And for that reason they do not call him Gregory, as is his papal name, nor even Hildebrand, his name in life, but "Hellebrand", which in German means the burning embers of hell.

Theodore Bibliander, in his *Chronicle*, would have it that the same Gregory is the very prince of Gog and Magog, and all other heretics of this time detest no Pontiff more than him. Above all Tilman Hesh clearly lies about the evils he relates concerning Gregory VII contained in his book of monks, Popes and their flatterers.[2] Still neither Tilman nor the Centuriators advance any witness apart from one: the testimony of a Cardinal Benno who lived in that time and left behind a written life of Gregory VII.

Reading the book of this Benno, and discovering it to be full of the most impudent lies, I am persuaded of one of two possibilities: either Benno never wrote any such book in that time and instead some Lutheran is really the author of this book, who published it under the name of Benno; or certainly that Benno did not so much write a life of Gregory VII, as under the name of Gregory, because he wished to depict what the worst Pontiff would do, in the manner in which Xenophon wrote a life of King Cyrus of Persia, not so much to relate what Cyrus did, as much as what the greatest ruler ought to do.

At any rate one must not put any trust in this work of Benno, and that is clear from the contrary works published on the matter of all other authors who lived at that time, in whom one must place greater trust. Both because they are many and he is only one, but also because Benno was created a cardinal by the antipope Clement III, whom the Holy Roman Emperor set up in hatred of Gregory,[3] not by the true Pope as Bibliander falsely relates in his *Chronicle,*[4] where he falsely depicts Benno as an intimate of Gregory. Since he was the cardinal of an antipope, he could not speak well on the true Pope. Moreover, these other authors were of a neutral party confined by some benefice and therefore judged more correctly. That what the rest write is contrary to the things which Benno wrote, can be easily proven.

---

[1] *Cent.* 11, ch. 10

[2] *De Ecclesia*, lib. 1 ch. 9.

[3] Onuphrius, *de Pontificibus.*

[4] Tabul. 13.

There are four claims to which everything that Benno writes can be reduced. 1) That Gregory VII seized the pontificate by military force without either the vote of any Cardinal or a consensus of the clergy and people. But St. Anselm, the bishop of Lugo (who lived at that time), wrote a letter to Wilbert, a man in schism with the antipope Clement III, saying: "That I might speak on our Father, Blessed Gregory, what St. Cyprian wrote about Cornelius: He was made a bishop by the judgment of God and Christ, by nearly all the clergy, and, that I might speak more truly, absolutely by the acclamation of all, from the suffrage of the people who were then present, to the gathering of the elder priests and good men, since it happened that no man before him, since the place of Alexander, that is, the place of Peter, and the step of the sacerdotal chair was vacant, etc." The Abbot of Ursberg relates this epistle in his *Chronicle*, and adds that this Anselm was a very learned and holy man, and was glorified with miracles in life and after death.

The form of election of this Pope is extant in Platina, in these words: "We, cardinals of the Holy Roman Church, clergy, acolytes, subdeacons, priests, with bishops, abbots and many other ecclesiastics present, as well as laity, elect today, 22 April, in the Basilica of St. Peter in Chains, in the year of our Savior 1078, as the true vicar of Christ, Hildebrand the archdeacon, a man of much doctrine, great piety, prudence, justice, constancy, religion, who is modest, sober and continent, etc." Such a form appears to have been preserved by divine providence to argue against the lies of Benno. Likewise, all other authors write the same, whom we will cite below.

2) Benno writes that Gregory VII excommunicated Henry IV even though he was innocent (as the Centuriators make bold to assert).[5] But Stephen, the bishop of Halberstadt, a holy and learned man, wrote in that time these words to bishop Walram, as Dodechinus witnesses in his addition to Marianus Scotus, in the year 1090, as well as Trithemius in his *Chronicle*: "Listen to what is true, not shams; listen to what is more steadfast, not jokes; anyone that sells spiritual dignities is a heretic (simoniac); but the Lord Henry, whom they call king, sells episcopates and abbacies. Indeed Constance, Bambergen, Moguntia and many others, for money; Regensburg, Augsburg and Strasburg for a sword; the Abbacy of Fuldens for adultery; for the episcopate of Munster, which is unlawful to say and hear, he sold for foul sodomy. If you were to impudently deny these things, with heaven and earth as a witness, even all those responding from the furnace with a little knowledge shall deduce this: the Lord Henry is a heretic. For such unlawful evils he was excommunicated by the Apostolic See; he can exercise no power over us, because we are Catholic."

---

[5] *Cent.* 11, cap. 6, colum 264.

Marianus Scotus, who lived in the time of Henry IV says: "Catholic men, seeing and hearing these crimes, as well as wicked and unheard of matters like unto them that were done by King Henry, were constituted with zeal in the Church, being zealous, like the prophet Elijah, for the house of Israel. After messages had been directed to Rome to Alexander the bishop of the Apostolic See, they bemoaned by letters, as by a groan and affliction of the living voice, these and other deeds which were a great many that were said and done by the insane heretical simoniacs, having King Henry as their author and patron."[6]

Likewise, Dedechinus, the continuator of Marianus, in the year 1106 says: "Henry was a perverse man and it is manifestly certain that he was cast out from the Church by a just judgment; for he sold all spiritual things." The same author in the year 1090 and 1093 relates many crimes of Henry IV. Also, St. Anselm of Canterbury wrote an epistle at the same time to Walram, which preceded his book on unleavened bread, where he calls Henry the successor of Nero, Domitian and Diocletian. Next, Lambert of Schaffnaburg relates not a few crimes of Henry, as well as the Abbot of Ursberg,[7] Albert Kranz,[8] Joannes Aventinus,[9] to which authors the Centuriators usually attribute much. But what does Calvin confess on the matter? He writes thus: "The Emperor Henry, the Fourth of that name, was a capricious and bold man, of no counsel, but great boldness and dissolute life. He had the episcopates of the whole of Germany in his halls, some for sale, others abandoned for plunder."[10]

3) Benno writes that Pope Gregory was a Berengarian heretic; that is, he did not believe for certain that the body of Christ was present in the Eucharist. But certainly nothing less true can be said about this Pope. For (that I might omit the fact that he is called a saint by all writers, that Leo IX and Nicholas II, who condemned Berengarius, always communicated with him, that no approved author, not even Sigebert who had little love for him, has dared to advance such a thing) Gregory himself, while presiding at the Council of Turin as a legate of the Pope condemned the same Berengarius. Guitmundus writes the following: "The Church herself soon condemned the fabrications which had arisen from Berengarius through Pope Leo. Thereupon, he convicted him in the Council of Turin, through the one who is now our blessed Pope Gregory when he was an archdeacon of the same Roman See. Moreover, as it seemed Berengarius himself was corrected, he [Gregory] mercifully received his hands in the Sacrament.

---

[6] Chronicle for the year 1125.

[7] In *Chronico.*

[8] *Metropolis*, lib. 5 et *Saxoniae* lib. 5.

[9] *Annalium Boiorum*, lib. 5.

[10] *Instit.* Lib. 4, ch. 11, § 13.

When Berengarius later returned to his vomit, Pope Nicholas of holy memory again refuted him in the general council at Rome."[11]

But lest they might say that Gregory, when he was an archdeacon, was Catholic, but then a heretic when he was made Pope, let Thomas the Waldensian be read where he relates word for word the opinion of this seventh Pope Gregory, which he imposed in the Roman Council against Berengarius in the sixth year of his pontificate, from which it will appear most clearly that Benno is lying.[12]

4) Benno writes that Gregory was a most wicked man, a simoniac, a magician, an adulterer, a murderer, that he covered up all his crimes; and he relates certain histories of which there is not a vestige extant in good authors, and still Illyricus and Tilman pass them off as oracles from heaven.

Nearly every other author who lived in that time, and in later ages wrote the contrary. Now, I will advance the Germans alone. Trithemus in his Chronicle, writes on the council of the emperor: "William, the Abbot of Hirsau, was called to this wicked council, he scorned to do so, for indeed he knew that the vicar of Christ was holy and innocent." Otho of Frisia says: "Hildebrand was always constant in ecclesiastical rigor."[13] And in the same work, he says: "The form of the flock became what he taught by word, he showed by example; being strong, he did not fear to place himself as a wall for the house of the Lord through all struggles."[14] Again: "The Church, bereaved of such a pastor, who among all priests and Roman Pontiffs, was of outstanding zeal and authority, had no little sorrow."[15] Kranz says: "Henry IV encroached upon the laws of the Church, establishing bishops at will, forsaking the Supreme Pontiff Gregory VII, and he persecuted that holy man."[16]

The Abbot of Ursberg does not seem to have dared to praise Gregory VII too openly, yet still, in three places, he shows his opinion. Firstly, where he reproaches Henry IV in clear words: "In the year of our Lord 1068, King Henry, having used the freedom of adolescence, began to dwell in Saxony alone from all the Empire. He despised princes and oppressed nobles, while raising those of lower rank on high, and devoted himself to hunting, soft living, and other exercises of this sort, more than to justice which needed to be done, as he has been condemned. He married daughters of nobles to anyone of obscure birth; he

---

[11]   *De Eucharistia*, lib. 3.

[12]   *De Sacramentis*, tomo 2, ch. 43.

[13]   *Histor.*, lib. 6, ch. 32.

[14]   Ibid, ch. 34.

[15]   Ibid, ch. 36.

[16]   *In Metropoli*, lib. 5, c. 20.

set up private guards, not trusting the powerful very much.... This last end, ruin and lot of Henry was to be known as the fourth Roman emperor under that name by his own; but by Catholics, that is, by everyone united to Blessed Peter and his successors, preserving trust and obedience to Christian law, he was called the chief of pirates, together with heresiarch, apostate and persecutor more of souls than of bodies." There, while he teaches that Henry sunk from adolescence into tyranny, he shows that the judgment of Gregory against the same king was just.

Next, below that, when he cited the words of the assembly against Gregory, and then the defense of St. Anselm for the same Gregory, the Abbot so adds: "bishop Anselm wrote these things exceedingly contrary to his earlier opinion, a man clearly erudite in letters, with a keen intellect, particular eloquence, and what is best of all, he was most noted in the fear of God and holy conversation, to the point that both in life and after death, he is glorified by the relation of miracles." Certainly, it is no wonder if he who places those that praised Gregory before the condemners, also, seems to tacitly praise Gregory.

Later, he speaks about the successor of Gregory VII: "Desiderius, a Roman cardinal, abbot of Cassino, and true servant of Christ, although he struggled much in heart together with his body. But laboring with great infirmity, he was brought forth to this supreme apex and he obtained by prayers, that he would be taken from this life in a few days." Who could question that this Desiderius, if he was a true servant of Christ, would never have approved the cause of Gregory, unless he recognized it was most just?

Nauclerus, in his *Chronicle*, says: "Gregory was a religious man, fearing God, a lover of equity and justice, constant in difficulties, who, on account of God, did not fear to complete anything in those matters which pertain to justice."[17]

Marianus Scotus, a monk of Fulda, who lived in the time of Gregory VII, says: "Having heard the just complaints and cries of Catholics against Henry, as well as the barbarity of his crimes, burning with the zeal of God, Gregory then pronounced excommunication on the aforesaid king, particularly due to simony. What he did greatly pleased many Catholic men, although the simoniacs and flatterers of the king were greatly displeased."[18]

Dodechinus the abbot, the continuator of Marianus, adds for the year 1085: "Urban himself confirmed the writings and declarations of the venerable Pope Gregory against the schismatics." And, in the year 1090, names Gregory "Pope of blessed memory".

---

[17] *Chron.*, gener. 37.

[18] *In Chronico,* anni MLXXV

Lambert Schaffnaburg, who lived in the same time, in his history of German affairs, says: "The constancy of Hildebrand, his spirit unconquered against avarice, excluded all arguments of human fallacy... The signs and wonders that were done more frequently by the prayers of Pope Gregory and his most fervent zeal for God and ecclesiastical laws sufficiently fortified him against the poison tongues of his detractors."

Likewise, he relates the death of William, bishop of Utrecht, who opposed Gregory together with Benno: "Immediately seized by a grave illness, he uttered miserable cries in the presence of all; then, by a just judgment of God, lost the present as well as eternal life, because he had offered to the king his devoted labor for all things which he had so criminally done, and also in the hope of his favor, knowing the grave contumelies against the most holy Roman Pontiff, a man of apostolic virtues, even calling for penalties against him when he was innocent."

Next, he says in the same place: "The Pope, after he celebrated a solemn Mass, advanced upon the king with the Lord's body in his hand and clearly declared: 'For too long I have been accused by you and your flatterers that I took possession of the Apostolic See by simony and that I have stained my life with other crimes. Therefore, I am cutting short such satisfaction, that I shall take away every scruple from every scandal; I ask God that, by his judgment, he might absolve me from the suspicion of the adjacent crime, if innocent, or that I might be killed immediately if guilty.' Then he took up part of the Lord's body and ate. This being freely done, since the people rejoiced in the innocence of the Pope and applauded him in praises of God for a considerable time, he turned to the king and said: 'Please, do what you have seen me do.' The king, after procuring a postponement, refused to cleanse himself or his injustices in this manner; for after he went back to his own, he returned to his normal character and would not rest until he had expelled St. Gregory from the city and substituted Gilbert of Ravenna in his place."

John Aventinus remains from the Germans, who wrote in our century. Although he writes many things on Gregory from some author without a name, and for that reason is without authority, still he was occasionally overcome by truth. He condemned Henry and praises Gregory: "Henry burned with the infamies of sexual affairs, lovers, unchastity and adultery, which even his friends do not deny."[19] And in the same place: "Gregory emerges as a most holy steadfast man. Paul Bernrietensis, who recounts his life in two books, and his remaining shrewd champions, advance his side."

---

[19] *Annalium Boiorum*, lib 5, pag. 563.

Thus we have the innocence of Gregory proven three-fold: by the testimony of writers, the testimony of dying adversaries, and the testimony of God, when invoked by the Pontiff. Only one calumny remains, namely, that of Sigebert in his *Chronicle*, where he writes that Gregory VII thought that, should priests who had concubines wish to carry out sacred functions, they could not really consecrate, and for that reason, forbade Christians to communicate with priests who had concubines.

I respond: Sigebert was among the secretaries of Henry IV, as Trithemius relates in his *Catalogue of Writers*, and therefore he interpreted the interdict of Gregory in a perverse manner. Moreover, what Gregory commanded is far better and more faithfully related by St. Anselm, who is older and holier than Sigebert. He says: "On the priests who are publicly reproved and show themselves to God cursed by carnal relations, it must altogether be feared that apostolic providence constituted an ecclesiastical and just rigor, without a doubt, it is by no means fitting that there one might reverently assist where they, making a stench with impudent lust, scorn the prohibition of God and the saints, and forsake sacred altars; nay more, they do not merely forsake them, but they have foully defiled them in the same measure. Not in the way in which someone will scorn those things which he treats, but rather he thinks those treating them so must be cursed just like those who do not reverence the presence of God and angels, or are repulsed by the detestation of men; they must cease to contaminate sacred things."[20] He correctly explained the decree of Gregory that was published in his own time.

Now, it is fitting to ascribe a catalogue of those authors who wrote honorably about Gregory VII. First, Leo Hostiensis wrote in the age of Gregory himself (around the year 1080) many things on his sanctity in which there are also heavenly revelations and visions of approved servants of God.[21] In the same time period, Marianus Scotus wrote on Gregory as a holy Pope from the year 1075 even to the year 1083.[22] Likewise Lambert Schaffnaburg,[23] and St. Anselm of Canterbury.[24] St. Anselm of Lucca in his epistle to Guibert and Stephen Halberstatensis in his epistle to Walramus found in Dodechinus, in an addition to Marianus Scotus. Bernard Corbeiensis[25] which Trithemius witnesses in his

---

[20] Epist. 8 ad Gulielmum Abbatem.

[21] *Historiae Cassinensis*, lib. 3.

[22] Lib.3 Chronici.

[23] *Historia Germanica*, near the end.

[24] Epist. 8 et initio libri de azyma.

[25] *In Apologia pro Gregorio*.

Catalogue of Writers, as well as Guitmundus.[26] Next, Paul Berniensis, and Gerochus Reichersperg, who wrote on behalf of Gregory and for that reason suffered exile, as John Aventinus witnesses.[27] These, therefore, constitute ten holy and learned writers who defended Gregory while he was alive. The only one who accuses him from these writers is the pseudo-cardinal Benno.

Next, around the year 1100 we have Sigebert, in his *Chronicle.* We already noted how he favored the Emperor Henry IV; still, he never dared to ascribe any crime to Gregory of the sort which Benno and the Centuriators relate; he only attributed to him inconsiderate zeal, and error concerning the ministers of the Sacrament, about which Anselm sufficiently exculpates him. Next, the same Sigebert, in the same place, is not silent that Anselm of Lucca wrote for Gregory, and God showed the sanctity of this Anselm by signs and wonders, which certainly pertains to the great praise of Gregory. Not long after, Gratian, in the year 1150, referred to the decree of Gregory.[28] Otho of Frisia, outstanding for his race, erudition and most noble in integrity of life, wrote for our Gregory.[29] Likewise, William of Tyre around the year 1180[30] and Gottfried Viterbiensis.[31]

Conrad, the Abbot of Ursberg in his Chronicle around the year 1200, although he does not clearly praise Gregory, does not reproach him either but he praises him (as we said above) more secretly in many ways, but does not condemn him. In the same time Dodechinus, in an addition to Marianus Scotus, openly praises Gregory, and reproaches Henry. Vincentius, around the year 1250, witnessed that Gregory VII was famous for miracles and the gift of prophecy. St. Thomas cites the same man with honor.[32] Martin Polanus, around the year 1300, in the life of the same Gregory. And John Villanus,[33] Blondus around the year 1400,[34] Matthew Palmerius in his *Chronicle* and Thomas the Waldensian.[35] St. Antoninus around the year 1450,[36] Platina, in the life of Gregory, as well as Aeneas Sylvius (Pope Pius II) in the compendium of Blondus.

---

[26] *De Sacramento Eucharistiae,* lib. 1&3.

[27] *Annal. Boiorum.,* lib. 5.

[28] 15 quest., 6, canon *Nos Sanctorum.*

[29] *Hist.,* lib. 6.

[30] *De bello sacro,* capite 13.

[31] *Chronicus universalis,* parte 17.

[32] Vincentius, *Speculum Historiale,* lib. 25, cap. 44.; 2.2. quaest. 12, art. 2.

[33] *Hist. Florentinae,* lib. 4, cap. 21.

[34] *Decade* 2, lib 3.

[35] Tomo 2, cap. 43.

[36] *Secunda Parte Summae Historialis,* tit. 16, cap. 1 § 21

John Trithemius, around the year 1500 in his *Chronicle*. John Nauclerus in his *Chronicle*, Albert Kranz[37] and Sabellicus[38] as well as Volaterranus.[39] They all clearly describe him as a holy man. These are thirty-two authors, whom we oppose to the one witness of Benno, so as to blunt the impudence of the Centuriators and Tilman and certainly to refute the lie of Tilman, who made bold to write that the "crimes" of Gregory VII were brought to light by Monks and flatterers of the Pope, when we have shown the contrary: that Gregory was praised by all.

---

[37] *Metropolis*, lib. 5

[38] *Enneade* 9, lib. 3

[39] *Anthropologiae* lib. 22; *res gestas Gregorii.*

CHAPTER XIV
On the Remaining Popes to Whom Error in Faith is Falsely Attributed

HE THIRTY-SECOND is Alexander III. In the chapter *Cum esses* (on wills), he says it is foreign to divine law and the custom of the Church that more than three witnesses would be required for wills, and in the same place he commands under penalty of excommunication that no one may rescind a will made with three witnesses. But the contrary is in practice throughout the whole Christian world; nor are wills held as ratified unless seven witnesses were applied. The same Pope Alexander, in the chapter *Licet*, on a spouse of two people, says that certain predecessors judged that Matrimony contracted through words in person, but still not consummated, could be invalidated through another matrimony; but he thought the contrary. From which it follows that either Alexander or his predecessors erred.

I respond: To the first with the Gloss of Canonists; Alexander did not publish that law except for men subject to himself in temporal as well as spiritual affairs; and hence that canon does not disparage civil laws, nor the practice of the remaining Christian world. Or if he passed down a law for all Christians, it ought to only be understood for pious reasons, concerning which the Church judges; that is, the Pontiff wished that wills, not all, but only those which make either the Church or a local pious person their heir, that they should be valid even if it were made with only three witnesses applied. To the second, I say that neither Alexander nor his predecessors defined anything, but only expressed what they thought.

The thirty-third is Celestine III, whom Alphonsus de Castro asserts could not be excused from heresy in any way, because he taught matrimony could be so dissolved by heresy and that it would be lawful for one to enter into another marriage when his prior spouse had fallen into heresy.[1] Even if this decree of Celestine were not extant, still it was formerly in ancient decretals, in the chapter *Laudabilem*, on the conversion of infidels, which is the decree Alphonsus says that he saw. Moreover, that this teaching of Celestine is heretical is clear, because Innocent III taught the contrary on divorce,[2] and the Council of Trent also defined the same thing.[3]

I respond: Neither Celestine nor Innocent stated anything certain on the matter; but each responded with what seemed more probable to them. That is manifestly gathered from the words of Innocent who, when he says his

---

[1] *De Haeresibus*, lib 1 cap. 4

[2] Cap. *Quanto.*

[3] Sess. 24, can 5.

predecessor thought otherwise, shows in his opinion that the whole matter was still being thought out. On the other hand, Alphonsus says the epistle of Celestine was at one time among the epistles in the decretals. While certainly that is true, it cannot thence be gathered that a plainly apostolic decree was made by Celestine, or even one *ex cathedra*; since it is certain that there are many epistles in the decretals which do not make any matter *de fide*, but only declare to us the opinions of the Pontiff on some affair.

The thirty-fourth is Innocent III, who in the chapter, *Per venerabilem*, concerning who might be legitimate sons, teaches the old law was not yet plainly abrogated: "Clearly, since Deuteronomy means the second law, it is proved from the force of the word, that what is discerned there ought to be observed in the New Testament." But this decree of Innocent is opposed to a decree of St. Paul in Acts XV.

I respond: Innocent, in that place, did not wish to say that Deuteronomy ought to be preserved even today by the letter, but insofar as what was said there was a figure of the New Testament. Therefore, Innocent thought Deuteronomy was called second law, because it contained figuratively pertinent matters to the new law.

The thirty-fifth is Nicholas IV, who in the Chapter *Exiit*, on the meaning of the words *in Sexto*, defined that Christ in word and example taught perfect poverty which consists in the abdication of all things, with no ownership being left to himself, neither in particular nor in common, and hence such poverty is holy and meritorious. Yet John XXII taught that this is false and heretical in his *Extravagantes*,[4] on the title of the meaning of the words. For in *Extravagantes*, to the fashioner of the canon, he teaches it is impossible that such poverty whereby someone should swear off all ownership in matters pertaining to the use of consumable things, while only retaining the use; and again in *Extravagantes*, where among several points, he declares it heretical to say that Christ taught such poverty by word and example. Also in *Extravagantes*, under the title of *Quia quorundam*, he teaches the same thing, and more amply drives home the point. Juan Torquemada tries in all things to reconcile these Popes, just as even John himself attempts to show himself to disagree with Nicolas.[5]

But certainly, unless I am greatly deceived, in all things they cannot be reconciled. And therefore, we must observe that John and Nicholas treat three questions. 1) Whether in matters in regard to the use of consumables one can

---

[4] Translator's note: *Extravagantes* refer to papal decrees not contained in certain canonical collections which were obligatory for the Church, but not in the corpus of medieval canon law. There were several by this title.

[5] *Summae*, lib. 2, cap. 112.

separate use from ownership. 2) Whether poverty, which removes all ownership from itself, being left behind only in use, may be holy and meritorious. 3) Whether Christ taught such poverty by word and example.

Pope John himself responds to the first in the following manner: One cannot separate use from ownership in matters of this sort, for to have ownership is to be able to destroy a thing. Hence it is impossible that one can destroy a thing by use, such as by eating bread, and not be the master of that thing. But Nicholas teaches it can be done, and rightly, for afterward, Clement V clearly taught the same thing in *Clementina*, "*Exivi de paradiso*," on the meaning of the words of Nicholas, and the reasoning is clear. He argues that because one is a master, he is not able to destroy anything in any manner; but he can freely destroy a thing after someone might have wanted it, and even given, sold, commuted etc. Furthermore, it is certain that all true religious have the use of the bread which they eat, and the wine which they drink; still they cannot give, sell, change or throw them away, etc. Now, you might say, then Pope John must have erred. I respond, it is true, but not in the matter itself; for this question does not pertain to the faith, as John himself says in *Extravagantes*, because it is of certain worldly things; and even more, there are different opinions of teachers on this matter.

On the second question, Nicholas thought that poverty is holy and meritorious; John denied it. Furthermore, on each point Nicholas thinks better, yet Nicholas neither defined this as though it were an article of faith, nor did John directly oppose it. For John, in those matters discussed in *Extravagantes*, to the fashioner of the canons, only intends to renounce the mastery of those things which are given to Franciscans, and, as Nicholas asserted, these things were the Roman Pontiffs'; moreover, John could renounce a law of this sort.

On the third question (which is the most serious of all and pertains to faith), Nicholas and John do not disagree. For Nicholas says that at some time Christ taught that most perfect poverty by word and example: moreover, at some time he showed poverty was less rigid by example, just as the common father and teacher of all. Furthermore, John defined it heretical to assert that Christ had nothing of his own here on earth, neither in particular nor in common. These two propositions are not opposed to each other. Nicholas does not deny Christ at some time had something of his own at least in common; rather he denies that Christ always led such a life. John also does not deny that Christ at some time had nothing of his own, neither in particular nor in common, but denies that Christ always led such a life.

That Christ taught each by word and example is proved; for he taught poverty by every means in Matthew X, when he says: "Do not possess gold, nor silver, nor money in your belts, nor a hat or two tunics, nor shoes or a staff."

Neither relates whether these words sound like a precept, or a counsel, and whether they might be expressed otherwise than on abdication of all ownership. For it is enough to preserve the opinion of Nicholas, what this doctrine of Christ might be, and what this sense is not opposed to, as really it is not opposed. Although Christ added: "The laborer is worth his wage," he obligated the people to sustain preachers, and hence conceded to preachers that they might rightly furnish sustenance from the people. Still, he did not oblige those preachers that they should furnish something as though it were due, as is clear from Paul in 1 Corinth. IX, but he permitted them to live on their own labors, even to receive just as a gift without any usurpation of ownership, what is due to them from justice. It happens that in this sense, St. Francis received these words and the institutions; God approved this man with many miracles, as well as the common consensus of the universal Church.

The Lord also shows the same thing in this very example, as is clear from Matthew 8. "The Son of Man does not have a place where he might recline his head," as well as that of Luke 8: "Women followed him, who ministered to him from their resources." For then the Lord lived on the almsgiving of others with the Apostles without a blemish.

The Lord also taught another type of life by his example, which is clear from John 13, where we read that he had places from which he lived in common with his disciples; nor is there a doubt whether they had ownership of certain monies, at least in common, seeing that they had been accustomed to distribute alms, as is clear from the same place. The faithful who were in Jerusalem later imitated such a life,[6] just as nearly all orders of religious. For with the exception of the Franciscans, all have, at least in common, ownership of moveable things.

The thirty-sixth is Pope John XXII, who is condemned by many, and especially by William of Ockham[7] and by Adrian,[8] because he had taught that the souls of the blessed were not going to see God before the resurrection. Erasmus himself affirms this with an addition.[9] He says: "In such an error it appears was Pope John, the twenty-second of that name, being compelled by works of the theologians of Paris to recant in the presence of Philip the king of the French, not without embarrassment. John Gerson says this in his sermon on Easter."

Calvin adds that the same Pope John taught that souls are mortal. "But if they would have the privilege which they claim to be confirmed, they must

---

[6]   Acts 4:32-36.

[7]   Opus 93, dierum.

[8]   *Quaestio de Confirmatione.*

[9]   Prefatione ad li. 5 Irenaei.

expunge from their list of pontiffs John XXII who publicly asserted that the soul is mortal and perishes with the body until the day of resurrection. And so, that you would observe that the whole See with its chief props then altogether fell, none of the Cardinals opposed his madness, only the Faculty of Paris urged the king to insist on a recantation. The king forbade his subjects from communion [with him], unless he would immediately recant; he published an interdict in the usual way by a herald. Thus necessitated, John abjured his error." Yet Calvin does not prove from any source, but placed in the margin: "John Gerson, who then lived, was the witness."[10]

I respond: first, to Adrian. John, at that time, really thought that souls would not see God unless it were after the resurrection: others so reckoned when still it was lawful without danger of heresy, since still no definition of the Church had gone before him. John, moreover, wished to define the question, but while still preparing and in consultations, died, as Benedict XII, his successor, witnessed in *Extravagantes* which begins: *Benedictus Deus*; the whole of which Alphonsus a Castro relates.[11]

Furthermore, John Villanus relates that Pope John, before his death, partly declared and even partly recanted his opinion.[12] First, it is on good evidence that he never had it in his mind, although he had spoken on this matter, to define the question, rather only to treat it so as to discover the truth. Next, he added that John already thought the opinion was the more probable that asserts the souls of the blessed enjoy the divine vision even before the day of judgment, and he embraced this opinion, unless at some time the Church would have defined otherwise, and he subjected all his teachings freely to its definition. This retraction simply teaches that the mind of Pope John XXII was always good and Catholic.

To Calvin I say, he most impudently tells five lies in but a few words. First, John Gerson did not live at the same time as John XXII. It is certain from John Villanus[13] and all other historians that John XXII died in the year 1334, while Gerson was born in 1363.[14] Therefore, Gerson was not yet born when Pope John died.

The second lie is that Gerson might have said Pope John denied the immortality of the soul. For Gerson says nothing on the errors of John, except in a sermon on Easter, which is held in volume 4, which alone is cited by all

---

[10]   *Institut.* Lib 4 cap. 7, §28.

[11]   *Contra Haeres.*, liber 3 in verbo Beatitudo.

[12]   *Histor.* lib. 11 Capite 19.

[13]   Lib. 11, ch. 19.

[14]   Trithemius, *de viris illustribus.*

against the error of John. There, moreover, Gerson says: "He did this, to the thief, who seems not yet to have fulfilled the penance for all his sins, yet was beatified and saw God face to face at that proper hour, just as the saints in Paradise. For that reason the falsity of the doctrine of Pope John XXII on that point appears." He neither expresses more what such a doctrine was, but when he said: "There appears the falsity of the doctrine of Pope John," the very reason that the thief crucified with Christ soon after death saw God, manifestly shows Pope John erred in this, because he believed the souls of the saints do not see God immediately after death. Yet, neither Gerson nor anyone else who wrote before Calvin, not even William of Ockham, a most hostile enemy of that Pope, asserts that John XXII denied the immortality of the soul.

But I see why Calvin devised such a dreadful lie, because the error of Pope John on the vision of God is not an error for Calvin, but rather a doctrine. For he says only Christ is in heaven; the rest of the saints await in a type of hall even to the end of the world.[15] He adds: "The saints after death are still joined together with us. But if they have faith, therefore they do not see God."[16] Therefore, because Calvin saw what others condemned in Pope John, he could not condemn him; still, he refused to pass over the occasion to accuse a Pope, so he fled to his teacher, the father of lies, and from him changed the whole affair into a characteristic calumny.

The third lie is that no cardinal opposed the teaching of John. This is clearly false, because neither Gerson nor any other says this, and because many thought the contrary, as was clear from the definition which was made by Pope Benedict XII after the death of John from the consensus of all Cardinals which is clear in the epistle of Benedict. Nor was there a reason why these, who thought the contrary, should fear to oppose John while he was living. Benedict XII, in his *Extravagantes*, asserts that Pope John severely commanded the cardinals and others, all teachers, that they should give their true opinion so that the truth would be discovered. Next, John Villanus, who did live at that time, writes that the greater part of the cardinals opposed the opinion of Pope John while he lived.[17]

The fourth lie of Calvin is that the king of France forbade his subjects communion with John. The fact that King Philip of France believed the Parisian Theologians more than John as a private teacher on that question, is witnessed by Gerson in the cited place; but how, on that account, he would have

---

[15]   *Institut.* lib 3, cap. 20.

[16]   Ibid, §24.

[17]   *Histoiria*, lib. 10, cap. ult.

excommunicated the Pope, no one tells, nor is it believable that a Christian king at that time would have dared to do such a thing.

The fifth lie is that the Pope abjured his error. This, also, neither Gerson writes, nor any other nor ought the Pope abjure error, when he never fell into error. He retracted his opinion the day before he died, but by the advice of those close to him, not at the command of the king. [18] Nor is it true that John was compelled to repent, and it is much less true that it happened in the presence of King Philip.

The thirty-seventh is John XXIII (anti-pope), who at the Council of Constance, sess. 11, is accused of a very pernicious heresy; for it is said that he denied the future life, and resurrection of the body. I respond: John XXIII was not a Pope, and it is certain and undoubted, hence it is not necessary to defend him at all. There were in those times three men that claimed to be Pope, Gregory XII, Benedict XIII, and John XXIII. It could not easily be determined who among them was the true and legitimate Pope, since none of them lacked very learned men as patrons. I add in addition that it is very probable and nearly certain that the error is falsely attributed to this anti-pope John. For in the first place when in that session of the council the articles that he objected to were enumerated, they first placed 53 articles, which all pertain to custom, and all these were confirmed by certain witnesses. Next, others are advanced without certain witnesses, and the second to last of these is the one on which we are now arguing.

Therefore, this point was not proven, except by common rumor, which, because people saw John was of dissolute life, they began to reckon and even say that he did not believe in the future life or the resurrection of the body. But who does not see that heresy is not truly gathered from bad deeds? How many can be counted who believed rightly and lived a most degenerate life? Next, in sess. 12, the definitive opinion of the council against John also briefly reviewed the reasons for his condemnation and deposition, but no mention is made of error, or of heresy. Certainly the argument is evidence that it cannot be proven that this "Pope John" was an object of heresy. For if it could have been proved, it ought to have been reviewed in the first place among the reasons of condemnation, since there is no more just cause of judging a Pope than the note of heresy; nay more, there is no other reason why a Pontiff can justly be judged.

The thirty-eighth Pope is Benedict XIII, whom the Council of Constance condemns in the name of heresy. [19] But this Benedict was not a legitimate Pope,

---

[18] cf. John Villanus, lib. 11 cap. 19, wherein the calumnies of Erasmus may also be detected.

[19] Sess. 37.

since he succeeded Clement VII, who had invaded the papal seat while Urban VI was still alive, but still he was not truly a heretic. The only thing objected against him is that he did not believe a council had greater power than the Supreme Pontiff, in which affair Benedict did not err at all.

The thirty-ninth is Eugene IV, whose pontificate was abrogated by the Council of Basel,[20] because he had fallen into heresy. But he also did not err in any truth. Wherefore, the Council of Lausana continued his earlier acts and Nicholas V, the successor of Eugene, was venerated as a true Pope, as can be recognized from the letter of the same Nicholas, which is usually attached to the Council of Basel in the volumes of councils.

The fortieth Pope to be accused of error is Innocent VIII, who seems to have sinned because he permitted the Norwegians to celebrate the sacrifice without wine, as Raphael Volateranus relates.[21] But this can be answered easily. For in the first place he did not publish a decree wherein he declares something for the universal Church, namely that it is lawful to offer the sacrifice of the Mass without wine. Therefore, if he erred, he erred in fact, not in doctrine. Next, he did not permit another liquor to be confected in place of wine, which would pervert the matter of the Sacrament; he only permitted that they might consecrate the Eucharist only under the species of bread on account of extreme necessity, since in that region wine cannot be preserved, thus it quickly sours. But certainly there is either no error, or certainly the error was not explored. It happens that it is baffling that in that time they did not have the use of wine, or could not preserve it, since in our time it is so frequently used because the heretics do not wish to communicate without it.

---

[20] Sess. 34.

[21] *Geographiae*, lib. 7.

CHAPTER XV

A Question is Proposed: Whether the Supreme Pontiff Has Jurisdiction that is Truly Coercive, so that he can Make Laws Which Oblige in Conscience as well as Judge and Punish Transgressors?

SO FAR we have proven that the Supreme Pontiff is a judge of controversies which arise in the Church and that he is certain and infallible in his judgment. Now follows the third question: *Whether the Supreme Pontiff can compel the faithful to believe or do that which he has judged.* The same thing is understood about other bishops, save for proportion. But before we come either to our arguments or those of our adversaries, it will be worthwhile to record a few things on the state of the question, as well as the opinion of our adversaries.

Therefore, first it must be noted that we do not speak about the Pope as a temporal prince of a certain province. In this manner, it is certain that he can impose laws on his subjects and also turn to them with the sword. The heretics do not deny this in regard to the arrangement wherein the Pope is a temporal prince, although they deny it is fitting for him to exercise such a rule. We will speak more on that matter in the next book. Therefore, now we only treat on the Pontiff as he is the Pontiff of the whole Catholic Church. Moreover, we ask whether he may have true power over all the faithful in spiritual matters just as temporal kings have in temporal affairs, to the extent that, just as they can make civil laws, so also the Pope can make ecclesiastical laws truly obliging in conscience as well as punish transgressors with spiritual penalties at least, such as excommunication, suspension, interdict, irregularity, etc. We will treat on temporal or civil power which the Pope has either directly or indirectly in the following book. At present we are only discussing the spiritual or ecclesiastical, whose end is eternal life.

Secondly, it must be noted that we are only treating on just laws. Unjust laws are not properly called laws, as Augustine teaches.[1] Moreover, four conditions are required for a law to be just. 1) On the side of the end, that it is ordained to a common good; for as a king differs from a tyrant,[2] in that the former seeks the common advantage, while the latter seeks his own, so also a just law differs from a tyrannical one. 2) On the side of the agent, that it should be from one having authority, for no one can impose a law except upon a subject. 3) On the side of the matter, that it should not forbid virtue, nor command a vice. 4) On the side of form, that a law should be clearly

---

[1] *Libro arbitrio*, lib. 1, cap. 5.

[2] Aristotle *Ethici*, lib. 8, cap. 10.

promulgated and constituted in a measure and order due to it, so that a law would preserve that proportion in the distribution of honors and imposition of burdens which subjects have in rank toward the common good.

For if the Pontiff would command that boys as well as grown men, the strong and the weak, healthy and sick should fast during Lent the law would be unjust.[3] Likewise, if he would establish that only the rich and nobles could be admitted to the episcopacy, but not the poor or commoners even if they be otherwise more learned and better, it would be absolutely unjust; although we must note that somewhere at some time, on account of some circumstance it *could* be just. But even if an unjust law is not a law and from its force does not oblige in conscience, nevertheless, a distinction must be made concerning laws. For unjust laws by reason of the matter, that is, which are contrary to divine, natural or even positive law, do not only not oblige, but they even ought to not be observed in any way, according to what we read in Acts V: "It is proper to obey God more than men." Jerome,[4] Augustine,[5] and Bernard also teach that.[6] But even those laws that are unjust regard to their end, or authority, or even to their form and manner of promulgation must be observed when scandal would follow. This can be deduced from what we read in Matthew, "He who would constrain you to walk a mile, go with him even another two, but if he would ask you for a tunic, give him your cloak also."[7] The sense is not that we should always do this but that we should be prepared to do it and whenever it will be necessary for the glory of God. Likewise, from 1 Peter: "Slaves be subject to your masters, not only to the good and modest, but even to the wicked."[8]

Lastly, it must be noted that the opinion that teaches there is no authority in the Church to make laws that oblige the faithful in conscience pleases many heretics. So formerly the Waldenses thought, as St. Antoninus attests.[9] Marsilius of Padua taught the same thing in a book titled *Defender of Peace*, against which Albert Pighius wrote;[10] John Wycliffe taught the same thing,[11] from where it was

---

[3] Until the imposition of the 1983 Code of Canon Law, Catholics in normal conditions had to fast (only one full meal) every day of Lent. –Translator's note.

[4] *Ad Ephesios*, in cap. 6.

[5] In Psal. 124, serm. 6 *de verbis Domini*.

[6] *De praecepto, et dispensatione*.

[7] Matthew 5:40.

[8] 1 Peter 2:18.

[9] 4 part tit. 11, cap. 7, §2 *Summae Theologicae*.

[10] Liber V, *hierarchia Ecclesiastica*.

[11] 38 damnato sessione 8 Concilii Constantiensis.

gathered that the decretals of the Popes were apocryphal, and only stupid men devoted themselves to recognizing them. Jan Hus later taught the same thing, as John de Wessalia notes in a little book on his condemnation that was made at Moguntium, in 1479, the first of which was that the prelates of the Church could not make a law which obliges in conscience but could only exhort men to keep the commandments of God.

Thereafter in our own times, all Lutherans and Calvinists teach the same thing. Above all Luther in his book *On the Babylonian Captivity*, in the chapter on Baptism: "By what right does the Pope constitute laws over us? Who gave him the power of placing the liberty that was given to us through Baptism captive, when neither the Pope nor a bishop nor any man should have the right to constitute one syllable over a true Christian unless it were done by the consent of the same." He teaches similar things in his book on Christian liberty, which Iodocus Clicthouseus refutes,[12] as well as John of Rochester [Fisher] in his attack on the assertion of article 27.[13] Yet Luther most vehemently treats it in his explication of the vision of Daniel, and that he might condemn ecclesiastical laws even by his deeds, in the year 1520 he publicly burned the whole body of canon law, as John Cochlaeus writes in the life of Luther.[14]

Melanchthon teaches the same thing in the Augsburg Confession and in his defense of the same;[15] so does Calvin;[16] the opinion of all of them is nearly the same, and can be reduced to certain headings.

1) They teach that bishops and hence even the Pope can constitute a certain order in the Church to preserve useful discipline, such as to define on what day men should go to church, who should sing the Psalms and how, or the Scriptures that must be read in the Church, etc.; but still, such constitutions do not oblige in conscience, except by reason of scandal, so that one would be free to keep or not keep these laws in a manner without scandal to others. But the Pope or bishops cannot constitute any true law which is not expressly in Scripture.

2) They teach that not only can the Pope or bishops not make a new law, but neither can they compel Christians to keep the law of God by a command from

---

[12] Lib. I sui Anti-Lutheri.

[13] *Assertionis Lutherani Confutatio,* in assertione articuli 27.

[14] Translator's note: Cochlaeus' works have rarely made it to English translation, but his life of Luther was translated along with Melanchthon's encomium in the following work: *Luther's Lives: Two Contemporary Accounts of Martin Luther,* Manchester University Press.

[15] Art. 28.

[16] *Instit.,* cap. 10, 11, et 12.

authority. Even if it occurs in the form of judgment in proceeding against transgressors, still they can only resort to exhortation, advice and rebuke to make men preserve the law of God.

3) They teach that while there is a power of excommunicating in the Church (that is, of rejecting incorrigible men from the body), nevertheless, they do not mean this power is in the Pope or the bishop per se, but only in the Church, which for them means the body of ministers along with the consent of the people. This should not be a wonder, since they deny the Pope is greater than a bishop, or a bishop greater than a priest in regard to authority. Moreover, they grant nothing to priests except that they can preach and minister the Sacraments to those men over whom a secular magistrate commands.

But in the Catholic Church it has always been believed that bishops over their dioceses (as well as the Roman Pontiff over the whole Church), are true ecclesiastical princes, who can impose laws that oblige in conscience, judge in ecclesiastical cases, and at length, punish by the custom of others—all without the consensus of the people or the counsel of priests. We will briefly prove these things.

CHAPTER XVI

That Popes can Make True Laws is Proven from the Testimony of the Word of God

HEREFORE, the Catholic teaching is proven from many kinds of arguments, but first from Sacred Scripture. The first passage in Scripture is Deuteronomy 17: "He who will be proud, refusing to obey the command of the priest who ministers unto the Lord your God in that time, that man will die by the decree of the judge, and you will take away evil from Israel." This passage ought also to be understood concerning Christian bishops either by a similitude, or from the greater. For just as the Jewish people was then the people of God, so now the Christian people. We cannot say that an ecclesiastical prince in the New Law ought to be of lesser authority than the priests in the Old Law were, since in the former we see all the greater and more august things. Nevertheless, the precepts of the Jewish priest were true commands, not admonitions or encouragements, as is clear from the words: "the command of the priest," and they obliged the conscience. Otherwise transgressors would not have been severely punished. If they who did not obey the precept of the Priest did not in fact sin then they would seem to have been killed for no reason.

Our adversaries respond, from this and similar passages that can be gathered, that those men who condemn their superior sin in conscience, because they refuse to obey due to pride. Hence it does not follow that they sin in conscience when they do not keep such laws on indifferent things short of contempt and scandal.

But we have especially, at least in the Pope, true authority to command that is of the kind that a political prince has; the very thing that the Waldenses, Marsilius of Padua and others denied. Next, from this we evidently deduce that the laws of the Pope oblige in conscience, even without regard to contempt and scandal. Whoever can command can also make an indifferent act necessary by his precept, and good in itself; to omit an act that is necessary and good in itself is to sin in conscience even without regard to contempt and scandal.

We prove the proposition. An indifferent act, if it is commanded, will now be necessary; otherwise it is commanded in vain. And this same thing is proven from the fact that it would follow that even the positive laws of God do not oblige in conscience. For why did circumcision oblige the Jews, and Baptism us, when they ought to be acts that are indifferent in themselves? Does not the fact that they are commands of God make them necessary acts of religion? Likewise, why were the Jews obliged in conscience to not eat pork to the extent that the Maccabees would prefer death to eating that meat, if the matter of pork were indifferent? Would it not be that because it is a precept of God abstinence is a necessary act of temperance? But God did not do this insofar as he is God, but insofar as he is the law-giver. Therefore every true law-giver (even one who commands in the name of God) can do this same thing. But the Pope can command, as we have already shown, and will also show again below therefore he can make an indifferent matter necessary and oblige in conscience, even without regard to contempt and scandal.

The second passage is Matthew 16. "Whatsoever you will have bound on earth will be bound in heaven." These words can and should be referred to all things that are said to be "bound" according to the use of Scripture. Generally, when the Lord speaks, he does not say: "Whatever you will have bound." We discover, however, in Matthew 23:4 that the word "to bind" means to impose a law: "They bind heavy burdens that cannot be lifted and place them upon the shoulders of men, but they refuse to move a finger to help them." Therefore, the Lord promised to Peter that whatever he will have bound, that is, some obligation he would impose upon the faithful by command, should be bound in heaven, in other words it will be valid there. The precept of Peter is, consequently, the precept of Christ, and one who does not comply sins. It is confirmed by the testimony of Jerome commenting on the words *Whatever you will have bound* in Matthew 18:4, "He granted power to the Apostles to understand who is condemned by such things; the human judgment is fortified by the divine."

The third passage is John 21:17, "Feed my sheep." There, when Christ shows Peter what he promised in Matthew 16:18, he uses royal vocabulary, ποί μαινε τὰ πρόβατάμου.

The fourth passage is John 20: "Just as the Father sent me, so I send you." Chrysostom says on this passage: "He left behind his ministry to them." Likewise, Theophylactus says: "Take up my work." Thus, the Lord left behind his place to the Apostles and willed that they would exercise authority by governing in his kingdom. This is also confirmed from that which is written in Luke 10: "He who hears you, hears me, but he who spurns you, spurns me." Cyprian[1] and St. Basil[2] teach that these words properly pertain to the Apostles and their successors. Moreover, Christ was sent from the Father with power, not only to preach and administer the Sacraments, but also to command and judge, as everyone affirms; consequently he himself granted the same thing to the Apostles, and especially Peter. One cannot respond to this that these words were said to all the Apostles together, but not as individuals, since the Apostles were soon going to separate from each other and journey to different parts of the

---

[1] Lib. 4, epist. 9

[2] *Constitutiones monastici*, cap. 23

world, and the Lord was not ignorant of that. Hence, without a doubt, what he gave to all, he meant to give even to separate individuals.

The fifth passage is Acts 15. There, Peter, along with the other Fathers of the Council, writes to the Gentiles converted to the faith: "It seemed to the Holy Spirit and to us to impose no further burden upon you beyond what is necessary: to abstain from what has been sacrificed to idols, from fornication, and from strangled meat and blood."[3] Here, the Apostles made a new law, as Chrysostom remarked, because Christ gave no precept concerning suffocated animals and blood, nor are these good or evil in the law of nature, but indifferent, such things that the heretics teach the Church cannot make necessary.

Moreover, the fact that this was a true law of the Apostles obliging men in conscience (at least in that time in which they lived), is proven: 1) because the Apostles call them burdens when they say, "to impose no further burden." 2) Because they say, "beyond what is *necessary.*" For that reason it necessarily had to be observed as constitutions of the Church that must be kept—and not freely, as the heretics would have it. 3) Luke absolutely calls these precepts at the end of the chapter, when he says that Paul "went through the cities and commanded them to preserve the commands of the Apostles and of the elders,"[4] as well as in the next chapter, "They handed down to them decrees to be kept, which had been decreed by the Apostles and the elders in Jerusalem."[5] 4) We see from the testimony of St. John Chrysostom that he says, "See this short epistle having neither arguments nor syllogisms, but commands,"[6] since it was the legislation of the Spirit.

Next, because in the canons of the Apostles, can. 62, the heaviest penalty is imposed upon those failing this precept; for eating blood or suffocated animals clerics were deposed while the laity were excommunicated. That was renewed in the Second Council of Arles, can. 19 and 20. But so atrocious a penalty cannot be imposed unless it is for mortal sin.

Calvin responds that the Apostles commanded nothing new with this law, but only that what was always a precept of divine law, for no one to offend by giving scandal to the weak in the eating of food either sacrificed to idols, mixed with blood, or from a suffocated animal. Hence Christians were not obliged in conscience to abstain from these things, but only not to scandalize anyone.[7]

---

[3] Acts 15:28-29.

[4] Acts 15:41.

[5] Acts 16:4.

[6] Homil. 33 in Acta.

[7] *Instit.*, lib. 4, cap. 10, §21 and 22.

Calvin also tries to show this in three ways: 1) The scope of the apostolic decree was to free the Gentiles from the yoke of the Jewish ceremonial law; consequently, they would overturn this decree if they obliged them to the same ceremonies. 2) This precept was not kept, because the reason of scandal ceased; therefore, only scandal was prohibited by this precept. 3) Paul, who was present at this Council of the Apostles, and understood this matter the best, so explained it in 1 Corinthians 8 and 10, that it is not illicit to eat food sacrificed to idols, unless the weak would be scandalized. He says in chapter VIII, "Some still think of such meat as something belonging to idolatrous worship when they eat it, having a false god in their mind and their conscience, being weak, is defiled. ... See to it lest perhaps your liberty might become a stumbling-block to the weak. If anyone sees one with more knowledge sit to eat meat in the temple of an idol, will not his conscience, being uneasy, be emboldened to eat those things which are sacrificed to idols? And will the weak brother perish, for whom Christ died, due to your knowledge?"[8] And in chapter 10: "But if someone says 'This has been sacrificed to idols, it is a matter of conscience and he that told you not to eat it. I say conscience, meaning not your own, but the other man's."[9] But this epistle was written after that Council of the Apostles, as is clearly gathered from the Acts of the Apostles, because Acts 15 relates the Council, next Acts 18 tells first of Paul's entry into the city of Corinth. Furthermore, it is certain that this epistle was written later than Paul preached to the same Corinthians. For he said in chapter 2: "And when I came to you, brethren, I came not in the grandeur of speech, etc."

Still, this is easy to refute. For even if the end of the Apostolic precept was that the weak should not be scandalized, still that precept did not end in the avoidance of scandal, but on abstinence from burnt offerings, blood and suffocated animals, which was the means to that end. In the same way the end of all divine precepts is charity, and still those particular precepts to not steal and kill do not oblige one to love, but they do oblige a man to keep his hands off another's goods as well as not to harm another. And although the reasoning of each law, as the lawyers say, might be the spirit of the law; generally, when the reasoning for it should cease then the purpose of the law also ceases, hence the law ought to be abrogated and cease. In any event, when the reasoning of the law does not cease, except in some particular case, the law is still valid; when it is general, it obliges all even in that case when the reason or purpose of the law cannot be discovered. The law of fasting proves to be a perfect example.

---

8   1 Corinth. 8:7, 9-10.

9   1 Corinth. 10:28-29.

The purpose of fasting is the castigation of the flesh against the spirit of concupiscence; therefore, when this reasoning will universally cease, which will be after the resurrection, the law on fasting will also cease. Yet at the present, although the purpose of this law may not have place in one case or another, still these are held to fast because the law is still in force and is general.

Moreover, the matter still stands in this apostolic law on meat immolated to idols, blood and suffocated animals. Firstly, Chrysostom says this is the new law, and taken from the ceremonial precepts of Moses; but to not scandalize is an ancient precept, and a moral one; therefore it is not scandal, but specific foods that were prohibited by the Apostles. Secondly, in the whole decree of the Apostles there was no mention of avoiding scandal, yet it is absolutely commanded that they should abstain from meat sacrificed to idols, blood and suffocated animals; so the precept falls upon these three. Otherwise it would be lawful to overturn all laws, even divine ones.

Next, the Fathers thus understood this precept of the first churches. For Tertullian, in his *Apologeticus*, says: "We do not even have blood in our meals, on that account we abstain also from suffocated animals and those found dead, lest they might be contaminated with blood, or have it buried in their entrails. Next, among the trials of Christians are even sausages filled with blood, for it is certain they are altogether illicit for them."[10] Note here that Tertullian does not say Christians abstain from blood on account of scandal, but lest they be contaminated. Certainly they thought blood was unclean, though not by their nature (as the Manicheans thought) but on account of the apostolic prohibition, just as many animals are said to be unclean because they are forbidden.

Note also the fact that the pagans, knowing that it was unlawful for Christians to eat blood, tried to compel them to eat it. From this it is clear that Christians simply thought that blood was prohibited to them by the Apostles, not simply on account of scandal of the horrified Jews. There could be no scandal when the pagans tempted them, for the pagans freely fed upon blood.

Likewise, Origen,[11] disputing on forbidden foods, says that Christians abstain from meat immolated to idols, blood and suffocated animals by the prescription of the Apostles; yet he makes no mention of scandal to the Jews. St. Cyril of Jerusalem also says: "Confirm your soul for certain, lest you might eat what has been offered to idols." There, Cyril disputes on foods and says that meat and wine are indifferent, and can be rejected well or wrongly; indeed rightly if it was done on account of the maceration of the body, or another good end, but wrongly if it was done from the opinion that meat and wine might be

---

[10] *Apologeticus*, cap. 9.

[11] Lib. 8 *contra Celsum*

unclean. But where he comes to that which was immolated to idols, or blood and suffocated animals being forbidden by the Apostles, he places no distinction but absolutely teaches they must not be eaten, because without a doubt they were simply illicit by apostolic precept.

Eusebius relates that when the pagans objected to Christians, because they secretly ate the flesh and blood of infants, the holy martyr Blandina responded: "You err very much, O men, in that you think they eat the flesh of infants, who do not even eat the blood of silent animals."[12] In such words, St. Blandina indicated that Christians would not use blood even secretly where there was no occasion of scandal.

St. Augustine asks the question, whether a traveler overcome with hunger, if he discovered nothing else but food in the service of idols, where there is no other man, ought he rather die of hunger than eat that food? He responds: "Either it is certain that it was sacrificed to idols, or it is not, or he does not know. If it is certain, it is better for a Christian to reject it for the sake of virtue, but if he does not know, or is ignorant, without any scruple of conscience in the use of necessity he eats it."[13] But certainly, in this case what St. Augustine proposes leaves no place for scandal, and Augustine still judges that it is better to abstain from meat sacrificed to idols. His reason seems to be no other than the authority of the apostolic precept. It is similar to what St. Leo the Great writes, where he says that those must do penance who knowingly eat meat which was immolated to idols, or even did it from fear of force, or compelled by the necessity of hunger.[14]

Next, the Council of Gangra says (cap. 2) that they have no hope of salvation who eat the meat that was immolated to idols, as well as blood and suffocated animals, while those who eat other meats maintain hope of salvation. It cannot in any way be explained that those who do eat these foods should not because of scandal, because even those who eat any meat and any other food, but give scandal to others, sin. The Apostle says, "Wherefore, if meat scandalize my brother, I will never eat it, lest I should scandalize my brother."[15] Therefore, we have an apostolic precept that truly obliges in conscience, even without regard to scandal.

Now I respond to the first argument of Calvin, to not oppose the obligation of this precept with the scope and end of that decree. For the Apostles decreed that the Gentiles ought to be free from the observance of the Mosaic law, but

---

[12] *Historiae*, lib. 5, cap. 1.

[13] Epistol. 154 *ad Publicolam*.

[14] Epist. 70 *ad Nicetam*, cap. 5.

[15] I Corinthians 8:23.

not from obedience to their prelates. Furthermore, this precept on the abstinence from meat immolated to idols, blood and suffocated animals was not imposed as from the law of Moses, but as apostolic and ecclesiastical. Besides, the Apostles freed Christians from the observance of innumerable ceremonies. They commanded only one thing, and an easy thing, and to endure for a short time.

To his second argument I say the reason that precept is not observed now is not because the reason of scandal has ceased in every possible way, but because it ceased in general and now (especially in the West), that law was abrogated.

To the third, some respond that in that time in which St. Paul wrote that epistle, the apostolic law began to be abrogated, and for this reason Paul advised the Corinthians that they may eat from meat offered to idols, but should avoid scandal, but this reason is not solid. For it is not in any way credible that such a law could so quickly be abrogated, especially when still in that time the reason on account of which the law was broadly imposed was still present. Nay more, that this law endured for many centuries is clear from the many cited authorities.

Therefore, I respond in two ways. 1) Perhaps in that time in which Paul wrote to the Corinthians, the precept of the Apostles had not yet come to the Corinthians on abstinence from meat offered to idols, blood and suffocation. For the Apostles only wrote to the churches of Syria and Cilicia. Thus he begins his epistle: "The Apostles and elder brothers to those who are at Antioch, Syria and Cilicia from the nations, greetings." But Corinth is not in any of those places, which are in Asia, but in Greece. Besides, if the Corinthians had the apostolic precept on abstinence from meat offered to idols, I ask, would they have sought a letter from Paul on whether it was bad to eat such meat? What they asked is clear from 1 Corinthians 8. Thus, I say that the Corinthians did not have this precept at that time. Since they had not received it from the Council of the Apostles and since Paul knew they were very superstitious he showed it was still not expedient to hand this down to them. So, instead he gave them a response which one should have according to the law of nature, that they were not held to such abstinence except by reason of scandal and danger to the weak.

2) I also respond that perhaps the Corinthians had the precept of the Council of the Apostles and just the same some of them, trusting in their own knowledge whereby they knew idols were nothing and hence they could not be infected by food offered to idols, rashly ate from such. This was related to Paul, and he wrote back chiding them and giving the reason of that Apostolic precept, because without a doubt he rightly forbade the use of meat sacrificed to idols, and on account of the danger of idolatry. Therefore, the whole disputation of Paul is treated not on precept, but on the reason for the precept. Nor does it

follow that Paul said that meat immolated to idols was not bad in itself, except for scandal and danger, therefore if scandal was not present, nor danger, then they could lawfully partake. I say this does not follow. For although it would not be bad, unless on account of those two causes, still they could absolutely forbid it. For many lawful things are forbidden lest they drag us down to illicit things, and in that prohibition these are absolutely illicit.

The sixth passage is Romans 13:1-2. "Let every soul be subject to higher powers; for there is no power but from God and those that are, are ordained of God. For that reason, he that resists the power, resists the ordinance of God. And they that resist, purchase to themselves damnation." This passage is not only understood concerning secular princes but also ecclesiastical ones. What Calvin declares is manifest from this,[16] since the Apostle speaks in general on all powers when he says, "For there is no power but from God," because they are equal in that all power is from God. Moreover, the same Apostle Paul teaches that there is some ecclesiastical power, and Paul teaches the same thing in 2 Corinthians 13:10, "I write these things while I am away so that when I will be there I will not deal more severely, according to the power which the Lord has given me." And although Paul speaks in the literal sense on the secular powers, still in a similar fashion, the same thing must be understood on the greater, which is ecclesiastical power.

That their laws are provided with power and oblige in conscience is clear from the words "he that resists the power, resists the ordinance of God. And they that resist, purchase to themselves damnation." Everyone shows this to be on a damnation that is both temporal and spiritual, such as Chrysostom, Oecumenius, Theophylactus, Ambrose and even the Calvinist Peter Martyr himself commenting in this passage. Likewise, from the verses, "Therefore it is necessary to be subject," that is, this is not free, but necessary, and from: "Not only on account of wrath, but even on account of conscience." In other words, necessarily you must obey, and understand that not only on account of fear of punishment, but even on account of fear of sin which you incur with the witness of conscience.

---

[16] "For if we must obey princes not only from fear of punishment but for conscience's sake, it seems to follow that the laws of princes have dominion over the conscience. If this is true, the same thing must be affirmed of ecclesiastical laws. I answer, that the first thing to be done here is to distinguish between the genus and the species. For though individual laws do not reach the conscience, yet we are bound by the general command of God, which enjoins us to submit to magistrates. And this is the point on which Paul's discussion turns—viz. that magistrates are to be honored, because they are ordained of God." *Instit.*, lib. 4, cap. 10, §5.

Now what Chrysostom, as well as Theophylactus and Oecumenius who followed him, understood about conscience in this passage is not opposed to what we have said since they speak of conscience of good deeds. This is, as it were, necessarily that one must obey princes not only because of anger, that is, their retribution, but also on account of conscience, because you are aware of the many benefits you receive from kings. This, I say, is not opposed, for the common exposition is on the conscience of sin, as Theodoret, Ambrose, Bede, Anselm and others say on this place of Scripture, as well as Augustine;[17] and our adversaries, both Calvin and Peter Martyr, receive the same exposition. And the Apostle always receives this term (conscience) in this sense.

Yet, Calvin responds to this that the obligation of conscience, about which the Apostle speaks here, does not refer to the individual laws of princes but to the general precept of God in which we are held to honor princes and also the purpose of their laws, that is, peace and love of neighbor.[18]

Yet, we especially showed above that it clearly follows from this that we are held to obey superiors, because we are also held in conscience to keep their laws, even short of contempt and scandal. Next, when the Apostle says: "Be subject from necessity, not only because of anger, but also on account of conscience," certainly what extends to "on account of anger," also extends to "on account of conscience." Moreover, "on account of anger," the Apostle extends, not only to avoid contempt and scandal, but even to the observation of laws in particular. For a prince not only punishes one who scorns his laws, but even those who do so in particular; for he kills a thief by hanging, and punishes a murderer by cutting off his head. He commands forgers to be burned, even if it was not from contempt of the prince, rather it is certain they sin from the lust for money. Consequently, for the same reason (but on account of conscience), that ought to be extended to the violation of laws. For Paul did not say be subject from necessity, not only on account of anger in the observance of particular laws, but on account of conscience in the observance of a general command concerning not scorning the prince, but simply and without any distinction he joins the two: "Not only on account of anger, but also on account of conscience."

And besides, that it is wicked to disdain and scorn a superior is so clear that it was not necessary for St. Paul to drive this point home so often in as many words. Therefore, he teaches so that there could be no doubt among Christians on the matter; they are also held in conscience to observe the precepts and laws even of temporal princes, as Chrysostom and other interpreters rightly remark.

---

[17] Epist. 54 *ad Macedonium*.

[18] *Instit.*, lib. 4, cap. 10 §5.

The seventh passage is 1 Corinthians 4, where Paul says: "What do you want? That I should come to you with the rod, or in a spirit of meekness? Here with the word "rod" Chrysostom, Augustine,[19] and all other interpreters of this place understand as the power to punish sinners. For Christ, as king of the Church, has the rod, which in Psalm 2 is called the "iron rod," because it is inflexible, and in Psalm 44 (45) it is called the rod of direction, which is a Hebrew phrase meaning the straight rod, because it punishes justly. But he shares this rod with the bishops who rule the Church in his name. Therein, St. Augustine reconciles a certain contradiction that appears in Matthew and Mark. In Matthew 10, he gives a command to the Apostles that they not bear the rod. Mark 6 says that he commanded them that they should bear it. Augustine reconciles these so that Matthew speaks on the corporal rod, but Mark on the spiritual one, that is on the apostolic power, on account of which sustenance ought to be given to the Apostles by the people.[20] Just as taxes are due to a king on account of the royal rod, so tithes are due to the bishop on account of a similar rod.

Peter Martyr responds to this argument that while certainly the Church has the rod to punish, still it is not in one particular man, like the Pope, or a bishop, but in the body of the Church.[21] For Paul, in 1 Cor. 5, means that a certain incestuous man was to be killed by the ecclesiastical rod when he said: "When you are gathered, my spirit is with you," etc.

But the same Peter Martyr says in the same place that the Apostolic rod also pertained to the death of Ananias and Sapphira, the blinding of Elymas and similar punishments that the Apostles afflicted. Yet certainly, only Peter slew Ananias and Saphyra by his word, and only Paul blinded Elima, not the body of the faithful, who did not even give counsel. Besides, only Paul handed him over to Satan, that is, excommunicated him, and permitted Alexander and Himenaeus to be vexed by the devil, as he himself says in 1 Tim. 1:20. He also says in 2 Corinth. 13:10, "I forewarn you that if I will come again, I will not spare," and: "That I will not do it any harder in person, according to the power which the Lord gave me."

Certainly the rod and power are the same, and Paul affirms that he was given the power, not the body of the faithful. I omit the fact that Ambrose excommunicated Theodosius by himself, and we can advance countless examples of this sort.

---

[19] Lib. 3, cap. 1, *contra epist. Parmeniani.*

[20] *De consens. Evangel.,* lib. 2, cap. 30

[21] In comment. cap. 5 *primae ad Corinth.*

That verse, "When you are gathered," is not opposed to this, for Paul did not mean that they should gather so as to deliberate, or that this incestuous man ought to be excommunicated, but that the excommunication would be published publicly and solemnly. Solemn excommunications are conducted in the same manner; when some men are excommunicated by name, they are not imposed except in the presence of the Church, but still they are imposed by the authority of the prelate alone. For this reason even while Paul was absent and without a vote of the Church, he had already decreed the man be handed over to Satan, and he writes to the Corinthians, not counseling them in this matter, but commanding them, that with the Church gathered they might promulgate that excommunication.

The eighth passage is 1 Timothy 3:2, where the Apostle established a law that men who married twice should not be ordained. Such a law obliged in conscience, even if it was clearly positive and ecclesiastical law, for it is clear both from the practice of the Church, which never dared to ordain the twice-married, and from the Fourth Council of Carthage,[22] where a bishop, who knowingly ordained a twice-married man, was seriously punished with deprivation of the authority to ordain.

The ninth passage is 1 Timothy 5: "Do not receive an accusation against a priest unless it is made with two or three witnesses." Here the Apostle clearly teaches that the bishop should have his tribunal even outside the forum of conscience, and to hear accusations and proofs in the fashion of judges as well as to judge according to testimony and proofs. Chrysostom reasonably understands by the word *presbyter* any elder you like, whether priest or laity. From that we gather that even the laity are judged in the external forum by a bishop for some crimes. But Ambrose understands by this term a priest, and perhaps more correctly. Nevertheless, this exposition does not exclude the laity from the forum of a bishop but very clearly includes them. For the Apostle means (as Ambrose shows) that the accusers of the laity are more easily admitted and can be heard, but against a priest, on account of the dignity of the order, it ought not be done unless two or three witnesses are present. Apart from these there are many other passages less to the point, but that still have efficacy.

The tenth is Luke 10:16, "He who hears you, hears me," which Cyprian teaches is properly understood about bishops.[23]

The eleventh passage is 1 Corinthians 11:2, "I praise you because you keep my precepts," and 1 Thessalonians 4:2, "You know what precepts I have given

---

[22] Can. 69.

[23] Lib. 4, epist. 9, cf. St. Basil, *in constitutionibus*, cap. 22.

you." And in the same place: "If anyone will not obey our word, mark this man through by epistle, and have nothing to do with him."

The twelfth passage is Hebrews 13:17, "Obey those placed in charge of you, be subject to them, for they keep watch as they are going to render account for your souls." Chrysostom, writing about this passage, says that it is better not to have one in charge than to have one, and to not obey a superior because he has none, for he only suffers the loss of pastoral direction; but for one who has a superior and does not obey him, he suffers the same loss and also sins and will be punished by the Lord. Basil says the same thing explaining that in this passage the Apostle added: "For it is not useful to you," that he might show the serious loss as well as sin and punishment which comes upon those who do not obey their superiors.[24] For in the Greek text it is not put in the negative (it is not expedient for you), but in the positive, that it is harmful, ἀλυσιτελὲς γὰρ ὑμῖν τοῦτο. So, Basil interpreted what it is harmful or detrimental as the punishment due for the fault of transgression.

Thus we conclude the Scriptures. Now in the second place, it is proven from the tradition of the Fathers as well as from the fact that there is almost no council that does not command something, or forbid under penalty of anathema, or deposition. For equal reason, the epistles of the Popes are full of precepts and censures that can be read either in the volumes of councils or in the body of canon law. Above,[25] we also brought to bear particular passages from the epistles of the ancient Pontiffs, Leo I, Gelasius, Hilary, Anastasius and Gregory I. Therefore, passing these over, we advance the testimony of the Fathers, only on one ecclesiastical law which the heretics especially condemn, and what we will prove for that one will be the same proof for all the others.

Therefore, that the law of fasting during Lent, or on Ember Days, or vigils is clearly positive and ecclesiastical law our adversaries affirm, but all the Fathers teach the fact that it obliges the faithful in conscience even without regard to contempt. Canon 68 of the Apostles bids a cleric to be deposed and a layman to be excommunicated if he would fail to observe an appointed fast. Likewise, the Council of Gangra, can. 29, bids those who absolve men from the appointed fasts without necessity to be excommunicated. Also, the 8th Council of Toledo, can. 9, deprived those who violated the fast of Lent of Holy Communion on Easter and commanded them to abstain from meat for a whole year. Here we must notice that the council did not speak of contempt, but rather of those who do not fast from intemperance.

---

[24] *Constitutionibus*, cap. 22.

[25] Volume 1, book 2, ch. 29.

St. Basil says: "All, equally, both hear and receive the precept with joy. ... See lest you incur damnation due to a little desire for food, and make yourself guilty of the crime of a turn coat."[26] St. John Chrysostom, says, "When the season of fasting arrives, even if someone will exhort a thousand times and countless things may torture and compel him to take a little wine or taste something which is forbidden by the law of fasting, he should prefer to suffer all these things rather than taste forbidden nourishment."[27] And in homil. 2 on Genesis he says that Lent bends everyone's conscience—even that of the emperor—to obedience.

St. Ambrose says: "It is no light sin to violate the Lent appointed for the faithful, and to break the holy fasting by the voracity of his belly."[28] St. Jerome says: "We fast according to the tradition of the Apostles in a time that is not agreeable to us. There is no time through the whole year except in Pentecost that it is not lawful to fast, but it is on the one hand a necessity, on the other a duty of the will to offer it." Note the word: *necessity*. St. Augustine says: "On other days it is a remedy to fast, or a recompense, but in Lent it is a sin not to fast."[29] Pope Leo the Great said: "It is pious to do what is not appointed, but impious to neglect what has been decreed."[30]

Next, Epiphanius[31] and Augustine place Aërius among the heretics for the reason that he said that one must fast, but not because of a precept of the Church, but whenever it pleases. Aërius says (quoted in Epiphanius): "Fasts must not be commanded because this is Jewish and under the yoke of servitude, for the just law is not placed upon anyone. But if one altogether fasts from the will, and I may choose any such day for myself, then I will fast on account of my liberty." The same speech is customary for the Lutherans.

In the third place, the case is made from reason. Some true laws are necessary to govern the Church well, apart from divine and civil laws, for every true law has coercive force. Consequently, coercive ecclesiastical laws are necessary in the Church, but there are not, nor ever were in the Church ecclesiastical laws other than those which the Supreme Pontiffs (or councils confirmed by the Popes), published; consequently, the laws of Popes and councils of this kind are coercive laws and truly and properly oblige in

---

[26] Orat. 2 de ieiunio.

[27] Homil. 6 to the people of Antioch

[28] Serm. 25.

[29] Serm. 62 de tempore.

[30] Serm. 3, de ieiunio decimi mensis.

[31] Haeresi 75; haeres. 63.

conscience. But the proposition must be proved, and the assumption of the first syllogism, for upon that everything depends.

Thus, that some ecclesiastical laws are necessary can easily be proven. By the same reasoning in which laws are necessary for the Church, so they are also for the state. The reason why laws are necessary in every state is because men ought to live according to reason so that they might live well, and still, because they are composed of body and spirit, and reason and sense, they can scarcely be without affectation following the lead of reason alone. For that reason, laws are discovered which contain nothing but the judgment of reason, that when men are compelled to follow them they are compelled together with reason to follow them. Now this reasoning has place in the Church. Although Christians are freed from sin by the grace of Christ, still they are not freed from concupiscence and the passions that perpetually oppose reason.

You will say that Christians have the law of the Gospel to follow. I respond: They certainly have that, but that is very broad and insufficient to direct all of our actions, except that it be done through determinations of ecclesiastical rulers in some mode of a particular. In the same way, the state also has the natural law and yet, because that is too general, it does not suffice unless it is deduced to particulars through determinations of the prince.

For that reason, to the extent that civil laws (being like conclusions deduced from natural law) are necessary, so also in the Church ecclesiastical laws apart from the law of the Gospel are necessary since they are like conclusions deduced from the principles or determinations of the Gospel. For example, the Gospel says: "He who would minister to me, let him follow me."[32] There, the Church deduces as a conclusion that it will be useful to ratify a law, lest they might be admitted to sacred ministry who refuse to be continent. Likewise, the Gospel bids the Eucharist to be received but it does not determine how or when; accordingly, the ruler of the Church determines that it must be taken at least during Easter, and the Apostles made a law that it should be taken before all other food, without a doubt while fasting. Hence Augustine says: "He [the Lord] did not prescribe the order in which it was to be observed, since he reserved this for the Apostles through whom he intended to arrange all things pertaining to the Churches."[33]

Now it remains that the assumption be proven, namely that every true law is coercive. This is proven from natural law itself, since a law is a certain rule

---

[32] John 12:26.

[33] Bellarmine gives the citation for this as: *Epist. 118, cap. 6*, but subsequent to his time this has been revised in the collection of Augustine's works and is found in Migne's edition of Augustine's works under *Epistle 54*, no. 8. –Translator's note.

over human actions constituted either immediately or mediately by God. To deviate from the rule is to sin. This is why Aristotle says: "Law is a discourse set out from some prudence and mind, having the force to compel."[34] Therefore, the essence of a law is placed in this, that it should bind and compel, so that it would be a sin to do otherwise. Likewise, what the definition of sin shows, for what is a sin but the transgression of law? For sin is thus defined by the Apostle, ἁμαρτία εστιν ἡ ἀνομία.[35] Nor can it be said that a law does not oblige one to not scorn it. For a law, which obliges one not to scorn a prince, is a certain general and divine law. But this, on which we are treating, is a particular and human law, as when the Pope says that fasting during Lent does not oblige you to not neglect a superior, but to fast.

---

[34] Ethic. lib. 10, ca. 9.

[35] "Sin is lawlessness." I John 3:4. Translator's note: Bellarmine here quotes the Greek because the Vulgate has "All sin is iniquity."

CHAPTER XVII

The Arguments Advanced by our Adversaries from the Testimony of Scripture are Answered

IT REMAINS to answer the arguments. 1) They take the first from the last chapter of Matthew: "Baptize all nations in the name of the Father, and of the Son and of the Holy Spirit, teaching them to keep all things which I have commanded you." Here our adversaries note, that it was not said teaching *your* commands, but *mine*. Thence, they gather that it is not lawful for bishops to give commands. This is the argument of John de Wessalia. I respond: In those things which the Lord commanded is included obedience to the commands of prelates, for the Lord said: "He who hears you, hears me, etc."

2) It is said in Deuteronomy, "You will not add to the word which I speak to you, nor will you take from it."[1] The issue in this verse is ceremonial precepts, as well as judicial ones. For in the verse just before this one, it begins with: "Listen, O Israel, to commands and judgments." And in chapter 12: "These are the precepts and judgments, etc." If God already commanded the Israelites that they should add no precept to those which are in the Scripture of the Old Testament, would one not correctly suppose that it commands Christians all the more not to add anything to the Gospel, which is by far more perfect than the Old Testament? This argument Luther, Calvin and nearly all others make. And Peter Martyr thought it was so good that in the commentary on chapter 8 of 1 Corinthians, he wrote in the margin: "Note, a good argument."

I respond: addition or subtraction in regard to a precept can be understood in two ways. In the first, that which is added is a precept to a precept, so that if two other precepts were added to the number of ten, or if two precepts were taken away from the number of ten, that would make twelve or only eight. In the second way, it is done without the multiplication of more or fewer precepts than the precept itself may command, e.g., if when God commanded families to eat one lamb at the Pasch, some family were to eat two lambs, or only a half. Therefore, I say that Scripture does not prohibit the addition of the first type, but it does of the second type, that is, it does not forbid an addition to the number of precepts, but an addition to the work of a specific precept. I prove the fact, because we discover that the Jews added to the number of precepts both ceremonially and judicially.

On ceremonial additions there are many examples. For Esther says, "Mordochai wrote that on the fourteenth and fifteenth of the month of Adar they should receive the fourteenth and fifteenth day of the month Adar for holy

---

[1] Deuteronomy 4:2.

568

days, and always at the return of the year should celebrate them with solemn honor.... The Jews took upon themselves their seed, and all who would join them in their religion, so that it would be lawful for no one to spend these two days without solemnity."[2] Likewise Judith, in the last chapter, "The day of this victory is a festival for the Hebrews in the number of their holy days, and the Jews have venerated it from that time even into the present day."[3] Likewise 1 Maccabees: "Judas decreed, along with his brethren and all the assembly of Israel that the day of the dedication of the altar should be observed from year to year for 8 days."[4] Such a feast, although new and added to the old, the Lord still honored with his presence, which is clear in John 10:22.

On judgments we have the example of 1 Kings, where David made a new law that it would be just in war for those going down to the battle to remain with the baggage train: "And this came to pass," it says in the Scripture, "from that day it was constituted and determined just as a law in Israel."[5] Now, that it says "as a law" is not opposed to what we are saying, for in Hebrew it does not say "as a law" but only לתק ול משפט [le-taq ul mishpat] (an authoritative judgment), and those two words are also contained in Deuteronomy 4 and 12. Therefore, the Scripture does not forbid new precepts to be added but prohibits the adding or taking away on one's own authority. This is confirmed by Deuteronomy 4 and 12, where Moses does not speak of princes, whose job it is to make laws, but the people, who must obey; therefore, he only commands that which is fitting to be commanded of the people, namely that they should fulfill completely the works that were commanded, not by adding or by subtracting. Moses more clearly explains this in Deuteronomy 5, where he says on the same issue: "Do those things which the Lord God commanded you, and do not turn to your right or to your left." For it is certain here that Moses speaks on the fulfillment of precepts, not on the impositions of new laws.

Moreover, it must be observed in this place that when Moses commands that nothing is to be added to what the law prescribes, this must be understood on an addition that corrupts the law, not one that accomplishes the work that was commanded. For when the law says: "You will not steal," one who does not abscond someone else's things but also gives from his own does more than what the law commands. Still, it is not said he added, because he did not destroy the precept; rather, he kept it better. But when the law says you will only sacrifice clean sheep, oxen and birds, if anyone would also sacrifice dogs, pigs and men,

---

[2] Esther 9:20-21, 27.

[3] Judith 16:31.

[4] 1 Maccabees 4:59.

[5] 1 Kings (1 Samuel) 30:25.

he adds to and corrupts the precept. And this example is placed in Deuteronomy 12 where addition is forbidden, lest anyone might sacrifice their sons as the Gentiles did.

Moreover, we can answer with a second argument. Even if we were to admit the Scripture forbids an addition of new laws, nevertheless, this prohibition should be understood only on the addition of laws contrary to the prior laws, as St. Thomas profitably teaches,[6] and it is clear from the laws added later, as we have already shown.

A third argument can also be made, that the plan of the Old and New Testament is not the same. For the law of the Old Testament was given to only one people, at a certain time, even to the coming of Christ; it could easily determine all things for an individual, just as it did. In individual cases it prescribes all things which both pertain to the worship of God as well as judgments and public contentions. And therefore it would be little wonder if it forbade other laws from being added. But the Law of the Gospel is given to the whole world, that is, to peoples of very different nations, and it is going to endure even to the end of the world. Hence, it cannot determine all things concerning each individual with such ease that other laws would not also be necessary, both civil and ecclesiastical. The same laws and rites are not suitable to a very diverse people. So, God judged it better that in the Gospel he would hand down what was common to all as the most common laws on the Sacraments, articles of faith and the like, while other more special cases for the diversity of times and places he left to be established by the Apostles and their successors.

3) Calvin takes up an argument from Isaiah 33:22 where we read, "The Lord is our judge, the Lord is our lawgiver, the Lord is our king." These words are equivalent to the Lord is our only Judge, Lawgiver and King, which is certain from the epistle of James: "There is one legislator and one judge; it is he who can destroy and set free."[7]

I respond: Isaiah and James speak on the primary legislator who can judge and make laws by his own authority; but we do not say the Supreme Pontiff is such an authority, but rather God and Christ alone. The Pope is not the king, nor the judge, nor the primary legislator but the vicar of the king and judge, that is of Christ the legislator, and he can make laws on Christ's authority. St. Cyprian also speaks this way when he says that the Pope is the judge in place of Christ.[8]

---

[6] In cap. 1 ad Gal. lect. 2 et 3.

[7] James 4:12.

[8] Lib. 1 epist. 3.

Yet, you might argue that when James says, "There is one legislator and judge, who can destroy and set free," he gives the reasoning why all men ought to keep the laws and not give them. Hence he excludes all other legislators since they would oblige consciences, punish sinners and save the obedient. For he says in the previous verse: "Do not detract from one another. For whoever detracts from his brother, judges his brother, and detracts from the law and thus judges the law." That is, he who detracts from a brother doing a good, like one who condones injuries, "detracts from the law," which commands that good: "If you judge the law, you are not a maker of law, but a judge. For there is one Legislator, and Judge who can damn and save." There it is understood in one proposition after those words: "But if you judge the law, you are not a maker of law, but a judge," certainly you ought, O man, to be a maker of law, not a judge. And the reason is added: "There is one Lawgiver, and Judge."

I respond: James speaks about all men, insofar as they are under some laws, and he means no man is allowed to judge the law of his superior when in fact only the latter is a legislator and judge that is so supreme and distinguished that only he should give laws but not receive them. It is he who can so destroy and save, and consequently he fears no one and does not hope for something from anyone. Hence the Pope, and the other bishops, although they judge and can impose laws, still they must also be judged by God and must keep the laws of God.

4) Calvin takes up a fourth argument from Isaiah, "For that reason this people glorifies me with their mouth and their lips, but their heart is far from me, and they fear me in the commands and doctrines of men, behold I will add to it; I will see to it that admiration shall be in this people by a great and resounding miracle; their wise men shall lose wisdom and understanding shall be hidden from their prudent men."[9] There the Lord complains because the people of Israel fear the commands of man, that is, the fear or worship and religion of God they constituted in commands to be kept by men. Similar things are contained in Matthew 15 and Mark 7.

I respond: The commands of men in Scripture are not called mere precepts of men, but only those which are altogether human, meaning that they were constituted neither from God's command, nor inspiration, nor his authority in any fashion. Such are two-fold: a) Some contrary to divine commands; b) Some altogether vain and useless. That is clear from all the citations where precepts are called human law, such as Isaiah 29, Matthew 15, Mark 7, Coloss. 2, 1 Timothy 4, and Titus 1. Moreover, the Lord is found three times to have condemned the Pharisees for human traditions. Firstly, in Matthew 15 where he

---

[9]   Isaiah 29:13-14.

argues with them because they preserved human commands contrary to the Divine Law. For after he said that the Pharisees commanded that sons should give to the temple what was due to the care of their parents, he added, "You make void the law of God on account of your tradition," then adding the passage cited in Isaiah. This is why St. Irenaeus explaining these citations, says they must be understood on the precepts of the Pharisees against divine laws.[10]

Secondly, in Mark 7, he condemns traditions or commands of men, that is, certain useless and frivolous ceremonies proceeding merely from a human spirit, which the Jews did so much, that they placed them before divine commands. In other words, leaving behind the commands of God you hold traditions of men, the baptism of jugs and chalices, and you do other things similar to these.

Thirdly, he condemns the same things in Matthew 23:3, because they had made certain good laws out to be more important than the divine law. There, he does not call these laws precepts of men, but says it is fitting to do them rather than omit them. They only sinned in that they constituted those ceremonies as the chief point of religion although they were merely external. What they did was similar to the dog of Aesop, who on account of the shadow of the bread left behind the bread itself, as Irenaeus beautifully alludes to concerning the Valentinian heretics, who preferred a certain angel as creator, instead of God.[11]

Next, pontifical and ecclesiastical commands, although they can be called human because they are not immediately from God, still are never called "traditions of men" in the Scriptures. Furthermore, they cannot be condemned when they do not oppose divine commands; they are not useless, nor do we place these ahead of divine law, rather we say they ought to be placed second to divine precepts.

5) They take up a fifth argument from the words of Paul, whereby it is asserted that Christians are free from the laws of men. In 2 Corinthians 3:3, he says: "Where the Spirit of the Lord is, there is freedom." And Galatians 4:31 "We are not the sons of the maidservant (Hagar), but of the free woman (Sarah), in such liberty Christ freed us." And again: "Stand and do not again be bound under the yoke of servitude."[12]

I respond: Christian freedom is constituted in three ways. Firstly, in the freedom from the servitude to sin, whereby Paul says in Romans: "Freed from sin, you are slaves to justice."[13]

---

[10] Lib. 4 cap. 25 and 26.

[11] Lib 2, cap. 12.

[12] Galatians 5:1.

[13] Romans 6: 18.

Secondly, in the freedom from the servitude of the divine moral law. For the law cannot be fulfilled without grace and still it threatens a penalty unless it is fulfilled, and moreover, it presses and holds men just as slaves. Yet the grace of Christ frees us from that fear and servitude, not by freeing us from the obligation of fulfilling the law, but by inspiring us with charity whereby we may easily and joyfully fulfill the law. The Apostle speaks of this in 2 Corinthians when he says: "Where the Spirit of the Lord is, there is freedom,"[14] and again in Galatians: "Christ redeemed us from the curse of the law, being made a curse for us."[15] For this reason, Augustine says: "We are not under the law which indeed commands a good but still does not give it, rather we are under grace which, making us love that which the law commands, is able to command the free."[16]

Thirdly, in the freedom from servitude to the ceremonial and judicial precepts of the Mosaic law. This is said in Acts: "Why do you tempt God by placing a yoke upon the necks of the disciples, etc."[17] And Galatians: "Stand and do not again be bound by the yoke of servitude."[18] We never read, however, that we are freed from obedience to prelates, but rather the contrary, when Paul exclaims: "Obey those placed over you."

For this reason, Peter and Paul, foreseeing in spirit the heretics of our time who under the pretext of freedom bear neither the fasts appointed by the Church nor any other law it imposes, frequently drive home that we must be obedient to superiors, even to the pagans. Let us show this: "Be subject to every human creature on account of God; ... Just as free men who do not have liberty as a veil of malice."[19] Next, Peter speaks on heretics, "Promising them freedom when they are in fact servants of corruption."[20] Then Paul says, "You are called to freedom, but do not give an occasion to the flesh by that freedom."[21]

---

[14] 2 Cor. 3:17.

[15] Gal. 3:13.

[16] *De continentia*, cap. 3.

[17] Acts 15:10.

[18] Gal. 5:1.

[19] 1 Peter 2:13, 16.

[20] 2 Peter 2:19.

[21] Gal. 5:13.

CHAPTER XVIII

The Argument is Answered by a Comparison of Laws

E CONTINUE with the arguments of our adversaries.

6) If God meant for Christians to be free from Jewish ceremonies and other positive laws of the Old Testament, then he also meant from the ceremonies introduced by the Popes and from all other human laws. For if we ought to have positive laws then divine laws excel human laws; besides, we would gain no benefit but harm by that liberation from the Jewish law, since those laws are called "an unbearable burden," by St. Peter,[1] both on account of their multitude, and on account of the obligation under pain of sin. Otherwise these individual matters in themselves were not grave, nor unbearable. On the other hand, positive laws of Christians are ten times more than were those of the Jews, as is clear from examining the volumes of canon law,[2] and the volumes of councils, with the Mosaic Pentateuch. Therefore, if all these laws oblige under pain of eternal punishment it would be far better for us to have the laws of Moses.

Calvin confirms his argument with the testimony of St. Augustine, who complains about ecclesiastical rites introduced rashly, saying, "They so oppress the very religion which God wished in his mercy to free [men] from servile burdens in the fewest and most manifest Sacraments by way of celebration that the condition of the Jews would be more tolerable since, even if they did not recognize the time of freedom, still they were subjected to legal burdens rather than human presumptions."[3] Calvin also adds: "If this holy man lived in our time, would he not deplore this with such complaint, which is now servitude? For the number is ten times greater, and individual points a hundred times more rigid than were driven out at that time. So it usually happens where once these perverse legislators seize control, there is no end of command and prohibition, until they arrive to the end of pedantry."[4]

I respond: Christ wished us to be free from the ceremonies and judicial precepts of Moses because these ceremonies were figures of the New Testament; hence, they ought to cease in our present reality. Moreover, the precepts

---

[1] Acts 15:10.

[2] Translator's note: The reader should keep in mind that before the Pio-Benedictine reform of 1917, canon law was a difficult discipline, having multiple volumes and requiring a wide knowledge of what laws had been superseded and what laws were still in force, and these occupied many volumes and commentaries.

[3] Ep. 119, ch. 19.

[4] *Instit.*, lib. 4, cap. 10 §13.

pertained to the rule of the people of God according to their state; for that reason after that state was changed, it was necessary for the precepts to be changed, "Since the priesthood has been transferred," says the Apostle in Hebrews, "it is necessary that for the transference of the law to happen."[5] It does not follow that we ought to have no civil and ecclesiastical laws, if we do not have the law of Moses.

Now to that argument about the number and weight of the Popes' laws, I respond: pontifical laws are, without any comparison, lighter than those of the Mosaic law. Hardly any laws can be discovered that are imposed upon all Christians except for four: 1) To observe feast days; 2) To observe fasts; 3) To go confession once a year; 4) To go to communion during the Easter Season. All the rest, in which the volumes of councils and books of canon law are full, are either not laws but admonitions, or pious institutions without obligation under penalty of sin. A great many of the rites of Christians are of this sort. Unless it were done out of contempt, nobody sins who does not recite the Hail Mary three times a day, or who does not take a palm branch on Palm Sunday, or sprinkle themselves with holy water when they enter a Church, or who does not strike their breast at the elevation of the holy Eucharist etc., and still, these and like things Calvin decries as a burden to the Church. There are also conditional laws, those that are placed upon men who wish to be admitted to Holy Orders, such as celibacy, which do not burden the Church, since no man is bound to become a cleric or a monk. Some rules are not prescribed for all Christians, but only ecclesiastical judges, so that they would follow these prescriptions in the judgment of cases. Some of these are censures and penalties imposed upon those who violate divine law, without which there is no other way to preserve discipline. There are also explications of dogmas of the faith, either of divine law, which do not even impose a new burden upon Christians. But the Mosaic law was imposed upon every individual Jew; they were innumerable on purifications, sacrifices, the eating of foods, etc. Therefore, it is not fitting to compare the Pentateuch with volumes of councils and the books of canon law, but with a small Catechism, since a Christian can be saved if he only knows a small Catechism.

Now for what deals with the gravity of laws, there is also no comparison between the severity of the Jewish law and levity of ecclesiastical law. From our four laws, there is not one which would not be rather more a determination of divine law than an altogether new law. For we are held by divine law to dedicate some time to the worship of God, and at some time to fast, confess and communicate. Therefore, the Popes have merely determined the times; hence

---

[5]   Hebrews 7:12.

if there is some difficulty in these laws it should be referred to divine law instead of the law of the Popes and especially regarding the precept of confession, which is held to be the hardest of all. Indeed, the confession of sins is hard for some people, not because it ought to be done at such and such a time, but simply because it has to be done at all. There is no doubt on that fact.

Next, the determination of the time of feasts and fasting done by the Popes has the mildest obligation. For they are not obliged to fast unless they can, for which reason children, the old and sick are excepted. Likewise, we are held to abstain from servile work in feasts as well as to hear Mass, but with many exceptions, for they ought not cease necessary work or those disciplines of great advantage to men, such as the trade of doctors, apothecaries, cooks, etc. For equal reason those who are impeded by a just cause and not present at Mass are not judged to have sinned. But the Jews were so very severely held to be idle on the Sabbath that they could not even light a fire or cook food—even a man that merely gathers wood on the Sabbath was stoned at God's command.

Now, I speak to Augustine. Calvin means to maliciously abuse his words, for he does not complain about the rites established by Popes, but about certain particular customs of common and unlearned men that little by little obtained the force of law, such that when they rose too much, they ought to be abolished and abrogated by the authority of bishops. He says: "Where the authority is granted, I think without any doubt that all things that are not contained in the authority of the Holy Scriptures, nor discovered in the statutes of councils of bishops, nor fortified by the custom of the universal Church, but vary so innumerably in the diverse customs of diverse places that hardly can any reasoning ever be discovered which men followed in establishing them, these must be pruned and cut back. For although how they are against the faith may not be discovered, still religion itself, which in the fewest ..." then the rest as above.

Therefore, you see that Augustine altogether meant to keep the laws that bishops established in councils, or that the custom of the universal Church had fortified and even all those of the kind we call ecclesiastical laws. For they would not be preserved in the volumes of councils or in the volumes of canon law unless they were from bishops, but I know of no private laws imposed broadly by ordinary men.

576

CHAPTER XIX
The Argument Taken from Examples is Answered.

E CONTINUE with the arguments of Calvin.

7) He takes this argument from three examples, which are contained in the Scripture. 4 Kings (2 Kings) 16:11 relates the deed of Achaz the King and Uriah the high Priest, who added one altar to another in the temple. Although it seems that he did that to adorn the temple, still because God did not command this, it was condemned as a human invention. Next, in chapter 17:24-26, it is related that those whom the King of Assyria had brought from Babylon into Samaria were punished by God by having lions sent in among them because they worshiped God with new ceremonies that the Lord had not commanded. Next, in 4 Kings 21:3, it is related about King Manassah, that he especially sinned because he built altars in the temple, which the Lord had not commanded.

I respond: The impudence of Calvin here is admirable. For when he teaches that Achaz, Manassah and Babylonians sinned in that they established ceremonies that God had not commanded. In reality the Scripture clearly says that all of these men sinned because of idolatry. Truly, Achaz is condemned, not because he built a new altar in the temple, but because he raised an altar to the likeness of the altar of idols which were then in Damascus,[1] and because he not only removed the altar of the Lord from its place, but also refused to allow sacrifices to be offered on the altar of the Lord, rather they could only be offered on the new altar consecrated to an idol.

Furthermore, that it would not have been bad to raise another altar in the temple, even if the Lord had not commanded it is clear from 3 Kings where we read that Solomon, when he saw the bronze altar of the Lord did not hold all the holocausts which were offered, sanctified another place in the temple, and there also offered holocausts.[2] For God neither commanded Solomon to do this, nor condemned him. It must be said that he rather approved of it, since in the following chapter he appeared to Solomon in a dream and praised him, promising many good things to him.

---

[1] 4 Kings (2 Kings) 16:10.

[2] 3 Kings (1 Kings) 8:64.

Next, it is certain that those Babylonians who lived in the region of Samaria were idolaters. For the Scripture thus speaks in 4 Kings, "And when they began to dwell there, they did not fear the lord and the Lord sent lions among them that killed them. ... Each nation made its god, and placed them in high temples ... And when they worshiped the Lord, they also worshiped their false gods according to the custom of the Gentiles that were brought over into Samaria."[3] Thus, the Scripture condemns the sin of idolatry that they practiced in those citations, not that they worshiped God with new ceremonies.

---

[3] 4 Kings (2 Kings) 17:25, 29, 33.

CHAPTER XX

Two Arguments of Calvin from the Reasoning of Conscience are Answered

CONTINUATION of Calvin's arguments.

8) The eighth argument of Calvin is that Paul in no way permitted the faithful to consciously be reduced to the servitude of men. For he says in 1 Corinthians, "You are bought for a price, do not become slaves of men."[1] There, Paul does not command that slaves not obey their masters in exterior things, for in Ephesians 6 he says: "Slaves, obey your human masters with fear and trembling."[2] Nor does he command lest those who are free not be made slaves, for he also says, "Have you been called a slave? Do not be troubled, but even if you could be free, use [the opportunity] more."[3] That is, even if you could be free, it is better for you that you serve and use your servile condition to preserve humility. Therefore, it remains that he forbade them to serve men with fear of sin as well as to be anxious for their conscience, in the way that they must serve God alone.

I respond: In that place, Paul only commands that we do not serve men on account of their being men, rather on account of God, so that we might serve God in those men, rather than the men themselves. For Paul explains himself in Ephesians, "Slaves, obey human masters with fear and trembling, in the simplicity of your heart, just as Christ, serving not by appearance to please men, but as servants of Christ doing the will of God from your heart, serving with good will just as it were the Lord, and not men."[4] Therefore, they are made slaves of men (which the Apostle forbids) who have human respect and serve them, even if they command sins and flatter them, even when they act wrongly. See Chrysostom in I Cor. 7, as well as Jerome's commentary on Ephesians 6.

9) The ninth argument of Calvin. Conscience pertains to the forum of God alone. For he is the one who scrutinizes hearts and minds. Consequently, men cannot oblige in conscience. This argument is confirmed by the fact that a man cannot damn anyone to hell, as a result he cannot oblige him to keep a law under penalty of eternal death. For it would be ridiculous were anyone to oblige under a penalty they could not inflict.

I respond: Conscience that pertains to the forum of God alone can be understood in two ways. 1) Because only God can see the consciences of men and judge on their internal actions, which are not clear on the outside nor have

---

[1]   1 Cor. 7:23.

[2]   Ephesians 6:5.

[3]   1 Cor. 7:21.

[4]   Ephesians 6:5-6.

other witnesses than God and the conscience of the agent; in this way it is quite true that the conscience pertains to the forum of God alone. 2) It can be understood that conscience pertains to the forum of God alone, because clearly only God could bind men with such laws that if they would not do what has been commanded, he himself would judge that they have done wickedly by their own conscience. And in this mode it is false that the conscience does not pertain to the forum of men. It is not required for someone that would oblige another in conscience in this manner that he be able to see the conscience, nor that he search hearts and minds, nor be judge over internal actions. It is enough that he can legitimately command him and by commanding him thus, oblige him to carry out an external work so that if he would not do it, he would certainly understand, or certainly could understand that he acts badly.

Therefore, John Calvin is deceived in the equivocation (or desires to deceive others) when he speaks in this way: "The business of our consciences is not with men, but with God alone. Hence the common distinction between the earthly forum and the forum of conscience. When the whole world was enveloped in the thickest darkness of ignorance, it was still held like a small ray of light which remained unextinguished that conscience was superior to all human judgments. Although this, which was acknowledged in word was afterwards violated in fact, still, God was pleased that there should even then exist an attestation to liberty, exempting the conscience from the tyranny of man."[5]

But when we say that conscience is superior to all human judgments we mean nothing other than that a man who is well aware of himself ought not to fear that God will damn him, even if all men who do not see his heart judge otherwise concerning his affairs. To what end? For that reason, shall a man not sin who violates ecclesiastical laws by the testimony of his conscience?

I respond in the affirmative; human law does not oblige under the penalty of eternal death, except insofar as by the violation of human law God is offended. His ministers are princes, not only ecclesiastical, but also political; whoever transgresses the laws of a viceroy consequently offends the king and can be punished by the king, even by the kind of penalty that a viceroy perhaps could not inflict. Likewise, a man that does not keep the just laws of princes also offends God and is punished by him with the eternal penalty of death since princes are indeed also ministers of God.[6] Therefore, if we were to pretend that God is not in the nature of affairs, those who will violate just laws will also sin in conscience, but will neither offend God, nor will they be condemned to hell.

---

[5] *Instit.* lib. 4, cap. 10, §5.

[6] *cf.* Wisdom 6:1-9, Romans 13:1-7, 1 Corinth. 4:1-2.

You will say: If that is so, it follows that human law inasmuch as it is human, does not itself oblige that transgressors should be said to sin mortally. I respond: if by a human law, inasmuch as it is human, you mean a thing that is not properly divine then I deny that a transgressor of human law, inasmuch as it is human, does not sin mortally. But if a human law, as human, you would understand that which a man imposes by an authority not received from God, but conferred on his own authority or that of men alone, I affirm that transgressors of such a law do not sin mortally. A law of this sort is null. For all true power is from God,[7] and without true power no true law can be made.

---

[7]   Romans 13:1.

CHAPTER XXI
An Argument from the Fathers is Answered

E NOW proceed to arguments from the Fathers.

10) The tenth argument is taken from several testimonies of the Fathers that Juan Torquemada refers to by name.[1] The first is of Origen who, while explaining Matthew 20, "The kings of the nations lord it over them, with you it is not so," says: "Just as carnal matters are placed in necessity but not in the will, so the spiritual things are in the will, not in necessity, so even spiritual princes. Their rule ought to be placed in love of their subjects, not in corporal fear."[2]

I respond: Origen does not exclude from ecclesiastical rule coercive power, but only advises princes of this sort about their duty. For there is a difference between a secular and ecclesiastical prince, because the secular prince has for his temporal end also the external peace of the state; therefore his end is attained when his subjects live in peace, whether they wish to, or against their will. The spiritual prince, however, has for his end eternal life and external peace which is internal for his subjects, and for that reason he ought to altogether procure that his subjects are rather more led by love than by fear, although where he cannot command that they live joyfully and from love, he also ought to apply coercive force, at least from fear of penalty not to disturb the external peace of the Church. For this reason, Gregory says: But towards their subjects there ought to be in the hearts of rulers both mercy giving comfort in justice, and justice dealing wrath with pitifulness."[3]

The second is St. John Chrysostom, where he compares the Pope with a pastor of irrational sheep and says: "For it is not possible to doctor all men with the same authority with which the shepherd treats his sheep. For in this case it is also necessary to bind and to restrain them from food, and to use cautery or the knife; but the reception of the treatment depends on the will of the patient, not of him who applies the remedy."[4] And he also says: "For Christians above all men are not permitted to forcibly correct the failings of those who sin. Secular judges indeed, when they have captured malefactors under the law, show their authority to be great and prevent them even against their will from following their own devices; but in our case the wrong-doer must be made better, not by force, but by persuasion. For neither has authority of this kind for

---

[1] Lib. 2 capit. 45.

[2] Tract. 12 *in Matthaeum.*

[3] *Moral.* lib. 20, cap. 6.

[4] Lib. 2 *de sacerdotio*, no. 3.

the restraint of sinners been given us by law, nor, if it had been given, should we have any field for the exercise of our power, inasmuch as Christ will give them an eternal crown who abstain from evil by their own choice, not of necessity."

Juan Torquemada responds that Chrysostom speaks on those who are outside, that is the pagans, whom the Church cannot compel to the faith. But Chrysostom also speaks clearly on the sheep who are within, and who are consigned to the bishop. Therefore, it must be said that Chrysostom never meant to deny the coercive power of the Pope when he eloquently asserts this. For in homily 70, to the people, he forbids Christian subjects to call certain foolish women to themselves, who are usually put out to weep at funerals, and says: "Lest I would compel them to weep over their true and proper evils ... Were we not heeded, God forbid we would be compelled to go from threats to serious business, castigating you with ecclesiastical laws, such as will correspond to the threats; ... Nobody will despise any ecclesiastical bonds. For he who binds is not a man but Christ who conferred this power to us, and constituted us masters of such an honor." And in Epistle 1 to Pope Innocent, he asks him to compel Theophilus, the bishop of Alexandria as well as others by ecclesiastical laws, since they had expelled him from his see unjustly. And in homily 83 on Matthew, speaking to priests he says: "If any general or consul you like were adorned with a diadem but should be present unworthily, confine and compel him. You have greater power than they do, but if you dare not to drive them out, you ought to speak with me for I will not permit such a matter to pass." Therefore, we see that Chrysostom sensed prelates can bind their sheep and drive them out of the Church and severely punish them, which he seemed to deny beforehand.

Next, I respond to those words in two ways. Firstly, this distinction between the shepherd of irrational sheep and rational ones was placed by Chrysostom so that when he treated on the natural sickness of the sheep, he could heal the sheep even if they refuse; but when he treated on that voluntary sickness of the sheep, he cannot cure it unless they wish, and therefore, the latter is more, difficult than the former. I say it is likewise in regard to the secular power. For a secular judge treats on external actions, and therefore can compel a man against his will so that he will change his manners, but it is certainly external; yet a bishop treats on internal manners, which cannot be changed against the will of one who has them. For even if the bishop can excommunicate and inflict other penalties, still these things are of no profit unless he who is punished should be willing. I understand those words of Chrysostom in this way since authority of this kind for the restraint of sinners has not been given us by law, but the bishop does not have the authority to compel men to change their heart, just as a judge has to compel a man to change his external manners. Secondly, it can be said on this citation that Chrysostom deals with the priestly power in the forum of conscience. There we cannot correct the penitent unless he wishes to be corrected; the chief thing we can do is to dismiss him without absolution.

The third testimony is of St. Augustine, where he defines sin in this way: "Sin is called either a deed or coveting against the eternal law of God."[5] From this it is deduced that the transgression of human law is not a sin. It is also similar to the definition of Ambrose: "Sin is a prevarication of divine law."[6] I respond: Every sin is against the law of God, not the positive law, but the eternal, as Augustine rightly teaches. For every justly enacted law, whether it is given by God or by man, is derived from the eternal law of God. There is, moreover, an eternal law that it is evil to violate a rule.

The fourth testimony is of St. Bernard: "Those who say this will not show, I believe, where anyone of the Apostles you like sat as a judge of men. I read that they stood to be judged; I do not read that they sat in judgment."[7] I respond: St. Bernard speaks on judgment in civil cases. For otherwise he says in the same place: "Why do those who will judge angels in heavenly matters not think so little of judging about little earthly possessions of men? Therefore, your power is over crimes, not over possessions. Because on account of the former, not the latter, you received the keys of the kingdom of heaven." Add the fact that Bernard did not dispute whether it was lawful, but fitting, for the Pope to judge on earthly lawsuits.

---

[5] *Contra Faustum*, lib. 22, cap. 27.

[6] *Libro de paradise*, cap. 8.

[7] *De Consideratione*, lib. 1.

CHAPTER XXII

The Last Question is Proposed: Whether Christ Conferred Ecclesiastical Jurisdiction Immediately to the Supreme Pontiff and to Him Alone?

HE LAST question remains concerning the derivation of ecclesiastical power from the Supreme Pontiff to the other bishops. It must be known that there is a threefold power in the Pope and the other bishops: 1) of order; 2) of interior jurisdiction; 3) of external jurisdiction. Of these the first refers to the confecting and administration of the Sacraments; the second to ruling the Christian people in the interior forum of conscience; the third to rule the same people in the exterior forum.

On the first and second there is no question on our side, but only on the third, since the first point is certain among all authors, that bishops, and the Supreme Pontiff himself, have the power of order equally and immediately from God, since it is conferred through a certain consecration that works in the same measure in one man and in another.[1] On the second point there is some dissent among the authors, for Abulensis thinks this power is conferred to all priests immediately by God when they are ordained.[2] But just the same, not simply any priest can absolve any Christian, or bind them, that is a fact; because to remove confusion, the Church divides dioceses and subjects one people to one bishop, and one bishop to another. But Torquemada teaches that this power is not conferred by God from the force of ordination, but by man through a simple command; still both authors agree in that the use of this power depends upon external jurisdiction and therefore it will be enough to treat on that external jurisdiction.[3] Besides, the first two powers pertain properly to the matter on the keys of the Church, which we shall not dispute in this place.

Therefore, only the third has to be argued wherein we also treat on the above questions. And indeed they are all fitting in that the jurisdiction of bishops is at least in general by divine law. For Christ himself so arranged the Church that in her there would be pastors, teachers, etc. The Apostle says this, "He gave some to be Apostles, some prophets, others pastors and teachers."[4] And besides, unless that were so, the Pope could change this order and institute that there would not be any bishop in the Church, something he certainly cannot do. But the question is whether bishops canonically elected would receive their jurisdiction from God, just as the Supreme Pontiff does, or on the

---

[1]   See on this power in Juan de Torquemada lib. 1, cap. 93.

[2]   In a book which he calls *Defensores*, part 2, cap. 62.

[3]   Lib. 1, *summae*, cap. 96.

[4]   Ephes. 4.

other hand from the Pope. Moreover, there are three opinions of theologians on this matter.

1) Of those who would have it that both the Apostles and the remaining bishops received and do receive jurisdiction immediately from God. Francis Victoria[5] and Alphonse à Castro[6] teach this.

2) Of those who would have it that the Apostles received jurisdiction not from Christ but from Peter, and that bishops do not receive jurisdiction from Christ, but from the successor of St. Peter. Torquemada[7] supposes this as does Dominic Jacobatius.[8]

3) The third is the middle of those two and would have it that the Apostles indeed received all their authority immediately from Christ, while the bishops do not receive it immediately from Christ, but from the Supreme Pontiff. For this opinion are Cajetan,[9] Domingo de Soto,[10] Francis Vargas (in a little book on this very question), Hervaeus,[11] and Gabriel;[12] and the same seems to be the opinion of the old Scholastics, St. Bonaventure, St. Albert and Durandus, as well as others commenting on book 4 of the Sentences of Peter Lombard, distinction 18, or 20, and even 24; which is the truest opinion, and therefore must be briefly confirmed.

---

[5] In relect. 2 *de potestate Ecclesiae.*

[6] Lib. 2, cap. 24 *de justa haereticorum punitione.*

[7] Lib. 2, cap. 54 *summae de Ecclesia.*

[8] Lib. 10 *de Conciliis,* arctic.7.

[9] *Tractatus de auctoritate Papae et Concilii,* cap. 3.

[10] 4 dist. 20, quaest. 1, arctic. 2.

[11] *De potestate Papae.*

[12] In canonem Missae, lect. 3.

CHAPTER XXIII

The Apostles received all jurisdiction from Christ.

HEREFORE, the fact that the Apostles received their jurisdiction immediately from Christ is witnessed: 1) from the words of the Lord in John 20, "Just as the Father sent me, so I also send you." The Fathers, particularly Chrysostom and Theophylactus, explain that by these words the Apostles were made vicars of Christ; nay more, they even received the duty of Christ and His authority.

St. Cyril adds on this passage that the Apostles were properly created as such by these words, as well as teachers of the whole world, so that we would understand that all ecclesiastical power is contained in the apostolic authority; therefore, Christ added, "Just as the Father sent me." Accordingly, the Father sent the Son provided with supreme power. St. Cyprian says, in his book *De Unitate Ecclesiae*: "The Lord says to Peter, 'I will give you the keys of the kingdom of heaven,'" and after the resurrection he said to the same: 'Feed my sheep.' And although he gave equal power to all the Apostles after his resurrection, and says: 'Just as the Father sent me, even I send you,' still, to manifest unity, he constituted one chair, etc." There you see the same thing is given to the Apostles through the words: "I send you," because it was promised to Peter through that promise, "I will give you the keys," and after it was fulfilled through that command, "Feed my sheep." It is certain, however, through the former "I will give you the keys," and through the latter "feed my sheep" that the fullest jurisdiction is understood, even external. But how this does not impede the primacy of Peter, we have shown often enough elsewhere.

2) The election of Mathias into the apostolate shows the same thing. For in Acts I we read that Mathias the Apostle was not elected by the Apostles, nor was any authority given to him, but after the election that which they implored and prayed through divine agency, soon he was numbered among the Apostles. Certainly if all the Apostles had jurisdiction from Peter, he ought to have shown the fact especially in the election of Matthias.

3) It is proven from Paul, who expressly teaches that he had authority and jurisdiction from Christ, and this is what he uses to prove himself a true Apostle. For in Galatians I he says: "Paul, an Apostle not by men, nor through a man, but through Jesus Christ and God the Father." And in the same passage, to show he did not receive authority from Peter or the other Apostles, he says: "When it pleased him who separated me from the womb of my mother, he also called me through his grace, and I did not right away acquiesce from flesh and blood, nor did I come to Jerusalem to those who were Apostles before me, but I went away into Arabia, and again went back to Damascus. Next after three

years I came to Jerusalem to see Peter, etc." And in Chapter 2: "Those who seemed to me to be something, conferred nothing."

4) It is proved by the evidence of reason. The Apostles were constituted such by Christ alone, as is clear from Luke 6, "He called his disciples, and he chose twelve from them, whom he called Apostles," and in John 6, "Did I not choose you twelve?" Moreover, the fact that the Apostles have jurisdiction is clear both from the deeds of Paul, who excommunicates[1] and everywhere constitutes laws,[2] and because the Apostolic dignity is the first and supreme dignity in the Church, as is clear from 1 Corinthians 12 and Ephesians 4, "And some he placed in the Church, first Apostles, then prophets, etc."[3] Moreover, the fact that before the passion of Christ they were Apostles, but still were not bishops or priests, nor had any jurisdiction is not to be marveled at. The Lord conferred various powers upon the Apostles at various times. And in John 20 he especially finishes what he had begun before the passion.

---

[1] 1 Cor. 5:1-5; 9-12.

[2] 1 Corinthians 6:1-7, 7:1-40, 11:1-34, 14:1-40 and other places.

[3] See St. Thomas in chapter 12 of First Corinthians.

CHAPTER XXIV
All bishops Receive Jurisdiction from the Pope

E ARE going to prove the fact that all ordinary jurisdiction of bishops comes down immediately from the Pope.

1) From a figure in the Old Testament. In Numbers we read that when Moses could not rule the whole people alone, God commanded seventy elders to be present and taking from the spirit of Moses, he gave to them that together with him they would rule the people. Here it must be noted with Augustine,[1] that this taking of the spirit from Moses does not mean a decrease of the spirit in Moses, because then it would not have benefitted Moses to have helpers if on that account he was made weaker. Rather, it means the derivation of the power of the elders from the power of Moses. For God wished to show that the whole authority resided in Moses, but if others were to have something, they had it from Moses. Moreover, it is certain that the Pope has the same place in the Church that Moses had among the people of the Jews.

2) The ecclesiastical government is a monarchy, as we showed above, consequently, the authority is in one and is derived from him to others. For all Monarchies are constituted in this way. They respond that ecclesiastical government is monarchy, but it is tempered by aristocracy. Therefore, apart from the monarch there are also other lower prefects, who are not vicars of the monarch, but absolute princes. For they would be vicars only if they received their authority from him.

But on the contrary, the aristocracy of the Church requires also that bishops must be princes and not simple vicars; yet it does not require that these princes would be instituted by God and not the Pope, but only that the Pope is compelled by divine law in various parts of the Church to constitute diverse ecclesiastical princes. It works just as if the king should be held to not constitute governors or presidents in one place or in some province but true dukes and princes, who would rule their province but still have their dependence on the king.

3) It is proved from four similitudes, which Cyprian uses in his book *The Unity of the Church*, where he compares the see of Peter to the head, root, font, and sun. In every body the strength of the members is derived from the head, in every tree the strength of the branches arises from the root, and in every river water flows from the font, and last of all the light of the rays is from the sun.

4) Fourthly it is proven from the inequality of jurisdiction. For if God immediately confers jurisdiction on bishops then all bishops would have equal

---

[1]   Q. 18 in librum Numeri.

jurisdiction, just as they equally have the power of order. For God did not ever determine the jurisdiction of bishops, but only that one bishop should have one city, another should have hundred cities, another should have many provinces. Therefore, jurisdiction of this sort is not given by God, but by man. For that reason, one rules a great, while another rules a little people, because it so pleases the one that gave jurisdiction, that is, the prince of the whole Church.

5) If the bishops had their jurisdiction immediately from God, the Pope could not change it or take it away. For the Pope cannot do anything against the ordination of God; but it is certain what the Pope can do, and often has done. For this reason St. Bernard says: "The Roman Church can ordain new bishops wherever they have not been hitherto; it can reduce those who are and elevate others, according to what reason dictates, so that he may create an Archbishop from a bishop, and if it would seem necessary vice versa."[2]

They respond that bishops have jurisdiction from God, but they are still under the Pope, and therefore, the Pope is permitted to abolish or change it.

On the other hand, the Apostles had power under Peter, and still because they had it immediately from Christ, Peter could not take it away or diminish it. Besides, they all have the power of the order of priesthood under the Pope, and still because they have that from God, the Pope cannot so take it away that they cannot use it if they wish. For even if he excommunicates a priest, suspends him, interdicts him or lowers him, still, if the latter wishes he could truly consecrate. Next, clergy and people in any city you like are subject to a bishop, and still if anyone from the clergy or the people has some authority immediately from the Supreme Pontiff, the bishop cannot abolish or diminish that authority. In the same way, if the bishops have their authority from Christ, then a vicar of Christ could not take that away or diminish it; or our adversaries should say that the Lord so subjected the bishops to the Pope that he also meant for those things which he himself had conferred upon them to be able to be changed.

They respond: At least the Pope can take away from the bishop the matter subject to him, that is, subject his people to another bishop, and for that reason he does not properly take the jurisdiction given by God away from him, but causes that indirectly so as to destroy it. But when power of jurisdiction means a relation of prelate to subject, from relation to one placed or elevated, and on the other it is placed or taken away, if jurisdiction cannot be taken from a bishop, it cannot happen that the people would not be his subject. Next, it would be quite a wonder if divine providence, which sweetly disposes all things, would

---

[2] In epist. 131 ad Mediolanenses.

not allow jurisdiction to be given by him through whom he would wish it to be increased, diminished and also utterly taken away.

6) If the bishops have their jurisdiction from divine law then they ought to show something in the Word of God whereby this jurisdiction of theirs is founded. But they advance nothing, nor can our adversaries advance anything but the words of the Lord spoken to the Apostles, that to them is given the fullest jurisdiction in the Church by those words which certainly our adversaries do not concede to the bishops. Therefore, they see in what ground they defend their opinion.

7) Next we advance very serious testimonies of two Fathers and holy Popes. Innocent I, in his epistle to the Council of Carthage, which is the 91st among the epistles of Augustine: "The episcopate itself and the whole authority of this name emerged from Peter." And in an epistle to the Council of Milevitanus, which is 93rd among the epistles of Augustine: "I think all our brethren and co-bishops ought not to be brought to any but to Peter, that is the whole authority of this name and honor." St. Leo the Great: "If he wished there to be something in common with him and the others princes, whatever he did not refuse others he never gave except through himself."[3] And Epistle 89, "The Lord so wished the Sacrament of this office to pertain to the duty of all the Apostles that in St. Peter the Apostle he principally placed the greatest of all, that some of his gifts would diffuse just as if from the head into the whole body."

Furthermore, the fact that the Apostles did not receive jurisdiction from Peter is not opposed to our position, since here Leo speaks on the ordinary mode whereby God conferred to princes of the Church, that is the bishops, their gifts and says they are conferred ordinarily through Peter. For the Apostles by an extraordinary privilege received their jurisdiction from Christ.

Last of all come the words of the Pope which he uses to create bishops. For he says: "We provide to the Church such and such a person and we put him in charge as a father, pastor and bishop of the same Church, entrusting to him the administration in both temporal and spiritual things, in the name of the Father, and of the Son, and of the Holy Spirit. Amen."

---

[3] Serm. 3 *de assumptione sua ad Pontificatum.*

CHAPTER XXV
The arguments of our Adversaries are Answered

UT on the other hand, our adversaries object: 1) That our opinion destroys itself. For bishops succeed the Apostles, as the Roman Pontiff Peter; therefore, if the Apostles have jurisdiction from Christ, as our first conclusion asserts, it also follows that bishops have from Christ what the second conclusion denies. And on the other hand, if bishops have jurisdiction from the Pope, as the second conclusion asserts, consequently, the Apostles have from Peter what the first conclusion denies. For the successor has from his jurisdiction from the one from whom the predecessor has it, otherwise he does not truly succeed but is instituted in another order. But St. Augustine teaches that bishops succeed Apostles for he explains that: "Sons are born to their fathers, the Apostles are sent; sons are born for the Apostles, they are constituted bishops."[1] Moreover, the Council of Florence and the Council of Trent teach that bishops succeed in the place of the Apostles.[2]

I respond: There is a great difference between the succession of Peter and of the other Apostles. For the Roman Pontiff properly succeeds Peter, not as an Apostle, but as the ordinary pastor of the whole Church, and therefore the Roman Pontiff holds jurisdiction from the source whence Peter had it. But bishops do not succeed the Apostles properly speaking, because the Apostles were not ordinary, but extraordinary, and just as delegated pastors they are not succeeded in such powers.

Still, bishops are said to succeed the Apostles, not properly in that mode whereby one bishop succeeds another, and one king another, but by a twofold reason. 1) First by reason of episcopal order; 2) Through the same similitude and proportion: because just as while Christ was living on earth the first twelve Apostles were under Christ, then the seventy-two disciples, so now the first bishops are under the Roman Pontiff, after these the priests, then deacons, etc.

But even for bishops to not otherwise succeed Apostles is proven, for they have no share of true apostolic authority. The Apostles could preach in the whole world, and found churches, as is clear from the last chapter of Matthew, as well as of Mark, but bishops cannot do this. Likewise, the Apostles could write the canonical books, as all affirm, the bishops could not do this. The Apostles had the gift of tongues and miracles; the bishops do not. The Apostles had jurisdiction over the whole Church and the bishops do not. Besides, one does not properly succeed unless he succeeds someone that precedes him, but

---

[1] In Psal. 144.

[2] Florence, *instruct. Armenorum*; Trent, Sess. 23, cap. 4.

the Apostles and the bishops were together in the Church as is clear from Timothy, Titus, Evodius and many others. Therefore, if the bishops succeeded the Apostles, which Apostle did Titus succeed, or Timothy? Next, the bishops succeed the Apostles in the same mode in which the priests do the seventy-two disciples, as is clear from Anacletus[3] and from Bede.[4] But it is certain that priests do not properly succeed the seventy-two disciples, except through a similitude. For the seventy-two disciples were not priests, nor of any order, but they received the jurisdiction from Christ. Accordingly, Philip and Stephen, and the five other deacons ordained by the Apostles in Acts 6 were from the seventy two disciples, as Epiphanius teaches.[5] Certainly they were not ordained Deacons if they were already priests beforehand.

Secondly, they object with the citation, "Attend yourselves to every flock in which the Holy Spirit has placed you as bishops to rule the Church of God."[6] Likewise Ephesians 4, "He gave some Apostles, others prophets, others pastors and teachers." There, by the name of pastors and teachers, bishops are understood, as Jerome says on that passage. It is also confirmed by the Fathers, for Dionysius says in the book *On Ecclesiastical Hierarchy*, chapter 6, that the hierarchy of bishops ends immediately in Jesus, just as the lower orders of priests and deacons and others are ended in the bishops. Cyprian says that bishops are made by Christ, by whom the Apostles were created;[7] while deacons were instituted by the Apostles, and not by Christ.

St. Bernard also says: "You err if as the highest, you think only your Apostolic power was established by God."[8]

I respond: To the first citation it can be said that bishops are constituted by the Holy Spirit not immediately, but mediately, because the Apostles constituted them bishops by the inspiration of God and the power received from the Holy Spirit. But how in Acts 15 do they say: "It has been seen by the Holy Spirit, and us," and still they speak on human law. Likewise Romans 13: "There is no power but from God," certainly mediately or immediately.

To the second, I say there, the general order of the Church is expressed, without a doubt on divine law. For God is the one who established that in the Church there would be Apostles, prophets, pastors and teachers, even if he did not immediately give authority to all.

---

[3] Epist. 2.

[4] In cap. 20 Luc.

[5] Haeresi 20, which is of the Herodians.

[6] Acts 20:28.

[7] Lib. 3 epistola 9, ad Rogantium.

[8] Liber 3 de consideration.

To the third, I say, Dionysius speaks on the order of bishops, not on their jurisdiction.

To the fourth I say, Cyprian meant the order of bishops established from Christ himself; hence (by divine law), it was introduced into the Church. But the order of deacons was first devised by the Apostles. The later part of the opinion some theologians of the School commonly reject, but whether it may be true or false, it does not avail to our proposition.

To the fifth proposition I say, Bernard speaks in that mode in which Paul speaks to the Romans when he says: "There is no power but from God."[9]

Thirdly they object that if bishops have jurisdiction from the Pope, consequently after the Pope dies the authority of the bishops would cease, just as all the limbs die when the head is cut off. I respond: There is a great distinction between the natural head and the mystical head. In fact, the members of the natural cannot be preserved unless they receive a continual flow from the head; but the members of the Mystical Body, especially the ministerial and external, depend upon the head that they should come into being, but still not that they be preserved. Therefore, once episcopal jurisdiction has been conferred, it is not lost when the one who gave it dies, but when the one who receives it dies, or when someone who is able should take it away.

Fourthly they object that to exercise the order of episcopacy, jurisdiction is necessary; for that reason, God who confers order, confers also jurisdiction. I respond: Both are conferred by God, but one immediately, the other mediately. 1) The power of order requires the character and grace, but only God can cause these; 2) jurisdiction only requires the will of a superior.

Fifthly they object that the Supreme Pontiff calls bishops *brothers and colleagues*, therefore they are put in charge of the Church by one common father. *I respond*: They are primarily called brother by reason of the episcopal order in which they are equals. Secondly, by reason of jurisdiction, because the bishops are raised up by the Pope to assist him in his burden, not to some lower ministry.

Sixthly they object that if all bishops ought to receive jurisdiction from the Pope then a great many bishops were not true bishops because the Roman Pontiff did not create all the bishops, especially in Asia and Africa.

I respond: It is not necessary that the Pope immediately create bishops, rather it is enough if it is done mediately, through patriarchs and archbishops. Therefore, from the beginning Peter constituted the Patriarch of Alexandria, as well as Antioch, who, receiving authority over the whole of Asia and Africa, could create archbishops, who afterward would create bishops.

---

[9] Romans 13:1.

BOOK V
ON THE TEMPORAL POWER OF THE POPE

CHAPTER I
A Question is Proposed on Temporal Power

ONLY the last part of our disputation on the Pope remains, which is on his temporal power, in which we discover three opinions of the authors. 1) That the Supreme Pontiff has the fullest power over the whole world from divine law, both in ecclesiastical matters as well as political. Augustine Triumphus teaches that,[1] as well as Alvarus Pelagius[2] and many lawyers, such as Hostiensis,[3] Panormitanus[4], Sylvester and not a few others.[5] Moreover, Hostiensis has another teaching, that through the coming of Christ all dominion of the princes of the infidels was transferred to the Church and resides in the Supreme Pontiff, so that as the vicar of Christ, the greatest and true king, namely the Pope, should he wish, can even give the kingdoms of infidels by his own right to some of the faithful.

2) The next opinion is on the other extreme and teaches two things. a) That the Pope, as Pope, has no temporal power by divine law and he cannot command any secular princes in any way; he may not deprive them of their kingdom or rule, even if they otherwise deserve it; b) This view teaches that it is not lawful for the Pope to receive the temporal dominion of other bishops, which they now have in some cities and provinces, whether they were given dominion of this sort or whether they usurped it. Divine law forbids the spiritual and temporal sword from being consigned at the same time. All the heretics of our time teach this, especially Calvin,[6] Peter Martyr,[7] and Brenz in his prolegomena against Pedro de Soto. The Centuriators of Magdeburg[8] place among the marks of Antichrist that the Pope bears two swords in all directions and they condemn this more than anything else among "the vices of the Popes".[9]

The third opinion, which is in the middle, is common to Catholic theologians. The Pope, as Pope, does not have any temporal power directly or immediately, but only spiritually. Still, by reason of the spiritual power, he at least has indirectly a certain power and that is supreme in temporal affairs.

---

[1] *Summa de potestate Ecclesiae*, quaest. 1, art. 1.

[2] Lib. 1 *de planctu Ecclesiae*, capite 13.

[3] In cap. *Quod super his*, on vows and the fulfillment of vows.

[4] In cap. *Novit*, de iudiciis.

[5] In *Summa de Peccatis*, verbo Papa, §2.

[6] *Instit.*, lib. 4, cap. 11, § 8-14.

[7] In cap. 13 ad Rom.

[8] *Cent.* 1, libro 2, cap. 4, colum. 435.

[9] *Centur.* 8-11, cap. 10.

Henricus and the following writers think the same:[10] John Driedo,[11] Juan de Torquemada,[12] Albert Pighius,[13] Thomas Waldensis,[14] Peter de Palude,[15] Cajetan,[16] Francisco Victoria[17] Domingo de Soto,[18] and Nicholas Sanders.[19]

What St. Thomas Aquinas thought is not so certain. For at the end of his commentary on the sentences he says that the Pope is the apex of both powers. Still, in his commentary on chapter 13 to the Romans, he says that clerics are exempt by privilege from the taxes of the secular powers, and he says that prelates can administer wars insofar as it is ordered to the spiritual good, which is the purpose of that power.[20] From this it is gathered that he does not think differently than other theologians.

We therefore will treat three things. 1) We will show the Pope by divine law does not directly have temporal power; 2) That he has in some way, that is by reason of his spiritual monarchy, supreme power even in a temporal manner; 3) That it is not against divine law that bishops should also directly have actual temporal jurisdiction over cities and provinces given to them by kings, or otherwise acquired by just title.

---

[10] *Quodlibet* 6, quaest. 23.

[11] *De libertate Christiana*, lib. 2, cap. 2.

[12] *Summae*, lib. 2, cap. 113 et sequentibus

[13] *Hierarchia Ecclesiastica*, lib. 5.

[14] Lib. 2 *Doctr. Fid.* arctic. 3 cap. 76-78.

[15] In libro *Potestate Ecclesiastica*.

[16] *Apologia*, caput 13 ad 6.

[17] Quaest. *de potestate Ecclesiae*.

[18] In 4, dist. 25, quaest. 2, art. 1.

[19] Lib. 2, cap. 4, *Visibilis Monarchiae*.

[20] S.T., II IIae, quaest. 40, art. 2.

CHAPTER II

The Pope is not the Lord of the Whole World

E WILL endeavor to prove three things in order. 1) The Pope is not the lord of the whole world. 2) That he is not lord of the whole Christian world. 3) That he is not the lord of any province or town, and has no jurisdiction that is merely temporal *by divine law.*

In the first place it is proven that the Pope is not the Lord of those provinces which the infidels obtained because the Lord consigned to Peter only his sheep.[1] Next, the Pope cannot judge infidels. "Why is it for me to judge those who are outside?"[2] Therefore, infidels are the true and supreme princes of their own kingdoms; for dominion is not poured out in grace, or faith, but in free will and reason. Nor does it descend from divine law, but the law of nations, as is clear from the fact that God approves the Gentile nations in both the Old and New Testament. "You are king of kings, and the God of heaven has given you a kingdom and dominion, etc."[3] "Render to Caesar those things which are Caesar's."[4] *Note,* "render," not give those things which are Caesar's, that is, because they ought to be given by law. And in Romans 13: "Render all things due, tribute to whom it is due, a tax to whom a tax is due." He commands in the same place to obey pagan princes on account of conscience. But certainly we are not held in conscience to obey someone who is not a true prince.

Therefore, the Pope is not the lord of those provinces that the infidels obtained and it follows that he is not the lord of the whole world, unless one would say that these provinces do not pertain to the whole world.

Our opponents will say, we are held to obey infidel princes, because all princes are vicars of the Pope. *Sed contra*, the Pope would not wish to have such vicars, even if he could freely give kingdoms of infidels to the princes of the faithful. Moreover it would be ridiculous for God to have given to the Pope rights over the kingdoms of the whole world and not to have given him any faculty of using a right of this sort.

But they will say that the Pope is the spiritual monarch over the whole world, and still he never could exercise this rule in the whole world. I respond: The Pope is called a spiritual monarch over the whole world, not because he is in charge of all men who are in it, but because he is in charge of all Christians diffused throughout the world. And again, even hypothetically because if the

---

[1] John 21.

[2] 1 Corinth. 5:12.

[3] Daniel 2:37.

[4] Matth. 22:21.

whole world would be converted to the faith, then the Pope would plainly be over the whole world in regard to spiritual jurisdiction.

They will add: But Alexander VI recently divided the world between the kingdom of Spain and Portugal.[5] I respond: He did not divide for the purpose that these kings should set out to make war upon all infidel kings of the new world and seize their kingdoms, but only that if preachers were to add them to the Christian faith they would protect and defend both those preachers and the Christians that they convert. At the same time, he sought to impede contentions and wars of Christian princes who wished to trade in those new regions.

---

[5] Translator's note: This is the *Treaty of Tordisillas.* Many popular historians today falsely hold that this treaty divided the whole world between the Spanish and Portugese, but this is to take what Spanish jurists argued as a fact when, in reality, no such right was ever granted by the Pope, as Bellarmine shows here.

CHAPTER III

The Pope is Not the Lord of the Whole Christian World

INDEED, what was proposed in the second place, that the Pope is not the lord of the whole Christian world, is proved. First, because if the matter stood otherwise, as some would have it, then it ought to be certain from the Scriptures, or certainly from the tradition of the Apostles. We have nothing from the Scriptures except that the keys of the kingdom of heaven were given to the Pope, but no mention is made about the keys of an earthly kingdom. Likewise the Apostolic tradition advances nothing for the side of our adversaries. Besides, Christ did not take away, nor does he take away kingdoms from those who owned them; for Christ does not come to destroy those things that were good, but to fulfill therefore, when a king is a Christian, he does not lose the earthly kingdom which he lawfully obtained but acquires a new right to the eternal kingdom. Otherwise the good of Christ would be opposed to kings, and grace would destroy nature. It is also confirmed from a hymn of Sedulius, which the whole Church publicly sings:

O Herod, impious enemy,
Why do you fear Christ's coming?
He does not snatch up mortal things,
But gives heavenly kingdoms.[1]

In like manner, if the Pope is the lord of the whole Christian world, consequently, individual bishops are temporal princes in the cities subject to their episcopate. Accordingly, that which the Pope is in the universal Church, each bishop is in his particular one. But that bishops are lords of the cities of which they are bishops, our adversaries do not concede, and it is clearly false. For St. Ambrose says: "If it were tribute, what the emperor asks is not denied, the fields of the Church give tribute."[2] And in a letter of St. Athanasius, treating on the solitary life, he quotes Hosius of Cordoba as saying to the Emperor: "God consigned to you rule, but to us Christ consigned those matters which are of the Church."

Next, it is proven from the confession of Popes. Leo affirms that the emperor Martianus was chosen by God to command[3] and also that his authority is from

---

[1] Translator's note: This hymn is used for Vespers on the feast of the Epiphany.

[2] *In oratione de tradendis basilicis.*

[3] Epist. 38 ad Martianum.

God.[4] He writes similar things in nearly all the epistles to Theodosius, and Martianus, while Leo's successors wrote the same in turn to their emperors. Pope Gelasius says in his epistle to the Emperor Anastasius,[5] "There are two things, O august Emperor, whereby this world is ruled; the sacred authority of Popes, and the royal power, etc." There it must be noted, that Gelasius does not only speak on the execution, but on power itself; and by authority (lest our adversaries might say the Pope does indeed have each power), rather demands execution from others.

St. Gregory the Great writes: "Power over all men of my lords was given from heaven for the sake of piety."[6] And Nicholas the Great clearly says: "Do not ask a precedent from the Church of God. By all means she bears no precedent to your rule ... The same mediator of God, and the man of men Christ Jesus, thus distinguished the duties of each power from the proper acts and distinct dignities of each, so that Christian emperors would need Pontiffs for eternal life, and Pontiffs would merely use imperial laws for the course of temporal matters."[7] Here, the Pope speaks not only on the execution but also on the power and dignity. And even if he were to speak on the execution alone, that would be enough for us. For whatever the emperors have, says Nicholas, they have from Christ. Therefore, I ask, can the Supreme Pontiff take away from kings and emperors this execution just as if he were supreme king and emperor, or can he not? If he can, then he is greater than Christ; if he cannot, then he does not truly have royal power.

Besides, Pope Alexander III was asked whether an appeal might be made from a secular judge to the Pope, and responded, "Indeed, those who are subjects of our temporal jurisdiction can, but we believe others cannot according to the inflexibility of the law."[8] Likewise he says, "We, being attentive to what pertains to the king and not to the Church, judge on such possessions, etc."[9]

Next, Pope Innocent III, speaking on authority and obedience, says: "To the firmament of heaven, that is, the universal Church, God made two great lights, that is, he established two dignities which are papal authority and royal power, but the former is in charge of the two, that is, the greater is in spiritual matters, the lesser rules carnal affairs. By the same difference that is understood between the sun and the moon, so also between Popes and kings, etc." Note here, to the

---

[4] Epist. 43

[5] Found in the decretals, d. 96, can. *Duo sunt*

[6] Lib. 2, epist. 61 ad Mauritium.

[7] Epist. ad Michaelem.

[8] Cap. *Si duobus*, §. *denique, extra de appellationibus.*

[9] Ibid, cap. *Caussam*, 2. extra, *qui filii sint legitimi.*

extent that the sun and moon are not the same, and just as the moon does not make the sun, but God, so also, the papacy and empire are not the same thing, nor does one absolutely depend upon the other. He says the same thing in another canon,[10] that the Pope only has full power in his temporal domains, but on all other accounts he does not have the same power outside of them: "Although the king recognizes no temporal superior, still he could submit himself to our judgment without injuring another's right. It seemed to some that by himself, not as a father to his children but rather as the prince, that he could issue a dispensation to himself. You, however, know that you are subject to another and so you may not appeal to us and not at the same time injure them, unless first they would offer assent to us, nor could you grant such a dispensation yourself."[11]

---

[10] Per venerabilem, extra *qui filii sint legitimi.*

[11] Ibid.

CHAPTER IV
The Pope Does not Have any Temporal Jurisdiction Directly

NOW it remains that we show that the Pope is the temporal lord of no land by divine law. Moreover, it will be manifestly proven by this reasoning that Christ, as man, while he lived on earth did not receive nor wished to have any temporal dominion; but the Supreme Pontiff is the vicar of Christ, and represents Christ for us, and since Christ was of that sort while he lived among men then the Supreme Pontiff, as the vicar of Christ, should also be as Christ was and thus, has no temporal dominion.

Each proposition of this argument must be proven. 1) From the false principle (that Christ was a temporal king), two errors arise; from this they deduce, just as from a particular foundation, that the Pope, who is the vicar of Christ, is king and priest at the same time. On the other hand, the followers of John Wycliffe[1] deduce from this very same principle that kings are greater and more worthy than Popes, because kings are vicars of Christ the king, and Popes are vicars of Christ the priest. Moreover, Christ was more king than priest, for he descended from the royal tribe of Judah and the family of David, not from the tribe of Levi and the family of Aaron. And hence, he was a king by hereditary succession, not a priest.

Therefore, so as to explain and prove this principle, I say Christ was indeed always (as Son of God), king and lord of all creation in the manner in which his Father is, but this is an eternal and divine kingdom; it does not abolish the dominions of men, nor can it fit the Pope. Besides, Christ as man was the spiritual king of all men, and had the greatest spiritual power over all, both faithful and infidel alike in the order of eternal salvation, so that he could oblige them to receive faith and his Sacraments. After the day of judgment this spiritual kingdom of Christ is going to come into being; it will also be sensible and manifest and so the glory of this kingdom, even as the glory of this kingdom began in Christ our head when he rose from the dead.

In other respects, this is not a temporal kingdom, such as of our kings, nor can it be shared with the Pope because it presupposes the resurrection. Next, Christ the man could (if he had wished), have obtained that he be seen to receive royal authority but he refused and hence did not receive it. He also did not have either the execution of dominion and rule, or the power of any temporal king. That fact is proven, for if he had such it would either be from hereditary succession, election, the right from war, or a special gift of God. For

---

[1] Walld. lib. 2, doctr. fidei, art. 3, cap. 76.

every king acquires his kingdom from some of these ways, either heredity, election of the people, right of war, or the gift of one higher.

Christ as man did not have a hereditary kingdom. For although he descended from the royal family, still it is not certain whether he was closer to David than many others who were from the same family. Besides, at that time, God willed that the kingdom be taken from the family of David; he also foretold this from the family of Jechonia whence Christ descended,[2] that there was never going to be a king, certainly not temporal, in the way in which David and his successors had been. In Jeremiah we read about Jechonia: "Thus says the Lord, write that this sterile man is a man who will not prosper in all his days. For there will not be a man from his seed who shall sit upon the throne of David, and have power beyond Judah."[3] It is also certain from Matthew that Christ descended from this Jechoniah.

It follows from this that Christ could not have temporal rule by hereditary succession, unless the prophecy which had foretold the matter with eloquent words were false, that no man ever had power in Judah from the line of Jechoniah; nor can it be responded that his posterity had the right to rule, still from the fact that he did not sit on the throne of David. For to what end is a right that no one ever used? Furthermore, it is confirmed from the Fathers. Jerome, commenting on this passage, as well as Ambrose,[4] asked how this prophecy of Jeremiah is not opposed with the prophecy of the Archangel Gabriel in Luke 1, when he says, "The Lord God will give him the throne of David his father." They responded that it is not opposed because Jeremiah spoke on the temporal and physical reign, but Gabriel on the spiritual and eternal kingdom. In this Augustine agrees: "Such a people were going to lose the kingdom but Christ Jesus our Lord is going to reign over it not carnally, but spiritually."[5] Christ was also not a temporal king by the title of election, as is clear from Luke 12: "O man, who set me up as a judge or as a candidate among you?" In other words, neither an emperor nor a republic has chosen me as a judge. Also from that in John 6: "When he knew that they were going to come to take him and make him a king, he fled again to the mountain alone." Therefore, it seems he refused to accept his election as king.

Next, he also was not a temporal king by the right of war for his war was not with mortal kings but with the prince of darkness, as is clear from John 12:

---

[2] Matthew 1:16.

[3] Jeremiah 20:24.

[4] Lib. 3 in Luc. cap. 1.

[5] *de Civitate Dei*, lib. 17, cap. 7.

"Now the prince of this world is cast out."[6] And in Colossians: "Despoiling the principalities and powers he cut them down boldly, triumphant in himself over them."[7] And in 1 John 3: "In this the Son of God appeared that he would break the works of the devil." Therefore by right of war Christ acquired a spiritual kingdom to rule over our hearts through faith and grace, where beforehand the devil ruled through vice and sin.

Next, the fact that he was not a temporal king by a special gift of God is clear from John 18: "My kingdom is not of this world." and: "My kingdom is not of this place." The Fathers, such as Chrysostom, Theophylactus, Cyril, Augustine and Ambrose, all show in this place that Christ meant to free Pilate from suspicion by these words, by which he could believe that he feigned a temporal kingdom of the Jews. For that reason the sense is: I am indeed a king, but not like Caesar and Herod; for my kingdom is not of this world, that is, it does not consist in honors, wealth or worldly power, etc. And this argument is confirmed by the fact that Christ never exercised royal power in this world. He came to minister, not be ministered to, to be judged, not to judge. Therefore, were he to receive royal authority it would be in vain since power is useless if it is never brought to act.

They respond that Christ exercised this power when he cast out those buying sheep and oxen from the temple in John 2. But to cast men out from the temple is not the duty of a king, but the priest. For if the priests threw out the king himself from the temple, as they did with Uzziah and by force,[8] how much more easily could he throw out merchants? Besides, it must be known that Christ did not cast those men from the temple as the priests, or with royal power, but after the custom of the Prophets with divine zeal, such as Phineas who killed the fornicators, and Elijah the prophets of Baal. And for that reason the Jews said to the Lord: "What sign do you show us, that you do these things?" In other words, how will we know you are a Prophet and sent from God with such power?

Secondly, it is confirmed for the same reason. For royal authority was not necessary for Christ, nor useful, but plainly redundant and useless because the purpose of his coming into the world was the redemption of the human race, but to this end temporal power was not necessary, rather spiritual power. Accordingly, he could even dispose of temporal affairs by that spiritual power in the way he judged it expedient for the redemption of the human race. The fact, however, that such merely temporal power was useless for Christ can be

---

[6] John 12:31.

[7] Colos. 2:15.

[8] 2 Paralip. (Chronicles) 26:17-20.

understood for the very reason that Christ ought to persuade men to have contempt for glory, delights, wealth and all earthly things, which kings of this world most especially abound in: "Those who are clothed in soft raiment, they are in the houses of kings."[9]

Lastly, it is confirmed for the reason that nearly all passages of Scripture which treat on the kingdom of Christ ought necessarily be understood concerning a spiritual and eternal kingdom; hence, it cannot be deduced from Scripture that Christ was ever a temporal king. Psalm 2 treats on the kingdom of Christ, where it says: "I have been constituted a king by him," and in the same place it is added: "Preaching his command;" that a spiritual kingdom is shown. Likewise in Daniel 2:44, "In the days of those kingdoms God will raise the kingdom of heaven, which will never be destroyed," and in Luke 1:33, "And of his kingdom there will be no end."

But temporal kingdoms are not eternal, and if Christ was king of the Jews, by human custom, while he lived on earth, certainly he would cease to reign in that way when he ascended to the Father. Therefore, how will there be no end to his kingdom? And when the same kingdom was seized a little after by the Romans, then the Saracens, and now is held by the Turks, which, since that has happened, how does it fulfill what Daniel said, that his kingdom will not be given to another? Therefore, Christ was not the temporal king of Judah, but the spiritual king of the Church, of whose kingdom the temporal reign of David and Solomon were but a figure. It is for this reason that the Father gave to Christ the seat of David his father, that he would reign in the house of Jacob forever.

But now the assumption of the first argument must be explained. We said the Pope has that office which Christ had when he lived among men in human custom on earth. For we cannot attribute to the Pope the duties which Christ has as God, or as immortal and glorified man, but only those which he had as a mortal man. Because the Church consists of men, it needs a visible head, by the custom of living men. Therefore, Christ, when he ceased to live in human fashion (that is, after the resurrection), left Peter behind in his place to show us that the reign of Christ is visible and human which the Church had before the passion of Christ, as is clear from those words of John 20: "As the Father sent me, I also send you."

Add that the Pope does not have all the power which Christ had when he was a mortal man. For he, because he was God and man, had a certain power which they call an excellence, through which he was over both the faithful and the infidels; but he consigned only his sheep to the Pope, that is, the faithful. Besides, Christ could establish the Sacraments and do miracles by his own

---

[9]   Matthew 11:8.

authority, which the Pope cannot do. Likewise he could absolve from sin without the Sacraments, something the Pope cannot. Therefore, he only communicated that power to the Pope which he could share with a pure man, and which was necessary to govern the faithful so that they might be able to obtain eternal life without hindrance. The fact follows that Christ, as a mortal man, did not have any temporal kingdom, nor does the Pope, as vicar of Christ, have such a kingdom.

CHAPTER V

The Arguments to the Contrary are Answered

ET some oppose this and object: 1) From the words of the Lord in Matthew, "All power in heaven and earth has been given to me."[1] From there it seems to be understood that Christ had spiritual and earthly dominion. Moreover, he gave the keys of both kingdoms to Peter, as Pope Nicholas I says in his epistle to the emperor Michael: "Christ consigned to Blessed Peter the key-bearer of eternal life together with earthly life and the laws of the heavenly kingdom."

I respond: The Lord did not mean temporal power such as of earthly kings, but only spiritual, as St. Jerome and Anselm say, who understood the sense of the words: "All power in heaven and earth has been given to me," in other words, just as in heaven I am the king of angels, so through faith the ruler over the hearts of men, or (as Theophylactus adds) it is a certain supreme power over all creatures, not temporal but divine, or like to the divine, which cannot be communicated to mortal man.

Now, to the testimony of Nicholas I say in the first place that is cited by Gratian,[2] but is not discovered among the epistles of Pope Nicholas. Secondly, I add that if it really was the opinion of Pope Nicholas, it has this sense, that Christ consigned to Peter the right of earthly empire at the same time with the heavenly; that is, Christ conceded to Peter that which he would loose or bind on earth, should be loosed or bound in heaven. For Nicholas alluded to the words of the Lord in Matthew 16.

Nor could we explain it otherwise, even if we would have it that Nicholas opposed himself when he taught so eloquently in the same epistle that Christ distinguished acts, duties and dignities of Pope and emperor, lest either the Emperor would presume to usurp the rights of the Pope or vice versa.

2) They object secondly with the Scripture, in which the Lord conceded two swords to Peter.[3] For when the disciples say, "Behold there are two swords here," the Lord does not say it is too much, but it is enough; for this reason St. Bernard[4] and Pope Boniface VIII[5] deduce from this passage that the Pope has two swords from the establishment of Christ.

---

[1] Matt. 28:18.

[2] Distinc. 22, can. *Omnes.*

[3] Luke 22:38.

[4] *De consideration*, lib. 4.

[5] *In extravaganti, Unam Sanctam, de maioritate et obedientia*

I respond: In the literal sense, no mention is made in that passage of the Gospel of the spiritual or temporal sword of the Pope; rather the Lord merely wished to advise the disciples with those words that they were going to go through crises and fear in the time of his passion, in which men usually sell their tunic to buy a sword as is gathered from Theophylactus and other fathers. Hence, St. Bernard and Pope Boniface mystically interpreted this passage, but they did not mean to say that the Pope has both swords in the same manner, but in one way and another, as we shall explain a little later.

3) All quarrels and contentions, both spiritual and temporal, pertain to the judgment of the Supreme Pontiff. For that is held expressly in the canon *Quicunque litem* and the canon: *Quaecunque contentions*, 11. quest. 1.

I respond: From those two canons the first is of the Emperor Theodosius, who conferred that out of piety, but not from an honor due to the Church. Besides, in that canon he did not give the right to judge civil cases to the Pope alone, but to all bishops if these should be brought to them. Next, these canons were already abrogated by other canons, as the Glossa asserts in the same place. It is evident that the second canon says that it is not for a prince to fashion laws but for a particular bishop; yet it is of uncertain authority, which is why it is marked by the term *Palaea*. Besides it can be understood in a correct manner, that is, concerning all contentions which cannot be settled by the secular judges, whether because the judge does not want to administer justice, or the other party does not wish to obey, for then the cases fall upon the judgment of the Church through the way of fraternal correction, as Innocent III rightly teaches.[6]

4) The fourth argument is that when the ruler is away, the Supreme Pontiff succeeds in administration, and uses imperial power until another emperor has been elected, as was held by Innocent III,[7] and the Council of Vienne.[8] For that reason, it is a sign that imperial power flows from the Supreme Pontiff just as from a supreme temporal prince.

I respond: The Pope succeeded the emperor when the throne was vacant, but not in all matters, rather only in the authority to judge and settle those cases which the emperor usually judged, and those matters which do not easily suffer delay. But the reason for this is not that the Pope is a supreme temporal prince, but that all cases cannot be settled by temporal judges come down to the spiritual judge, as we will say below and have said for our part.

---

[6] *Novit*, de iudiciis.

[7] Cap. *Licet*, de foro competenti.

[8] *Clement. pastoralis, de sententia et re iudicata.*

CHAPTER VI
The Pope Indirectly Holds Temporal Power

HE TEACHING of the theologians must be expressed and then also proved. Thus we assert: 1) the Pope as Pope, even if he does not have any merely temporal power, still has the supreme power to manage the temporal affairs of all Christians for the sake of the spiritual good. Many explain this by means of a similitude to the art of bridle making and the equestrian art and similar things. For as these two arts are different among themselves, because they have more distinct objects and subjects and actions, nevertheless, because the end of one is ordered to the end of the other therefore, one is in charge of the other and prescribes laws for it; so the ecclesiastical and political powers seem to be distinct, and still are subordinated to one end, because the end of one is referred to the other.

But this similitude is not altogether agreeable. For in those arts the inferior exists only on account of the superior, to the extent that if you take away the superior you immediately get rid of the inferior. For if there was no equestrian art, certainly the makers of bridles would be redundant. But political power does not exist only on account of the ecclesiastical, for even if the ecclesiastical did not exist, still the political would exist, as is clear among the infidels, where true temporal and political power exists and still without being ordered towards some true ecclesiastical and spiritual power.

Therefore, another similitude is by far more suitable for us, which St. Gregory Nazianzen gives in an oration to a people demoralized by fear and an angry emperor. For as the flesh and the spirit exist in a man, so the two powers exist in the Church. Flesh and the spirit are like two republics, which can be found separated and joined. The flesh has the sense and the appetite in which acts and proportionate objects correspond, and the immediate end of all these is health and the good constitution of the body. The spirit has the intellect, will, acts and their proportionate objects for the purpose of health and perfection of the soul. The flesh is discovered without the spirit among the brute animals, and the spirit is discovered without the flesh among the angels.

From such it appears that neither exists precisely on account of the other, for flesh is found joined to the spirit in man where, because they make one person, necessarily they hold a subordination and connection. For the flesh is subject while the spirit is preeminent, although the spirit does not mix itself in the actions of the flesh, but corrects it to exercise all its actions, as it exercises in brute animals. Yet, when these impede the end of the spirit itself, the spirit commands the flesh, and castigates it if it must, commands fastings, and other afflictions, even with some detriment and weakness to the flesh itself. It also compels the tongue not to speak, the eyes not to see, etc. For equal reason, if to obtain the end of the spirit some operation of the flesh would be necessary—and even death itself—the spirit can command the flesh that it should expose itself, as we see in the martyrs.

So political power has altogether its princes, laws, judgments etc., and likewise the Church has its bishops, canons and judgments. The former has for its end temporal peace, the latter, eternal salvation. Sometimes they are found separated, as formerly in the time of the Apostles, and sometimes they are found joined, as even now; but when they are joined, they make one body, and therefore ought to be connected, the lower subjected to the higher, and subordinated.

Therefore, the spiritual does not mix itself in temporal business, but permits all things to proceed as before they were joined, provided it does not hinder the spiritual end, or those things necessary to obtain it. But if it should be necessary, the spiritual power ought also to coerce the temporal in every way in which it appears necessary.

Now, let us explain all these matters in more detail. The spiritual power of the Pope must be compared with the persons of judges, or of secular princes, with their civil laws and with their forum and judgments.

Inasmuch as it concerns persons, the Pope, as Pope, cannot ordinarily depose temporal princes, even for a just cause, in the way in which he deposes bishops, i.e., just as an ordinary judge; yet he can take a kingdoms away from one and bestow it on another as the supreme spiritual prince if it would be necessary for the salvation of souls, as we will prove.

Insofar as it concerns laws, the Pope cannot ordinarily, as Pope, make civil law, or strengthen or weaken the laws of princes, because he is not the political prince of the Church. Still, he can do all those things if some civil law would be necessary to the salvation of souls and still, kings would not wish to make such a law, or if another would be injurious to the salvation of souls but still kings do not wish to abrogate it.

Therefore the best law is that which the Glossa hands down which is:[1] When imperial laws are discovered contrary to papal ones on the same matter, and the matter of the law concerns danger to souls, the imperial law is abrogated by the pontifical law. And in this way pontifical law, which is contained in the chapter *Finali*, on the prescriptions, abrogated an imperial law which is contained in the Codex on prescriptions that were thirty or fifty years old; it was also made with bad faith, because it could not be preserved without mortal sin. But when the mater of the law is a temporal affair that does not

---

[1] Ad cap. *Possessor*, de regula Juris in Sexto.

concern the salvation of souls, pontifical law does not abrogate the imperial, but each is preserved, the former in the ecclesiastical forum, the latter in the civil forum.

Insofar as judgments are concerned, the Pope cannot as Pope, ordinarily judge on temporal affairs. St. Bernard rightly says to Pope Eugene: "These low and earthly matters have their own judges, kings and princes of the earth. Why do you invade foreign boundaries? Why does your sickle stretch out to a foreign harvest? ... your power is in crimes, not in possessions."[2] But, just the same, in those cases which are necessary to the salvation of souls, the Pope can also assume temporal judgments, when, without a doubt, there is nobody who could judge, e.g., when two supreme kings contend, or when those who can and ought to judge will not pass judgment. For that reason, the same Bernard said: "It is one thing to sally into those matters per chance as an incident requires, but another to press on in such affairs, as if the nature of such things merited such a focus.." And Innocent III, says that the Pope exercises temporal jurisdiction only accidentally.[3]

---

[2] *De consideration*, lib. 1

[3] cap. *Per venerabilem*, on those who would be legitimate sons.

CHAPTER VII
The Teaching of the Theologians is Proven by Reason

HEREFORE, this teaching can be proven in two ways, by reasoning and examples.

a) The civil power has been subjected to the spiritual power when each part is of the same Christian republic. Therefore the spiritual prince can command temporal princes and dispose of temporal affairs for the sake of a spiritual good. For every superior can command an inferior.

Moreover, that political power, not only as it is Christian, but even as it is political, would be subjected to the ecclesiastical power. This is so for three reasons: a) It is proven from the end of each. For the temporal end is subordinated to the spiritual end, as is clear because temporal happiness is not absolutely the final end, and therefore, ought to be referred to eternal happiness; besides it is certain from Aristotle that as the faculties are subordinated, so are the ends.[1]

b) Kings and Popes, clergy and laity, do not make two republics, rather one. This is one Church, for we are all one body[2] but in every body the members are connected and there is a dependency of one upon the other. Moreover, it is not rightly asserted that spiritual matters depend upon temporal ones; rather temporal matters depend upon and are subjected to the spiritual.

c) If the temporal administration impedes a spiritual good, the judgment of all is that the temporal prince must change that mode of governance, even to the detriment of the temporal good; therefore it is a sign that the temporal power is subject to the spiritual.

Nor would the response of some satisfy, namely that the prince is held to change the plan of his governance, not on account of subjection or subordination to the spiritual power, but only due to the order of charity, in which we are held to put the greater goods ahead of lesser ones.

This is because one state is not held to suffer detriment for the sake of charity, lest another more noble state suffer a detriment. And one private man who is held to give all his goods for the conversion of his state is not still held to do likewise on account of a foreign state, although it would be nobler. Therefore, when a temporal state is held to suffer detriment on account of the spiritual power, it is a sign that these two are not different, but parts of one and the same, and one is subject to the other.

---

[1] I *Ethic.* lib. 1, cap. 1.

[2] Romans 12:4-8; 1 Cor. 12:4-31.

Nor would it avail if one were to say that a temporal prince is not held to suffer detriment for the spiritual good; not because of the subjection to the spiritual state, but because otherwise he would harm his own subjects for whom it is evil to lose spiritual things for the sake of temporal ones. This is because even if they are not subjects, but men of another kingdom who suffer notable injury in spiritual matters on account of the temporal administration of some Christian king, that king is held to change his mode of governance; for which matter no other reason can be given but that they are members of the same body, and one subject to another.

2) The ecclesiastical state ought to be perfect, and sufficient to itself for the sake of its end, just as are all well established states; therefore, it ought to have all the power necessary to attain its end. But the power of using and disposing in regard to temporal affairs is necessary to a spiritual end, otherwise wicked princes could foster heretics with impunity as well as overturn religion. Therefore, the ecclesiastical state has this power.

Likewise, each state can (because it ought to be perfect and sufficient unto itself) command another state that is not subject to it, and compel it to change its administration, nay more, even depose its prince and institute another, when it cannot otherwise defend itself from his injuries. Therefore the spiritual state can command much more than the temporal state subject to it, and compel it to change administration as well as depose its princes, and also to institute others when it cannot safeguard its spiritual good. And in this way the words of St. Bernard[3] and Pope Boniface VIII[4] must be understood, where they say that both swords are in the power of the Pope. For they mean the Pope has in himself properly the spiritual sword, and because the temporal sword is subject to the spiritual, the Pope can command a king, or interdict the use of the temporal sword when the necessity of the Church requires it.

These are the words of St. Bernard, which Pope Boniface imitated: "Why do you (he says addressing the Pope) again try to usurp the sword, which you once bid to be sheathed? Still, anyone who would deny this it seems does not sufficiently attend the word of the Lord, saying 'put your sword back in its sheath.' Therefore, yours must be sheathed at least by your nod, if not by our hand; otherwise in no way does it pertain to you and that, while the Apostles were saying: 'Behold here there are two swords,' the Lord would not have responded: 'It is enough,' but "it is too much". Therefore, the Church has each sword, the spiritual and the material, but it is on behalf of the Church. Moreover, the Church must exercise it. The one at the hand of the priest, the

---

[3] *de Consideratione*, lib. 4.

[4] *loc. cit.*

other at the hand of the soldier, but rightly at the nod of the priest, and the command of the emperor." There it should also be noted that when the heretics condemn Pope Boniface's teaching as erroneous, arrogant, tyrannical (for thus they say in all their works about him), they ought to be warned that they should think the same about the words of St. Bernard in the books of *de Consideratione*, where he so spoke without flattery that Calvin said that truth itself seems to speak.[5]

3) Christians may not tolerate an infidel or heretical king if he would try to drag his subjects to his heresy or infidelity. Yet, to judge whether the king forces to heresy or not pertains to the Pope, to whom the care of religion was consigned. Therefore, it is for the Pope to judge whether a king ought to be deposed or not.

The proposition of this argument is proved from chapter 17 of Deuteronomy, where the people are forbidden to choose a king who would not be from their brethren, that is, not a Jew, lest he would compel the Jews to idolatry;[6] consequently, Christians are prohibited to choose a king that is not Christian.

That is a moral precept and it rests upon natural justice. Again, to choose a non-Christian or not depose a non-Christian pertains to the same danger and injury that we have noted; thus, Christians are held not to suffer a non-Christian king over them if he would try to turn the people away from the faith. I add this condition, on account of infidel princes who had their rule over the people before the people converted to the faith. For if such princes do not try to turn the faithful away from the faith, then I do not believe they can be deprived of their dominion, although St. Thomas thought the contrary.[7] But if these same princes would try to turn the people from the faith, all agree they can and ought to be deprived of their dominion.

But if Christians in ancient times did not depose Nero, Diocleatian, Julian the Apostate and Valens the Arian, as well as many like them, that was because Christians lacked temporal strength. That they could lawfully do it just the same is clear from the Apostle when he bids new judges constituted by Christians for the sake of their temporal affairs, lest Christians be compelled to make their case in the presence of the judge who might be a persecutor of Christ.[8] As new judges could be constituted, so even new princes and kings for the same reason, if they were to possess sufficient strength to do so.

---

[5] *Instit.* lib. 4, cap. 11 §10.

[6] Deut. 17:15.

[7] *II IIae*, quaest. 10, article 10.

[8] 1 Cor. 6:4-5.

Besides, to tolerate a heretical or infidel king trying to drag men to his own sect is to expose religion to the clearest danger, as we read in Ecclesiasticus, "For those who live in the city will be like unto its ruler,"[9] and from that: "The whole world is conformed to the example of the king." And experience teaches the same thing; when King Jeroboam was idolatrous a great part of the kingdom began to worship idols.[10] After the coming of Christ, during the reign of Constantine, Arianism flourished; during the reign of Julian, Paganism again flourished; even in our times in England, during the reign of Henry VIII and afterward Edward VI, the whole kingdom apostatized from the faith in a certain measure. Under Mary, again the whole kingdom returned to the Church, while under the reign of Elizabeth Calvinism again began to rule and banished the true religion.

But Christians are not held, nay more, ought not tolerate an infidel king when there is evident danger to religion. For when divine and human law are opposed, divine law should be preserved and human law omitted. Moreover, to keep divine law is to keep true faith and religion, which is one, not many, but concerning human law it is merely that of this or that king.

Next, why can a faithful people not be free from the yoke of an infidel king, and free from being dragged to infidelity, if a wife who is Christian is free from the obligation of remaining with an unbelieving husband without injury to faith (outside of those issues involved in divorce), provided that he does not wish to remain with a Christian wife, as is clearly deduced from Paul?[11] For it is no less a power of a spouse over spouse, than of a king over his subjects, albeit in a greater degree.

4) When kings and princes come to the Church to become Christian, they are received with the explicit or tacit agreement that they will subject their scepters to Christ and promise that they are going to preserve and defend the faith of Christ, even under the penalty of the loss of their kingdom. Therefore, when they become heretics or harm religion, they can be judged by the Church and even deposed from their rule; nor is any injury done them if they are deposed. One who is not prepared to serve Christ and to lose whatever he has on account of him is not suited to the Sacrament of Baptism, for the Lord says, "If anyone comes to me, and does not hate father and mother, wife and sons, even his life, he cannot be my disciple."[12] Besides, the Church would grievously

---

[9] Ecclesiasticus (Sirach) 10:2.

[10] 3 (1) Kings 12:26-33.

[11] 1 Cor. 7:12-26; Innocent III, cap. *Gaudeamus.*

[12] Luke 14:26.

err if she were to admit some king who willed to foster some sect with impunity, as well as defend heretics and overturn religion.

5) When it was said to Peter: "Feed my sheep,"[13] all faculty was given to him which is necessary for a shepherd to guard the flock which is threefold:

a) Concerning wolves, to ward them off by any means they can; b) concerning rams, that if ever they harm the flock with their horns, he can enclose and forbid them lest they go any further ahead of the flock; c) concerning the remaining sheep, that he should give agreeable food to each one, therefore the supreme Pontiff has this threefold power.

From here, three arguments are deduced from this passage. Firstly, wolves who devastate the Church of the Lord are heretics, as is clear from Matthew, "Beware of false prophets, etc."[14] Therefore, if some from the sheep or rams would become a heretic, that is, go from being Christians to heretics, the shepherd of the Church can ward them off with excommunication and at the same time bid the people not to follow them, and hence deprive a man of dominion over his subjects.

Secondly, the pastor can separate and enclose furious destructive rams from the flock, and a prince is a furious destructive ram in the sheepfold when he is of the Catholic faith but is exceedingly wicked and does great harm to religion and the Church, such as if he were to sell episcopacies, destroy churches, etc. Consequently, the shepherd of the Church can enclose him, or return him to the rank of the sheep.

The third argument is that the pastor can and ought to so feed all his sheep as is fitting for them. Therefore, the Pope can and ought to command these things from Christians and compel them to each of those things to which they are held according to their state in life. That is, to compel individuals that they should serve God in the way in which they ought to according to their state. Moreover, kings ought to serve God by defending the Church and punishing heretics as well as schismatics, as St. Augustine, St. Leo and St. Gregory teach.[15] Therefore, he can and ought to command kings that they should do this, and unless they will have done it, he will compel them through excommunication and other fitting measures.[16]

---

[13] John 21:17.

[14] Matthew 7:15.

[15] Epist. 50 *ad Bonifacium*; epist. 75 *ad Leonem Augustum*,; Gregory lib. 2 epist. 61 *ad Mauritium*.

[16] See more in Nicholas Sanders, *de visibili Monarchia*, lib. 2, cap. 4. There you will discover many of those things we said above.

CHAPTER VIII
The Same thing is Proved by Examples

OW we come to examples. 1) We read in 2 Chronicles 26 that King Uzziah, when he had usurped the office of the priests, was cast out of the temple by the high priest, and when on account of the same sin he was struck with leprosy by God, he was also compelled to leave the city and resign the kingdom to his son. Moreover, he was not deprived of the city and administration of the kingdom by his own will, but by the judgment of the priest. For we read in Leviticus, "Whoever has been stained with leprosy, being set apart at the judgment of the priest, he will live alone outside the camp."[1] Therefore, when this law was in Israel, and at the same time we read 2 Chronicles 26, that the king dwelt alone outside the city in a solitary house, and his son judged the people of the land in the city, we are compelled to say that he was separated at the judgment of the priest, and consequently, deprived from the authority of rule. So, if because of corporal leprosy the priest could once judge and deprive a king of rule, why could he not do that in the case of spiritual leprosy, or in other words because of heresy, which is prefigured through leprosy as St. Augustine teaches;[2] especially when Paul says that everything happened to the Jews in figure?[3]

2) In 2 Chronicles 23 we read that when Athalia tyrannically occupied the kingdom and fostered the worship of Baal, Jehoiada, the high priest, called sergeants and soldiers, and commanded them to kill Athalia, which they also did and created Joas king in her place. There, the high priest did not persuade, but commanded, and it is clear from the words of 4 Kings, "And they made sergeants according to all things which the priest Jehoiada commanded them."[4] And likewise from 2 Chronicles, "Jehoiada the high priest went out to the sergeants and chiefs of the army; he said to them: 'Lead her (Queen Athalia) outside the precincts of the temple,' and she was killed outside with a sword."[5] The fact is that the reason for this deposition and killing of Athalia was not only that she was a tyrant, but because she also fostered the worship of Baal, which is clear from the words which are placed immediately after her death: "Therefore, all the people went into the house of Baal, and destroyed it, and

---

[1] Leviticus 13:45.

[2] In questionibus Evangel., lib. 2, quaest. 40.

[3] 1 Cor. 10:6, 11.

[4] 4 Kings (2 Kings) 11:9.

[5] 2 Paral. (Chron.) 24:14-15.

621

broke both the altars and the idols; they also killed Mathan, the priest of Baal, before the altar."

3) The example of Blessed Ambrose. When he was bishop of Milan he was also the pastor and spiritual father of the Emperor Theodosius, who ordinarily kept court at Milan. First, he excommunicated the emperor on account of the slaughter which he had commanded his soldiers to make at Thessalonika, then commanded him to impose a law to invalidate the death sentences or the confiscation of goods but for thirty days from the pronouncement of the sentence, so that what had been commanded from anger should be so drawn up that within the space of as many days it could be recalled.[6]

Yet, Ambrose could not excommunicate Theodosius for that slaughter, unless he knew and judged the case beforehand; although were it a criminal case it would have pertained to the external forum. Moreover, he could not know and judge a case of this sort unless he was also the legitimate judge of Theodosius in the external forum.

Besides, to compel an emperor to impose a political law and to prescribe for him the form of law, does not this manifestly show that a bishop can use temporal power now and again, even over those who received power over others? If a bishop can do it, how much more the prince of bishops?

4) Gregory I conceded a privilege to the monastery of St. Medard, which is contained at the end of the epistles: "If anyone, be they kings, bishops, judges or any other secular person, should violate the decrees of this apostolic authority and of our precept, no matter how great his dignity and highness might be, he shall be deprived from that honor."

5) Gregory II excommunicated the emperor Leo the Iconoclast and forbade taxes to be paid to him from Italy, and hence he punished him with a fine in part of his empire. Even the Centuriators affirm this,[7] but they condemn Gregory and call him a traitor to his own country. But they advance no writer who censures the deed of Gregory, while on the other hand we have many writers who praised this deed as holy and legitimate, such as Cedrenus, Zonaras[8] and all other historians who wrote on the deeds of these times.

6) Pope Zachary, who was asked by the nobles of France to depose Childeric and create Pepin, the father of Charlemagne, as king in his place. The reason was that due to the inaction of Childeric, it seemed that religion and the very kingdom in France were on the verge of ruin, as is clear from Cedrenus in the

---

[6] Theodoret, *hist.* lib. 5, cap. 17.

[7] Cent. 8 cap. 10 *in vita Gregorii* II

[8] In *Vita Leonis Isauri.*

life of Leo the Isaurian, Paul the Deacon,[9] and St. Boniface in his epistle to Pope Zachary.

The heretics also acknowledge this deed and condemn it, such as the Centuriators who say that Pope Zachary violently assumed quasi-divine authority to himself.[10] Still, there is no ancient author that can be found who condemned this deed, moreover we have a great many more approved authors on our side, such as Ado, Sigebert and Rhegius;[11] but on this matter we spoke enough previously against Calvin.[12]

7) Leo III translated the empire from the Greeks to the Germans, for the reason that the Greeks could advance no help to the labor of the western church. From this it came to pass, that although imperial dignity must not be considered to absolutely come from the Pope, but from God by means of the law of nations (as we showed above from Gelasius, Nicholas and Innocent III), nevertheless emperors at the time of Charlemagne owed their rule to the Pope.

The fact that this power is now with the Germans is due to the Pope, and although it is not absolutely necessary that the Pope would confirm the emperor, or that the emperor furnish an oath of fidelity to the Pope, still from the time of the translation of the empire to the Germans, each is required, as is clear from Innocent III,[13] and this is not required unjustly. Whoever could confer the empire upon the Germans for the safety of the Church could also link certain conditions to it, on account of the same cause, lest it would happen that a heretic or schismatic be created emperor.

Our adversaries respond to this example in two ways: a) Some deny the fact that the Pope transferred the empire from the Greeks to the Germans; the Centuriators are clearly in this number of those that say: "This translation is clearly among the miracles of Antichrist."[14] Theodore Bibliander says that Leo III, having usurped authority, transferred the empire from the Greeks to the Germans.[15] b) Others assert that it was done by law, but the Pope was not the agent, rather it was the Roman people. Marsilius of Padua thinks thus, as Albert Pighius relates.[16]

---

[9] Lib. 6, cap. 5 de gestis longobardorum.

[10] Cent. 8, cap. 10.

[11] In *Chronicles.*

[12] Book 2, ch. 17.

[13] Cap. *Venerabilem, extra de electione* and *Clementina unica de jurejurando.*

[14] *Centur.* 8 cap. 10, colum. 751.

[15] Tabula 10 *suae Chronologiae.*

[16] Lib. 5 *Hierarch. Ecclesiasticae,* cap. 14.

To the first I respond: It is a certain fact that this translation was done lawfully and legitimately. Firstly, from the consent of the whole Christian world, because all Christians held Charlemagne for their true emperor as well as his successors; there was never any Christian king who wished to go before the emperor, even if their power and kingdom were more ancient. The Lutherans were the first to despoil the people from faith and religion and also plotted to topple the emperor from his seat.[17]

Secondly, we consider the happy event of this translation. God adorned Charles with many victories to show this fact; he made this kingdom the most flourishing and useful to the Church. Thirdly, from the confession of the Emperor of the Greeks, who at one time did not concede that the Roman Pontiff could do this, but later did. For in the first place when the Empress Irene heard that Charles had been called emperor by Leo, not only did she not protest, but even wished to marry Charlemagne, and she would have but for the impudence of a treacherous eunuch, as Zonaras writes as well as Cedrenus in the life of the same Irene.

Next, after Irene died, Emperor Nicephorus, who succeeded her, sent legates to Charlemagne, as though he were emperor, as Ado writes in his chronicle for the year 803; and a little after the death of Nicephorus, Michael succeeded him, and likewise sent legates to Charlemagne, who clearly greeted him as emperor, which Ado writes in his Chronicle for the year 810. Not only the Greeks, but even the Persian legates sent gifts to the emperor, as Rhegius[18] and Otho of Frisia write.[19] Again, Immanuel, the Emperor of the Greeks, when he heard that Pope Alexander III was reduced to extreme necessity by Emperor Frederich, offered help to the same Pope, as well as give a vast sum of money if he would return the Empire of the West to the emperors of Constantinople. But the Pope responded that he would not unite what his ancestors had divided even for the best and most advantageous reasons. There, it must be noted that Immanuel did not want any more from the Pope than the title of Emperor. He knew well enough that the Pope could not give actual possession; rather it would have to

---

[17] Translator's note: Here, Bellarmine refers to the attempt to get the archbishop of Cologne to convert to Lutheranism so as to have enough electors to elect a Lutheran prince over the Empire. The archbishop was given to hunting and the trappings of aristocracy, but was not a theologian, and went in that direction until the maneuvering of Charles V destroyed the Smalkaldic league and made that impossible. A detailed account from primary sources can be found in *St. Peter Canisius*, by Broderick, S.J., in chapter 3.

[18] Lib. 2.

[19] Lib. , cap. 31; see also Blondus lib. 5, decadis 2, and Platina *in vita Alexander III.*

be acquired by force of arms. But he would not have wanted to buy the title for such a price if it were empty, or even false, or if he believed it was illegitimate.

To the others, who say the author of the translation was not the Pope, but the Roman people, it is easy to respond. In the first place the Roman people almost never had the power to create the emperor. The ancient emperors either had rule by hereditary right, such as Octavian, Tiberius, Gaius [Caligula], or were created by the army as was Claudius, Vespasian and others. It was the ordinary custom, that the Emperor be created by the army, as St. Jerome witnesses in his epistle to Evagrius.

For that reason, we read an extant canon[20] from the time of Charlemagne, that there was no army of the Romans who could create him emperor. In Italy there were only the armies of the Greeks and the Lombards and all these were hostile to Charlemagne. It is also certain that he did not have any hereditary right to rule.

Next, if the Roman people ever had any authority in the election of an Emperor, they lost it when the seat of the empire was transferred to Constantinople. Thereafter, for nearly five-hundred years from Constantine the Great even to Charlemagne, the Senate and the Roman people never did anything in regard to the creation of an emperor.

Besides, all authors who write on this matter, such as Zonaras and Cedrenus,[21] Paul the Deacon,[22] Ado,[23] Albert Krantz,[24] Odo of Frisia,[25] Marianus Scotus, Hermannus Contractus, Lambertus, Sigebert, Rhegius, Palmerius, Blondus, and all others, *Chronicles* or *Histories* of Leo III assert that he transferred the Empire from the Greeks to the Franks (Germans). Innocent III teaches the same thing when he says: "The right and power of this sort comes to them from the Apostolic See, which transferred the empire from the Greeks to the Germans in the person of the magnificent Charles."[26] And he adds that the princes of Germany certainly recognize it. Charlemagne himself did not treat this ambiguously when he wrote his testament, wherein he leaves behind his sons as heirs of the empire. He sent it to Pope Leo that it would be confirmed by him, as Ado writes in his *Chronicle* for the year 804. Next, the same is clear from the confession of the Greek emperor Emmanuel, as was noted above.

---

[20]   Dist. 93.

[21]   In *vita Irenae.*

[22]   Lib. 23 *Rerum Romanarum.*

[23]   In *Chronico anni DCCC.*

[24]   In *Metropoli*, lib. 1, cap. 14

[25]   Lib. 5, cap. 31

[26]   Cap. *Venerabilem, de electione.*

8) Gregory V published a law on the election of the emperor by seven German princes, which is preserved even to our day. That this is so, many historians assert;[27] even the Centuriators acknowledge this in these words: "Gregory was going to adorn his country with some notable dignity, so he ratified that the law of choosing a king was in the power of the Germans alone, so that after the emperor had received the crown from the Roman Pontiff, he would be called Augustus. Electors were constituted as at Moguntianum, Trier, the archbishop of Cologne, the Marquise of Brandenburg, the Count Palatine of the Rhine, the Duke of Saxony and the king of Bohemia."[28] Whether the Pope had done this lawfully, they do not disclose. But if they were to say it was done lawfully, then they would be compelled to affirm that the Pope is superior to emperor and princes, as is clear; but if they would say it was not lawful but done tyrannically, they would injure their patrons and protectors, such as the Duke of Saxony, the Count of the Palatine and the Marquis of Brandenburg. For what do they have that is greater than an electorate? But it would not have been done rightly if he who gave it could not give it. Moreover, that the Pope gave it is beyond controversy.

Here we must note that Onuphrius writes against the common opinion of the historians,[29] in that this decree on the election of the emperor was not of Gregory V but Gregory X. I rather think that even if the matter was so, concerning which we now treat, it would cause no harm. Still it is not true, for Innocent III, who sat 70 years before Gregory X, indicates that it had already been conceded by the Apostolic See a long time before for specific German princes to have the right to elect the emperor.[30] Heinrich Hostius, who lived before the times of Gregory X, says in his commentary on the chapter of Innocent we just mentioned, that Innocent speaks of the seven electors. Pelagius Alvarus, who lived a little after the times of Gregory X, also mentions everything Gregory X did but affirms that the election of the Emperor which is now in use was established by Gregory V, and he enumerates the seven electors in the same place which we had named above.[31]

9) Gregory VII deposed Emperor Henry IV and bid another to be chosen, and even the Centuriators affirm this event.[32] That this deed was done with the

---

[27] Blondus, decade 2, lib. 3; Nauclerus, *generat.* 34; Platina *in vita Gregorii V.*

[28] Cent. 10, cap. 10, col. 546

[29] Lib. *de comitiis imperialibus.*

[30] In that chapter *Venerabilem.*

[31] Lib. 1 art. 41, de planctu Ecclesiae.

[32] Cent. 11, cap. 10, in *vita Gregorii VII.*

approval and applause of all good men we have already shown in the previous book, where we defended the Popes from so many calumnies of the heretics.[33]

10) Innocent III deposed Otho IV in a similar fashion, as is clear from Blondus.[34]

11) Innocent IV, at the general council of Lyons (with the consent of all the Fathers), deposed Frederick II and declared the empire vacant for 28 years, as Matthew Palmerius records in his *Chronicle*. The whole sentence imposed on Frederick is extant.[35] Innocent IV was also a coadjutor to a certain king of Portugal to administer the kingdom, seeing that the negligence of the king was to the detriment of the state and religion in Portugal.[36]

12) Clement VI deposed Emperor Louis IV who had been excommunicated by John XXII and Benedict XII. You can see his history in the works of Albert Pighius,[37] and Robert Arboricensis.[38]

The arguments of our adversaries were partly answered in book 2 of this work, and can partly be answered from the foregoing with scarcely any labor. See Juan de Torquemada,[39] and Albert Pighius;[40] there they answer certain arguments, but they are light and easy.

---

[33] Book 4, ch. 12.

[34] *Decade* 2, lib. 6.

[35] Cap. *ad Apostolicae de sentential et re iudicata, in sexto.*

[36] That is found in the chapter *Grandi,* on the supplying for the negligence of Prelates, in the sixth.

[37] Libro *Hierarch. Ecclesiasti.* 5, cap. 14 et 15.

[38] *De utroque gladio,* tomo 2, theoremate 7.

[39] *Summae,* lib. 2, cap. ult. et penultimo.

[40] Lib. 5, cap. 15.

CHAPTER IX

It is Not Opposed with the Word of God that one man Would be an Ecclesiastical Prince and a Political one at the Same Time

SO WE proceed unto the third part of the question, since our adversaries teach two specific things on the temporal rule which the Supreme Pontiff has.[1] 1) That he occupies the possession by mere theft; 2) even if he did have a just title, he cannot lawfully retain it because it is opposed with spiritual rule, as Calvin so argues.[2] It behooves us to show both, so as to prove that it can be fitting for the Pope to have and possess a sovereignty of this sort, both really and justly, which he has and does possess.

Therefore, that it is not opposed for the Pope to be at the same time a spiritual prince and the prince of some province, is proven first from the examples of the saints who were found to be both kings and priests. For in the law of nature Melchisedech was a king and a priest, as is clear from Genesis 14 and Hebrews 7 and more to the point, once the first born son was both king and priest, as St. Jerome teaches.[3]

It is also certain that Noah, Abraham, Isaac and Jacob were both in charge of those matters that pertained to religion as well as those which pertained to political life.

Next, that Moses was both a temporal high prince and the High Priest is clear from Scripture. For in Exodus 18 it is said: "Moses sat to judge the people." And in chapter 32 he commanded a great number of the people to be slain for idolatry. In chapter 40 he burnt incense to the Lord, which was the proper office of the priest in particular.[4] Likewise in Leviticus 8, Moses consecrated Aaron into the priesthood, sanctified the tabernacle and altar, offered sacrifices and holocausts, something that only the priest can do. Therefore, Philo of Alexandria says at the end of his *Life of Moses*: "This is the life, this is the death of Moses the king, lawgiver, priest and prophet."[5] Gregory Nazianzen, in his oration to Gregory of Nyssa, says: "Moses, the prince of princes, and priest of priests, used

---

[1] Translator's note: The temporal sovereignty refers to the Papal States, which the Pope ruled since ancient times, and that he continued to hold through Bellarmine's time even until 1870. While in modern times this discussion might be said to be redundant, still there are important principles which Bellarmine discusses here.

[2] *Instit.*, lib. 4, cap. 11, §8 and 11.

[3] *Hebrew Questions*, on Genesis 49, *Ruben primogenitus meus.*.

[4] 2 Chronicles, 26:18.

[5] Philo, *de vita Moysis*, lib. 3.

Aaron for a tongue." Next, Augustine said about the reign of Moses: "He sat alone in judicial loftiness, while all the people stood about."[6] On his priesthood, he says, "Together they were high priests, Moses and Aaron."[7]

Additionally, Heli was both priest and a judge in state for forty years, as is clear from 1 Kings (1 Samuel) I and IV. Then the Maccabees, Judas, Jonathan, Simon, John and the rest, even to Herod who was at the same time high priest and head of state, as is clear from the book of Maccabees, and from Josephus.[8]

Secondly, it is proved by reason. a) ecclesiastical power and political power are not contrary, but both are good, both are from God, both are praiseworthy and one serves the other, so they are not opposed in and of themselves. Therefore, they can be in the same subject.

b) Peace and war are more diverse than temporal and spiritual goods, but one and the same king at the same time is over the senate and the army, civilians and combatants, so one can be much more in charge in both temporal and spiritual matters.

c) One king can govern a very diverse realm, even if it should have very different customs, rites, laws, and traditions, and for equal reason one bishop can rule a great many churches, as is clear from the ancient patriarchs (that I might omit the Roman), each of which had a great number of bishops under him; therefore one man can rule one episcopate, and one realm. Thus, it is either more difficult to rule an episcopate than a realm, easier, or equally difficult. If more difficult, then if one man rules two episcopates, he will rule one episcopate and one dominion from the greater of the two; if it is easier, then he rules two dominions so he will rule one dominion and one episcopate from the greater of the dominions; if it is equally difficult then if one man rules two dominions or two episcopates, in a similar fashion he will be able to rule one episcopate and one dominion.

d) Those who donated their temporal rule to the bishop of Rome and other bishops were pious men, and for that reason they were especially commended by the whole Church, as is clear in the example of Constantine, Charlemagne and Louis his son, who was thereafter called the pious. Even our adversaries praise them, and on the other hand, when some rulers tried to take away a temporal dominion of this sort, such as King Aistulphus of the Lombards, Henry IV and V, Otho IV, Frederick I and II, then all historians regarded them as impious and sacrilegious.

---

[6] Q. 68 in Exod.

[7] Q. 23 in Levit.

[8] *Antiquit.* lib. 12, et sequentibus.

Ado writes thus about Aistulphus in his *Chronicle*: "Aistulphus, the king of the Lombards, was treacherous and gave the resources of the Roman Church to his own soldiers... Aistulphus, as a faithless man, always lied... by divine judgment, while he went on a hunt, right away he was struck and died."[9] Not only the historians, but a saint remarks on this. St. Bernard vehemently rebuked the Roman people because they had departed from obedience to Pope Eugene; the reason for this departure had been, according to Platina and other historians, that the Roman people refused to be under the Pontiff in temporal affairs, but wished to be governed by the ancient custom through republican consuls. On Henry IV, see what we said above.[10]

Nor were the best princes only those who so gave an inheritance to the Holy See, but even a great many of those who received wealth and dominion of this sort. Platina writes that Leo IV was glorified by miracles. All writers call Leo IX a saint, and Sigebert as well as Otho of Frisia write that he was glorified with miracles. Lambert Schaffnaburg wrote that Gregory VII was glorious with miracles, and one of the best men. As we have related many things about him above,[11] we will omit the rest. Peter from Aliacus, the bishop of Cambrai describes the life of Celestine V as very holy and glorified by miracles. Next, Adrian I, Leo III, Nicholas I, Innocent III and several others are praised by all writers, though it is certain enough that they administered both the earthly dominion together with the pontificate.

e) Lastly, it is shown by experience. Even if it were to be brought to bear that priests only treat spiritual things, and kings temporal, still, on account of the malice of the times experience declares that not only advantageously, but even necessarily, some temporal dominions were given to the Pope and even to other bishops by the singular providence of God. Moreover, if there were no prince bishops in Germany, then to this day none would have remained in their sees, just as in the Old Testament when there were priests without temporal dominion.

Moreover, in the last times of the Old Testament, religion could not survive and be defended except that the priests were also kings, namely in the time of the Maccabees. So also we see it happened in the Church, that it was not necessary to guard its majesty with temporal dominion in the first times, but now it seems necessary.

Indeed, the fact that the Supreme Pontiff lawfully has the temporal dominion he has can easily be proven because he had it from the gift of princes.

---

[9] *Chronicus anni* DCC. XXVIII.

[10] Book. 4, ch. 13.

[11] *Ibid.*

For thus Ado writes in his *Chronicle* for the year 727: "King Pepin, when he was over Ravenna, handed over the whole of the ten cities to the holy Apostles Peter and Paul."

Moreover, a decree of Louis I, the son of Charlemagne, is extant with Gratian in this form: "I, Louis, august emperor of the Romans, establish and concede through this accord of our confirmation to Blessed Peter, the prince of the Apostles, and through you his vicar the lord Paschal, the Supreme Pontiff, and his successors in perpetuity, just as it was in the power of your predecessors even to now it is your power, the dowry you hold and you have laid down over the city of Rome with its dukedom, and suburbs, mountain territories, coastal territories, ports or all cities, castles, towns and villas in the parts of Thuscia."[12]

Likewise, Leo, the bishop of Hostia, says: "The same celebrated king (Pepin) made with his sons a concession to Blessed Peter and his vicar the designated boundaries concerning the cities of Italy and its territories. From Luna with the island of Corsita, thence in Suranum in Mount Bardo, Vercetum, Parma, Rhegius, Mantua, and the mountain of Silicis, and at the same time the whole exarchate of Ravenna, just as it was more anciently, with the provinces of the Veneto and Histria, and the whole duchy of Spoleto and Benevento.... At length, the same king together with the Roman Pontiff coming into Italy subjected Ravenna and twenty cities taken from Aistulph to the Apostolic See."[13] The same Leo also writes, "In the year of the incarnation of the Lord, 1079, Count Matilda, fearing the army of the emperor Henry, devoutly offered the provinces of Liguria and Thuscia to Pope Gregory."[14]

The authentic documents of these donations and similar ones are extant at Rome. But even if none of these were extant, then by far the prescription of 800 years would be sufficient in itself. For even if the kingdoms and dominions were acquired by theft, at length they become legitimate after a long time. Otherwise, by what right would Julius Caesar have occupied the Roman Empire? And still, in the time of Tiberius, Christ said: "Give to Caesar that which is Caesar's."[15] By what right did the Franks invade France, the Saxons invade Britain, or the Goths Spain, and yet the kingdoms constituted by them in this time are still said to be legitimate?

---

[12] Dist. 63.

[13] *Chronici Cassiensis*, lib. 1, cap. 9

[14] loc. cit., lib. 3, cap. 48.

[15] Matth. 22:21.

CHAPTER X

The Contrary Arguments are Answered

IT REMAINS to answer arguments. The first is of John Calvin, who objects with a verse from Matthew 20: "The kings of the nations lord it over them, but it is not so with you." There he notes, "The Lord means the office of pastor is not only distinct from the office of a prince, but the matter is too separated to be composed in one man."[1] And because Calvin saw the example of Moses could be offered in refutation he added: "Although Moses held both together, in the first place it came to pass from a rare miracle; second it was temporary, until a better state of affairs could be arranged. Thus a certain form was prescribed by the Lord, thus civil governance was relinquished to him [Moses], while he was bidden to resign the priesthood to his brother, and rightly, for it is beyond nature for one man to sustain the burden of both."

I respond to both arguments. 1) In this passage the Lord only established mere ecclesiastical princes, and to teach them that, such as they are, they ought to be over their subjects not in the fashion of kings and masters, but in the fashion of fathers and pastors. Thence, it does not follow that one and the same man cannot be both bishop and prince.

Moreover, the example of Moses, which Calvin tries to evade, altogether convicts him. For what he says, that it came to pass by a rare miracle, is shown to be manifestly false by the examples we have already mentioned of Melchisedech, Heli, Judas Maccabaeus and others. What he adds, that it was only done until that time when Aaron was consecrated, has been shown as false by St. Augustine.[2] Commenting on Leviticus, he says that in that time Moses and Aaron were priests together, and it is proved from the fact that Moses deposed Aaron as high priest and consecrated Eleazar, the son of Aaron, in his place in Numbers 20. And besides, if after Aaron was ordained dominion and priesthood could no longer be combined in any one person, then how was Heli both a priest and ruler for 40 years? How were the Maccabees such for more than a hundred years?

Secondly, I say, with those words the Lord did not prohibit rule to bishops of the kind that is exercised by pious kings and princes, but the kind that is exercised by kings ignorant of God, who are more tyrants than kings. That much is clear from the propriety of the Greek words. For Matthew does not say: κυριεύουσιν αὐτῶν, that is, that they rule simply, but κατακυριέυουσιν, that is to dominate violently. Just as in 1 Peter 5: "Not lording it over the clergy," which

---

[1] *Instit.*, lib. 4, c. 11, §8.

[2] Q. 23 in Levit.

is: μηδ᾽ ὡς κατακυριεύοντες τῶν κλῆρον. In Joshua 15 we read, "Caleb said: 'Whoever will have struck Cariath-Sepher, and take it, etc.,'" but in Greek it is καὶ κατακυριεύσει αὐτῆς, that is, where this had been dominated, etc. Wherefore, 2 Peter 2 as well as in the Epistle of Jude 1:8, we see the heretics are condemned because they scorn κυριότητα (dominion).

Secondly, Calvin objects[3] from a verse in Luke where it says, "O man, who constituted me as a judge or as a distributor among you?"[4] This shows that the Lord rejected the office of judgment as though it were not fitting for the duty of a preacher and minister of the word, just as the Apostles: "It is not right for us to leave behind the Word of God and to wait on tables." One who is a prince, however, cannot reject these duties.

A response can be made to the words of the Lord. While the Lord received the person of the priest in this world, and not of a temporal prince, still by these words he warned simple priests not to mix in foreign business. But it can be said better, that generally in each place the Popes and princes are admonished lest they so busy themselves in trifling and vile duties that they are compelled to omit greater things. In this manner Jethro, when he saw Moses sat for the whole day to judge,[5] wisely admonished him not to lay aside political rule and only serve the Church, but so that he would constitute the lesser judges to satisfy the people in lighter matters, as well as that they would refer serious matters both political and ecclesiastical to him. Thus St. Bernard also exhorts the Pope with the same words of the Lord,[6] and by that medium he exhorts the Pope to delegate judgments on temporal matters to others, though he knew the Pope was a temporal prince.

Thereupon, though the Apostles omitted the care of waiting on tables in Jerusalem in this way, they still presided over temporal matters for the whole Church. For that reason, in Galatians 2:10, Peter, James and John are anxious for their brothers who were in Jerusalem, and they ask Paul and Barnabas that they would be mindful to gather some alms to send to Jerusalem. But they did that and brought money that they had collected themselves, not to deacons who were put in charge of tables, but to the elders, as it is contained in Acts 11:30.

Thirdly, Calvin objects using the words of St. Bernard: "Rule was forbidden to the Apostles; go, therefore, and dare to usurp or dominate the apostolate, or

---

3   Ibid, §9.

4   Luke 12:14.

5   Exodus 18:27.

6   Lib. 1 *de Consideratione*.

apostolic dominion. The apostolic model is this, rule is forbidden, ministry is proclaimed."[7]

I respond: Bernard speaks about the Pope as Pope of the whole Church and according to that which he has from the institution of Christ. For a little earlier he said: "Be so that you defend yourself in any other cause, but not by apostolic right, for what he did not have and could not have has not been given to you, etc." Consequently, Bernard meant that as pastor of all, he ought not exercise dominion over them, but to feed the flock; but just the same, just as a political prince rules the same sheep, insofar as they are citizens of his state, so also the Pope can exercise dominion over them for the same reason, if he were their political prince.

Fourthly, Calvin objects[8] with the words of St. Gregory, who says anathema to a bishop who commanded to be given the title to some field by a fiscal custom.[9] I respond: Little wonder if Gregory refused bishops and even those in charge of the patrimony of the Roman Church to use fiscal custom to recover fields for the Church. For the Church did not yet have a political prince, but possessed temporal goods by its custom in the way that private citizens possess such. Therefore, it was just that fields which the Church sensed were its own, if by chance they were to be seized by others, should be returned by a legitimate judgment, but not sold to her on her own authority by some fiscal custom.

Fifthly, others object with 2 Tim. 2:4, "No man in God's service should get mixed up in secular business." Such words are said to a bishop. But a prince cannot not fail to mix himself in secular business. I respond: In this passage, secular business is not called political rule, but care of preparing provisions, merchandise and like things. In Greek it is: "τοῦ βίου πραγματείαις, which means "in the business of life," or provisions. It must also be noted that the word "God" is not contained in the Greek or even in all Latin codices, rather the Greek has: οὐ δεὶς εστιρατευόμενος ἐμπλέκεται ταῖς τοῦ βίου πραγματέιαις.

And the sense is: *I have sent you as laborers just as a good soldier of Christ.* Hence, a good soldier is not anxious for the provisions and care of the body, but eats and drinks when he can, and how he can, sleeps on the ground, is clothed more in iron than soft garments, etc. Therefore, the apostle does not forbid political rule, but exceeding care over bodily life; and as Chrysostom rightly warned, these are said by Paul both to a bishop and to other men; for all, both the laity as well as kings, ought to be soldiers of Christ.

---

[7] Ibid § 11; Lib. 2 *de consid.*

[8] Ibid, §14.

[9] Lib. 4, epist. 44.

Sixthly, they object using the words of Nicholas I in his epistle to the Emperor Michael where he says that before the coming of Christ certain kings were also priests, but Christ the true king and priest separated these: "When in fact he came, he did not take to himself as an emperor any laws beyond the pontificate, nor as pontiff did he usurp the name of emperor, etc."

I respond: Nicholas refused to deny that some temporal rule can be fitting to the Pope, for he was a political prince of Rome and Ravenna, and his predecessors had long ago received the rule of these cities from their emperors. He only meant to say that it is not fitting that the same man should be the Pontiff of the whole world and at the same time emperor of the whole world, not that it is opposed to the Gospel and in no way could it be done. Since Christ willed to preserve humility, he willed that the Pope should require the defense of the emperor in temporal matters, and at the same time the emperor required the direction of the Pope in spiritual matters. Moreover, what Christ wished is clear from the fact that he left the empire behind to Tiberius, and upon Peter only conferred the pontificate.

End of the Third General Controversy

ON THE PRIMARY DUTY OF THE SOVEREIGN PONTIFF
From a Letter of St. Robert Bellarmine to Pope Clement VIII

Translated from:
EPISTULÆ FAMILIARES ROBERTI BELLARMINI
S.R.E. Cardinalis e Societate Jesu
Pragae, 1753

THE SUPREME PONTIFF bears a threefold person in the Church of God. He is the pastor and ruler of the universal Church; He is bishop of his own city of Rome; he is the temporal prince of the ecclesiastical patrimony. Yet, among all his duties the solicitude for every Church holds the first place. This is the first, the most unique and greatest. It is first because the Apostle Peter was made pastor of the Lord's entire flock long before he was bishop of Antioch or Rome. It is unique because there are many other bishops over very noble cities, and there are many temporal princes, but there is only one Pontiff of the who world that is vicar of Christ, and general pastor of the universal Church. Lastly, it is the greatest, because the episcopate of the city of Rome has its own defined limits, and these are narrow enough just like the Church's temporal rule. But the Supreme Pontiff has no limits except those that the world itself has.

Next, the Supreme Pontiff can easily fulfill this duty both ancient and great, singular and both proper to himself and necessary for the Church, if he will put good bishops over every Church, and take care to satisfy his duty that they will be good. Accordingly, good bishops choose good parish priests, good preachers, and good confessors. Therefore, the salvation of souls will be assured so long as he will stand for them.

But if by chance, due to the negligence of bishops or parish priests, some souls should perish, their blood will be required from the hand of the pastors. Moreover, the Supreme Pontiff will liberate his soul, naturally, should he have done what was due to him to make sure these souls would not perish. If, on the contrary, the Supreme Pastor himself would give to particular churches either bishops that were less good, or should he not see to it that they exercise their office; then indeed the blood of these souls will be required at the hand of the supreme Pontiff.

This consideration so vehemently terrifies me that I have compassion for no man more than the Supreme Pontiff, whom most men envy. What St. John Chyrsostom writes with a great sense of mind about bishops, specifically that only a few of them would be saved because of the extreme difficulty of giving a good account of the souls committed to their care, certainly applies much more to the occupants of St. Peter's throne. Nor ought we to flatter ourselves with the excuse of a good conscience or right intention on holy works, since the

Apostle Paul said: *"Nihil mihi conscius sum, sed non in hoc justificatus sum."*[1] For that reason, supported by apostolic kindness, I lay aside in the bosom of the most pious Father, or rather more at his feet, my scruples, which do not allow me to rest.

Therefore, it seems to me there are six matters which require reformation and cannot be overlooked without great danger. The first is the long vacancy of churches. There is an epistle of St. Leo I to Anastasius, the bishop of Thessalonika, in which the Pope bid that he provide for the churches without delay lest the Lord's flock should suffer from want of pastoral care. There are also extant many things in St. Gregory's epistles, wherein he admonishes those who have the right of election to choose a pastor as soon as possible. And if, by chance, some delay were necessary, the same Pope commended the vacant Church to a neighboring bishop to enjoy the fruits but to manage it in the meantime for the sake of that Church. Therefore, the holiest and most prudent Popes were zealous to immediately provide for vacant churches, lest matters should be effected for souls which, on account of the absence of a pastor, would cause them to perish. For it would be difficult to explain to a few how great a detriment the widowed churches cause; in such the flock falls headlong in suddenness of vices while it lacks a pastor; just as the Lord's vineyard becomes a forest while it lacks a farmer.

The next matter is the promotion of less useful pastors; for they ought to provide for the Church from their personal goods, but not for their person from the goods of the Church. Still, I affirm the best provision is when each can be together, that well deserving persons should be provided to a vacant church. And, so as to pass over other things, the Council of Trent clearly declares that all those who are in any way responsible for the appointment of a bishop would commit mortal sin if they do not choose the men whom they consider most suited for the office and the most likely to be of good service. That is also the common opinion of all Doctors. St. Gregory says it is right order that men be sought for the episcopacy. And St. Bernard says: "One that asks for himself has already been judged. ... round up and compel all those who refuse."

I confess that I have been terrified when I have seen several times persons promoted to cardinalatial sees in consistitories although from their advanced age, bad health or lack of episcopal virtues they could hardly be thought fit or of any use so as to have the charge of souls. Nevertheless, custom demands, you may say, that these churches be given to the cardinal priests, in order of seniority, whether they would have the necessary abilities or not. I do not

---

[1] "For I am not conscious to myself of anything. Yet I am not justified in this; rather the one that judges me is the Lord." 1 Corinthians 4:4.

believe custom would ever persuade us to entrust our bodies to aged physicians if through senility or any other cause they were less capable of doing us good. If we take such precautions when our perishable bodily health is at stake, why will we not take them for the sake of immortal souls? I omit the fact that in our time many are ambitious of the episcopal dignity, nay more, they ask and demand it in public, not knowing what they ask for as our Lord says.

Another matter is the absence of bishops from their dioceses. What benefit is it to elect a suitable man if he is never to be at home? The Council of Trent declares that by divine precept bishops must know their flocks, preach the Word of God to them and feed them by the administration of the Sacraments and the example of all good works. bishops are counted among those who are apostolic Nuncios; some of whom have not seen their own churches for many years. Some, since they have left behind the ministry to shepherd the souls entrusted to them, manage secular offices. Many, after they have left behind their sheep, busy themselves in affairs at Rome that can be done suitably by others. I do affirm however, that some bishops are excused from residence through obedience, nor do I deny that the Pope can exempt some bishops from residence for certain reasons and for a certain period of time. Yet I do not know whether God is pleased when such a number of bishops are absent from their churches for such a long time and with such a detriment to souls—it is clear that they certainly cannot satisfy their office.

Printed in Great Britain
by Amazon

24164670R00368